CW01466593

Elegant Complexity

A Study of David Foster Wallace's *Infinite Jest*

Greg Carlisle

Sideshow Media Group
Los Angeles / Austin

SIDESHOW MEDIA GROUP
Los Angeles / Austin
www.sideshowmediagroup.com

ISBN 978-0-9761465-3-7

FIRST EDITION

10 9 8 7 6 5 4 3 2 1

Manufactured in the United States of America

Acknowledgments

Participating in the Wallace-l listserv throughout the composition of this study has helped me clarify what I have to say about *Infinite Jest* and has led me to important reference works. For example, a post from Mark Brawner led me to the 1996 Wallace interview on the *Bookworm* radio program, which provided the inspiration for the structure of the study. Also, a dozen or so of the more elusive connections in the study were taken from postings on the Wallace-l listserv, many from George Carr's posts for the *Infinite Jest* Slow Read (IJSR).

I want to thank John Bucher of Sideshow Media Group and all those who reviewed earlier drafts of the study, including: Tricia Farwell, who offered meticulous chapter-by-chapter comments; Nick Maniatis; Greg Maupin, who suggested a couple of interesting references and who originally loaned me *The Bloomsday Book*; Steven Moore; Layne Neeper, who helped me clarify the Introduction; and Kyle Ware, who illustrated the E.T.A. grounds. I especially want to thank Matt Bucher for his support and editorial guidance.

for Laurie, Brian, and John

and

for Caroline

Contents

Elegant Complexity

Introduction

David Foster Wallace's *Infinite Jest* (1996) invites commentary because Wallace has not only written a fluid and immensely enjoyable novel of extraordinary depth and compassion that is funny, wise, and profoundly moving; he has created a book that also engages its readers by challenging them to connect the disparate plot threads that run through the novel's fragmentary episodes as they navigate shifts in chronology, location, and narrative perspective. To further heighten the reader's engagement, Wallace uses endnotes to provide comments and relevant information best placed outside the main text, to explore narrative tangents, and to make meta-narrative comments. "Although the interaction of reader and text is a relationship fraught with ambiguity and misunderstanding, since there are so many choices for interpretation, it is nevertheless the vital energizing force that keeps the story alive. Interpretation is open and never complete, yet that is also the very source of its vitality" (Boswell, p. 61). *Infinite Jest* holds a mirror up to our vulnerable natures and illuminates the necessity of making hard choices if we are to navigate successfully the ambiguities, missing information, multiple perspectives, temptations, obstacles, fears, and obsessions that make up our experience. The reader of *Infinite Jest* is rewarded not by passive acceptance of easy answers or tidy resolutions, but by an active engagement with ongoing narratives. The "elegant complexity" of the novel makes it "almost addictively compelling" (*Infinite Jest*, p. 322).

This study provides complete scene-by-scene summaries of *Infinite Jest* and investigates the novel's structure and thematic unity in commentaries that accompany the scene-by-scene summaries. Readers interested in the evolution of the novel will wish to familiarize themselves with *Infinite Jest*, and this study joins a growing body of scholarship concerning Wallace and his signature work. Marshall Boswell, essaying Wallace's fiction, identifies Wallace as a member of a "third wave of modernism," following in the wake of Joyce and Barth (Boswell, p. 1). Another excellent resource for readers interested in Wallace and *Infinite Jest* is Nick Maniatis's comprehensive website, www.thehowlingfantods.com/dfw, named for a phrase used in the novel. Maniatis's site includes links to the Wallace listserv (Wallace-l, which regularly features commentary on *Infinite Jest* and a wide range of other topics) and to works of scholarship, criticism, and opinion on Wallace's oeuvre. A reader's guide (Burn) and a reader's companion (Dowling and Bell) to *Infinite Jest* are also available. A brief discussion of the nature, structure, and scope of this study follows. Unless otherwise indicated, page numbers refer to *Infinite Jest*.

The Nature of This Study:
Its Inspiration, Its Intended Audiences and Functions, Its Length

The primary inspiration for this study is Harry Blamires's *The Bloomsday Book*, which was of great assistance to my reading of *Ulysses*. Although my first reading of *Infinite Jest* was easier than my first reading of *Ulysses*, I constantly flipped back through *Infinite Jest* to keep the multitude of plots, characters, and themes present in my mind. This study is designed to help readers flip back efficiently and, in the words of Blamires, to "enable the reader to get from his first reading . . . an understanding which, without my guide, it might have taken him several readings to arrive at" (Blamires, p. xi).

The study is intended to help first-time readers of *Infinite Jest* stay oriented as they progress through the novel scene-by-scene, summarizing and connecting various narrative and thematic threads without revealing information that is yet-to-come. Another intention is to provide readers, students, and critics with a reference work that supports scholarly investigations of the novel's structure and thematic unity by gathering information, making connections, and asking questions. The study's running commentaries are placed after the running narrative summaries to respect those readers who want help flipping back to track plots, characters, and chronologies, but who prefer to stay in the flow of an already complex story rather than take time out for commentaries.

Wallace's writing is precise, efficient, and detailed, regardless of whether the situation he describes is clear or ambiguous. Therefore, the summaries and commentaries provided by this study are often lengthy in order to minimize the oversimplification or misinterpretation of Wallace's text. A system for tracking plots, characters, and themes (described below) has been devised to assist readers in their navigation of this lengthy study.

Structure in *Infinite Jest*:
"It'll help your attitude to look for evidence of design" (p. 113)

Infinite Jest is divided into "chapters" marked by 28 centered, shadowed circles (❍) that appear in the main text of the novel (pp. 3-981). Another centered, shadowed circle is placed before the notes and errata (pp. 983-1079). The hardcover and paperback versions of the novel as published in the United States have the same pagination. Some changes made after publication of the first edition will be noted in the study. Within each chapter of the novel, a triple line-space designates division of the text into "subchapters" or "sections," of which there are 192, frequently introduced by a heading. In creating an Outline for *Infinite Jest*, this study suggests that the novel could be grouped into six relatively equal "units":

I.	Chs. 1-15	pp. 3-181	179 pages and nn. 1-59
II.	Chs. 16-21	pp. 181-321	141 pages and nn. 60-119
III.	Chs. 22-24	pp. 321-489	169 pages and nn. 120-207
IV.	Chs. 25-26	pp. 489-619	131 pages and nn. 208-256
V.	Ch. 27	pp. 620-808	189 pages and nn. 257-336
VI.	Ch. 28	pp. 809-981	173 pages and nn. 337-388

In the first unit of the novel, plots, characters, and themes burst forth continually in a frenetic sequence of shorter chapters. In the second unit, the length of chapters and sections extends to include more details about the characters, and a keener awareness of narrative patterns can be attained. In the third and fourth units, the interrelation of plots, characters, and themes becomes more apparent as narrative tensions increase. The fifth unit achieves a "chaotic stasis" (n. 61, p. 996) of narrative tensions; and although the sixth unit is not a denouement, there is a sense of stillness and reflection that balances the ongoing narrative tensions. This study will summarize and comment on the main text and associated notes of each section of the novel. Brief commentary on the thematic unity of each chapter of *Infinite Jest* will be provided at the end of each chapter of the study. Brief commentary on each unit of the novel will be provided after the last chapter of that unit.

The Structure of This Study

Centered headings mark the beginning of each chapter, and left-justified headings identify each subchapter or section of the study. The first line of the section heading identifies the subchapter, section number, and page numbers of the corresponding section of the novel; the middle line (if applicable) identifies the notes and page numbers of the notes associated with that section of the novel; and the last line identifies the time during which the events of the section occur. Because sections are not identified numerically in the novel, references to page numbers will be the primary means of identification in the study. The Outline at the back of the study provides a complete match of the novel's page numbers to subchapters and section numbers used in the study.

Each summary begins with an orientation to help readers keep track of plot threads, characters, and chronologies. Chronological shifts, shifting points of view, a variety of narrative approaches, and the memory lapses and errors of the characters or the narrator(s) create intentional mysteries and ambiguities to challenge the reader; and the study will call attention to these challenges (cf. that Wallace wrote "All typos intentional" on a draft version of *Infinite Jest* (Moore, commentary on draft pp. 315-21)). The main text and the text of the notes are quoted often to ensure the accuracy of the summaries. For readability, the convention of using ellipses to identify missing text will be applied in the middle of quotations, but usually not at the beginning or end. For example, you would often see "and . . . but . . . so"; but ". . . and but so . . ." would almost always be identified as "and but so" instead. Also, the study uses double quotation marks for dialogue, whereas Wallace uses single quotation marks in the novel; but the study follows Wallace's convention for dates: e.g., 8 November 2007. References to the page numbers of quoted text will usually only be identified for text *outside* the section being summarized. In an effort to minimize spoilers for first-time readers, the summaries rarely reference events that will occur later in the novel, but often reflect on what has come before. Occasionally, brief mention is made of Wallace's narrative approach or use of a particular convention. A single line-space divides each section's summary and commentary.

The commentaries begin with lists of the most relevant plot, character, and thematic threads for that section. Plot threads are usually listed in order of significance to the section, and thematic threads are listed in the order that they are discussed. Themes are generally intertwined, requiring the simultaneous discussion of several themes, sometimes in the space of a single sentence. (For easy reference, the reader may wish to keep handy the lists of plots, characters, and themes identified below.) Spoilers will be minimized just as in the summaries. Textual references to art, literature, movies, television, mythology, and philosophy are often identified. Although the commentaries are exclusively concerned with *Infinite Jest*, frequent brief references or comparisons are made to television programs, movies, or literary works such as *Hamlet*, *Ulysses*, or *1984*. The commentaries also address—or question the reader about—mysteries and ambiguities in the text.

CHAPTERS 1-28 of the study provide summary and commentary for each section of the corresponding chapter of the novel, and conclude with a thematic assessment of the entire chapter. Unit Commentaries appear after Chs. 15, 21, 24, 26, 27, and 28. The back of the study features MORE QUESTIONS, a discussion of some of the novel's major mysteries; a brief INTERPRETATION of the novel; a thematic OUTLINE with titles for each unit, chapter and subchapter of the novel; CHRONOLOGIES, including a more-or-less chronological ordering of *Infinite Jest* by subchapter that serves as a timeline for the novel; an E.T.A. SPATIAL ORIENTATION that gathers information about one of the novel's primary settings; charts and lists that identify CHARACTER ASSOCIATIONS for many of the novel's characters; and a listing of the study's REFERENCES to other works.

The Scope of This Study:
Tracking Plots, Characters, and Themes

Like *Ulysses*, the scope of *Infinite Jest* is vast; no study of its content can be definitive or exhaustive. The system used to track plots, characters, and themes as a means of focusing this particular study is now described. First-time readers may wish to come back to this part of the Introduction after becoming more familiar with the novel.

In a 1996 radio interview, Wallace said that the structure of the unedited first draft of *Infinite Jest* was based on a fractal object called a Sierpinski Gasket (cf. p. 213), generated geometrically by an iterative process of cutting smaller triangle-sized holes out of larger triangles. In the first iteration, one large triangle becomes three smaller triangles and one smaller-triangle-sized hole. In the second iteration, the smaller-triangle-sized hole remains, and the three smaller triangles each become three even smaller triangles and one even-smaller-triangle-sized hole (cf. Bourke). In analogy to viewing a Sierpinski Gasket, readers of *Infinite Jest* construct narrative interpretations "as much out of what's missing as what's there" (p. 681).

In order to comment on *Infinite Jest* systematically and efficiently, 16 categories of plot and character and 16 categories of theme that recur throughout the novel have been identified below in groups of four. Plot and character categories have been grouped into four major concerns of the novel: Hal Incandenza's relationships with his brothers and his experiences at the tennis academy he attends; the legacy of Hal's father, James Incandenza; abuse, addiction, and recovery, especially as it pertains to Don Gately and residents of the house for recovering addicts down the hill from the tennis academy; and backgrounds for and threats to the North American political and cultural environment as represented in the novel. Thematic category groupings are represented by prepositions that imply motion, distance, and conflict: a lack of connection or resolution. Explanations are provided for individual plot and theme categories.

As a tribute to the Sierpinski Gasket, these categories have been arranged into two large groups-of-triangles—one for plot and character, one for theme (on p. 24 of the study)—each made by dividing one triangle into four triangles which are then each divided again into four triangles. (Of course, an actual Sierpinski Gasket after two iterations would be represented by nine small triangles, three small holes, and one big hole, not by 16 small triangles.) As stated above, a listing of the most relevant categories of plot, character, and theme will begin the commentaries of each section of the study.

PLOT AND CHARACTER

The Brothers Incandenza

E.T.A.: history, philosophy, and events associated with the Enfield Tennis Academy and its students, administration, and staff

Orin

Hal

Mario

Jim's Life and Work

Avril

Jim

Art/Ent: theories and examples of art and entertainment, especially Jim's work

Tech: O.N.A.N.ite media and technology and Jim's technical achievements

Abuse, Addiction, and Recovery

Joelle

Ennet: Ennet House or the Enfield Marine complex; Ennet House administrators, staff, counselors, and residents

Gately

AA&R: abuse, addiction, and recovery outside Ennet House; meetings; illicit drugs

Politics and Terror

Samizdat: Jim's *Infinite Jest* used or discussed as an object of terror

U.S.O.U.S.: the United States Office of Unspecified Services, especially Steeply

O.N.A.N.: politics, environment, business, and culture in the Organization of North American Nations

A.F.R.: *Les Assassins des Fauteuils Rollents*, especially Marathe; other Canadian terrorist organizations

THEME

Between

Inf/Reg: infants, regression, adult regression to an infantile state, pleasure, compulsion, selfishness, self-obsession, and self-absorption

Phys/Ob: physical disabilities, obstacles, objects, bodies

Choice: discipline, surrender, the ability to refuse fatal pleasures, action

Non-Action: a lack of activity, passivity, being horizontal

Around

His/Father: personal or family history, especially concerning fathers

Cycles: circles, cycles, annulation, rituals, routines, motion, nested loops

Recur: a category applied to a range of concepts and images—the color blue, teeth, old TV shows, missed connections, weeping, dancing, vestiges of the primitive, etc.—or to less relevant recurrences of other themes in a particular section

Time: slow motion; being frozen; periodicity; an addict's experience of time; the simultaneity of past, present, and future

Under

Memory: the burden of memory or the fluidity and ambiguity of memory

Secrets: lies, hiding, masks, disguises, costumes, betrayal

Fear/Obsess: fears, obsessions, anxieties, neuroses, horrors, desires, pain

Dreams: dreams and nightmares

Away

Waste: toilets, trash, filth, mold, vomit, and other human or environmental waste

Loss: loss, depression, sadness, abandonment

Boundaries: physical, mental, spiritual, geographic, or philosophical barriers or limits

Isolation: loneliness, separation, retreat, cages, distance, an inability to communicate

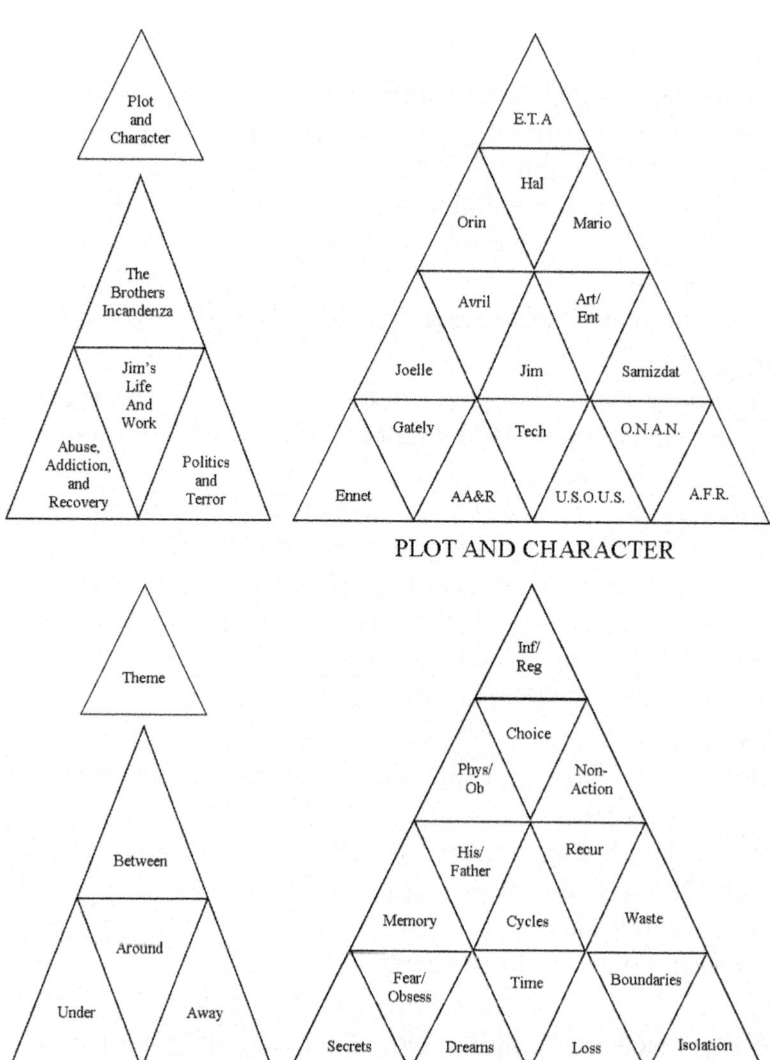
Plot
and
Character
The
Brothers
Incandenza
Jim's
Life
And
Work
Abuse,
Addiction,
and
Recovery
Politics
and
Terror
E.T.A
Hal
Orin
Mario
Avril
Art/
Ent
Joelle
Jim
Samizdat
Gately
Tech
O.N.A.N.
Ennet
AA&R
U.S.O.U.S.
A.F.R.
PLOT AND CHARACTER
Theme
Between
Around
Under
Away
Inf/
Reg
Choice
Phys/
Ob
Non-
Action
His/
Father
Recur
Memory
Cycles
Waste
Fear/
Obsess
Time
Boundaries
Secrets
Dreams
Loss
Isolation
THEME

Chapter 1

Surrounded by Heads and Bodies

Chapter 1.1, Section 1, Pages 3-10
November Y.G.

Although *Infinite Jest* accurately takes the pulse of the United States around the turn of the third millennium, many historical and political realities are altered in the novel. The heading "YEAR OF GLAD" (Y.G.) refers to a calendar year. Beyond a certain historical date, years are no longer referenced numerically. Also, the United States, Canada, and Mexico are united politically into the Organization of North American Nations (O.N.A.N.). Other organizations have been renamed accordingly; for example, O.N.A.N.C.A.A. has replaced the old N.C.A.A. (Wallace uses acronyms and slang throughout the novel. Dowling and Bell provide lists of these in their reader's companion.) All five sections of this first chapter are narrated in first-person by Hal Incandenza, who provides vivid, perceptive descriptions of his experiences. However, the majority of the novel consists of third-person narration, which ranges from objective reporting to extreme empathy for one or more characters, sometimes within a single section of text. Instances of radical narrative shifts within a section or of first-person narration will be noted. Wallace uses single quotation marks when characters speak, which may be simply a conventional choice or may imply that the entire novel is spoken (is in double quotation marks), that no narrator speaks from a position of pure objectivity.

It is November in the Year of Glad (cf. "the November heat," p. 3), and Hal Incandenza is eighteen. Hal attends and plays tennis for (and his brother attended and played tennis for) a boarding school: the Enfield Tennis Academy (E.T.A.) in Enfield, Massachusetts, part of the greater Boston area (cf. Hal's reference to Boston traffic, p. 15). Hal's uncle, Charles Tavis (C.T., Hal's "mother's half-brother"; p. 3), is headmaster of E.T.A.; and Hal's mother is also an administrator. Hal is an excellent junior tennis player and is currently seeded third in an annual tennis tournament in Arizona, the WhataBurger Southwest Junior Invitational, where he also excelled last year (p. 14). Hal, Tavis, and "Academy prorector" Aubrey deLint are meeting with five administrators about the possibility of Hal's attending the University of Arizona and joining their tennis program after graduation from E.T.A.:

- Dean of Admissions: lean, yellowish, fixed smile, at left
- Dean of Academic Affairs (Students): Sawyer, shaggy lion, at center
- Dean of Athletic Affairs: Bill, avarian, freckled scalp, at right
- Director of Composition: more than the normal number of eyebrows
- Tennis Coach Kirk White

The administrators are concerned that Hal's complex and adjective-inspiring essays (with impressive titles, cf. p. 7) and his high (but falling off in the last year) E.T.A. grades do not gel with his low standardized test scores. Hal—whose thoughts are often concerned with language, grammar, and usage—imagines telling the administrators that the essays in question are old and that recent essays "from the last year" would look "like some sort of infant's random stabs at a keyboard." Hal is concerned about being misperceived and does not speak. He would talk if the sounds he made could be what the administrators heard. The administrators ask Tavis and deLint to leave so that they may talk to Hal alone. When Hal does finally speak to the administrators he says that he cannot make himself understood. He says to call it something he ate.

PLOT AND CHARACTER: Hal
THEME: Inf/Reg, Isolation, Recur

Communication issues (the inability to communicate, missed- or non-connections) and infantile regression or self-absorption are recurring themes of the novel. O.N.A.N. recalls the Biblical masturbator and suggests that the novel occurs in a self-focused cultural and political environment. In this section Hal compares his current writing ability to that of "an infant's random stabs at a keyboard." Hal, an eloquent thinker who is keenly aware of his environment, is nevertheless isolated and does not speak to the others in the room. Other recurrent themes and images that appear in this section are spiders ("spidered light," p. 3); light; moving shadows (p. 5); a smile as a warning, teeth, and vestiges of the primitive (a "fixed smile" on p. 3, "radiant" teeth on p. 5, "lips drawn back" on p. 6, "broad expanses of recessed gum" on p. 7); something going away or receding (Tavis's voice, p. 8); and waste (the "defecatory posture," p. 9). Wallace, like Hal, is concerned with grammar and usage; cf. "Authority and American Usage," from his essay collection *Consider the Lobster.*

Chapter 1.2, Section 2, Pages 10-11
November Y.G.

Hal thinks of an incident that he doesn't remember from his childhood in Weston, MA. The incident was reported to Hal by his older brother Orin (O., who now plays in the NFL; p. 14) and involves Hal, Orin, and their mother, nicknamed the Moms. (Nicknames and variations in the spelling or initials of characters' names occur throughout the novel.) In March or early April of the year that Hal was around 5 according to Orin, Hal took a bite from a horrific patch of mold. Hal's mother, who "feared and loathed more than anything spoilage and filth," ran around the garden yelling "God! Help! My son ate this!" after Hal showed her the mold and said "I ate this."

PLOT AND CHARACTER: Hal, Orin, Avril
THEME: Memory, Fear/Obsess, Waste, Cycles

This section is a flashback to a significant incident in Hal's childhood that he doesn't remember but that he does remember his brother describing. Hal's mother has a fear of spoilage and filth (waste), and both she and Hal repeat phrases over and over and run laps around the garden in this section. Are we to infer from the lead-in to this section—"Call it something I ate" (p. 10)—that this incident with the mold approximately thirteen years ago has something to do with Hal's current communication trouble?

Chapter 1.3, Section 3, Pages 11-13
November Y.G.

Hal attempts to inform the administrators of his complexity: e.g.; he consumes libraries, he opines about philosophers. Hal says, "I'm not a machine. I feel and believe." The administrators do not understand what Hal says; they are frightened by the sounds and gestures Hal makes. As Hal tries to tell them that he is okay, they subdue him violently amid protests from deLint who re-enters the room. The administrators' reactions include "*God!*" and "*Help!*" (cf. Hal's mother's reaction to Hal's eating the mold).

PLOT AND CHARACTER: Hal
THEME: Phys/Ob

Hal's communication obstacles result in his being physically restrained. Why does Hal say that Dennis Gabor, inventor of holography, "may very well have been the Antichrist" (cf. Hal's essay on holographically mimetic cinema, p. 7)?

Chapter 1.4, Section 4, Pages 13-15
November Y.G.

Hal has been transferred to a men's room. The administrators give Tavis graphic descriptions of Hal's attempts to communicate with them, which from their perspectives are visceral and extreme.

Hal looked like a "writhing animal with a knife in its eye"; he was flailing and making a "sort of awful reaching drumming wriggle"; and his actions looked like "a time-lapse, a flutter of some sort of awful . . . growth." The administrators have not heard what Hal said as Hal reported it to the reader in the previous section. An ambulance is on the way. Tavis states that Hal is "fine" and is an "excitable kid" who "reads like a vacuum. *Digests* things." Hal's narration is calm in the face of the conflict happening around him.

PLOT AND CHARACTER: Hal
THEME: Waste, Cycles, Isolation, Inf/Reg, Time, Recur

Several of the novel's scenes occur in men's rooms, locker rooms, and toilet stalls—places in which waste is produced. Tavis is "a truly unparalleled slinger of shit." Disorder "revolves all around" as Hal remains on the floor in isolation. Hal's "trouble communicating" is described by the administrators as both primitive and infantile. Altered perceptions of time and a flutter as a symbol of danger or horror will recur throughout the novel. If the administrators' perceptions are accurate, how is Hal able to play tennis so well? Coach White has "seen him play. On court he's gorgeous. Possibly a genius."

Chapter 1.5, Section 5, Pages 15-17
November Y.G.

Hal is being put in an ambulance. DeLint attempts to comfort him, as an outraged Tavis stabs his cell phone's antenna skyward. Hal's only other visit to an emergency room was almost exactly one year ago; he was on a "psychiatric stretcher," restrained and immobile as he is now. Hal thinks of several people, characters that will be encountered or discussed during the course of the novel: Cosgrove Watt, the hypophalangial Grief-Therapist, the Moms, Himself, John N. R. Wayne (who would have won this year's Whataburger), Donald Gately (who helped Hal dig up Hal's father's head as Wayne stood watch in a mask), blind tennis-player (and Hal's predicted next opponent) Dymphna, Petropolis Khan, and other predicted tournament semifinalists Stice and Polep. Hal considers synonyms for the word "*unresponsive*." He predicts that someone will come by soon and ask him "what's *your* story?"

PLOT AND CHARACTER: Hal
THEME: Recur, Inf/Reg

The color blue is featured prominently throughout the novel (and on the cover). Note here "blue sky," "blue jaw," and "blue-collar." Hal thinks of a plane as making an incision in the sky, and there is another reference to a knife: "I once saw the word *KNIFE* finger-written on the steamed mirror of a nonpublic bathroom." There is another reference to Hal's infantilism: "I have become an infantophile." C.T.'s voice is again "receding." Masks will recur throughout the novel. Stories (personal or family histories) are also a recurring motif of the novel; and at the end of this introductory chapter, Hal expects someone to prompt him for his. Why was Hal digging up his father's head? Who is John N. R. Wayne; why is he wearing a mask; and why isn't he at the Whataburger?

Chapter 1: Surrounded by Heads and Bodies

In this chapter, Hal is disconnected from the other characters and sees the other characters as "heads and bodies" (disconnected). The actions of Hal's body are apparently disconnected from the thoughts in his head. There is a marked difference between Hal's thorough, sensitive narration and the brusque, frantic (disconnected) reactions of the other characters as reported by Hal. From the administrators' points of view, Hal's unnatural sounds and gestures suggest that he needs care. Yet Tavis states that Hal is fine, and Hal's communication problems in no way affect his ability to play tennis. Shifting points of view between Hal and the administrators create a sense of mystery or uncertainty for the reader.

Hal has much in common with Hamlet. He talks to his audience. He has an uncle in a position of authority over him. He has a penchant for introspection and attention to detail. He has a complex nature that is by turns passionate and reasonable. He is misunderstood or even regarded as insane by other characters. His father is dead. He participates in a graveyard scene. Hal has a significant memory of (Orin's report of) an event from his childhood in this chapter; Hamlet's memory of his childhood with Yorick prompts the monologue from which the novel's title is taken (*Hamlet*, V.i.178-89).

Chapter 2

An Immobility That Seemed Like The Gathering Of A Force

Chapter 2, Section 6, Pages 17-27
Note 1, Page 983
unspecified Y.D.A.U.

Chapter 2 of *Infinite Jest* occurs in a different year: the Year of the Depend Adult Undergarment (Y.D.A.U.). The third-person narrator of this single-section chapter (one of four: the others are Chs. 3, 4, and 14) is describing the thoughts and actions of a man named Erdedy. Geographic references to (for example) Cambridge and Marlborough Street place Erdedy in Boston and therefore near the Enfield Tennis Academy described in Ch. 1. References to teleputers and to land barges emptying dumpsters are examples of the uses of technology in the slightly altered reality of *Infinite Jest*. Page 23 references the first of 388 notes that comprise pp. 983-1079 of the novel. Note 1 simply states that methamphetamine hydrochloride is also known as crystal meth. Wallace uses notes (here and in other works) to provide relevant information best placed outside the main text, to explore narrative tangents, to make meta-narrative comments, and to heighten the reader's engagement with and participation in the reading experience.

In the first paragraph, Erdedy is watching an insect and waiting for a "woman who said she'd come." He is afraid to kill the insect and afraid to tie up the phone line since the woman might call him just as he calls her, which might prompt her to take "what she promised him somewhere else."

The second paragraph reveals that what the woman promised Erdedy is marijuana and that Erdedy has tried to stop smoking marijuana 70 to 80 times before. He is careful not to create ethical dilemmas for people by always seeking out new people to obtain for him the marijuana that he will smoke "one more last time." He is aware of the phone and that the insect has disappeared into a hole.

In the third (five-page) paragraph, Erdedy, though still afraid of taking up time, tries to call the woman using "just audio" and gets her "audio" answering device. The woman was to buy the marijuana from a guy with a harelip who lives and keeps snakes in a trailer out on the Allston Spur. Erdedy, always casual in his requests to purchase marijuana because he is afraid to show how much it matters to him, fears he has been too casual with the woman, who might think it wouldn't matter to Erdedy if she forgot to get the marijuana or to call. Erdedy notices that the insect is back on the shelf and feels that he is similar to it but is unsure how he is similar. Erdedy takes several courses of action each time he smokes marijuana for the last time: he isolates himself, stocks up on things that will add to the experience, and rids himself of things that will subtract from the experience. This includes renting film cartridges from the InterLace entertainment outlet. InterLace also makes teleputers (TPs), one of which Erdedy has in his bedroom. Erdedy's counselor, Randi, told him that he was "insufficiently committed" to removing substances from his lifestyle. Erdedy continues to be aware of the phone and of whether the insect is on the shelf or in the hole. He grows disgusted with himself that he is waiting anxiously for something that has stopped being fun and catalogues the negative effects of marijuana. He decides he will use his willpower to make this experience so unpleasant (by forcing himself to become ill from smoking too much) that he will never want to smoke again. He will insure himself against asking the woman for marijuana again by being rude to her after paying for what she promised to bring.

In the fourth (four-page) paragraph, Erdedy reflects upon the last woman he involved in his smoking marijuana for the last time. Erdedy's attention to the insect sitting on the shelf "with an immobility that seemed like the gathering of a force" intrudes upon his reflection of the last woman, who had come at precisely the time she had promised. He hears the sound of a dumpster being emptied into an

E.W.D. (Empire Waste Displacement, p. 121) "land barge." He goes into the bathroom, consciously choosing not to look at the insect or the phone. In the bathroom, his throat closes and he weeps hard for two or three seconds before abruptly stopping. The woman was over four hours late. He is unable to use the bathroom. He puts "a whole stack of film cartridges into the dock of the disc-drive" of the "huge teleputer" in his bedroom, but he cannot stay with any of them for more than a few seconds due to an irrational panic over missing something more entertaining on another cartridge. He answers the phone when it rings, but it is not the woman. Ideas come to him about what to do while he waits. He does not react to them, but watches as they float away. He does not have time to consider how this image of impulses floating away relates to either himself or the insect, because his telephone rings and his front door buzzes at the same time. He tries to move toward both at once, "flung, splayed, entombed between the two sounds, without a thought in his head."

PLOT AND CHARACTER: AA&R
THEME: Inf/Reg, Waste, Isolation, Fear/Obsess, Cycles, Secrets, Non-Action, Recur, Loss

The Year of the Depend Adult Undergarment is a symbol of adults regressed to an infantile state with respect to waste. Land barges for waste displacement are referenced in this section. Like the insect retreating into a hole, Erdedy retreats into his home and into himself (isolated from others, preferring masturbation to intercourse) for his compulsory binges, which make him "stare raptly like an unbright child at entertainment cartridges." Erdedy is afraid and obsessive. He is in a cycle of quitting marijuana; he has tried to quit "70 or 80 times." His binges are secret, and he deceives those he involves in his procurement of marijuana. Erdedy watches his impulses float away without acting on them and is "caught in the middle," inactive, "entombed between the two sounds." In addition to the recurrence of a moving shadow (cf. p. 5), this chapter initiates the recurring ideas of a person (usually a parent, here the woman) who does not come, of the weeping addict (Erdedy weeps hard on p. 25) experiencing the loss of a substance, and of the click and whir of machinery (p. 25).

Chapter 2: An Immobility That Seemed Like the Gathering of a Force

Like Hal in Ch. 1, the narrator for Erdedy provides a detailed account of moment-to-moment perceptions mixed with memories and reflections. Like Hal in Ch. 1, Erdedy is isolated and unable to communicate or to choose: he does not make connection with the woman; and he is stuck between the phone and the door, immobile. Most of the characters in *Infinite Jest* are addicted to some substance or activity that drives them to some level of obsession or desperation or "paralyzed stasis" (p. 72). As Erdedy's desperation and anxiety move him to a state of immobility in which his ability to make a decision recedes, narrative tension increases without resolving, and the narrator's paragraphs bulge. As narrative tension builds throughout the novel, the chapters will lengthen. Often—in this chapter, throughout the novel, in his other works—Wallace concludes a narrative sequence in "chaotic stasis" (n. 61, p. 996) or at a moment of maximum tension. The force of the narrative tension gathers in the stasis of the narrative sequence; i.e., in the immobility of the narrative sequence with respect to its resolution. This quality of creating tension that remains open-ended or achieves chaotic stasis is a signature feature of Wallace's work, present even in his first novel, *The Broom of the System* (which stops in the middle of a sentence), and in some of the stories in his first collection, *Girl with Curious Hair*.

Chapter 3

Are You Hearing Me Talking, Dad?

Chapter 3, Section 7, Pages 27-31
1 April Y.T.M.P.

This third chapter occurs in a third different year—the Year of the Tucks Medicated Pad (Y.T.M.P.)—and features a third different narrative approach. Chapter 3 is almost exclusively dialogue, with narrative interjections limited to sound effects of soda cans being tapped or opened. Sound effects related to drinking soda are placed inside quotation marks. At the end of the chapter and throughout the rest of the novel, an ellipsis by itself in quotation marks indicates that one of the characters does not respond verbally. Hal says that he is ten and will be "eleven in June," which places Y.T.M.P. seven years before Y.G., when Hal will be eighteen in his November interview at the University of Arizona in Tucson—a city in which Hal's father used to live—and Hal's father will be dead (cf. p. 17). The first edition of *Infinite Jest* states that Hal is twelve (twice on p. 30) and will be turning thirteen in June (p. 27). Wallace corrected Hal's age for subsequent printings (cf. Moore, commentary on draft pp. 1-5).

Hal's father is disguised as a "professional conversationalist" and is attempting to communicate with his son. Hal, who has low salivary output, is offered lemon soda by the conversationalist. Young Hal is a "tennis and lexical prodigy" who also has an interest in Byzantine erotica. Hal's father (Himself) often hallucinates (perhaps because he "drinks Wild Turkey at like 5:00 A.M.") that Hal is unable to speak. Hal's father is "a towering figure in optical and avant-garde film circles and single-handedly founded the Enfield Tennis Academy." Hal's mother is a "mover and shaker in the prescriptive-grammar academic world" (cf. Hal's essays on erotica, cinema, and grammar; p. 7).

As Hal becomes suspicious of the conversationalist, he is accused of having a connection with the "intra-Provincial crisis in southern Québec." Hal's family is accused of having a "sordid liaison with the pan-Canadian Resistance's notorious M. DuPlessis and his malevolent but allegedly irresistible amanuensis-cum-operative, Luria P——." The conversationalist believes that the leaking of said liaison to the press resulted in the deaths of two people. At this point the conversationalist begins to believe Hal is not responding to him. The conversationalist also believes that Hal's mother has weekly "assignations" with a "bisexual bassoonist in the Albertan Secret Guard," cavorts with over thirty "Near Eastern medical attaches," and introduces steroids into Hal's cereal that are not dissimilar to his father's "hypodermic 'megavitamin' supplement." ("Mondragonoid" refers to Hal's mother's maiden name. "Interdependence Day," analogous to Independence Day, is a November celebration for the now-united North American nations.)

As Hal informs the conversationalist that his mustache is askew and that his face is running, the conversationalist states that the materials composing the tennis racquets Hal uses are identical to the materials composing items that have been implanted in Hal's father's head: a "gyroscopic balance sensor and *mise-en-scene* appropriation card and priapistic-entertainment cartridge." The items were implanted after a series of detoxifications and various operations on Hal's father's internal organs. A stained argyle sweater-vest leads Hal to realize that the conversationalist is his father and prompts Hal to ask whether this meeting is an April Fools joke. Hal's father laments that his son is as silent as his own father was (Hal's grandfather would turn the *Tucson Citizen* into "the room's fifth wall"), while Hal tries to tell his father that he is speaking: "Are you hearing me talking, Dad?"

PLOT AND CHARACTER: Hal, Jim
THEME: His/Father, Secrets, Fear/Obsess, Recur

Parent-child relationships are as significant in *Infinite Jest* as they are in *Hamlet.* Hal's father had trouble communicating with

Hal's grandfather and believes he must resort to a disguise to communicate with Hal. Hal's father is obsessed with the idea that Hal is silent. He also fears his wife is involved with secret Canadian organizations and Canadian and Near Eastern lovers. Hal's mother, like Hamlet's mother, is accused of infidelity by (the memory/ghost of) his father. Hal's dental issues will recur throughout the novel as will his father's alcoholism and communication problems.

Is what Hal's father says about his mother true? If so, do/did the steroids in his cereal affect Hal? What is the significance of the items supposedly implanted in Hal's father's head? Do these items have something to do with Hal's digging up his father's head in Y.G. (p. 17)?

Chapter 3: Are You Hearing Me Talking, Dad?

Like Erdedy in Ch. 2, Hal's father has a problem with an addictive substance. Like the administrators in Ch. 1, Hal's father has trouble communicating with Hal. Over seven years from now (after Hal's father has died), the administrators will hear subanimalistic noises and sounds (p. 14) from Hal. Although Hal's father understands Hal in the first half of this chapter, in the second half (and on other occasions) he hears only silence.

Chapter 4

The Connection Was Cut

Chapter 4, Section 8, Pages 32-33
9 May Y.D.A.U.

This chapter occurs in the same year as Ch. 2. Hal has another older brother, Mario, with whom he shares a room at E.T.A. Hal's regular routine is to leave his room before 0600 (military time is used in *Infinite Jest*) for dawn drills, and he often does not return until after supper. His brother Mario, who has a "small hunched shape" and an "oversized skull," does not drill and cannot play tennis.

As Hal packs his bags for the whole day quietly in the dark as not to wake Mario, he receives a brief, cryptic telephone call from his brother Orin. Orin says "I want to tell you" and "My head is filled with things to say." Hal says "I don't mind" and "I could wait forever." Orin says "That's what you think." Hal hears janitors Brandt and Kenkle down the hall and shoves Dunlop tennis racquets into his complimentary gear bag. When Mario, now awake, asks who it was on the phone, Hal replies "No one you know, I don't think" as he deactivates the ringer on the phone.

PLOT AND CHARACTER: Hal, Mario, Orin
THEME: His/Father, Secrets, Recur

This section begins with the phrase "Another way fathers impact sons," which may imply that the events of the previous section have significance for Hal in terms of his relationship with his father. Hal keeps a secret from Mario. The "hunched shape" is an image that will recur. Scenes of Hal and Mario in their room will recur, as will scenes of Hal and Orin on the phone.

What is the significance of the cryptic, menacing conversation between Hal and Orin? Is it significant that they are quoting George Harrison lyrics from the Beatles album *Revolver*? What does Orin want to tell Hal? Why doesn't Hal tell Mario that Orin was on the phone?

Chapter 4: The Connection Was Cut

Again in Ch. 4, communication is mysterious, desperate, abrupt, and incomplete. Ch. 1 progressed in a linear sequence, and Chs. 2-4 were not divided. However, now that Wallace has prepared the reader for changes in time, location, and narrative approach and for mysteries and ambiguities in the narrative; he will gradually expand the chapters and subchapters, broadening the range of plots, characters, and themes explored in the novel and patching together a fragmented but unified narrative like a quilt. The next eleven chapters will introduce a flood of new information and characters.

Chapter 5

Fatally Pretty

Chapter 5.1, Section 9, Pages 33-37
1 April Y.D.A.U.

Chapter 3 occurred on 1 April Y.T.M.P. This section occurs on 1 April Y.D.A.U., about 5 ½ weeks before Orin calls Hal with his cryptic message on 9 May (Ch. 4), and features a medical attaché who is one-half ethnic Arab and Canadian (Québecois) by birth and residence (cf. p. 30: Did Hal's mother have a relationship with this man?). The medical attaché is a special consultant to the personal physician of the Saudi Minister of Home Entertainment, who is treated by the attaché for chronic "*Candida albicans*" (which leads to "yeasty sores" in his mouth) and who is here with his legation to cut a deal with InterLace TelEntertainment—an organization with a hub of manufacture in Phoenix AZ and a hub of dissemination in Boston MA. The attaché normally divides his practice between Montreal and the Rub' al Khali, and this is his first return to the U.S.A. since his residency eight years ago. He is staying in "sumptuous apartments he had his wife sublet in districts far from the legation's normal . . . digs."

Normally, the medical attaché's wife wordlessly attends to his every need as he simultaneously eats and watches the teleputer until he falls asleep in a recliner that automatically turns into a bed. However, tonight is Wednesday, the night his wife and other legation wives are permitted to play tennis; so the medical attaché views the "spontaneous disseminations" of the "InterLace Subscription Pulse-Matrix," which include an episode of the Mr. Bouncety-Bounce children's program and a session from the aerobics series of Ms. Tawni Kondo, InterLace's aerobics-guru. (Conjunction strings like "and but so" on p. 35 will appear throughout the novel; cf. also "and then but" on pp. 28, 39.)

The only entertainment cartridges in the house are those that have arrived in the mail and have been left on a sideboard underneath a triptych of Byzantine erotica (cf. p. 29 for Hal's interest in Byzantine erotica). In the stack of mail is a cartridge in a plain brown and untitled case which has been mailed in a featureless white three-day standard mailer sent with "routine O.N.A.N. postage" rather than the diplomatic seal used by the Prince's legation. The package was postmarked Phoenix AZ but had no return address. In place of the return address there was the term *"HAPPY ANNIVERSARY!"* and a "small drawn crude face, smiling." The attaché and his wife were married in "October, four years prior" and are therefore not celebrating their anniversary at this time. The cartridge has another circular smiling head where the registration and duration codes should be. The attaché begins viewing the cartridge in his recliner at 1927h. (7:27 P.M.)

PLOT AND CHARACTER: Tech, Samizdat
THEME: Inf/Reg, Cycles, Recur

In Y.D.A.U., the "self-congratulating idol" of the United States, the "Libertine statue," wears an "enormous adult-design diaper" (as does Mr. Bouncety-Bounce, cf. p. 648). The attaché normally requires that his wife attend to him as if he were an infant, so that "he may enjoy his hot dinner without having to remove his eyes" from the entertainment he watches. Normally he puts the teleputer on "a recursive loop," so that it will play on as he falls asleep in a recliner that automatically turns into a bed. There is reference to a popular children's program (Mr. Bouncety-Bounce), and like a child the Prince has an "inability to control his appetites" with respect to Toblerone chocolate. With InterLace, the Boston-Arizona cycle recurs in this section: cf. Bostonian Hal interviewing in Tucson in Ch. 1 and Hal's Bostonian father's memory of childhood in Tucson in Ch. 3. Also, the medical attache's practice cycles between Montreal and the Rub' al Khali. The novel is rife with vomiting characters; here the attache's duties are "sort of nauseous."

Chapter 5.2, Section 10, Pages 37-38
unspecified Y.T.-S.D.B.

This section occurs in yet another year—the Year of the Trial-Size Dove Bar (Y.T.-S.D.B.)—and features another rare instance of first-person narration, the use of which Wallace reserves for either Hal or an unknown narrator with two notable exceptions: both Clenette in this section and yrstruly in Ch. 12.2 narrate in voices that are markedly different from that of the other narrators.

Reginald asks Clenette to help him retrieve Wardine from the back of a closet, where she sits crying to recover from the latest beating-with-a-hanger she has received from her mother. Wardine's back is "all beat up and cut up"; it makes Clenette "[s]ick down in [her] insides to look at it." Wardine's mother's "man," parolee Roy Tony, does "business" at the playground at the Brighton Projects and comes to where Wardine sleeps at night and says quiet things and breathes. Roy Tony's brother, who is "gone," is Wardine's father (and Clenette's father if Wardine's reference to Clenette being her "half Sister" is literal); Roy Tony is presumably the father of "Roy the baby"; and presumably either Roy Tony or his brother is also the father of Wardine's mother's other children, William and Shantell.

Wardine begs Clenette and Reginald not to tell their mothers about her problems with her mother and Roy Tony. Clenette will not tell her mother—Clenette's mother is afraid of Roy Tony because Roy Tony killed Columbus Epps (presumably the father of Clenette's double-dutch partner, Delores Epps) "for Love" of Clenette's mother—but Clenette fears that Reginald will confront Roy Tony, that Roy Tony will kill Reginald, and that Wardine's mother will beat Wardine to death. "And then nobody know except me. And I am gone have a child."

PLOT AND CHARACTER: AA&R
THEME: His/Father, Cycles, Fear/Obsess, Recur

The characters in this section are interconnected in a familial cycle of fear and abuse. The fathers in this section are either unknown, absent, or abusive. The women live in fear. This is the first of many occurrences of child abuse in the novel, often manifested as a cyclical continuance of previous abuse. How will Clenette's child fare in this environment?

Chapter 5.3, Section 11, Pages 38-39
unspecified

This section is undated and spans several years. It tells the tale of Bruce Green, who fell in love with flaxen-haired and "fatally pretty" Mildred Bonk in eighth grade, witnessed her change of personality and associated teasing and gelling of flaxen hair into finger-in-electric-socket hair by tenth grade, and was living with Mildred and "tiny incontinent Harriet Bonk-Green" in a housetrailer with Tommy Doocey "by the year of what would have been graduation." Tommy Doocey is a "harelipped pot-and-sundries dealer who kept several large snakes" in a trailer just off the Allston Spur and was referenced by the woman who said she would come to Erdedy in Ch. 2 (p. 19). Like Erdedy, Mildred "got high in the afternoon and watched serial cartridges, . . . and for a while life was more or less one big party."

PLOT AND CHARACTER: AA&R
THEME: Recur, Waste, Phys/Ob

Mildred Bonk is described as being "fatally pretty" and like a "wraith" who glides through dreams. Both of these ideas will recur. Bonk's "bored mask of Attitude" is another reference to masks. Harriet Bonk-Green is specifically described as "incontinent." Doocey's harelip is a physical obstacle that keeps him from smelling his unclean snakes.

Chapter 5: Fatally Pretty

This chapter briefly examines the relationships of characters from three different cultures to entertainment and/or drugs—both of which can be fatally pretty, in that an abusive consumption of either promotes a dangerous disconnection from reality. Each section introduces new characters and creates a sense of fatality, describing the moments before impending calamities. The attaché begins to watch the mysterious cartridge; Clenette fears that her two friends will die soon; and there is the sense that Green and Bonk's "big party" will not end well. Although the attaché unwinds "without chemical aid," he becomes as self-absorbed as an addict when he watches his entertainment. Substance abuse features prominently in the environments of both Clenette (Roy Tony's "business") and Green and Bonk. Bonk regresses into a life of drugs and "serial-cartridges." Consider the roles of women in this chapter: the attache's wife is generally servile; the women in Clenette's world are objects of love or lust and are beaten and afraid (fatally pretty); and Bonk—although put on a pedestal—is won by Green when he develops "a will." Later in the novel, a female character will appear who is veiled like the attache's wife, who has scarred flesh like Wardine, and who is fatally pretty and a drug-user like Mildred Bonk.

Chapter 6

After Himself Passed Away

Chapter 6.1, Section 12, Pages 39-42
unspecified Y.D.A.U.

Like Ch. 3, this section is a dialogue between two characters; and like Ch. 4, it is a scene in Hal and Mario's room. It is midnight on an unspecified date in Y.D.A.U. Mario (nicknamed Booboo) is keeping Hal awake with a discussion about Hal's defeat of another tennis player and whether it made Hal feel like Hal believed in God, something Mario asks Hal about "once a week." Hal expresses his problem with God's pro-death stance versus his own anti-death stance and says "We countenance each other from either side of some unbridgeable difference on this issue" before attempting to get Mario off the subject by telling a joke.

Mario asks Hal why the Moms never cried when Himself passed away, recalling that he, Hal, and C.T. all cried; Hal while listening to *Tosca* over and over. Mario asks Hal whether he thinks the Moms seemed to get happier after Himself passed away. Mario notes that the Moms stopped traveling to corporate-grammar and library-protest things. Hal counters that since Himself's death the Moms never goes anywhere. She just travels between the Headmaster's House and her office via a tunnel and is more of a workaholic and obsessive-compulsive than she ever was which doesn't seem happier to Hal. Mario notes that she "laughs at C.T. way more than she laughed at Himself" and from "lower down inside," and asks Hal why she never got sad. Hal says that she just got sad in her way instead of in Hal's or Mario's way: "She's plenty sad, I bet."

PLOT AND CHARACTER: Hal, Mario, Avril
THEME: Loss, His/Father, Isolation, Fear/Obsess

Hal and Mario discuss their mother's reaction to the loss of their father, which was to isolate herself on the E.T.A. grounds and to become even more obsessive. Hamlet's mother married her husband's brother, who became the new king, after her husband's death; Hal's mother seems happier with her own "half-brother" (p. 3), who became the new headmaster, after her husband's death.

Chapter 6.2, Section 13, Page 42
1 April Y.D.A.U., 2010h.

Forty-three minutes after the end of Ch. 5.1 (p. 37), "the medical attaché is still watching the unlabelled entertainment cartridge."

PLOT AND CHARACTER: Samizdat
THEME: Isolation, Non-Action

This short, two-line section creates a sense of importance or mystery by isolating a particular moment, like a quick-cut in a film. The attaché sits in his recliner: isolated, inactive.

Chapter 6.3, Section 14, Pages 42-49
Note 2, Page 983
October Y.D.A.U.

About five months after his phone call to Hal (Ch. 4), Orin wakes up in his Phoenix AZ condominium at 0730h. to find a note "with phone # and vital data" of his latest Subject (sexual conquest) on the other pillow. He sweats every night in his sleep. As he sits outside and eats breakfast at his condo complex's central pool, he hears cartridge-viewers going from behind closed windows ("that aerobics show every morning"; probably Tawni Kondo, cf. p. 35). He ponders whether the dead bird that fell into the Jacuzzi last week was a bad sign.

Enormous roaches often come out of the drains in Orin's bathroom. They are large and create a mess when killed, so Orin keeps big glass tumblers in the bathroom with which to trap and asphyxiate them. He then discards both roach and tumbler (in separate Ziplocs) into an E.W.D. dumpster. "Orin's special conscious horror, besides heights and the early morning is roaches." They "give him the howling fantods." It was the mobile flying roaches that fed on the mucus in babies' eyes and the flooding that caused dead bodies to slide down the hill on which Orin lived in New Orleans that prompted his request to be traded to another NFL team. Orin's father's "conscious horror" was of "black widows and their chaotic webs," which are all over the place both in Phoenix and Tucson, the city his father left as "an unhappy youngster." Orin has inherited none of his mother's (Avril M. T. Incandenza's) "phobias about disorder, hygiene" (cf. p. 11).

Orin often has "spider-and-heights" dreams and finds it hard to get through the day. Many of Orin's dreams begin with a competitive-tennis situation. Last night's dream may have involved Ross Reat or Walt Flechette or M. Bain (whose sister has been a Subject of Orin's) from Orin's Academy days. Later in that dream, his mother's disconnected head is strapped tight to his own, face-to-face, like an overtight helmet that he can't get out of. Orin doesn't see a therapist, and his interpretations of his dreams are therefore surface-level (n. 2).

Orin awoke one morning from "a night of horror-show dreams" to find a previous Subject (an Arizona State University grad student and mother) watching a Spontaneous Dissemination of an old "late-millennial" Canadian news documentary in which a paranoid schizophrenic believes radioactive fluids invade his skull and machines are programmed to pursue him, make brutal sport of him, and bury him alive. The injection of radioactive dye and subsequent P.E.T. scan procedure then documented in horrific detail seem to justify the schizophrenic's fears. The Subject (who keeps Toblerone—a favorite of the Saudi Prince's (p. 34)—in Orin's freezer) noted that the P.E.T. scans referenced in the documentary had been replaced by "Invasive Digitals."

Since the dead bird fell in Orin's jacuzzi five days ago, he has come under pressure from the Arizona Cardinal football administration to submit to personality-profile interviews with *Moment* magazine, in which he must answer personal background questions. The "unexamined stress" of the impending interviews has driven him "to start calling Hallie again," which he equates to reopening a "whole Pandora's box of worms."

Orin shaves as he was taught.

PLOT AND CHARACTER: Orin
THEME: Dreams, Fear/Obsess, Recur

This section documents Orin's nightmares and his fears of early morning, heights, spiders, and roaches; his father's fear of spiders; his mother's fear of disorder and hygiene; and Fenton's fears of invasive radioactive fluids and malevolent machines. Orin's method of roach removal is somewhat obsessive. There are many recurring images in this section: Orin is "fetally curled" and has a "fetal spasm"; his complex is a "ring"; the pool is "blue"; Orin has "feelings of being submerged and not knowing which way to head for the surface and air"; and Orin dreams of being attached to his mother's "disconnected head" (cf. Hal digging up his father's head, p. 17).

Orin's nightmares are called "horror-show" dreams, which is a phrase used in Anthony Burgess's novel *A Clockwork Orange*, which was made into a film by Stanley Kubrick. Kubrick's film of Arthur C. Clarke's novel *2001: A Space Odyssey* featured an all-knowing machine with human qualities named Hal (cf. our Hal: "I'm not a machine," p. 12). Orin's analogy of the day being climbed (p. 46) recalls the Sisyphus myth. The New Orleans flooding which exhumed dead bodies recall Horatio's tale of tenantless graves in *Hamlet* (I.i.118-9). Hamlet reminded Horatio of the "special providence in the fall of a sparrow" (*Hamlet*, V.ii.215-6). Is the fall of a bird into Orin's jacuzzi significant? The bird is "undistinguished," "[n]ot a predator," and like "a wren [O-rin], maybe."

Chapter 6: After Himself Passed Away

The death of their father is still in the minds of Hal, Mario, and Orin. Hal and Mario discuss the effect of their father's death on their mother in this chapter; and Orin has moved to "metro Phoenix, in a kind of desiccated circle, near the Tucson of his own father's desiccated youth." Orin has inherited (although to a lesser degree) his father's fear of spiders. The film that the attache watches was made by the boys' father and still has the capacity to captivate viewers after their father's death.

Chapter 7

Overlooked

Chapter 7.1, Section 15, Pages 49-54
Notes 3-10, Pages 983-984
October Y.D.A.U.

The section begins "Here's Hal Incandenza, age seventeen," which places Y.D.A.U. as the year immediately before the Year of Glad in which Hal was eighteen in November (p. 3). Since Hal has passed his seventeenth birthday, it must be June or later (cf. p. 27). Hal is dreading Interdependence Day (8 November) and the erection of the Lung—which makes it possible "for outdoor tennis" during the "winter months"—"at some point soon." The narrative perspective in this section moves fluidly from Hal to Avril to an objective report of E.T.A. grounds back to Hal. In addition to using symbols in the text (like # in the previous section), Wallace also uses abbreviations like "Bldg." and undefined acronyms like ATHSCME. He substitutes slang names like "Bob Hope" for marijuana and often represents a character by a variety of names or nicknames. Here, "Avril I." may call attention to the significance of "April 1" to the novel so far. Later in the novel, the narrator will misspell words to better represent particular characters. Wallace also uses phrases that could double as jabs at his narrative approach: e.g., "it all gets too abstract and twined up to lead to anything."

In this section, Hal (like Erdedy in Ch. 2) is secretly getting high and reflecting in detail upon the processes and materials best used for secretly getting high and upon who knows or might know that he secretly gets high. He is as attached to the secrecy as he is to getting high, "though he's never given much thought to why." Hal's mother Avril has a "dread of hiding or secrecy" with respect to her sons, according to her "adoptive brother" (previously referenced as her half-brother) Charles Tavis and E.T.A. psych-counselor Dolores Rusk. Avril is aware that Hal drinks but is not "crazy about the idea," given the way Hal's father and paternal grandfather (in "AZ and CA") drank (cf. the Wild Turkey, p. 30). However, Avril attempts to be "concerned but unsmothering" about "the two high-functioning of her three sons," doesn't "wring her fine hands" over the drinking, and prefers that Hal drink rather that take drugs with "reptilian" Pemulis and "trail-of-slime-leaving" Struck, both of whom give her the howling fantods.

The Enfield Tennis Academy sits on top of a hill, is laid out in the shape of a true cardioid (a heart, cf. also the Lung in this section), and is traversable by underground tunnels of varying diameter, some of which require hunching or knuckle-dragging or crawling postures for navigation. E.T.A. was designed by "Avril's old and very dear friend" A. Y. Rickey (n. 3). Avril rarely travels above ground (cf. p. 42) and takes a tunnel from the Headmaster's House to the Community and Administration (Comm.-Ad.) Building, where she has an office next to Tavis. The sublevel of the Comm.-Ad. Bldg. houses the weight room, sauna, and shower areas with a large tunnel leading from the shower to the laundry room and smaller tunnels leading from the sauna to the subbasements of buildings housing classrooms and subdormitories (the buildings—not the subbasements—house the classrooms and subdormitories, which despite the "sub" are located on the upper floors of E.T.A. buildings). These smaller sublevel tunnels also are used as hallways between the private rooms of E.T.A. prorectors, "younger staffers who double as academic and athletic instructors" (n. 4). The subbasements are in turn connected by even smaller tunnels to the optical and film-development facilitics of Leith, Ogilvie, and Hal's late father (Dr. James O. Incandenza, headmaster of E.T.A. before Tavis) and to the offices of the Physical Plant, which sits beneath the tennis courts at the center of the E.T.A. complex. The Physical Plant offices are connected by tunnel to the Lung-Storage and -Pump Rooms. The Lung refers to a dome (erected and serviced by employees of TesTar and ATHSCME) that is kept inflated over the center courts between November and March by the upside-down-spider-shaped Pump Room and that between March and November is stored in the Lung-Storage Room, during which time Hal may use the Pump Room to get high in secret between afternoon matches and conditioning, activities that occur before E.T.A.'s communal supper.

Many E.T.A. players use drugs, although a "decent percentage" do not. "Some persons can give themselves away to an ambitious pursuit and have that be [enough, but] American experience seems to suggest that people are virtually unlimited in their need to give themselves away, on various levels. Some just prefer to do it in secret." Although much of the drug use at E.T.A. is "good clean temporary fun," a small number of players are reliant on the drugs to manage the demands of their hectic E.T.A. lifestyle. The habits and rationale of drug-use at E.T.A. are described, and various drugs are described and classified in the main text and in nn. 5-9. Interesting information can be found buried in these drug-specific notes. Troeltsch feels that Tenuate helps his "sports-color-commentary loquacity" and "promotes" Tenuate capsules from his roommate Pemulis, "which secret promotions Pemulis knows about" and for which Pemulis is preparing retaliation (n. 5.a, endnotes to endnotes appear regularly in *Infinite Jest*). In n. 8, "DMZ/M.P."—which will soon become significant—is described as "a CNS [central nervous system]-rattler."

Although the use of alcohol and drugs is cause for expulsion at E.T.A., enforcement is left up to the alumni prorectors ("eight" here refers only to the male prorectors); who are "depressed or traumatized about not making it into the Show" (the professional tennis circuit), who are often away trying to make money playing tennis, and who sometimes get high themselves. Therefore, the drug enforcement "tends to be flaccid." Since the Pump Room is connected by tunnel to the prorectors' rows of housing units, Hal can navigate his way into a men's room and eliminate all trace of his drug use before going to supper. His obsession with secrecy, although not based on "fear per se, fear of discovery," is "almost irresistible in its force." "Like most North Americans of his generation, Hal tends to know way less about why he feels certain ways about the objects and pursuits he's devoted to than he does about the objects and pursuits themselves."

PLOT AND CHARACTER: Hal, E.T.A., AA&R
THEME: Isolation, Secrets, Fear/Obsess, Cycles, Recur

In this section, Hal isolates himself so that he can get high in secret, a process that involves obsessive rituals; and Hal's obsession that nobody know is "almost irresistible in its force." Hal is "underground," and his process is "covert." The use of "alcohol or illicit chemicals" at E.T.A. is forbidden, and therefore must be done in secret. Troeltsch secretly steals capsules from Pemulis, who secretly knows he does so. Navigating drug use and optimum on-court performance at E.T.A. is described as a "gradual cycle" and a "circular routine." Avril fears Hal could join his grandfather and father in a cycle of alcoholism, but does not express this fear to Hal (does not "wring her fine hands"—cf. Hamlet to Gertrude: "Leave wringing of your hands," *Hamlet* III.iv.34). Since the death of her husband, Avril isolates herself to the E.T.A. grounds and fears secrets and hiding with respect to her children. The cardioid design and extensive interconnected tunnels of E.T.A. reflect a complexity born of obsession. Analogous to the recurrent imagery of submersion in water, "Hal can take every iota [of smoke] way down deep and hold his breath forever." Also, Hal has to "hunch" in the tunnels, and the Pump Room resembles a spider.

Chapter 7.2, Section 16, Page 54
Note 11, Page 984
2 April Y.D.A.U., 0015h.-0020h.

Two hours after Ch. 6.2 (p. 42), the medical attaché's wife is just leaving the fitness center; and the medical attaché is "still viewing the unlabelled cartridge," now "configured for a recursive loop." He has "wet both his pants and the special recliner."

PLOT AND CHARACTER: Samizdat
THEME: Waste, Non-Action, Isolation, Cycles, Fear/Obsess

The attaché sits in his recliner, in his own waste, inactive, alone, watching a cartridge in a recursive loop. The attaché's ominous obsession with viewing the cartridge is resonant with Hal's obsession with secrecy in the previous section.

Chapter 7.3, Section 17, Pages 54-55
May Y.D.A.U.

Mario is eighteen in May Y.D.A.U., the month that Hal did not tell Mario that Orin called (cf. Ch. 4). Mario will be nineteen in November (p. 589), and his "designated function" (cf. that Mario is not one of "the two high-functioning of [Avril's] three sons," p. 50) at E.T.A. is to film tennis drills so that Coach Schtitt and the prorectors can use the film for student instruction.

PLOT AND CHARACTER: Mario, E.T.A.
THEME: His/Father, Cycles

Unlike Orin and Hal, Mario has inherited an interest in making film from his father. Coach Schtitt can use an isolated moment of Mario's film in a recursive loop to instruct students. The viewing of film connects this section to the previous section.

Chapter 7.4, Section 18, Pages 55-60
Notes 12-20, Pages 984-985
Autumn Y.D.P.A.H.

This section occurs in the autumn of a fifth year—the Year of Dairy Products from the American Heartland (Y.D.P.A.H.)—and features "twenty-seven-year-old oral narcotics addict" Don Gately, who is "the size of a young dinosaur, with a massive and almost perfectly square head" (Hal, in Y.G., remembered digging up his father's head with Gately, p. 17). Gately and his associate, Trent ("Quo Vadis") Kite (n. 13), burglarize homes to support their drug habits. Gately once spent 92 days in jail on "a North Shore Assistant District Attorney's circumstantial suspicion." As revenge for this "impromptu detox," Gately and Kite burgled this A.D.A.'s house while the A.D.A. and his wife were away, and later sent pictures of themselves in Halloween-clown masks with toothbrushes belonging to the A.D.A. and his wife protruding from their bottoms. (This is one of at least three instances in which urban legends make their way into the *Infinite Jest* narrative.)

Now, in Brookline, Gately and Kite (wearing clown masks) are burglarizing the home of Guillaume DuPlessis (James Incandenza referred to his "family's sordid liaison" with DuPlessis on p. 30; DuPlessis's home is neo-Georgian, like the E.T.A. buildings (p. 51) designed by Avril's friend A.Y. Rickey (n. 3)), "the right hand man to probably the most infamous anti-O.N.A.N. organizer north of the Great Concavity." "Québecer Separatists and Albertan ultra-rightists [are] united only in their fanatical conviction that the U.S.A.'s Experialistic 'gift' or 'return' [as opposed to an Imperialistic acquisition] of the so-calledly 'Reconfigured' Great Convexity to its northern neighbor and O.N.A.N. ally constituted an intolerable blow to Canadian sovereignty, honor, and hygiene." The U.S.A.'s "gift" of land to Canada (re)configured a new cartographical Concavity on U.S.A. maps and a new cartographical Convexity on Canadian maps (cf. p. 1018). The environmentally ominous nature of this area is implied by the phrases "post-feral-hamster meadow" and "what's left of the Berkshires."

Gately did not think that DuPlessis was home and does not realize that DuPlessis has a cold. Although Gately is "not often inclined toward violent crime," he chooses to allow the nonviolent burglary to become a violent robbery because of his need for narcotics, binds the "rhinovirally afflicted" DuPlessis to a chair, and gags him. Gately cannot understand French and does not realize that DuPlessis's cold will not allow him to breathe while gagged. Included in the items stolen by Gately and Kite are film cartridges which Kite thinks may be of value (n. 18; n. 16 foreshadows some danger associated with these cartridges). After the robbery, DuPlessis is discovered dead. Because Gately used his signature method of killing power to houses (the same method used on the A.D.A.'s house in North Shore) and because the A.D.A. is on the lookout for Gately due to the toothbrush incident, Gately is now in the sort of "deep-shit mess that can turn a man's life right around."

PLOT AND CHARACTER: Gately, AA&R, O.N.A.N., A.F.R.
THEME: Inf/Reg, Fear/Obsess, Recur

Like an infant, Gately's head is big in proportion to his body. Gately's compulsive need for narcotics leads him to make a significant choice that will alter his life. The A.D.A.'s wife, post-burglary pictures, is obsessed with cleaning her teeth (she needs "Valium even just to floss"). Masks are worn in this section. The following phrases are associated with DuPlessis's death: "receding" thunder, his vision's "circle," and passed "bluely" from this life. DuPlessis's safe is behind a "seascape," and he has an "Impressionist landscape." References to art and artists recur throughout the novel, as does an aversion to fluorescent lighting (n. 20). DuPlessis's Frenchman-with-a-cold speech "doesn't even sound like human speech to Gately," which resonates with Hal's inability to communicate with the administrators in Ch. 1. Hal's drug use (and neo-Georgian buildings) connects this section to Ch. 7.1, and film and cartridges connect this section to Chs. 7.2 and 7.3.

Chapter 7.5, Section 19, Page 60
unspecified Y.D.A.U.

This section is a nine-line description of the features, components, capabilities, and accessories associated with a particular Y.D.A.U. model of InterLace teleputer, including "screens so high-def you might as well be there."

PLOT AND CHARACTER: Tech
THEME: Isolation, Non-Action, Inf/Reg

The "Virtual-capable media cards" and body-attachment accessories of this teleputer promote isolation of the user into a private world that requires an absolute minimum of active behavior or connection with people and events outside the self: a regression to an infantile state of feeling like all needs are met. Hal in the Pump Room and the attaché in his chair experience this kind of isolation, passivity, and self-absorption.

Chapter 7.6, Section 20, Pages 60-61
Notes 21-22, Page 985
3 November Y.D.A.U., after 0745h.

Jim Troeltsch, age seventeen, is not at "the B-squad's 0745h. drills" (Hal's A-squad drills begin at 0600h., p. 32) with his roommate Pemulis because he is sick with an illness (a "rhinovirus" like DuPlessis's, p. 56) that "came out of nowhere." He keeps "promoted" Tenuate capsules (cf. n. 5.a) in a Seldane bottle "where the Peemster would never think to check" (cf. Hal's secret drug use). He is "in bed now, supine," (cf. the attaché in his recliner) "watching digitally recorded professional tennis" alone, but is too sick to call the action (cf. Troeltsch's "sports-color-commentary loquacity," n. 5.a). He hears "ATHSCME displacement fans," the pock of tennis balls, and his vaporizer as he drifts in a feverish half-sleep state "where your mind's still working and you can ask yourself whether you're asleep even as you dream." It's the kind of sleep from which you awaken "convinced there's someone unauthorized in the dorm room with you." Troeltsch looks up at a blanket glued to the ceiling's corners that "billows, hanging, so its folds form a terrain, like with valleys and shadows."

PLOT AND CHARACTER: E.T.A.
THEME: Dreams, Recur, Secrets, Fear/Obsess, Isolation

A state of shifting between dreams and reality and water metaphors like "cast adrift on rough seas" are ideas that will recur throughout the novel, as will the ideas of nested secrets (secretly stolen Tenuate secreted in a Seldane bottle, Rader might have "pretended to pretend") and fears associated with the "squeak of . . . bedsprings," "someone unauthorized in the . . . room with you," billowing motion, and shadows. The phrases "out of nowhere" and "out of the . . . blue" will also recur. Troeltsch's "circle-stained pillow" is reminiscent of Orin's sweating in his sleep (p. 43). Troeltsch's isolating himself to pursue his addictions recalls both Hal and the attaché.

Chapter 7.7, Section 21, Pages 61-63
unspecified, flashback to April-May Y.T.-S.D.B.

The unsettling imagery of Troeltsch's fitful half-sleep and the idea of "someone unauthorized in the dorm room with you" (p. 61) in the previous section lead to a first-person description of a nightmare in this section. Although Hal recounts having April-into-May nightmares of a "face in the floor" on p. 254, perhaps the unidentified first-person narrator of this section is meant to signify the universality of nightmares at E.T.A. or to signify that more than one E.T.A. dreamer sees the face in the floor. The narrator recalls his "first nightmare away from home and folks [on his] first night at the Academy" when he was "almost twelve," which—assuming the narrator is Hal—places this event in Y.T.-S.D.B., just over one year after the "professional conversation" of Y.T.M.P. in Ch. 3 (cf. the partial chronology of years constructed in the Ch. 8.1 summary). Since Hal has been "in residence at [E.T.A.] since age seven" (p. 4), presumably Hal lived with his parents in the Headmaster's House for about four years before moving one night at age eleven into a dorm room in the Comm.-Ad. Bldg. He considered this night his "first night at the Academy" because it was his first night "away from home [the Headmaster's House] and folks," even though physically he had only moved from one Academy building to another.

The first-person narrator suggests that the "sensation of the worst nightmares, a sensation that can be felt asleep or awake," is the realization that the "essence and center [of the nightmare] has been with you all along, even awake: it's just been . . . *overlooked*." You dream that you awake from a deep sleep and "that there is a distillation of total evil in this dark strange subdorm room . . . for you alone." You search the room with your flashlight, noticing all its details, except overlooking and then realizing that you have overlooked a face of pure evil in the floor. You awake from the dream of being awake, grab your flashlight, and search the floor for the face "just as in the dream." You can't find the face, but you're "not sure all night forever unsure you're not missing something that's right there."

PLOT AND CHARACTER: Hal
THEME: Cycles, Dreams, Fear/Obsess, Recur

The narrator has a nightmare within a nightmare. After the dream, he can't stop looking for the face in the floor (cf. the attaché who can't stop looking at the cartridge), the same activity he pursued in the dream. The dreamer's fear has prompted obsessive looking. There are recurrences here of symbols, teeth (the face's "eyebrows' \ / and horrid toothy smile"), and Tawni Kondo. Another way that Hal, who has experienced face-in-the-floor dreams, is like Hamlet is that he has bad dreams: "I could be bounded in a nutshell and count myself a king of infinite space—were it not that I have bad dreams" (*Hamlet*, II.ii.254-6).

Chapter 7: Overlooked

Hal's drug use at E.T.A. goes unrecognized or overlooked by most people. Hal himself does not examine (he overlooks) the reasons he feels the way he does with respect to his use of drugs. The cartridge has cast a spell over the attaché; he can't escape looking. Coach Schtitt oversees player development with the help of Mario's footage. Realizing that "like 90% of people with wall-safes" DuPlessis has a safe behind his seascape makes Gately feel like he is "in possession of certain overlarge private facts" (like he is looking over human behavior from a higher vantage point), but Gately overlooks that DuPlessis has a cold and that he (Gately) can be identified as a burglar by his signature M.O. Teleputers and their accessories maximize a person's capacity to look at a screen. Troeltsch thinks Pemulis will overlook the Tenuate capsules in his Seldane bottle. With respect to his nightmare, the narrator of Ch. 7.7 speaks of "that horrific interval between realizing what you've overlooked and turning your head to look back at what's been right there all along."

Chapter 8

A Great Loss In At Least Three Worlds

Chapter 8.1, Section 22, Pages 63-65
Notes 23-25, Pages 985-994
As Of Y.D.A.U.

Information about Hal's family has been extracted from the text and put into outline-resume form below.

James O. Incandenza, Sr. (Hal's paternal grandfather)

- former top U.S. junior tennis player and then promising young pre-Method actor
- became a disrespected and largely unemployable actor
- driven back to his native Tucson AZ
- dipsomaniacal: experiences an insatiable, often periodic, craving for alcohol
- obsessed with/by: death by spider-bite, stage-fright, bitterness towards Method
- decided to build a promising junior athlete of his son in AZ basement workshop

Dr. James Orin Incandenza, Jr. (Hal's tall father)

- used his tennis scholarships to finance private secondary and higher education
- obtained a doctorate in optical physics, fulfilling something of a childhood dream
- top applied-geometrical-optics man for U.S. and O.N.A.N. government agencies
- designed neutron-scattering reflectors for thermo-strategic weapons systems

- developed gamma-refractive indices for lithium-anodized lenses and panels
- indices are one of the big discoveries that made possible cold annular fusion
- made a fortune on several patents after an early retirement
- patents include holographic greeting cartridges and videophonic Tableaux
- built and opened the U.S.T.A.-accredited and pedagogically experimental E.T.A.
- ceded most of E.T.A. operations to half-brother-in-law, Charles Tavis, Ed.D.
- created a body of "apres-garde" experimental- and conceptual-film work
- films are surreal, abstract, CNS-rendingly melodramatic (cf. CNS-rattler drugs, n. 8)
- gradually spiraled into the crippling dipsomania of his late father
- committed suicide at the age of fifty-four in the Year of the Trial-Size Dove Bar
- burial in Québec's L'Islet County twice delayed by annular hyperfloration cycles
- interview posthumously included in a book on the genesis of annulation

Dr. Avril Mondragon Incandenza (Hal's tall mother)

- nonviolent involvement with Québecois-Separatist Left while in graduate school
- as a result, placed on "*Personnes a Qui On Doit Surveiller Attentivement*" List (note: the name of this list was not italicized in the first edition of *Infinite Jest*)
- held Macdonald Chair in Prescriptive Usage, Royal Victoria College, McGill U.
- met Incandenza at U. Toronto conference on Reflective vs. Reflexive Systems
- even after marriage, experienced problems obtaining Visas and Green Card
- birth of first child, Orin, had been at least partly a legal maneuver

As of Y.D.A.U., E.T.A. "has been in accredited operation for three pre-Subsidized years and then eight Subsidized years," which means that Y.D.A.U. must be the eighth Subsidized year. Using this information and the completion and distribution dates from n. 24's filmography of James O. Incandenza, eight of the nine Subsidized years—and the sections which have occurred in those years so far—are identified below. The latest-referenced B.S. (Before Subsidization) year in n. 24 is 1997 (pp. 986-7), so Subsidization must begin after 1997.

1. Year of the Whopper (Y.W.)
2. Year of the Tucks Medicated Pad (Y.T.M.P.), Ch. 3
3. Year of the Trial-Size Dove Bar (Y.T.-S.D.B.), Ch. 5.2, Ch. 7.7
4. (Y.P.W.), first referenced in n. 24 on p. 987
5. (Y.W.-Q.M.D.), first referenced in n. 24 on p. 992
   Year of Dairy Products from the American Heartland (Y.D.P.A.H.), Ch. 7.4
8. Year of the Depend Adult Undergarment (Y.D.A.U.), various
9. Year of Glad (Y.G.), Ch. 1

The filmography of n. 24 is from a journal article on Anticonfluential *Apres Garde* filmmakers written by Comstock, Posner, and Duquette and published in Y.D.P.A.H. (n. 24.a; footnotes a-f to endnote 24 are associated with the "cited" filmography, whereas the endnotes to endnotes 5, 8, and 12 are associated with an *Infinite Jest* narrator). The authors provide up to nine categories of information for each of the 78 works listed in the James O. Incandenza filmography. Incandenza's works—including unfinished, unseen, and unreleased works—are listed in their "probable order of completion," but the authors state that the "order and completeness" are "not definitive" given the "archival challenges" listed below:

- there were large shifts in film venue over Incandenza's 12 years of activity
- Incandenza is identified as working in ten different film genres

- Incandenza eschewed registration and formal dating before Subsidized Time
- Incandenza often had several works in production at the same time
- Incandenza's private production company underwent at least four name changes
- some projects were titled and subjected to critique but never filmed

Jim Incandenza produced six of his earliest experimental works under the name Meniscus Films, Ltd. "Meniscus" is defined as a "concavo-convex lens" and is derived from a diminutive of the Greek word for "moon." These films include the first of the series of Cage films, the first of the series of *Infinite Jest* films (unfinished and unseen), and two documentaries, one concerning "the public Steven Pinker-Avril M. Incandenza debate on the political implications of prescriptive grammar during the infamous Militant Grammarians of Massachusetts convention." Under the name of Heliotrope Films, Ltd., Jim produced six more early documentaries on tennis, annular fusion, or annular holography. "Heliotrope" is defined as a plant that turns toward the sun and is derived from Greek words meaning "sun" and "turn." "Heliotropism" is growth or movement toward or away from the light of the sun.

Beginning with *Widower*, the first of fifteen films to feature Cosgrove Watt (thought of by Hal in Y.G., p. 16), Jim produced films under the name of Latrodectus Mactans Productions through the end of the first Subsidized Year of the Whopper (two films were also produced in the subsequent Y.T.M.P.). Latrodectus Mactans is the species name of the black widow spider (which Jim fears, cf. p. 45) and the name of a disease whose symptoms include violent cardiac pain, fearful screams of pain, gasping for breath, fear of the loss of breath and of death, and skin as cold as marble. The earliest films credited to this production company deal with pain, fear, obsession, communication problems, intense medical procedures, and romantic betrayal. More films in both the *Cage* and the *Infinite Jest* series were produced during this period. Jim also uses holography, animation, and claymation during this period. (Hal believes the inventor of holography, Dennis Gabor, may have been the Antichrist; p. 12.) Early in Y.T.M.P., Jim renamed his production company Poor Yorick Entertainment Unlimited. Poor Yorick was to Hamlet "a fellow of infinite jest" (*Hamlet*, V.i.178-9).

Many people associated with E.T.A. can be found in these film credits, including Ross Reat (in *Widower*, p. 987; cf. p. 46), Marlon Bain (first in *Death in Scarsdale*, p. 987; cf. p. 46), Brandt and Kenkle (in *Zero-Gravity Tea Ceremony*, p. 988; cf. p. 32), Leith (first in *Cage II*, p. 987; cf. p. 51), and Ogilvie (first credited for holography for *"The Medusa v. the Odalisque,"* p. 988; cf. p. 51). Coach Schtitt (cf. pp. 9, 52, 55) appears in T*he Man Who Began to Suspect He Was Made of Glass*, about which Hal may have written an essay (cf. p. 7) and which was the first film produced after the advent of Subsidized Time, an event that was accompanied by political and ecological realignment and strife. Subsequent films concern "the F.L.Q.-incited anti-O.N.A.N. riots of January/Whopper," "the inception of North American Interdependence and Continental Reconfiguration" (cf. pp. 58-9), Troy NY's "bombardment by miscalibrated Waste Displacement Vehicles [and] subsequent elimination by O.N.A.N. cartographers," the "New New England Chemical Emergency of Y.W.," and an "outsized feral infant."

Twenty-three of the 78 films are listed as "unfinished" and "UNRELEASED"—five of those 23 are also "*Untitled*"—and therefore have no production company credit. These include the eight "films" of the *Found Drama* series ("conceptual, conceptually unfilmable"; note the gaps in the numbering of the series) and the final films in the *Cage* series: *Web* and *Infinite Jim.*

Many of Jim's films are based on incidents from his life. *As of Yore* is based on the basement workshop talk (referenced in the main text of this section) given to Jim by his father. In *(At Least) Three Cheers for Cause and Effec*t, the wife of the "headmaster of a newly constructed high-altitude sports academy" has an affair with the "renowned mathematical topologist who is acting as the project's architect" played by "Hugh. G. Rection" (cf. Avril's "old and very dear friend" A.Y. Rickey, n. 3). In *It Was a Great Marvel That He Was in the*

Father Without Knowing Him, a father "suffering from the delusion" that his son is "pretending to be mute" poses as a "professional conversationalist" (cf. Ch. 3). Events in the life of at least one actress can be traced through the credits as well. In *Dial C for Concupiscence*, a woman played by Soma Richardson-Levy-O'Byrne falls in love with a Near Eastern medical attaché played by Ibn-Said Chawaf. In her next credit, the actress is listed as Soma Richardson-Levy-O'Byrne-Chawaf.

Jim used three different actresses in his *Infinite Jest* series: Hearn was replaced by Heath, who was replaced by "Madame Psychosis." The first film that definitively credits "Madame Psychosis" is *Low-Temperature Civics*, in which Cosgrove Watt's character "has an ecstatic encounter with Death ('Psychosis') and becomes irreversibly catatonic" (Heath played "Death as a lethally beautiful woman" in *Mobius Strips*). Other roles played by "Madame Psychosis" include "a beautiful cadaver," a woman whose "face is grotesquely mangled by an outboard propeller," and a "veiled nun." Although "no scholarly synopsis or report of viewing exists" for *Infinite Jest (V?)*—"Incandenza's last film"—two essays about the film have been published. One archivist lists the film as privately distributed under the provisions of Jim's will, while all others list the film as "either unfinished or UNRELEASED, its Master cartridge either destroyed or vaulted *sui testator*." The only definitive data is that it features "Madame Psychosis."

PLOT AND CHARACTER: Jim, Tech, Avril, Art/Ent
THEME: His/Father, Cycles, Recur, Fear/Obsess, Boundaries

This section features information about Hal's family, especially his father. One of Jim's technical discoveries helped make "cold annular fusion" possible ("annulation" is the act or process of forming rings, or a ringlike structure or segment). Jim's technical patents involve concepts that recur throughout the novel: mirrors, light, holography, videophonic Tableaux, maps ("homolosine-cartography [even-mapping] software"), an aversion to fluorescence, and film equipment. Jim's technical interests and his films reflect his fears and obsessions—cages, mirrors, light, tennis, annulation, holograms, spiders, marital infidelity, incommunicability, etc.—and the novel's recurring themes. Hal and other characters will have recurring nightmares about their teeth, which resonates with Jim's *Fun with Teeth*; death as the elimination of a map resonates with Jim's *No Troy* (which has a mythological resonance that will come up again); and the novel's missed-connection motif resonates in Jim's *Dial C for Concupiscence*. The title of the journal article which includes Jim's filmography features the phrase "Movement Toward Stasis," which is another of the novel's recurring concepts. Recall Hal's essays on holographically mimetic cinema and heroic stasis (p. 7). Jim's *Found Drama* series challenges the boundaries of what constitutes film.

Jim chose names associated with *Hamlet: Infinite Jest* and Poor Yorick Entertainment Unlimited. Just as the authors introduce their filmography by listing ten genres in which Jim worked, Polonius introduces the players by announcing their skill in ten genres, including "poem unlimited" (*Hamlet* II.ii.392-6). The Concavity/Convexity region, like the Polish land in *Hamlet*, is "a little patch of ground/That hath in it no profit but the name" and that is "not tomb enough and continent/To hide the slain" (IV.iv.18-9, 64-5). Jim's burial in the Concavity region was "twice delayed by annular hyperfloration cycles." Like Molly's "Met him pike hoses" in *Ulysses*, *Infinite Jest*'s Madame Psychosis is a play upon the word "metempsychosis," defined as the transmigration of souls (cf. Blamires, p. 26).

Chapter 8.2, Section 23, Pages 65-66
1 November Y.D.A.U.

Soon after the October events of Ch. 6.3, Orin is in Denver CO suffering the humiliation of one of the NFL's (presumably pregame) promotional schemes. The section begins "I hate this," which sounds like Hal's "I ate this" (p. 11). Orin is dressed as an actual cardinal with a beak, and is required to float down from the top of the stadium to the field along with other members of his team and members of the opposing team, who are dressed as broncos. Orin has not told anyone involved with the Arizona Cardinals organization about his fear of heights and high-altitude descent. Orin feels that being required to give personal interviews (cf. p. 48) is bad enough, but that this "crosses every line!" given that he is "paid to punt!" Clayt's reference to an "Oiler" may just be nostalgia, or it may imply that in *Infinite Jest*, the Houston Oilers organization did not move to Nashville to become the Tennessee Titans.

PLOT AND CHARACTER: Orin
THEME: Fear/Obsess, Boundaries, Recur

Orin must overcome his fear of heights to participate in the pre-game flying activity that he considers to cross the boundary of what is required of him. Orin's falling in a cardinal costume recalls the dead bird that fell in his Jacuzzi in Ch. 6.3. Images of beaks and claws, ludicrous here, will recur throughout the novel in images more primitive and ominous.

Chapter 8: A Great Loss In At Least Three Worlds

This chapter contrasts Jim and Orin. Jim had a multifaceted career in optics, tennis pedagogy, and experimental film, while his son Orin's NFL career requires public humiliation. Jim inherits his father's fear of spiders, but Orin is more afraid of roaches (and heights) than spiders. Jim experienced a "very gradual spiral into the crippling dipsomania of his late father"; Orin "doesn't loop or spiral like the showboats" descending to the field. Although Jim's death "was held a great loss in at least three worlds," his accomplishments are primarily technical and conceptual ("cold annular fusion," anticonfluential film), appealing to the intellect rather than to the emotions of most people. Recall the cold fact that Orin's birth "had been at least partly a legal maneuver." Orin's behavior often perpetrates losses of emotional significance in the worlds of his family and of his romantic partners.

Chapter 9

The Lines That Bound And Define Play

Chapter 9.1, Section 24, Pages 66-67
unspecified Y.D.A.U.

This unspecified section is assumed to occur in Y.D.A.U. Michael Pemulis (mentioned by Mario, p. 40; considered "reptilian" by Avril, p. 50; roommate of Troeltsch, p. 60) is leading "a pre-dinner 'Big Buddy' powwow, where the littler [E.T.A.] kids receive general big-brotherly-type support and counsel from an upperclassman." Pemulis, however, is lecturing (without notes) on the structure, properties, and "psycho-spiritual effects" of a mushroom "revered by the aboriginal tribes of what's now southern Québec and the Great Concavity" (cf. pp. 58-9) while the little kids engage in various activities either to stay alert or to amuse themselves.

PLOT AND CHARACTER: E.T.A., AA&R
THEME: Recur

A "semi-sleep-like trance with visions" is an experience that recurs throughout the novel. Recall Troeltsch's "fugue-state" on p. 61.

Chapter 9.2, Section 25, Pages 67-68
Notes 26-27, Page 994
unspecified, flashback to the year Hal turns 16

Hal (presumably) provides a first-person description of a dream (as he presumably did in Ch. 7.7) after continuing a brief discussion (begun by the narrator of Ch. 7.1) of the "gradual cycle" and "circular routine" of drug use at E.T.A. (cf. p. 53), here described as a "vicious circle." Hal, "having taken certain vows early on concerning fathers and differences, didn't even get downwind of [his] first bit of Bob Hope" until he was nearly sixteen. In n. 27, other "subdialectical argot" for marijuana is provided, including "kif," which is avoided by the attache (p. 34) but smoked by his wife (p. 54). In n. 26, Y.P.W. is identified as the Year of the Perdue Wonderchicken.

Hal's first use of marijuana, prompted by Bridget Boone, was for the purpose of sleeping through a recurring dream. Although using marijuana "worked like a charm," the dream still recurs "every now and then." In the dream, Hal prepares to play tennis but "there are lines going every which way [like] rivers and tributaries and systems inside systems . . . . The whole thing is almost too involved to try to take in all at once." His mother is in the crowd, "fist upraised and tight in total unconditional support." Although, theoretically, he plays, he cannot see his opponent across "the horizon of the distant net" on the huge court "for all the apparatus of the game."

PLOT AND CHARACTER: E.T.A., Hal, AA&R
THEME: Cycles, Dreams, Boundaries, Recur

The "vicious circle" of E.T.A. drug use is described, and the lines of the court in Hal's dream are like systems inside systems. Hal describes another of his recurring dreams, in which the "lines that bound and define play" are complex. Recurrences in this section include water imagery (rivers, tributaries); a "blue-blazered" umpire; a crowd in "tableau, motionless, and attentive"; and Avril's sitting in a small "circle" of "shadow." Orin also dreams of his mother (pp. 46-7).

Chapter 9: The Lines That Bound And Define Play

This chapter deals with complex boundaries, represented by the "lines going every which way" on the court in Hal's dream and by drug-related choices and their effects. Drawing the lines between recreational drug use and drug abuse is complex even for adults (cf. Erdedy in Ch. 2), and in this chapter those lines are being navigated by "littler kids" and their Big Buddies, by twelve-year-olds and those who are nearly sixteen. The mushroom described by Pemulis induces boundary-blurring "alterations in consciousness," which include a "semi-sleep-like trance with visions." Innocent use of marijuana to relieve bad dreams leads to secret sessions in the Pump Room for Hal (cf. Ch. 7.1).

Chapter 10

Paralyzed Stasis

Chapter 10.1, Section 26, Pages 68-78
Notes 28-30, Page 994
unspecified Y.D.A.U.

The narrator of this section specifically describes the sensory environment of a psych ward and the appearance, condition, and medical history (including one series of electro-convulsive treatments) of 21-year-old Katherine Ann Gompert of Newton MA from the perspective of a doctor (a resident) on a twelve-week psych-ward rotation. This is Gompert's "[f]ourth hospitalization in three years, all clinical depression, all unipolar." She has a history of abusing her prescribed medication, and has attempted suicide three times. The doctor maintains "a professional manner somewhere between bland and deep" and continually attempts to question and respond to his patient in a way that encourages her to continue talking about her situation. Because of the doctor's thick glasses, other patients "had sometimes complained that they sometimes felt like something in a jar he was studying intently through all that thick glass" (cf. that glass facilitates the asphyxiation of Orin's bathroom roaches, p. 45).

Discussing her most recent suicide attempt, Kate says, "I didn't want to play anymore. . . . I'd rather feel nothing than this. . . . The feeling is the *reason* I want to die." The doctor asks if she associates this feeling with her other depressions. She says that depression is a "blue kind of peaceful state" but that she has a feeling all over her body that she can't "get outside enough" to call anything. "It's like horror more than sadness. . . . It's like something horrible is about to happen, [and] there's the feeling that there's something you have to do right away to stop it but you don't know what . . . and then it's happening . . . it's about to happen and also it's happening, all at the same time. . . . I fear this feeling more than I fear anything." She compares the feeling to nausea not just of the stomach but "[a]ll through you," and "you [feel] that way all the time."

Kate's feeling of horror arises about two weeks after Kate stops smoking pot (she knows a drug dealer "with snakes in a tank in a trailer in Allston," also known by Erdedy's woman and Bruce Green; pp. 19, 39). Kate, like Hal on p. 67, refers to pot as "Bob Hope." The doctor is careful not to betray that he doesn't know what she is talking about because "[c]lassic unipolars were usually tormented by the conviction that no one else could hear or understand them when they tried to communicate" (cf. Jim's *Insubstantial Country* and *It Was a Great Marvel That He Was in the Father Without Knowing Him*, pp. 992-3). Kate explains the meaning of the term and says of pot, "But I love it so *much.* Sometimes it's like the center of my life." Her descriptions of smoking in secret and wondering if people know recall Hal in Ch. 7.1, and her description of repeatedly trying to quit recalls Erdedy in Ch. 2. A couple of weeks after she quits, though, the feeling "starts creeping in." She tries to deny it, because she fears the feeling more than anything. Soon, she's "totally inside it." She doesn't want to do anything. She doesn't "want *anything* except for the feeling to go *away*. But it doesn't. . . . It's not wanting to hurt myself it's wanting to *not hurt.*"

Although Kate is describing withdrawal from marijuana, "[n]one of the clinical literature the doctor had read for his psych rotation suggested any relation between unipolar episodes and withdrawal from cannabinoids." Kate says, "I just want you to shock me. Just get me out of this." The doctor records this on his chart and adds "*Then what?*" as Kate (like Erdedy on p. 25) begins "weeping for real."

PLOT AND CHARACTER: AA&R
THEME: Isolation, Non-Action, Loss, Fear/Obsess, Recur

This section explores the isolation and "paralyzed stasis" (non-action) of clinically depressed patients. Consider that "sarcasm and jokes were often the bottle in which clinical depressives sent out their most plangent screams for anyone to care and help them," but that "[c]lassic unipolars were usually tormented by the conviction that no one else could hear or understand them when they tried to communicate." Also, the "normal paralyzed stasis" of clinically depressed patients "allowed these patients' own minds to chew them apart." Erdedy (Ch. 2) and the medical attaché (Chs. 6.2, 7.2) were described in states of paralyzed stasis. Screams for help, fears of non-communication, paralyzed stasis, and chewing as a fearful image recur throughout the novel. Kate describes her feeling as one of "horror," and she fears this feeling more than anything. The feeling occurs not when she is using marijuana but shortly after she stops using it. Kate says, "I can't stand feeling like this another second, and the seconds keep coming on and on." The horror of stopping substance abuse, the withdrawing user's experience of time, and the withdrawing user's ambiguous expression of looking "either pained or trying somehow to suppress hilarity" also recur throughout the novel.

This section is rife with recurring images: Kate's blue jeans and dark-blue sneakers, the staffer's blue gum, Kate's description of depression as a blue state, and Kate's hair "like a cell's glossy bars." There are "cages" over the lightbulbs in Kate's room and "no locks" on the "toilet" door. Kate's room has a smell of waste and urine. Kate is "fighting for breath"; she makes a "circle" of her arms; and she is "fetal." Her mother found Kate "chewing the rug" and hallucinated her "as a newborn." Kate says when she feels as she does every sound "has teeth." Kate has "a frightening smile" and has "classic inattention to oral hygiene." Like many addicts throughout the novel, Kate weeps. Another artist (Watteau) and film (*One Flew over the Cuckoo's Nest*) are referenced, and Kate incorrectly refers to Jack Nicholson as Nichols.

Chapter 10.2, Section 27, Pages 78-79
2 April Y.D.A.U., just before 0145h.

Continuing the narrative thread of Ch. 7.2 (p. 54), the medical attaché's wife returns home to find her husband staring straight ahead and can get no response from him. Noting that "the expression on his rictus of a face nevertheless appeared very positive, ecstatic, even," the section ends with her "turning her head and following his line of sight to the cartridge-viewer."

PLOT AND CHARACTER: Samizdat
THEME: Isolation, Recur, Waste

Cutting the narrative of this short section as the attaché's wife turns her head is analogous to an ominous filmic quick-cut, an isolated moment. The attaché's wife is unable to communicate with (she is isolated from) her husband. The attaché's recliner is in a "soiled condition."

Chapter 10.3, Section 28, Pages 79-85
Notes 31-36, Page 994
unspecified Y.D.A.U.

Gerhardt Schtitt is the Head Coach and Athletic Director at E.T.A. and has been at E.T.A. for nine years. He has blue eyes, wears shiny black boots and epaulets, rides a motorcycle, and has a reputation as a strict disciplinarian; although "he's become mostly a dispenser of abstractions rather than discipline." Mario Incandenza often rides with Schtitt in the sidecar of his motorcycle on trips to acquire gourmet ice cream. The narrator says of Mario that he waves "his claw" and that "he can't even grip a stick," that he is "leptosomatic" (thin-bodied) and "brady-kinetic" (slow-moving), but that he is "the one kid at E.T.A. . . . with whom Schtitt speaks candidly." By contrast, Schtitt is formal with prorectors Aubrey deLint and Mary Ester Thode. Mario is described as "a born listener. One of the positives to being visibly damaged is that people can sometimes forget you're there, even when they're interfacing with you." In conversation with Mario, Schtitt challenges the myth that efficiency requires moving in a straight line and asks, "But what then when something is in the *way*"?

Wallace challenges the reader to question traditional fictional conventions: the efficiency of moving in a straight line (the chronology of his narrative arrangement is not linear) and the formality of spelling out rather than abbreviating words (cf. "w/r/t" in n. 31 and "w/o" on p. 81). The narrator also embraces ambiguity by stating that Charles Tavis is either Avril's "half-brother or adoptive brother, depending on the version" and breaks narrative flow mid-paragraph to tell the reader that a passage about Schtitt "should not be rendered in exposition like this, but Mario Incandenza has a severely limited range of verbatim recall."

James Incandenza recruited Schtitt because Schtitt, like Incandenza, "approached competitive tennis more like a pure mathematician" and knew that tennis was not about order but "*limit*, the places where things broke down, fragmented into beauty." The beauty and art of match-play tennis is found not in reducing chaos to pattern but in expansion: "the aleatory flutter of uncontrolled, metastatic growth" (cf. "a flutter of some sort of awful . . . growth," p. 14). Match play is a "continuum of infinities of possible move and response, . . . mathematically uncontrolled but humanly *contained*, bounded by the talent and imagination of self and opponent." This is resonant with Hamlet's "I could be bounded in a nutshell and count myself a king of infinite space—were it not that I have bad dreams" (*Hamlet*, II.ii.254-6).

Schtitt's values of "honor and discipline and fidelity to some larger unit" clash with the modern "experialist and waste-exporting" U.S.A., which is described as a "sloppy intersection of desires and fears, where the only public consensus a boy must surrender to is the acknowledged primacy of straight-line pursuing this flat and shortsighted idea of personal happiness." Schtitt describes this as "the happy pleasure of the person alone."

Schtitt believes that the boundaries of tennis are not defined by baselines but by the player himself, the opponent being more a partner in the dance than a foe. "You compete with your own limits to transcend the self in imagination and execution. . . . You seek to vanquish and transcend the limited self whose limits make the game possible in the first place. It is tragic and sad and chaotic and lovely. All life is the same, as citizens of the human State: the animating limits are within, to be killed and mourned, over and over again." Schtitt remarks that "junior athletics is but one facet of the real gem: life's endless war against the self you cannot live without." In the first section of this chapter, suicidal Kate Gompert said, "I didn't want to play anymore" (p. 72). Here, Schtitt says that the difference between tennis and suicide is "the chance to play."

PLOT AND CHARACTER: E.T.A., Mario
THEME: Cycles, Boundaries, Choice, Isolation, Recur

Schtitt regards both tennis and life as a tragic cycle of vanquishing and transcending limits. Schtitt's philosophy of tennis is based on choice, on navigating an "infinite system of decisions and angles and lines." Schtitt pushes boundaries by experimenting with choices of ice cream, while Mario plays it safe. References to dancing recur in *Infinite Jest.* Here Schtitt describes an opponent as "a partner in the dance" and does "a dance-floor dip" to catch Mario when he stumbles after bumping into a dumpster. The "short-sighted idea of personal happiness" that leads to isolation and the "happy pleasure of the person alone" (secret drug use, reclined and incontinent viewing of a mysterious cartridge, etc.) will continue to be explored. Schtitt's "mentally rewinding and replaying" his thoughts recall the recursive loop of the attaché's cartridge.

Analogous to Schtitt's tennis philosophy, Wallace's writing philosophy questions the myth of straight-line efficiency—there are chronological gaps and disparate narrative threads in this novel—and favors narrative "*limit*, the places where things [break] down [and fragment] into beauty," over the narrative order that would promote decision-free reading of a novel that required no need for "mentally rewinding and replaying" as it moved linearly toward complete resolution. For more about Georg Cantor and infinity (n. 35), cf. Wallace's book *Everything and More: A Compact History of ∞*.

Chapter 10.4, Section 29, Pages 85-87
early November Y.D.A.U.

In this section, Tiny Ewell (who really is tiny) takes an early November taxi ride through East Waterfield, "the same district he grew up in." The ride is a "straight-line easement" (cf. Schtitt in the previous section on the myth of straight-line efficiency) from St. Mel's detox to a halfway house in Enfield MA. In detox, Tiny banged at imaginary mice with his shoes and so was talked into wearing Happy Slippers "of green foam rubber with smiley-faces embossed on the tops" (cf. the "circular smiling heads" of the attaché's cartridge, p. 36). This is Tiny's first day out of Happy Slippers (and detox) in two weeks. Tiny Ewell's roommate of the last three days is still in detox. "He has been watching the air conditioner all day. His face produces the little smiles and grimaces of a person who's being thoroughly entertained" (cf. the attaché's "rictus of a face," p. 79). Tiny is taking a taxi to Unit #6 in the Marine VA Hospital Complex. When the cabbie asks if Tiny is sick, Tiny replies, "So it would seem."

PLOT AND CHARACTER: AA&R
THEME: Recur, Phys/Ob

This section includes many recurring images. Because Tiny runs around "hunched," killing imaginary "rodents," he is assigned slippers with "smiley-faces." Tiny's ex-roommate sits in a "blue" chair gazing at the "horizontal" vents of an air conditioner that "hums" and causes curtains to "billow." His profile appears in a shatterproof "mirror." Throughout the novel, an addict's physical appearance is often affected either directly or indirectly by substance abuse. Tiny's ex-roommate "has the rouged-corpse look that attends detox from late-stage alcoholism" and is "burnt-yellow beneath his flush, from chronic hepatitis." Coffee in Styrofoam cups, cigarettes, and brownies are recurring props for recovering addicts.

Chapter 10.5, Section 30, Page 87
2 April Y.D.A.U., mid-afternoon

In addition to the medical attaché and his wife (cf. Ch. 10.2), there are now six more people watching the cartridge, including two "pamphleteers" whose curiosity brought them through the unlocked door. All eight people are "still and attentive, looking not one bit distressed or in any way displeased, even though the room smelled very bad indeed."

PLOT AND CHARACTER: Samizdat
THEME: Non-Action, Waste, Cycles, Recur

Now eight people are inactive ("still and attentive") and incontinent, passively viewing the cartridge in a "recursive loop." The image of heads separate from bodies (as seen by pamphleteers here) recalls Hal in the first sentence of the novel, "surrounded by heads and bodies" (p. 3).

Chapter 10: Paralyzed Stasis

Schtitt describes the United States as promoting the "happy pleasure of the person alone": encouraging isolation and self-absorption without sacrifice to "the larger imperatives of a team" or acknowledgment of the necessity of transcending limits in a "war against the self you cannot live without." People become obsessed by their desires (substances, entertainment) and do not have the necessary discipline to wage "a war against the self" to transcend those desires. They are in state of paralyzed stasis in which both smiles of pleasure and the pain of not transcending can be seen on their faces. Kate Gompert isolates herself and becomes obsessive if she gives in to her desire for marijuana but then experiences depression and fear after quitting marijuana because she is unable to transcend her desire for it. She has "a frightening smile" and looks "either pained or trying somehow to suppress hilarity." Tiny's ex-roommate—so marred by alcoholism that he has become obsessed by an air conditioner—"produces the little smiles and grimaces of a person who's being thoroughly entertained." Although the attaché does not abuse substances, he has a strong desire for entertainment and pampered comfort. Although he sits in his own waste watching the cartridge, "his rictus of a face nevertheless appear[s] very positive, ecstatic." A dangerous quality of the "happy pleasure" environment is the ease with which people are drawn into it: many young people at E.T.A. use substances without questioning their long-term effects, and even random visitors to the attaché's apartments get caught up in the entertainment and cannot look away. They too are in a happy, paralyzed stasis, without even the discipline to remain continent.

Chapter 11

Limits And Rituals

Chapter 11.1, Section 31, Pages 87-92
Notes 37-41, Pages 994-995
30 April Y.D.A.U.

This section occurs four weeks after the previous section (in which eight people were captivated by the mysterious cartridge) and nine days before Orin's mysterious phone call to Hal (Ch. 4). As the sun sets behind the Tortolita mountains (there are three misspellings in the first edition: "Totolita" on pp. 88, 94, and 97), Rémy Marathe, a native of Québec's Papineau regions, sits in a wheelchair atop a high outcropping near Tucson AZ (in "U.S.A. area code 6026"—Tucson's current area code is 520; one of Phoenix's is 602). The setting sun causes large shadows (monster- or wraith-shadows, n. 38) of Marathe to be cast over whole counties below the outcropping. Marathe is joined by Hugh Steeply, who is employed by the United States Office of Unspecified Services (U.S.O.U.S.: in Québecois, the *Bureau des Services sans Specificite*, or B.S.S.). Steeply is dressed as (and attempts to behave as) a woman. Marathe "must release the machine pistol under his blanket to grab Steeply's bare arm" to keep Steeply from sliding off the edge of the outcropping. Steeply asks, "How in God's name did you get up here?"

Marathe is a member of *Les Assassins des Fauteuils Rollents* (the A.F.R.), "Wheelchair Assassins, pretty much Québec's most dreaded and rapacious anti-O.N.A.N. terrorist cell" (n. 39.a). Fortier is Marathe's A.F.R. superior and "the former boyhood friend of Rémy Marathe's late older brothers, both struck and killed by trains" (n. 39). Fortier believes that Marathe is pretending to betray the A.F.R. to Steeply (that he is pretending to be a "double agent" that is betraying the A.F.R. and so therefore a "triple agent," cf. n. 40) in order to secure medical care for his wife (who does indeed need care). However, Marathe is only pretending to pretend, and is actually betraying the A.F.R. to Steeply (and is therefore a "quadruple agent"), which is why meetings between Steeply and Marathe are conducted in English, even though "Steeply's Québecois was better than Marathe's English" (note the skewed syntax of the narrator for Marathe in this section).

Steeply wants to know if Marathe and the A.F.R. had anything to do with sending a "cartridge-copy" of what Steeply calls "the Entertainment" to the medical attaché. Steeply knows that the Entertainment (which caused a total of 23 people to be "lost for all time") was routed through the desert Southwest and that the A.F.R.'s "dissemination-scheme's routing mechanism is proposed for somewhere between Phoenix and the border down here." Steeply also notes that the "mischief" occurred in Boston, Marathe's "so-called Ops-area," and that the medical attaché has Canadian citizenship, "born in the hated-by-you Ottawa." Steeply adds that the attaché was "connected to a major buyer of trans-grid entertainment" and was possibly involved with the "widow of the *auteur* . . . responsible for the Entertainment," also called "the *samizdat*." Steeply notes that the "[f]ilm director's wife'd taught out at Brandeis where the victim'd done his residency" and that "the wife was fucking just about everything with a pulse. . . . Particularly a Canadian pulse" (cf. Jim to Hal on Avril's infidelity with medical attachés, p. 30). The wife is a Québecer "from L'Islet county" (where Jim is buried, cf. p. 65), and Steeply's superior is aware that she spent three years "on Ottawa's '*Personnes Qui On Doit*' list" (cf. p. 64). Marathe says, "Civilians as individual warnings to O.N.A.N. are not our desire."

Steeply's superior is "Rodney Tine, Sr., Chief of Unspecified Services, acknowledged architect of O.N.A.N. and continental Reconfiguration." He holds the ear of the White House, and his stenographer is Luria Perec (also of of L'Islet county), who "had long doubled as" the stenographer of DuPlessis, the "former asst. coordinator of the pan-Canadian resistance" (accidentally killed by Gately in Ch.

7.4). Tine's connection to Perec prompts speculation about whether his loyalties are to the U.S.A. or to Québec.

PLOT AND CHARACTER: Samizdat, U.S.O.U.S., A.F.R.
THEME: Secrets, Recur, Phys/Ob, Cycles, Boundaries

The narrative style of this section is one of tension and secrecy. In another correlation with *Hamlet*, this section initiates a narrative thread concerned with spies and secret schemes (cf. Polonius's schemes and Claudius's use of Rosencrantz and Guildenstern, for example). Because of its scope, size, structure, and chaotic nature, Infinite Jest is often compared with Thomas Pynchon's *Gravity's Rainbow* (1973), which also features a discussion of *Brockengespenstphanom* ("monster-shadow phenomenon", n. 38) in paragraphs 4-8 of its 33rd episode (the fourth episode of part 3). This 31st section of *Infinite Jest* features several references to shadows, a sign of tension or danger throughout the novel. Often danger (or understanding) happens "without warning or motive. Out of the blue," as it did for the attaché. Marathe says there are no "below-the-surface connections" between the attaché and the A.F.R. Marathe and other A.F.R. members must overcome physical obstacles to perform their jobs successfully. Marathe and Steeply (and perhaps Tine and Perec) are involved in a cycle of nested secrets and blurred loyalties (boundaries). Steeply pretends to be a woman, and Marathe pretends to sniff (as Kate Gompert does, cf. p. 76). Marathe and Steeply must work through communication barriers with respect to language, politics, and trust. The connection between Phoenix-Tucson and Boston is highlighted again through Marathe and the A.F.R. What is the A.F.R.'s dissemination-scheme?

Chapter 11.2, Section 32, Page 93
unspecified

A "herd of feral hamsters" is moving across "the southern reaches of the Great Concavity in what used to be Vermont." To the east are "the annularly overfertilized forests of what used to be central Maine." After "the Experialist migration in the subsidized Year of the Whopper," these territories became "property of Canada." Since an environmental problem serious enough to create feral hamsters and "uremic-hued" clouds in the area of the Great Concavity has occurred, it makes sense that Canadian extremist factions would not be pleased with the U.S.A.'s "gift" of this territory to Canada (cf. pp. 58-9). Rome NNY (New New York), Glens Falls NNY, and Beverly MA are cited as "border" metropolises. At "bordered points" between these cities, ATHSCME fans atop "hugely convex protective walls" blow "drooling and piss-colored" Concavity clouds back into Canadian territory.

PLOT AND CHARACTER: O.N.A.N.
THEME: Waste, Boundaries, Recur

The Great Concavity is a wasteland (cf. "piss-colored" clouds), the boundaries of which are carefully delineated and must be actively contained. Old TV shows and characters, like Ward and June from *Leave It to Beaver* here, will be referenced throughout the novel. Wallace's first novel, *The Broom of the System*, is also concerned with boundaries and hygiene, and features occasional references to old TV shows and a wasteland called the Great Ohio Desert.

Chapter 11.3, Section 33, Pages 93-95
Note 42, Page 995
30 April Y.D.A.U.

The meeting between Marathe and Steeply continues from Ch. 11.1. Marathe still has a firm grip on the pistol beneath his blanket. Steeply, compelled by "obsessive caution," questions Marathe about the details of the report Marathe will give to Fortier. Marathe questions the suspicious circumstances of DuPlessis's death (but the "inept burglary and grippe" are consistent with Ch. 7.4). Steeply asserts that DuPlessis always suspected Tine "tried to hold back on the information he passed sexually to Luria." Marathe says that if "Tine's betrayal were incomplete" "Luria would be aware," because of Tine's "caution." The "desert U.S.A.'s light had become now sad";

and as dusk settles, Steeply examines a scratch on his arm, "his rouged lips rounded with concern."

PLOT AND CHARACTER: U.S.O.U.S., A.F.R.
THEME: Fear/Obsess, Secrets, Recur

Steeply fears betrayal and is obsessed with caution and secrecy. It makes sense that people who spy for a living would have these character traits. The narrative focus on changes in light and shadow helps build the tension of the scene.

Chapter 11.4, Section 34, Pages 95-97
3 November Y.D.A.U., 1640h.

This section—which occurs six months after the meeting between Marathe and Steeply—begins by listing the typical daily events scheduled for E.T.A. students. After playing challenge matches and working in the weight room, several students are in the Comm.-Ad. Bldg.'s males' locker room at 1640h. Troeltsch, who was not at A.M. drills because he was sick (Ch. 7.6), is asking whether people realize they feel—or even if they feel—unhappiness. It turns out Troeltsch is asking about an exam question which Hal says was "about the syntax of Tolstoy's sentence, not about real unhappy families." General locker room behavior is exhibited. John Wayne, a Canadian, farts; Ted Schacht makes "ghastly sounds" in one of the stalls; and Pemulis sends a loogie into the sink. Everyone is "stunned with fatigue," although Ortho Stice and John Wayne seem "less fatigued than detached . . . , removed, for a moment, from the connectedness of all events."

Troeltsch asks about the difference "between your historical broadcast TV set and a cartridge-capable TP" to prepare for a test which will be given the next day by Disney Leith, who worked with Jim (cf. n. 24) and whose courses include "certain high-level esoteric Optics things you needed Permission of Inst. to get into." The ensuing conversation concerns "advances in home communications." Troeltsch next asks for a definition, which Hal immediately recites, prompting both awed and sarcastic responses from the other guys. As the section ends, Hal sits on the floor, "thinking it's nice finally to breathe and get enough air."

PLOT AND CHARACTER: E.T.A., Hal, Tech
THEME: Waste, Recur

This section occurs in a room where waste is made and documents Wayne's fart and Schacht's "ghastly sounds." Recurrences in this section include references to breathing problems, circles, light, and nicknames. Hal apparently had trouble breathing earlier. In Ch. 10.1, Kate Gompert, who also uses marijuana, "seemed both to be fighting for breath and to be breathing rapidly" (p. 69). "Halation," a "halo-shaped exposure pattern around light sources seen on chemical film at low speed," is used as a nickname for Hal in this section.

Chapter 11.5, Section 35, Page 97
30 April Y.D.A.U.

This section returns briefly to the meeting in Arizona (continuing from Ch. 11.3), where the temperature has fallen, Steeply still examines his scratch, the last "digitate spikes of the radial blades of the sun" are seen, and there are "rustlings of small living things that wish to come out at night, emerging. The sky was violet."

PLOT AND CHARACTER: U.S.O.U.S., A.F.R.
THEME: Boundaries

This section highlights the shift from day to night (the crossing of a boundary), and the section's brevity holds that shift in stasis, like a photograph, although the change itself is more like a moving picture. The sky, in transition from daytime blue to nighttime black, moves through violet. The blurred boundary of the switch from day to night is occurring in the chapter's other main thread at E.T.A six months later, highlighting "the connectedness of all events" (p. 96) across the boundaries of geography and time. In the locker room, the day's activities are complete, but nighttime activities have not yet begun. Also, the discussion of "Analogs v. digitals" in the previous section (p. 96) resonates with the "digitate spikes" of the sun.

Chapter 11.6, Section 36, Pages 97-105
Note 43, Page 995
3 November Y.D.A.U.

Continuing from Ch. 11.4, some of the younger E.T.A. kids have joined the others in the locker-room. Each E.T.A. player in the 18-and-Unders category has four to six 14-and-Unders to look out for. "Charles Tavis instituted the practice and calls it the Big Buddy System" (cf. Ch. 9.1). Big Buddies are scheduled to meet with their charges "twice a week, in the interval between P.M. challenge matches and dinner." Big Buddies must balance keeping prorectors informed of kids that "can't hang" and remaining trustworthy to their charges. One of Trevor Axford's charges, Evan Ingersoll, is now under Hal's care (and one of Hal's charges, Possalthwaite, is under Axford's care), due to Axford's struggling against a compulsion to be cruel to Ingersoll (although Hal struggles with a similar compulsion). Hal enjoys meeting with his charges, unless he's had a bad afternoon session on the courts and would rather go off by himself "in underground ventilated private" (cf. Ch. 7.1). On most days that he doesn't travel or meet with his charges, he does go off by himself and "carries Visine AC, mint-flavored floss, and a traveller's toothbrush in a pocket of his Dunlop gear bag" for this purpose.

Information about several individual E.T.A. students is provided throughout this section. Hal looks "ethnic" (he has "a great-grandmother with Pima-tribe Indian S.W. blood," and his late father had "high flat Pima-tribe cheekbones") and requires no sunscreen, whereas players who can tolerate using Lemon Pledge use it as a sweat-resistant sunscreen to avoid the uneven tanning associated with frequent match play. All but three of the junior players in the room are ranked in the top 64 continentally. Pemulis is one who is not in the top 64. The players express their fatigue in hyperbolic fashion and look forward to reduced schedules on Saturday ("Interdependence Day Eve," four days from now) and Sunday (on which day a "Gala" will be held). Ortho Stice speaks of being "skeletally stressed," and Hal's ankle is "faintly swollen" (cf. "The bad ankle hasn't ached once this whole year," p. 16). Players are "rhythmically squeezing tennis balls with their racquet-hands, as per Academy mandate" (Orin still does this, cf. p. 44).

"And time in the P.M. locker room seems of limitless depth; they've all been just here before, just like this, and will be again to-morrow. The light saddening outside, a grief felt in the bones, a sharpness to the edge of the lengthening shadows" (cf. the sad desert light and the shadows of Marathe and Steeply, p. 94). Aware of Schacht's feet under a stall door, Hal considers the "hunched timeless millennial type of waiting, almost religious" exemplified by the "defe-catory posture" (cf. p. 9) and imagines the "mute quiescent suffering of generations" of people in that posture, going back to "shaggy-browed men in skins hunched just past the firelight's circle." The sec-tion ends with "the roar of a high pressure toilet" (cf. "the leonine roar of a public toilet," p. 15).

PLOT AND CHARACTER: E.T.A.

THEME: Cycles, Waste, Recur

The commonality and cyclical nature of human experience is represented here by daily occurrences of a sad twilight and by the uni-versality of the "defecatory posture." For more on "mute quiescent suf-fering" and the "defecatory posture," cf. Wallace's "The Suffering Channel," from his story collection *Oblivion.* In addition to the "hunched" posture, the firelight's "circle," and the "toilet" roar; there are recurrences of mirrors (p. 104), blue crush carpet, blue steel lockers, the lighter-blue eyes of Avril and Orin, and the blue tinge of Hal's swollen ankle. The "French-painting tits that sort of like *tumble* out" recall Steeply's "ridiculous tits" (p. 92). Pemulis's line to Struck, "Look. . . . It's trying to think," was also used by Miguel Ferrar's character to insult Michael Ontkean's character in the first season of *Twin Peaks*, a television series created by Mark Frost and David Lynch, which also featured a government agent in drag in its second season. Lynch is an avant-garde filmmaker (cf. Jim's apres-garde films, n. 24) about whom Wallace wrote in "David Lynch Keeps His Head," from his essay collection *A Supposedly Fun Thing I'll Never Do Again.*

Many of the ideas found in *Infinite Jest* resonate with ideas found in Don DeLillo's *White Noise* (1985) and William Gaddis's *The Recognitions* (1955). Early in Ch. 12 of *White Noise*, DeLillo writes of "the connectedness of events" and of a feeling in the bones at dusk: "It was the time of year, the time of day, for a small insistent sadness to pass into the texture of things. Dusk, silence, iron chill. Something lonely in the bones." *The Recognitions* describes "this transition from day to night: a grotesque time of loneliness" (Gaddis, p. 265).

Chapter 11.7, Section 37, Pages 105-109
Notes 44-45, Page 995
30 April Y.D.A.U.

Continuing from Ch. 11.5, Marathe and Steeply are now in a "dusk-shadow." Steeply ponders whether Rod Tine and Luria Perec have a timeless, immortal love. This leads to a discussion of Paris and Helen and the "horse: the gift that was not a gift. The anonymous gift brought to the door. The sack of Troy from inside" (cf. other gifts that were not gifts: the Entertainment to the attaché and the wasteland to Canada). Marathe states that the "love" of Paris and Helen was an excuse for a war that was really about the Greeks wanting to take over sea trade routes from Troy and that wars are started over political and not romantic concerns. Steeply says that those close to Tine say he would sacrifice O.N.A.N. and "die twice" for Luria and that this has a "tragic element that transcends the political." Marathe says that it is only tragic if Tine "were not responsible for choosing it, as the insane are not responsible" and that Tine's love for Luria is fanatic (meaning "worshipper at the temple"), an "attachment not carefully chosen."

Marathe says that to die for one person who could either betray you or die is crazy and that "[y]our nation outlives you. A cause outlives you." This prompts Steeply to ask about Marathe's wife (for whom Marathe has decided to betray his country). Marathe knows of Steeply's "recent divorce" and of his "fanatically beloved car," a "green sedan subsidized by a painful ad for aspirin upon its side." He asks Steeply, "Who teaches your U.S.A. children how to choose their temple? What to love enough not to think two times? . . . All other . . . *free* choices follow from this: what is our temple. What is the temple, thus, for U.S.A.'s? What is it, when you fear that you must protect them from themselves, if wicked Québecers conspire to bring the Entertainment into their warm homes?" (cf. the "dissemination scheme," p. 90). Steeply counters, "What if sometimes there is no choice about what to love? . . . What if you just *love*? without deciding?" Marathe: "Then in such a case your temple is self and sentiment. . . . [Y]ou are a fanatic of desire, . . . a citizen of nothing." Marathe says this is sentimental rather than tragic, but he later uses the phrase "tragically, unvoluntarily, lost."

Marathe thinks of "his victory over the train that had taken his legs" (Recall that both Marathe's older brothers were "struck and killed by trains," n. 39. Both n. 39.a and n. 45 refer to n. 304, assuring the reader that more will be said about these trains.) and of the "remote embryonic disseminatory Ops base down here in Southwest U.S.A. [which] seemed to him like the surface of the moon."

PLOT AND CHARACTER: Samizdat, U.S.O.U.S., A.F.R.
THEME: Choice, Boundaries, Recur

This section initiates a major theme of the novel: the significance of making a voluntary choice rather than following an involuntary compulsion. When does recreational drug use, like that of the E.T.A. students or Erdedy or Gompert, become addiction? This boundary is often blurred. Mythological references and references to the moon occur here and throughout the novel. Black Widow spider webs recall Jim's (and his father's) fear of spiders. Steeply's bra has cut into his flesh, analogous to the "abdominal stripe" left by Stice's jock (p. 96, cf. "the connectedness of all events" on the same page). Steeply also farts, like Wayne on p. 95.

Chapter 11.8, Section 38, Pages 109-121
Note 46, Page 995
3 November Y.D.A.U.

Since the events of Ch. 11.6, E.T.A. students have moved from the locker room to the various locations of seven Big Buddy sessions. Hal is in Viewing Room 6 (V.R.6) with Arslanian, Beak, Blott, and Ingersoll. As background for Hal's meeting, motivational images of tennis strokes play in a hypnotizing loop on a viewer that is "huge and almost painfully high-definition; it hangs flat on the north wall like a large painting; it runs off a refrigerated chip." Hal's charges lie "limp and splayed, supine, jaws slack, eyes wide and dim, a relaxed exhausted warmth." In considering why students endure the grueling E.T.A. lifestyle, the kids suggest the rewards of the Show (the professional tennis tour) or of college scholarships; but Hal counters that only one junior in twenty makes the Show and hardly anyone at E.T.A. needs a scholarship. The kids infer that Hal means the students endure it for love of the game. Hal says, "They sure must love something" (cf. Marathe and Steeply on love in the previous section).

Hal says that the ritual of bitching and moaning at E.T.A. is a planned and expected part of the curriculum. The academy pits each student against the other students in competition for specific spots in a hierarchy. Hal says, "We're all on each other's food chain. . . . Welcome to the meaning of *individual.* We're each deeply alone here. It's what we all have in common, this aloneness." Complaining in the locker rooms and elsewhere engenders a sense of community to fight loneliness and to unite players against teachers and coaches. "This is their gift to us" (cf. "the gift that was not a gift" in the previous section). "Nothing brings you together like a common enemy." Coaches inspire more unity (more community bitching) by getting even stricter before important competitions, like the upcoming "Port Washington meet. I[nter]. D[ependence]. Day. The Tucson WhataBurger the week after" (actually Thanksgiving weekend, so almost three weeks after). "It'll help your attitude to look for evidence of design. . . . You guys ever see evidence of the tiniest lack of coolly calculated structure around here?" (Hal references Lyle on p. 114, of whom more will be said in Ch. 12.1.)

Hal reflects upon the physical effects his body experiences in relation to getting or not getting high on a regular basis, like needing to spit now because he hasn't gotten high. His use of smokeless tobacco "started almost as an excuse to spit, sometimes." Hal wonders again "why he gets off on the secrecy of getting high in secret more than the getting high itself, possibly. He always gets the feeling there's some clue to it on the tip of his tongue."

In V.R.5, as John Wayne stretches, Lamont Chu speaks to Wayne's other charges—McKenna, Peterson, and van Vleck—about reaching higher plateaus (Canadian Wayne insists on the plural "plateaux") of achievement through "frustrating mindless repetitive practice and patience and hanging in there." Chu identifies the types who "don't hang in there" as Despairing, Obsessive, and Complacent. In V.R.2, Pemulis is card-sharping students, two of whom are Lord and Possalthwaite (who should be with Axford given Hal's trade of Possalthwaite to Axford for Ingersoll, cf. p. 98). In V.R.3, Schacht is lecturing his charges on oral hygiene using large visual aids. Troeltsch, still sick and holding his meeting in his room in Subdorm C (but cf. his room in Subdormitory B, p. 60), assures his charges that, until they are somewhere between thirteen and fifteen, their time at the academy is about "sheer mindless repeated motions. The machine-language of the muscles. Until you can do it without thinking about it, play." This frees up a "whole shitload of head-space you don't need for the mechanics anymore . . . . Until then you might as well be machines . . . going through the motions." In V.R.8, Struck, a prized tactician, holds a Q&A in which on- and off-court responses to an opponent's unethical behavior and the pros and cons of on-court farting are discussed with Gopnik, Tallat-Kelpsa, Traub, and Whale. Stice, in the "foyer off the front door to Subdorm C," is reiterating to Wagenknecht and his other charges Schtitt's philosophy of tennis: "It's about discipline and sacrifice and honor to something way bigger than your personal ass. . . . He'll say it's how to learn to be a good American during a time, boys, when America isn't good its own self."

The narrative moves back to Struck, who advises that those who "want to hang for the long haul" should hold their farts on-court; then to Schacht, still lecturing on oral hygiene; then to Pemulis, who is suggesting double or nothing; and finally to Hal, who considers going down to the tunnels before the "communal dinner" prepared by E.T.A.'s cook, Mrs. Clarke. Thinking about limits and rituals, he wonders whether there is "a quantifiable difference between need and just strong desire." Sitting up to spit, he experiences "a twinge in a tooth on his mouth's left side."

PLOT AND CHARACTER: E.T.A., Hal
THEME: Cycles, Boundaries, Choice, Isolation, Recur

E.T.A. philosophies concerning rituals and limits are the subject of many of the Big Buddy meetings in this section. Repetition is essential to achieving success as a player. In Hal's meeting, the video loop features Stan Smith hitting strokes "over and over again." Chu (for Wayne) says that to achieve higher plateaux (to transcend limits, to cross boundaries) requires "mindless repetitive practice." Troeltsch advises making strokes "over and over and over again." Stice tells his kids that they will hear Schtitt profess his philosophy of "discipline and sacrifice and honor" (being willing—choosing—to give) "over and over." Hal tells his kids that the ritual of bitching and moaning is purposeful and necessary to stave off isolation by creating a common enemy, to unify players who—pitted against one another—are all "deeply alone here. It's what we all have in common, this aloneness." In response to this, Ingersoll muses, "*E Unibus Pluram.*" Insight into Wallace's fiction-writing philosophy can be gleaned from "E Unibus Pluram: Television and U.S. Fiction," from his essay collection *A Supposedly Fun Thing I'll Never Do Again.*

The monotony of the E.T.A. routine is draining and hypnotic: cf. "unhappiness every day and day after day of tiredness and stress and suffering"; the state of Hal's kids—"limp and splayed, supine, jaws slack, eyes wide and dim"; and the "hypnotizing" loop of strokes on the viewer with "gauzy and dreamlike" (boundary blurring) transitions. Troeltsch advises "mindless repeated motions" ("machines . . . going through the motions") until "you can do it without thinking about it," until "the mechanics are wired in," freeing up "head-space" which will then allow you to think "a whole different way now, playing. The court might as well be inside you." Then "chinks in the mental armor" start to matter. Hal says, "The physical stuff's just pro forma. It's the heads they're working on here, boys. Day and year in and out."

There are recurrences in that Stan Smith is "hunched" and that Stice will play "hunched" to keep from farting (another example of the novel's ever-present concern with waste). There is another reference to Mr. Bouncety Bounce. Peter Beak has a dream in which his "eyes roll up"; a new image that will recur, as will the ideas of the "common enemy" and of a memory being "on the tip of [the] tongue." Schacht is obsessed with oral hygiene, and Hal has a twinge in a tooth. Tallet-Kelpsa is blue-eyed. Stice's charges sit in a circle.

Struck uses the phrase "me droogies" (p. 118), which like "horror-show" (p. 46) is from Burgess's novel *A Clockwork Orange* (and Kubrick's film; cf. Wallace's novel and the fictional Incandenza's film, *Infinite Jest*). Burgess invented a unique speaking style for the characters (droogies; i.e., buddies) in his novel. Immediately after "me droogies" appears in this section of *Infinite Jest*, Wallace invents the unique word "kertwanging."

Chapter 11.9, Section 39, Pages 121-126
mid-October Y.D.A.U.

The heading for this section goes beyond the standard identification of day, month, and year to announce "MARIO INCANDENZA'S FIRST AND ONLY EVEN REMOTELY ROMANTIC EXPERIENCE, THUS FAR." A few weeks before the Big Buddy sessions of the previous section, strolling through thickets of trees and bushes on the E.T.A. grounds, Hal left Mario to "go off by himself briefly" as "a certain kind of melancholy sadness was insinuating itself into the grounds' light," which becomes violet. (Recall the sad desert light and violet sky of 30 April on pp. 94 and 97, and the saddening light outside of 3 November on p. 104.) An "Empire Waste Displacement displacement vehicle whistle[s] past overhead."

Mario is approached by the U.S.S. Millicent Kent, who he has filmed "for staff-analysis on several occasions" (cf. Ch. 7.3). Kent, "#1 Singles on the Girls 16's-A squad and two hundred kilos if she was a kilo," informs Mario that she has seen a telescoping tripod set up in the middle of the thicket "for no visible reason" and with no footprints leading to it. Mario asks technical questions about the tripod as Kent flirts with him and confides to him intimate details (cf. Mario's affinity for "diary-type private reveries indulged out loud," p. 80) of her childhood: her passion for modern dance and the antics of her cross-dressing father. Twice during this exchange, Mario hears crackling sounds that he is sure are not being made by Hal.

Eventually, Kent transitions from flirting with to making a serious move on Mario that is complicated by his "vest with extendable police lock he used for staying upright in one place," which overlaps his trousers. Hearing ticklish Mario's high-pitched laughter, Hal finds the duo and begins walking back with them. On the way, they stumble across the tripod, the finding of which Mario relates to a word on the tip of your tongue (cf. Hal on p. 114) that pops into your head when you stop trying to remember it.

PLOT AND CHARACTER: E.T.A., Hal, Mario
THEME: Recur, Phys/Ob

Kent's intentions are not understood by Mario (a recurrence of the missed-connection motif), and the police lock that assists Mario with his physical obstacles is an obstacle to Kent's intentions. Note that the tripod is an obstacle stumbled upon when taking "the most direct route" (cf. Schtitt on straight-line efficiency, p. 80). The cross-dressing of Kent's father recalls Steeply; his diaper-wearing (p. 125) recalls Mr. Bouncety-Bounce (cf. p. 648). There are recurrences of the related concepts of "a word on the tip of your tongue" and "out of the blue"; the displacement vehicle has a "blue alert-light"; there are two bird references (omens?); Kent leads Mario in "slightly diminishing circles"; Kent had a passion for modern dance; Kent's father looks in a mirror; and another artist (Titian) is referenced.

This section, like Ch. 10.3 with Mario and Schtitt, makes use of a meta-narrative interjection. Note the reference to "chill dusk" (p.

122), followed eight lines later by the statement that Mario "hadn't literally said 'chill dusk.'" Also, Kent "referred to her father as her Old Man, which you can just tell she capitalizes." Compare the narrator's attention to punctuation with Wayne's attention to the pronunciation and spelling of "plateaux" on p. 115. The use of a centered heading to enhance the narrative recalls the "Aeolus" chapter of *Ulysses*. Centered headings, which recede in Ch. 12 of *Infinite Jest*, will bulge in Ch. 13.

Chapter 11.10, Section 40, Pages 126-127
Notes 47-48, Page 995
30 April Y.D.A.U.

Continuing from Ch. 11.7, Steeply suggests that the A.F.R. chose Boston as an Ops center because it is "the place of the supposed Entertainment's origin." Marathe, whose "wheelchair squeaked very slightly whenever he moved," suggests the alternate logic of having an Ops center in Boston because it is the closest U.S.A. city to the Convexity and therefore closest to Québec. *Le Front de la Liberation de la Québec* (the F.L.Q.), another anti-O.N.A.N. group, has adopted "certain cultural customs, musics and motifs associated with Hawaii" to suggest Québec's post-Reconfiguration affinity with Hawaii, an "annex or territory of the U.S. . . . separated from its real captor-nation" by unbridgeable differences (n. 47). Steeply wonders if "they [presumably the F.L.Q.] actually do have copies" of the Entertainment and whether there was an "anti-Entertainment . . . made to counter the lethality." Steeply suggests that "this really could be some sort of game for you and the F.L.Q., to hold out the promise of the anti-Entertainment as a chip for concessions." Marathe implies that the "anti-film" is a crazy rumor.

"Marathe's wife was dying slowly of ventricular restenosis," a "narrowing of one of more cardiac sinuses . . . rare before continental Interdependence" and now a leading cause of death on both sides of the Concavity (n. 48). Marathe asks Steeply why he is always disguised when he is sent into the field, and the narrator for Marathe observes that "U.S.A. persons' shrugs are always as if trying to lift a heavy thing." Marathe's superiors, Fortier (to whom this meeting with Steeply will be meticulously reported) and Broullîme, believed him to have perfect recall; but "Marathe, who could remember several incidents of crucial observations he had failed later to recall, knew this was not true." (Marathe observed, then forgot to report some observations, then remembered that he forgot.)

PLOT AND CHARACTER: Samizdat, U.S.O.U.S., A.F.R.
THEME: Secrets, Memory, Recur

Steeply, in disguise, seeks to uncover secrets from Marathe, who hides a gun and whose loyalties, like his memory, are susceptible to fluctuation. The squeak of an A.F.R. wheelchair and "trying to lift a heavy thing" will recur.

Chapter 11.11, Section 41, Page 127
30 April Y.D.A.U.

Continuing from the previous section, this section of only two lines notes that several times "Marathe called U.S.A. to Steeply 'Your walled nation' or 'Your murated nation.'"

PLOT AND CHARACTER: U.S.O.U.S., A.F.R.
THEME: Memory, Boundaries

This section seems like an afterthought, but may signify, given the end of the previous section, observations forgotten by Marathe in his report to Fortier but then later remembered. The boundaries of memory fluctuate and are not always reliable. Marathe suggests that the U.S.A. is a nation of walls, of boundaries (cf. the "protective walls" near the Concavity, p. 93).

Chapter 11: Limits And Rituals

Marathe, who like Mario has physical limitations, regularly (ritually) meets with Steeply, who always (ritually) disguises himself in the field. Steeply practices ritual feminine behaviors, and Kent's father practiced private cross-dressing rituals. In the spy game, ritual caution is the result of limited trust. Marathe, whose memory is limited, refers to the U.S.A. as a walled nation (a nation that enforces limits), which seems appropriate in the case of the protective walls with ATHSCME fans on top, which mark the boundaries of the Concavity and limit the path of Concavity clouds. E.T.A. students participate in daily locker room rituals and regular Big Buddy sessions in which the benefits of ritual bitching and moaning and repetitive practice (rituals) are explained. E.T.A. students are encouraged to transcend their limits as players in order to reach higher plateaus of achievement. A sad light accompanies the ritual change from day to night. Human experience across time features many recurring rituals and ideas that range from defecatory postures to mythologies of timeless love. Kent seeks to initiate Mario into a rite of passion. Marathe, who equates love with attachment and warns of choosing attachments carefully, espouses a philosophy that maximally limits self-indulgent choices.

Chapter 12

A Weight Greater Than Their Own Weight

Chapter 12.1, Section 42, Pages 127-128
unspecified Y.D.A.U.

This section, assumed to occur in Y.D.A.U., features an unknown first-person narrator (if Hal were narrating, he probably would refer to his father as Himself rather than as "Dr. Incandenza") and serves as an introduction to Lyle (who was referenced by Hal on p. 114), an "oiled guru" who sits "in full lotus on top of the towel dispenser . . . about a meter off the rubberized floor of the weight room" at E.T.A. Some E.T.A. players allow Lyle to lick (with a tongue "like a kitty's") the sweat off their arms and forehead in exchange for nuggets of wisdom like "Let not the weight thou wouldst pull to thyself exceed thine own weight." The narrator says, "Everything he sees hits him and sinks without bubbles. He just sits there. I want to be like that. Able to just sit all quiet and pull life toward me, one forehead at a time. His name is supposedly Lyle."

PLOT AND CHARACTER: E.T.A.
THEME: Recur

Lyle, in the weight room, promotes the avoidance of "a weight greater than [your] own weight" (something you can't control), which could serve as metaphorical advice against the use of substances (cf. also Steeply's shrug "as if trying to lift a heavy thing," p. 127). There are recurrent images in that Lyle "smiles," that he's "like a baby," and that he "just sits there" "all quiet" (cf. Hal, "I simply lie there, listening," p. 15). There is more water imagery in that everything Lyle sees "hits him and sinks without bubbles."

Chapter 12.2, Section 43, Pages 128-135
24 December Y.D.P.A.H.

This section is narrated in first person by "yrstruly," whose narration features colloquial slang, slurs, misspelled words, and the misplacement of apostrophes. However, words are usually misspelled in ways that are phonetically resonant with the correct spellings: "on-nings" for awnings, for example. Months after Gately accidentally kills DuPlessis (Ch. 7.4), yrstruly and C and Poor Tony are spending Christmas Eve Y.D.P.A.H. (confirmation of this year will occur later in the novel) attempting to obtain two days' worth of drugs so that they can make it through Christmas Day, traditionally a hard day on which to obtain drugs. They begin by crewing on—beating up (as a minimum) and robbing someone in order to obtain the means by which to purchase drugs for those (the crew) doing the beating and robbing—an older homosexual of Poor Tony's "old acquaintance from like the Cape." Although C would like to "elemonade the Patty's map for keeps," he settles for breaking his jaw and cutting off his ear, which is thrown into a dumpster. The crew then "go back to the Brighton Projects" and "cop half a bundle from Roy Tony" (a menace to Clenette and Wardine, pp. 37-8) and "go down to the library at Copley"—where they normally stash their drugs—and get high in the bathroom.

Back at Harvard Square, Poor Tony decides to "hang for lunch time with his red leather fags"; so yrstruly and C go to Central Square instead, steal and get "messed up on" NyQuil, rob a "foran slope studn type kid," and talk with "Eckwus" and Purpleboy, who warn them that Stokely Darkstar (McNair, who was in Jim's *Accomplice!*; cf. n. 24, p. 992) has "the Virus" and doesn't care who might contract "the Virus thru trancemission" as a result of sharing needles with him. Yrstruly and C then go back to Harvard Square and locate Poor Tony. Lolasister and Susan T. Cheese accompany the crew to the Bow&Arrow, where they wait for a "foran studn stuck here for Xmas" to leave alone in order that they may "crew" and "cop before 2200." They note that an inebriated older man is leaving alone and ask Lolasister and Susan T. Cheese to leave (Lolasister is opposed to bloodshed, or "wet work," which is guaranteed if C is crewing). Poor Tony, who wears a "feather snake around his neck," coaxes the older man into an alley, and then yrstruly and C "crew on the individual and roll him" for "400 $" and more. C leaves the man "in no condition to eat cheese" (rat on the crew, cf. p. 202). C would like to set the man on fire, but doesn't.

By the time the crew reaches the Brighton Projects, Roy Tony is "not open for comerce." Poor Tony's suggestion to try to cop from Delphina is denied on grounds of finding more quality dope, especially given that they now have a good amount of money. C suggests copping from Dr. Wo in Chinatown, who has "excellent skeet." Poor Tony says they have enough money to "stay straight . . . for Xmas" if they don't blow it in Chinatown tonight, but C is determined to go. On the way to Chinatown, yrstruly and C almost rape a nurse, and Poor Tony tells the others that he was involved in a situation in which Dr. Wo was "burnt" and would like to stay low profile in Chinatown and not see Wo. But "C is Wos' former acquaintance from crewing with slopes on the North shore for Whitey Sorkin in the days of his youth. C is not 2Bdenied." As Poor Tony waits nearby, yrstruly and C go into Hung Toys, Wo's place of business. Wo takes a "longer than avrege time" to prepare three bundles in the back behind a curtain. Yrstruly wonders whether Poor Tony has been seen outside and secretly reported by an employee of Wo's. Wo comes out and sits down with them, something he never does, and asks whether they have seen Poor Tony and Susan T. Cheese. C says that they "fucked up [Poor Tony's] map and Cheese and Lolasisters' map in a beef and didn't crew with fags" anymore, which Wo says is excellent. Wo says that if they see Poor Tony to wish him prosperity and "a thousand *blisses*." Outside, yrstruly and C find Poor Tony down the street "tryng to be low profile in his red coat and heels" and feather boa, while surrounded by "subservants of Wo."

Back at the library behind Copley Square, as C and yrstruly cook up the first bundle, yrstruly notices unusual behavior from Poor Tony: he's neither whining nor looking at the "skeet." Yrstruly gets a bad feeling about this and lets C shoot up first. It turns out that the drugs were laced, probably with Drano given the effects of C's horrific, violent death, which ends with C shitting his pants. Poor Tony had put his boa in C's mouth to stifle C's screams. When Poor Tony asks yrstruly to help him into the dumpster in which C has been thrown for the purpose of retrieving his boa, yrstruly decides to go back to Wo and eat cheese (trade information about Poor Tony) for more drugs, since all three bundles were laced and therefore unusable. But Wo was not at Hung Toys the next morning; Poor Tony "departed for green pastures and ate cheese"; and yrstruly spent two days "Kicking the Bird" (experiencing painful withdrawal) in the hall outside his mother's apartment (she had locked him out) before he could "start to thearize" on what to do next.

PLOT AND CHARACTER: AA&R
THEME: Phys/Ob, Recur, Waste

An addict's desperate physical need for substances drives the addict to face obstacles and risk danger: "Like C said any thing would count in your mind when your' sick and had copped and was minus works and Darkstar [from whom a user could contract the HIV virus] had works." Yrstruly fears that Wo might have laced the skeet, but he prefers to see the evidence of what happens to C (to risk C's life) because yrstruly will have to wait to shoot the skeet if they stop to discuss that it is potentially bad but will not have to wait if it turns out to be good. The use of cough syrup (here, NyQuil) to get high is a desperate action that will recur. Getting high in a bathroom is also a desperate move (Hal does this when the Lung is up, and Gompert does this at work; cf. pp. 52, 76). Death expressed as the elimination of a map (a face) will also recur. C's death is accompanied by the release of waste: "the hot air blowergate is blowing small bits of fart and blood and missty shit up into our maps." Poor Tony pisses while C cooks up. Earlier, Poor Tony had "hunched behind a lightpoal" waiting near Hung Toys. There is a missed connection if yrstruly and C, who were trying to avoid Poor Tony's "red leather fags," do not realize that two of the prostitutes they run into, Eckwus and Stokely Darkstar, fit that description (cf. p. 690). The Drano was "blue," there was "a blue string" at the back of C's popped-out eye, and upon his death C "turned lightblue."

When Wo was gone on Christmas morning, yrstruly, like other addicts throughout the novel, "almost was cryng."

The section begins "It was yrstruly and C and Poor Tony," which is similar to the syntax by which Alex in *A Clockwork Orange* introduces his droogs, who are as (ultra)violent as the characters in this section. Alex narrates in first person, referring to himself as "your humble narrator," and often describes himself as a victim. Yrstruly says "its' a never ending struggle its' a full time job to stay straight and there is no vacation for XMas at anytime. Its' a fucking bitch of a life dont' let any body get over on you different." By mentally correcting yrstruly's linguistic anomalies (e.g., "onnings" to awnings) in this section—and by navigating copious endnotes, chronological jumps and gaps, and shifting narrative perspectives and approaches throughout the novel—the reader of *Infinite Jest* becomes a more active participant in the reading experience, as does the reader who translates the lingo Burgess invented for his characters in *A Clockwork Orange*. This heightened activity, along with yrstruly's first-person narration, brings the reader closer to yrstruly, an uncomfortable place to be given that yrstruly—like Alex in *A Clockwork Orange*, a first-person narrator who is a pretty nasty character—uses racial slurs (note the misspelled "Nigers" for one) and almost rapes a nurse. Some of the more extreme names, character traits, and events in *Infinite Jest* (like those in this section) are reminiscent of those in "Girl with Curious Hair," from Wallace's story collection of the same name, which features Sick Puppy, a first-person narrator who refers to himself as "yours truly" and enjoys burning people.

Chapter 12: A Weight Greater Than Their Own Weight

Lyle "lives off the sweat of others" in a positive way, exchanging wise advice for literal sweat. C's crew lives off the sweat of others in a negative way by exchanging bloodshed—"wet work"—for money and goods, what their victims have figuratively sweated to earn. Lyle takes wet sweat and gives intangible advice; C's crew makes wet blood, takes tangible items, and gives nothing. Lyle's nugget of wisdom, "Let not the weight thou wouldst pull to thyself exceed thine own weight," warns one not to take on what one can't control. C's crew is driven to desperation (out of control) by a figurative weight (addiction) greater than their own weight. Lyle is still and calm; C's crew is in constant motion.

Chapter 13

Working Alone

Chapter 13.1, Section 44, Pages 135-137
3 November Y.D.A.U.

Although he doesn't know why, "Hal never liked talking on the phone after he'd gotten high in secret" (Hal has given in to the impulse documented in Ch. 11.8, pp. 120-1). However, Hal answers a phone call from Orin (two days after Orin's game against Denver, Ch. 8.2), to whom he enjoys lying about meaningless details, although (again) he doesn't know why. Hal considers for the first time whether Orin might also be lying about meaningless details to him. Orin "had abruptly started calling again this spring." Perhaps Ch. 4 (9 May Y.D.A.U.) documents this abrupt start. Orin complains about the heat, and Hal mentions studying for SATs, for which "Pemulis is less and less helpful on the math." When Orin says he may pursue becoming E.T.A.'s Kleenex vendor to profit from Hal's (presumed by Orin) excessive masturbation, Hal cuts with "That of course would mean actually contacting C.T. and the Moms." When Orin says he met "a possibly very special somebody," Hal implies that he must go to dinner: "Triangle's a-clangin' over in West" (cf. "Sometimes Mrs. Clarke in the kitchen lets Mario ring a triangle with a steel ladle," p. 120). Orin stops Hal with "Kidding aside for a second" (recall Orin's view of women as Subjects, Ch. 6.3) and asks about Canadian Separatism.

PLOT AND CHARACTER: Orin, Hal
THEME: Isolation, Recur

Hal has returned from his isolated activity in the Pump Room to speak with Orin, who has isolated himself from his family; but in a city near Tucson, where his father used to live. He accuses Hal of "self-abuse," an isolated activity. Orin speaks of the city in which he lives as "made of glass and light" and of a pith-helmeted "Phoenician felled by the heat." This conjuring of a primitive image resonates with the introduction of mythology into Marathe and Steeply's conversation (Ch. 11.7), also held near Phoenix. The felled Phoenician "hit the pavement," which is another recurring image.

Chapter 13.2, Section 45, Pages 137-138
Notes 49-51, Page 995
unspecified

The Ennet House Drug and Alcohol Recovery House (redundancy *sic*, n. 49) was founded in Y.W. and "originally renovated, furnished, and decorated" with stolen items by an old "recovered addict/alcoholic" who underwent "a sudden experience of total self-surrender and spiritual awakening." Valuing the Alcoholics Anonymous tradition of anonymity, the man (who was not named Ennet) was known in the Boston AA community as the Guy Who Didn't Even Use His First Name. Ennet House is located "in the Enfield Marine Public Health Hospital Complex, managed by the United States Veterans Administration." Recall that Tiny Ewell was travelling to Unit #6 of this complex in early November Y.D.A.U. (p. 87). "Ennet House is equipped to provide 22 male and female clients a nine-month period of closely supervised residency and treatment." The old founder's AA circle was the White Flag Group of Enfield, whose members referred to "tough old Boston galoots" like Ennet's founder as "The Crocodiles" (n. 50). The nameless founder's death "went unremarked outside the Boston AA community."

The old founder died in the Year of the Yushityu 2007 Mimetic-Resolution-Cartridge-View-Motherboard-Easy-To-Install Upgrade For Infernatron/Interlace TP Systems For Home, Office Or Mobile (syntax *sic*, n. 51), which this study abbreviates as "YUSHITYU." All nine subsidized years have now been referenced (one by abbreviation only), and the order is known for all but two: YUSHITYU and Y.D.P.A.H. (cf. Ch. 8.1 summary). Note that "2007" is included in the name of this subsidized year, the faulty syntax of which "helped drive" Avril—a "mover and shaker in the prescriptive-grammar academic world" (p. 30)—"to help found the Militant Grammarians of Massachusetts" (n. 51; but cf. the B.S. existence of the organization in Jim's *Union of Theoretical Grammarians in Cambridge*, p. 987).

PLOT AND CHARACTER: Ennet, Avril
THEME: Choice, Isolation

Total surrender to addiction is via compulsion, whereas total surrender to sobriety is via an active choice, which requires discipline and sacrifice. The old founder "required incoming residents to attempt to eat rocks . . . to demonstrate their willingness to go to any lengths for the gift of sobriety." The old founder lived and died in relative anonymity (isolation).

Chapter 13.3, Section 46, Pages 138-140
26 June Y.D.P.A.H.

This section is introduced by a 6-line descriptive heading. A claims adjuster emails three fellow employees a copy of a letter (note the ten-digit zip codes) received on 21 June (months before Gately robs DuPlessis, Ch. 7.4) from Dwayne R. Glynn, who is seeking compensation for an accident that occurred on 27 March. The adjuster notes that Glynn's blood-alcohol level was .3+ (which means that the company is clear of liability) and that witnesses have confirmed the events. Glynn states that the accident at the brickyard where he works happened because he was "trying to do the job alone."

PLOT AND CHARACTER: AA&R
THEME: Isolation, Recur

Glynn's accident is attributed to his isolation. The description of the accident reads like farce or like cartoon violence and is based on an urban legend (cf. Mikkelson). In light of the accident, consider Lyle's advice: "Let not the weight thou wouldst pull to thyself exceed thine own weight" (p. 128). This section presents only the first page of the accident report, leaving the narrative in chaotic stasis.

Chapter 13.4, Section 47, Pages 140-142
21 February Y.P.W.

In this section, a 13-line heading introduces an essay Hal wrote for Mr. Ogilvie in seventh grade. The heading notes that 21 February Y.P.W. is four years after the demise of broadcast television and one year after the death of James Incandenza, which places Jim's death in Y.T.-S.D.B., one year after the professional conversationalist incident of Ch. 3. Details about the grade the essay received and Ogilvie's comments must be provided in the heading as the essay is reproduced as written without additional narrative comment. This essay (or a later draft of this essay) was cited by the administrators in Y.G. (cf. "The Emergence of Heroic Stasis in Broadcast Entertainment," p. 7).

The essay compares a modern 1970s-era television hero, Steve McGarrett of "Hawaii Five-O," with a "post"-modern 1980s-era television hero, Frank Furillo of "Hill Street Blues." McGarrett is a hero whose "field of action is bare of diverting clutter." In contrast, Furillo is "a hero whose virtues are suited to a more complex and corporate American era. I.e., a hero of *re*action." Furillo is "a genius for navigating cluttered fields" and is "usually one part of a frenetic, moving pan by the program's camera." Hal concludes the essay by predicting a future television "hero of *non*-action, the catatonic hero, the one beyond calm, divorced from all stimulus."

PLOT AND CHARACTER: E.T.A., Hal, Art/Ent
THEME: Isolation, Recur, Non-Action

Both TV heroes are isolated by their responsibilities. McGarrett is described as "a lone man of action riding lonely herd in paradise." Furillo, "responsible to everyone" and "'trapped' in . . . reactive moral ambiguity," wears a "lonely face." In the last episode of the first season of "Hill Street Blues," Furillo is revealed to be a recovering alcoholic when he is seen at an AA meeting (which resonates with the subject matter of Ch. 13.2); in the fourth episode of the second season, Grace Gardner references Byzantine erotica (cf. Hal's interest, p. 29). This is one of many sections to reference old TV shows and characters. The phrase "double binds," pertaining to difficult choices, will recur. The "hero of *non*-action" is also a significant idea that will recur. The hero (or at least the protagonist) of non-action is an idea that resonates in Samuel Beckett's novels *The Unnamable* (written in the dawn of the rise of broadcast television) and *Company* (written just before "Hill Street Blues" began its run).

Chapter 13.5, Section 48, Pages 142-144
10 August Y.D.A.U.

Essential information is introduced in the 11-line heading of this section. Wallace has chosen the heading of this section as the place to inform the reader that James Incandenza "TOOK HIS OWN LIFE BY PUTTING HIS HEAD IN A MICROWAVE OVEN." Jim's death occurred five years ago in Y.T.-S.D.B., not four as stated in the heading (cf. Ch. 8.1 and Ch. 13.4 summaries). With respect to Jim's death, the five-year span between Y.T.-S.D.B. and Y.D.A.U. often will be identified incorrectly as a four-year span. Also, it turns out that Hugh Steeply was in feminine disguise in Ch. 11 (30 April Y.D.A.U.) because he was on a field assignment for the U.S.O.U.S. as "Helen" Steeply, a "journalist." This section documents "her" "ONLY PUTATIVE PUBLISHED ARTICLE" (10 August) before profiling Orin for *Moment* magazine. Recall that Orin was stressed about upcoming interviews with *Moment* magazine in October (pp. 48-9) and on 1 November (p. 66). Is Steeply the "special somebody" Orin mentioned on 3 November in Ch. 13.1?

Steeply's article is about a woman with restenosis (like Marathe's wife, cf. p. 126), who received a "Jarvik IX Exterior Artificial Heart" which she kept "portably installed" in her purse. The woman died because her purse was snatched by a transvestite (like Steeply) with a "tattered feather boa" in Harvard Square (Poor Tony from Ch. 12.2). Steeply's report also laments that the fates of victims are "frequently kept from the light of public knowledge" (cf. the fates of the 23 victims who viewed the Entertainment cartridge on 1-2 April that are being kept from public knowledge by the U.S.O.U.S.).

PLOT AND CHARACTER: U.S.O.U.S., Orin, Jim, Tech, AA&R
THEME: Secrets, Phys/Ob, Recur, Time

Steeply writes under the guise of a secret identity. Poor Tony's victim, a woman with physical obstacles, sought the use of a machine to extend her life, while Jim used a machine to end his life. There is another missed connection in that the people on the street hear the victim's shouts for help (another recurring motif) to stop the person who stole her heart as figurative rather than literal.

Like the narrator of the heading, Hamlet gets confused about the amount of time that has passed since a father's death: Hamlet says "But two months dead—nay, not so much, not two" (I.ii.138) and then refers to the amount of time as one month throughout the rest of that speech. Later, Hamlet's sarcastic "my father died within's two hours" is countered by Ophelia's "Nay, 'tis twice two months my lord" (III.ii.125-6).

Chapter 13.6, Section 49, Page 144
unspecified

This section is introduced by a 5-line descriptive heading and lists alphabetically the seven anti-O.N.A.N. groups considered terrorist in nature. The list indicates which groups are Québecois, environmental, and/or separatist and which groups are considered violent or extremely violent. Marathe's group, *Les Assassins des Fauteuils Rollents*, is indicated as Québecois, separatist, and extremely violent, as is the F.L.Q. (cf. p. 126 and n. 47). Recall that DuPlessis, accidentally killed by Gately (Ch. 7.4), was the Boston-based liaison and "general leash-holder" for these groups (p. 58).

PLOT AND CHARACTER: O.N.A.N., A.F.R.
THEME: Isolation

These groups are in "OPPOSITION TO INTERDEPENDENCE" and want to separate from both Canada and O.N.A.N.

Chapter 13.7, Section 50, Pages 144-151
By Y.D.A.U.

This section is introduced by a page-length descriptive heading that indicates this section will explain why over 90% of private telephone users prefer "VOICE-ONLY TELEPHONIC INTERFACE" to "VIDEOPHONY," an activity that enjoyed only brief popularity (cf. Erdedy "using just audio," p. 18).

First, audio-only phone conversations made use of a "marvelous delusion . . . countenanced only in the context of its loss." The conversations "let you enter a kind of highway-hypnotic semi-attentive fugue" and allowed you "to believe you were receiving somebody's complete attention without having to return it," an illusion which in hindsight "appears arational, almost literally fantastic: it would be like being able both to lie and to trust other people at the same time." The advent of "[v]ideo telephony rendered the fantasy insupportable" because callers now found they had to pay attention or risk appearing "childishly self-absorbed," which caused the callers stress.

Second, videophony did away with the "answer-as-you-are informality" of audio-only conversation. Users could even play back conversations to view how they looked on video, which was described in a survey as "*untrustworthy, unlikable*, or *hard to like*" by almost 60% of respondents. This eventually resulted in users having masks of their "enhanced facial image[s]" made to use while on the phone and which hung from hooks by the phone when not in use. The use of masks made users "suddenly reluctant to leave home and interface personally with people who, they feared, were now habituated to seeing their far-better-looking masked selves on the phone." Soon, Transmittable Tableaux were developed: "high-quality transmission-ready photographs [were] fitted with a plastic holder over the videophone camera, not unlike a lens-cap" (recall that Jim had a patent on these videophonic Tableaux, p. 64). "[M]asking could now be dispensed with altogether and replaced with the video-transmitted image of what was essentially a heavily doctored still-photograph, one of an incredibly fit and attractive and well-turned-out human being," often "infomercial-level celebrities hard-pressed by the declining fortunes of broadcast television advertising" (cf. the demise of broadcast television, referenced in the heading on p. 140).

Third, the Tableaux brought phone-usage full circle (the "annular" shape of "the beyond-short-term viability-curve of advances in consumer technology" brings to mind Jim's influence on "annular" fusion, p. 64) in that they allowed users again to believe "that they were the objects of a concentrated attention that they themselves didn't have to exert." Soon, users realized that this was the same advantage provided by aural-only telephoning. Therefore, "videophony was mostly abandoned," and the market for videophonic services fell off, resulting in "massive shirt-loss for precipitant investors." Still, "the bulk of U.S. consumers remained verifiably reluctant to leave home and teleputer to interface personally," which "served to open huge new entrepeneurial teleputerized markets for home-shopping and -delivery."

PLOT AND CHARACTER: Tech
THEME: Inf/Reg, Secrets, Cycles, Isolation

For audio-only phone users, the "bilateral illusion of unilateral attention was almost infantiley gratifying from an emotional standpoint." Before the advent of masks and Tableaux, videophonic appearance-checks were "no more resistible than a mirror." Masks appear again in this section. Users of videophony (video phony) hide their fears about themselves behind flattering masks of themselves or behind images of others (videophonic Tableaux, patented by Jim). After the cyclical rise and fall of videophony, consumers remained in isolation, "verifiably reluctant to leave home."

Chapter 13: Working Alone

Characters in this chapter isolate themselves, surrender their identities, lie, and/or use masks. Orin, separated from his family, calls Hal to ask about Separatism and accuses Hal, who lies to Orin on the phone, of masturbation (sexual isolation). The founder of Ennet lived and died in relative anonymity and built a place where troubled people could isolate themselves and surrender to sobriety. Glynn's accident, described in an email probably sent from an individual isolated in an office to three individuals isolated in three other offices, is attributed to his working alone. Both of the TV heroes in Hal's essay are isolated by their responsibilities. Steeply and Poor Tony mask or surrender their male identities by dressing as women. The anti-O.N.A.N. groups are separatist groups, opposed to interdependence. Videophony customers, reluctant to leave home, hide behind masks and use Tableaux to change identities. The disparate sections of this chapter—a conversation, reports, an email, essays, and a list—are usually preceded by headings that are integral to the narrative (like the headings of the "Aeolus" chapter of *Ulysses*, but longer). Each of these sections stands alone as having a distinct narrative approach relative to the other sections of the chapter.

Chapter 14

Closely Monitored

Chapter 14, Section 51, Pages 151-156
Notes 52-55, Pages 995-996
15 October Y.D.A.U.

Four times a year, any E.T.A student "ranked higher than #64 continentally in his or her age-division" must submit a urine sample to an O.N.A.N.T.A. Juniors Division official. "An impressive percentage of the kids at E.T.A. are in their divisions' top 64," of which about a fourth of those over the age of "say, fifteen" cannot pass a standard urine scan. Therefore, Pemulis and Axford become "quarterly urine vendors," selling "little Visine bottles of urine out of an antique vendor's tub for ballpark wieners" to students in "two long lines that trail out of the locker rooms" all the way back to the Comm.-Ad. Bldg. lobby. Mario films "the congregated line and social interactions and vending operation of the urine-day lobby." The day after "urine-sample day," Visine bottles are emptied from individual wastebaskets into dumpsters behind E.T.A. Ennet House (cf. Ch. 13.2) is located at the bottom of one side of the hill on which E.T.A. stands, and some Ennet residents "do nine months of menial-type work [at E.T.A.] for the 32 hours a week their treatment-contract requires." Pemulis gets young E.T.A. players and Mario to retrieve the Visine bottles from dumpsters and then to sterilize and box the bottles. Urine from younger, drug-free players can then again be collected and stashed during the three months before the next O.N.A.N.T.A. visit.

Pemulis and Axford have priority use of a truck for which Hal and Jim Struck have also chipped in because the truck's registration and insurance is "paid for out of quarterly urine-revenues." The truck is emblazoned with the "O.N.A.N. heraldic ensign—a snarling full-front eagle with a broom and a can of disinfectant in one claw and a Maple Leaf in the other wearing a sombrero and appearing to have about half-eaten a swatch of star-studded cloth."

Pemulis is from Allston MA, "a grim section of tract housing and vacant lots," and his "pre-E.T.A. home life was apparently hackle-raising." Hailed as a "tennis prodigy at ten," Pemulis was "recruited up the hill at eleven," is "E.T.A.'s finest Eschatonic marksman" (Eschaton is a nuclear-conflagration game played on tennis courts, n. 53), but is "way lower-ranked than he could be with a little hard work." Although "Pemulis's real enduring gift is for math and hard science," he needs Hal's help with verbal classes such as Literature of Discipline, taught by Soma R.-L.-O. Chawaf (the matrimonially undisciplined actress featured in Jim's films, cf. pp. 990-3). Pemulis is the sole recipient of the "James O. Incandenza Geometrical Optics Scholarship," which "gives him sanctioned access to all the late director's lenses and equipment, some of which turn out to be useful to unrelated enterprises." Pemulis has a bond with Mario, "the only other person sharing the optic-and-editing labs off the main tunnel" (although Leith and Ogilvie used to work in these facilities, cf. p. 51).

Hal is "a late-blooming prodigy and possible genius at tennis" who is currently ranked sixth continentally. His "head, closely monitored by deLint and Staff, is judged still level and focused" (cf. "It's the heads they're working on here, boys," p. 113). Hal's father "was revered as a genius in his original profession [optics], without anybody ever realizing what he really turned out to be a genius at [film], even he himself, at least not while he was alive" (the grammatical arrangement of these words suggests that no one, including Jim, realized that Jim was a filmic genius until after Jim's death).

Pemulis is described as "nobody's fool" and requires callers purchasing substances to demand that he "Please commit a crime" (cf. Gompert: "One kid makes you ask him to please commit a crime," p. 75) and to threaten him with violence in order to protect himself from "the potential eater of cheese, the rat."

PLOT AND CHARACTER: E.T.A., Hal, Mario, AA&R
THEME: Waste, Cycle, Recur

Pemulis's urine-vending service is maintained by an efficient three-month cycle. The O.N.A.N.T.A. toxicologist wears a blue blazer, and the carpet in the E.T.A. Comm.-Ad. Bldg. lobby is royal-blue shag. What are the implications of the fact that "Mario and his brother Hal both consider Pemulis a good friend, though friendship at E.T.A. is nonnegotiable currency"?

Chapter 14: Closely Monitored

In this chapter, E.T.A. players are closely monitored by O.N.A.N.T.A. with respect to substance abuse; Mario monitors the "urine-day" activities by filming them; the efficient maintenance of Pemulis's urine-vending cycle requires close attention; Hal's head is closely monitored by deLint and Staff; and Pemulis's substance-deal requirements are intended to protect him from any secret monitors.

Chapter 15

Managed Fear

Chapter 15.1, Section 52, Pages 157-169
Winter 1960

This section begins with James Incandenza, Sr. (Hal's grandfather) talking to James Incandenza, Jr. (Hal's father, age 10; identified as Jr. on p. 64) outside the shared garage of the Tucson AZ trailer park where they live (James Sr. is a Tucson native, but he and his wife lived in California before James Jr. was born). The reader must determine James Jr.'s responses from James Sr.'s commentary, because the section is presented as a monologue (quotation marks are not placed around James Sr.'s speech), the last paragraph of which comprises approximately ten pages. The events of this section were referenced earlier (cf. p. 63, where the garage is called a "basement workshop") and were the basis of James Jr.'s film, *As of Yore* (cf. p. 991). James Sr. espouses a philosophy of tennis based on the transcendence of limits and the relationship between head and body (cf. Schtitt in Ch. 10.3 and Chu (for Wayne) and Troeltsch in Ch. 11.8), and he asserts that the relationship between external objects and the body should be one of efficiency and consideration, a measure of a person's character.

Sr. attempts to instruct Jr. about the importance of people's "relations with their own bodies and the everyday objects and bodies around them," a relationship that Jr.'s mother doesn't understand: "She treats bodies outside herself without respect or due care. She's never learned that treating things in the gentlest most relaxed way is also treating them and your own body in the most efficient way." Sr. believes his wife's disrespect of bodies outside herself is done in tribute to "slouching slob-type" Marlon Brando, but she "never intuited the gentle and cunning economy" behind Brando's approach. Brando "really touched whatever he touched as if it were part of him. Of his own body." He was "playing the equivalent of high-level quality tennis" and knew "what the great tennis player knows, son: learn to do nothing, with your whole head and body, and everything will be done by what's around you." Sr. predicts that Jr. will be a great tennis player, even though today will be Jr.'s first lesson. Sr. has observed "the way you already adjust your overlarge and apparently clumsy child's body" and therefore knows that Jr. will "overshadow and obliterate" him with regard to tennis. Sr. tells Jr. that Jr. "will be poetry in motion" when Jr. learns to transcend "that overlarge head" and "to move just the way you already sit still. Living in your body."

Sr. coaches Jr. to open the garage door with respect and speaks in admiration of his 1956 Mercury Montclair, "a machine," once inside the garage. "It's an object, Jim, a body, but don't let it fool you, sitting here, mute. It will *respond.* If given its due. With artful care." Countering his wife's praise of Jr.'s "scientific-prodigy's mind," Sr. says that "those thoughts in your mind are just the sound of your head revving, and head is still just body . . . : you're a machine a body an object, Jim." Sr. prompts Jr. to kill a spider ("*Latrodectus mactans*, Jim. Widow"; cf. Latrodectus Mactans Productions, n. 24) before noting that "a tennis ball is the ultimate body. Perfectly round. Even distribution of mass. But empty inside, utterly, a vacuum. Susceptible to whim, spin, to force—used well or poorly. It will reflect your own character. Characterless itself. Pure potential. . . . [A]pply the lessons of today to yourself as a physical body. . . . Imagine what it feels like to be this ball, Jim. Total physicality. No revving head. Complete presence." Sr. admires as a body and treats with care the flask from which he has offered Jr. a drink and chastises Jr. for dropping, rather than placing on the floor, the *Columbia Guide to Refractive Indices Second Edition*. Jr., upset by this chastisement to the point of having his "eyes slant and goggle like some sort of mongoloid child's," is told that he must "learn to control this sort of oversensitivity to hard truths." Concerning the flask, Sr. asks Jr. to hear "the sound of threads moving through well-machined grooves" as he is "less unscrewing, here, than guiding, persuading, reminding, the silver cap's body what it's built to do, machined to do." The cap leaves the flask with "just a snick, . . . not a harsh brutal Brando-esque rasp of attempted domination but a snick a . . . nuance [like the] never mistakable *ponk* of a true hit ball."

Jr. is again chastised because he is upset, presumably over his book. Sr. again predicts that Jr. will have "a tennis career that'll put his busted-up used-up old Dad back square in his little place," although with respect to his place Sr. himself is "harking one last attempted time to that celluloid siren's call" when the family moves back to California in the spring, giving Sr. his "last shot at a life with any meaning at all." Sr. has announced the move well in advance to provide Jr. with "plenty of notice," given how upset Jr. was over "this last move to this trailer park" (previously, the family lived in a "house it was clearly my fault we couldn't afford anymore" and "the Club's staff quarters I got us removed from"): "so say adios to that school and that fluttery little moth of a physics teacher and those slumped chinless slide-rule-wielding friends" (one of Jr.'s teachers urged his parents to nurture Jr.'s "optical knack with physics"). Sr. tells Jr. that his crying becomes less effective with each use, although "we know it'll always work on your mother" (a "poor dumb patient" woman), who looks "like she's burping some sort of slumping oversized obscene bow-tied infant" when she comforts the crying, book-holding Jr.

Sr. relates a story from 1933 about his father (Jr.'s grandfather, Hal's great-grandfather), who "never acknowledged I even existed." Unlike his father, Sr. goes "way, *way* out of my way to let you know I *see* you recognize you am aware of you as a body." Although Sr.'s father had never come to see Sr. play tennis, Sr.'s mother (Hal's great-grandmother "with Pima-tribe Indian S.W. blood," p. 101) "never missed a competitive match," and therefore "it ceased to mean anything that she came." However, on a day that Sr. was playing the son of one of Sr.'s father's clients, Sr.'s father "came for the client, to put on some sham show of fatherly concern." Sr., elegant and magnificent ("because I knew myself as a body"), was "handing the dandy his pampered ass" ("you could see the straps of his jock biting into the soft ass I was handing him") as the client drank "the lemonade my mother had brought for me" and said that Sr. was good.

Sr. says of tennis: "You play right up to your limit and then pass your limit and look back at your former limit and wave a hankie at it, embarking. You enter a trance. You feel the seams and edges of everything." When "playing with such ease and total mindless effortless effort and and and entranced concentration you don't even stop to consider whether to run down every ball. You're barely aware you're doing it. Your body's doing it for you and the court and Game's doing it for your body. You're barely involved. It's magic, boy. . . . Facts and figures and curved glass and those elbow-straining books of yours' lightless pages are going to seem flat by comparison." "Talent is its own expectation, Jim: you either live up to it or it waves a hankie, receding forever. Use it or lose it, he'd say over the newspaper" (Years later, Jr., talking to his ten-year-old son Hal, will accuse Sr. of turning a "newspaper into the room's fifth wall," p. 31).

Sr. says he was going after a drop-shot another man would have let "dribble, conceded the affordable, not tried to wave a hankie from the vessel of his limit" when he heard his father say, in response to the client, "Yes, But He'll *Never Be Great*," but that "[w]hat he said in no way made me fall forward." Sr. says he doesn't know what he slipped on—"it could have been either a daytime *latrodectus* or some pus from a palm frond" (1933 was the year "of the Great Bisbee Palm-Rot epidemic")—but that he slipped because of "a *foreign* body, or substance, not my body." Sr. admits he may have gotten careless listening for what his father, who he respected, might say. Sr. says "you kids today somehow don't know how to *feel*, much less love, to say nothing of respect. [Your parents are] just bodies to you." Kids today cannot "imagine our absence. We're so present it's ceased to mean. We're environmental. Furniture of the world."

Sr. says, "God I'm I'm so *sorry*, Jim. You don't deserve to see me like this. I'm so scared, Jim. I'm so scared of dying without ever being really *seen*. Can you understand? . . . That I was *in* there [cf. Hal: "I am in here," p. 3], out there in the heat, listening, webbed with nerves? A self that touches all edges, I remember she [Sr.'s mother?] said." One minute Sr. was running for the ball, and the next minute he came down on his knees and slid "desperately forward toward the net," leaving "twin tracks of brown red gray white like tire tracks of bodily gore." Sr.

heard his "father pronounce my bodily existence as not even potentially great at the moment I ruined my knees forever [but] I do not insist that the judgment and punishing fall are . . . were connected, Jim." "I learned what it means to be a body, Jim, just meat wrapped in a sort of panty-ho, son, as I fell kneeling and slid toward the stretched net, myself seen by me, frame by frame, torn open. [I'm] telling you what I learned, son, my . . . my love, too late, as I left my knees' meat behind me . . . . I felt the religion of the physical that day . . . . It's a pivotal, it's a seminal, religious day when you get to both hear and feel your destiny at the same moment."

PLOT AND CHARACTER: Jim, AA&R
THEME: Boundaries, Phys/Ob, His/Father, Cycles, Inf/Reg, Recur, Loss

James Sr.'s tennis philosophy concerns the transcendence of limits (boundaries, obstacles) and the relationship between head and body and between objects and body. James Jr. will pass on this philosophy (and intensive training, cf. Ch. 15.3) to Hal and will hire Schtitt, a man with similar ideals, to coach at E.T.A. There are numerous other correspondences between fathers and sons that cycle through generations of Incandenzas. Sr. and Jr. share the same name; their middle name will be passed on to Orin. Sr. refers to his father as "Himself"; Jr. will also be called this by his sons. Sr.'s father's fear of spiders is passed down to Sr. and then again to Jr. (spiders and spiderwebs loom large in this section: cf. pp. 157, 159, 162, and 164-7). Sr., Jr., Hal, and Orin are all skilled tennis players. Sr. and Jr. are both interested in physical properties; Sr. has (and Jr. will have) a physical affinity with objects and motion, while Jr. has a mental affinity with understanding and manipulating the properties of light. Sr. is an actor; Jr. will become a filmmaker, as will his son Mario (cf. Ch. 15.3). Sr. and Jr. both abuse alcohol; Hal is in danger of abusing marijuana. Sr. describes himself as "knocking lamps over, overshooting my reach" (p. 168) and tells Jr. that if Jr. applies "the lessons of today" Jr. will have no more "overshot reaches, shattered plates, tilted lampshades" (p. 160). Sr. says that Jr. has an "overlarge and apparently clumsy child's body." Does this resonate with Hal's movements in Ch.

1? (Jr.'s "overlarge head" and "big flat face" recall Gately's "massive and almost perfectly square head," p. 55.) Sr. calls his father's appearance at the 1933 match selfish, a "sham show of fatherly concern," and Sr.'s talk to Jr. in the garage here is extremely one-sided. Jr. dominates the professional conversation with Hal in Ch. 3 (also a sham show, given Jim's disguise). Here, Sr. is bitter about his father's inability to communicate and, attempting to be a good father, laments his inability to communicate with Jr. (who is clearly sensitive to what Sr. says, though). As the professional conversationalist, Jr. is bitter about Sr.'s inability to communicate and, attempting to be a good father, laments that Hal does not speak (although Hal clearly does speak; Jr. does not listen). Sr. cycles between AZ and CA throughout his life. Jr. moves from AZ to Boston, but Orin eventually cycles from Boston back to AZ (and Hal is attempting to move to AZ in Y.G.). Sr.'s mother attended all his matches; Hal dreams that Avril is at his match (Ch. 9.2), and Orin dreams Avril's head is attached to his on-court (Ch. 6.3).

Sr. compares Brando to "a moody child" and "a moody infant," says that Jr. has an "overlarge and apparently clumsy child's body," chastises Jr.'s pre-crying face as being "like some sort of mongoloid child's," and chastises his wife's infantilizing treatment of Jr. Other recurring themes in this section include betrayal by a parent who does not come when needed; machine sounds, often associated with the head ("those thoughts in your mind are just the sound of your head revving"); tennis as a dance; the sense of loss associated with "receding forever"; and the ominous nature of shadows. Sr.'s father "cast a long shadow"; Sr.'s father smoked "in the waggling fronds' shadow"; and Sr. (drunk) sees Jr.'s "long shadow grotesquely backlit" at the top of the stairs.

Chapter 15.2, Section 53, Pages 169-171
Notes 56-57, Page 996
4 November Y.D.A.U., around lunchtime

The day after meeting with his Little Buddies (Ch. 11.8), Michael Pemulis (in "his Mr. Howell hat" with detachable lining) takes in downtown Boston, "[h]aving indulged in 150 mg. of very mild 'drines post-transaction." After "slow and tortured" research, Pemulis had decided to purchase "incredibly potent DMZ." One user compared the effects of DMZ to "plowing at high knottage through time itself, kinetic even in stasis, plowing temporally ahead, with time coming off him like water" (n. 57). "The incredibly potent DMZ is synthesized from a derivative of fitviavi, an obscure mold that grows only on other molds" (cf. the fly agaric muscimole, n. 56 and pp. 66-7). The drug sent one "Sandoz chemist into early retirement and serious unblinking wall-watching" (which resonates with the attaché's experience), has a "reputation as the single grimmest thing ever conceived in a tube," and is the second hardest "recreational compound to acquire in North America after raw Vietnamese opium." The drug is sometimes referred to as *Madame Psychosis*—cf. "CNS [central nervous system]-rattler" DMZ/M.P. (n. 8) and the actress in Jim's films (n. 24)—after a popular cult radio personality admired by Mario and "Eschaton game-master [cf. n. 53] Otis P. Lord." Pemulis is both Big Buddy to Lord (p. 117) and "E.T.A.'s finest Eschatonic marksman" (p. 154).

To protect himself, Pemulis takes precautions against "the slightest possible chance of pursuit" downtown, "has a rigid policy about not transacting with E.T.A. employees who come up the hill" from Ennet House (cf. p. 122), and requires that clients like Hal (who will again answer the phone "Mm[m]yellow," cf. pp. 32 and 135) ask him to "Please commit a crime" (cf. p. 156). Hal sits in a chair with the Riverside *Hamlet* (he told Mario he would read it and "help with a conceptual film-type project," cf. the next section for a transcript of one of Mario's projects) under an Alexandrian mosaic (Byzantine erotica, cf. p. 29) *Consummation of the Levirate*s (a levirate marries his brother's widow) with SAT-prep guides ("SATs are six weeks away and Pemulis is less and less helpful on the math," p. 136) at his feet, "waiting very casually" (like Erdedy in Ch. 2) by the phone. Pemulis calls at lunchtime.

PLOT AND CHARACTER: E.T.A., Hal, AA&R
THEME: Time, Waste, Recur

The user of DMZ has a radically altered perception of "his relation to the ordinary flow of time." DMZ is derived from mold (waste), and Pemulis's code phrase to Hal is "The turd emergeth," the archaic suffix of which is appropriate given that Hal is sitting with *Hamlet*. Mr. Howell is another old TV character (from *Gilligan's Island*), and Pemulis's attire includes a blue sport-coat and gray-and-blue shoes, worn under a sky of "pilot-light blue."

Chapter 15.3, Section 54, Pages 172-176
April YUSHITYU

A 13-line heading introduces the text of *Tennis and the Feral Prodigy*, a digital entertainment cartridge (with footage of Jim) created by Mario and narrated by Hal, which received an honorable mention in April YUSHITYU (presumably 2007), "ALMOST EXACTLY THREE YEARS" after their father died. Recall that Jim died in Y.T.-S.D.B. (cf. Ch. 13.4 summary) at the age of 54 (p. 64) and that Jim was ten (p. 159) in the winter (Jan.-Mar.) of 1960. Therefore, the reader now has all but one bit of information to determine the sponsors and chronology of Subsidized Time, here updated from the Ch. 8.1 summary with conversion to pre-subsidized dating.

2002 Year of the Whopper (Y.W.)
2003 Year of the Tucks Medicated Pad (Y.T.M.P.)
2004 Year of the Trial-Size Dove Bar (Y.T.-S.D.B.)
2005 Year of the Perdue Wonderchicken (Y.P.W.)
2006 (Y.W.-Q.M.D.)
2007 Year of the Yushityu 2007 . . . (YUSHITYU)
2008 Year of Dairy Products from the American Heartland (Y.D.P.A.H.)
2009 Year of the Depend Adult Undergarment (Y.D.A.U.)
2010 Year of Glad (Y.G.)

Note that the days of the week for 2009 match the days of the week for Y.D.A.U.; consider for example "Tuesday, 3 November" (p. 95).

Hal's narration addresses the philosophy, grueling activities, and sacrifices associated with achieving success at E.T.A. Images of Jim and Hal on the cartridge resonate with images of Jim and his father from Ch. 15.1: "Hit about a thousand serves to no one while Himself sits and advises with his flask" and "Have Himself hunch down . . . and tell you that his own father had told him that talent is sort of a dark gift, that talent is its own expectation: it is . . . either lived up to or lost" (cf. p. 168). Hal also wears a bow tie to the small openings of his father's films (cf. the "bow-tied" ten-year old Jim, p. 163). Hal observes that his father "lived up to his own promise and then found thing after thing to meet and surpass the expectations of his promise in, and didn't seem just a whole hell of a lot happier or tighter wrapped than his own failed father," which leaves Hal in "a kind of feral and flux-ridden state with respect to talent."

Hal speaks of "practicing and playing until everything runs on autopilot [cf. Troeltsch, pp. 117-8] and talent's unconscious exercise becomes a way to escape yourself, a long waking dream of pure play" (cf. pp. 67-8 for Hal's dream of play). Compare Hal's discussion of "how to play with personal integrity" with respect to line-calls with Struck's advice in the Big Buddy session (pp. 118-9). Hal advises, "Try to learn to let what is unfair teach you," both with respect to bad line-calls and the "rough dreams [that] come with the territory": "Keep a flashlight by your bed. It helps with the dreams" (cf. pp. 61-3).

Hal's advice for success at E.T.A. includes: "be *on guard*" against seductive detours; "be no one"; use rankings to "determine where you are not who you are"; and "learn the pragmatics of expressing [rather than invoking] fear." "How promising you are as a Student of the Game is a function of what you can pay attention to without running away." Hal says that nets, fences, and opponents are mirrors; that "the Game is about managed fear [and] its object is to send from yourself what you hope will not return." Hal closes with a prescription of how players can ease the suffering inherent in playing the game and in attempting to meet the expectations of well-intentioned parents "who just wanted to make sure you didn't miss anything they got."

PLOT AND CHARACTER: E.T.A., Hal, Jim
THEME: His/Father, Recur

In addition to the father and son images that resonate with Ch. 15.1, there are many other familiar images: the embarrassment of a tight jock strap making "bulged ridges in your butt" (cf. the dandy's "soft ass," p. 165), Hal's intentional "fall forward into the court" (contrast Jim's father's unintentional slip) to scoop keys that he still keeps on the floor "years after the man's death" (Hal's keys were on the floor on p. 171), the incessant squeezing of tennis balls, and Hal's becoming "a walking lunging sweating advertisement for Dunlop, Inc." (cf. pp. 30, 32, and 101 for references to Dunlop and Hal's complimentary gear bag). Note the recurring mouth-words "smile," "vomit," and "breathe" (all in the middle of p. 173); Jim's "hunch down"; Hal's weeping over his "torn blue ankle"; and reference to "mirrors."

Chapter 15.4, Section 55, Pages 176-181
Notes 58-59, Page 996
4 November Y.D.A.U, 1300h.-1500h.

A 6-line heading identifies this section as "SELECTED TRANSCRIPTS OF THE RESIDENT-INTERFACE-DROP-IN-HOURS [which occur shortly after Pemulis calls Hal, p. 171] OF MS. PATRICIA MONTESIAN," the executive director of Ennet House (picking up the Ennet thread from Ch. 13.2 and the threads of at least three other characters). This section is composed of twenty snippets separated by single line-spaces.

Nell (cf. snippet three) owns her part of an "occurrence" involving a fork.

Someone who is "not *in denial*" asks Montesian to define "alcoholic." Note reference to "the Kemp and Limbaugh administrations."

Nell's victim, also harassed by Minty and McDade, speaks: "I know part of the process is learning to live in a community. . . . But is it not also supposed to be . . . a *safe* and *nurturing* environment? I have seldom felt less nurtured than I did impaled on that table." "Gately [over a year after the events of Ch. 7.4] and Diehl had to pull the fork out of my hand and the tabletop both."

Someone wonders if there is a "prayer for when you want to hang yourself."

Alfonso says, "I fear I do not stop when I admit I am Alfonso, powerless. . . . My head it is crazy from this fearing of no power. . . . Is hope of power the bad way for Alfonso as drug addict?"

Someone tells Pat that "Division called" with an ultimatum about the vermin.

Someone notifies Pat that something in the toilet upstairs "won't flush."

Someone implies that McDade (cf. snippet three) ate his pudding.

Someone with a dissolved septum speaks of wanting "to stop the coke": "but then so how come I can't stop, if I want to stop, is the thing."

Upon learning that trailer-mate Doocy (note that the narrator of Ch. 5.3 spells this name differently than Bruce Green, cf. p. 39) had "been like sexually abusing fowls," Green moved to a shelter with his girlfriend, who soon left with another man, taking their daughter with her: "I was still trying to deliver ice to machines at gas stations [cf. Leisure Time Ice, p. 39]. Who wouldn't have to get high just to stand it?"

Someone asks, "You're *ordering* me to pray?"

Someone with facial tics purports to be fine.

Someone with job interview problems resists expulsion ("Where'm I suppose to *go* to?"), suggesting Pat ask Clenette (here at Ennet five years after the events of Ch. 5.2) and "that Thrale girl" to confirm that she's "*trying*."

Someone objects to being punished for using mouthwash: "It's like 2% proof!"

Someone registers a complaint about a farter.

The definition seeker (cf. snippet two) continues.

The mouthwash user (cf. snippet fourteen) continues.

Someone says, "I'll come back when you're free."

Someone says, "It's back. For a second there I hoped. I had hope. Then there it was again."

Someone says, "First let me just say one thing."

PLOT AND CHARACTER: Ennet
THEME: Cycles, Phys/Ob, Recur, Waste

Pat hears an ongoing cycle of complaints from Ennet residents, who experience physical and mental obstacles as part of their recovery process. Nell stabs another resident with a fork because the drumming of his fingers on the table is to her the "sound of a fucking mind coming apart." Alfonso's "head it is crazy from this feeling of no power." A dissolved septum and wanting to stop does not keep one resident from being able to stop using cocaine. The similarity of residents' complaints is highlighted by the fact that the last three snippets could potentially be attributed to more than one resident. Nell's flight across the table adds to the images of forward motion in this chapter and is described as horizontal. The thing in the toilet that won't flush is a recurrence of waste and recalls Pemulis's "The turd emergeth" earlier in the chapter. Like problems associated with addiction, "It won't go away." Also, a resident complains about someone farting. Another resident grinds teeth. What is the status of Clenette's child (cf. p. 38)?

Chapter 15: Managed Fear

A fear of spiders is an ever-present concern of James Sr.'s, the origin of which may be tied to his slipping (his falling "desperately forward") in 1933. James Sr. manages his fear with the contents of his flask and admits to his son: "I'm so scared, Jim." Pemulis manages his paranoia with unnecessary travel (moving desperately forward), the ingestion of 'drines, research of a potent substance before ingestion, and strict policies of behavior and business practice. Hal's narration climaxes with the observation that "the Game is about managed fear [and] its object is to send from yourself what you hope will not return." Ennet House is a place where people can potentially learn to manage their fears of substance dependency, fears expressed when Alfonso says "I fear I do not stop" and another resident asks "how come I can't stop, if I want to stop," fears of moving desperately forward, fears of not being able to send from themselves what they hope will not return.

Infinite Jest I

Disconnected: Dangers, Addictions, Deceptions, Boundaries, Bad Dreams

Chapters 1-15 of *Infinite Jest* provide numerous examples of the different ways human beings are disconnected from each other and from themselves. Hal has trouble communicating with the administrators and with his father. Jim, addicted to alcohol like his father, attempts to communicate with Hal via deception and then stops being able to hear him. Hal lies to Orin on the phone and to Mario about Orin's call. Both Hal and Orin have bad dreams and dreams about their mother. Hal and his mother are both obsessed with secrecy. Orin deceives women. Marathe and Steeply are professional deceivers who live dangerous, secret lives. Erdedy deceives people to obtain marijuana before isolating himself to use the drug; so does Gompert, who like Erdedy cannot quit taking the drug, a condition shared by residents of Ennet House. Hal secretly uses marijuana and is in danger of becoming like Erdedy and Gompert. There is a potentially dangerous culture of drug use at E.T.A., and Pemulis runs an industry of deception to help people avoid being caught with substances. C and his crew deceive and brutalize others to obtain addictive substances.

Anything that inspires addiction or obsession—substances, entertainment, beauty, secrecy—is dangerous in that it can lead to isolation, self-absorption, and disconnection, to paralyzed stasis: an immobility that gathers like a force (p. 24). Therefore, attachments should be carefully chosen (p. 107). A technological society addicted to pleasing itself could end up like the attaché, paralyzed and incontinent. Boundaries (limits, discipline, ritual behavior) can be set to help a person contain excessive attachments (as at Ennet) or to frame an infinity of possibilities (as in tennis), but boundaries (walls) can also foster obsession and disconnection.

These chapters are presented in sections—threads—that document memories and events from 1933 to Y.G. in chronologically fragmented fashion, that feature an ever-expanding cast of characters, and that might not seem to be weaving a unified narrative; but the reader will become increasingly aware of "the connectedness of all events" (p. 96). Even as the last section fragments into even smaller pieces of text, loose threads of characters making their second appearance are woven together: Clenette, Bruce Green, and Don Gately are all at Ennet House, and other characters will be found there in Ch. 16.

Chapter 16

Circulars and Catalogues

Chapter 16.1, Section 56, Pages 181-193
Notes 60-66, Pages 996-997
22-23 October Y.D.A.U., just before 0000h. to just after 0101h.

This section opens with a segment from the program "right before Madame Psychosis's midnight show on M.I.T.'s semi-underground WYYY" radio station (Pemulis's incredibly potent DMZ is sometimes referred to as Madame Psychosis, pp. 170-1), which features a student parodying his father in the voice of "some really silly cartoon character." The program for Thursday, 22 October Y.D.A.U. concerns a 73-yard punt from "eight seasons back" (recall that Orin is an NFL punter). The entire M.I.T. Student Union is "a great hollow brainframe," designed in exact detail by A. Y. Rickey (n. 3), the architect of E.T.A. (which is heart-shaped—a cardioid—and makes use of a "Lung"). The "soft latex-polymer roof is cerebrally domed," and its "bulging rooftop" looks "wrinkled" from the air.

The WYYY late-shift student engineer checks sound levels for Madame Psychosis, whom he never sees because she "probably takes the elevator" (unlike the student engineer) and sits behind a "jointed triptych screen" in the "chilly shadowless [fluorescent] light" of the studio (although her "shadow is just visible outside the [engineer's] booth's thick glass"). There are clocks over her left screen, including a numberless one "to designate the annularized Great Concavity's No-Time." Madame Psychosis's contract stipulates that there be five minutes of dead air preceding her show, which enjoys "rock-solid" ratings and "inelastic" audience demand. To open the 22 October show (airing after midnight on what is technically 23 October), "she says what she's said for three years of midnights."

Madame Psychosis's monologues "seem both free-associative and intricately structured, not unlike nightmares." She is "exceptionally conversant w/r/t avant-garde celluloid and avant- and apres-garde digital cartridges, anticonfluential cinema, Brutalism, Found Drama, etc. Also highly literate on U.S. sports, football in particular." Note 61 states that anticonfluential cinema is "characterized by a stubborn and possibly intentionally irritating refusal of different narrative lines to merge into any kind of meaningful confluence." Contributors to the genre include J. O. Incandenza (middle period). Recall that Madame Psychosis was an actress in some of Jim's films, including *Infinite Jest* (n. 24). "The show kind of flies itself. She could do it in her sleep, behind the screen. Sometimes she seems very sad." Tonight, Madame Psychosis reads extensively from a "circular," listing examples of the kinds of people invited to join the Union of the Hideously and Improbably Deformed (U.H.I.D.), including the "dermally wine-stained or carbuncular or steatocryptotic or God forbid all three."

Scenes from the Headmaster's House (HmH) at E.T.A.—where Mario is listening to Madame Psychosis's broadcast—begin to interweave with scenes from the M.I.T. Student Union at the bottom of p. 187. The marriage of Avril and Jim is described as an "evolved product of concordance and compromise" (a phrase used by Madame Psychosis in her sound check). Avril "quit M.I.T. entirely and went down to half-time at Brandeis" (cf. p. 91) to design E.T.A.'s academic curriculum. The curriculum is rigorous in a classical sense (as n. 64 explains after a meta-narrative comment: "Not 100% clear on this"), and therefore E.T.A. is not simply a "jock-factory." Some classical requirements have been adapted to E.T.A.'s unique mission, but without any loss of academic rigor. Jim stipulated in his will that Mrs. Pricket (his sound engineer), Ogilvie, Leith, and Soma R.-L.-O.-Chawaf have an "endowed-for-perpetuity presence on the academic payroll." Mario sits close to the radio because Avril "gets the howling fantods from any voice that does not exit a living corporeal head." Because of Avril's "issues of enclosure" there are no interior doors between rooms at the Headmaster's House. Her second floor bedroom is right next to Tavis's. A stairway runs from her study down to the tunnels, so she "can commute over to E.T.A. below ground" (cf. p. 51).

Madame Psychosis's accent is "the accent of someone who's spent time either losing a southern lilt or cultivating one." Her voice is "strangely empty, as if she were speaking from inside a small box. It's not bored or laconic or ironic or tongue-in-cheek." Madame Psychosis invites both medusas and odalisques to join U.H.I.D. (cf. Jim's film, "*The Medusa v. the Odalisque*," p. 988). Listeners are invited to leave, for example, their "TP Tableaux" (cf. Ch. 13.7) and come "don the veil of type and token. Come learn to love what's hidden inside." The music she is using "is weirdly compelling. You can never predict what it will be, but over time some kind of pattern emerges, a trend or rhythm." The music is described as making one see "something heavy swinging slowly" (cf. "the rhythm of long things swinging" from the sound check). The music is periodic (a word that pops into Mario's head eleven lines before it is used to describe the music) and haunting. "It suggests expansion without really expanding." Madame Psychosis's voice strikes Mario as "familiar and oddly sad," and he is "sure Madame Psychosis cannot herself sense the compelling beauty and light she projects over the air." Her "cued musics stir very early memories of Mario's father." A random caller to the program asserts that in its revolution around the earth the moon does not itself revolve, that "it just stays there, hidden and disclosed by our round shadow's rhythms, but never revolving. That it never turns its face away."

Sometimes on their visits to the Headmaster's House, Hal and Mario bring John Wayne (like Avril a Canadian), whom Avril "likes and speaks to animatedly even though he rarely says anything." Tonight Hal "disappeared for about half an hour" before the visit (while Mario waited for him) and says he will "blast down the hill for a bit" before going home, although that may just be something he says as part of the "ritualistic and almost hallucinatory . . . post-prandial farewell routine."

PLOT AND CHARACTER: Joelle, Mario, Hal, Avril
THEME: Fear/Obsess, Isolation, Loss, His/Father, Boundaries, Cycles, Secrets, Recur

Sixty Minutes More Or Less With Madame Psychosis is a program with obsessively devoted listeners. The moon, obsessed with the earth, "never turns its face away." Mario listens to Madame Psychosis fanatically—"almost religiously" (p. 171)—sitting "right up close to one of the speakers." Because of Avril's "issues of enclosure" there are no interior doors between rooms at the Headmaster's House (presumably this includes the adjacent bedrooms of Avril and Tavis), but she travels by tunnel below ground. Madame Psychosis is alone and sounds "as if she were speaking from inside a small box" (a cage?). She is twice described as sad, and her "cued musics stir very early memories of Mario's father" (the show before Madame Psychosis's is born out of a sense of loss and miscommunication with respect to fathers). Her music "suggests expansion without really expanding," somewhat analogous to Schtitt's discussion of tennis boundaries (p. 82). The music is periodic: "over time some kind of pattern emerges, a trend or rhythm." Hal and Mario make periodic visits to HmH, where the farewell "routine" is "ritualistic." Madame Psychosis "sometimes reads circulars and catalogues" as she does tonight, inviting listeners to "Come learn to love what's hidden inside." The caller asserts that the moon is "hidden and disclosed by our round shadow's rhythms." Madame Psychosis is hidden from the engineer, who can only see her shadow outside his booth, and speaks for the U.H.I.D. (you hid) organization. In addition to the recurrence of ominous shadows and the unnatural quality of fluorescence (which eliminates shadows), there are other recurrences of circles (annulation, a cold-fusion ring, a halo-ish ring), dancing ("Look at that fucker *Dance*"), blue (an emergency ladder, the Charles), hunched figures (tunnel posture, U.H.I.D. invitees), and a primitive description of Mario's hands as claws.

Chapter 16.2, Section 57, Pages 193-198
Note 67, Pages 997-998
early November Y.D.A.U.

Ennet House (cf. Ch. 13.2) is the sixth of seven units in the Enfield Marine Public Health Hospital complex. This was Tiny Ewell's destination in early November (Ch. 10.4), and the last Ennet thread (Ch. 15.4) occurred on 4 November, which makes early November a convenient assumption for the time period of this section. From E.T.A.'s hilltop, the E.M.P.H.H. complex "resembles seven moons orbiting a dead planet." Unit #1 counsels and "dispenses various pacifying medications" to Vietnam vets. Unit #2 is a methadone clinic. In the mornings, 50 or 60 people wait in line at Unit #2 "and yet still [manage] to appear alone and stand-offish." Unit #3 is being reconditioned for lease. Unit #4 is a repository for Alzheimer's patients with VA pensions. When Don Gately—who "graduated treatment [after nine months, p. 137] and took the offer of a live-in-Staffer's job at Ennet House"—was "in the very early part of his Ennet House residency" (presumably just after the events of Ch. 7.4, over one year ago), he was almost discharged for his part in a prank played on the customers of Unit #2, similar to the prank played "[n]ot six weeks ago" on the "ancient retired Air Force nurse [who] does nothing but scream 'Help!' for hours at a time" in Unit #4.

Unit #5 is for "catatonics and various vegetablish, fetal-positioned mental patients" and is referred to as The Shed. Note 67 explains that a couple of Enfield Marine cops (who were extras in two of Jim's films) call Unit #5 The Shed "because its residents don't seem housed there so much as more like *stored* there" and call the Shed's residents "objay darts." The cops sometimes frequent The Unexamined Life tavern (cf. p. 50) and will relate anecdotes about The Shed's catatonic residents if Hal is there, because Hal is "the only E.T.A. who seems truly interested." The cops tell of a woman who is debilitatingly phobic, "almost psychotically terrified of the possibility that she might be either blind or paralyzed or both," sitting completely still with her eyes shut tight so she can at least hope that she may not be blind or paralyzed (because her non-action allows those conditions to go untested). The "common unifying symptom of most of the Shed's objay darts is a terror so terrifying it makes the object of the terror come true" (cf. Fenton, pp. 47-8). Gately sometimes watches a catatonic who touches a tree, illuminated by "light that spills down from the snooty tennis prep school overhead on its hill." He tries not to associate his empathy for her with "watching his mother pass out on some piece of living-room chintz."

Unit #6 is Ennet House. The front office is the director's office, and the house is divided into male and female sides. Unit #7 teeters on an eroding ravine. It is "boarded up and unmaintained." Entering Unit #7 "is cause for immediate administrative discharge" of Ennet residents, since former residents have been known to sneak in and "secretly relapse." Behind Unit #7 is the biggest hill in Enfield, at the top of which is E.T.A. Almost half the Ennet House residents negotiate this hill (rather than taking the longer "legit route") on the way to their jobs, including those who have "custodial and kitchen jobs at the rich tennis school for blond gleaming tennis kids" (cf. Avril's displeasure with respect to this shortcut, p. 122). During construction of E.T.A, debris fell down the hill and damaged Unit #7 (cf. Jim's *(At Least) Three Cheers for Cause and Effect*, p. 991), for which (unbeknownst to Gately) E.T.A. "still has to pay full rent, every month, on what it almost buried."

PLOT AND CHARACTER: Ennet, Gately
THEME: Phys/Ob, Isolation, Inf/Reg, Fear/Obsess, Non-Action, Recur

Residents of the units of E.M.P.H.H. face severe physical and mental obstacles. The customers of Unit #2 ("alone, brooding, solo acts") are described as participants in a balletic "isolation-in-union" in which they are "doing everything but truly congregating." Unit #4's residents have a "toddlerish aspect"; Unit #5's residents are "vegetablish, fetal-positioned mental patients," who are terrified to the point of catatonia (non-action) and who inspire the cops' compulsive interest. There are recurring images here of orbits (circles), the dance motif of Unit #2's ballet of isolation (which includes "standing on first one foot and then the other" "like hyper-conditioned rats"), an eliminated map, literal blue collars, and getting high in secret.

Chapter 16.3, Section 58, Pages 198-200
Note 68, Page 998
6 November Y.D.A.U., 1610h.

Two days after their phone conversation (Ch. 15.2), Pemulis and Hal (who spits "into an old NASA glass") are with several of their peers in the E.T.A. weight room, where Lyle (cf. Ch. 12.1) helps Graham Rader understand that Rader is not the "paralyzed perfectionist" he claims to be. Pemulis impersonates people at the behest of Troeltsch and winces "whenever Kornspan and Freer roar at each other" as part of their weight-lifting ritual.

PLOT AND CHARACTER: E.T.A.
THEME: Phys/Ob, Non-Action, Recur

In this section, E.T.A. players work with "various resistance-systems" (obstacles, weights). Lyle assures Rader that Rader is not a "paralyzed perfectionist" who would stand in a state of self-absorbed non-action, unable to make a choice (like Erdedy at the end of Ch. 2). Some students do exhibit self-absorbed qualities. Carol Spodek is "intent on the mirror," and Freer watches himself "walk toward the mirror." Pemulis's "eyes roll way up," behavior that signifies pleasure or pain throughout the novel.

Chapter 16.4, Section 59, Pages 200-211
Notes 69-72, Page 998
beginning 4 November Y.D.A.U.

The first part of this section is a 5 ½ page catalogue of truths you will learn if "you ever chance to spend a little time around a Substance-recovery halfway facility" like Ennet House (last described in Ch. 16.2). If you are enslaved to a Substance, you will "pray to be allowed literally to lose your mind" and "leave it in an alley" when the Substance is taken away from you (recall Kate Gompert's request for shock treatment in Ch. 10.1). Anything can be an addictive escape "according to some hard-line schools of 12-Step thought" (n. 70). This philosophy inspires local stories of people so advanced in their recovery "they end up sitting in a bare chair, nude, in an unfurnished room, not moving but also not sleeping or meditating or abstracting." (This resonates with Hal's hero of non-action essay in Ch. 13.4.) Other truths include: "loneliness is not a function of solitude"; "logical validity is not a guarantee of truth"; "concentrating intently on anything is very hard work"; "no single, individual moment is in and of itself unendurable"; and "it is often more fun to want something than to have it." A person "will do things under the influence" that he "would not ever do sober," and "some consequences of these things cannot ever be erased or amended. Felonies are an example of this. As are tattoos."

As an example the way recovering people temporarily lose their minds when their "enslaving Substance" is taken away, the second part of the section tracks the particular obsession with tattoos of "new resident Tiny Ewell" ("the little attorney"). His first obsession was "with the exact definition of *alcoholic*" (on 4 November, p. 177). As the narrator catalogues their various tattoos, most current Ennet residents and counselors are introduced or reintroduced. Characters associated with Ennet House so far are listed at the end of this summary by category and in order of their appearance. The Five-Man Room (5MR, cf. p. 194) houses "the newer male residents." This brings the Ennet House residency up to its stated capacity of 22 (cf. p. 137), although Skull "lasted only like four days" (over a quarter of incoming residents get discharged within thirty days, p. 195).

Note the misspelling of Minty's tattooed racial slur (p. 207; cf. yrstruly's misspelling, p. 129) and that "St. Elizabeth's Hospital is just two blocks down from the House." If the description of Tiny's "two-month" obsession with tattoos (p. 210) is not an exaggeration, he will approach Gately about jailhouse tatts in January Y.G. Gately considers getting an unwanted tattoo a minor mistake "compared to some of the fucked-up and *really* irrevocable impulsive mistakes [he'd] made as an active drug addict and burglar" (cf. Ch. 7.4), which Gately is "trying to accept he'll be paying off for a real long time."

ADMINISTRATION	RESIDENTS	RESIDENTS
Pat; Chs. 15.4, 16.2	Erdedy (5MR), Ch. 2	Thrale, Ch. 15.4
House Manager, Ch. 16.2	Green; Chs. 5.2, 15.4	Day (5MR)
	Clenette; Chs. 5.3, 15.4	Hanley
LIVE-IN STAFF	Gompert, Ch. 10.1	Cortelyu
Gately; Chs. 7.4, 15.4, 16.2	Ewell (5MR), Ch. 10.4	Foss
Foltz	Glynn, Ch. 13.3	Lenz (5MR)
	Nell, Ch. 15.4	Treat
COUNSELORS	Diehl, Ch. 15.4	Belbin
Gene M; Chs. 15.4, 16.2	McDade, Ch. 15.4	Didi N.
Thrust, Ch. 16.2	Minty, Ch. 15.4	Tingly
Steenbok	Alfonso, Ch. 15.4	Skull (5MR)

PLOT AND CHARACTER: Ennet, AA&R
THEME: Fear/Obsess, Inf/Reg, Loss, Secret, Recur

The obsession that drives an addict back to his or her "enslaving Substance" is equated with a "kind of interior psychic worm that cannot be sated or killed." "50% of persons with a Substance addiction suffer from some other recognized form of psychiatric disorder, too." Most "Substance-addicted people . . . have a compulsive and unhealthy relationship with their own thinking," which is about themselves and about bad things happening to them. Tattoos are a measure of "the chilling irrevocability of intoxicated impulses." The recovering addict becomes familiar with loss in the form of hurt and loneliness. A secret doesn't have to be ominous if it involves doing "something nice for somebody" and is "almost its own form of intoxicating buzz."

There are recurring references here to waste (skin as an "excretory organ" and the equivalence of male and female discussions of "eliminatory functions"), sexually abused children (who are later "arrested for drug- and alcohol-related offenses"), people that look like "rodents," a screen that "fills your whole vision," "Boundary Issue[s]" over tattoos in private female areas, water imagery (tattoos that look like they're "just under the surface of a murky-type pond" and faded to "a kind of underwater blue"), "blue-collar" tattoos, "*BLUEYED BOY*" on Skull's tattoo, and the "blue ink" that makes jailhouse tatts "night-sky blue." The Millennial Fizzy appears to be a popular beverage, consumed by recovering addicts and the WYYY student engineer as well (cf. p. 182). Also linking this section to Ch. 16.1 are the "Madame Psychosis-like harmonies" that one can weave around the sound of "a cheap vacuum cleaner." The "terse and hateful single word [tattoo] *PUSSY*" links this section to the previous section in which Pemulis whispered "Pussy" to Kornspan.

Chapter 16.5, Section 60, Pages 211-219
Notes 73-77, Pages 998-999
4-5 November Y.D.A.U

Before Ch. 15.2 (which occurs "post-transaction," p. 170), Pemulis had purchased "thirteen incredibly potent 50-mg. artifacts of the B.S. 1970s" from "reputed former Canadian insurgents" (one of whom was "cradling a broom") at "a cut-rate mirror, blown-glass, practical joke 'n gag, trendy postcard, and low-demand old film-cartridge emporium called Antitoi Entertainment." This section begins "close to 1430h." on Wednesday 4 November, shortly after Pemulis calls Hal at the end of Ch. 15.2, and ends "the next academic day," which is the day before "the inter-academy thing with Port Washington tomorrow" (p. 217; cf. pp. 103, 112). The intensity of the locker room activity on 6 November (Ch. 16.3) is perhaps due to anxiety about the Port Washington meet, set to occur later that day (on Friday 6 November, not Tuesday as Pemulis incorrectly states on p. 212).

Pemulis is in his room talking with Hal and Trevor Axford about the DMZ he purchased while his roommates Schacht and Troeltsch are "down at lunch" (cf. "still at lunch," p. 171). Pemulis says of the tablets that the last lots "came off the line in the early 70s" and points out "the little trademark on each one, with the guy in bell-bottoms and long sideburns," a "tiny mod hipster in each center wishing the viewer peace" (cf. also the iconic 70s smiley-face on the attaché's cartridge, p. 36). The tablets were used in "certain shady CIA-era military experiments" that "got out of control": "Subjects locked away in institutions and written off as casualties of peace." As proof of the DMZ's potency, Pemulis cites a Moment magazine (employer of Steeply, p. 142) article which states that an Army convict "literally lost his mind, like the massive dose picked his mind up and carried it off somewhere," when injected as part of an Army experiment (recall that literally losing one's mind is also what is prayed for when enslaving Substances are taken away, p. 201). He was "found later in his Army cell, in some impossible lotus position, singing show tunes in a scary deadly-accurate Ethel-Merman-impression voice." Axford suggests Pemulis may have found "a possible explanation for poor old Lyle and his lotus position" and gestures toward the weight room with his "bad right hand." The DMZ is "stashed deep in the toe of an old sneaker that sits atop the aluminum strut between two panels in subdorm B's drop ceiling, Pemulis's time-tested entrepot," for safekeeping.

"Over the course of the next academic day" (Thursday 5 November), it is decided that Pemulis, Hal, Axford, and maybe Struck will "sample the potentially incredibly potent DMZ in predeterminedly safe amounts" themselves before "unleashing it on" others. Before sampling the drug, Hal's requires that someone must go to a "medical library and physically verify that the compound is both organic and nonaddictive." Pemulis believes they will need "36 hours of demand-free time"—during which Axford and Hal will not be required to go to 0500 (0600 on p. 32) drills—to "rally from whatever meninges-withering hangover the incredibly potent DMZ might involve." Pemulis will need a couple of weeks to do the medical research, so "the window of opportunity looks to be 11/20-21" after "the big End-of-Fiscal-Year fundraising exhibition" with teams from Québec. This is "the weekend right before Thanksgiving week and the WhataBurger Invitational in sunny AZ," where Hal is "apt to face Wayne in the semis" (n. 75). Recall that it is during the Y.G. WhataBurger tournament one year from now (the tournament Wayne "would have won," pp. 16-7) when Hal says that he was in the hospital "almost exactly one year back" (p. 16). Will Hal try the DMZ? Will that be the reason he goes to the hospital? Why won't Wayne be in the Y.G. WhataBurger? Does it have something to do with Wayne's "standing watch in a mask as Donald Gately and [Hal] dig up [Jim's] head" (p. 17)?

Note 76 states that Hal was gifted "as a toddler" "in the early B.S. 1990s." Given that Hal is eighteen (cf. p. 3) in November Y.G. (2010, cf. Ch. 15.3 summary); he was born in June (cf. p. 27) 1992, was a toddler in the early 1990s as stated here, and was almost five in "March or early April" 1997, at the time of the mold incident described by Orin (Ch. 1.2). Therefore, Hal was gifted before he ate the mold, "though part of this high cerebral rank was because [the] diagnostic tests weren't quite so keen when it came to distinguishing between raw neural gifts and the young Hal's mono-maniacally obsessive interest and effort, as if Hal were trying as if his very life were in the balance to please some person or persons, even though no one had ever hinted that his life depended on seeming gifted." In winning public competitions of intellectual prowess as a toddler, Hal felt "that same pale sweet aura that an LSD afterglow conferred . . . like almost a halo of approved grace" (cf. the aura or luminescence Hal feels after a night of hallucinogens, p. 218). Axford describes an LSD hangover as leaving you "utterly empty, a shell, void inside, like your soul was a wrung-out sponge."

PLOT AND CHARACTER: E.T.A., AA&R, Hal
THEME: Inf/Reg, Recur, Fear/Obsess

Hal compulsively asks a question about the DMZ "knowing he sounds greedy but unable to help himself." Pemulis compares the DMZ to a "gargantuan feral infant." There is another instance of a communication problem in that Pemulis "speaks no French" and must therefore negotiate the DMZ transaction "in dumbshow." The afternoon light is described as being "the slightly sad color of early winter P.M." (cf. Ch. 11.9 summary). An alcohol hangover will make your eyes feel like they are "bulging and receding." Hal's "halo of approved grace" is a circle of light (cf. halation, p. 97). Pemulis has "an enormous hand-drawn Sierpinski gasket" (cf. the Introduction to the study) on his wall. To what degree does the "obsessive interest and effort" of Hal's childhood still affect him? Presumably, Hal was naturally gifted as a toddler (n. 76), but cf. that Jim references Avril putting steroids into ten-year-old Hal's cereal (p. 30). If Avril had been giving Hal steroids since he was a toddler, could that have affected his abilities? Consult Ch. 9.b of Wallace's *The Broom of the System* for more on increased intelligence resulting from the introduction of substances into baby food.

Chapter 16: Circulars and Catalogues

Madame Psychosis, reading from a circular, provides a catalogue of people who are invited to join U.H.I.D. The architectural features of the M.I.T. Student Union are catalogued. Madame Psychosis's music is "periodic." Hal and Mario periodically visit HmH and participate in farewell rituals there. A caller speaks of the moon's revolution about the earth. Ennet is the sixth of "seven moons orbiting a dead planet." The E.M.P.H.H. Units are catalogued in Ch. 16.2. The pre-match ritual activities of E.T.A. students are catalogued in Ch. 16.3. Ch. 16.4 begins with a catalogue of truths ("exotic new facts") and ends with a catalogue of tattoos. Pemulis provides a catalogue of facts about DMZ (also called Madame Psychosis) and is able to determine a window of opportunity based on his knowledge of E.T.A. events, which follow a regular yearly pattern. As a child, Hal felt an aura "like almost a halo of approved grace" (cf. the "halo-ish ring" on the M.I.T. Student Union brain, p. 186).

Chapter 17

Veiled Veils

Chapter 17.1, Section 61, Pages 219-223
7 November Y.D.A.U.

It turns out that Madame Psychosis (cf. Ch. 16.1) is Joelle van Dyne, "the daughter of a low-pH chemist and homemaker from western Kentucky," who not only appeared in Jim's films, but knew Orin as well. She is "sitting by herself under what used to be her window" at a party hosted by Molly Notkin "to celebrate [Molly's] passing her Orals in Film & Film-Cartridge Theory" at M.I.T. The chairs at the party are "molded in the likeness of great filmmakers from the celluloid canon." Joelle met Molly in this doctoral program "before her retreat into broadcast sound." It turns out that even if Joelle did not sit behind a screen at WYYY, the student engineer would still not see her face, because as a member of U.H.I.D. (Joelle read from this organization's circular on her show in Ch. 16.1) she wears a veil. The partygoers wear "disguises and whiskers," which from Joelle's point of view are "veiled veils." Joelle intends to commit suicide by drug overdose at this party. Joelle "sits alone in her linen veil" and listens "to bits of conversation she reels out in the overall voices' noise." She can "call up everything from all times." She sees her life running before her like film projected on "the white screen" before her eyes: "from Uncle Bud and twirling to Orin and Jim and YYY, all the way up to today's wet walk here . . . on this last day before the great O.N.A.N.ite Interdependence revel."

Joelle traces her walk "from the Red Line's Downtown stop, walking the whole way from East Charles St." to this "third floor cooperative apartment on the East Cambridge fringes of the Back Bay" above "both river and Bay's edge." During her walk in the rain (past

I.W.D.—not E.W.D.—dumpsters), people look at her like they "look at the blind, naked gazes, not knowing she could see everything at all times." Everything is "milky and halated [cf. n. 76] through her veil's damp linen, . . . her legs on autopilot, she a perceptual engine." People ask "about the deal with the veil" and "where's the wedding at." One of the people she encounters is a "sooty wheelchaired man" who wears a cap that says "NOTRE RAI PAYS" (our spoken country), has a "puffed red cut" across his palm, and says nothing after receiving Joelle's money.

"The rain's wet veil blurs things like Jim had designed his neonatal lens to blur things in imitation of a neo-natal retina, everything recognizable and yet without outline." Joelle is "excruciatingly alive and encaged" and feels that there "isn't an exit. The ultimate annular fusion: that of exhibit and its cage. Jim's own *Cage III: Free Show* [cf. p. 988]. It is the cage that has entered *her*, somehow. . . . The Fun has long since dropped off the Too Much" (cf. *Too Much Fun*, one of Jim's unfinished films; p. 993).

Joelle buys a cigar for the tube that holds it and buys a "Pepsi Cola in a blunt plastic bottle" since there was no "Big Red Soda Water." She intends to use these items to get so high that she will "fall down and stop breathing and turn blue and die, clutching her heart." She has "lost the ability to lie to herself about being able to quit, or even about enjoying it, still." She, like Erdedy, Gompert, and other Ennet residents, "wanted to stop and also couldn't stop." She first came to this realization after the show with "that caller and the moon" (cf. p. 192), when she had "gone home and at least finally not turned her face away from the situation . . . . She had in a way done as they'd made Jim do near the end and admitted powerlessness over this cage, this unfree show, . . . weeping and veilless and yarn-haired, like some grotesque clown, in all four mirrors of her little room's walls."

PLOT AND CHARACTER: Joelle, AA&R, Jim
THEME: Loss, Isolation, Secrets, Boundaries, Time, Inf/Reg, Recur

Joelle feels sadness (loss) at the end of a party, when "voices recede down the hall." Yet Joelle is in isolation even during Notkin's party: she "sits alone in her linen veil" (the other partygoers are also in disguise). As an addict, she feels that she is in a cage, a recurring image of isolation, especially in this chapter. The boundaries of her cage have lost definition: "It is the cage that has entered her, somehow. . . . [Using her substance] no longer delimits and fills the hole. It no longer delimits the hole." She is also blending past, present, and future: she "can call up everything from all times." She remembers her past as she sits in a chair ("feeling like a child") observing the party and planning her suicide, that "most self-involved of all acts, self-cancelling" (also described as the elimination of a map). She secretly plans a suicidal overdose because she has "lost the ability to lie to herself about being able to quit" but still cannot quit. Her realization was prompted by the caller who said the moon "never looked away" and occurred when she was "veilless" before "four mirrors" ("blindingly open" vs. "hidden," p. 220). As with Erdedy (cf. p. 25) and Gompert (cf. p. 78), Joelle's realization is accompanied by weeping (loss). Other recurrences here include the water imagery of "utter silence in the party's wake" and Notkin's party overlooking the river and the bay, Notkin's "fear of direct light" and her boyfriend's guilty erections (fears and obsessions), another annular fusion reference, the waste encountered on Joelle's wet walk, "blue shoeless limbs" on that walk, and Joelle's vision of turning "blue" upon her death.

Chapter 17.2, Section 62, Page 223
Note 78, Page 999
unspecified Y.D.A.U.

This section confirms the chronology of Subsidized Time constructed for the Ch. 15.3 summary and identifies Y.W.-Q.M.D. as the Year of the Whisper-Quiet Maytag Dishmaster. Rights to the Year of Glad are subject to "ratification of final contract" on 15 December Y.D.A.U. (n. 78). We know from Ch. 1 that the contract will indeed be ratified.

PLOT AND CHARACTER: O.N.A.N.
THEME: Time, Secrets, Inf/Reg, Waste, Isolation

With the year-long subsidization (support) of time by O.N.A.N.ite corporations, the old B.S. system of numerical years has subsided (receded, sunk, become hidden) from the consciousness of the O.N.A.N.ite citizenry. The compulsions and regressions inherent in O.N.A.N.ite society can be traced through the sponsors of Subsidized Time. The Whopper is a symbol of gluttony (and a whopper is a big lie). Tucks Medicated Pads combat the hemorrhoids that develop at a source of waste, often prompted by the stress that accompanies obsession. Trial-Size Dove Bars are used to clean the body of waste (and bite-size Dove bars promote impulse snacking). The Perdue Wonderchicken is presumably large and boneless, encouraging both gluttony and minimal dining effort. The Whisper-Quiet Maytag Dishmaster is a machine used for cleaning residual food (waste) that minimizes both the human dish washer's activity and environmental stimuli (noise). The Yushityu TP Upgrade promotes isolation and physical passivity. Dairy Products from the American Heartland include cheese—the "eater of cheese" betrays and isolates himself from his companions—and milk, sustenance of infants. The Depend Adult Undergarment symbolizes an adult regressed to a state of infancy with respect to waste. Glad flaccid receptacles are used to seal (isolate) food. A Year of Glad is an extremely long period of unbroken happiness (also represented by the smiley-face on the attaché's cartridge), symbolizing fanatic (compulsive) attachment or freedom from care and responsibility, like an infant.

In *Infinite Jest*, as in *Hamlet*, "The time is out of joint" (I.i.196). As in 1984, military time is used: "It was a bright cold day in April and the clocks were striking thirteen" (Book One, Ch. 1). As in *The Sound and the Fury*, a novel that also takes its title from Shakespeare, the narrative is fragmented with respect to point of view and chronology. Also, the clock in the final part of Faulkner's novel is three hours off (cf. Wallace's phrase: "a kind of doomed timeless Faulknerian feel," p. 957).

Chapter 17.3, Section 63, Pages 223-226
Note 79, Page 999
7 November Y.D.A.U.

Joelle continues (from Ch. 17.1) to reflect on her life and her walk to the party. After passing a "statue of Boston's Colonel Shaw . . . draped in a large Québecois fleur-de-lis flag" she then sees, on the street outside F.A.O. Schwartz, a 2-D display of a man in a wheelchair with an ecstatic expression holding a case for a cartridge that is "conspicuously unlabelled." There is no way to determine what the display is advertising: "It's some kind of anti-ad. To direct attention at what is not said. . . . The film-cartridge itself would be a blank, too, or the case empty . . . . Joelle removes it and looks at it and puts it back. She's had her last fling with film cartridges." Joelle hasn't made a film since Jim "filmed her at prodigious and multi-lensed length, and refused to share what he'd made of it, and died w/o a note." Therefore, Joelle doesn't realize that the display is presumably an advertisement for the very film she just remembered making. When she puts the cartridge back, a young dealer "calls her Mama and asks where's the funeral at." Does the ad with the man in the wheelchair suggest that the A.F.R. is "conspir[ing] to bring the Entertainment into [the] warm homes" (p. 108) of Bostonians? Is there a dangerous cartridge in the case, like the one viewed by the attaché?

"For a while, after the acid [and "after taking the veil"], after first Orin [a "dodger of flung acid extraordinaire"] left and then Jim came and made her sit through that filmed apology-scene and then vanished and then came back," Joelle "liked to get really high and clean." Joelle thinks of cleaning as imitating "the wife and mother they both declined to shoot." (Joelle twice thinks of Jim as being dead for over four years on p. 225. He has actually been dead for over five years.)

Joelle recalls smoking "freebase cocaine this A.M. for the last time," after which she "had wept and imprecated at the mirrors and thrown away her paraphernalia again for the final time" (like Erdedy) before leaving to get more from Lady Delphina (also spoken of by yrstruly on p. 131) an hour later. At her T-stop platform, an older black man tells Joelle that he has seen "one or two of these linen veils before" and that he was curious. She ties the origins of U.H.I.D. —"designed to afford the scopophobic empathic fellowship and the genesis of sturdy resources through shame-free and unconstrained concealment"—to a comment made by Winston Churchill.

PLOT AND CHARACTER: Joelle, AA&R, Jim, Samizdat
THEME: Memory, Fear/Obsess, Recur

In this section, Joelle remembers her "own personal Daddy," Orin, Jim, her film work, and some of her activities on this day prior to arriving at Notkin's party. Orin's five-holed lemon pledge masks recall videophony masks on hooks (p. 148). Joelle's obsession with cleaning is resonant with Avril's fear of "spoilage and filth" (p. 11). U.H.I.D. members are "scopophobic." There is a missed connection when Joelle doesn't realize that the "anti-ad" is for the last film she did with Jim. The figure in the anti-ad has "his eyes on the blue harlequin-patches of the post-storm sky." Joelle walks past "revolving doors." The boys nearby are "so black they're blue, horrifically skinny and young, little more than living shadows."

Chapter 17.4, Section 64, Page 227
unspecified Y.D.A.U.

This section provides the "PUTATIVE CURRICULUM VITAE OF HELEN P. STEEPLY." It spans the ten years of "her" journalism "career," from graduate intern at *Time* to her current position at *Moment* magazine in Erythema AZ, where she has been for 15 months. If it is now November Y.D.A.U., Steeply has been on this U.S.O.U.S. field assignment since August Y.D.P.A.H., just before Gately robbed DuPlessis (Ch. 7.4). He is in this disguise when he meets Marathe on 30 April Y.D.A.U. (Ch. 11). Steeply's first *Moment* article was published on 10 August Y.D.A.U. (Ch. 13.5).

PLOT AND CHARACTER: U.S.O.U.S.
THEME: Secrets

Somewhat analogous to Joelle's use of a veil, Steeply works (lives) undercover, his identity known only to some members of the U.S.O.U.S. and unknown by the general public.

Chapter 17.5, Section 65, Pages 227-240
Notes 80-81, Pages 999-1000
7 November Y.D.A.U.

From her T-stop (Ch. 17.3, p. 226), Joelle proceeds to Upper Brighton for a meeting with Lady Delphina (imagined on pp. 225-6) and then "from the Red Line's Downtown stop" (p. 221) begins her wet walk (pp. 221-5) to "the cooperative Back Bay-edge brownstone she had lived in once with Orin and performed in with his father and then passed on to Molly Notkin," who is still dressed as Karl Marx a day after obtaining A.B.D. status with a "devastating oral critique of post-millennial Marxist Film-Cartridge Theory from the point of view of [and dressed as] Marx himself." After being greeted by Notkin, Joelle sits alone in her chair and watches the partygoers as she reflects on her life and the trip to Notkin's apartment (pp. 219-226).

Notkin has "no idea that Joelle's been in a cage since Y.T.S.D.B. . . . or that Joelle even now lives hand-to-lung on a grossly generous trust willed her by a man she unveiled for but never slept with, the prodigious punter's father, infinite jester, director of a final *opus* so *magnum* he'd claimed to have had it locked away." Jim saw the name of one of Avril's lovers (presumably) reappear in the steam of Avril's car's window on his way "to this very brownstone, to shoot Joelle in the weird wobble-lensed maternal 'I'm-so-terribly-sorry' monologue-scene [cf. "God I'm I'm so *sorry*. Jim" from James Sr.'s monologue, p. 168] of the last thing he'd done, and then never shown her, and had ordered the cartridge's burial in the brass casket w/ him in the same testament in which he'd willed Joelle an absurd (and addiction-enabling) annuity." This may have given Avril the impression that Jim and Joelle were lovers, but Orin knew they were not lovers (n. 80). Jim told Joelle that this final film ended up breaking his heart by being as entertaining as he'd always wanted to make it. (If this cartridge went with Jim to his grave, how did a copy get to the attaché?) Joelle was Orin's "only lover for twenty-six months and his father's optical beloved for twenty-one" (but cf. Ch. 20.1 summary for more on Joelle's time with Jim). Joelle never got to know Mario "because Orin had disliked him."

The dancers at the party are doing the "Minimal Mambo" and appear "to be just this side of standing still." Some of their "movements are so tiny they are evocative and compel watching." Joelle watches a beautiful female dancer "watching herself with unselfconscious fascination" in a mirror Jim had "cut for the scenes of that last ghastly thing he'd made her stand before, reciting in the openly empty tones she'd gone on to use on-air." Joelle notes the "absence of shame at the self-obsession." When the dancer announces to "the whole dancing mass" that her "*tits*" are "*beautiful*" (vs. Steeply's "ridiculous tits," p. 92), there is "something so heartbreakingly sincere in what she says Joelle wants to go to her" and "tell her it is and will be completely all right." Joelle realizes that the dancer has taken Ecstacy. Joelle is "an academic generation ahead of most of these candidates, and rather feared, even though not many know she is an Aural Personality, feared for quitting instead of failing [Joelle quit the Ph.D. program, but she obtained an M.A. and published one monograph; p. 234], and because of the connection of the memory of Jim, and she is given a certain wide social berth, allowed to delay and orbit and stand unengaged at the fringes of shifting groups."

"Was the allegedly fatally entertaining and scopophiliac thing Jim alleges he made out of her unveiled face here at the start of Y.T.S.D.B. a cage or really a door? Had he even cut the tape into something coherent? There was nothing coherent in the mother-death-cosmology and apologies she'd repeated over and over, inclined over that auto-wobbled lens propped up in the plaid-sided pram. He never let her see it, not even the dailies. He killed himself less than ninety days later. . . . Did she kill him somehow, just inclining veilless over that lens?" Joelle's "last facial-expression memory" of Jim is his "frightened look" when Joelle laughed at his choice of "that skull-fragment out of the *Hamlet* graveyard scene" as the title of his "unseen last cartridge."

Joelle listens "to bits of conversation she reels in" (p. 220). Comstock and Duquette, co-authors with Posner of n. 24's filmography, are referenced on p. 233: "Comstock says if it even exists it has to be something more like an aesthetic pharmaceutical. Some beastly post-annular scopophiliacal vector. Suprasubliminals and that. Some kind of abstractable hypnosis, an optical dopamine-cue. A recorded delusion. Duquette says he's lost contact with three colleagues. He said a good bit of Berkeley isn't answering their phone." (Is something akin to the events of 1-2 April in Boston happening in Berkeley now?) Another partygoer asserts, "This ultimate cartridge-as-ecstatic-death rumor's been going around like a lazy toilet since Dishmaster." A film-scholar asserts: "Fans do not begin to keep it all in the Great Convexity. . . . You cannot give away your filth and prevent all creepage, no? Filth by its very nature it is a thing that is creeping always back. Me, I can remember when your Charles was cafe with cream. Look at it now. It is the blue river." This prompts: "I think you mean Great Concavity, Alain."

Joelle has "the pre-suicide's classic longing: Sit down one second, I want to tell you everything [cf. Orin to Hal, p. 32]. My name is Joelle van Dyne, Dutch-Irish, and I was reared on family land east of Shiny Prize, Kentucky, the only child of a low-pH chemist and his second wife [Joelle later thinks of her father's third wife, "her stepmother in the Locked Ward"]. I now have no accent except under stress [cf. p. 189]. I am 1.7 meters tall and weigh 48 kilograms ["Helen" Steeply is "1.93 M., 104 KG."; p. 227]. I occupy space and have mass. I breathe in and breathe out [cf. Hal: "I am in here," p. 3]."

In Notkin's bathroom, Joelle recalls that freebasing cocaine "had been simply too much fun, at the start" and that "Orin had neither disapproved nor partaken." Jim's "Too Much was neat bourbon, and he had lived life to the fullest, and then gone in for detoxification, again and again." Joelle "always sees, after inhaling" (cf. "the arrow's best descent," p. 240) Bernini's "Ecstacy of St. Theresa" (cf. Jim's *Pre-Nuptial Agreement of Heaven and Hell*, p. 988), which she never got to see on display. Joelle hears "Molly's laugh which sounds like a shriek" "as an enormous glass crash sounds off in the living room" (cf. "C.T. always drops at least one plate out in the kitchen and then bellows," p. 193). Joelle "turns on the [fluorescent] light over the medicine cabinet's mirror" to remove the "shadows of her hands over what she needs." Joelle's freebasing ritual involves a series of meticulous procedures. The "vividly blue" river rolls away far below the windowless bathroom, and a projectile of waste arcs toward a yellow-brown cloud in the distance that "looks like a not very pretty sort of wastebasket, waiting."

"The only other thing . . . she'd ever come close to feeling this way about" was watching movies with her father as a child. Her father used to tell her "over and over again" that she was prettier than the movie stars on the screen, "her hand in his lap and their big box of Crackerjacks in her hand" or "his hand in her lap her hand in the box and rooting down past candy for the Prize." Standing in line with her father made her feel "*taken care of*." Orin did not make her feel this way, but "starting in with this lover, cooking and smoking it, [more than] five years back, before Incandenza's death" did. Unlike Orin, the cocaine "made her feel about to be entered by something that didn't know she was there and yet was all about making her feel good anyway, coming in."

Joelle's "unveiled face in the dirty lit mirror is shocking in the intensity of its absorption." "Her glass of juice is on the back of the toilet, half-empty." She is "[d]eliberately setting about to make her heart explode" (cf. p. 230: "How much must a person want out, to put his head in a microwave oven?"). She is "like a diver preparing for a long descent." Post-inhalation, she is "uprightly fetal," her limbs "removed to a distance where their acknowledgement of her commands seems like magic." After loading and smoking again, Joelle hears someone trying to get into the bathroom as she vomits "muddy juice and blue smoke and dots of mercuric red" into the "cool blue tub."

PLOT AND CHARACTER: Joelle, AA&R, Jim, Samizdat
THEME: Secrets, Isolation, Memory, Inf/Reg, Waste, Recur, Cycles

Joelle secretly plans to commit suicide by secretly freebasing cocaine in the bathroom of Molly Notkin, who is disguised as Karl

Marx and throwing a party for other costumed guests. "[T]he hours before a suicide are usually an interval of enormous conceit and self-involvement" (p. 220); and Joelle sits alone, veiled and "in a cage," remembering events in her life and observing partygoers rather than interacting with them. Partygoers dance before the mirror used to film the final *Infinite Jest*, a film that, like a drug, captivates and fuels the isolation and self-absorption of its viewers with the help of Joelle, whose openly empty tones and maternal nature are captivating even on radio. (Some films have the capacity to captivate viewers like a drug, as did the films of Joelle's youth, albeit without the overwhelming power of the final *Infinite Jest*.) Melinda, under the influence of Ecstacy, watches herself "with unselfconscious fascination" and without shame in this mirror, displaying a "heartbreaking openness" that triggers Joelle's maternal instincts. Melinda's innocent, self-focused discovery (of beautiful tits) prompts Joelle's only impulse to interact with anyone at Notkin's party. Joelle's self-focused suicide plans involve setting free "the encaged rapacious thing inside" (her inner feral infant?), unveiled before "the mirror that illuminates." Joelle likes freebasing cocaine "more than anyone can like anything and still live." Post-inhalation, she becomes "uprightly fetal" (cf. the harrowing images of addicts regressed to fetal positions that close Darren Aronofsky's 2000 film, *Requiem for a Dream*).

Joelle ends up in a bathroom, vomiting back up what in its original form looked like "shit from a goat" (the "Prettiest G.O.A.T."?). Barrels of waste arc toward a yellow-brown "wastebasket" cloud. One partygoer tells a story of projectile vomiting. Another asserts that the creepage of filth has turned the brown Charles blue. In addition to the blue river, there are other recurrences of water metaphors: Melinda is in "a blue-and-white-striped sailorish top"; an Ecstacy hangover makes a freebase hangover look like "a day at the emotional beach" (cf. p. 218 for more on hangovers); at the party Joelle is "memorizing every detail like collecting empty shells"; and in the bathroom Joelle is "like a diver preparing for a long descent." Joelle's suicidal dive recalls Ophelia's. There are several references to cycles: Joelle is allowed to "orbit" (p. 231); the filth that goes around comes back around (p. 233); Jim's last film is speculated to be "rotating whorls" (p. 233); Jim went to detox again and again (p. 235); and Joelle's father told her she was prettier than movie stars "over and over again" (p. 237). The shadow-motif recurs with reference to "a kind of wraith- or phantom-like" quality and elongating sunlight "in transit across the coop's eastern wall" (pp. 233-4). The teeth-motif recurs with references to "dentures" and "soft rock's grim dental associations." Notkin's "phalloneurotic New Yorker" (cf. p. 220) provides another example of obsession. Examples of non-action are found in the dancers of the Minimal Mambo, who are "just this side of standing still"; in the gulls that are "stamped to the cleared sky, motionless as kites"; and in the fact that "everything eventually has to fall" (hit the ground or become horizontal), as the mirror used in *Infinite Jest* presumably does on p. 235.

Another character name is found to have variant spellings: cf. "Prickett" on p. 229 with "Pricket" on p. 188. Joelle, who impersonated Death for Jim (cf. pp. 991, 993), "looks like death" under her veil and will "eliminate her own map." Partygoers reference various filmmakers and theorists, and someone references an old TV show (*The Brady Bunch*). There are several more recurring images: a phrase (*THE END?*) "pops into [Joelle's] head"; her "mouth twitches and writhes" when she is high; there is a crash accompanied by a shriek-laugh; the partygoer outside the bathroom stands "on one foot then the other"; Melinda's sailorish top is white and blue; the Charles is two shades of blue; Notkin's bathroom is vividly blue; the tub is lacquered blue; Joelle creates pale blue smoke; and Joelle "seems to see . . . fat fingers of blue light from one sky, searching."

As stated in the Ch. 11.6 commentary, many of the ideas found in *Infinite Jest* resonate with ideas found in William Gaddis's *The Recognitions* (1955), a novel about forgery, loss, and obsession that features missed connections (or non-recognitions), water imagery, references to *Hamlet* and *Tosca*, and other similarities. Snatches of conversation about art and literature are heard in the party scenes in Gaddis's novel, which recall this chapter of *Infinite Jest.* In Chapter V of Part I, someone attributes to Guy de Maupassant the phrase "I mask myself among masked people" (p. 177); and there are references to "an unconscionably persistent smile" (p. 188), time (pp. 188, 201), St.

Teresa (p. 197), and a crash (p. 201; although a person crashes, not a mirror). An ellipsis is used to signify nonverbal response (p. 192). Esme, an addict (p. 196), sits "alone in the room like the woman in that painting whose beauty cannot be assailed" (p. 193). A partygoer notes that "somebody passed out in the tub" and that "there's blood all over the place" (p. 199). Parallels to *Infinite Jest* occur throughout *The Recognitions*. Consider the following from Chapters V-VI of Part II: "Everything is either concave or convex" (p. 526); "The haggard face hung over the back of the booth like a separate floating entity" (p. 535); and (similar to Erdedy) "the telephone and the doorbell both rang at once. [Maude] shuddered right through her frame, put out a hand in each direction, and finally got to the door" (and to the phone, p. 557).

Chapter 17: Veiled Veils

Joelle is a member of an organization (U.H.I.D.) whose members literally wear veils. Joelle is also figuratively veiled in that she is secretive and tends to isolate herself. She attends Molly Notkin's costume party, where the partygoers wear "disguises and whiskers": "veiled veils." The subsidizers of time inspire Liberty's costumes (cf. "the colossal Libertine Statue, wearing some type of enormous adult-design diaper," p. 33). A ten-year history has been crafted to help Steeply better disguise himself as a female journalist. This chapter is dominated by women; it is primarily about Joelle and also references Lady Liberty, Lady Delphina, "Helen" P. Steeply, Molly Notkin, and breast-admiring Melinda. U.H.I.D., "designed to afford the scopophobic empathic fellowship and the genesis of sturdy resources through shame-free and unconstrained concealment," was inspired by Winston Churchill's disrespect of an English lady.

Chapter 18

Probing for Details

Chapter 18.1, Section 66, Pages 240-242
unspecified Y.D.P.A.H.

This one-paragraph section serves as an orientation to the city of Enfield MA and is narrated in first person (cf. "I" in the fifth line from the bottom of p. 241). Enfield is "a township composed almost entirely of medical, corporate, and spiritual facilities. A kind of arm-shape extending north from Commonwealth Avenue and separating Brighton into Upper and Lower [site of the "brooding Brighton Project high-rises," where Roy Tony does business; p. 129], its elbow nudging East Newton's ribs [Gompert is from Newton, p. 69] and its fist sunk into Allston [Pemulis is from Allston, p. 154]." Some of Enfield's facilities are St. Elizabeth's Hospital (two blocks from Ennet House, p. 209), the E.M.P.H.H. Complex (cf. Ch. 16.2), part of Sunstrand Power and Light (whose signs warn that extremely dangerous "annular-generated amps are waiting underground for anyone who digs"), ATHSCME corporate headquarters, E.T.A., Leisure Time Ice (where Green worked, p. 39), the National Cranio-Facial Pain Foundation, and "regional shiny-truck, land-barge, and catapult facilities ["block-long catapults that make a sound like a giant stamping foot as they fling great twine-bundled waste-vehicles into the subannular regions of the Great Concavity"] for the O.N.A.N.-subsidized Empire Waste Displacement Co."

E.T.A., which has "32 asphalt tennis courts and sixteen Har-Tru composition tennis courts," "occupies probably now the nicest site in Enfield, some ten years after balding and shaving flat the top of the big abrupt hill that constitutes a kind of raised cyst on the township's elbow" (the hill was shaved flat in 1998 (cf. p. 949), the year before E.T.A. was accredited (cf. p. 63), placing this section in Y.D.P.A.H. or later). A wraparound view of the city of Enfield is provided by E.T.A.'s hilltop, including a view "into the complexly decaying grounds of Enfield Marine."

PLOT AND CHARACTER: O.N.A.N., E.T.A.
THEME: Phys/Ob, Recur

The "whole flexed Enfield limb" is reminiscent of E.T.A.'s cardioid (heart) shape (n. 3), of E.T.A.'s use of a "Lung" over some of its tennis courts (p. 52), and of M.I.T.'s Student Union "brainframe" (p. 186). All of the preceding are examples of objects represented as (parts of) bodies (cf. Jim Sr. to Jim Jr. in Ch. 15.1). There is a reference here to "the haze-haloed Boston sun," reminiscent of the Student Union's "halo-ish ring" (p. 186) and Hal's milky "halo of approved grace" (n. 76). The catapults "that make a sound like a giant stamping foot" recall O'Brien to Winston Smith: "If you want a picture of the future, imagine a boot stamping on a human face—forever" (*1984*: Book Three, Ch. 3). The original city of Enfield was flooded to create the Quabbin Reservoir (Burn, p. 55; Dowling and Bell, p. 35; cf. Quabbin Recovery Systems, p. 797).

Chapter 18.2, Section 67, Pages 242-258
Notes 82-84, Page 1000
5 November Y.D.A.U.

This section—occurring shortly after the discussion of the window of opportunity for taking DMZ (Ch.16.5) and the day before the weight room activity (Ch. 16.3) preceding the 6 November Port Washington meet—documents a phone conversation between Hal and Orin (recall that Orin called Hal two nights ago and asked about Separatism, Ch. 13.1) and is presented entirely as dialogue (cf. Hal and Mario in Ch. 6.1) except for the few lines of narration that bookend the section. From statements Hal makes throughout the call, it is clear he is unimpressed with Orin's callous seduction of women who have small children, with Orin's not attending their father's funeral, and with Orin's attitude and behavior concerning their family. Twice (pp. 244, 249) Hal mentions that Orin went two years without contacting his family. Hal frequently sidetracks the conversation by reporting strategies employed and progress made with respect to "clipping his nails into a wastebasket that sat several meters away."

Hal compares his success at clipping toenails into the wastebasket to being "in The Zone" on court, which leads to a discussion of the superstitions that accompany an athlete's attempt to extend "can't-miss intervals." Hal extends the discussion to primitive rituals. The Ahts of Vancouver "tried to fill up ancestors' bodies completely with virgin-blood to preserve the privacy of their own mental states [believing that] 'The sated ghost cannot see secret things.'" "After a burial, rural Papineau-region Québecers [like Marathe and his wife, p. 88] purportedly drill a small hole down from ground level all the way down through the lid of the coffin, to let out the soul, if it wants out."

Orin says that he thinks he is being followed by people in wheelchairs, one of whom had on "some kind of domino-mask." Hal suggests the possibility of "[v]ery shy fans." Orin admits, "It's probably my imagination. A dead bird fell in my jacuzzi" (i.e., the ominous event (last month, p. 44) triggered his suspicious imagination). Orin is calling Hal for help with "family-background questions" for a profile in *Moment* magazine, which Hal describes as "a supermarket-checkout-lane-display magazine" that "recently did a thing on the little blind Illinois kid" (cf. Hal's likely November Y.G. opponent, Dymphna, who is blind; p. 17). Orin believes the profile will be "some sort of memorial to the Stork [Jim] as patriarch" to which Hal says, "He always did cast a long shadow, you said" (cf. Jim Sr. talking about his father to Jim Jr.: "He cast a long shadow, Jim," p. 164). Orin describes his female interviewer, Helen (Steeply), as "physically imposing. Large but not unerotic." Orin says he's "also thought of referring her to Bain" (Orin's E.T.A. classmate, p. 46). Hal suggests a brief outline for the profile (p. 247), which would include discussion of "nonexistent films."

In answer to Orin's first question, Hal tells Orin that Tavis moved into the upstairs room next to Avril two or three days before Jim killed himself. Orin asks if Hal, Tavis, or Avril talk about Jim. Hal asserts that Orin is forgetting about Mario, and that Mario sometimes talks about Jim (recall Ch. 6.1). Orin asks who found Jim "at the oven," and Hal says that he did "on April First" (at eleven years and nine months old, not thirteen as Hal states on p. 248). Recall that 1 April is also the date on which the attaché received the package with "*HAPPY ANNIVERSARY!*" in the return-address box (p. 36), five years to the day after Jim's death (note also the similarity of "Avril I." and "April 1"). Hal asks, "[W]hy this sudden interest after four years 216 days, and with two years of that not even once calling?" In response, Orin reminds Hal of what he said earlier: that he can't "avoid being forthright about the Stork material unless [he knows] what the really forthright answers would be." (Presumably Orin stopped calling in the Spring of YUSHITYU and "had abruptly started calling again" on 9 May Y.D.A.U. (cf. pp. 32, 136). The span of time from 1 April Y.T.-S.D.B. to 5 November Y.D.A.U. is five years 218 days. Two days from now on 7 November Y.D.A.U., Joelle cites this period as "four years seven months six days past" (p. 225).)

Orin asks if the P.G.O.A.T. (cf. p. 239) was there, and Hal says, "Joelle hadn't been around the grounds since you two split up. You knew about that. Himself met her at the brownstone, shooting [cf. p. 237 and n. 80]. I'm sure you know way more about whatever they were trying to make. Joelle and Himself. Himself went underground too. C.T. was already doing most of the day-to-day administration. Himself was down in that little post-production closet off the lab for like a solid month [March Y.T.-S.D.B.]. Mario'd bring food and . . . essentials down. Sometimes he'd eat with Lyle." In the third week of this underground month of editing, Jim had "flown off somewhere for three days, for what the impression I get was work-related business. Film-related. If Lyle didn't go with him Lyle went somewhere, because he wasn't in the weight room. I know Mario didn't go with him and didn't know what was up. Mario doesn't lie." About "a week after he came back" from his trip and resumed his underground editing, Jim made "a trip out to Belmont to McLean's for a two-day purge and detox." "The Moms herself emerged and risked exterior transit and took him herself, so I gather it was urgent." (Two weeks ago, Joelle had done "as they'd made Jim do near the end and admitted powerlessness over this cage" (p. 223). Two days from now, Joelle recalls that Jim "made her sit thorough that filmed apology-scene and then vanished and then came back but only to [die]" (p. 225).) Hal had "been around the lab door right after lunch [on 1 April] and [Jim] wasn't back." "It was unclear whether [Jim had] finished whatever he was editing [before he] stopped living on April First." Responding to the discussion of the detox, Orin counters that Jim quit drinking in January as a condition of Joelle's working with him: "She called even after we'd agreed not to call and told me about it even after I'd said I didn't want to hear about him if she was going to still be in his things." (Presumably, this request is not prompted by sexual jealousy, given that Orin knows—but Avril does not know—"Himself never had eyes for anybody but the Moms," cf. also n. 80.) Hal responds, "By this time it was hard to tell whether he'd been ingesting anything or not. Apparently at a certain point it stops making a difference."

Around 1630 on 1 April Y.T.-S.D.B., Hal "came around HmH to do an emergency load of laundry before dinner . . . and noticed something right away," before even entering the kitchen. It is difficult to determine exactly what happened in the kitchen. Apparently, Jim, a man noted for his "technical ingenuity," had "used a wide-bit drill and small hacksaw to make a head-sized hole in the [microwave] oven door, then when he'd gotten his head in he'd carefully packed the extra space around his neck with wadded-up aluminum foil" (Joelle also uses aluminum foil in her suicide attempt, p. 238). The "field pathologist who drew the chalk lines around Himself's shoes on the floor . . . said the pressure build-up [equivalent "to over two sticks of TNT. . . . Hence the need to reconstruct the scene"] would have been almost instantaneous. Then he gestured at the kitchen walls. Then he threw up." From Hal's descriptions, Orin infers "that Himself's head had popped like an uncut spud," but cf. that Hal "found Himself with his head in what was left of the microwave" and that Hal and Gately will dig up Jim's head (cf. p. 17). Perhaps the internal pressures created by the microwave traveled quickly from Jim's head throughout his body (analogous to the poison entering the ghost's ear but then coursing swiftly through his body to initiate a grisly death, *Hamlet* I.v.61-73) and took more of a toll on Jim's body and the microwave than on his head, given the presumed explosion of Jim's body onto "the kitchen walls," the "chalk lines around Himself's shoes" rather than around his body, and "what was left of the microwave."

Hal says there was a half-full bottle (cf. Joelle's half-empty glass of juice, p. 239) of Wild Turkey (analogous to "juice of cursed hebenon," *Hamlet* I.v.62) on the counter in the kitchen of the Headmaster's House where Jim was found "with a large red decorative giftwrappish bow on the neck" (another "gift which was not a gift," p. 105). Hal chastises Orin for asking if there was a note, since Orin knows there wasn't; for "criticizing [Jim] and making sobriety-claims when [Orin wasn't] anywhere near the scene or the funeral"; and for using the word "deconstructed," because Orin knows Jim hated that word.

Hal relates how he was sent to a therapist—who "never once turned his face away" (cf. the moon; pp. 192, 223), who subjected Hal to "six weeks of full-bore professional conversation" (cf. Jim as professional conversationalist, p. 28), and who had hands "no bigger than a four-year-old girl's" (cf. Hal's memory of "the hypophalangial Grief-Therapist," p. 16)—to deal with his trauma and how he experienced difficulty for the first time in his life (cf. n. 76) in "delivering the goods" to the therapist (i.e., telling the therapist what he wanted to hear so that Hal could get back to playing tennis), making the therapist Hal's "worst nightmare." Hal: "I even tried telling him I really didn't feel anything." Orin: "Which was a fiction." Hal: "Of course it was a fiction." (Compare this with Jim Sr.'s assessment of the unfeeling attitude of Jim Jr.'s generation toward their parents, pp. 167-8.)

Hal says that during the six weeks that he saw the therapist in April and May "the nightmares started. I kept dreaming of a face in the floor." Hal had "his first nightmare away from home and folks [on his] first night at the Academy" (p. 62)—i.e., in a dorm room instead of with folks at HmH and therefore seemingly spending his first night at the Academy (cf. Ch. 7.7 summary). If Hal were living in a dorm room before his father's death, he presumably would have switched to using the "mammoth laundry room below the West

Courts" (p. 51) instead of using "HmH to do an emergency load of laundry." Like Hamlet, within a month of his father's death Hal's uncle has moved into his father's place; Hal is distanced from his mother; and Hal has bad dreams.

With some library work prompted by Lyle's advice—"empathize with the grief-therapist" and discover "what he was professionally required to want"—Hal was able to determine what he needed to say to the therapist. Orin asserts, "The Lyle my class knew wasn't a how-to-deliver-the-goods-to-authorities-type figure." At his next session, Hal "presented with anger at the grief-therapist" and used "foul language and slang" and "certain loaded professional-grief-therapy terms." In a "textbook breakdown into genuine affect and trauma and guilt and textbook earsplitting grief, then absolution," Hal forgave himself for thinking that something smelled delicious right before he found his father. (Did Hal really think this? What did Hal mean when he said he "noticed something right away" on p. 250?)

Orin wants Hal to "thumbnail-sketch the overall feeling" for him, so he can "say something generic but convincing about loss and grief for Helen for *Moment*." Instead Hal loops the conversation back to his toenail clippings and says "that human nails are vestiges of talons and horns," which resonates with the primitive rituals Hal cited earlier. Orin asks whether his "probing for details" has reactivated Hal's grief and says that he will "call back when you're more yourself." At the end of the conversation, Hal holds the phone next to his foot so that Orin will hear the nail clippers, a sound that Orin said he hated at the beginning of the conversation.

PLOT AND CHARACTER: Hal, Orin, Jim
THEME: Memory, Secrets, Fear/Obsess, Recur

In this section, Orin is "probing for details" in Hal's memory. Presumably, Hal can be taken at his word about the family secrets he divulges in this section, because he only lies "about meaningless details to Orin on the phone" (p. 136); whereas the details of this conversation are significant, except for the toenail-clipping activities, and Hal even admits lying about that (p. 248). Many secrets remain at the end of this section: the length of Jim's period of sobriety, the events of his business trip, the condition of his body after his death, and the events that prompted Jim to have a Wild Turkey bottle with a "gift-wrappish" bow immediately after his detox. The identity of Orin's wheelchaired followers is a secret to him. Early in the conversation, Hal references two primitive burial rituals: one is done so that "[t]he sated ghost cannot see secret things," and the other is done "to let out the soul, if it wants out." Late in the conversation, Hal asserts that "human nails are the vestiges [from a Latin word for "footprint," cf. the stamping foot imagery of the previous section] of talons and horns," a reminder of our primitive natures.

Hal applies the athletic metaphors of the E.T.A. staff to events both trivial and significant. The "magical feeling" of playing "out of your head" (deLint) or "in The Zone" (Loach) is here applied to Hal's toenail clipping and to his sessions with the Grief-Therapist (p. 256). Hal's "self-consciousness and fear" about "delivering the goods" to the therapist had to be overcome: "self-consciousness . . . kills the magic" and leaves one "frozen." Once Hal had "a sense of where the lines were" (Schtitt, cited by Orin), he successfully won his game with the therapist. Hal cites a "celluloid moment" (from *Star Wars*) as an example of a "magic feeling."

Recurrences in this section include the "domino-mask" worn by one of the "wheelchaired figures" following Orin; images of chewing (Hal's chewing through books; cf. "The boy reads like a vacuum. Digests things," p. 15); and Hal's retreat to "the men's room," laughing hysterically and stamping his feet (cf. the giant stamping foot, p. 241). There are several misunderstandings here, too. Hal believes that Jim didn't want *Infinite Jest* released because it "turned out so bad," but Jim told Joelle that it was "entertaining" and that it "had broken his heart" (p. 228). Orin misinterprets and corrects Hal's purposeful substitution of "telemachry" for "telemetry." Hal waits until the end of the conversation to correct Orin's frequent mispronunciation of "asphyxiated," a word that is misspelled in Orin's dialogue here but is spelled correctly on p. 45 by the narrator for Orin.

Chapter 18: Probing For Details

Details about the city of Enfield (the geographic heart of the novel, home to both Ennet House and the heart-shaped E.T.A.) and details about Jim's last work done in the last month of his life (the heart of the novel's mystery, to paraphrase *Hamlet* III.ii.357) are provided in this chapter. After Jim's death, the Grief Therapist probed Hal for details, and Hal in turn probed library books for details on how to diffuse the therapist's probing. Hal needs no help in diffusing Orin's probing for details years later. Probing for details can be dangerous: "annular-generated amps are waiting underground for anyone who digs" around Sunstrand in Enfield. Orin believes his probing has initiated a change in Hal (who speaks ominously of human nails as the primitive vestiges of talons and horns), a possible reactivation Hal's grief, about which Orin wants to know to satisfy the probing of Helen Steeply. Wheelchaired persons are also probing for details by following Orin, and their probing could pose a danger to Orin.

Chapter 19

Trying to Locate Patterns in Each Other's Rhythms

Chapter 19.1, Section 68, Pages 258-270
Notes 85-89, Page 1000
6 November Y.D.A.U.

After working in the weight room earlier in the day (Ch. 16.3), E.T.A. players are now in Long Island for the Port Washington meet. There are six people on a junior tennis team, ranked 1-6. There are six singles matches and three doubles matches per team (usual doubles team pairings: 1-2, 3-4, 5-6; but cf. the exception of Schacht and Troeltsch). There are four teams (Boys A, Boys B, Girls A, Girls B) competing in each of three divisions (18 and Unders, 16 and Unders, 14 and Unders). Nine matches each for twelve teams is 108 matches. (Mathematicians unhappy with the odds given for a 54-54 tie: cf. the first error discussed in Mike Strong's "Dubious Math In *Infinite Jest.*") Thirty-six of the Port Washington courts are under a Lung, whereas E.T.A.'s Lung is only "over the sixteen Center Courts" ("in four rows of four"; presumably these are the sixteen Har-Tru courts, cf. p. 241) and usually goes up "the fourth Monday of November," which would be 23 November Y.D.A.U.

Hal, who has experienced a "competitive explosion" this year, is #2 on the 18 and Unders A team, behind John Wayne, "formerly of Montcerf, Québec." Wayne's father is an asbestos miner who "wears triple-thick masks," hoping to retire when John becomes successful (cf. Jim Sr.'s prediction about the success of Jim Jr.'s tennis career, p. 162). Wayne was first spotted by Jim when he was filming *Homo Duplex* (cf. p. 988). Wayne's father later made Jim take out John's segment in the film. Last spring Wayne was recruited by Schtitt and deLint to join E.T.A, after which Canada "disowned him as an emigrant." Wayne "tends to eat and study alone," although he is "sometimes seen with two or three expatriate E.T.A. Nucks [Canucks]." Wayne is "all business," and his game has "a kind of automatic beauty."

Schacht (#3-B, 18's) is helping Pemulis (#6-B, 18's) to his match. Pemulis, who gets nervous before matches (cf. pp. 154 and 218-9), is throwing up in a bucket of old tennis balls. He assures Schacht that he is not hung over. "It strikes Schacht as odd that Pemulis makes such a big deal of stopping all substances the day before competitive play but never connects the neurasthenic stomach to any kind of withdrawal or dependence." "This match is an all-out must win for [Pemulis] in terms of the WhataBurger," which occurs "over Thanksgiving" (p. 267) and so three weeks from now rather than "in a couple weeks" (p. 259). Presumably, Mario's "final footage" of this year's WhataBurger for his "annual documentary . . . that every year gets distributed to E.T.A. alumni and patrons and guests at the pre-Thanksgiving fundraising exhibition and formal fête" (p. 265) will be edited in (and the documentary distributed) after the fête.

Schacht's game has "improved slightly in the two years since he stopped really caring," "since first the Crohn's and then the knee at sixteen" (cf. p. 112). Schacht's take on Schtitt's tennis philosophy is that to win "you have to both care a great deal about it and also not care about it at all. Schacht does not care, enough, probably, anymore" and is "already in his heart committed to a dental career" (cf. his Big Buddy session on pp. 117, 120), interning at the National Cranio-Facial Pain Foundation in east Enfield (cf. p. 241). Schacht doesn't have "to worry about obsessive training like Inc or Stice or get sick so often from the physical stress of constant 'drines like Troeltsch or suffer from thinly disguised psychological fallout like Inc or Struck or Pemulis himself. The way Pemulis and Troeltsch and Struck and Axford ingest substances and recover from substances and have a whole jargony argot based around various substances gives Schacht the creeps." Schacht "doesn't say a word about Hal's devolution from occasional tourist to subterranean compulsive, substance-wise" but thinks there is "a psychic credit-card bill for Hal in the mail, somewhere, coming."

PLOT AND CHARACTER: E.T.A., AA&R
THEME: Recur, Fear/Obsess

Several themes and images recur in this section. The "reptilian tinge" of the players' skin in the light of the court (a "seasick-type pallor") and Hal's having "grown a beak" via the probing and pecking that constitute the evolution of his game recall the primitive and probing motifs of the previous section. High-hit balls cast "many shadows in the tray of lights hung from the ceiling's insulation." The applause of patrons behind a panel "like an aquarium's glass" sounds like "something tapping for help at a great depth." DeLint "squashes his nose flat against the glass" of the panel. Wayne hits a "balletic winner," and Schacht's nervous opponent makes "dancerly flourishes." Wayne looks mean "in a kind of distant way," and Mario plans a shot in which players "gradually recede into a kind of doomed mist of low exposure." Wayne's father wears "triple-thick masks," and on-court Wayne's face is rigid "with the hypertonic masking of schizophrenics and Zen adepts." Port Washington players wear "light-blue" shirts and use "light-blue" racquet covers; there is a "dull blue" brace on Schacht's racquet; and the Lung plans are "draftsman-blue." Schacht and Troeltsch have been doubles partners since they were "incontinent toddlers." Pemulis vomits, hunched over a bucket. The sun at the WhataBurger is "a retinal horror-show." Schacht assesses his fellow students' cycle of drug ingestion and recovery. Hal's training is described as obsessive. Hal fears what he sees as Schacht's interior decline, but admires and envies Schacht's "air of something other than failure," which is "something you can't quite define, the way you can't quite remember a word that you know you know, inside."

Chapter 19.2, Section 69, Pages 270-281
Notes 90-91, Pages 1000-1003
6 November Y.D.A.U.

This section occurs around the same time as Chs. 16.2 and 16.4, from about 0825-0835 on what is presumably Friday, 6 November (the date of the other sections of this chapter), given that "the [Ennet] House Manager has driven Jennifer Belbin to a court appearance downtown" (presumably on a weekday) and staffer Johnette Foltz "is at a Narcotics Anonymous convention in Hartford for the long Interdependence Day weekend" (presumably 6-8 November). "Gately has been completely Substance-free for 421 days today." This would place Gately's first day of sobriety as 12 September Y.D.P.A.H. Presumably the DuPlessis incident occurred just before this date in late Summer Y.D.P.A.H. (although the incident is said to occur in Autumn Y.D.P.A.H., p. 55). Presumably 12 September Y.D.P.A.H. is also the date Gately entered Ennet House for his nine-month residency (cf. p. 137). Gately has "been on live-in staff here four months now" (almost five if the job began immediately after the end of his residency). Today, Gately has come in from his "work janitoring [mopping shit] down at the Shattuck Shelter till 0700." He is downstairs with Ennet residents "that either aren't working or don't have to be at work early." He is again described as "just huge" and as having "a massive square head" (cf. p. 55). He is "almost twenty-nine" and "paying off restitution schedules in three different district courts" (p. 277).

Geoffrey Day (cf. p. 203), on his sixth day as a resident at Ennet House, is complaining that he is now expected to live his life by clichés. Gately has been advised to consider Day "an invaluable teacher of patience and tolerance," so he reminds himself "that this is all an Ennet House residency is supposed to do: buy [residents] time, till they can start to get a whiff of what's true and deep, almost magic, under the shallow surface of what they're trying to do." Day reported on his Intake that he "manned the helm of a Scholarly Quarterly." Volunteer alumni counselor Eugenio Martinez (Gene M; cf. pp. 177, 196) once advised Gately that "newcomers with some education are the worst [because they] identify their whole selves with their head, and the Disease [of substance addiction] makes its command headquarters in the head." Note 90, a snippet of an 11 November conversation between Gately and Day, is referenced as an illustration of what Gene M meant. "If Day ever gets lucky and breaks down, finally, and comes to the front office at night to scream that he can't take it anymore and clutch at Gately's pantcuff and blubber and beg for help at any cost, Gately'll get to tell Day the thing is that the clichéd directives are a lot more deep and hard to actually *do*. To try and live by instead of just say. But he'll only get to say it if Day comes and asks."

Gene M, Gately's counselor during his "nine residential months" (September-June), "hooked up with the House under the original founder Guy That Didn't Even Use His First Name [cf. pp. 137-8], and had about ten years clean" (so Gene was clean for over two years before Ennet was founded in Y.W., cf. p. 137). "Gene called the Disease The Spider and talked about Feeding The Spider versus Starving The Spider." "Gately, albeit an oral narcotics man from way back, has committed himself to AA" instead of Narcotics Anonymous (NA). "Gately personally is not hot on NA: so many relapses and unhumble returns . . . . There's a difference between abstinence v. recovery, Gately knows. Except of course who's Gately to judge what works for who. He just knows what seems like it works for him today." Gately's current AA sponsor, Ferocious Francis Gehaney (cf. p. 209), is one of the White Flag Group Crocodiles (cf. p. 138 and n. 50), "old guys with suspended bellies and white crew cuts and geologic amounts of sober time."

This section introduces one-month (working on two months; cf. "Burt Smith did it in September," p. 539) Ennet resident Burt F. Smith, age 45, who "got mugged and beaten half to death in Cambridge on Xmas Eve of last year, and left there to like freeze there, in an alley, in a storm, and ended up losing his hands and feet." Smith is the "older type individual" crewed on and rolled and left "in no condition to eat cheese" by C and yrstruly (p. 130). This section also marks the first reference to "Annie Parrot the Asst. Manager" of Ennet House.

Randy Lenz (cf. pp. 207, 209) is "a small-time organic coke dealer . . . of keen interest to both sides of the law." It's "obvious that Lenz is here mostly to hide out." Lenz's "obsessive compulsions include the need to be north, a fear of disks, a tendency to constantly take his own pulse, a fear of all forms of timepieces, and a need to always know the time with great precision." "One of Gately's jobs is to keep an eye on what's possibly brewing among residents" (analogous to an E.T.A. Big Buddy); and a "beef may be brewing" between

Lenz and Day, who are now "in the 3-Man together, since three guys in one night missed curfew . . . and got bounced on the spot," which got Day "moved up in his first week from the 5-Man room to the 3-Man." Presumably Skull (cf. pp. 208-9) was one of the three guys bounced. Although Gately's recollection of sharing the House with "twenty-one other" residents is in line with the stated 22-resident capacity (p. 137), it seems that this limit is not always strictly enforced, presumably because the House wants to be able to continue operating at full capacity even after, say, three people are bounced in one night. Adding Burt F. Smith and two bounced guys to the resident list in the Ch. 16.4 summary would bump the number of residents to 25, now 22 again. However, even though the House is now operating at capacity, "Exec. Director Pat M. is due in at 0900 [for] application interviews with three people, 2F and 1M."

PLOT AND CHARACTER: Ennet, Gately
THEME: Loss, Isolation, Fear/Obsess, Time, Recur

Gately "often feels a terrible sense of loss, narcotics-wise, in the A.M., still, even after this long clean," and Ferocious Francis G. commended Gately "for his candor in breaking down and crying like a baby and telling [Francis G.] about it early one A.M. over the pay phone, the sense of loss. It's a myth no one misses it." Alternately, the isolation of people who "identify their whole selves with their head" is exemplified by Day, who "is scanning the room for somebody else to engage and piss off so he can prove to himself he doesn't fit in here and stay separated off isolated inside himself . . . . You can almost hear his Disease chewing away inside his head, feeding." Addicts in the novel are usually plagued with other obsessions as well, especially Randy Lenz, whose host of obsessions include "a need to always know the time with great precision." "Ennet House reeks of passing time." "Gately remembers his first six months here straight: he'd felt the sharp edge of every second that went by. And the freakshow dreams. Nightmares beyond the worst D.T.'s you'd ever heard about."

In addition to an addict weeping, nightmares, a head isolated from a body, and ominous images of chewing (and spiders), there are other recurrences here. The philosophy of asking for help is espoused, which resonates with the Air Force nurse of p. 196. There is water imagery in the phrases "deepens like the lobster-waters" and "under the shallow surface" (p. 271). The varied list of Gately's fellow residents (p. 273) that highlights the universality of addiction resonates with Joelle's all-inclusive list of U.H.I.D. invitees (Ch. 16.1). Smith is "hunched." The waste motif is represented by Gately's job mopping shit, by Smith's farting in "Morris" Code, and by Gately's farting in the Ennet House living room. Gately stares at the ceiling, makes reference to "getting assaulted by sidewalks," and refers to Lenz's face as a map.

Chapter 19.3, Section 70, Pages 281-283
Note 92, Page 1003
6 November Y.D.A.U. to 7 November Y.D.A.U., 0030h.

This section documents the bus ride home from the Port Washington meet (Ch. 19.1). "Schacht and a conspicuously energized Jim Troeltsch rallied for the big win in 18-A #2 dubs." Pemulis's opponent had to default because he "had gotten weirdly lethargic and then disoriented in the second set after Pemulis had lost the first in a tie-break" (cf. Pemulis joking about tossing DMZ into Gatorade barrels at Port Washington, p. 212) and later made a spectacle of himself at "the post-meet mixer and dance." Mario and Coyle play rock-paper-scissors, "trying to locate patterns in each other's rhythms of choices of shapes, which they both decided there weren't any." "Charles Tavis sat way in the back with John Wayne and beamed and spoke nonstop in hushed tones to Wayne as the Canadian stared out the window." "Everyone was tired in a good way." The "whole mammoth travelling squad" got to stop at Denny's when they got back to Enfield.

PLOT AND CHARACTER: E.T.A., AA&R
THEME: Recur

The recurring interest in or use of drugs by E.T.A. students is documented again in this section. Schacht's "eyes roll up in his head" when injected with a pain killer for his swollen knee, prompting Axford and Struck to start "kibitzing Barry Loach about their knees were feeling punk as well" in hope of obtaining similar injections.

Chapter 19: Trying To Locate Patterns In Each Other's Rhythms

E.T.A. players are conscious of patterns in their games and in their opponents' games and of their hierarchical rankings: "Competitive tennis is largely mental" (but it is given expression by bodies). Schacht considers the patterns of his fellow students' drug use. Ennet House, in which a group of more experienced drug users resides, has housing policies which keep residents conscious of their seniority, their hierarchy. Gately considers the patterns of behavior exhibited by the residents in his charge, aware that "the Disease makes its command headquarters in the head" (but it ravages the body, too). Although the tennis matches are over, the bus ride home to Enfield includes a variety of games and plots and plans. Although Mario and Coyle try "to locate patterns in each other's rhythms" as they play rock-paper-scissors, "they both decided there weren't any."

Chapter 20

Both Destiny's Kisses and Its Dope-Slaps

Chapter 20.1, Section 71, Pages 283-299
Notes 93-101, Pages 1003-1004
unspecified Y.D.A.U.

This section is a Y.D.A.U. discussion (note that "last year's" Fall term Convocation at E.T.A. was 31 August Y.D.P.A.H., p. 287) of Orin's life and athletic career from his "competitive peak" in tennis at age thirteen to his junior season of football at Boston University at age twenty. "At late seventeen" (p. 283), Orin was still an E.T.A. senior (Spring 2001). After "tennis practice had started" (p. 288) in Orin's freshman year at B.U. (Fall 2001), Orin (now eighteen, p. 289) decided he wanted to switch from tennis to football and was attempting to do so "by the third week of his freshman year" (p. 288). Since 18-year-old Orin "got out of competitive tennis when Hal was nine and Mario nearly eleven," this places Orin's eighteenth birthday between Hal's ninth birthday (June 2001, cf. p. 27) and Orin's switch to football (September 2001), which was before Mario's eleventh birthday (25 November 2001, cf. p. 589). "Orin had been seven years old" at Mario's birth (p. 901). Orin's "unlikely defection" from tennis to football "was during the period of great pre-Experialist [i.e., before the "gift" of the Concavity to Canada, cf. pp. 58-9] upheaval and the emergence of the fringe C.U.S.P. [Clean U.S. Party, cf. p. 382] of [President; cf. pp. 65, 106] Johnny Gentle, Famous Crooner, and the tumescence of O.N.A.N.ism."

Shortly after Orin hit his competitive peak, "he'd suffered athletically from the same delayed puberty that had compromised his father when Himself had been a junior player" (Schtitt attributes Orin's decline to an "unwillingness to risk . . . temporary failure for long-term gaining" rather than to puberty, pp. 293-4). Although Orin had developed a phenomenal lob shot—in part due to his role as the first game-master of Eschaton, the nuclear-conflagration game (n. 53) popular at E.T.A.—it was clear that upon leaving E.T.A. he should continue to play tennis at the collegiate rather than at the professional level. Orin decided to play college tennis at Boston University, the close-to-home institution preferred by Avril, who "for six weeks would flee any room Orin entered" to keep from influencing his choice. "Avril's adoptive-slash-half-brother Charles Tavis" knew the tennis coach at B.U. and flew down from Canada (presumably around 1 October 2000) in order to introduce Orin and Avril to the coach, who was enthralled by Avril "in a tight black skirt and levantine jacket with kohl around her eyes and a moussed tower of hair."

Instead of returning to Canada, Tavis "at Avril's urging" stayed on at E.T.A. as Assistant Headmaster, since "both in- and external travels took J. O. Incandenza away from Enfield more and more often." Jim's death "3 ½ years" later (1 April 2004) occurred at a time when E.T.A. was dealing with several administrative crises (pp. 286-7), and "*someone* [Tavis] had had to come in and fill the void" (several reasons are given in justification of Avril's not becoming Headmistress, p. 288). Given that "on 4 July Y.D.P.A.H." Orin "declined his fifth straight [2004-2008] invitation back to Enfield and his family's annual barbecue," Tavis understands that he "might, by some grieving parties, be viewed as some kind of interloping usurper." Tavis announced at the 31 August Y.D.P.A.H. Convocation on the Center Courts—at which "everybody still wore [black armbands] to keep from forgetting" (cf. p. 65) and at which flags were flown at half-mast (cf. p. 42)—that he "fully accepted the stress and the resentment" that accompanied the job, even "four years" after Jim's death. (On 7 November Y.D.A.U., Hal "hasn't even seen [Orin] in four years" (p. 1015); so Orin presumably has not been back to E.T.A. since Y.P.W. (2005) and, given his annual decline of Tavis's barbecue invitation, probably not since his father's death a year earlier.)

By the third week of Orin's freshman year at B. U., he "was attempting an extremely unlikely defection from college tennis to college football" in order to be near a sophomore who twirled batons in support of the football team (Joelle, pre-veil). Orin and his doubles partner dubbed the twirler "the P.G.O.A.T., for the Prettiest Girl Of All Time" (cf. p. 239). She was so pretty that "she was almost universally shunned" because of what U.H.I.D. later described as a "fear of transhuman beauty." She had "a mid-Southern accent in her oddly flat but resonant voice. . . . When she danced, at dances, it was with other [girls], because no male had the grit or spit to ask her."

Orin's football tryouts (obtained with the help of phonecalls from Orin's former B.U. doubles partner's Dad) "were too pathetic to describe," but then a "destiny-grade event" occurred ("almost nothing important that ever happens to you happens because you engineer it"). A punt was blocked into the shadow of the exit-tunnel, where Orin had been ordered to go by the coach after his unsuccessful tryout. Rather than walk up the sideline and back "under the distant green gaze of the twirler who owned his CNS," Orin, who had never kicked a ball before in his life, kicked the ball all the way back to the coach at midfield. As the punter had been injured when his punt was blocked, Orin immediately was drafted to replace him, and within weeks his punting average had reached 69 yards. "In his initial Home start" (presumably September 2001), against "a Syracuse team that had no idea it was in its last season of representing an American university" (cf. also that U. Vermont and UNH are "history" by Orin's junior season), Orin "had a book-long of 73 yards" (cf. the discussion of the punt on the 22 October Y.D.A.U. radio show that preceded Joelle's, p. 181). "By Halloween his control was even better than his distance." Watching a cartridge of one of Orin's games, Schtitt observed that "Orin was still just only lobbing."

After the game with Syracuse ("the second home game," cf. the B.U. schedule on p. 293), Joelle "seemed to begin somehow directing her glittering sideline routines at Orin in particular. So and then the only really cardiac-grade romantic relationship of Orin's life took bilateral root at a distance, during games, without one exchanged personal phoneme, a love communicated [through] dances of devotion to the spectacle they were both . . . trying to make as entertaining as possible." Orin told Joelle, in "an increasingly revealing conversation after kind of amazingly she had approached him at a

Columbus Day Major Sport function . . . that he believed it wasn't all athletic, punting's pull for him, that a lot of it seemed emotional and/or even, if there was such a thing anymore, spiritual." In contrast to tennis, during football games Orin experienced "[a]udience exhortations and approvals so total they ceased to be numerically distinct and melded into a sort of single coital moan, one big vowel, the sound of the womb, the roar gathering, tidal, amniotic, the voice of what might as well be God." On the field, Orin was "transformed, his own self transcended as he'd never escaped himself on the court."

By the end of his first semester, Orin had moved with Joelle "into an East Cambridge co-op three subway stops distant from B.U." (where *Infinite Jest* would be filmed and which would be "passed on to Molly Notkin," p. 227). Orin showed Joelle, who majored in Film/Cartridge studies, "The Mad Stork's own *Pre-Nuptial Agreement of Heaven and Hell*, which had a major impact on her." (The film features a character "obsessed with Bernini's 'The Ecstacy of St. Theresa'" (p. 988). Joelle thinks of Bernini's work at Notkin's party (p. 235).) Orin and Joelle spent Thanksgiving with Orin's family and Christmas with Joelle's family in Shiny Prize, KY. "Right after Thanksgiving Himself let the P.G.O.A.T. understudy with Leith on the set of *The American Century as Seen Through a Brick* in return for getting to film her thumb against a plucked string." In late December, Orin participated in B.U.'s "nonvictorious but still unprecedented appearance at Las Vegas's dignitary-attended K-L-RMKI/Forsythia Bowl." Back in Shiny Prize on "the last P.M. Before Subsidization" (New Year's Eve 2001), Orin "saw Joelle ingest very small amounts of cocaine" ("her ingestion then was recreational").

The following year, after Orin's sophomore Y.W. football season, Orin flew with Joelle to Toronto to watch Jim work on his film, *Blood Sister: One Tough Nun*. (Presumably Joelle was not filmed at this time, but note that the compilers of Jim's filmography cite Madame Psychosis's possible appearance in *Infinite Jest (IV)*, which is listed immediately after *Blood Sister* (p. 990). If Joelle was filmed at this time, did any footage of the pre-veil, "heart-stopping," prettiest girl of all time end up in *Infinite Jest (V)*?) Jim would take Orin and Joelle out after work, "and then later Orin would shepherd the two of them back to their Ontario Place hotel, stopping the cab to let them both throw up . . . . Himself showed them . . . where he and the Moms had first met. This might have been the end's start, gradually, in hindsight." Presumably, Orin means the end of his relationship with Joelle.

In the summer (presumably May or June) of Y.T.M.P., Joelle "let Himself give her a stage name and use her in rapid succession in [three films—playing Death, a beautiful cadaver, and a fiancée with a grotesquely mangled face; cf. pp. 991-2], travelling with Himself and Mario while Orin stayed in Boston recuperating from minor surgery." Mario does not seem to connect the Madame Psychosis of his father's films to the Madame Psychosis of his beloved radio program (cf. p. 190). Recall that "Joelle was Orin Incandenza's only lover [but cf. the staff at the hospital where Orin was recuperating filing "for legal separation from their husbands, with custody"] for twenty-six months [October 2001 to December Y.T.M.P., one year after the Toronto visit and just before Joelle filmed the final *Infinite Jest*, during which Joelle called Orin even after they "agreed not to call" (p. 249)] and his father's optical beloved for twenty-one" (p. 229). Presumably, Joelle added a year in reckoning her time as Jim's optical beloved on p. 229 (she subtracted a year in reckoning the time since Jim's death—a common error—on p. 225) and actually is referring to a period of nine months, since her time as Jim's optical beloved began in May/June Y.T.M.P., not May/June Y.W. (but cf. that her thumb had been filmed after Thanksgiving 2001 and footage for *Infinite Jest (IV)* may have been filmed after the Y.W football season), and ended in January/February Y.T.-S.D.B.

Joelle "no longer twirled" and therefore was able to film Orin's games throughout his sophomore and junior seasons, "sometimes with Leith in attendance (never Himself)." "The P.G.O.A.T.'s real ambitions weren't thespian, Orin knew, is one reason he hung in so long." (Orin and Joelle's relationship ended at the close of Orin's junior season. Why would thespian ambitions matter to Orin?) The clips were of Orin exclusively, and Orin found that he "sat rapt" watching them "over and over," seeing "something different each time he rewound, something more." The clips "seemed to reveal him in ways he could never have engineered." By junior year, the clips had sound (in part due to a gift of equipment from Orin) and color. "She gets his timing; a punt's timing is minutely precise, like a serve's; it's like a solo dance." Orin watches a clip of the one time all year that the center oversnaps the ball and Orin is "just about to get personally contacted and knocked out of his cleats." The "disk-drive [stalls] at the terminal byte and Orin's chin-strapped plastic-barred face is there on the giant viewer, frozen and High-Def in his helmet, right before impact, zoomed in on with a quality lens. Of particular interest are the eyes" ("Orin knows too well the light on the side that means Zoom," p. 65).

PLOT AND CHARACTER: Orin, E.T.A., Joelle
THEME: Isolation, Recur, Inf/Reg, His/Father, Fear/Obsess

Both Orin and Joelle experience adulation in isolation. Orin, isolated from his teammates and protected from his opponents, experiences the gathering roar of audience approval when he punts. Joelle's "transhuman beauty" isolates her from men, who adore her but are afraid to approach her (to orbit in close); she dances with other girls at parties (but does not dance, years later, at Notkin's party). At first, Orin admires Joelle "from a distance," and their love "took bilateral root at a distance." Joelle practices "baton-aloft splits in a heart-rendingly distant way," and Tavis's voice is again described as "distant and receding" (cf. p. 8). At first, Orin and Joelle's love was communicated through "their respective little dances of devotion to the spectacle . . . they were both trying to make as entertaining as possible." When Orin punts, "it's like a solo dance." Orin prefers watching clips of himself over and over at home in self-obsessed isolation to "herd-like spectation," although he considers "his own self transcended" in the adoring roar of the crowd that makes "the sound of the womb . . . amniotic." Orin avoided the "sense of arrested adolescence and reality-avoidance" of a prorector position at E.T.A., but did not have the courage "to risk the temporary failure and weakness for long-term gaining" (delayed gratification) in his game, which supposedly suffered "from the same delayed puberty that had compromised his father." It is noted that Leith attended football games in support of Joelle's camera work, but "never Himself" (cf. Orin's great-grandfather, who "never came" to his grandfather's matches, except once in a "sham show of fatherly concern"; p. 164). Joelle (like Avril) is obsessed with cleaning (cf. p. 225); and Orin, "like many children of raging alcoholics and OCD-sufferers," has "internal addictive-sexuality issues."

A "short interest-piece" on Orin discussed his applied use in Eschaton of the Pink$_2$ DOS program. Although "by Y.D.A.U. it's kind of a dinosaur" (n. 95), the program is still listed as a feature of the Y.D.A.U. teleputer described on p. 60. Tavis's reference to "a 2-D cutout image of a person" recalls the advertisements Joelle saw on her walk to Notkin's party (p. 224). Joelle, also called Madame Psychosis, was "the twirler who owned [Orin's] CNS." DMZ, also called Madame Psychosis, is described as a CNS-rattler (n. 8); and Jim's work, which often features Madame Psychosis, is described as "CNS-rendingly melodramatic" (p. 64). Orin told Joelle that she was "prettier than the women in the films" they watched (n. 101); so did her father (p. 237). Jim's "freakish gift" for hailing cabs was remembered by Joelle on her walk to Notkin's party (p. 225). Orin's popcorn "tends to burn as the foil top inflates," and his punter's stance "is not unlike a diver's"; at Notkin's party, Joelle heats foil and is "like a diver preparing for a long descent" (pp. 238-9). Orin hears the sound of the crowd as "tidal" and meets Joelle's eye without "drowning." In addition to images of dancing, there are recurrences of a "glassy blue" sky (p. 287), vomiting (Jim and Joelle, p. 297), the "high-pitched noise" of machinery (p. 298), and a sense of "powerlessness over the really meaningful events" of life (p. 291).

Tavis feels that "some grieving parties" might consider him a usurper (p. 287), like Claudius in Hamlet or Blazes Boylan in Ulysses. Tavis explains that "Salic law'd nothing to do" with Avril's not taking charge of E.T.A. Avril was too busy with other duties, including "marathon multireadings of e.g. Orwell's 'Politics and the English Language.'" Salic law was cited by the French to oppose King Henry (formerly Prince Hal) in *Henry V* (I.ii). U.H.I.D.'s term for the "fear of transhuman beauty" inspired by Joelle is "the Actaeon Complex." Actaeon was changed into a stag by Artemis and torn into pieces by his own hounds for staying to watch Artemis bathing in a stream (Graves, pp. 84-5).

Chapter 20.2, Section 72, Pages 299-306
Notes 102-103, Page 1004
14 November Y.D.A.U.

This section occurs seven days after Molly Notkin's party (Ch. 17) and eight days after the Port Washington meet (Ch. 19). Since "last Xmas" 10 ½ months ago, Emil (yrstruly in Ch. 12.2) had Poor Tony "marked for de-mapping as a consequence of that horrid thing with Wo and Bobby C," and Poor Tony "hadn't dared show one feather" in parts of Enfield "even after Emil simply dematerialized from the street-scene." Emil Minty (who wears an "orange mohawk"; cf. pp. 275, 303) has rematerialized as an Ennet House resident alongside Burt F. Smith, the man he and C left for dead last Christmas Eve. Neither man seems to recognize the other at Ennet (cf. p. 275). And now "since 29 July" Poor Tony "couldn't dare wear anything comely, not even the Antitoi brothers' red leather coat, not since that poor woman's bag had turned out to have a heart inside." In the 10 August issue of *Moment* Magazine, Steeply reported on the heart stolen by Poor Tony (Ch. 13.5). Pemulis purchased DMZ from the Antitois on 4 November (p. 215).

Because of the incidents with Wo and the stolen heart, Poor Tony had "no way to cop for himself" and therefore had to rely on others to cop for him. "Stokely Dark Star [McNair] died in a Fenway hospice" (cf. that McNair had "the Virus for sure" last Christmas Eve, p. 129); and in October, Poor Tony's last friend and drug connection "Lolasister went down with hepatitis-G." Hiding in a dumpster, Poor Tony "began to Withdraw From Heroin," which prompted "[f]luids of varying consistency . . . to pour w/o advance notice from several openings." After being kicked out of his dumpster by an E.W.D. land-barge crew, he relocated to a library men's room and "tried to keep Withdrawal at some sort of bay" with bottles of cough syrup, which only "slowed up time." "Time began to pass with sharp edges" (cf. "the sharp edge of every second," p. 280). Poor Tony experienced "time with a shape and an odor" (cf. the reek of passing time, p. 279). "It would not keep still and it would not end." "Poor Tony had become an hourglass: time moved through him now" "in the form of endless gushing liquid shit that he could not flush enough to keep up with." Often, Poor Tony thinks of his deceased father, particularly an image of him "tearing his sportshirt in filial woe," presumably upon learning of his son's sexual orientation.

"Toward the end of the second syrupless afternoon," Poor Tony "began to Withdraw from the cough syrup's alcohol" and now has taken the Gray Line train with the intention of trying to cop from the Antitoi brothers, "hapless political insurgents he'd twice availed of services through the offices of Lolasister." He is keenly aware of his appearance and has "simply never in his life felt so unattractive or been so sick. He wept silently in shame and pain." He had "consumed upwards of sixteen little Eighty-Proof bottles of Codinex per day for eight days, and so was cruising for a real neurochemical bruising when he just up and stopped." Poor Tony hallucinates that ants are crawling on him and that his limbs are floating away, and then he soils himself and has a seizure on the train. "He heard a rushing train-roar that was no train on earth." He recalls Bobby "C's blood misting upward in the hot wind of the Copley blower" and has more hallucinations (many involving his father), apparently prompted by paramedics that have arrived on the scene. "Poor Tony convulsed and drummed and gasped and fluttered" and swallowed his tongue. His last worry as he feels his legs spreading is that his father "could see up his dress, what was hidden."

PLOT AND CHARACTER: AA&R

THEME: Secrets, Time, Waste, His/Father, Recur

An addict is "a thing that basically hides" (p. 932). Poor Tony hides from Minty and Wo and those who might connect him with the stolen heart. He hides in a dumpster and then in a men's room. He apparently saw his father's funeral "through dark glasses from a distance." In seizure, he imagines his father will see "up his dress, what was hidden." In n. 103, the narrator cites an uncredited (a hidden) source. Poor Tony's slow and painful experience of time as endless and unbound is tied to his experience of waste: "time had become the shit itself." Poor Tony smells, and he sees time as a "wingless fowl hunched incontinent atop the stall" in which he sits hunched and incontinent, in a men's room "full of old men . . . whose flatulence smelled of cabbage." Poor Tony thinks often of "his sonless father," who is clearly not just a body or furniture (cf. p. 168) to Poor Tony. Wallace explores the prolonged effect of a men's room environment on a father-son relationship in his story collection *Brief Interviews with Hideous Men* ("B.I. #42," pp. 73-7).

Most of the addicts in the novel have other fears or obsessions; Poor Tony's is a fear of ants, stemming from childhood, which manifests itself in his hallucinations. Like many of the novel's addicts, Poor Tony also weeps (p. 304). In other recurring images, Poor Tony "stamp[s] his foot," hallucinates that his limbs float away (separation of head and body), and remembers that his father wore a mask. A squeak, convulsions, and fluttering are again harbingers of danger or horror.

Chapter 20: Both Destiny's Kisses And Its Dope-Slaps

This chapter contrasts the fortunes of Orin Incandenza and Poor Tony Krause. Both men experience isolation in public: Orin is adored by fans in a stadium; Poor Tony is avoided by commuters on the T. Orin heard the crowd "roar gathering, tidal, amniotic, the voice of what might as well be God." Poor Tony heard "a rushing train-roar that was no train on earth and felt a vascular roaring rushing that until the pain hit seemed like the gathering of a kind of orgasm of the head." Orin watched "little ten-second clips of [his punting] over and over [which] unfolded like time-lapsing flowers and seemed to reveal him in ways he could never have engineered." Time spoke to Poor Tony of "the same things, over and over. They were unrepeatable. Nothing in even Poor Tony's grim life-experience prepared him for the experience of time with a shape and an odor." Orin's late father never supported Orin's football career; Poor Tony's late father "rended his own clothing in symbolic shiva in the Year of the Whopper in the kitchen of the Krause home," presumably to express that his "gender-dysphoric" son was dead to him.

Chapter 21

The Only Thing of Importance, Choosing

Chapter 21.1, Section 73, Pages 306-312
Notes 104-112, Pages 1004-1022
7 November Y.D.A.U.

Ted Schacht and Hal are attending Saturday classes taught by E.T.A. prorectors on the day after the Port Washington meet (Ch. 19.3). At "like 1435-1445h." the results of the meet are being announced in classrooms via the intercom system that Jim Troeltsch is allowed to use for his "pseudo-radio program." Schacht is taking a class in "pathologic double-bind-type quandaries" from Mary Ester Thode, who is giving a midterm exam today. The first item of the exam may be summarized as follows: What is a kleptomaniac agoraphobic who lives alone to do?

Hal is taking Thierry Poutrincourt's "Separatism and Return: Québecois History from Frontenac Through the Age of Interdependence." "Hal sees no way of Orin's knowing he was taking [this class] when he called to ask for help with Separatism [beginning 3 November, p. 137], which Orin's asking for help from him with anything was strange enough." "It was the establishment of O.N.A.N. and the gerrymandering of the Great Convexity [Concavity] that turned the malevolent attention of Québec's worst . . . insurgents south of the border." "The earliest unignorable strikes involved a then-unknown terrorist cell [the A.F.R. "of the E.W.D.-receptacle-festooned Papineau region of southwestern Québec," n. 112] that . . . dragged huge standing mirrors across U.S. Interstate 87," causing numerous accidents to "[n]aïvely empiricist" U.S. motorists (attempting to avoid the car in the mirror) before the crash of a suicidal (non-car-in-mirror-avoiding) motorist "brought to light the first tangible evidence of an anti-O.N.A.N. ill will way worse than anything aroused by plain old historical Separatism, up in Québec."

Note 110 documents Hal's activities "later in the same day" (around 1600h., p. 1009), requires more than seventeen pages, and is the only note to be divided into sections like a chapter. Note 110.1 (pp. 1004-5) finds Hal soaking his ankle in his room after "skipping a quick trip down to the Pump Room," reflecting on both the phone message Orin left earlier (at 1412h. with "professional-locker-room sounds in the background") and on his special plans for this evening—made possible by tomorrow's "day of total mandatory R&R" in honor of Interdependence Day—which include a trip to The Unexamined Life (cf. n. 67). "Mario has been closeted with Disney Leith all day preparing things for [tomorrow's] post-prandial gala and filmfest." Hal is rummaging through a shoebox of "mementos and postal correspondence Mario's rescued from wastebaskets and recycling bins and dumpsters." "None of the Hush Puppy box's snail-mail letters are to or from Mario." Two of the items found in the shoebox are a Y.W.-Q.M.D. letter from Avril to Orin (n. 110.2: p. 1006 and endnotes a-f on p. 1021) and an example of then-New-Orleans-Saint Orin's impersonal responses to Avril's letters (n. 110.3: p. 1007 and endnote g on p. 1021). Orin "quit mailing the Moms the pseudo-form-replies" in YUSHITYU (p. 244).

Note 110.4 (pp. 1007-21 and endnotes h-l on pp. 1021-2) documents another phone call from Orin to Hal. Orin called recently on the 3rd (Ch. 13.1) and on the 5th (Ch. 18.2) of November. First, two of Orin's seduction strategies are discussed. As usual, Hal chastises Orin's lack of both human decency and word-choice/ pronunciation skills. Then there is general conversation about a toothache Hal feels is starting (Orin blames Hal's use of oral tobacco, which prompts Hal to spit into an old NASA glass (p. 1005, cf. p. 198). However, Hal claims "The caries are Himself's legacy."), current events on the E.T.A. courts, Orin's possible attendance if Hal makes the WhataBurger semifinals in Arizona this Thanksgiving, and the fact that Orin hasn't seen any wheelchaired stalkers in days. After a "half-dozen or so" conversations "with a certain Subject," Orin needs "considered-sounding responses to two basic questions" and wants Hal's feedback. Hal quickly discerns that the Subject is Orin's *Moment* profiler, Helen, who is "en route" (p. 1012) to Enfield. Hal has said he will let Orin know if there are "sightings of any journalists," but predicts that Schtitt will not allow "her" to talk to any E.T.A. students.

In answer to Orin's first question, Hal defines *samizdat* as a combination of "self" and "to publish," used generically as "any sort or politically underground or beyond-the-pale press or the stuff published thereby." Hal supposes "ultra-radical Québecois and Albertan stuff could be considered O.N.A.N.ite samizdat" if it advocated violence or "anti-O.N.A.N. terrorism." Regarding their father's name being used in connection with the word *samizdat*, Hal says that though a "lot of Himself's stuff was self-distributed . . . [h]is interest in politics was subordinate to form. Always. And none of it's banned." When Orin begins to move the line of questioning to Québecois Separatism, Hal implies that Orin should contact their mother, "who's really the person to chat with about all issues Canadian."

To begin the second question, Orin wonders "why the whole Québec-Separatisteur collection up there [cf. p. 144] dropped the original Québec-independence objective like a rock and switched seemingly overnight to putting everything into agitating [for all of Canada] against O.N.A.N. and the Reconfiguration and forcing the return of the Concavity to our map." Terrorism "especially directed at Ottawa" included the "Crétien [spelled without an "h"] assassination ["a railroad-spike through Crétien's eye"]. 'Notre Rai Pays [cf. the wheelchaired man's cap on Joelle's walk today, pp. 221-2].' Terrorists in plaid flannel." But "suddenly everything changes . . . with the advent of O.N.A.N.," and "in *immediate unison* all the various different Separatist groups drop secession and independence like rocks . . . and now insurge against O.N.A.N. on behalf of the same Canada they'd spent decades treating like the enemy. Does this seem a little bit odd?"

Hal again reminds Orin that their mother, "ashamed of even hurting over" her lack of contact with Orin, would be overjoyed to hear from him and that she is an excellent source for these questions given her dual citizenship. Hal remarks on the irony of President Gentle's Reconfiguration "bringing Canada together at our expense, when it was pretty obviously meant to bring us [the U.S.] together at Canada's expense," but adds that "Québec's hatred of anglophone Canada transcends anything they could work up against O.N.A.N." Orin says that "the Subject [Helen] concurs" and that she "seems to imply the anti-O.N.A.N. thing is some sort of anomalous dodge or something."

Hal wonders about Orin's interest in the large "profiler you just last week were preparing to fend off about Himself." Hal suggests that Orin's "rapacious fetish for young unmarried mothers he can strategize into betraying their spouses and maybe damaging their kids for all time" comes from Orin's blaming "the whole affair of Himself" on their mother, and notes that Orin "won't interface with [Avril] or worse even acknowledge her," present in Hal's mind given what he has just seen in Mario's shoebox. (Compare Orin's comment—"Chortles are good. We like chortles"—with a statement from Avril's letter on p. 1006: "Chortling is good. We like chortling.") After a brief return to the second question (If independence from Canada is the goal, why would the Québec groups "dissipate themselves" engaging in anti-O.N.A.N. terrorism? If the Québec groups don't get along, why this "united concerted switch" of terrorist tactics?), Hal lambastes Orin mercilessly about his behavior, but then apologizes and says "I hate losing the temper," citing his toothache as a source of intense irritation. At this point, Pemulis enters the room and becomes an ever-increasing obstacle to the phone conversation.

Hal suggests that Québec's hatred of O.N.A.N. is due to the fact that "three-quarters of the Concavity's northern border runs contiguous to Québec" and that Québec bears the brunt of the environmental horrors associated with the region, including "kids the size of Volkswagens shlumpfing around with no skulls," "green sunsets and indigo rivers" (cf. the Charles, p. 233), "feral-hamster incursions" (cf. p. 93), and lobsters "like monsters in old Japanese films." Both Orin (via Steeply) and Hal believe Québec will not get Gentle to take back the Concavity and that Canada will not oppose O.N.A.N; therefore, the "little anti-O.N.A.N. campaigns and gestures"—mirrors stretched across U.S. highways (cf. pp. 311-2 in this section), fleur-de-lis banners hung from U.S. monuments (Joelle passes by one today, pp. 223-4), moose-guano rained upon New Haven, etc. (pp. 1015, 1021)—have just been "hopeless and pathetic." Pemulis interrupts to exhort Hal to get "Mr. *Hope*" so that he and Hal can go down and join their friends in the truck and begin "the I.-Day-Eve expedition and supper out." In response to Hal's protestations of rolling "a zeppelin out of *my* part of the Hope," Pemulis assures Hal that it will be sorted out and that Hal will not be exploited.

As Hal attempts to get dressed to go out with his free hand, Orin gives Hal something to ponder for their next phone conversation. Orin (via Steeply) wonders why Québec—instead of trying to return the Concavity to the U.S.—doesn't ask Ottawa for sole responsibility of the Concavity in exchange for independence from Canada. The reason could be that Québecois terrorist groups (with some help from the Albertan ultra-rightists, cf. p. 144) think it will be more effective to create the illusion of "pan-*Canadian* anti-O.N.A.N.ism"—thereby inciting the anger and potential retaliation of the U.S. and Mexico against all of Canada—and then "use the U.S. and Mexico as levers on Ottawa": if Ottawa gives Québec independence, which is "still the Québecer insurgents' real goal," Québec will admit to being solely responsible for all anti-O.N.A.N. terrorism and then intensify/increase the incidents of terror in order to achieve de-Reconfiguration. Hal says that pondering is not required because, as stated earlier, "the total anti-U.S. insurgency so far's been too hapless and small-potato for [Helen's] theory to work." Orin says that's what he told her, but then "she raised this *samizdat*-word in connec—" (Pemulis, who had been eyeing the phone console for two paragraphs, breaks the connec[tion] between Orin and Hal). Given Orin's first question, surely he was about to say that the word was raised in connection with their father.

PLOT AND CHARACTER: E.T.A., O.N.A.N., A.F.R., Hal, Mario, Orin, Avril

THEME: Choice, Secrets, His/Father, Cycles, Waste, Recur

Ms. Thode's course explores double-binds: difficult choices. Troeltsch must make creative choices to achieve variety in his "broadcasts." Québecois Separatists believe that their ancestors had no choice in a "forced property-transfer" (p. 1014) and want to rectify that situation by choosing independence. Orin hides from contact with his mother, who secretly longs to have contact with him. Orin deceives women with his seduction strategies. Steeply deceives Orin and Orin's teammates by pretending that he is a woman. "Separation is still the Québecer insurgents' real goal, and their anti-O.N.A.N. insurgency is not what it appears." The Separatists secretly use the Concavity as the means by which they will take back land they believe is rightfully theirs, just as Fortinbras perhaps secretly uses the Polish ground (like the Concavity, "a little patch of ground/That hath in it no profit but the name," *Hamlet* IV.iv.18-9) as a means to obtain passage into Denmark so that he can take back land he believes is rightfully his. Fortinbras, like Hamlet and Hal and Orin, is haunted by his father's death. Orin, like Hamlet, seems to blame his mother to some degree. Orin has inherited a fear of spiders from his father (pp. 45, 1010), and Hal has inherited dental problems (pp. 27, 1010). Ted Schacht is another character who has lost his father (p. 308).

Note 110.4 is another example of how Wallace slowly (through 14 pages) builds the narrative to a state of high tension or "chaotic stasis" (n. 61, p. 996) and then truncates it. By the time Pemulis disconnects the phone, Hal is getting dressed with one hand, being pressured by Pemulis, and on the verge of an important discovery with Orin. The reader remains alert and active because the reader never experiences an end to the narrative, only separation and return. Earlier, the reader was separated from Erdedy when he was caught between choices in chaotic stasis on p. 27 and then returned to him in his Ennet residency on p. 209. Using endnotes also fosters separation and return. When n. 110 (which features a dozen additional endnotes, the first two of which are meta-narrative interjections) has run its course, the reader returns to p. 311 and continues from there. Resonances of the text of Ch. 21.1 are found in n. 110. Thode's exam contains an item concerning a hypothetical agoraphobic; Hal speaks of Emily Dickinson as an "agoraphobic poet." Troeltsch speaks metaphorically of a "spike into the right eye"; the A.F.R. "put a railroad-spike through Crétien's eye." Orin and Hal speak of the terrorist tactic of stretching mirrors across highways, incidents of which are described after the return to p. 311.

Other terrorist tactics include causing moose-guano to rain on New Haven, symbolic of Québec getting "splatted when the E.W.D. vehicles overshoot the Concavity." The Separatists want Gentle of "The Clean U.S. Party" (n. 110.k) to "acknowledge the [Concavity's] waste as fundamentally American waste." The terrorists "only barely get foiled from injecting anaerobic toxins into jars of Planters peanuts," a subject explored by Wallace in "Mister Squishy," from his story collection *Oblivion*. Who were the "O.N.A.N.ite V.I.P.s" shot on U.S. soil; i.e., who were the "demapped officials" (pp. 1015, 1021)?

In addition to a resurgence of Hal's chronic tooth problems, there are several other recurrences: "stuporous passivity" is regarded as "venemous" at E.T.A. (n. 106); Orin asks for help; Troeltsch speaks of a boot to a toadstool (a stamping foot); huge mirrors are stretched across highways; Pemberton moves in wobbled and diminishing circles (pp. 1004, 1009); net-shadows elongate across courts (p. 1005); Avril writes of "her maternal beak [pressed] to the terminal window's glass" (p. 1006); Orin uses the name of an old TV character, Jethro Bodine of *The Beverly Hillbillies*; Hal greets Orin with "E Unibus Pluram" (cf. Ch. 11.8 commentary); Orin imagines a blue "pilot-light of passion" and Hal imagines the "Subject" of Orin's passion as having a "big blue eye" (pp. 1007, 1012); Orin and Hal will miss a connection when Orin travels to play the Patriots at the same time Hal will be at the WhataBurger in Arizona; Pemulis makes a claw of his hand (three times), rolls his eyes, and makes motions of rending and chewing (pp. 1016, 1017, 1020); "Hal is hunched" (p. 1016); Pemulis holds a "Constantine bust" (p. 1018); and two artists are referenced—Rubens (pp. 1014, 1015, 1020) with respect to Steeply's femininity and Munch (p. 1016) with respect to Hal's "tooth-episodes."

Chapter 21.2, Section 74, Pages 312-317
Notes 113-119, Page 1022
unspecified Y.D.A.U.

This section provides a biographical sketch of Mario, "[f]ive years" after his father's death. "The first birth of the Incandenzas' second son was a surprise," occurring on a "November evening in the seventh month of a hidden pregnancy." The second birth may refer to Mario's emergence from incubators after "many weeks," or may refer to the birth of Hal if Mario is Tavis's biological son. "Avril's half-brother Charles Tavis" had been on an extended visit with the Incandenza's in the Back Bay brownstone—where or close to where Orin and Joelle lived, *Infinite Jest* was filmed, and Notkin lives now (cf. "the Back Bay-edge brownstone," p. 227)—that "they were soon to leave" for a home in Weston before moving again to E.T.A., "their third and final home." Tavis had been visiting since spring and therefore could have gotten Avril pregnant in April. Avril hid her pregnancy, and Mario is the "object of some weird attracto-repulsive gestalt for Charles Tavis" (cf. n. 98). Mario's "thin lank slack hair . . . looked at 18+ like" Tavis's, "his possible half-uncle."

Mario was named for his golf-addicted (cf. p. 163) great-grandfather, who one day in 1933 watched Jim Sr. play tennis as a boy (Ch. 15.1). Recall that Jim Sr.—whose first two careers were tennis player and pre-Method actor (p. 63)—told Jim Jr. in 1960 that "we're headed for the big time again" with respect to the family's upcoming move to CA (p. 162). In 1962 (n. 114), Jim Sr. became "the first of two actors to portray the Man from Glad" (p. 494) and served until 1964 ("for two years," p. 492). Jim Sr. was able "to retire from a sad third career as the Man From Glad in sandwich-bag commercials" upon his father Mario Sr.'s death, shortly after Mario Sr. "made a small fortune" by inventing *X-Ray Specs!* and selling the copyrights to AcmeCo. Jim Sr. moved back to Tucson—fatherless and sonless since Jim Jr. had already "[grown] up and fled east," presumably at the age of 14 (he was 10 in 1960, p. 159). Recall that Jim Jr. "used tennis scholarships to finance, on his own, private secondary and then higher education at places . . . far away from the U.S. Southwest" (p. 63). Jim Sr. drank himself "to a cerebral hemorrhage" and "dropped dead on a set of stairs."

Mario's "incomplete gestation and arachnoidal birth left the kid with some lifelong character-building physical challenges." Mario has a small body and a large head, "perfectly square" feet, and "withered-looking" arms that curl "out in front of his thorax in magiscule S's and [are] usable for rudimentary knifeless eating"; some parts of his body do not grow as fast as others; his movements are of an exaggerated slowness; and he "uses four pillows minimum" due to "dangerously slow breathing during sleep" (n. 115). Mario is resistant to pain, a condition that was frequently exploited by Orin in their youth. Mario's skin is "an odd dead gray-green" (compare this with Tavis's "gray-green-complected scalp") that looks "reptilian" (contrast this with Hal's appearance, p. 101). His fingers are "talon-esque," and he is homodontic: "all his teeth are bicuspids and identical, front and back." He has an "involuntarily constant smile." Although Mario is "technically, Stanford-Binet wise, slow," he is not "retarded or cognitively damaged."

Mario "and his late father had been . . . inseparable," and Mario's "dad let him into his heart's final and best-loved love." Mario "carried the late Incandenza's film and lenses and filters in a complex backpack . . . for most of the last three years of [Jim's] life, attending him on shoots and [sharing] the same motel room as Himself and occasionally [getting] Big Red Soda Water [cf. p. 228] and taking it to the apparently mute veiled graduate-intern down the motel's hall, fetching coffee and joe and various pancreatitis-remedies and odds and ends and props and helping D. Leith out with Continuity." If Joelle was not called "Madame Psychosis" on set and Mario thinks of her as "apparently mute," then perhaps this is why he does not identify the host of his beloved radio program as someone he actually knows (cf. p. 190). Presumably Joelle's being "veiled" is in reference to the filming of *The Night Wears a Sombrero* (p. 992), in which she played a veiled nun.

Mario is "inclined ever forward." "When required to stand upright and still," like when he's filming, Mario uses "a .7-meter steel pole that extends from a special Velcroed vest and angles . . . down and out to a slotted piece of lead blocking." Mario "stood thus buttressed on sets Himself had him help erect and furnish and light, . . . getting a thorough technical grounding in a cinematic craft he never imagined being able to pursue on his own" until Jim arranged for Mario to receive, on the Christmas after Jim's death, a camera that Jim had designed and built especially for Mario's ease of use. "Mario's facility with the head-mount Bolex attenuates the sadness of his status here, allowing him to contribute via making the annual E.T.A. fundraising documentary cartridge [cf. p. 265], videotaping students' strokes [cf. p. 55] and . . . the occasional challenge match . . . plus producing more ambitious, arty-type things that occasionally find a . . . following in the E.T.A. community." Mario's camera was "forwarded from the offices of Incandenza's attorney." Did Jim instruct his attorney to mail anything else after his death?

Mario was born in 1990. He will be nineteen on 25 November Y.D.A.U. (p. 589), nearing his twentieth Christmas. The Christmas after his father's death (in 2004) would have been Mario's fifteenth Xmas (or fourteenth if his first Christmas in an incubator doesn't count), not his "thirteenth Xmas" as stated on p. 315. In this section, E.T.A. is said to have been erected around summer 2000, "when Mario was nine [ten in November] and Hallie eight and Orin seventeen and in his one E.T.A. year B-4 Singles [2000-2001]." Recall Orin's "relegation to a middle spot on the Academy's B-squad" when "E.T.A. opened" (p. 284). But E.T.A. "has been in accredited operation for three pre-Subsidized years [1999-2001] and then eight Subsidized years" (p. 63). Presumably then, E.T.A was in accredited operation before its erection was complete in 2000. Or perhaps there is confusion due to an unfocused narrator, who interjects that he "overshot the place to mention" and "also overshot the place to include" (nn. 117, 119) facts about Mario. Presumably the place to mention and include these facts was on p. 314.

Mario is a favorite of Lyle's, and trainer "Barry Loach all but kisses the kid's ring, since it's Mario who through coincidence saved him from the rank panhandling underbelly of Boston Common's netherworld and more or less got him his job." Schtitt often "lets him ride in his surplus sidecar" (cf. p. 79), and E.T.A. players "vie to see who gets to cut up" his food at Denny's. Hal idealizes Mario and, "showing a striking lack of insight into his Mom's psyche," "fears that Avril sees Mario as the family's real prodigy." However, it was "Avril, not Hal, who insisted that Mario live . . . with Hal in an E.T.A. subdorm"; and "it was Hal, not [Avril]" who turned away "the veiled legate from the Union of the Hideously and Improbably Deformed" who came to see Mario. "Hal, brandishing his Dunlop stick, told the guy to go peddle his linen someplace else."

PLOT AND CHARACTER: Mario, Jim, Avril, Orin, Hal, E.T.A.
THEME: Secrets, Phys/Ob, His/Father, Choice, Time, Recur

Mario's birth was "a complete surprise," the culmination of "a hidden pregnancy." If Tavis is indeed Mario's biological father, that fact has been kept secret. Mario was born with "character-building physical challenges," but he is able to surmount these obstacles, in part due to a healthy relationship with his father (the next section will also address the importance of a father's influence). Rather than doing things for Mario and cultivating passivity, Jim applied his creativity in ways that inspired Mario to take action, "to contribute," to choose. Mario was "buttressed on sets," not just by the stability of his police lock, but because "Himself had him help erect and furnish and light" those sets. Jim made a complex camera that Mario would be able to use and had it mailed to Mario after his death, "attenuat[ing] the sadness" of Mario's status at E.T.A.: physically challenged in a place that rewards physical excellence. An "involuntarily constant smile" is a warning of danger in the novel; but not in Mario's case, because Mario transcends the self-absorbed pleasure-seeking that leads to dangerous passivity. Resonant with constant smiles and passivity is the fact that Jim's father portrayed "the Man From Glad" of "The Glad Flaccid Receptacle Corporation." What is implied by the fact that Glad is the "sponsor of the very last year of O.N.A.N.ite Subsidized Time" (n. 114)?

Jim had a strained relationship with his father (who "dropped dead on a set of stairs"), but he managed to be a good father to Mario (whose birth began on a staircase), even though he was an alcoholic who staged a grisly suicide. Jim's father moved in a circle—from AZ (tennis) to CA (acting) to AZ (Ch. 15.1) to CA (Man From Glad) to AZ (death)—but Jim's son Mario is "inclined ever forward." Mario also moves with "an exaggerated slowness that both resembles and permits extremely close slow attention to whatever's being done" (n. 115), resonant with the slow-motion motif exemplified (for example) by the dancers of the Minimal Mambo at Molly Notkin's party.

Mario's birth caused Avril to "turn in toward herself . . . hunched" in pain; Jim "saw the whole slow thing in a light like he was Vermeer," "ragged from an afternoon of Wild Turkey and low-temperature holography." On set, Jim used lighting that was "almost blinding, sunbursts of angled mirrors and Marino lamps and key-light kliegs" (Incandenza, a virtuoso of incandescence). Mario was found "spiderishly clinging" to Avril's womb and has a "reptilian/dinosaurian" (primitive) look. He has a large head and must use multiple pillows, like John Merrick, subject of a film by David Lynch, subject of an essay by Wallace. There are missed connections concerning Mario's failure to identify his acquaintance Joelle as radio's Madame Psychosis, Hal's keeping Mario from possibly meeting Joelle again via U.H.I.D., and Hal's "lack of insight into his Mom's psyche." Hal's "God-type issues" were documented in Ch. 6.1, and his "being shunted around for assessment of possible damage" was documented in n. 76. "People who're somehow burned at birth, withered or ablated way past anything like what might be fair, they either curl up in their fire, or else they rise": cf. "Incarnations of Burned Children," from Wallace's story collection Oblivion.

Chapter 21.3, Section 75, Pages 317-321
30 April / 1 May Y.D.A.U.

This section returns to the meeting between Marathe and Steeply, last documented in Ch. 11. Marathe asserts that the "appetite for the appeal" of "this Entertainment cartridge" comes from the "U.S.A. drive for spectation, which your culture teaches. This I was saying: this is why choosing is everything. When I say to you choose with great care in loving . . . you make ridicule" (cf. p. 107). Marathe asks Steeply to consider whether the U.S.A. can "hope to survive for a much longer time," given that its people "choose nothing over themselves to love" and "would die" and let their children die for this film, "would die for this chance to be fed this death of pleasure with spoons, in their warm homes, alone, unmoving: . . . forget for a moment the Entertainment, and think instead about a U.S.A. where such a thing could be possible enough for your Office to fear." Marathe asks how the U.S.A. can survive and "exercise dominion over other nations" if these nations consist of people "who still know what it is to choose? who will die for something larger? who will sacrifice the warm home, the loved woman at home [but recall that Marathe is betraying the A.F.R. for his wife, p. 89], their legs, their life even, for something more than their own wishes of sentiment? who would choose not to die for pleasure, alone?"

Marathe asserts that Québecers "will force nothing" on U.S. citizens but will "make only available. Entertainment. There will be then some choosing, to partake or choose not to" (cf. the display Joelle sees, p. 224). "How will U.S.A.s choose? Who has taught them to choose with care? How will your Offices and Agencies protect them, your people?" Marathe wonders whether the situation will be handled as ineffectually as drug wars were handled by the U.S.A. in the past. Steeply argues that, unlike drug-dealers who just want money, the A.F.R. "seem to want us dead. Not just the Concavity redemised. Not just secession for Québec." Marathe counters, "You cannot kill what is already dead. . . . This appetite to choose death by pleasure if it is available to choose . . . *this* is the death." The "collapsing" is a "formality only." Marathe says this is what Guillaume DuPlessis (accidentally killed by Gately, Ch. 7.4) "taught the cells," though only the A.F.R. understood: Steeply and others cannot save the American people; they "can only delay" the inevitable, because the Entertainment exists. The incident with the medical attaché is "more proof" that it exists.

Marathe says that Gentle's Reconfiguration was done "to delay this splitting apart [of the U.S.]. To keep you together, the hating of some other": a common enemy. (Hal, in his capacity as Big Buddy, will speak to his charges on 3 November about the application of the common-enemy tactic to improve performance at E.T.A. (p. 113). Orin and Hal will speak of Gentle's common-enemy tactic in their 7 November phone conversation (p. 1013).) But, Marathe says, it is "not someone outside you, this enemy. Someone . . . killed your U.S.A. nation already, Hugh. [Someone] let you forget how to choose, and what. Someone let your peoples forget it was the only thing of importance, choosing. . . . Someone taught that temples are for fanatics only [cf. p. 107] and took away the temples and promised there was no need for temples. And now there is . . . no map for finding the shelter of a temple," only a "confusion of permissions. The without-end pursuit of a happiness of which someone let you forget the old things which made happiness possible."

Steeply shudders at "what a separate Québec would be like. Choose what we tell you, neglect your own wish and desires, sacrifice. For Québec. . . . There are no choices without personal freedom, Buckeroo. It's not us who are dead inside. These things you find so weak and contemptible in us—these are just the hazards of being free. . . . Now you will say how free are we if you dangle fatal fruit before us and we cannot help ourselves from temptation. And we say 'human' to you. We say that one cannot be human without freedom." But Marathe warns that "[n]ot all compulsion comes from without" and calls U.S.A. freedom a "freedom-**from**: no one tells your precious individual U.S.A. selves what they must do. . . . What of freedom-**to**. How for the person to freely choose? How to choose any but a child's greedy choices if there is no loving-filled father to guide, inform, teach the person how to choose?" Would a good father allow "his child to choose only what is sweet, eating only candy" in the name of freedom? "Marathe could believe he could hear some young U.S.A. voices shouting and laughing . . . out on the desert floor below."

Steeply "stamp[s] a high heel in frustration" and says, "Human beings are not children." Steeply predicts Marathe will say that there is no difference if Americans "cannot choose to resist it, the pleasure, and cannot choose instead to live" and that Americans are "bullies but still children inside, and will kill [themselves] if you put the candy within the arms' reach." (Steeply, analogous to Hal's fixed-smile Dean (p. 3), relates Marathe's side of the story for him, to him.) Marathe says, "You speak to yourself, inventing sides. This itself is the habit of children: lazy, lonely, self."

Neither man mentions how he expects to get off the mountain.

PLOT AND CHARACTER: A.F.R., U.S.O.U.S., Samizdat
THEME: Isolation, Non-Action, Inf/Reg, Choice, His/Father, Cycles, Recur

Marathe and Steeply are at a remote, isolated location. Americans have become isolated and passive ("alone, unmoving"), living amid a "confusion of permissions" from which they are unable to "choose with great care in loving," because someone "took away the temples"; leaving Americans with only their "precious individual U.S.A. selves" to worship, unable to sacrifice, addicted to pleasure (entertainment, substances), ready "to die for pleasure, alone" in a state of infantile regression (a "death of the head by pleasure," "children inside"), making only "a child's greedy choices," "eating only candy": "lazy, lonely, self" (non-action, isolation, inf/reg). To "choose with great care" "something larger" than self and sentiment and pleasure requires the assistance of a "loving-filled father to guide, inform, teach the person how to choose" (or a place like Ennet that inspires "total self-surrender and spiritual awakening," p. 137).

But is the A.F.R. justified—if they "find a Copy-Capable copy and copy it and disseminate it"—in taking advantage of American "infants" simply because they find them "weak and contemptible"? Perhaps, as Steeply implies, it is the Québecois terrorists who are dead inside, unable to accept "the hazards of being free." Under the "blue stars," Marathe's chair squeaks (danger) as he speaks of "your walled-up country" (cf. p. 127), and Steeply stamps "a high heel in frustration" (a stamping foot). Marathe makes "emphatic circles" and Steeply makes "a circular flourish" (p. 318) as they go round and round with no way "up or down from the mountainside's shelf."

Chapter 21: The Only Thing Of Importance, Choosing

Without choice there is passivity or paralyzed stasis. If Thode's hypothetical agoraphobic kleptomaniac fails to choose, he or she will be double-bound, caught between choices, separating from one choice only to return to another in a mental loop or cycle, static, passive, troubled, never deciding (like the drug-addicted Erdedy on p. 27). Québecois Separatists believe that historically they were victims of a "forced property-transfer" and have sought independence through separation from Canada ever since. They now also seek to return land that Ottawa chose for them as part of Reconfiguration. Orin is caught in a cycle of seducing women who are mothers to young children, presumably because he will not choose to admit that he blames his mother for his father's death. Mario's relationship with a "loving-filled father," who dared to help Mario find a way out of himself through filmmaking, ensured that Mario is "inclined ever forward," able to choose, to contribute, not caught in a cycle of stasis or passivity, even though Mario's father was caught in a cycle of alcoholism. Marathe, discussing double-binds in a cyclical argument with Steeply, warns that America's enemy, the person at fault for America's problems, is "not someone outside you." Someone let Americans "forget it was the only thing of importance, choosing," and now Americans find themselves in a "confusion of permissions" with no temple, no map, and no happiness. Steeply says that although freedom is hazardous, there are "no choices without personal freedom"; "that one cannot be human without freedom"; and that, being human, "we cannot help ourselves from temptation." Marathe asks Steeply how an American can "choose any but a child's greedy choices if there is no loving-filled father to guide, inform, teach the person how to choose? How is there freedom to choose if one does not learn how to choose?"

Infinite Jest II

Details, Patterns

Beginning with Chapter 16, the reader encounters lengthier sections that build on the plots and characters already introduced and that provide details by which the disparate narrative threads of the novel can be recognized as parts of an interconnected weave. Like with the Madame Psychosis show, "over time some kind of pattern emerges, a trend or rhythm": a pattern of separation from and return to various interconnected narrative threads.

Chapter 16 introduces the rituals of the legendary Madame Psychosis show on WYYY and of the Incandenza family's late suppers at E.T.A., which include Mario's listening to Madame Psychosis, whom he should know from her work with his father but seems not to. Both the M.I.T. Student Union, which houses the Madame Psychosis show, and E.T.A. were designed by A.Y. Rickey. A brief description of each of the seven units of the Enfield Marine Public Health Hospital complex is provided. General facts about life in a Substance-recovery halfway facility are provided, and a more personal introduction to the residents of Ennet House (E.M.P.H.H. Unit #6) than was provided in Ch. 15 is gained by a description of their choices with respect to tattoos. Don Gately, who accidentally killed a coordinator of violent Québecois Separatists, has graduated treatment and become live-in staff at Ennet House. A date of significance—the window of opportunity for trying Pemulis's mysterious DMZ, also called Madame Psychosis in reference to the radio show—is determined.

In Ch. 17, it turns out that Madame Psychosis is named Joelle van Dyne, who not only worked with Jim but dated Orin. Some of her memories of Jim and his suicide are woven into the story of her walk to a party in her old apartment where she lived with Orin and then worked with Jim and now plans to commit suicide herself. Cut into her story is the first overtly stated chronology of Subsidized Time and the resume created for Hugh Steeply, who is undercover as journalist Helen Steeply and interviewing Orin.

Because of those interviews, Orin is calling Hal for information about their father. In Ch. 18, significant details about a crucial event—Jim's death—and Hal's experiences afterwards are provided. Orin also reports that wheelchaired persons (the A.F.R., Québecois Separatist terrorists) are following him. Ch. 18 also features an overview of the novel's geographic center, Enfield MA.

In Ch. 19, the patterns and rhythms of E.T.A.'s competition with Port Washington are described, and part of Schacht's story is told, with bits about Wayne and Hal and Pemulis thrown in. A normal morning at Ennet is described, and a better picture of the friction between residents is provided.

Chapter 20 features Orin's story and provides more information about his football career, his relationship with Joelle, and his choice to separate from his family. In Ch. 12, a snapshot of Poor Tony's violent life as an addict was provided. It turns out an old crewmate (Minty) and a victim (Smith) from that night are both now at Ennet. In Ch. 20, the story of what happens to addicts who don't choose Ennet is told: Poor Tony's horrific withdrawal and seizure are described.

Chapter 21 focuses on a central concern of the novel: choice vs. stasis or passivity. The story of the logic behind the Québecois Separatists' choice to use terrorist tactics against the U.S.A. is provided, with a hint that Jim's last film (featuring Joelle) may play a part in those tactics. Mario's story is one of surmounting physical obstacles with the help of a "loving-filled father," who helped him make active choices by designing special equipment so that he too could create films. Mario is "inclined ever forward," not in stasis. The story of the 30 April / 1 May meeting between Marathe of the A.F.R. and Hugh/Helen Steeply of the U.S.O.U.S. continues to thread its way through the novel, examining some of the novel's major themes. Here, Steeply asserts, "There are no choices without personal freedom." Marathe counters, "How is there freedom to choose ["any but a child's greedy choices"] if one does not learn how to choose" from "a loving-filled father"?

Chapter 22

Triggering Situation

Chapter 22.1, Section 76, Pages 321-342
Notes 120-130, Pages 1023-1025
8 November Y.D.A.U., 1400h.-1600h.

The heading indicates that 8 November Y.D.A.U. is Interdependence Day and includes the Latin phrase "*GAUDEAMUS IGITUR*," which means "let us rejoice therefore." Interdependence Day is "a day of total mandatory R&R" (p. 1005) at E.T.A., and the afternoon has been reserved for the playing of Eschaton, a "nuclear-conflagration game" (n. 53), beginning at 1400h. (p. 1011). "Eschatology (from the Greek **eskhatos**, "last") is Christian theology's doctrine of the Last Judgement—or what your present behaviour will earn in the future" (Appignanesi, p. 168). Eschaton is "nearly incomprehensible" (according to the description of Jim's *Baby Pictures of Famous Dictators* on p. 991) and "almost addictively compelling." The game's appeal is attributed to its "elegant complexity" and "complete disassociation from the realities of the present." Eschaton is played by "maybe a dozen of the kids between maybe like twelve and fifteen," but originally it was played by upperclassmen. Recall that "Orin was Eschaton's first game-master at E.T.A." (p. 284). The narrator of this section claims that no one is sure who brought Eschaton to Enfield, but the narrator of Ch. 20.1 states that "a Croatian-refugee transfer" brought the game up from "the Palmer Academy in Tampa" (p. 284). Pemulis was "E.T.A.'s finest Eschatonic marksman" (p. 154), helped make the game "way more compelling," and "is far and away the greatest Eschaton player in E.T.A. history." He therefore "has a kind of unofficial emeritus power of correction" over thirteen-year-old

Otis P. Lord, who as this year's Eschaton game-master (first described as such on p. 171) "Wears the Beanie" and "more or less [has] to play God" during the course of the game.

Pages 321-326 and n. 123 describe the conditions, preliminary calculations, set-up, objectives, and Situations (both World and Triggering) required for an Eschaton game. Eschaton requires eight to twelve players, 400 tennis balls (each representing "a 5-megaton thermonuclear warhead"), "four contiguous tennis courts" ("representing the whole rectangular projection of the planet earth"), "a head for data-retrieval and coldly logical cognition," a computer for game calculations, and a "wide array of tennis paraphernalia." There are (usually) six teams, called Combatants, in Eschaton: AMNAT (America/NATO: 3 players, which today are President Chu, Supreme Commander Possalthwaite, and McKenna); SOVWAR (Soviet/Warsaw Pact: 3 players, which today include Premier Peterson and Air Marshal Kittenplan); REDCHI (Red China: 1-2 players); IRLIBSYR (Iran-or-Iraq/Libya/Syria: 1-2 players, represented today by Ingersoll); SOUTHAF (South Africa: represented today by Gopnik); and INDPAK (India/Pakistan: represented today by J. J. Penn). "Pieces of tennis gear are carefully placed within each Combatant's territories to mirror and map strategic targets." Players can launch "warheads" only with their tennis racquets, which helps players (e.g., Orin) "develop terrific lobs." The "most favorable ratio of points for INDDIR—Infliction of Death, Destruction, and Incapacitation of Response—to SUFDDIR—self-evident" determines a "given Eschaton's winning team." A "quorum of the day's Combatants" must endorse both the World Situation (Pemulis's "teams won most games before the first lob landed" due to his negotiating skills) and the Triggering Situation determined by the game-master.

Before Pemulis, "Combatants' balls were simply doled out by throws of shiny red Yahtzee-dice." But now Pemulis has incorporated "stats-cruncher software" on a computer linked "by cellular modem to a slick Yushityu portable with color monitor out on the courts' nuclear theatre." Pemulis has introduced complicated mathematical formulas into the game so that the effects of real-world military, political, religious, economic, environmental, and battle conditions may be approximated with maximum precision. In n. 123, Pemulis explicates (with graphs labeled "PEEMSTER" and "HALSADICK," rather than the standard Figure 1 and Figure 2) the Mean-Value Theorem for Integrals and its relevance to the distribution of tennis-ball warheads in Eschaton. The second error discussed in Mike Strong's "Dubious Math In *Infinite Jest*" concerns Pemulis's application of the Mean-Value Theorem to his Eschaton calculations. Strong asserts that the theorem does not offer a method of finding a specific mean value. It is indeed difficult to follow exactly how Pemulis applies the theorem to the calculations discussed in n. 123, because Pemulis does not work through a specific example involving representative continuous functions associated with a particular Combatant across two Eschatons. However, the same abstracted form of the theorem used by Pemulis—the integral of f(x)dx on the interval [a, b] = f(x')(b-a)—is used in Calculus books to determine a specific mean value for a continuous function. For example: the integral of f(x) = x^2 on the interval [1, 4] divided by (4-1) yields a specific value of f(x') = 7 at x' = 2.65; i.e., at x' = the square root of 7. That is, the integral of f(x) = x^2 (which is $(x^3)/3$) on the interval [1, 4] divided by (4-1) = $[((x=4)^3)/3-((x=1)^3)/3]/3$ = $[(4^3)/3-(1^3)/3]/3$ = [64/3-1/3]/3 = [63/3]/3 = 21/3 = 7 (Munem and Foulis, p. 306). (The sign for the integral from a to b in the abstracted formula Pemulis uses is missing in the first edition of *Infinite Jest* (cf. Strong's "third, minor error"). This sign was added to subsequent editions, and the line that indicates division was properly placed immediately under "2π" on p. 328. Also, the shading in the "HALSADICK" graph was removed for Back Bay's 1997 paperback edition of *Infinite Jest* but then shaded again in Back Bay's 10th anniversary paperback in 2006.) Pemulis asserts that the Mean-Value Theorem also can be used in calculations involving tennis-court boundaries and drug urine-level ranges.

Pemulis got Hal to write a complex rulebook for Eschaton in Y.P.W. Note 123, perhaps an excerpt from that rulebook, was written by Hal in third person as a verbatim transcription (after the event) of Pemulis's dictation ("Pemulis here") to Hal, who added "occasional verbal flourishes" and fourteen indications that he was letting errors stand. When Pemulis suggests using the size of Hal's penis as a constant in a formula, Hal also inserts an addendum into the transcription. At one point, Pemulis asks that Hal "pass that certain item back on over here." Of course, Pemulis could just be asking for a pencil with which to draw the graph that follows; but if he is asking Hal for marijuana, n. 123 was probably written after the Y.P.W. rulebook, given that Hal "didn't even get downwind of [his] first bit of Bob Hope until fifteen, more like nearly sixteen" (p. 67), which would have been in Y.D.P.A.H. In fact, n. 123 may have been written coincident with the main text of Ch. 22.1. During the explication of the Triggering Situation for today's Eschaton, a meta-narrator (via n. 127) interjects, "A lot of these little toss-ins and embellishments are Inc amusing himself," implying that Hal may be writing the main text of Ch. 22.1 in third person, too (cf. "But if Hal had" and "but for Hal's synoptic purposes here," pp. 322-3). Note 127 may even be another transcription by Hal of a comment by Pemulis, given that both n. 123 and n. 127 end with Pemulis-style parting shots ("P.S."s). Of course, a meta-narrator or Hal-in-third-person could just be parodying Pemulis's style.

Pages 327-332 document today's game so far, played on "E.T.A.'s four easternmost tennis courts." Hal, who yesterday was in class with Poutrincourt and on the phone with Orin (Ch. 21.1, including n. 110), watches the game with Struck, Axford, Troeltsch, and Pemulis. Someone in a "mint-green advertorial Ford sedan" watches the game from "behind West House." This is Steeply: cf. his "green sedan subsidized by a painful ad for aspirin upon its side" (p. 107) and the fact that yesterday Hal referred to Helen as being "en route" (p. 1012) to E.T.A. The Eschaton players are "almost parodically adult" in shouldering "the awesome weight of their responsibilities." Otis P. Lord "has to keep legging it from one continent to another, pushing a rolling [food cart] with a blinking Yushityu portable on one shelf and a [diskette case] on the other, the shelves' sides hung with clattering clipboards." It's "a nerve-racking job, he's more or less having to play God." From the "pavilion outside the fence along the south side of the East Courts," Struck and Axford are drinking "suspiciously bracing Gatorades" and passing a "psychochemical cigarette of some sort" between them. Hal is spitting in his NASA glass, feeling a twinge in an upper left tooth, and fighting the urge to get high for a second time today in front of people which would include Little Buddies. Pemulis and Troeltsch have both taken Tenuate. Pemulis scrutinizes the game, and Troeltsch "call[s] the action into a disconnected broadcast-headset." The following is a possible representation of the East Courts and the Eschaton map (note the square of Courts 13-16 nested inside the square of Courts 1-12), although it may put Court 12 too far from the Eschaton map:

03	04	05	06	Pacific C. America	N. America
02	14	15	07	S. America Africa	Atlantic Europe
01	13	16	08	Africa	Europe Asia
12	11	10	09	Australia	Asia
Gate		Pavilion			

By 1515h., the game has entered an "actionless diplomatic interval" in which SOVWAR is negotiating terms with AMNAT and "Lord tear-asses back and forth between Courts 6 and 8, food cart clattering." Struck, "who as usual has made a swine of himself with the suspiciously bracing cups of Gatorade, is abruptly ill all over his own lap and then sort of slumps to one side in his patio-chair with his face slack and white." Hal finds himself "smoking dope in public without even thinking about it or having consciously decided to go ahead." Pemulis is "completely absorbed."

Pages 332-336 describe the "most crucial phase" of today's game, initiated by Otis P. Lord's donning of the white beanie "that signals a temporary cessation of [Spasm Exchanges] between two Combatants but allows all other Combatants to go on pursuing their strategic interests as they see fit." It begins to snow. "Yesterday it had been warmer and rained" (during Joelle's walk to Molly Notkin's party, Ch. 17). Struck threatens to "fall out of his chair"; Pemulis keeps "tallies via pencil and clipboard"; the "idling Ford sedan is conspicious"; Hal, Axford (who "has a total of only three-and-a-half digits on his right hand), and Troeltsch share "what looks to the Combatants like a suckerless Tootsie-Roll stick"; and in West House, Mrs. Clarke can be heard "preparing the Interdependence Day gala dinner, which always includes dessert" (cf. "Mrs. Clarke's confectionary day in the sun," p. 1009).

At this point, REDCHI attacks INDPAK; but Lord, busily crunching numbers, has a "lapse of omniscience" and doesn't see it. J. J. Penn of INDPAK creates a distraction by claiming that the snow will affect the conditions of the game, which prompts Pemulis to yell, "It's snowing on the goddamn *map*, not the *territory*, you *dick!*" This "theatre-boundary-puncturing threat" to "the game's whole sense of animating realism" leads to a "metatheoretical fuss" as Struck falls out of his chair. As Hal leans over to spit, he becomes "lost in a paralytic thought-helix" of "marijuana thinking." Meanwhile, Ingersoll of IRLIBSYR realizes that "IRLIBSYR's highest possible strategic utility lies in AMNAT and SOVWAR failing to come to terms." As Pemulis warns against "letting asswipes like Jeffrey Joseph Penn run roughshod over the delimiting boundaries that are Eschaton's very life-blood," Hal watches Ingersoll "fire a ball . . . straight as if shot from a rifle and [strike] Ann Kittenplan [who is "butch and suspiciously muscular"] right in the back of the head." Everyone freezes. Ingersoll claims that he has taken out the entire launch capacity of SOVWAR and AMNAT, unless the "kill-radius is somehow altered by the possible presence of climatic snow." Pemulis and Kittenplan begin hurling "anti-Ingersoll invectives."

Pages 336-342 document the game's devolution into "Utter Global Crisis," signified by Otis P. Lord's donning of the red beanie for only the second time in Eschaton history. Pemulis castigates Lord for reacting to Ingersoll's "obvious instance of map-not-territory equivocationary horseshit." There is considerable debate about the rules and underlying theory of Eschaton, in which Pemulis shouts that the exemption of players as targets (players are part of the map, not the territory) "is like the one ground-rule boundary that keeps

Eschaton from degenerating into chaos." Pemulis warns Lord against compromising "Eschaton's map for all time." During this Hal spits; the idling Ford emits exhaust; and three EWD vehicles are propelled north with a "sudden tripartite whump."

Kittenplan can contain herself no longer and strikes back at Ingersoll. This prompts other players to attack Ingersoll with cruelty. Hal, "paralyzed with absorption," cannot spit; and Struck, who lies motionless, "looks to have wet his pants in his sleep." Troeltsch makes to stop the carnage, but Pemulis blocks him. Troeltsch asks about the "Nunhagen-Aspirin-adverting Ford" but is ignored. Kittenplan is attacked at close range; Lord (to signify the worst possible situation) "flicks the red beanie's propeller, never before flicked"; and from this point the players begin fighting for real. Troeltsch says he "wouldn't be just sitting and lying there if any of the Little Buddies under his own personal charge were out there getting potentially injured," but Hal is too "absorbed" to respond. As Axford attempts to relight the "cigarette," Hal notes that "this is the third anniversary of Axhandle losing a right finger and half his right thumb."

Attempting to get off-court with the cart, Lord is hit by another player, and the equipment flies off the cart high into the air. Lord attempts "to save hardware that's now at the top of its rainbow's arc. It's clear Lord won't make it. It's a slow-motion moment." Lord trips over vomiting Lamont Chu "and is spectacularly airborne." A face appears in the Ford's window. Axford shakes the lighter. Kittenplan bashes a player's face into the fence. "The color monitor lands on its back with its screen blinking ERROR," and Lord goes "headfirst down through the monitor's screen, and stays there, his sneakers in the air." A distant siren sounds to mark 1600h. and "is creepily muffled by the no-sound of falling snow."

PLOT AND CHARACTER: E.T.A., Hal
THEME: Boundaries, Waste, Non-Action, Inf/Reg, Recur

In this section, Ingersoll breaches "the one ground-rule boundary that keeps Eschaton from degenerating into chaos," and the map of an imagined conflict becomes the territory of an actual conflict. Metaphorical map elimination has been used throughout the novel to symbolize death; literal map elimination here may compromise Eschaton "for all time." J. J. Penn's original boundary-blurring question was inspired by the snowfall, which "makes everything gauzy and terribly clear at the same time" (like the lens Jim used to film *Infinite Jest*?). Pemulis is often concerned with boundaries and waste, which is expelled at the boundaries of the body: where what is internal to the body meets what is external. In addition to being violently upset by the boundary breaches of Penn and Ingersoll, Pemulis uses the words turd, urine, Unit, HALSADICK, dick (a boundary-breaching organ), asswipe, and horseshit throughout this section. (The boundary of the Concavity is also determined by waste.) The slow pace of a standard round of Eschaton appears "almost narcotized-looking" to outside observers. Pemulis is "completely absorbed" by the game. Hal is "paralyzed and absorbed," a victim of "marijuana thinking." Only Troeltsch has the impulse to help the Little Buddies on court, but Pemulis keeps him from taking action. Struck lies motionless and wets his pants like an infant. Pemulis berates the selfishness of Ingersoll's willingness to "eliminate Eschaton's map for keeps for one slimy cheesy victory in just one day's apocalypse."

E.T.A. features a "circular drive" (pp. 327, 338), and when Ingersoll is hurt he "begins to limp around in small circles"; Axford "is hunched coughing" (p. 329) from overindulgence; there is "a tiny whirring sound" (p. 335) in Ingersoll's head; Kittenplan's face is "a stony Toltec death-mask" (p. 336); Struck and Chu throw up; Lord's race to save airborne hardware is "a slow-motion moment"; and when Pemulis and Kittenplan beginning yelling at Ingersoll "the trees' crows take slow flight," perhaps another bird omen. Hegel (n. 120), artists Durer (p. 323) and El Greco (p. 334), and mythological hero Achilles (p. 325) are referenced. Other textual recurrences include Axford's hatred of Ingersoll (pp. 326, 340; cf. p. 98), the multi-emblazoned tow truck (p. 331, cf. p.153), Pemulis's nickname Penisless (p. 333, cf. p. 1019), Pemulis's penchant for dosing someone's water jug (like at Port Washington) or voltaging their door-knob (n. 129), and Thode's vitaminish stink (p. 339, cf. p. 306). Wallace again leaves a narrative section at a moment of chaotic stasis. Note that the playful narrator responds to Troeltsch's "Oh, my" with "O. Lord" (p. 334) and that "Lord" is "more or less having to play God."

Chapter 22.2, Section 77, Pages 343-367
Notes 131-141, Pages 1025-1026
8 November Y.D.A.U., 2000h. (p. 344) to the end (p. 367) of the 2045h. break (p. 360)

This section begins about four hours after the Eschaton debacle, and picks up the thread of Don Gately and the Ennet residents, last documented in Ch. 19.2. Pages 343-352 detail Boston AA procedures and typical events that lead an addict to seek out AA. Each Boston AA Group holds its regular meeting once a week (and uses as many capitalized phrases as Eschaton uses military abbreviations), at which (almost always) speakers address the audience. Often beginners' meetings occur a half-hour before regular meetings (n. 131). The speakers at one Group's regular meeting are always from another Boston AA Group participating in what is called a "Commitment." Groups trade Commitments, and therefore travel often. The White Flag Group of Enfield, MA (Ennet House's founder's group, n. 50) meets on Sundays in the cafeteria of the Provident Nursing Home close to the Enfield Tennis Academy and tonight is hosting a Commitment from the Advanced Basics Group of Concord. The White Flaggers will reciprocate by traveling to Concord on Friday. Speakers spread "the message that despite all appearances AA works," especially to newcomers. Ennet House residents are required to attend "a designated AA or NA meeting every single night of the week" accompanied by a House Staff member, which tonight is Gately, who is "so huge no one sits behind him for several rows." The goal of the audience is "to Identify [with other] instead of Compare [with self]" when listening to a speaker. "[A]ll the speakers' stories of decline and fall and surrender are basically alike."

Tonight's first speaker (introduced by "the Advanced Basics member who's chairing this evening's Commitment") is John L., who like most speakers recounts Losses suffered and Denials made before finally choosing to try AA. John L.'s specific story is interconnected with the narrator's general description of the addict's spiral: asking "why can't I quit if I so want to quit, unless I'm insane?" (cf. p. 179), being "in a cage" (like Joelle in Ch. 17), and finally seeing the Substance (after it removes "its smily-face mask") as "the Face In The Floor, the grinning root white face of your worst nightmares [cf. pp. 62 and 254], and the face is your own face in the mirror, now." "All these speakers' Substance-careers seem to terminate at the same cliff's edge," "this cliffish nexus of exactly two total choices, this miserable road-fork Boston AA calls your Bottom." The addict then makes the choice to either "eliminate [his or her] own map for keeps" or to call AA. Everybody "Comes In dead-eyed and puke white" and is told "You are not unique . . . : this initial hopelessness unites every soul." Later, people are united by the shocked realization that AA works (keeps them Substance-free). "The newcomers who abandon common sense and resolve to Hang In and keep coming and then find their cages all of a sudden open, mysteriously, after a while, share this sense of deep shock and possible trap." But if "you keep getting ritually down on your big knees every morning and night asking for help [from God or your Higher Power], and like a shock-trained organism without any kind of independent human will you do exactly like your told, you keep coming and coming, nightly, . . . you Hang In and Hang In [cf. "unbridgeable gaps of experience" for E.T.A. players who hang in and stick it out "for years and years" (p. 98)], meeting after meeting, . . . not only does the urge to get high stay more or less away, but more general life-quality-type . . . things seem to get progressively somehow, better." Concerning general life-quality-type things, the speaker after John L. is an Irishman who "wax[es] lyrical about his first solid bowel movement in adult life."

Pages 352-360 describe Don Gately's experiences in particular, including his relationship with the "Crocodiles" (White Flag longtimers) and an "epiphanic dream." The narrator for Gately misspells as Gately would misspell: cf. "orevwar" on p. 353. Gately's "biggest asset as an Ennet House live-in staffer" (besides his size) is his "ability to convey his own experience about at first hating AA to new house residents who hate AA and resent being forced to [listen to] clichéd drivel night after night." ("Why is the truth usually not just un- but *anti*-interesting?") Gately informs new residents that they can't "get kicked out, not for any reason. Which means you can say *anything* in here." At 30 days clean, Gately tried to get kicked out of AA by "spraying vitriol" at a meeting, but that just prompted some White Flaggers to "Identify with the deeply honest feelings he'd shared." After one of Gately's vitriolic outbursts, one of the Crocodiles called Gately "a ballsy little bastard" and advised him to "just Keep Coming" and to "shut the fuck up and just listen." Gately often rides with the Crocodiles to speak at Commitments. (The Crocodiles meet at a diner "next to Steve's Donuts," where C threw an ear into a dumpster last Christmas Eve (p. 129).) On one of these trips, the Crocodiles invited Gately "to see the coincidence of long-term contented sobriety and rabidly tireless AA activity as not a coincidence at all." Without this activity, there is a danger of drifting away from the Group, entering another cycle of addiction, and finding yourself "back in the Disease's cage all over again." Eventually, Gately joined the White Flag Group and asked Crocodile "Ferocious Francis" Gehaney to be his sponsor. Although "Boston AA stresses the utter autonomy of the individual member" (cf. "no one tells your precious individual U.S.A. selves what they must do," p. 320), Francis G. "compares the totally optional basic suggestions in Boston AA to [the suggestion that] if you're going to jump out of an airplane . . . you wear a parachute" (cf. "How to choose any but a child's greedy choices if there is no loving-filled father [or AA sponsor] to guide, inform, teach the person how to choose?" on p. 320).

Gately's counselor when he was an Ennet House resident, Eugenio Martinez (Gene M.), calls the Disease *The Spider* and tells Gately, "The will you call your own ceased to be yours as of who knows how many Substance-drenched years ago. . . . You have to Starve The Spider: you have to surrender your will. . . . You have to want to surrender your will to people who know how to Starve The Spider." During his residency at Ennet, Gately had "an epiphanic AA-related nocturnal dream" in which he and "row after row of totally average and non-unique U.S. citizens" were kneeling on cushions in a church basement whose "walls were of this like weird thin clean clear glass." If someone stood up, they would be "yanked backward with terrible force" by a hooked stick and sucked out "through the soundless glass membrane." The stick was held by an "authoritative figure" that "radiated good cheer and abundant charm and limitless patience" and that wore a "mask that was simply the plain yellow smily-face circle that accompanied invitations to have a nice day." After this dream, Gately realized that AA doesn't need a Sergeant at Arms to enforce order at Group meetings because "AA's patient enforcer was always and everywhere Out There," urging you to "have a nice day. Just one more last nice day. Just one." It was after this dream that Gately first took the AA suggestion to get on his knees and "Ask For Help from something he still didn't believe in, ask for his own sick Spider-bit will to be taken from him."

On pp. 360-367, Gately keeps track of the Ennet residents, who are under his watch this evening. During breaks at the 45-minute mark of the 90-minute White Flag meetings "Gately usually stands around chain-smoking with the Ennet House residents, so that he's casually available to answer questions and empathize with complaints," like those of Ken Erdedy ("who came into the House about a month ago") and Joelle van Dyne. It turns out that Joelle did not die from her overdose at Molly Notkin's party last night (Ch. 17.5). Gately apparently has been told that Joelle "just showed up two days ago right after supper" after being "up at Brigham and Women's for five days." But of course Joelle "entered the House just today," "as of Interdependence Day A.M.'s discharge from B&W" (n. 134). Gately knows that Joelle "got in overnight under some private arrangement with somebody on the House's Board of Directors," that there's "been no talk of a humility job for her," and that "Pat's counseling the girl personally." Joelle is "the first veiled resident Gately's had under him, as a Staffer," but he knows of "one male veiled U.H.I.D. guy that's an active White Flagger, Tommy S. or F." "Gately's had the U.H.I.D.-and-veil philosophy explained to him in passing a couple of times but still doesn't much get it, it seems like a gesture of shame and concealment, still, to him, the veil." Gately observes the other Ennet residents as well. Given that "the couple of residents that are black" are Clenette and Didi N. (p. 208), all current residents are mentioned except Cortelyu, Thrale, and Tingly, all of whom will appear again later. The addition today of Joelle (and of Amy J., p. 475) therefore brings the resident count to 24, two over the 22 the House is "equipped to provide" (p. 137).

During the break, Joelle points out (as might Avril) the grammatical senselessness of the subjunctive, counterfactual phrase "I'm here But For the Grace of God" and wants "to put her head in a Radarange at the thought that Substances have brought her to the sort of pass where this is the sort of language she has to have Blind Faith in." (In this section, the narrator speaks for Joelle ("counterfactual," p. 366), for Gately (who remembers Joelle's word as "countersexuals," p. 367), and for himself ("I," p. 357).) Gately finds Joelle's voice "familiar in a faraway way" even though he's never met her before. Gately has "nothing in his huge square head to Identify with her with and latch onto or say in encouraging reply, and . . . his own heart grips him like an infant rattling the bars of its playpen, and . . . for a second the blank white veil leveled at him seems a screen on which might well be projected a casual and impressive black and yellow smily-face, grinning." (In addition to the Sergeant at Arms of Gately's dream, recall the "small drawn crude face, smiling" on the *Infinite Jest* cartridge and package opened by the medical attaché on p. 36 and Joelle's participation in this film as Madame Psychosis.) The "moment hangs there, distended" (cf. how the "still moment hangs" at the end of Eschaton, p. 342) until the break ends "and the infant leaves its playpen alone inside him."

PLOT AND CHARACTER: AA&R, Gately, Ennet, Joelle
THEME: Choice, Inf/Reg, Dreams, Boundaries, Secrets, Recur

To surrender to a Boston AA Group, like the appropriately named White Flag Group, is an active choice: it is "asking for help," after which things get better. If you surrender to the Disease—The Spider (alcoholics Jim Sr. and Jim Jr. both feared spiders), eventually you will find "the Substance has devoured or replaced and become *you*" and you will reach a "miserable road-fork Boston AA calls your Bottom": "You are in the kind of a hell of a mess that either ends lives or turns them around" (cf. p. 60). Addiction is again associated with being in a cage, and Gately's fear of getting high again (going "back in the cage") manifests as "an infant rattling the bars of its playpen." Those in Gately's dream who do not continue to choose to surrender (to stay on their knees) are pulled "out through the soundless glass membrane." The protective boundary for addicts is tenuous and is only effective while the addict chooses to surrender. Ennet House staffers rotate Dream Duty, "to be awake and on-call in the front office all night" for residents who "get hit with real horror-show dreams."

Realization of addiction is associated with masks coming off at the P.M./A.M. boundary ("it's midnight now and all masks come off"); and addiction is likened to "a beckoning taloned hand" or "It" or an authoritative figure in a "smily-face mask," who in Gately's dream is bound only by an addict's will to surrender to AA. Midnight is also the hour at which the Madame Psychosis show begins. Gately does not realize (misses the connection) that Joelle's voice is the voice of Madame Psychosis, and he imagines a "black and yellow smily-face, grinning" "might well be projected" on the screen of her veil. The figure's mask is a circle and he moves his hook in circles; one of the places he can be found is "in the astringent fluorescence of pharmacies" (pp. 358-9). Addicts roll their eyes and "hobble sideways like a crab" (pp. 352-3). Addicts are in a shit-storm (p. 344), vomiting, incontinent (p. 346), in puke-crusted T-shirts (p. 347), and puke-white (p. 349). Crocodiles smoke "turd-like cigars" (p. 354). Banners are emblazoned with AA slogans in blue and gold (p. 344); "tatt-obsessed" (p. 352) Tiny Ewell wears a blue suit (p. 362); and Joelle wears an "overlarge blue coffee-stained sweater" (p. 365) on Interdependence Day. Recall Jim's "special Interdependence-Day-celebratory-dinner argyle sweater vest," also stained (p. 31).

Chapter 22.3, Section 78, Page 367
unspecified

Liberty is a "gigantic Lady" (Steeply is another gigantic U.S.A. "lady") who "holds aloft a product" instead of a torch since the advent of Subsidized Time. "The product is changed each 1

Jan." In Y.D.A.U., she wears "some type of enormous adult-design diaper" (p. 33). See p. 223 for a list of each Subsidized year's product.

PLOT AND CHARACTER: O.N.A.N.
THEME: Cycles

Lady Liberty "has the sun for a crown" and has her product changed annually.

Chapter 22.4, Section 79, Pages 367-375
Notes 142-143, Page 1026
8 November Y.D.A.U., after the 2045h. break to 2130h. (p. 360)

The White Flag AA meeting of Ch. 22.2 continues after the break with three more Advanced Basic speakers. This section addresses two unspoken AA norms: speak "just the truth" without irony, a norm violated by the first speaker and upheld by the second speaker (pp. 367-370); and do not "blame your Disease on some cause or other" ("an appeal to exterior *Cause* . . . can slide, in the addictive mind, . . . into *Excuse*," p. 374), a norm violated by the third speaker (pp. 370-375). The first speaker appears to "deprecate the Program rather than the Self" in front of a crowd that is "very sensitive to the presence of ego" and that will punish "somebody by getting embarrassed for him, killing him by empathetically dying right there with him." A Boston AA meeting is an "[i]rony free zone" where "sly disingenuous manipulative pseudo-sincerity" will be recognized for what it is by "tough ravaged people" who remember their own "self-presenting fortifications." "This doesn't mean you can't pay empty or hypocritical lip service, however. Paradoxically enough. . . . It's called 'Fake It Till You Make It.'" Gately "tries to be just about as verbally honest as possible at almost all times, now."

The third speaker talks about running away from her foster home, where her foster mother "was in total Denial about her biological daughter's being a vegetable, and [insisted that the family treat] the invertebrate biological daughter like a valid member of the chordate phylum." The foster mother knelt daily before a "photo of some Catholic statue" ("The Ecstacy of St. Theresa") and "required daily that It [the biological daughter] be hoisted by the adopted daughter from Its never-mentioned wheelchair [and made] to approximate the same knelt devotion to the photo." (Recall that Jim's *Pre-Nuptial Agreement of Heaven and Hell* is concerned with "The Ecstasy of St. Theresa" and that this film had "a major impact" (p. 297) on Joelle, who thought of Bernini's work last night immediately "after inhaling, right at the apex" (p. 235) and who reacts now to the description of the photo (p. 376).) At night, the foster father would come into the bedroom that the daughters shared, place "a cheesy rubber Raquel Welch full-head pull-on *mask*, with hair" on his biological daughter's face, and "incestuously diddle" her while the adopted daughter kept her "face turned to the wall, in the room's next bed." The adopted daughter would then tidy up her foster sister afterwards. On the night that she noticed "the exact same expression ["of the statue's orgasm," p. 376] on the face of a catatonic who'd just been incestuously diddled, an expression at once reverent and greedy on a face connected by dead hair to the slack and flapping rubber visage of an old sex goddess's empty face," she left home and soon found herself at "that standard two-option addicted cliff-edge" (cf. pp. 348-9).

PLOT AND CHARACTER: AA&R
THEME: Inf/Reg, Recur

"A Boston AA is very sensitive to the presence of ego" and punishes self-focused speakers with "empathic distress." There is "empathetic distress at the look-what-happened-to-poor-me invitation implicit in the tale" of the third speaker, "a member of a splinter 12-Step Fellowship, an Adult-Child-type thing called [WHINERS]." She also worked at the Naked "I" Club out on Route "1."

The novel occasionally documents or hints at the sexual abuse of some of its younger characters. The abused foster sister of the third speaker here is also catatonic like the tree hugger and other residents of Unit #5 (pp. 196-7) and in a wheelchair like Marathe, who returns in the next section. She is incontinent and is forced to wear a mask. This section features another mythological reference, equating Self-Pity and Denial to minotaurs in the labyrinth of the

Disease. The meta-narrator of the notes points out terms that a character "doesn't actually" use three times in this chapter (nn. 130, 137, and 142) and points out that the last words of this section are "*Sic*" (n. 143).

Chapter 22.5, Section 80, Page 375
30 April / 1 May Y.D.A.U.

Marathe and Steeply are still on the outcropping of rock as they last were in Ch. 21.3. "Marathe remained unsure [what Steeply] wished to learn from him, or verify through Marathe's betrayal." "Near midnight" Steeply told Marathe that he was "back in the field" after "his recent divorce" and that his assignment (presumably since August Y.D.P.A.H., cf. Ch. 17.4 summary) was "to cultivate some of the Entertainment's alleged filmmaker's relatives and inner circles." Upon hearing Steeply's "cover's false name," Marathe expressed "humored doubts that [Steeply's face] would be responsible of launching even one ship or vessel." Six months after this meeting, Orin will be quite taken with "Helen" Steeply when Steeply begins interviewing him for *Moment* Magazine (cf. p. 227). A fragment of an interview with Orin from 3 November will be documented in an endnote to the next section.

PLOT AND CHARACTER: A.F.R., U.S.O.U.S.
THEME: Secrets, Recur

Marathe ("hunched slightly in his metal chair") and Steeply are concerned with betrayal and identity in this section. Marathe, who is betraying the A.F.R., wears a shirt that is "not of Hawaiian type," because a Hawaiian shirt is an identifying characteristic of rival separatists the F.L.Q. (n. 47). Steeply, recently divorced (betrayed), is assigned an identity to use in betraying those in Jim's "inner circles." Marathe again alludes to the mythological Helen of Troy (cf. pp. 105-6), a famous betrayer who prompted a famous betrayal.

Chapter 22.6, Section 81, Pages 375-376
Notes 144-145, Pages 1026-1028
unspecified, early Y.W.

On the "first brutal winter night" of the Year of the Whopper, "soon after the InterLace dissemination of *The Man Who Began to Suspect He Was Made of Glass*" (cf. p. 989), Jim laments to Lyle that critics find his "fatal Achilles' heel" to be plot. "Mario and Ms. Joelle van Dyne are probably the only people who know that Found Drama and anticonfluentialism both came out this night with Lyle."

Orin gives his version of the origin of Found Drama in a "TRANSCRIPT-FRAGMENT" (n. 145) of Steeply's 3 November Y.D.A.U. interview with him, conducted on the same day he called Hal to ask about Separatism (p. 137). Steeply's questions to Orin are not documented and are simply referenced as "Q"s, a convention Wallace uses elsewhere in the novel and in his story collection *Brief Interviews with Hideous Men*. According to Orin, Jim decided to "get revenge" on disgruntled critics who preferred "Neorealism" to his work, which the critics called "unentertaining formalism and unrealistic abstraction." Critics Duquette and Pos[e]ner, who co-authored Jim's filmography (cf. n. 24.a, p. 985) with Comstock, were "in on the revenge." However, unlike Mario and Joelle, the critics are unaware of the origins of Found Drama and list three Found Dramas as preceding *The Man Who Began to Suspect He Was Made of Glass* (p. 989). In addition, n. 146 states that *Pre-Nuptial Agreement of Heaven and Hell*—also listed as preceding *The Man Who Began to Suspect He Was Made of Glass* and therefore presumably made before his anticonfluential period—was "made at the acknowledged height of [Jim's] anticonfluential period" (n. 146). In the authors' defense, their article does qualify that "the list's order and completeness are, at this point in time, not definitive" (p. 986). Note also that Orin makes reference to anticonfluential directors who preceded Jim (p. 1027).

Jim would tear out a phonebook page, thumbtack it to a wall, and throw a dart at it. The name he hit would be the protagonist of the Found Drama. "The joke's theory was there's no audience and no director and no stage or set because . . . in Reality there are none of these things. And the protagonist doesn't know he's the protagonist." Nothing "got recorded or filmed"; there was only speculation about what the protagonist was doing or whether the protagonist was even alive. Even critics not in on the joke were calling Found Drama "the ultimate in avant-garde Neorealism, and saying maybe [Jim] deserved reappraisal." Eventually, Jim "unveiled" the hoax.

PLOT AND CHARACTER: Jim, Art/Ent, Orin
THEME: Recur

Another mythological reference is made in this chapter (to Jim's Achilles' heel, p. 375; cf. Lord's "bit of an Achilles' heel imagination-wise," p. 325). Orin slips and says Sad Stork instead of Mad Stork in reference to Jim (p. 1027), a slip also noticed by Joelle (p. 238).

Chapter 22.7, Section 82, Pages 376-379
8 November Y.D.A.U., after the 2045h. break to 2130h.

The White Flag AA meeting of Chs. 22.2 and 22.4 continues with the last Advanced Basics speaker, who accepts responsibility for her actions without attributing a Cause to her drug use. She speaks "about being pregnant at twenty and smoking Eightballs of freebase cocaine like a fiend all through her pregnancy even though she knew it was bad for the baby and wanted desperately to quit." Her descriptions of using freebase cocaine prompt a reaction from Joelle, who overdosed on the drug last night. The speaker "delivered of a stillborn infant" while "still compulsively loading up the glass pipe and smoking." The baby's "limbs were malformed and arachnodactylic" (like Mario, p. 314); it "had been poisoned before it could grow a face or make any personal choices" (cf. Marathe on choices, p. 320). When she came to "the next day and saw what still clung by a withered cord to her empty insides she got introduced to the real business-end of the arrow of responsibility" (cf. the arrow raised by the angel in "The Ecstasy of St. Theresa," p. 235).

In Denial about what she had done, she carried the decaying baby with her, even when she turned tricks, until "a pale and reeling beat-cop phoned a hysterical olfactory alert in to the Commonwealth's infamous Department of Social Services." The mother "finally broke down, emotionally and olfactorily, from the overwhelming evidence," and "a D.S.S. team closed in for the pinch." After four months in the hospital, she "wanted only tall smooth bottles whose labels spoke of Proof, and she drank and drank and believed in her heart she would never stop or swallow the truth, but finally she got to where she had to, she says, swallow it, the responsible truth." At that point, she called AA. "Gately tries not to think. Here is no Cause or Excuse. It is simply what happened. This final speaker is truly new, ready: all defenses have been burned away." The audience has "to consciously try to remember even to blink as they watch her, listening. I.D.ing without effort. There's no judgment. It's clear she's been punished enough."

PLOT AND CHARACTER: AA&R
THEME: Recur, Inf/Reg

Another addict "wanted desperately to quit" but couldn't. The speaker is "a round pink girl with no eyelashes at all and a 'basehead's ruined teeth." Her lashes were "lost in a Substance-accident; fire hazard and dental dysplasia go with the freebase terrain." The smooth-skinned speaker, whose "infant emerged all dry and hard like a turdlet" and who carried her "infant's corpse completely veiled and hidden [cf. Joelle] in a little pink blanket," "looks like she's the one that's the infant."

Chapter 22.8, Section 83, Page 379
Note 146, Page 1028
unspecified, c. 1999-2001

Lyle, Jim, and Mario often spent late-night hours in the "newly outfitted E.T.A. weight room," presumably beginning in 1999—the year of E.T.A.'s accreditation—or later. Once Mario heard Jim say that "if he had to grade his marriage he'd give it a C-." Lyle would read William Blake (author of *The Marriage of Heaven and Hell*) to Jim, "but in the voices of various cartoon characters, which

Himself eventually started regarding as deep," evidenced by "Incandenza's first narrative collaboration w/ Infernatron-Canada, the animated *Pre-Nuptial Agreement of Heaven and Hell* [c. 2001, cf. p. 988], made at the acknowledged [by whom?] height of his anticonfluential period" (n. 146). Earlier, anticonfluentialism was said to have come out of a conversation with Lyle on the first brutal winter night of Y.W. (Ch. 22.6, p. 376), months after the completion of *Pre-Nuptial Agreement of Heaven and Hell.* Either the authors of the filmography applied the term to Incandenza's pre-anticonfluential works, unaware of Lyle and Jim's conversation, or the chronology of the filmography is in error. Given the nature of the concept (against confluence), disagreement about the origin of Jim's anticonfluentialism seems appropriate.

PLOT AND CHARACTER: Jim, Mario, E.T.A.
THEME: Recur

Mario often "drifted in and out, slept upright and leaning forward." Recall Marathe's "head slightly forward in a practiced position that allowed him almost to sleep" (p. 375). Voices of cartoon characters were also used by the students who spoke of Orin's record punt on their 22 October WYYY radio show (pp. 181-2).

Chapter 22: Triggering Situation

Chapter 22 documents several turning points and crisis moments: boundaries at which a realization or choice is made and action is taken. In Ch. 22.1, Otis P. Lord experiences ascending levels of crisis in which he must make decisions that will affect the way Eschaton is played in the future. Hal smokes marijuana in public within view of Little Buddies. Actual fighting breaks out in what is supposed to be a game that only simulates (maps) fighting. In Ch. 22.2, addicts, at the fork in the road that AA calls their Bottom, have "exactly two total choices": they can either seek AA's help or die. The realization that the Substance has devoured or become you happens at midnight, a turning point when "all masks come off." Gately recounts his epiphanic dream of the Sergeant at Arms in the smily-face mask and experiences a crisis moment in which he imagines a smily-face projected onto the screen of Joelle's veil. Chapter 22.3 cites "1 Jan." as the yearly turning point at which Lady Liberty's product is changed. In Ch. 22.4, AA speakers recount the moments leading up to their Bottom or turning point. One speaker decided to leave home in the middle of the night after a mask came off the face of her foster sister. In Ch. 22.5, near midnight Steeply tells Marathe of his recent divorce and new cover. Helen of Troy and Achilles are referenced in this chapter, both of whom were involved in historical crisis moments. Chapter 22.6 documents a night that became a creative turning point for Jim. In Ch. 22.7, a speaker recounts having to face the arrow of responsibility: having to swallow the responsible truth and make "a blubbering 0200h. phone call" from "the old two-option welfare-hotel window-ledge." In Ch. 22.8, the E.T.A. weight room has been newly outfitted; Mario hears the potentially scarring information of how Jim would grade his marriage; Lyle inspires Jim with cartoon-voiced Blake; and Jim makes a film based on that experience that will trigger a response in Joelle (p. 297).

Chapter 23

Hygienic Stress

Chapter 23.1, Section 84, Pages 380-386
Notes 147-151, Pages 1028-1029
8 November Y.D.A.U., 1930h.-2018h.

Three-and-a-half hours after the Eschaton debacle (Ch. 22.1), the Interdependence Day gala supper is ending in the E.T.A. dining hall. Schtitt and Tavis have not yet learned of the Eschaton debacle. Avril does know about it and is deciding what action must be taken. Avril thanks God that John Wayne was not involved. Avril has also convinced Tavis that it is good publicity to let *Moment* journalist Helen Steeply (who secretly witnessed the earlier Eschaton from a distance) onto the grounds, given that Steeply's article is about an E.T.A. alumnus rather than a current student (but she neglected to tell Tavis that she thinks the article is about Orin). Although Tavis is concerned about the journalist's "impending arrival," he is in a festive mood tonight, as are most of the faculty and students. Almost everyone wears a hat, except a handful of Canadian students including John Wayne, who "keeps wiping his nose"; and the student athletes are allowed to eat dessert (cf. "Mrs. Clarke's confectionery day in the sun," p. 1009).

Three summers back, Mario made a 48-minute "film of a puppet show" (with puppets made in elementary classes taught by Pam Heath, one of Jim's actresses) based on his father's film *The ONANtiad* ("tendentiously anticonfluential political parody"). The film has "proved so popular that it gets shown annually now every 11/8" after supper, usually getting "under way about 1930h." (Yesterday, Mario was "closeted with Disney Leith all day preparing things for Sunday's post-prandial gala and filmfest," p. 1005.) Before the film is over, the White Flag AA meeting will begin nearby (Ch. 22.2). The early part of the film is about the rise of "Johnny Gentle, Famous Crooner" to the presidency of the United States (pp. 381-4) and his courting/manipulation of Canada and Mexico into an interdependent alliance (pp. 384-6).

Gentle was a "lounge singer turned teenybopper throb turned B-movie mainstay" so obsessed with cleanliness that he founded the "Clean U.S. Party." The C.U.S.P. political party, its "white-gloved finger on the pulse of an increasingly asthmatic and sunscreen-slathered and pissed-off American electorate," won the 2000 presidential election (and the Y.T.-S.D.B. and Y.D.P.A.H. elections, making Gentle the first president since FDR to be elected to a third term; cf. that Gentle has been "roundly disliked for over two terms now") during "a post-Soviet and -Jihad era" in which Americans had "no external Menace to hate and fear." In *Infinite Jest*, presumably Clinton-Gore sought reelection in 1996; but instead of running against Dole-Kemp, they ran against Kemp-Limbaugh, who won the election. After Kemp dies in an explosion (cf. "the poor late M. Kemp with his exploding home" (p. 422) and a poster of Limbaugh "from before the [presumably Kemp's] assassination" (p. 929)), Limbaugh becomes president (cf. "the Kemp and Limbaugh administrations" (p. 177) and "the pre-millennial Limbaugh Era" (p. 411)). In 2000, Gentle's C.U.S.P. party defeated incumbent Republican Rush Limbaugh and Democrat Hillary Clinton, due to "a surreal union of both Rush L.- and Hillary R.C.-disillusioned fringes."

At Gentle's first Inaugural Address (presumably January 2001), he wore a "Fukoama microfiltration mask" (Avril is wearing one at the I.-Day gala, n. 148), promised to "rid the American psychosphere of the unpleasant debris of a throw-away past," and said "he wasn't going to stand here and ask us to make some tough choices because he was standing here promising he was going to make them for us [and] asked us simply to sit back and enjoy the show." He swore he'd "find us some cohesion-renewing Other" and alluded to "a whole new North America for a crazy post-millennial world." The next part of Mario's filmed puppet show documents Gentle's inclusion of the President of Mexico and the Prime Minister of Canada in his cabinet during the "second year" (beginning January Y.W) of his first term, which marked "the rise of O.N.A.N. and U.S. Experialism." After a puppet "entr'acte," Mario documents an earlier meeting in which Gentle assures Prime Minister "J.J.J.C[hrétien]" that he will remove from Manitoba all NATO ICBMs: "those complete totalities of Canada's strategic capacity." Another puppet entr'acte follows.

PLOT AND CHARACTER: E.T.A., Mario, Art/Ent, O.N.A.N.
THEME: Fear/Obsess, Waste, Secrets, Recur

Gentle is obsessed with cleanliness (the removal or isolation of waste) and seeks to unite the country through fear of a common enemy. Gentle's helping Canada dismantle their strategic defenses seems driven by an ulterior motive to make Canada a defenseless common enemy. Gentle keeps his potential enemy close by inviting a Canadian to join the U.S. cabinet. Gentle's view of Canada as a common enemy has been spoken of by Hal and Orin (p. 1013) and by Marathe (p. 319). Gentle and Avril, both obsessed with cleanliness, are both described as wearing microfiltration masks in this section, and most of the gala attendees are wearing celebratory disguises: hats. Avril has not told Tavis about the Eschaton debacle or the subject of (the disguised) Steeply's article.

This section features references to chewing (p. 381), "inadequately nurtured children" (n. 149), annular agnation (p. 382), annular fusion (n. 150), and "the glass-walled Great Convexity" (p. 385), which recalls the glass walls in Gately's dream (p. 358). There is also another meta-narrative comment about an actual term employed by Gentle (n. 151). Although the attacks on the World Trade Center and the Pentagon presumably did not occur in O.N.A.N.'s post-Jihad era, Wallace addresses this event in "The View from Mrs. Thompson's," from his essay collection *Consider the Lobster.*

Chapter 23.2, Section 85, Pages 386-390
Notes 152-153, Page 1029
8 November Y.D.A.U., 1930h.-2018h.

As Mario's film is screened in the dining hall in West House, some students "make yellow-slickered wet-shoed migrations" to see

Lyle in the weight room in Comm.-Ad. The snow of 1600h. (p. 342) "has given way to rain" at the 1930h. start of Mario's film. Lyle counsels students about "the human pains of stunted desire," from which even he is not completely exempt. Lyle sometimes recalls "Orin's Academy doubles partner" Marlon Bain, who was "always wet" and "always doing his best to stay clean." (This section begins with "Though can any guru," not with "Can any guru," which gives the reader the impression that he or she is not privy to thoughts that occurred before the beginning of the section.)

LaMont Chu (who "doesn't mention the Eschaton") comes to Lyle and "confesses to an increasingly crippling obsession with tennis fame." He's "ashamed of his secret hunger for hype in an academy that regards hype and the seduction of hype as the great Mephistophelian pitfall and hazard of talent. A lot of these are his own terms. He feels himself in a dark world, inside, ashamed, lost, locked in." Chu seeks to give his "life some sort of kind of meaning" by getting his photograph in a tennis magazine like the players he admires, but Lyle says that doing so will not alleviate Chu's anxieties about fame and that these players are "trapped, just as you are." Lyle says, "LaMont, the truth is that the world is incredibly, incredibly, unbelievably old. You suffer with the stunted desire caused by one of its oldest lies. Do not believe the photographs. Fame is not the exit from any cage." Lyle asks Chu to "consider how escape from a cage must surely require, foremost, awareness of the fact of the cage."

As the storm dies down, Lyle sees other students, including Kent Blott (whom he advises "not to let the weight he would pull to himself exceed his own personal weight," cf. p. 128) and Anton Doucette, who is self-conscious "about the big round dark raised mole on his upper-upper lip, just under his left nostril" and fears "that some upperclassmen are referring to him behind his back as Anton ('Booger') Douchette." Lyle asks Doucette to come back with Mario after the gala (cf. n. 147). "Mario gets a fair number of aesthetic-self-consciousness referrals from Lyle" (cf. p. 316).

PLOT AND CHARACTER: E.T.A.
THEME: Fear/Obsess, Recur

Like Gentle and Avril and Joelle, Bain is obsessed with cleanliness. Students come to Lyle with various anxieties, fears, and obsessions. With respect to his anxiety, Doucette is described as "frozen" and "in a vicious cycle." There is a recurrence of cage imagery in this section, and sportscasters wear "blue I/SPN blazers."

Chapter 23.3, Section 86, Pages 391-394
8 November Y.D.A.U., 1930h.-2018h.

Mario's filmed puppet show continues with a mixing of "real and fake news-summary cartridges, magazine articles, and historical headers from the last few great daily papers, all for a sort of time-lapse exposition of certain developments leading up to Interdependence and Subsidized Time and cartographic Reconfiguration" throughout 2001 and early Y.W. (2002).

The headers include references to the "dismantling" of NATO and subsequent "CONTINENTAL ALLIANCE" of the three North American nations. Québec Separatists oppose the alliance, but "CANADA 'NUCK'LES UNDER" after pressure by Gentle to participate. A congenial post-"O.N.A.N. PACT" conversation between Gentle and "J.J.J.C[hrétien]" was presented earlier in Mario's film (pp. 385-6). Prime Minister Chrétien was assassinated when a "RAILROAD SPIKE" was implanted in his right eye, an event referenced yesterday in Hal and Orin's phone conversation about Québec Separatists (p. 1013). Gentle becomes the first chair of the Organization of North American Nations, and the "Mexican Presidente and new heavily guarded Canadian P. M." serve as co-Vice Chairs (these leaders will also become honorary members of Gentle's U.S.A. cabinet, p. 384). Gentle's first "State of the O.N.A.N. Address" was delivered on "the very last day of 'B.S.' solar time." If this Address was coincident with the State of the Union Address (in late January 2002, not 31 December 2001), then presumably references to January 2002 were changed retroactively (as in Orwell's *1984*) to the Year of the Whopper.

Gentle's instigation (to be documented in Ch. 23.11) of Subsidized Time (note the headline in which Burger King is "AWARDED RIGHTS TO NEW YEAR") came just after the decline of television advertising and the rise of InterLace (to be documented in Ch. 23.7). Note the references to InterLace in this section and the headline asserting that the Viney and Veals advertising agency (employers of Ken Erdedy, p. 360) is not to blame for bomb threats to ABC Television's headquarters.

Several headlines document extreme problems with environmental waste. Gentle "SPEAKS OUT ON A U.S. 'CONSTIPATEDLY IMPACTED ON CONTINENTAL WASTE'" and establishes "a blue-ribbon panel of waste experts to investigate the feasibility of mass landfill and conversion sites in northern New England." One headline concerns the method of waste conversion: "HOLOGRAPHY MAKES ULTRA-TOXIC [ANNULAR] FUSION GAMBIT SAFE FOR WORKERS." Gentle's personal and national obsessions with cleanliness contribute to his being "CONFINED FOR 'HYGENIC STRESS'" and to the eventual consideration of "RECONFIGURATIVE OPTIONS" (to be documented in Ch. 23.6).

PLOT AND CHARACTER: O.N.A.N.
THEME: Fear/Obsess, Waste, Cycles, Recur

Gentle's obsession with cleanliness causes him to make radical decisions concerning the environmental wastes that have been exacerbated by his obsessed decision-making. The headings in Ch. 13 were analogous to headings in the "Aeolus" chapter of Ulysses in that they outlined subsequent text. The headers in this section are the text, and Mario's fragmented narrative headers are analogous to Wallace's fragmented narrative sections. Note the ambiguity inherent in Mario's use of "real and fake" information. Mario's film is a tribute to Jim, whose annular fusion process, which involves holography, is the basis of the waste conversion used in the Concavity (Ch. 26.10).

Chapter 23.4, Section 87, Pages 394-395
8 November Y.D.A.U., 1930h.-2018h.

Lyle continues to see students in the weight room during Mario's film. Ortho ("The Darkness") Stice has come to Lyle because "he goes to sleep with his bed against one wall and then but wakes up with his bed against a whole nother wall." This morning "ball-cans [were] arranged in a neat pyramid in the dusty rectangle where his bed was supposed to normally be." Stice offers three possible explanations of this problem for Lyle's consideration. "*Do not underestimate objects,* [Lyle] advises Stice. Do not leave objects out of account. The world, after all, which is radically old, is made up mostly of objects." Lyle then tells Stice a story about a man who "bet people that he could stand on any chair . . . and then lift that chair up off the ground while standing on it." After winning the bet, the man would walk off, "leaving behind a dumbfounded crowd still staring up at an object he had not underestimated."

PLOT AND CHARACTER: E.T.A.
THEME: Phys/Ob, Recur

Lyle's advice about objects resonates with Jim Sr.'s talk with Jim Jr. about the disrespect of objects (Ch. 15.1). Lyle's familiar "advice about the pull-down station" is also referenced. Stice apologizes to Lyle for Krazy-Gluing his left buttock to the towel dispenser; Mary Ester Thode was also a victim of this prank (p. 385). Stice is powerless to stop his bed from moving. Themes of powerlessness and waste also resonate with the oncologist "dying of his own inoperable colorectal neoplastis" (cf. Jim's *Kinds of Pain*, p. 987), who bemoans his lack of "power over my own ravening colorectal cells." What is Coyle's "suspicious discharge"?

Chapter 23.5, Section 88, Pages 395-398
Notes 154-155, Page 1030
8 November Y.D.A.U., 1930h.-2018h.

Hal "has severe compulsion-issues around nicotine and sugar" as well as marijuana. He "tries to mollify" the nicotine cravings with smokeless tobacco (which he spits into his "cherished old childhood NASA glass"), but his "more serious problem is with sucrose." Lately too much sugar "induces odd and unpleasant emotional states that don't do him one bit of good on court." Even so, Hal now has "a mouth full of multilayered baklava" as he watches Mario's film, inspired by their late father.

Mario's film prompts Hal to consider two (and he doesn't want to think about a third) of his father's films which were made when Jim was "obsessed with the idea of audiences' relationships with various sorts of shows." (The films are said to be from Jim's "anticonfluential middle period," but n. 24 lists all three films as occurring before Jim's conversation with Lyle in early Y.W.; cf. Ch. 22.8 summary.) In "*The Medusa v. The Odalisque*" the audience watches a play in which "the mythic Medusa, snake-haired and armed with a sword and well-polished shield is fighting to the death or petrification against L'Odalisque de Ste. Thérèse [who holds a mirror], a character out of old Québecois mythology who was supposedly so inhumanely gorgeous that anyone who looked at her turned instantly into a human-sized precious gem, from admiration." As the combatants attempt to "de-animate each other with their respective reflectors . . . members of the playlet's well-dressed audience eventually start catching disastrous glimpses of the combatants' fatal full frontal reflections" and either get turned into gems or petrified. Viewers of the film never get "a decent full-frontal look at what it is about the combatants that supposedly has such a melodramatic effect on the rumble's live audience, and so the film's audience ends up feeling teased and vaguely cheated."

But audiences hated *The Joke* even more, a film in which Jim and Mario aimed cameras at the theatre audience and projected the images of the live audience onto the theatre's screen. The audience then watched themselves. When the last audience member left, the film was over; and Jim and Mario would fly to another city to set up for the next screening.

PLOT AND CHARACTER: Hal, Jim, Mario, Art/Ent
THEME: Non-Action, Recur

In "*The Medusa v. The Odalisque*" the audience inside the film is petrified; watching *Infinite Jest*, the audience outside the film is petrified. Similar to an odalisque or a medusa, Joelle captivates listeners as Madame Psychosis on the radio and captivates viewers as Madame Psychosis in *Infinite Jest*. The Odalisque holds a mirror, and both the Medusa and the Odalisque are holograms, choreographed by an "Oriental guy" who, like many others, "cottoned" to Avril right away. Although Jim liked that *The Joke* was "publicly static and simple-minded and dumb" (the narrator also describes Found Drama as "self-consciously dumb stasis"), the critics who (missing a connection) declared "that the simple-minded stasis was precisely the film's aesthetic thesis were dead wrong, as usual."

Chapter 23.6, Section 89, Pages 398-410
Notes 156-160, Page 1030
8 November Y.D.A.U., 1930h.-2018h.

Mario's filmed puppet show continues with headlines (at least some of which are phony) concerning Subsidized Time—a man is killed by a 5-ton cast-iron burger in a freak Statue of Liberty accident—and the problems with environmental waste that lead to Gentle's Reconfiguration of O.N.A.N. One news-cartridge clip is about toxic materials found in New Hampshire by EPA staffers who purportedly "stumbled on" the corroded receptacles when playing a casual game of softball. New Hampshire officials claimed that the receptacles were placed in their state "against statute by large men with white body suits [Gentle's new white-suited U.S.O.U.S., cf. p. 382] . . . in long shiny trailer trucks with O.N.A.N.'s official crest." Residents in New Hampshire and Maine claimed "that the incidence of soft-skulled and extra-eyed newborns in the toxicly affected area far exceed[ed] the national average." The next headline references a Vermont test site for annular fusion. The final headline of this sequence documents Gentle's declaration of U.S. territory from Syracuse to Ticonderoga NY to Salem MA as disaster areas incapable of being cleaned and his offer of federal aid to residents wishing to relocate. Reactions to Gentle's declaration are documented in the penultimate headline of this sequence.

Pages 400-405 document Mario's puppet version of the 16 January Y.W. Concavity Cabinet. "Just the mere thought" of "befouled and waste-impacted" territory has Gentle breathing pure oxygen while the meeting of cabinet secretaries is conducted by "his oral proxy" Rodney Tine, Chief of the U.S. Office of Unspecified Services. The Canadian prime minister—suspected in the preceding headlines of secret meetings with New England governors—is absent (he was present at an earlier Y.W. cabinet meeting, p. 384) and accused of pouting by Tine. After the Secretary of the Interior discusses the exorbitant "costs of detoxifying and/or deradiating the better part of four U.S. states [ME, NH, VT, and NY]," Tine suggests "the only viable option [is] to give it away." Secretary of State Billingsley responds, "You mean simply tell the truth? That . . . given the amount of additional waste annular fusion's start-up is going to start putting in circulation [Gentle's platform necessitates] transforming vast stretches of U.S. territory into uninhabitable . . . toxic-disposal sites? Concede publicly that those EPA softball games weren't casual or pick-up in the least? That you allowed Rod the God here to convince you to authorize . . . massive toxic dumping and skull-softening against local statute . . . essentially because New Hampshire and Maine didn't let C.U.S.P. on their Independent ballots . . . ? Give away the entire strategy the two of you . . . mapped out?" After insulting Billingsley, Tine says that by "give it away" the president means the territory.

Tine says, "Gentlemen, we're going to make an unprecedented intercontinental gift of certain newly expendable northeast American territories, in return for the *faute-de-mieux* continuation of U.S. waste-displacement access to those territories. Allow me to illustrate what Lur— just what the president means." Tine then exhibits pre- and post-Concavity maps (the post-Concavity map is described as having "an ascending and then descending line," which suggests that the map is being described from the Canadian—from Luria's—perspective) and asks the Secretary of Transportation to discuss resident-relocation scenarios. Note 156 suggests that Mario's film "comes down maybe a little hard on the implication that former O.C.D.-support-group-sponsor and later Clean U.S. Party campaign manager and now O.U.S. Chief Rodney P. Tine is the real dark force behind Reconfiguration," given that Tine's "O.C.D. has been documented to be ruminative rather than hygienic, not to mention that he's hopelessly smitten with the Québecer Luria P——" (cf. pp. 92, 94-5, 106-7). The narrator of n. 156 presumes that Tine would not wish for Reconfiguration, since Luria, a Québec Separatist, presumably would oppose it. But recall Orin and Hal's phone conversation just yesterday (n. 110.4) in which the theory was put forth that the Separatists could make use of the Concavity in a scheme for secession. Is it Gentle's idea to give away the unclean territory (it could create the "cohesion-renewing Other" (p. 384) he seeks, but note his confused breath on p. 405), or has Tine convinced Gentle to do so at Luria's request, because Luria sees the territory as an aid to Québecois Separatists? The Secretary of State suggests that the territory be kept and used as "our own designated disposal area," and the Secretary of Health, Education, and Welfare asks, "Why cede vitally needed waste-disposal resources to a recalcitrant ally?" Tine counters that the territories can be used "no matter whose nation's name they're in," given the new interdependent union of nations. Tine's reasoning seems to confuse both Gentle and the Mexican president. Tine assures the Mexican president that Gentle is capable of convincing the Canadian prime minister to accept the offer.

The speedier headlines of pp. 405-407 (accompanied by a 45-rpm playing of a 33-1/3-rpm disc, not a "1/3-rpm disc" as stated) document Canada's resistance to Gentle's gift, Gentle's "HISTORY OF 'EMOTIONAL INSTABILITY,'" and Gentle's inability to accept Canada's resistance to his "gift." The fact that Gentle "threatens to bomb his own nation" over this issue is recognized by some in Mario's audience as an allusion to "the dark legend of one Eric Clipperton," the explication of which begins on pp. 407-410. Compare Gentle "seated at his desk with his head in his gloves" with Clipperton's "hands spidered across both cheeks."

During "the very last couple years of solar, Unsubsidized Time" (concurrent with Gentle's rise, 2000-2001), Eric Clipperton—who had no Academy affiliation—"from his very first appearance ["as an unseeded sixteen-year-old" in 2000] on the East Coast jr. tour made clear his intention to blow his own brains out publicly, right there on court, if he should lose, ever, even once." Clipperton's first win was against Ross Reat (from Orin's Academy days, p. 46) of the "just-opened Enfield Tennis Academy" (cf. Ch. 21.2 summary). Since Clipperton held a Glock 17 to his own head during play, Reat—"strategically and emotionally all alone out there"—"opted for not even pretending to make an effort, given what the unseeded Clipperton seem[ed] willing to sacrifice for a win." Clipperton never loses, because no one wants "the sight of the Glock going off on his conscience."

Mario befriended Clipperton during the Summer of 2000 (Mario was nine, not eight as stated on p. 410. Orin turned seventeen that summer, presumably by "late July" (p. 410); cf. Ch. 20.1 summary.) while on tour with Jim, who was filming "under ostensible U.S.T.A. auspices a two-part documentary on jr. competitive tennis, stress, and light." (One of the two films Jim made with the U.S.T.A. is called *"There Are No Losers Here,"* documenting the 1997 tour; "*Light*" is found in the titles of two other early films (p. 986).) A test-cartridge shot for this documentary "contains the only available footage of the late Eric Clipperton," because "disturbing footage of Clipperton's suicide" was "designated Unviewable by testatory codicil" and buried with Jim in his casket, along with "perhaps half a dozen other emotionally or professionally sensitive cartridge-Masters" (including the *Infinite Jest* Master, n. 80). "As far as can be determined, only [Jim's] lawyers, Avril, Disney Leith, and perhaps Mario know that the cartridges were, in fact, along with his case of special lenses, interred right there with J. O. Incandenza's dead body"; "as far as Hal or Orin knows" the cartridge-Masters are "enclosed in some sort of vault-apparatus." Jim is buried "in the Mondragon-family-plot" of a cemetery "just over the border from what is now the eastern Concavity." The funeral was delayed and had "to be fit in between annulation-cycles" (n. 160, cf. p. 65).

PLOT AND CHARACTER: O.N.A.N., E.T.A., Jim, Mario
THEME: Fear/Obsess, Boundaries, Waste, Secrets, Recur

Gentle's obsession with cleanliness leads to his creation of boundaries for the containment of waste, secretly transferred to the Northeastern states. Tine, a "former O.C.D.-support-group-sponsor," supports the boundary-changing creation of the Concavity (probably secretly motivated by Luria) and continued secrecy about the administration's motives in the face of Billingsley's statements of truth. This section references blue-bellied flies (p. 403) and a blue-blazered umpire (p. 409); Mario's grammatical tribute to the Moms, who whips her hat around "in an enthused circle" as appreciation (n. 157); and Clipperton's hands "spidered" across both cheeks (p. 410). Gentle's breathing of pure oxygen (p. 400) resonates with a character from a David Lynch film: Frank in *Blue Velvet.* The years 2000-2001 are called "the very last couple years of solar, Unsubsidized Time"; the phrasing of n. 114 cites Glad as sponsor of "the very last year of O.N.A.N.ite Subsidized Time."

Comic book enthusiasts will note that advertising (cf. the next section) is also an imposing environmental feature in Frank Miller's *Hardboiled* and that Miller's *Give Me Liberty* features a president elected to more than two terms governing in the third millennium and a surgeon general obsessed with cleanliness. The headline referencing "SIN CITY" (p. 406) recalls another work of Miller's which was made into a film. Alan Moore's *Watchmen* (which like *Give Me Liberty* is drawn by Dave Gibbons) begins with blood on a smiley face.

Chapter 23.7, Section 90, Pages 410-418
Notes 161-168, Pages 1030-1031
8 November Y.D.A.U., 1930h.-2018h.

Hal continues to watch Mario's film. He has "smoked cannabis on four separate occasions" today, "twice w/others," and is in "shock from the afternoon's Eschaton debacle and his failure to intervene or even get up out of his patio-chair." He is experiencing discomfort "in the left-molar range" and is "sinking, emotionally, into a kind of distracted funk" after "swinishness with sugar." Mario's "puppet-film is reminiscent enough of the late Himself that just about the only more depressing thing to pay attention to or think about would be advertising and the repercussions of O.N.A.N.ite Reconfiguration for the U.S. advertising industry." Hal wrote a "mammoth research paper on the tangled fates of broadcast television and the American ad industry" as the final for the same class in which he wrote of the catatonic hero (Ch. 13.4) four years ago ("May of Y.P.W."). The demise of TV advertising—concurrent "with the waxing of the Gentle era and Experialist Reconfiguration Mario's puppet show makes fun of"—was complete by 2001, "four years prior" to Hal's paper.

In the late 1990s, the American Council of Disseminators of Cable (A.C.D.C., operating under the premise that over 500 channels is better than, say, four) was attacking the T.V. networks "right at the ideological root, the psychic matrix where viewers had been conditioned . . . to associate the Freedom to Choose and the Right to Be Entertained with all that was U. S. and true." Viney and Veals Advertising of Boston sponsored the A.C.D.C. campaign, but also "started taking advantage of the plummeting [Network] advertising rates to launch effective Network-ad campaigns for products and services"—like those provided by Nunhagen Aspirin Co., LipoVac Unltd., and NoCoat Inc.—"that wouldn't previously have been able to afford national image-proliferation."

Nunhagen Aspirin created advertisements—in association with "the Enfield-based National Cranio-Facial Pain Foundation" (cf. p. 241), who were sponsoring an "exhibition of paintings by artists with crippling cranio-facial pain about cranio-facial pain"—in which representations of pain were "so excruciating that [consumers] were buying the product but recoiling from the ads" (one painting "had particularly nailed nine-year-old Hal" (n. 162), but recall that in 1999, the "penultimate year of the millennium," Hal was seven; perhaps he didn't see the ad until 2001). This "compromised the ratings-figures for the ads that followed them and for the programs that enclosed the ads," given that viewers would quickly change the channel when confronted with an excruciating Nunhagen Aspirin ad. "Hal doesn't even want to think back on" the "ads with the more dental-pain-type paintings." The Nunhagen ads "awakened legions of these suddenly violently repelled and disturbed viewers to the power and agency their thumbs actually afforded them." LipoVac ads comprised "shots of rippling cellulite and explicit clips of [liposuction] procedures," which also drove away viewers but generated product sales that allowed LipoVac to purchase more spots. The networks needed money to compete with the cable companies and ran the ads in spite of their propensity to turn away viewers. NoCoat tongue-scraper (cf. pp. 151, 235) ads featured a "lingering close-up on [a pedestrian's] extended tongue that must be seen to be believed, coat-wise" followed by scenes of resultant rejection and humiliation experienced by the pedestrian.

In the aftermath of the NoCoat ads, advertisers switched from network to cable, which caused most networks such financial repercussions that they ceased broadcasting. ABC received bomb threats (cf. headline, p. 393) from citizens "homicidally tired" of "Happy Days" reruns who found themselves "with vast maddening blocks of utterly choiceless and unentertaining time" in "the penultimate year of the millennium." Organizations supporting network advertising, including Viney and Veals, also collapsed. But then Noreen Lace-Forche, "video-rental mogulette," convinced the networks to consolidate their combined resources behind her company, InterLace TelEntertainment, and hired P. Tom Veals—whose partner had jumped off a bridge in the aftermath of the networks' collapse—to orchestrate a new campaign against the cable companies. Lace-Forche and Veals appealed "to an American ideology committed the *appearance of freedom*" (n. 164) and argued that watching cable "was still just the invitation to choose which of 504 visual spoon-feedings ["504 infantile evils"] you'd sit there and open wide for." But InterLace asked "what if a viewer could more or less *100% choose what's on at any given time?* Choose and rent, over PC and modem and fiber-optic line, from tens of thousands of [entertainment options from] the Big Four's mammoth vaults and production facilities and packaged and disseminated by InterLace TelEnt. in convenient fiber-optic pulses that fit directly on the new palm-sized" cartridges offered by InterLace. The pulses were viewable on PC monitors via cartridges or on TV sets via coaxial cable. The viewer was therefore able to "*define* the very entertainment-happiness it was his/her right to pursue," choosing from pre-packaged factory-recordings of programming or from "'spontaneous dissemination' of viewer selected menu-programming."

"American mass-entertainment became inherently pro-active, consumer-driven. And . . . advertisements were now out of the tele-visual question." Advertising agencies desperately looked "for new pulses to finger and niches to fill." Ford was convinced for a short time to advertise on the side-panels of its cars (recall Steeply's "Nunhagen-Aspirin-adverting Ford," p. 341). InterLace bought out "the Networks' production talent and facilities" and began expanding its offerings, including the production and sale of "PCs with mimetic-resolution cartridge-view motherboards": teleputers, or TPs. P. Tom Veals was doing so well that "out of ennui and a sense of unlikely challenge" he "consented to manage PR for the fringe candidacy" of Johnny Gentle, the subject of the puppet-film Hal is watching. Gentle's "ranting about literally clean streets and creatively refocused blame and rocketing people's waste into . . . space" in 2000 got the attention of Coach Schtitt, who was "swept away with the athleto-Wagnerian implications of Gentle's proposals for waste, this business of sending from yourself what you hope will not return" (n. 168, cf. p. 176).

PLOT AND CHARACTER: Hal, O.N.A.N., Art/Ent
THEME: Choice, Non-Action, Inf/Reg, Fear/Obsess, Waste, Recur

Television "viewers had been conditioned . . . to associate the Freedom to Choose and the Right to Be Entertained with all that was U. S. and true" (cf. though "an American ideology committed to the *appearance of freedom*," n. 164). Given this philosophy, Marathe believes that for a successful offensive against the U. S., it is enough to "make only available [the] Entertainment. There will be then some choosing, to partake or choose not to" (p. 318). Marathe will have more to say about choice in the next section of this chapter. The "cable kabal" "derided the 'passivity'" (non-action) of viewers forced to choose between only four channels, and later InterLace suggests that choosing between 504 channels is still passive, because the viewers are accepting "visual spoon-feedings" of "infantile evils." Pleasure, like that provided by television—or to an extreme degree, *Infinite Jest*, which is labeled with a happy face—promotes passivity, but viewers were not passive when faced with pain. The Nunhagen ads "awakened legions of these suddenly violently repelled and disturbed viewers to the power and agency their thumbs actually afforded them," and unhappy days (watching reruns of "Happy Days," an old TV show) filled with "maddening blocks of utterly choiceless and unentertaining time" prompted viewers to bomb threats and suicides. However, there is an image of pain promoting passivity in the "painting that had particularly nailed nine-year-old Hal," which "had been of a deeply parlor-tanned [cf. Hal's complexion, p. 101] and vaguely familiar upscale male, a disembodied fist yanking a handful of brains out of the guy's left ear while the guy's overhealthy face, like most of the ads faces, wears a queer look of intense unhappy concentration" (n. 162). Jim explored pain in his films, too. Consider, for example, *Fun with Teeth* and *Kinds of Pain* (p. 987). The painful advertising was supposed to "create an anxiety relievable by purchase," but the NoCoat campaign became a "case-study in the eschatology of emotional appeals" and preyed upon "the vulnerable psyche of an increasingly hygiene-conscious U.S.A.," a U.S.A. that elected a president in part because of his "proposals for waste, this business of sending from yourself what you hope will not return."

This section features recurrences of dark, primitive, fearful, and violent imagery. The origin of Subsidized Time, like the story of Eric Clipperton, is a "dark legend" (pp. 407, 411). The tone of Hal's paper (which featured commentary from Ogilvie in the form of "a big red yawning skull") on advertising evoked "the misty remove of glaciers and guys in pelts," and the demand of Network overhead is compared to a "slavering maw." The financial demands are so great that the Networks are caught in the vicious cycle of running suicidal ads that drive away viewers because the sponsors are willing to pay the "obscene sums" the networks require to meet their financial demands. Ominous NoCoat ads featured a "nightmarish slo-mo" and cast "a shaggy shadow" across the ads that came before. Spiders symbolize fears or dangers (like addiction) in the novel, and InterLace conjures an image of a web, the interlaced strands of which have caught an American public addicted to entertainment and the illusion of choice. Noreen Lace-Forche is "The Killer-App Queen" (p. 415), and InterLace sells TPs with killer apps (n. 166, cf. p. 60). InterLace "hopp[ed] up and down on the B.S. 1890 Sherman Act with spike heels" (n. 165).

Chapter 23.8, Section 91, Pages 418-430
Notes 169-174, Pages 1031-1032
30 April / 1 May Y.D.A.U.

Marathe and Steeply's conversation was last documented in Ch. 22.5. The previous section's concern with choice now prompts a Marathe-Steeply interlude in which they discuss choice, as they did in Ch. 21.3. Regular features of the Marathe-Steeply sections recur here as well: reference to Marathe's wife and the loss of his legs (pp. 418, 429), "shreds of young laughter" below and the rustles of "small living nightly things" (p. 422), a "bonfire of young persons" (p. 423), and Marathe's "pretending to sniff" (p. 422).

Steeply's organization believes that if Marathe's organization "had one Achilles' heel it was their penchant for showing off, making a spectacle of denying any kind of physical limitation" by choosing extreme locations at which to hold covert meetings, such as the outcropping on which Marathe and Steeply currently sit and stand, respectively. Marathe's organization believes that there is "something latent and sadistic in [Steeply's organization's] assignments of fictional personae for its field-operatives," given the extremes to which those personae oppose the appearances of their operatives, an example of which is Steeply's current disguise featuring "high-heeled feet compellingly grotesque" and "the ugliest supposedly female feet" of Marathe's experience. Marathe believes that "the humiliations of [Steeply's] absurd field-personae" are used "as fuel for the assignment's performance" and that "Steeply welcomed the subsumation of his dignity and self" in the role.

Steeply cannot understand the motive behind the A.F.R.'s scheme to disseminate the Entertainment, which seems to be about "getting the Entertainment out there to hurt us" rather than about political goals. Steeply could understand if he had a context, "a field and a compass" (a map), if it was "just business"; but it seems "personal" to him. When Marathe remarks that the "U.S.A. has previously been hated" by various organizations and countries, Steeply counters that there was always "something they wanted from us." Marathe summarizes Steeply's logic: "For this is how one who is sane proceeds, [motivated by] some desire of self, and efforts expending to meet that desire."

When Marathe asks Steeply what the U.S.A. desires, Steeply says that his country's "whole system is founded on [an] individual's freedom to pursue his own individual desires" and that he and his countrymen want choice, to love and be loved, and the "little things" of which the recently divorced Steeply gives several examples, including a "wife who doesn't mistake your job's requirements for your own fetishes," and to which Marathe adds the "loyalty of a domestic pet" and "[h]igh-quality entertainment." Marathe relates these ideals to the classic philosophy of utilitarianism: "Maximize pleasure, minimize displeasure: result: what is good." Marathe wonders further whether "the best good" is the maximum pleasure of each individual or "the maximum pleasure for all the people." Steeply counters by saying "that each American seeking to pursue his maximum good results together in maximizing *everyone's* good."

Marathe asks Steeply to imagine that "there arises a situation in which your deprivation or pain is merely the consequence, the price, of my own pleasure" and offers a simple example in which he and Steeply are "both large and vigorous U.S.A. individuals" craving a single-serving can of Habitant soup. Steeply suggests that the person willing to pay the highest price should get the soup. When Marathe says that bidding is not relevant to the question, Steeply moves the discussion into the realm of politics by suggesting that Marathe is using the example of the soup as an analogy for the strained relationship between the U.S.A (population "310 million") and Canada. During this, Marathe thinks about his "favorite personal place of off-duty in the U.S.A.'s city Boston," the Public Garden, which includes a duck pond. Marathe sees "Barges of Land" below and thinks that although some waste will be vectored into Mexico, much will be launched into the Convexity. "Part of Marathe always felt almost a desire to shoot persons who anticipated his responses and inserted words and said they were from Marathe, not letting him speak. Marathe suspected Steeply of knowing this."

Marathe then moves the discussion back to "the example of you and me only, we two." Because maximum pleasure is dependent upon a community, Marathe cannot bonk Steeply on the head for the soup: "How am I able to think past this [moment of wanting] soup to the future of soup down my road?" Steeply says that mature Americans are able to understand the necessity of "delayed gratification" in service of "enlightened self-interest." Referencing Marathe's earlier example of the "little kid who'll eat candy all day," Steeply says, "You can't induce a moral sensibility the same way you'd train a rat. The kid has to learn by his own experience how to learn to balance the short- and long-term pursuit of what he wants." American children are taught not "what to desire" but "how to be free [and] how to make knowledgeable choices about pleasure and delay." Steeply admits that the system is imperfect—that it permits greed, crime, drugs, cruelty, ruin, infidelity, divorce, and suicide—and that not everybody learns "how to balance his interests," but that "this is just the price" of freedom.

Marathe asks why Steeply's government would work so hard to prevent dissemination of the *samizdat* "if you do not fear so many U.S.A.s cannot make the enlightened choices." Steeply objects that Marathe can't compare "this kind of insidious enslaving process" to soup. Marathe agrees there is no choice "after the first watching," but "to be this pleasurably entertained in the first place. This is still a choice, no? Sacred to the viewing self, and free? No? Yes?"

PLOT AND CHARACTER: U.S.O.U.S., A.F.R.
THEME: Choice, Phys/Ob, Secrets, Inf/Reg, Recur

In this section, Marathe and Steeply discuss desire and choice and the ability to delay self-gratification. Yet another reference to an

"Achilles' heel" is made, this time in reference to the A.F.R.'s denial of their physical obstacles in choosing to arrive at difficult meeting locations in secret. Steeply's "subsumption of his dignity and self" in his disguise is also a denial of self. Alternately, Steeply begins the section in a "self-embrace." A regression to an infantile state is accomplished by "Happy Patches" (n.169). Marathe asks for "the simplest of examples. The most child-like case," experiences a memory of childhood (p. 429), and refers to an infant's teeth as "fangs," implying that infancy is a regressed, primitive condition. Other primitive or fearful images include "an infant without a skull" (Marathe's wife, p. 429), the "hard tusks" of smoke from Steeply's nostrils (p. 428), "teeth and bared claws" (p. 424), the squeak of Marathe's chair (p. 421), references to a "caged rodent" (p. 422) and a "trained rat" (p. 429), and the "shadow of pain across the face of Steeply" (p. 425). Also, the "U.S.A. *fantods* are meaning fear, confusion, standing hair" (p. 420).

Marathe makes a "rotary gesture" (p. 425; cf. fellow-Canadian Avril's rotary gesture, n. 157), sees a ring of fire (p. 423), and rolls his head when he thinks of the circling sun, circling ducks, and round stones of the Public Garden (p. 427). "Part of Marathe" floats and hovers (p. 418), like Lyle. Steeply references a "chasm of different values" (cf. the "unbridgeable difference" between Hal and Mario, p. 41). Marathe farts mildly (p. 429), as Steeply did earlier (p. 108).

Chapter 23.9, Section 92, Pages 430-434
Note 175, Page 1032
8 November Y.D.A.U., 1930h.-2018h.

The narrative interlude concerning the dark legend of Eric Clipperton—concurrent with the events depicted (or depuppeted) by Mario's film, 2000-2002—continues from Ch. 23.6. Clipperton "was regarded by the U.S.T.A. as never having had a legitimate victory" and was therefore unranked. But with "the inception, in Clipperton's eighteenth summer, of Subsidized Time, the adverted Year of the Whopper, when the U.S.T.A. became O.N.A.N.T.A.," the new O.N.A.N.T.A. manager "didn't know enough not to treat Clipperton's string of six major junior-tournament championships that spring as sanctioned and real" and ranked Clipperton "#1 in Boys' Continental 18-and-Unders." Speculation then ensued about how Clipperton would respond to his ranking, "now that he's got what he's surely been burning over and holding himself hostage for all along."

Two days before the next scheduled tournament, Clipperton unexpectedly arrives at E.T.A. "pleading for entry and counsel" to "the cold-eyed part-time portcullis attendant from the halfway place down the hill." Over the objections of Schtitt and despite "strict and complex" rules about non-E.T.A. students being admitted on the grounds, Clipperton, with Mario's help, is granted "a few private minutes to obtain the counsel of Incandenza Sr. himself," provided Clipperton allow the meeting to be recorded out of concern over O.N.A.N.T.A. rules (recall that this recording was placed in Jim's casket, n. 160). At Jim's request, Lyle "was delotusing from the dispenser and making his way with sideways Lateral Alice to the emergency-type huddle" when Clipperton "eradicate[d] his map and then some" with his Glock 17, creating "an ungodly subsequent mess."

After Clipperton's funeral, Mario insisted "that no one else get to clean up the scene." It took him "all night and two bottles of Ajax Plus to clean the room with his tiny contractured arms and square feet." The "spotless room" has "been locked ever since," but Schtitt "holds a special key" and invites students who complain too much to spend some time in "the Clipperton Suite, to maybe meditate on some of the other ways to succeed besides votaried self-transcendence and gut-sucking-in and hard daily slogging toward a distant goal you can then maybe, if you get there, live with."

PLOT AND CHARACTER: E.T.A., Mario
THEME: Fear/Obsess, Recur

There is a vicious cycle in that "the very tactic that let [Clipperton] win in the first place kept the wins, and in a way Clipperton himself, from being treated as real." But then Clipperton went from being no one to No. 1. He got what he'd been "burning [obsessing] over and holding himself hostage for," and it killed him. Other tennis deaths in *Infinite Jest* include Ivan Lendl, also a suicide (p. 259), and

"M. Chang, lately expired" (p. 388). Recall Lyle's advice to LaMont Chu, "Fame is not the exit from any cage" (p. 389). Mario interfaced with Clipperton "through the bars" of the E.T.A. portcullis (p. 432) attended by an Ennet resident. Clipperton's mother was "a late-stage Valium addict."

Clipperton's visit was a significant event in Mario's life, and it prompted excitement over a rare instance of Lyle's being "outside the weight room upright and walking across the grounds" (but cf. too that Lyle is "a dewimpled Carmelite who works the kitchen day-shift," p. 437). Mario "has never spoken of what he got to sit in on [but cf. "Mario probably told Lyle all about everything"], not even at night to Hal when Hal's trying to go to sleep" (cf. Ch. 6.1). Clipperton's was "the first of [Mario's] two funerals so far." Less than two years after Clipperton's death, Mario's father, like Clipperton, "eradicates his map and then some," leaving "an ungodly subsequent mess."

Chapter 23.10, Section 93, Pages 434-436
9 November Y.D.A.U., 0430h. to 0801h.

Mario's cleaning of the Clipperton Suite leads into a section about Gately cleaning the Shattuck Shelter, presumably hours after Mario's film and the White Flag AA meeting (Ch. 22). Five mornings a week (presumably Monday through Friday), from about 0500h. to 0800h. (but cf. "0700," p. 272), Don Gately works as a janitor at the Shattuck Shelter For Homeless Males. "Janitoring the Shattuck for Stavros Lobokulas was the menial job Gately had landed with only three days to go on his month's deadline to find some honest job, as a resident, and he's kept it ever since," "for over thirteen months." Assuming Gately became an Ennet resident on 12 September Y.D.P.A.H. (cf. Ch. 19.2 summary), he would have had landed this job on 8 or 9 October Y.D.P.A.H.; and 9 November Y.D.A.U. would be the beginning of his fourteenth month on the job. Stavros Lobokulas has "an enormous collection of women's-shoes catalogues." What would Stavros have to say about Steeply's "high-heeled feet," "the ugliest supposedly female feet" of Marathe's experience (p. 419)?

"The inmates at the Shattuck suffer from every kind of physical and psychological and addictive and spiritual difficulty you could ever think of, specializing in ones that are repulsive." Gately wears a mask to clean the toilets and shower areas because "[h]alf the guys in the Shattuck are always incontinent. There's human waste in the showers on a daily fucking basis." There are "almost always one or two guys in the Shattuck who Gately knows personally, from his days of addiction and B&E, from before he got to the no-choice point and surrendered his will to staying straight at any cost."

PLOT AND CHARACTER: Gately
THEME: Inf/Reg, Waste, Recur

The metaphorically caged "inmates" of the shelter are incontinent and experience "impulse-control-deficit." "There are colostomy bags and projectile vomiting" and ejaculations. "A couple have those shaved little patches on their arms" (cf. Lenz, p. 276). "Guys in D.T.s treat the heaters like TVs" (cf. Tiny's ex-roommate at his air-conditioner, pp. 86-7). "The state employees who supervise the shelter at night are dead-eyed and watch soft-core tapes" (entertainment). To abide working at the shelter where he cleans waste, Gately wears a mask and "shuts his head off as if his head has a kind of control switch" (head separate from body). Like reading this novel, working at the shelter is "a better ad for sobriety at any cost than any ad agency could come up with."

Chapter 23.11, Section 94, Pages 436-442
Notes 176-177, Page 1032
8 November Y.D.A.U., 1930h.-2018h.

This section begins with a coda to the "Clipperton saga" (Chs. 23.6 and 23.9), documenting a kid from Fresno who, like Clipperton, was unaffiliated with an academy and who died from drinking "a big glass of Nestle's Quik laced with the sodium cyanide his Dad kept around for ink and drafting." The sodium cyanide, via successive mouth-to-mouth resuscitation attempts, kills each family member in turn. The family members were all trained in CPR but were unaware that the Quik would leave them dead.

After the "self-felonious Gentle/Clipperton comparisons" (cf. p. 407), "the Rodney-Tine-Luria-P.-love-rumor-and-Tine-as-Benedict-Arnold thing" (cf. p. 411), and a final sequence of headers, Mario's film concludes with a puppet enactment of the meeting at which Subsidized Time was established. The Tine-Luria P. plot is where Mario is most derivative of his father's original *ONANtiad*. Note 176 compares Mario's plot to that of the "claymation romance" of the ONANtiad, in which the affair is between Gentle and "the equally hygiene-and-germ-obsessed wife" [cf. Avril] of a Canadian who "hires a malevolent young Canadian *Candida albicans* specialist [cf. the medical attaché, p. 33] to induce in his wife a severe and more or less permanent yeast infection." She "throws herself across the tracks in front of a Québecois bullet-train" (cf. Marathe and his brothers), and Gentle takes "revenge on a macrocartographic scale."

The Subsidized Time meeting is held at a Chinese restaurant, excludes the Secretary of Mexico and the Secretary of Canada, and includes P. Tom Veals and Luria P——. Gentle is "fresh back from a goodwill appearance at a post-collegiate bowl game," and he enthuses to his cabinet about the punter in that game—obviously Orin, though Gentle can't remember his name. After folders outlining the enormous costs of Reconfiguration are distributed, Tine summarizes the administration's financial triple bind: "Outflows required, inflows restricted, balance demanded." As Gentle prepares "to announce some seminal, visionary insight," he references both "the Sino-epithetic calendrical scheme" of the restaurant placemats and "the Ken-L-Ration-Magnavox-Kemper-Insurance-Forsythia Bowl."

There's some "retroactive puzzlement," because the meeting that spawned Subsidized Time happened "sometime in Orin Incandenza's first major-sport year at Boston U., which ended in the Year of the Whopper, pretty obviously a Subsidized year." But Orin's first major-sport year of course began in the fall of 2001, pretty obviously an Unsubsidized year. At "the end of [Orin's] freshman fall," B.U. appeared "at Las Vegas's dignitary-attended K-L-RMKI/Forsythia Bowl" (p. 296). This bowl game occurred "just after Xmas" and before "what turned out to be the last New Year's Eve of Unsubsidized Time" (p. 915). Note that after the game, Orin spent his "Freshman New Year's Eve in Shiny Prize, far from the O.N.A.N.ite upheavals of the new Northeast, the last P.M. Before Subsidization" (p. 296). Given that Gentle's idea for Subsidized Time was initiated by the corporate subsidy of the bowl game in which Orin played and that Gentle is "fresh back" and has "just returned, at extremely high speeds" (p. 442) from this game at the Subsidized Time meeting, the meeting must have occurred in late December of 2001.

There is another chronology issue over which there should be "retroactive puzzlement," but there is none because it is taken for granted that "the advent of Subsidized Time is historically known to be a revenue-response to the heady costs of the U.S.'s Reconfigurative giveaway, which means it must have come after formal Interdependence, and indeed in the film it does come after." But Subsidized Time was actually initiated in December 2001 *before* Reconfiguration was initiated at the Concavity Cabinet of 16 January 2002. However, in Mario's film, this section's Subsidized Time meeting of December 2001 occurs *after* the Concavity Cabinet of 16 January 2002 (Ch. 23.6), and the "seminal experiment in Territorial Reconfiguration" being planned on 16 January is said to be progressing (p. 439, cf. p. 404) at this late December meeting. All U.S. secretaries are at the late December meeting (p. 439), but note that the "Reconfigurative giveaway" is new information to at least the Secretary of State on 16 January Y.W. (pp. 402-3). Therefore, Subsidized Time seems (at least originally) to have been more about the expense of moving "waste" (Gentle's first plank) and about "no new enhancements" (Gentle's second plank) than about Reconfiguration, although Reconfiguration might have been a strategy for Gentle's third plank: "find somebody outside the borders of our community selves to blame."

PLOT AND CHARACTER: E.T.A., O.N.A.N.
THEME: Recur

The accumulation of deaths in the Fresno kid's family is analogous to the accumulation of people around the attaché "lost for all time" (p. 92). The Fresno family's deaths are accompanied by blue faces and "rictus-grimaced mouths." The mother wears a "mud-mask and fluffy slippers." (Gentle wears a "Fukoama microfiltration mask" at the Subsidized Time meeting four pages from the end of the chapter, as he did at his first Inaugural three pages into the chapter.) Rusk screens "student athletes for their possibly lethal reactions to ever actually reaching the level they've been pointed at for years," but unlike Lyle, who warns of cages in the earlier sections of the chapter, she is "bird-of-prey-faced" (primitive looking) and makes "a cage of her hands." Hal's eyes are "rolling around in his head." In the *ONANtiad*, the "hygiene-and-germ-obsessed" woman is the wife of Canada's [MERDE]" (n. 176). A "yawning red skull . . . emblazons all bad-news memos in the Gentle administration" and is also used by Ogilvie on Hal's papers (p. 411). There is yet another reference to Achilles and also one to Cerberus (p. 441). A "high pitch" sound presumably accompanies Gentle's thinking (pp. 441-2). See n. 84 for another example of a multi-merger that resonates with the multi-sponsorship of the Forsythia Bowl.

Chapter 23: Hygienic Stress

In this chapter, obsessions with hygiene and waste removal are problematic and create stress; obsessions with fame or winning also create stress and occasionally lead to death. As Gentle ran a presidential campaign based on the removal of waste, television advertisements preyed upon "the vulnerable psyche of an increasingly hygiene-conscious U.S.A." Gentle's transport of waste to the Northeast leads to environmental problems that are so unbearable to him that he pawns his waste off on Canada and creates the Concavity. Lyle advises LaMont Chu, who is anxious about potential fame, that "Fame is not the exit from any cage." Getting what you desire can be dangerous, as it was for Eric Clipperton. In the aftermath of Clipperton's death, Mario cleaned the Clipperton suite with care, whereas Gately "shuts his head off" to make waste removal bearable.

A thread of secrecy (disguise, mystery) also runs through the chapter. There are frequent references to masks, and all the gala attendees wear hats. Lyle's advice to Stice is as mysterious as the events that prompt the advice. Marathe and Steeply are always secretive, and in this chapter they continue to debate choice and freedom. Themes of choice and freedom also play a part in Gentle's campaign and in the demise of television advertising. The chapter is also concerned with meta-narratives and nested narratives. Hal reflects upon films made by his father that are "obsessed with the idea of audiences' relationships with various sorts of shows": films that call attention to the action of the film itself. The Clipperton saga is a narrative enclosed within the narrative of Mario's film as a comment on an image in that film. The narrative of the career devolution of a meth-dependent headliner is nested in comments on the headers in Mario's film by the narrator of the chapter:

p. 391	last header	demoted
p. 392	8th header	in dutch again
p. 400	1st header	fired
p. 406	headers 1, 2, and 9	third daily in 17 months
p. 438	2nd header	reduced to working in Rantoul IL

The reader constantly is reminded that Mario's film is a puppet show, a comment on both his father's earlier film and on O.N.A.N.ite politics. The narrative of Mario's film (and therefore of the radical societal changes associated with the origin of O.N.A.N.) is nested in the narrative of the Interdependence Day gala (which includes Hal and—tangentially—Lyle), which is just one of the novel's many narrative episodes. The narratives of the novel are fragmented, perhaps creating confusion and stress; but they also are interdependent, as interludes featuring Marathe and Steeply and Gately attest. Below, a plot of Mario's film (left-justified) is juxtaposed with the other narratives of the chapter (right-justified).

MARIO'S PUPPET-FILM	**8 NOVEMBER Y.D.A.U.**	OTHER NARRATIVES

Ch. 23.1

from Gentle's rise to first Y.W. cabinet meeting in "cabinet's second year" (p. 384)
puppet entr'acte (p. 384)
Gentle meets with J.J.J.Chrétien post O.N.A.N.-pact, 2001 (pp. 385-6)
puppet entr'acte (p. 386)

Ch. 23.2

Lyle sees anxious students during film of Gentle's anxieties

Ch. 23.3

headers (pp. 391-3)
O.N.A.N. chair-agreement (p. 394), between Chrétien's death and first Y.W. cabinet meeting
first State of the O.N.AN. Address (p. 394), 31 December 2001 or late January Y.W.

Ch. 23.4

Lyle sees anxious students during film of Gentle's anxieties

Ch. 23.5

Hal ponders Jim's films (inspiration for Mario) while watching Mario's film

Ch. 23.6

headers (pp. 398-400)
second Y.W. cabinet meeting, the Concavity Cabinet, 16 January Y.W. (pp. 400-5)
headers (pp. 405-7)

begin Eric Clipperton interlude

Ch. 23.7

flash-cuts: erections and Tine-Luria P. in same restaurant as S.T. meeting (p. 411)

Hal ponders (choice and) advertising: fall is concurrent with rise of J.G. and S.T.

Ch. 23.8

choice interlude: Marathe and Steeply, 30 April / 1 May Y.D.A.U.

Ch. 23.9

the Eric Clipperton interlude concludes with Mario cleaning suite

Ch. 23.10

waste interlude: Gately cleans Shattuck Shelter, 9 November Y.D.A.U.

Ch. 23.11

coda to the Eric Clipperton interlude

headers (p. 438)
Subsidized Time meeting, late December 2001 (pp. 439-42)

Chapter 24

The Human Head

Chapter 24.1, Section 95, Pages 442-449
Notes 178-179, Page 1032
July Y.D.A.U.

In July Y.D.A.U. Gately, "at like ten months clean," admits before an AA audience that although "he takes one of AA's very rare specific suggestions and hits the knees in the A.M. and asks for Help and then hits the knees again at bedtime and says Thank You, [which] somehow gets [him] through that day clean," "when he tries to go beyond the very basic rote automatic get-me-through-this-day-please stuff [and] tries to achieve a Big-Picture spiritual understanding of a God as he can understand Him, he feels Nothing" and "he is afraid." After speaking, Gately is congratulated by a biker named Bob Death who tells him that it's "good to hear somebody new share from the heart about his struggles with the God component." Then Bob Death tells Gately "the one about the fish" in which, upon being asked "how's the water?" by a "wise old whiskery fish," three young fish "look at each other and go, 'What the fuck is water?' and swim away."

Boston AA neglects to mention that the way post-substance suicidal desperation gets better "is through pain. Not around pain, or in spite of it." They also neglected to tell Gately that "after the urge to get high magically vanishes" (after six or eight Substanceless months) he would suddenly start "to remember things he would just as soon not have," "to almost reexperience things that he'd barely even been there to experience, in terms of emotionally, in the first place."

Gately's "Estonian immigrant" father, Bulat, had "broken Gately's mother's jaw and left Boston when Gately was in his mother's stomach. Gately had no brothers or sisters." His mother, whose "maiden name was Gately," was next involved with "a former Navy M.P. who used to beat her up on a regular schedule" and who "logged each beer he drank carefully in a little spiral notebook he used to monitor his intake of alcohol." Gately remembers that at ten or eleven years old, he would drink most of his mother's remaining vodka after she passed out for the evening. At age seventeen, Gately "came in, after football, his last season" to discover his mother had experienced a cirrhotic hemorrhage. Shortly afterwards his mother was put in a "Long-Term place," to which Gately has been unable to go for "[t]en-plus years" because he "[c]ouldn't deal" and then because "he couldn't face her and try and explain why he hadn't come before now." His mother was first diagnosed with cirrhosis of the liver when Gately was nine, to which diagnosis Gately gave the Arthurian misinterpretation "Sir Osis of Thuliver." Since these memories started occurring in May and June, "when he mops Shattuck Shelter floors, he hears the Clopaclopaclop he used to make with his big square tongue as Sir Osis, then, riding."

After Bob Death's joke, Gately dreams that night that he is "under a sort of sea, at terrific depths, the water all around him silent and dim and the same temperature he is."

PLOT AND CHARACTER: Gately, AA&R
THEME: Memory, Choice, Fear/Obsess, Recur, Dreams

In this section Gately reexperiences memories of his abused mother, who like other addicts throughout the novel, weeps in withdrawal (p. 449). Boston AAs speak of "Release from Compulsion" and tell recovering addicts "to remember the pointless pain of active addiction and . . . that at least this sober pain now has a purpose. At least this pain means you're going somewhere . . . instead of the repetitive gerbil-wheel of addictive pain." Success in Boston AA is attributed to "staying rabidly Active." In this section, "the God-understanding stuff kind of makes [Gately] want to puke, from fear." Gately's mother tried to ward off blows from the former Navy M.P. "with a fluttered downward motion of her arms and hands." Fluttering is usually associated with fear or horror throughout the novel.

The former M.P. obsessively "logged each beer he drank carefully in a little spiral notebook."

The initials M.P. (Michael Pemulis, Madame Psychosis) recur again in this section. Gately "asks for Help" and is ready to eliminate his map as he abstains and recovers. Gately "feels like a rat" and like he wants to "stomp somebody into goo" (rats and a stamping foot are recurring images resonant with *1984*). Concerning cycles or circles, Gately's prayers are "rote automatic"; addictive pain is a "repetitive gerbil-wheel"; and the AA insignia is "a triangle inside a circle." Concerning water imagery, Bob Death tells a fish story, but not before Glenn K. puts "his own oar in." Memories of Gately's youth in a "decayed beach-cottage" "sank without bubbles" (cf. Lyle as described on p. 128), but later "came burpling greasily up." After Bob Death's story, Gately dreams he is "under a sort of sea." The church basement is "literally blue with smoke"; Ferocious Francis has "a little thin pale-blue plastic-like tube thing" under his nose; and memories come to Gately "[o]ut of the psychic blue." Herman the Ceiling That Breathed (p. 447) is a significant memory for Gately; and there was reference earlier to his mother's chintz couch (p. 197), which like Laura Palmer at the beginning of *Twin Peaks* was "wrapped in plastic." There is a missed connection in that Gately's mother calls her son "Bimmy or Bim," not realizing the nickname stands for "Big Indestructible Moron." There is both medieval and modern mythological resonance in Sir Osis of Thuliver and his use of a Light Saber.

A variation on Bob Death's fish story was used by Wallace in his May 2005 Kenyon College commencement address. The themes of this address, even nine years after the publication of *Infinite Jest*, resonate significantly with the themes of truth-telling and of choice vs. passivity explored in *Infinite Jest*.

Chapter 24.2, Section 96, Pages 449-450
Note 180, Page 1032
Very Late October Y.D.A.U.

The narrative now shifts from Gately's dream of water to Hal's "new recurring dream," in which his "teeth had become like shale and splintered when he tried to chew." Hal's old recurring dreams are of the face in the floor (cf. pp. 62, 254) and of competing on the "gargantuan tennis court" (cf. p. 67). Hal wakes from his dream alone because Mario, "weirdly agitated about Madame Psychosis's unannounced sabbatical," has been staying at HmH the last few nights (Joelle conducted one of her last radio shows in the first hour of 23 October, Ch. 16.1). Mario became agitated when he was taken by Corbett Thorp to WYYY, "where the only person who didn't talk like an angry cartoon character [was] a severely carbuncular man at the engineer's board" and where he discovered that Madame Psychosis used a screen during her broadcasts (n. 180, cf. Ch. 16.1). Could Mario's agitation spring from almost registering a connection between Madame Psychosis's screen and "the apparently mute veiled graduate-intern" (p. 315) for whom he fetched Big Red Soda Water while working with his father?

PLOT AND CHARACTER: Hal, Mario
THEME: Dreams, Fear/Obsess, Recur

In Hal's dream, there is "a general atmosphere of the splintering teeth being a symptom of something way more dire and distasteful that no one wanted to confront him about." The dream is "horrible," and Hal is "scared." The "static, momentumless music [played in Madame Psychosis's absence] as subject instead of environment is somehow terribly disturbing" and sounds to Hal "like somebody's mind coming apart right before your ears." There are recurrences of Hal's keys on the floor (cf. p. 172) and of a missed connection in that Mario is perhaps close to realizing the identity of Madame Psychosis. Madame Psychosis's replacement, Miss Diagnosis, reads critical theorists "Horkheimer and Adorno against a background of Partridge Family [old TV show] slowed down to a narcotized slur."

Chapter 24.3, Section 97, Pages 450-461
Notes 181-187, Pages 1032-1033
9 November Y.D.A.U., 0600h.-0730h.

Even on the morning after the I.-Day festivities (Ch. 23), E.T.A. students are required to attend drills. In the Headmaster's

House, Charles Tavis looks "southeast past West and Center Courts at the array of A-team players assembling" for drills, his "high forehead up against the window's glass." Asleep "next to the sound system with its claws on its chest and four pillows for bradypnea-afflicted breathing" is Mario—"the thing it's not entirely impossible [Tavis] may have fathered" (cf. pp. 312-4 and n. 98)—who began sleeping at HmH after Madame Psychosis left her radio show (cf. previous section). Tavis considers his job to be "cholesterol-raisingly stressful and complex" and "knows what James Incandenza could not have cared about less: the key to the successful administration of a top-level junior tennis academy lies in cultivating . . . a state of Total Worry." A summary of facts about the E.T.A. student population is given below:

Capacity	**Fall Y.D.A.U.**	**Drills, Scholarship, Housing**
80 boys	64 boys	2 sets of 32, 4 boys per 8 East Courts, 8 prorectors
68 girls	72 girls	3 sets of 24, 6 girls per 4 Center Courts, 4 prorectors
	136 students	(cf. p. 112) 95 paying, 41 scholarship
	12 available	+16 boys needed, -4 girls needed for capacity
148 total	148 total	

Presumably some B-team players participate in the 0600 drills, given that there are only two sets of drills for boys (with B- and C-team players participating in the "B-squad's 0745h. drills," p. 60). Which four girls are in the male dorms?

During drills, Schtitt is on an "iron transom players call the Tower that extends west to east over the centers of all three sets of courts and terminates w/ the nest high above the Show Courts." "When the E.T.A.s' strokes or play's being filmed for study, Mario Incandenza is positioned on the railing of Schtitt's nest." A prorector is at each of the courts being used for drills with "baskets of used balls, plus a ball machine." For the boys' drills, eight different drills are conducted on as many courts, four players per court. After Gatorade, impressions-so-far from Schtitt, additional wind sprints, and brief prorector instruction, conditioning drills are conducted on the eighth court.

Hal wears a "white alpaca tennis jacket that had been his father's," and his tooth continues to hurt, as it did last night. Evidence of Eschaton remains: "bits of glitter and broken monitor-glass in the frozen stuff up by the fences"; the absence of Penn "amid troubling leg-rumors"; bandages on Possalthwaite; and Otis P. Lord's return "from the emergency room at St. Elizabeth's last night with the Hitachi monitor over his head, still," which requires an expert for its removal. While awaiting "more overall impressions" from Schtitt, the players accept "clean towels from a halfway-house part-time black girl with a towel cart" (so from either Clenette or Didi N.).

Schtitt chastises the players for giving in to outside distractions like temperature. Referring to the tennis court as a second world, Schtitt says, "In that world is joy because there is shelter of *something else*, of purpose past sluggardly self and complaints about uncomfort." Schtitt continues, "You have a chance to *occur*, playing"; because in tennis there is "always only two of you, you and this other, inside the lines, with always a purpose to keep this world alive, yes?" Schtitt reminds the players that they have a choice between this second world and the "large external world where is cold and pain without purpose" (cf. Boston AAs to recovering addicts: "remember the pointless pain of active addiction and . . . that at least this sober pain now has a purpose," p. 446). Schtitt says, "Move. Travel lightly. Occur. Be *here*. Not in bed or shower or over baconschteam, in the mind. Be *here* in total. Is nothing else." Schtitt asks Hal "where you apply for citizenship in the second world." Hal says the human head is where "I'm going to occur as a player. The game's two heads' one world. One world, sir." Schtitt laughs aloud and says, "Play."

PLOT AND CHARACTER: E.T.A., Hal
THEME: Fear/Obsess, Recur, Boundaries

The obsessive Tavis cultivates "a state of Total Worry." There are four references to pain in Hal's tooth (pp. 452, 453 (twice), and 458) and two references to his stiff ankle that he injured at age fifteen (pp. 453, 457). "Tiny cries and a repetitive scream for help come up from someplace downhill to the east, presumably Enfield Marine" (cf. p. 196). "[L]ight-poles cast long thin shadows across the courts" (p. 453), and "you can almost see the light-pole and transom shadows rotating slowly northwest" (p. 455). Other recurrences include Tavis's "high forehead up against the window's glass" and references to the Charles normally being blue (p. 452) and to a glassy blue sky (p. 455). Final conditioning drills are called "Pukers" (p. 454, n. 182), and at one point during these drills Petropolis Khan "pitches forward onto the hard surface and lies very still." There is documentation of yet another character breaking wind: Brian van Vleck (p. 460). Artist Gaug[u]in is referenced (p. 460). Schtitt uses a weatherman's pointer like Tine (cf. p. 403), and the rising sun "gives his white head a pinkish corona" (cf. n. 76). Chu's obsessive picture clipping (cf. pp. 388-9) is noted by Schtitt, and reference is made to Stice's "mispositioned bed" and Coyle's "suspicious discharge" (cf. p. 394).

"[T]he monitor-glass bits' glitter shifts and dances along the opposite fence in a sort of sickening way." Schtitt makes "pirouettic" turns, and says of tennis that there are "always only two of you, you and this other, inside the lines, with always a purpose to keep this [second] world alive" (cf. "The competing boy on the net's other side: he is not the foe: he is more the partner in the dance," p. 84). Schtitt speaks of a "Different world *in*side" and delimits the boundaries of the second world as "this inside place inside the lines where is always the same." For more on Schtitt's declaration that "there are no conditions" in the second world, cf. Wallace's "Derivative Sport in Tornado Alley," from his essay collection *A Supposedly Fun Thing I'll Never Do Again*: Wallace learned to play tennis in his "home of Philo, Illinois"; drills with Gil Antitoi; and was at his "very best in bad conditions" (pp. 3-4, 17).

Concerning Schtitt's "promises of self-transcendence" (p. 453) and the boys' eyes "glazed with repetition" (p. 458), recall the Big Buddy sessions of six days ago, in which Stice spoke of Schtitt's philosophy of "discipline and sacrifice and honor to something way bigger than your personal ass" (p. 120) and Troeltsch spoke of "sheer mindless repeated motions" which "frees up your head" (p. 118). Hal speaks of occurring as a player in the "human head," but cf. deLint's phrase "Playing out of your head" (p. 242). Hal's "obsessive dislike for deLint" and his view of him as "just a cutout or projection" will change in November Y.G.: "The same Aubrey deLint I'd dismissed for years as a 2-D martinet knelt gurneyside to squeeze my restained hand" (p. 15).

Chapter 24.4, Section 98, Pages 461-469
Notes 188-197, Page 1033
8 November Y.D.A.U.

This section, like Ch. 24.1, is concerned with Gately and is assumed to occur on 8 November because Ch. 24.6 will continue this thread and occurs on that date. Because Gately "cooks the communal supper on weekdays" and "does the House's weekly shopping," he occasionally gets to drive Pat Montesian's black 1964 Ford Aventura. This is "a mark of serious regard or questionable judgement" on Pat's part, given that Gately "lost his license more or less permanently back in the Year of the Whisper-Quiet Maytag Dishmaster" (three years ago) for driving with a DUI-suspended license. As long as Gately maintains sobriety and reparations, driving with a DUI-suspended license is the only case (of many cases) against him that threatens to be taken off Closed-Without-Finding status ("it's only a matter of time"). This would require Gately to do a 90-day "bit at someplace like Concord or Deer Island," for which Gately is prepared given that he once did "17 months at Billerica." It is not the 90 days that Gately fears, but rather "[g]oing back to ingesting Substances," which are easy to acquire in prison. Even "the Nuck-VIP issue" (of about 14 months ago, cf. Ch. 7.4) was taken over by a federal bureau, rumored to be directing suspicions towards "shadowy Nucko-political bodies all the way up in Québec."

In Gately's application interview with Pat, he spoke with "grim honesty about his disinterest and hopelessness" with respect to staying clean. This honesty is what prompted Pat to admit him to Ennet House. In that interview, she described blackouts: "It's like your mind wasn't in possession of your body, and it was usually brought on by alcohol but could also be brought on by chronic use of other Substances, synthetic narcotics among them." "Everything mental for Gately was kind of befogged and prone to misprision for well into his first year clean."

"Pat Montesian was both pretty and not." Pat had "almost died from a stroke [cf. p. 278] during the D.T.s one A.M." and the "right side of her face was still pulled way over into this sort of rictus, and her speech [was] a kind of overenunciated slurring." Pat's "right arm had atrophied into a kind of semi-claw," and she dragged her right leg behind her "like something hanging on to her that she was trying to get away from." With the help of people like Pat, Eugenio Martinez (Gene M.), and "Ferocious" Francis Gehaney (a "Crocodile" with "geologic amounts of sober AA time"), after four or five months of being an Ennet resident Gately "realized that quite a few days had gone by since he'd even thought about" ingesting Substances. "It was the first time he'd been out of this kind of mental cage since he was maybe ten. . . . How could some kind of Higher Power he didn't even believe in magically let him out of the cage"? Now, "Gately usually no longer much cares whether he understands or not. He does the knee-and-ceiling thing twice a day, and cleans shit, and listens to dreams, and stays Active, and tells the truth to the Ennet House residents." When Gately was presented with a cake "on the September Sunday [13 September Y.D.A.U., the first Sunday White Flag meeting after 12 September; cf. Ch. 19.2 summary] that marked his first year sober, [he] had cried in front of nonrelatives for the first time in his life."

Gately has "eyes full of anxiety and hopes for everyone's full enjoyment" when he serves the dinners he cooks. The reactions to Gately's cooking of Ennet residents Lenz, Day, McDade, Glynn, Ewell, Cortelyu, and Smith are documented on p. 469. Lenz says that Gately's "food is the kind of food that helps you really appreciate whatever you're drinking along with it" (cf. Hal's description of the shaggy middle Dean's look, p. 6). Glynn is "still woozy and infirm from some horrendous Workers Comp. scam" (cf. Ch. 13.3). Tiny Ewell "never fails to thank Gately" (in the short time he has been a resident, cf. Ch. 10.4). Burt F. Smith "rolls his eyes with pleasure," as did Pat's dog when "Gately, who hadn't been told about Pat's thing about wanting her dog's petted [cf. p. 278], rubbed its scabby stomach" during his application interview.

PLOT AND CHARACTER: Gately, Ennet
THEME: Phys/Ob, Inf/Reg, Recur

Like Mario, Pat faces physical challenges. Pat's physical challenges arose from the stroke that "enabled her to finally Surrender." Also, Gene M.'s "left ear had been one of his Losses." Pat's pursuit of happiness through substances has pulled the right side of her face into a "sort of rictus" (analogous to the smiley face on the *Infinite Jest* cartridges). Addiction is infantilizing and negates mental processes (and therefore choice). In recovery, Gately is advised to treat AA like a box of cake mix and just follow "the childish directions." McDade leads "Glynn to the table by the hand, as if Glynn were a damaged child." Gately's mom's alcoholism led to the hemorrhage that "vegetabilized her brain." Addiction causes blackouts: mental shutdown and memory loss. In recovery, Gately prays "for his head to just finally explode already."

Pat has a "shadowy husband," and there are "shadowy Nucko-political bodies." The black paint of Pat's car "has the bottomless quality of water at night." Cases that are Closed Without Finding are Blue Filed. The eyes of both Pat's epileptic dog and of Burt F. Smith roll up (as a response to pleasurable stimuli). Gately thinks of prayer as "talking to the ceiling." Before prayer, Gately was rarely on his knees, except e.g. to "throw up." Gene M. drove Gately around in "aimless circles." Relief from addiction is again analogous to release from a cage. Pat chipped her incisors (cf. Hal's dream of splintered teeth earlier in the chapter) eating rocks for Ennet's founder (cf. p. 138). Twice in this section, endnotes reference earlier notes: n. 189 refers to n. 12, and n. 194 refers to n. 115. Compare Gately's "188 cm. and 128 kg." with Steeply's "1.93 M., 104 KG." (p. 227). Steeply returns to talk of pleasure centers in the brain in the next section.

Chapter 24.5, Section 99, Pages 470-475
Note 198, Pages 1033-1034
1 May Y.D.A.U.

Marathe and Steeply's conversation continues from Ch. 23.8. Steeply references a late 1970s experimental program by Canadian neuroscientists in which it was proposed that Briggs electrodes (like those used in pacemakers—Marathe's father had a pacemaker that required him to "[a]void all microwave ovens") implanted in the brains of epileptic patients could prevent seizures. During the trial and error implantation process (on rats), it was discovered that "certain parts of the lobes gave the brain intense feelings of pleasure," which the scientists dubbed *p*-terminals. A "*p*-terminal'd turn out to be right up next to some other neuron whose stimulation would cause pain, or hunger, or God knows what," and "soon the pleasure-stimulation phenomenon was its own separate radical experiment."

Steeply: The "Canadians found that if they rigged an auto-stimulation lever, the rat would press the lever to stimulate his p-terminal over and over, thousands of times and hour, over and over, ignoring food and female rats in heat, completely fixated on the lever's stimulation, day and night, stopping only when the rat finally died of dehydration or simple fatigue." Marathe: "Not of the pleasure itself, however." Steeply: Even upon removal of the apparatus, "the subject'd run around pressing anything that could be pressed or flipped, trying to get one more jolt."

The experiment was repeated on other animals. Eventually, the neuroscientists wanted to try the experiment on humans, but feared the legal issues associated and the risks involved. Marathe suggests that the Canadians could have asked the then CIA for subjects like those expended for "brainwashing experimentation with dangerous drugs . . . performed on persons who were not volunteers" in the U.S.A.'s 1950s MK-Ultra experiments (n. 198). When Marathe references illegal surgeries associated with these experiments, Steeply counters with a reference to "amputations for daring young train-cultists." Recall that Marathe lost his legs to a train (p. 108).

The neuroscientists' fears were unfounded, though, because when word about the experiment "up in Manitoba" was leaked, human volunteers began lining up to participate, "willing to trample one another to undergo invasive brain surgery and foreign-object implantation." Marathe: "Your point finally is Canadians also, we would choose dying for this, the total pleasure of a passive goat." Steeply: "A precedent [analogous to the Entertainment] in your own nation." Marathe: "Us, our nation is the Québec nation. Manitoba is—" Steeply: If Fortier "could get past the blind desire for harm against the U.S., [he] might be induced to see just what it is he's proposing to let out of the cage."

PLOT AND CHARACTER: Samizdat, U.S.O.U.S., A.F.R.
THEME: Inf/Reg, Recur

In this section, "invasive brain surgery and foreign-object implantation" brings to mind the contents of Jim's head (p. 31). Marathe's father having to "[a]void all microwaves" because they threatened his life brings to mind the fact that Jim used a microwave to take his life. Like the Manitobans, those who choose to watch *Infinite Jest* would be "[v]olunteering for fatal addiction to the electrical pleasure," presuming they understood the implications of the smiley face on the cartridge and the ecstatic expression of the man in the wheelchair in the street displays (p. 224).

Rat and cage imagery runs through this section. The experimental rats are caught in a cycle of compulsion. Note that even in recovery ("Release from Compulsion," p. 446), Gately says that when he prays "he feels like a rat that's learned one route in the maze to the cheese" (p. 443). Steeply warns Marathe about what Fortier is "proposing to let out of the cage." Pleasure centers in the brain are called rivers of reward (pp. 471, 474), and those experiencing the pleasure are "incontinent" and "pitching forward." Marathe twice makes "his rotary motion," his "slow circular gesture."

Chapter 24.6, Section 100, Pages 475-489
Notes 199-207, Page 1034
8 November Y.D.A.U., 1800h.

This section, which begins "Then tonight," continues the narrative of Ch. 24.4 and occurs just before the screening of Mario's film (at 1930h., Ch. 23) and just before Gately and the Ennet residents attend the White Flag AA meeting (at 2000h., Ch. 22). Two new residents have arrived at Ennet: Amy J. and Joelle van Dyne. Gately is amazed that the "Joelle v.D. girl seems to have like inordinate immediate weight and pet-status with Pat [cf. n. 134 and p. 364], who's already making noises about exempting the girl from the menial-job requirement, and wants Gately to [take Pat's car and] look for some kind of Big Red Soda Water [cf. p. 315] tonic for the girl, who's apparently still dehydrated." Recall that Joelle went to the hospital after overdosing at Molly Notkin's party last night.

On Gately's trip through Boston in Pat's car, he passes The Unexamined Life club (cf. n. 67) and the Brighton Projects (haunt of Roy Tony; pp. 37-38, 129). In the distance he sees the giant CITGO sign, "like a triangular star to steer by." He "likes to match a Green Line train at 75 k . . . and see how close he can cut beating it across the tracks at the Brighton Ave. split," a behavior that he likens to "a dark vestige his old low-self-esteem suicidal-thrill behaviors." He goes through Central Square to Inman Square (Poor Tony will be riding to Inman Square hoping to cop from the Antitois when he has his seizure on 14 November, Ch. 20.2). As Gately blows through Inman, a "tornado of waste" "whirls in his exhaust," and a "thick flattened M[illennial] F[izzy] cup" (the drink of choice for the WYYY engineer and Ennet addicts; pp. 182, 200) is "blown spinning all the way to the storefront" of the Antitois. Approximately halfway through the 3 ½ page paragraph of pp. 479-482, the narrative focus shifts from Gately to the Antitois.

The cup "hits the glass pane in the locked front shop door with a sound for all the world like the rap of a knuckle," which prompts Lucien Antitoi, who "opens up the front door with a loud hinge-squeak," to look for the source of the knock. Lucien holds a "sturdy broom he'd carved from a snow-snapped limb as a boy . . . and sharpened the tip of, as a sort of domestic weapon." Lucien's brother Bertraund is in the back "eating Habitant *soupe aux pois*" (cf. Marathe's example, p. 425). The Antitois are "borderline-incompetent" and "spurned by F.L.Q. after DuPlessis's assassination." The Antitois do not believe that DuPlessis's death (caused by Gately) was "an unfortunate burglary-and-mucus mishap" (although it was, cf. Ch. 7.4). The Antitois were sent to Boston "as a kind of primitive two-celled organism to establish a respectable front and abet malignant cells and to insurge and terrorize in small sad anti-experialist ways." The Antitois sell "exotic reflective glasswares and glass-blowing hardware" and have set "curved and planar mirrors at studied angles whereby each part of the room is reflected in every other part, which flusters and disorients customers." The Antitois deal in novelties "trucked over, along w/ the Saprogenic Greetings® treacly greeting and postcards, from the Waltham facilities of Acme Inc.," a company "owned by the Québec-sympathetic shadowy Albertan mogul who'd been such a force in the anti-broadcast A.C.D.C." (n. 204; cf. pp. 411, 414). Recall that the "X-ray spectacles" sold in the shop were invented by Jim's grandfather (p. 313). The Antitois also deal in "used and bootleg" entertainment cartridges, some of which "do not have labels, they're so obscure or illicit." "The pornographical cartridges [Lucien] finds nonsensical and views them in Fast Forward to get them over with as quickly as possible."

Since DuPlessis's death, Bertraund has shown a "flair for stupid wastes of time," including "hanging a sword-stemmed fleur-de-lis flag from the nose of a U.S.A. Civil War hero's Boylston St. statue when it would simply be cut down" (Joelle saw this yesterday, p. 223) and "branching out into harmful pharmaceuticals as an attack on the fiber of New New England's youth." Recall that four days ago (cf. p. 169) Pemulis visited Antitoi Entertainent (note that the narrator for Pemulis emended the spelling of the shop's name on p. 215), negotiated with Bertraund in dumbshow because Pemulis speaks no French, noted Lucien "cradling a broom," saw "a hardcore-porn cartridge going at five times the normal speed," and purchased DMZ: "thirteen incredibly potent 50-mg. artifacts" (p. 215), not eighteen as stated here. Bertraund had previously traded "an antique blue lava-lamp and a lavender-tinged apothecary's mirror" to "a wrinkled long-haired person of advanced years in a paisley Nehru jacket" for "650 mg." (13x50mg.) of DMZ and "a kitchen-can waste bag filled with crusty old mossy boot-and-leg Read-Only cartridges sans any labels."

Bertraund brought home two cartridges removed from "untended commercial displays" in "Saturday's chilling rain" (Joelle also passed by this display which featured a man in a wheelchair, p. 224) that were stamped "with a circle and arc that resembled a disembodied smile" (like on the attaché's cartridge, p. 36) and a slogan in

French. The tapes that were removed from the display as well as the "bartered tapes [Lucien] had removed from the waste bag" were "blank beyond static." "Unknown to the hapless Antitois, this doesn't mean that they're necessarily blank. Copy-Capable cartridges, a.k.a Masters, require a 585-r.p.m.-drive viewer or TP to run, and on a conventional 450-drive decline to give off so much as static, appearing rather empty and blank" (n. 205).

As Lucien looks out the shop window, he becomes aware that the shop is about to be attacked by the A.F.R. When he pulls his gun from his pants, a length of thread looped around the barrel causes his pants to rip and fall around his ankles. When Lucien goes to warn Bertraund he discovers that Bertraund has "a railroad spike in his eye" (like C[h]rétien; cf. pp. 392, 1013). The A.F.R. are wearing "plastic fleur-de-lis-with-sword-stem" masks, "except for one particular of the A.F.R., in an unpretentious sportcoat and tie and the worst mask of all, a plain yellow polyresin circle with an obscenely simple smily-face in thin black lines" (cf. the Sergeant at Arms in Gately's dream, pp. 358-9). This leader has "wiry hair and a small and strangely banal bald-spot." He says they have come to acquire a "Copy-Capable item" and asks if the shop has "a 585-rpm-drive TP somewhere about here, for running Masters." Lucien, whose sphincter has failed him, is "one of the very few natives of *Notre Rai Pays* [cf. p. 222] ever who cannot understand French" (p. 480) and therefore cannot answer the leader's questions.

As the A.F.R. search the shop, Lucien is killed violently with the broom that "he has loved and kept sharpened and polished and floor-fuzz-free since adolescence." The broom's passage "forms an obscene erectile bulge in the back of his red sopped johns, bursting then through the wool and puncturing tile and floor at a police-lock's canted angle to hold him upright on his knees, completely skewered." As "he finally sheds his body's suit, Lucien finds his gut and throat again newly whole, clean and unimpeded, and is free, catapulted home over fans and the Convexity's glass palisades at desperate speeds, soaring north, sounding a bell-clear and nearly maternal alarmed call-to-arms in all the world's well-known tongues."

PLOT AND CHARACTER: Gately, Joelle, A.F.R.
THEME: Recur, Cycles, Waste, Fear/Obsess, Inf/Reg

The narrator of this section asks, "Has anybody mentioned Gately's head is square?" which either implies that there are several narrators of *Infinite Jest* or that Wallace is making light of the frequency with which he mentions the size of Gately's head. Motion in this section, including the dance of light on mirrors and glass, is significant; and Wallace leaves the narrative in motion at the end of the section with Lucien "soaring north." Lucien, "who loves only to sweep and dance in a clean pane," "bobs and sweeps, and bobbing shafts of mirror-light gleam and dance, backed by night, in the locked door's pane." Lucien sees "in the carefully placed display mirrors' angles, spikes of light off rotary metal rotating" as the A.F.R. prepare for "encirclement" of the shop. "Gately's never had sex sober yet, or danced, or held somebody's hand except to say the Our Father in a big circle." In Pat's fast car, Gately raises a "tornado of waste" (other recurrences of waste imagery: the Irish are "puke-white"; the train has a "farty-sounding horn"; Lucien hears a nearby toilet flush; and Lucien's sphincter fails him). Lucien's "face's transparent image fills the glass," which is a figurative capture of the head by glass analogous to the literal capturing of Otis P. Lord's head by monitor glass at the end of Ch. 22.1 and which also is resonant with the recurring image of a forehead against glass, like Tavis's at the beginning of drills earlier in the chapter. The "disembodied smile" on the cartridge warns that the happy viewer's head will be captured by what it sees on the screen. This figurative disembodiment leaves the viewer trapped in a cycle; whereas Lucien's literal disembodiment, the shedding of "his body's suit," prompts a linear ascent: he is "soaring north."

Lucien does not understand the A.F.R.'s French, just as Gately did not understand DuPlessis's French and Pemulis did not understand Bertraund's French. There is "a blue-black shadow" at sunset; Bertraund eats "oblong blue-veined patties of meat"; the DMZ was traded for "an antique blue lava-lamp"; the twilight is "blue-shadowed"; and Bertraund has a railroad spike in his "former blue right eye." Fearful signs recur in association with the A.F.R.: their incessant squeaks; their being "like faceless rats, the devil's own hamsters"; and their masks, especially the "yellow empty smiling chewing face" of the leader. A pan drops, and a mirror shatters (cf. Tavis on p. 193 and Melinda on p. 235). Lucien is caught in a web spun by his unraveling pants. Lucien cleaned the shop obsessively; it resembled "a junkyard for anal retentives."

Usually, infant imagery is associated with regression or compulsion, but in this section it symbolizes Lucien's (relative) innocence. Consider the narrator's description of Lucien on p. 482: "He has that rare spinal appreciation for beauty in the ordinary that nature seems to bestow on those who have no native words for what they see." Lucien heard squeaks "naïvely like the babe." With his pants at his ankles, Lucien makes the "face a small child makes." His sphincter fails him. Attempting to reply to the A.F.R. leader, his movements have "a childlike pathos." When impaled, he makes "a natal gargle," sees "his crib," and is held on his knees "at a police-lock's canted angle" (associating Lucien with Mario, the most innocent character in the novel). There is a recurrence of water imagery in that the dying Lucien makes "landed-fish gasps," sounds "drowned," and sees "lake after lake after lake lit up by the near-Arctic sun and stretching out in the southeastern distance like chips of broken glass."

Chapter 24: The Human Head

The concerns of the previous chapter were hygienic or bodily, whereas this chapter is concerned with the mind (memories, dreams, functions of the brain) or with disembodiment: the separation of the mental or the spiritual from the physical. Gately struggles to understand God and spirituality as buried memories bubble back up into his head. Both Gately and Hal have vivid dreams. Hal makes a reference to "somebody's mind coming apart." Although drills are physical, Schtitt's philosophy espouses mental and spiritual discipline, and Hal declares that the human head is where he is going to occur as a player. Pat says of blackouts, "It's like your mind wasn't in possession of your body." Steeply discusses the stimulation of pleasure centers in the brain with Marathe. "Lucien's leonine head is tilted back" to facilitate his death, the shedding of "his body's suit." The attention to heads and bodies at the midpoint of the novel recalls Hal's opening phrase: "surrounded by heads and bodies" (p. 3).

Infinite Jest III

Interdependence

An even greater sense of the novel's interdependent structure is perceived as the stories of the characters continue to unfold and strands of the various narrative threads overlap and weave together in Chs. 22-24. Also, there is a tighter sense of structure than in the second unit of the novel, because most of the events of these three chapters occur in less than 24 hours: from Sunday afternoon through Monday morning. However, the fragmented style established in the first unit of the novel is retained in that events outside 8-9 November are shuffled into the narrative sequence, and even the sequence of events that does occur in this short period is shuffled around:

Narrative Order	Chronological Order
Ch. 22 Eschaton	1st, 8 November, 1400-1600
Ch. 22 White Flag AA meeting	4th, 8 November, 2000-2130
Ch. 23 E.T.A. I.-Day Gala	3rd, 8 November, 1930-2018
Ch. 23 Gately at Shattuck	5th, 9 November, 0430-0800
Ch. 24 E.T.A. drills	6th, 9 November, 0600-0730
Ch. 24 Gately drives by Antitois	2nd, 8 November, 1800

The sequence can be (inter)connected by the weather across the three chapters:

8 November

1600	p. 342	"falling snow"
1800	p. 475	"a weird-weather evening, both thundering and spitting snow"
	p. 484	"Light snowfall is bouncing back and forth"

1930 p. 387 "P.M. snow has given way to rain. . . . Thunder and lightning"
2000 p. 344 "shaking water off their outerwear"
p. 389 "thunder's died . . . spatter's gone random and post-storm sad"
p. 390 "without the sound of rain"
2045 p. 361 "wind is spattering goopy sleet against the broad window"

9 November
0600 p. 451 "the rainy melt of yesterday's snow"
p. 454 "frozen slush from I.-Day's snow and rain"

In Ch. 22, Jim is inspired to make a film that has a major impact on Joelle, who later works with Jim on the film that leads Steeply—who knows Marathe who was inspired by DuPlessis (also presumably known by Jim's wife) who was accidentally killed by Gately who is now at an AA meeting close to where Steeply observed Eschaton—to interview Orin, Jim's son who once dated Joelle, who now unsettles Gately and listens to the speakers recount their crisis moments on Interdependence Day. In Boston AA, "initial hopelessness unites every soul."

In Ch. 23, the events of Mario's film (also chronologically shuffled) ground the reader in the major interrelated events of 2000-Y.W. that establish the O.N.A.N.ite environment: the decline of advertising, the rise of President Gentle, Interdependence, Subsidized Time, and Reconfiguration. Gentle separates himself mentally and spiritually from physical waste.

In Ch. 24, the return of Gately's memory helps him thread together his past. The Antitois provide points of connection to previous events: Pemulis's purchase of DMZ in Ch. 16 and Joelle's rainy walk past a flag-draped statue and a 2-D display in Ch. 17. Gately's accidental killing of DuPlessis took away the Antitoi's protection, so it is appropriate that Gately causes the cup to "knock" at the Antitoi's door and foreshadow the A.F.R.'s entrance to the shop in search of what Gately (and Kite) presumably stole from DuPlessis, a cartridge that features Joelle, for whom Gately is obtaining Big Red Soda Water as he drives by the Antitoi's shop.

Ch. 24 focuses on mental processes (memories, dreams, functions of the brain); Ch. 23 focuses on physical processes (eating, transfer or licking or cleaning of waste, hygiene, rote behavior); and Ch. 22 documents mental triggers that prompt physical action: the interdependence of the mental and the physical. Gately's consistent physical action of getting on his knees to pray leads to the recovery of his memories and his mental stability. Gately's mind-body interconnection is presumably triggered by a spiritual force. Lucien's shedding of his body's suit places him completely in the spiritual realm, and makes him "newly whole, clean and unimpeded."

Chapter 25

Cycles: Orbits, Annulation, Attraction, Repulsion

Chapter 25.1, Section 101, Pages 489-491
1 May Y.D.A.U.

Marathe and Steeply's conversation continues from Ch. 24.5. Steeply mentions the A.F.R.'s plan to "recover this alleged Master copy [of the Entertainment] from the DuPlessis burglary" and says, "Nobody has this mysterious Master, but we've all got Read-Only's—all the anti-O.N.A.N. cells have at least one Read-Only, we're pretty sure." Marathe confirms that the A.F.R. has at least one copy, and Steeply assumes that the A.F.R. knows that the U.S.O.U.S. has "more than one." Marathe confirms, "Confiscated from razzles of Berkeley, Boston. But who can know what is on them? Who can study the Entertainment while detached?" The original Master was buried with Jim (n. 80), but clearly Read-Only copies and perhaps other Masters have been made. The previous section documents the A.F.R.'s attempt to recover a Master from the Antitois' shop six months from now on 8 November. Cartridges in the Antitois' shop from the street display and from the garbage bag are blank, but could be Masters that only seem to be blank (cf. p. 483 and nn. 205, 301). For the first time, Marathe mentions Berkeley in reference to an Entertainment problem. Recall that on 7 November, an attendee of Molly Notkin's party will report that "a good bit of Berkeley isn't answering their phone" (p. 233), perhaps alluding to a new "razzle" in Berkeley. (Steeply's reference to Dr. Brullent is presumably meant to be a reference to Broullîme, whose name is spelled "Brullîme" on p. 489.).

Steeply reports that "the developing theory" is that the Entertainment uses holography. Steeply cites Jim's use of holography "in the context of a kind of filmed assault on the viewer" (e.g., in *The*

Machine in the Ghost: Annular Holography for Fun and Prophet and "*The Medusa v. the Odalisque*" (p. 988); Hal reflected upon the latter film at the I.-Day gala (pp. 396-7) and believes the inventor of holography, Dennis Gabor, "may very well have been the Antichrist" (p. 12)). Marathe refers to Jim as "a maker of reflecting panels for thermal weapons, and an important *Annulateur*, also, and amasser of the capital from opticals" (cf. pp. 63-5). The U.S.O.U.S.'s theory is that the Entertainment's appeal is due to its having "the neural density of an actual stage play without losing the selective realism of the viewer-screen" thanks to "hologrammatical activity." Marathe says that his superior "finds the theories of content irrelevant."

PLOT AND CHARACTER: Samizdat, U.S.O.U.S., A.F.R.
THEME: Cycles, Recur, His/Father

"Around the bonfire, far out below upon the desert floor, rotated a ring of smaller and palsied fires, [young] persons carrying torches or fires" and possibly dancing (Burn describes this activity in terms of a May Day ritual, pp. 62-3). Marathe's father died when his pacemaker (cf. p. 470) was "damaged accidentally by a videophonic pulse [from a] video call, advertising the videophony" (cf. Ch. 13.7 and recall Jim's patent on videophonic Tableaux (p. 64)). The combined image of a death, an ongoing phonecall, and Marathe's mother's crying resonates with a powerful image from the first segment of the first episode of *Twin Peaks*.

Chapter 25.2, Section 102, Pages 491-503
Note 208, Page 1034
Winter 1963

The previous section's "Marathe committed all this to his memories" hands off to "I remember" in this section. The previous section's reference to Jim's technical achievements hands off in this section to Jim's Y.T.M.P. (2003) first-person narrative of a then 40-year old event that marks the first inspiration for those achievements. These events were also the subject of Jim's film, *Valuable Coupon Has Been Removed* (pp. 990-1). Note the reference to Sperber directly beneath the title of this film in n. 24.c. Jim's memoir was published in a Y.T.M.P. text on annular fusion edited by Sperber (n. 208). In addition to this memoir, there is also an "interview with Incandenza [that] was posthumously included in a book on the genesis of annulation" (p. 65). Three years have passed since the events of Ch. 15.1, and 13-year old Jim (cf. "Son, you're ten," p. 159) has moved with his family from Tucson AZ to Sepulveda CA.

After making a "tomato juice beverage," Sr. solicits Jim's help for a task in the bedroom, which is "very bright" and "the decor of which was white and blue and powder-blue." Jim's mother smokes and looks out the window (like Tavis before E.T.A. drills). Sr. has stripped the bed to look for the sources of its squeaks (like the A.F.R. makes). Jim often holds Sr.'s drink for him until he needs it (like Mario does for Jim). Sr. says the bed has areas that "gibber and squeak" (like the sheeted dead "a little ere the mightiest Julius fell" according to Horatio's speech just before King Hamlet's ghost appears, *Hamlet* I.i.117-9) "until we both feel as if we're being eaten by rats" (like Winston Smith's greatest fear in 1984). Sr. says that Jim needs to help him remove the mattress and box spring in order to expose the frame and find the bolts that are making the squeaks.

Sr. "was the first of two actors to portray the Man from Glad" (cf. the "alcoholic sandwich-bag salesman" of *Pre-Nuptial Agreement of Heaven and Hell* and the "sandwich-bag conglomerate" of *Low-Temperature Civics*; pp. 988, 991), a job he held for "two years" (1962-1964, since the Man from Glad originated in 1962; n. 114). As Sr. was just home from work during this task, he still wore a "rigid white professional wig" and "vaguely medical uniform of all white" (like a ghost?). Jim creates a "circular receptacle" for Sr.'s drink in the "deep-pile" "royal blue" carpet so they can begin the task of moving the mattress and box spring into the hall. Jim makes observations about this task relating to geometry and physics. Jim's "legs were trembling under the mattress's canted weight" (cf. Lyle's advice about weight). Sr.'s "old competitive-tennis injury," recounted in Ch. 15.1, still bothers him. Jim wears a bow tie (p. 496) as he did three years ago (p. 163).

After moving the mattress into the hall, Sr. darts "into the kitchen at the other end of the hall for a very brief errand" before moving the box spring out into the hall. While Sr. considers the frame for "a long silent interval," Jim observes how "the sun rose and crossed and fell outside the window, the room's daylight becoming staler and staler." Sr. makes pointed comments to Jim's mother about the dust on the frame and on the carpet under the bed and about the smell, before looking for potentially squeaky bolts on a frame that "moved noiselessly on its casters' submerged wheels."

After Jim's mother goes for a vacuum cleaner, "possible" bolts are discovered. Leaning over the frame, Sr. throws up into the dust. Jim notes, "It was not too uncommon for my father to be taken ill shortly after coming home from work to relax." Jim doubted that any of the "bolts were producing the sounds that reminded my father of rodents." Sr. then pitches forward into the dust, breaking the frame. Jim makes precise observations of his father and of the frame. Jim then helps his mother get the vacuum cleaner by the mattress and box spring in the hall, and goes to his room as she begins vacuuming because "the sound of vacuuming has always frightened me in the same irrational way it seemed a bed's squeak frightened my father."

As Jim dives onto his bed, he knocks over a lamp that hits the brass knob on the door to his closet. When the knob hits the wooden floor, Jim notices "two perfectly circular motions on two distinct axes." As the knob rolls on its own circumference, it traces the circumference of another circle on the floor, the center of which is marked by the hex bolt on the end of the knob. Making mathematical observations about this occurrence and noting its similarity to trying "to turn somersaults with one hand nailed to the floor," Jim "first became interested in the possibilities of annulation."

PLOT AND CHARACTER: Jim, AA&R, Tech
THEME: Memory, His/Father, Recur, Waste

Jim's memory of his dysfunctional family is described in unemotional prose dominated by geometry (circles, triangles, angles, rectangles, a cycloid) from a distance of 40 years and in a way that probably didn't make him question his own alcoholism. A possible indicator of a sexual disconnection between Jim's parents is the fact that Jim "didn't think [he]'d ever heard their bed squeak before." Jim's father on p. 500 is hunched, ill, and pitched forward (reminiscent of his fall on the court in 1933, p. 168). As for Julius Caesar and for victims of the A.F.R., a squeak is an omen for Jim's father's fall. The brushed steel of the cube lamp squeaks terribly, and the vacuum shrieks. Other recurring ominous omens are odors, waste, stillness, and light. Jim's "father's mood surrounded him like a field and affected any room he occupied, like an odor or a certain cast to the light." The dust had a "faint odor, sour and fungal" and looked like it had "taken root and grown on [the carpet] the way a mold will take root and cover an expanse of spoiled food." While Jim's "father seemed frozen in place," Jim observed how "the sun rose and crossed and fell outside the window, the room's daylight becoming staler and staler." When Jim knocks over his "high-intensity" lamp, it causes him to become interested in annulation which leads him to holography which may be the cause of *Infinite Jest*'s appeal (cf. previous section).

Jim's mother looks out her window as if from a cage. The bedroom features blue decor, a blue pillowcase, and royal blue carpet. Jim has an indigo comforter. Jim remembers the mattress moving "like the crest of a breaking wave." Over the bed frame, Jim's father moved like "a ship in high seas." The Man from Glad is the disguise that makes possible Jim's father's last career and was created by the same company that will sponsor the "very last year" (n. 114) of Subsidized Time.

Chapter 25.3, Section 103, Pages 503-507
9 November Y.D.A.U.

On the Monday night after an Interdependence Day picnic, "Ennet House staffer Johnette Foltz took Ken Erdedy and Kate Gompert along with her to this one NA Beginners' Meeting where the focus was always marijuana." Foltz "wanted Erdedy and Gompert to see how completely nonunique and unalone they were in terms of the Substance that had brought them both down" (cf. Chs. 2

and 10.1). The people at this Narcotics Anonymous meeting "took turns concurring on the hideous psychic fallout they'd all endured both in active marijuana-dependency and then in marijuana-detox," examples of which are provided on pp. 503-4.

When, after the meeting, everyone began hugging each other (cf. people trying to "hug on" Gately, p. 444), "Erdedy—who'd never particularly liked hugging—moved way back from the throng" and stood by himself. When "a tall heavy Afro-American fellow" attempts to hug Erdedy, he demurs, stating that he doesn't "particularly like to hug." It turns out the fellow is Roy Tony, former scourge of Clenette's neighborhood (Ch. 5.2) and Brighton Projects dealer (Ch. 12.2), who proceeds to take Erdedy to task for not hugging him: "And now you go and disres*pect* me in front of my whole clean and sober *set* just when I gone risk sharing my vulnera*bil*ity and dis*com*fort with you?" Roy Tony then threatens Erdedy, prompting a hug of such "vigor" that "it looked like Erdedy was trying to climb him."

PLOT AND CHARACTER: Ennet, AA&R
THEME: Non-Action, Isolation, Cycles, Recur

Symptoms of marijuana dependency include paralytic stasis (like Hal at Eschaton, "paralyzed with absorption"; pp. 335, 340), nightmares (which Hal also is having), and social isolation (cf. Erdedy at home in Ch. 2 and Hal in the Pump Room in Ch. 7.1). Although Foltz is trying to show the residents that they are "unalone," Erdedy tries to isolate himself from the "indiscriminate hugging" and causes Roy Tony to stand "frozen" for a moment. The chairs at the NA meeting are arranged in a "huge circle"; everybody holds hands "in a circle"; and Roy Tony's hair is in a "vertical cylinder." Erdedy cracks his knuckles (p. 504) like Sr. in the previous section (p. 494).

Chapter 25.4, Section 104, Pages 507-508
1 May Y.D.A.U.

Marathe and Steeply's conversation continues from Ch. 25.1. Steeply speaks of an "idiot-child intern" who "yielded to temptation" to watch the Entertainment, which caused the loss of the intern's supervisor, who "tried to go in after him and pull him out." This was Hank Hoyne, an "American adult of exemplary self-control and discretion," as opposed to the intern, "the sort of undisciplined selfish child you like to talk about, Rémy." Hoyne now begs to see the Entertainment, his "eyes wobbling around like some drug-addicted newborn."

As the "legs of the constellation Perseus were amputated by the earth's horizon," Steeply asks the legless Marathe if he ever thinks of what it would be like to watch the Entertainment. Marathe says, "We find its efficacy tempting. You and we are tempted in different ways." Marathe's chair "gave small squeaks when he shifted his weight upon it." Steeply says that Hank is in an "Inner world. Lost to us. You look in his eyes and there's nothing you can recognize in them." His eyes are "Empty of intent." Marathe says, "Us, of Québec's cause, we have never felt this temptation for the Entertainment, or knowing. But we respect its power. Thus, we do not fool crazily about."

PLOT AND CHARACTER: Samizdat, U.S.O.U.S., A.F.R.
THEME: Inf/Reg, Recur

Steeply refers to the "idiot-child intern" as "the sort of undisciplined selfish child you like to talk about, Rémy." Watching the Entertainment has regressed Hoyne to a state in which his "eyes wobbl[e] around like some drug-addicted newborn." There's "nothing you can recognize" in his eyes. This diminishment resonates with the fact that "the stars' light had paled" during Marathe and Steeply's all-night conversation. Hoyne lives in an inner world that "has collapsed into one small bright point," which resonates with the focused attention of tennis players, addicts, and spies. Describing constellations, the narrator references four mythological figures: Perseus, Pollux, Castor, and Hercules, whose "head was square" like Gately's.

Chapter 25.5, Section 105, Pages 508-527
Notes 209-221, Pages 1034-1036
10 November Y.D.A.U.

The day after the drills described in Ch. 24.3, Axford, Pemulis, Ann Kittenplan, and Hal are in the Headmaster's waiting room, presumably for "fallout from Sunday's horrendous Eschaton fiasco" (Ch. 22.1). Throughout the events of this section, Hal catalogues things that are blue. As Pemulis bobs in his chair, it produces "a kind of rapid rodential squeaking that [gives Hal] the howling fantods." The carpet in the waiting room has been "vacuumed against the grain." Recall that in 1963 (Ch. 25.2), Jim noticed the "white and blue and powder-blue" (p. 491) decor of his parents' bedroom; Jim's father was obsessed with a rodential squeak; and Jim's mother used a vacuum. Hal has just had a tooth removed by his dentist, Dr. Zegarelli (recall references to pain in Hal's tooth at Eschaton (p. 329) and in his tooth and ankle at the next day's drills (cf. Ch. 24.3 commentary)), and "he's drooling without being able to feel or stop it." Presumably this is a reaction to novacaine, but note that drooling is a symptom of marijuana withdrawal (p. 504). Ten-year-old Hal had just come from Dr. Zegarelli's office when he had the "professional conversation" with Jim, but at that time Hal had "low salivary output" (p. 27).

Avril, who serves as "E.T.A.'s Dean of Academic Affairs and Dean of Females," has a doorless office (Avril's "feelings about enclosure are well known") next to Tavis's office. She is conducting one of E.T.A.'s periodic "distaff community meeting[s] with all female players judged naïve and moppetish enough to be potential diddlees." Today's meeting includes seven-year-old Tina Echt and is unique because "diddle-checks" are usually conducted by E.T.A. psychologist, Dr. Dolores Rusk. Although Hal is "unaware of any particular reason for being uncomfortable around her," he "avoids ever mentioning Rusk's name." Also, Hal is aware that Pemulis "loathes Rusk" (Pemulis once "hooked a Delco battery up to the inside brass knob of her locked office door," cf. n. 129) and that Pemulis's "deepest dread is of academic or disciplinary expulsion and ejection" (n. 211). Tavis's administrative assistant, Lateral Alice Moore (a former airborne traffic reporter who, ever since a collision of two helicopters and "the cataclysmic fall to the rush hour's Jamaica Way six-laner below," can only move side to side—Joelle thinks of this accident on p. 238), responds to "powder-blue" "invitations to next week's WhataBurger Invitational" (the WhataBurger occurs over Thanksgiving weekend and is actually two-and-a-half weeks away, cf. Orin's citation of dates for the Y.D.A.U. Invitational on p. 1009; in Ch. 1 Hal is playing in the Y.G. Invitational), an event for which Pemulis needs to make the cut. Axford is "[s]inistral, his right hand missing digits from a fireworks accident three Interdependence Days past" (cf. p. 341).

Hal's "left ankle gives a sick squeak when he flexes it," and "his face feels like something far away that means him harm and is coming gradually closer." In the 48 hours since the Eschaton debacle (recall that Avril needed time "to figure out how upperclass heads" could roll "without those heads including that of Hal," n. 147), it "hadn't even occurred" to Hal to talk to either Tavis or Avril. In fact, Hal rarely thinks "about members of his immediate family as standing in relation to himself. It's a possible reason Hal avoids Dr. Dolores Rusk, who always wants to probe him on issues of space and self-definition" (other possible reasons are Rusk's role in the events after Jim's death (p. 252) and Hal's "curious inability to request aid" (n. 213)).

Charles Tavis is referenced in this section as Hal's "maternal half-uncle" (p. 516), "mother's adoptive brother" (p. 519), and "maternal uncle" (pp. 517, 520). In his former career as a civil engineer, Tavis specialized in "the accommodation of stress through patterened dispersal." "Mario's way of looking at it is that Tavis is very open and expansive and wordy, but so clearly uses these qualities as a kind of protective shield that it betrays a frightened vulnerability almost impossible not to feel for." As a child, Avril noticed that when Tavis was around a group of kids he would "lurk around creepily on the fringe, listening" (like Erdedy at the NA meeting, pp. 503-4). Tavis's smallness "resembles the smallness of something that's farther away from you than it wants to be, plus is receding." Tavis is described as "seeming to recede even as he bears down." "E.T.A.'s like to postulate that the mirrors [with "Objects In Mirror Are Closer Than They Appear" written on them—the source of Jim's "first unsettling entrepreneurial payday" (cf. p. 64)] had been inspired by the always foreshortened Charles Tavis" (n. 218).

While waiting, Hal wants "very much to go to the Pump Room and then to brush vigorously with his portable collapsible Oral-B" (a ritual first described in Ch. 7.1). Hal recalls that the last time he was "officially summoned" to the waiting room was in late August (after which he went to the Pump Room). Tavis had wanted Hal "to take temporary charge of a nine-year-old kid coming in from somewhere called Philo IL [home of Wallace, cf. Ch. 24.3 commentary], who was allegedly blind [Orin mentions this kid on p. 246]," and whose other unique qualities are described on p. 518. Due to a crisis, the kid "wasn't matriculating now until the Spring term." On that day in August, Tavis was "doing a late-day Intake interview" on Tina Echt in which he spoke metaphorically of "the court as a mirror" and of how E.T.A. "will take apart your skull very gently and reconstruct a skull for you." Misunderstanding these metaphors, seven-year-old Tina cries, which prompts Tavis to offer "a totally unthreatening lap" in the way of comfort. "Tavis's voice had assumed that stressed character of issuing from the end of a long corridor."

After a quick exchange with Ortho Stice on that day in August, Hal next encountered his mother Avril, who was wearing a "blue cotton" dress and "had this way of establishing herself in the *exact center* of any room she was in." "When Avril entered a room any sort of pacing reduced to orbiting, and Hal's pacing became vaguely circular around the waiting room's perimeter" (cf. the kids around the desert bonfire and the knob around its hexbolt; pp. 489, 502). Like Steeply and Jim's mother, Avril smokes. Since Hal is hungry, Avril insists (over Hal's objections) that Hal take an apple that he knows is "all you're going to eat between 12 and 23." "Orin and Hal's term for this routine is Politeness Roulette. This Moms-thing that makes you hate yourself for telling her the truth about any kind of problem because of what the consequences will be for her." Orin also said Avril "went around with her feelings out in front of her . . . and a Glock 9 mm. to the feelings' temple" (analogous to Clipperton). "Hal despised the way he always reacted, taking the apple, pretending to pretend his reluctance to eat her supper was a pretense" (phrasing analogous to a description of Marathe's convoluted loyalties in the next section). The apple "stimulated a torrent of saliva." When Avril invites Hal to have dinner later, he pretends that he has plans (he lies) so that he can "go get high in secret."

"The thing that's keeping things so tensely quiet" in the waiting room three months later on 10 November is that "there are historically at least two Charles Tavises"; and "if Tavis suddenly gets very quiet and very still," it is a "danger-sign" that he is "not to be fucked with." If this happens, there is a "depth-perspective skewing" because Tavis no longer seems to recede, but instead "seems, perspectively, to grow [and] to rush in at you, dopplering in at a whisper."

After the students are ushered into Tavis's blue-and-black-shag-carpeted office by Lateral Alice Moore, Clenette (narrator of Ch. 5.2)—"pretty-eyed and so black she's got a bluish cast"—exits. She is "one of the nine-month temps from down the hill" (either she or Didi N. was at drills yesterday, p. 457) and has emptied "Tavis's personal brass wastebaskets into her big cart." Also in the room are Dr. Dolores Rusk; Tavis, "who's sitting pulsing with swollen proximity" and later seems "direly to rise from his chair without getting up"; Otis P. Lord, "the Hitachi monitor still over his head [cf. p. 456] like the sallet of some grotesque high-tech knight"; and "the scrubbed young button-nosed urologist in [a blue] O.N.A.N.T.A. blazer, severely underdue at E.T.A." (cf. p. 151).

PLOT AND CHARACTER: E.T.A., Hal, Avril, AA&R
THEME: Recur, Fear/Obsess, Cycles, His/Father, Memory

E.T.A. is a haven for children who are gifted tennis players (some of whom are extremely young) and seeks to protect those players from adults who would abuse them sexually and from the abuse they can do to themselves with drugs. At her Intake interview, Tavis speaks to "pint-sized Tina Echt, just seven but a true cannibal off the backhand side"—and who wore "a plastic Mr. Bouncety-Bounce no-pierce earring"—of players "providing entertainment, engaging people's attention. As a high-velocity object people can project themselves onto, forgetting their own limitations in the face of the nearly limitless potential someone as young as yourself represents." Tavis offers Echt an unthreatening lap, and three months later she participates in one of E.T.A.'s regular "[a]dministrative diddle-checks." The allegedly blind kid with cranium-issues, who is slated to matriculate at E.T.A. in the Spring, is only nine and had been "one of the infantile natives of Ticonderoga NNY evacuated too late, [but was] still an extremely solid player."

Hal's attention to the color blue in this section resonates with the recurrence of the color blue throughout the novel. (The color blue recurs even more overtly throughout Mark Z. Danielewski's 2000 novel *House of Leaves*; in some printings of the novel, the ink used for the word "house" is always blue.) "Hal loathes the sky-and-cloud wallpaper" in the offices of both Tavis and Dr. Zegarelli ("fluffy cumuli arrayed patternlessly against an overenhancedly blue sky," cf. the U.S. covers of both the hardcover and paperback versions of *Infinite Jest*), "incredibly disorienting wallpaper" that makes Hal "feel high-altitude and disoriented and sometimes plummeting" (cf. Orin's experiencing a fear of heights, p. 66). Several recurring concepts are associated with Dr. Zegarelli's office: it exhibits a smell that is "the olfactory equivalent of fluorescent light" (cf. Tavis's "phobic thing about overhead lighting"); after a "cold stab" and "slow radial freeze," Hal felt "his face ballooning to become one of the frozen cumuli against the aftershave-blue of the dental wallpaper's sky" (separation of head and body); Zegarelli wears a "mint-blue mask"; and "his overhead light's corona" gives him a "medieval halo." Marlon Bain has a "corona of sweat" in one of the many still photos ("a lot" taken by Mario) "surrounded by locationless clouds and sky" in Tavis's office (n. 209, a thorough note referencing many current and former E.T.A. players that recalls the thorough note about hats worn by E.T.A. players at the I.-Day gala (n. 148)). There is a "halo-shaped metal brace" supporting the blind kid's head. Otis P. Lord's monitor is held "very carefully in place" by an E.T.A. nurse. Tina Echt at first fears E.T.A. will break open her head, and Hal wonders whether Echt will "lose her mind." "Avril has vividly white hair—as of the last few months before Himself's *felo de se*—that looks like it never went through the gray stage" (cf. incestuous Leland Palmer's hair turning white overnight in *Twin Peaks* and "you have committed incest" followed a page later by "an experience that will whiten your hair overnight" in the next-to-last paragraph of the second part of Faulkner's *The Sound and the Fury*). The pictures on Tavis's walls are "not in a straight line; they're more like chaotically placed" (analogous to the sections of the novel).

This section features many recurrences dealing with fears or obsessions. The sound of Lateral Alice's printer is like "supposedly unrippable fabric getting ripped, over and over, a dental and life-denying sound." Tavis has an "audible smile" because of "the thing with [his] teeth, about which maybe the less said the better." Is there some connection between Tavis's teeth and Mario's teeth (described in n. 119)? The doors of Tavis's office have "a jaw-like quality" (cf. "Tavis's office's maw"); whereas Avril, "whose feelings of enclosure are well known [and who taps her incisors with a blue pen], has no door on her office." "She has little sense of spatial privacy or boundary, having been so much alone so much when a child." After visiting the dentist, "the left side of [Hal's] face still feels big and dead." Although "not as drastic as a stroke-victim's face" (like, say, Pat's), "the two sides of [Tavis's] face didn't quite go together." "[O]ne half of Kittenplan's face" spasms at the "rodential squeaking" of Pemulis's chair. Hal's "left ankle gives a sick squeak when he flexes it." "Tavis's desk drawers have squeaky casters"; his "big seagrass chair" has a "sumptuous squeak"; and he has a "squeaky right Nunn Bush." The section references a "pet tarantula," a "cornered rat," "Tavis's window-lit shadow," and the urologist "seated back in the shadow." Given their obsessive personalities and habits, Tavis and Avril are "the Dynamic Duo of compulsion" (cf. p. 519).

Hal orbits his mother, "The Black Hole of Human Attention." They enact the ritual of their vocabulary game and play a game of "Politeness Roulette" over Avril's apple. Tavis bends his giant paperclip into "a sort of cardioid or else sloppy circle." There are "at least two Charles Tavises"; one that recedes and one that "seems, perspectively, to grow [and] to rush in at you, dopplering in at a whisper," analogous to an orbit. Hal's "face feels like something far away that means him harm and is coming gradually closer."

Hal experiences an "odd blankness about his family." When asked about family members other than Mario, sometimes his "mind will go utterly blank . . . as if the names were words on the tip of his tongue." Tina Echt says that she wants her Mommy and Daddy (absent parents) just before Hal is tempted away from the memory of his absent father by Avril's offer of an apple. Does this apple generate "tremendous amounts of saliva," or is the three-month old memory influenced by his current inability to stop drooling?

Chapter 25.6, Section 106, Pages 528-530
Notes 222-223, Pages 1036-1037
1 May Y.D.A.U.

Marathe and Steeply's conversation continues from Ch. 25.4. To provide examples of the universality of Entertainment-level temptation (as opposed to the temptation being simply a U.S.A. phenomenon), Steeply cites two myths. First, he cites an Oriental myth about a woman ("a mythic figure") who is "too exotic and intriguing or seductive to resist," even for "the young Oriental men happening upon her by some body of water" who know of the myth.

During this, Marathe thinks of both his father and his wife. "Marathe had reached the internal choice that he loved his skull-deprived and heart-defective wife Gertraud Marathe more than he loved the Separatist and anti-O.N.A.N. cause of the nation of Québec, making Marathe no better than M. Rodney 'the God' Tine [cf. pp. 106-7]. If Fortier knew of this, he would understandably drive a railroad spike through Gertraude's boneless right eye, killing her and Marathe both."

Steeply's "superiors did not know that Fortier knew that Steeply knew he (Fortier) knew Marathe was here" (cf. the phrasing of Hal's intentions toward Avril's apple, p. 523). In other words, Steeply's U.S.O.U.S. superiors believe Marathe is doubling; the A.F.R. believes Marathe is tripling; and Steeply, "very few" other U.S.O.U.S. operatives, and Marathe know that Marathe is quadrupling (cf. nn. 40-42). Marathe and Steeply danced around the possibility of Marathe's quintupling earlier (p. 94). "Steeply had volunteered to be liaison with Marathe's betrayal, despite language," meaning that Marathe's Québecois French "does not admit of easy coeval expression in English" (n. 222), which is the language the men are using. Although "Steeply's Québecois [is] better than Marathe's

English" (p. 89), Marathe still gets irritated with Steeply's pronunciation and syntax on the rare occasions Steeply uses Québecois French, but "rarely yielded to the temptation" to correct him.

However, Marathe corrects Steeply now by saying *"L'Odalisque de Sainte Thérèse"* when Steeply next cites "your own francophone myth of your Odalisk of Theresa," who is "so beautiful that mortal Québecois eyes can't take it. Whoever looks at her turns into a diamond or gem." Marathe: "In most versions an opal." Steeply likens her to a "Medusa in reverse . . . . Or like a combination of Medusa and Circe, your Odalisk." The narrator of n. 223 refers to Jim's *"The Medusa v. the Odalisque"* and says that it's "anybody's guess" "what the hell 'ALGOL' is" (presumably referring to Steeply's use of the acronym on p. 491) and that the acronym "isn't in any dictionaries or on-line lexical sources in the 2nd or 3rd IL/IN Grid." Whatever is meant by this, it seems to connect the narrator of n. 223 to Illinois/Indiana. Jim's *Pre-Nuptial Agreement of Heaven and Hell* (which features "an alcoholic sandwich-bag salesman obsessed with Bernini's 'The Ecstasy of St. Theresa,'" p. 988) had "a major impact" on Joelle (p. 297), who as Madame Psychosis is *Infinite Jest*'s irresistible beauty. Recall the associations of Bernini's work with sensual ecstasy from the perspectives of Joelle (p. 235) and of the sister of the sexually abused catatonic (p. 373-4), to whose "description of the statue's orgasm" Joelle reacts (p. 376).

Marathe posits that beauty and pleasure were not fatal temptations for the Greeks, who feared ugliness rather than beauty, and that "irony and contempt for selves . . . are part of your U.S.A. type's temptation." Steeply: "Whereas your type's a man of only actions, ends." Marathe realizes that his recurrent "pretended sniffing was for the purpose of alerting Steeply to the breaking of a silence" and says, "Soon I must leave."

PLOT AND CHARACTER: Samizdat, U.S.O.U.S., A.F.R.
THEME: Loss, Secrets, Cycles, Non-Action, Recur

The appeal of the Oriental mythic figure "seems to include a felt lack. A perceived deprivation." Marathe is keenly aware of the loss of his father and of his legs. Marathe and Steeply live in an environment of mistrust and secrecy. Steeply's not telling the U.S.O.U.S. about Fortier's knowledge "satisfied some U.S.A. desire to hold some small thing back from one's superiors, Marathe felt. Unless Steeply was deceiving Marathe about this. Marathe didn't know." "But Marathe knew quite well that Steeply was right-handed," even though Steeply held his cigarette in his left hand. Most of the desert life "remained hidden." "A hidden bird twittered." The "real Marathe" (as opposed to the hidden Marathe who usually speaks to Steeply?) says, "A false dawn."

The effects of dawn (an indicator of the cycle of the Earth's rotation) occur in "imperceptible degrees" and generate a quality of stillness in Marathe and Steeply's environment. "The softest light imaginable seeped into the desert . . . just below the ring of night." "In the American sky, the stars flutter[ed] like banked flames above a low-resolution seepage of glow. But [there was] none of the pinkening of genuine dawn." "The desert floor was brightening by imperceptible degrees." "No sun's top arc was appearing, and Marathe could cast no shadow yet on the shale behind them." "The whole imperceptibly lightening scene of the vistas had a stillness about it that suggested photography." "The distant construction site's payloaders were urine-colored and appeared frozen in the middle of various actions." Marathe and Steeply's conversation has continued until dawn, and they are "STILL" on the outcropping (cf. other recent headers in this thread: pp. 470, 489) going round and round. It is their "sixth or seventh" meeting. Those who succumb to the mythical Oriental woman are also still, "paralyzed with stasis by this intimate act," a "passive temptation."

Mythological references often recur in the Marathe-Steeply sections. In addition to the Oriental and francophone myths in this section, three other irresistible female figures are referenced: Venus, Medusa, and Circe. In the last section, Avril "smoked with her smoking-arm up and elbow resting in the crook of the other arm" (p. 522), as does Steeply here. Steeply also prods dust with the toe of his shoe, like Jim Sr. (p. 498).

Chapter 25.7, Section 107, Pages 531-538
11 November Y.D.A.U., 0450h.

Joelle could be added to the list of irresistible, mythological women discussed by Marathe and Steeply in the previous section by virtue of what happens to people who see *Infinite Jest*. In this section, Joelle's conversation with Gately is uninterrupted by narrative comment. All of Gately's documented thoughts about or interaction with Joelle before now occurred on 8 November (pp. 475, 364-6, 370, 376). Joelle either has the temporal disorientation of a recovering addict or has been up all night and still considers it to be the evening of 10 November, because she refers to "that Waltham NA thing" that Gompert and Erdedy attended (on Monday 9 November, pp. 503-4) as happening "last night." At 0450h., Gately has been up all night (p. 536) and is "getting ready to go mop shit with a shoe freak" (p. 538); he will presumably be late given that "he has to be on the Inbound Green Line by 0430h." (p. 434).

Gately tells a story about how one of the guys he was "crewing around with" was shot in a bar by someone who was "made small in front of his girl" by Gately's guy. In an attempt to keep the guy alive, Gately and crew, instead of taking him to a hospital, "walked him around in circles like some kind of O.D." The guy was dead when the ambulance arrived. Joelle relates a story with "an AA point" told by fellow resident McDade about a woman who "had this condition where each leg was shorter than the other." Then Gately asks about Joelle's veil, and she tells him that she has "almost four years in" the Union of the Hideously and Improbably Deformed (cf. that Joelle played a veiled nun in *The Night Wears a Sombrero* and "unveiled for" *Infinite Jest* more than four years ago; pp. 992, 228). U.H.I.D. is an organization about which Gately has asked Pat and Tommy S. (cf. "Tommy S. or F.," p. 364). Joelle—a sophomore (p. 289) at B.U. in 2001-Y.W. and the recipient of an M.A. degree in YUSHITYU (p. 234, n. 81)—would have been in the M.I.T. doctoral program (where she met Molly Notkin, p. 220) just before she joined U.H.I.D. four years ago (November Y.P.W.): "You're at a graduate wine-tasting party and improbably deformed and you're the object of stares" (presumably because you are unveiled).

Joelle: U.H.I.D. members "don the veil" to "declare openly that they wish to hide from all sight." No "mortal eye will see" the veil withdrawn. Gately: To join AA is to "finally step out of the cage and quit hiding." Joelle: Before joining U.H.I.D. you "feign acceptance of your deformity. You take your desire to hide and conceal it under a mask of acceptance," a "smile so wide it hurts." "In other words, you hide your hiding. . . . You're ashamed of your uncontrolled craving for shadow. U.H.I.D.'s First Step is admission of powerlessness over the need to hide. U.H.I.D. allows members to be . . . completely up-front and unashamed about the fact that how we appear to others affects us deeply, about the fact that we want to be shielded from all sight. U.H.I.D. supports us in our decision to hide openly." Gately says "Your voice gets different when you talk about this shit" and tells Joelle that "when you were talking about the veil you didn't sound like you to me." Recall that Joelle now has "no accent except under stress" (p. 234).

Joelle's sense is that Gately thinks (but she doesn't think) he's not bright, which "is fine, U.H.I.D. would say," but "the cycle becomes annular and insidious if you begin to be *ashamed* of the fact that being unbright shames you." Gately says that he "got kicked off of football my tenth-grade year for flunking English." Joelle perks up at the mention of football and says she "used to twirl a baton at halftimes. I went to a special camp six summers running" (but cf. that she "declined a sixth summer," p. 297). After Gately asks "Can I ask how you're deformed?" and Joelle mentions the NA meeting, there are mutual accusations of changing the topic or hiding. Joelle says, "I've already just completely opened up about my shame and my inability to be open and straightforward about this. You're exposing something I've already held up to view. It's your shame about being ashamed of what you're afraid might be seen as a lack of brightness that's getting to stay buried under this dead horse of my deformity that you're trying to whip."

When Gately explains that he is simply asking for "a straight-on Yes or No" to his question and stops short of complimenting

Joelle's "unhidden skin," Joelle says, "I'm so beautiful I drive anybody with a nervous system out of their fucking mind. Once they've seen me they can't think of anything else and don't want to look at anything else and stop carrying out normal responsibilities." (Is this why Joelle's stepmother is "in the Locked Ward" (p. 239)? Recall the range of responses to seeing Joelle without her veil: Orin and other men were infatuated with her beauty; the "wine-tasting crowd" tried not "to wince or stare" at her "deformity"; and viewers of *Infinite Jest* are paralyzed with stasis.) Gately thinks Joelle is being sarcastic and treating him like he is stupid. Joelle says, "I am deformed with beauty."

PLOT AND CHARACTER: Joelle, Gately, Ennet, AA&R
THEME: Loss, Secrets, Cycles, Recur

Gately wonders whether Joelle is "missing something" behind her veil, and Joelle thinks Gately fears being perceived to have "a lack of brightness." Joelle speaks of an "uncontrolled craving for shadow" and wanting to "hide your hiding," of how "the cycle ["the shame-circle"] becomes annular and insidious." Gately and crew walked their guy "around in circles." Gately's guy was shot because he made someone "small in front of his girl." Marathe is betraying his country for his wife. Gately's round-and-round with Joelle recalls Marathe's round-and-round with Steeply, and "hide your hiding" recalls Marathe's nested loyalties and Steeply's disguise. Gately gets irritated with Joelle for thinking she knows everything he's going to say; Marathe gets irritated with Steeply for putting words in his mouth.

Recurring images and ideas crop up in Joelle's phrases. She speaks of a "shithouse rat," a "smile so wide it hurts" worn as "a mask of acceptance," and a "deep slavering need." She speaks of "driving anybody with a nervous system out of their fucking mind," which recalls "the twirler who owned [Orin's] CNS" (p. 292) and reference to CNS-rattler DMZ as Madame Psychosis (n. 8). Grammar enthusiast Joelle subtly substitutes "fewer words" for Gately's "less words" (p. 535). Gately references videophones (cf. Ch. 13.7). Wallace has drug-addict Gately ask drug-addict Joelle to "Just say No" in reference to a "drug-unrelated question."

Chapter 25: Cycles: Orbits, Annulation, Attraction, Repulsion

In this chapter, Marathe goes round and round with Steeply; Gately goes round and round with Joelle, to whom most men are attracted; Jim becomes "interested in the possiblities of annulation"; Erdedy repels Roy Tony's hug before Roy Tony's threat compels Erdedy's attraction; and Hal orbits his mother. In Ch. 25.1, "hologrammatical activity" may account for the appeal of the "*Annulateur*"'s Entertainment. In Ch. 25.2, Jim's interest is sparked by "two perfectly circular motions." At Ch. 25.3's NA meeting, people "held hands in a circle" and Erdedy's retreat attracts Roy Tony. In Ch. 25.4, the stars move through their nightly cycles as Hoyne's attraction to the Entertainment is lamented. Two Charles Tavises are described in Ch. 25.5: one who seems to recede even as he bears down and one who no longer seems to recede, but instead "seems, perspectively, to grow [and] to rush in at you, dopplering in at a whisper." Hal's "face feels like something far away that means him harm and is coming gradually closer." In Ch. 25.6, the cycle of the Earth's rotation causes the desert floor to brighten "by imperceptible degrees" with "the softest light imaginable . . . just below the ring of night." Marathe and Steeply discuss mythological women who attract and then paralyze, like Madame Psychosis in *Infinite Jest*. In Ch. 25.7, Gately describes walking a man "around in circles" until the man died. Joelle is so beautiful she is deformed. She attracts and repulses.

Chapter 26

Powerless: Compulsion, Secrecy, Ritual, The Cult of the Infant

Chapter 26.1, Section 108, Pages 538-547
Notes 224-227, Page 1037
11 November Y.D.A.U.

This chapter begins on the Wednesday that "Bruce Green and Amy J. separately both [miss] curfew" (and ends there, too; cf. p. 601) but then jumps back to document how Lenz "found his own dark way to deal with the well-known Rage and Powerlessness issues that beset the drug addict in his first few months of abstinence." Lenz is "hiding from both sides of the Justice System" (cf. p. 276), wears a "white toupee and moustache" (cf. p. 363) when he goes out, and "walks back to the house [solo] after meetings" (cf. p. 277). Lenz's "panoply of strange compulsive habits" was documented on p. 279.

In the weeks leading up to 11 November, Lenz had taken to walking "abroad in the urban night, unaccompanied and disguised" between getting out of meetings at 2130h. or 2200h. and arriving back at Ennet House before the 2330h. curfew. One night Lenz discovered that killing a rat with a chunk of concrete was a way of "resolving internal-type issues." He then progressed to using food to lure a cat into a trash bag and watching "the wide variety of changing shapes the bag would assume as the agitated cat got lower on air."

Lenz recalls what Doony Glynn—who has diverticulitis and "physique-type issues from a load of bricks falling on his head" (cf. Ch. 13.3)—said about the effects of "a hallucinogen he'd refer to only as 'The Madame'" that turned the blue sky into a "dead deep-water gray-green" grid like a viewer-screen that ran "the Time and Celsius Temp to like serious decimal points." Lenz thinks sirens "always sound like they're terribly achingly far away, and receding, calling to you across an expanding gap." Lenz keeps cocaine in "the hollowed-out cavity" of a book (published by another multiple-merger company, n. 224) and has secretly gotten high since becoming an Ennet House resident.

Lenz discovered he could take a more active role in his issue-resolution process by swinging the cats in the trash bags against signs or poles. The next step was to resolve issues "inside the yards and porches of the people that owned" the cats. After an incident in which he was chased by a cat he had set on fire, Lenz decided to begin wearing his knife and using squares of Gately's meatloaf to establish a dog's trust before getting behind the dog and cutting its throat. Lenz agrees with a statement he read in his book: "the more basically Powerless an individual feels, the more the likelihood for the propensity for violent acting-out."

After visualizing a drunk he passes "both cut and on fire," Lenz becomes "inactive with pets" for a few days. He begins to enjoy the company of Bruce Green (a "quiet kid," p. 276) on his walks back to Ennet, but soon becomes agitated that Green's regular company is keeping him from resuming his issue-resolution. The cats that "lurk around Ennet House" (like the "nameless cat" on p. 278) are too risky—given that "female residents are always formulating attachments to them"—as are Pat's dogs. One day he was able to take "a miniature bird that had fallen out of some nest" and "put it down the garbage disposal," but this left him "impotent and largely unresolved."

PLOT AND CHARACTER: Ennet, AA&R
THEME: Recur, Secrets, Isolation, Inf/Reg, Cycles, Fear/Obsess

This section includes references to sirens that recede; a feral hamster, rats, and "godawful twittering squeaks"; and DMZ ("The Madame"), which turned Doony's "empty-grid accurate sky" into a "digital timepiece" the color of deep water. Lenz has begun a secret, isolated, compulsive ritual to resolve his issues of powerlessness and fear. (The ritual of switching parked cars referenced on p. 545 will become important at the end of the chapter. Joelle spoke of "powerlessness over the need to hide" on p. 535 in the last chapter.) Lenz is "unaccompanied and disguised," is obsessed with being north and with time, and is still using cocaine, which causes the physical obstacle of "his mouth twisting and writhing." Lenz once got high in secret "in the forbidden #7" (cf. p. 197). Lenz tests his knife "by dry-shaving a little patch of his tan forearm, which he loves" and which Gately has noticed (p. 276). A fallen bird activated Orin's ominous imagination (pp. 44, 245); Lenz doesn't pause to consider whether his fallen bird might be an omen.

Chapter 26.2, Section 109, Page 548
unspecified

With a few exceptions, "none of the doors inside Ennet House have locks, for predictable reasons" (cf. Ennet's "doorless dining room," p. 274).

PLOT AND CHARACTER: Ennet
THEME: Boundaries

Ennet's no-locks policy recalls Avril, "whose feelings about enclosure are well known" and who "has no door on her office" (p. 510). Presumably the no-locks policy is intended to minimize hiding and secrecy (but cf. that Lenz is able to hide his cocaine in a book), but it also may contribute to feelings of powerlessness among Ennet residents.

Chapter 26.3, Section 110, Pages 548-549
Notes 228-229, Page 1037
early November Y.D.A.U.

Chief of the U.S. Office of Unspecified Services (another merged entity, n. 228), Rodney Tine—referenced in Marathe and Steeply's long April/May conversation and in Mario's puppet film, which will be screened on 8 November—"measures his penis every A.M." with "a special metric ruler" or with "a special telescoping travelling model of the ruler" (cf. his "telescoping weatherman's pointer," p. 403) and records those measurements in a "little leather notebook" (recall that Gately's former Navy M.P. "logged each beer he drank" in a notebook, p. 447). Tine is in Boston to address the national security implications of the "unwatchable underground Entertainment-cartridge."

The cartridge "had popped up in Berkeley NCA, in the home of a film-scholar and his male companion" and had affected seventeen more people before the power to the Berkeley home was killed (cf. the razzle Marathe spoke of in May, p. 489). There were also incidents in New Iberia LA, Tempe AZ, and Boston MA (the incident with the Near Eastern medical attaché in April), and "[t]hree members of the Academy of D.A.S. had received unlabelled copies in the mail." The "head of D.E.A. and the Chair of the Academy of Digital Arts and Sciences" are with Tine now and first came to the U.S.O.U.S. "two summers past" with concerns about the cartridge. (Recall what Molly Notkin's party guests will say on 7 November: "This ultimate cartridge-as-ecstatic-death rumor's been going around like a lazy toilet since Dishmaster" (three years ago) and "Duquette says he's lost contact with three colleagues. He said a good bit of Berkeley isn't answering their phone" (p. 233). Does a second razzle occur in Berkeley in November?) Although the "Tempe and New Iberia cartridges are in custody, vaulted" (cf. Steeply: "We have more than one," p. 489), the "Berkeley cartridge had vanished from an S.F.P.D. evidence room an electron-microscopy toss of which had revealed flannel fibers" (Canadian terrorists?). Presumably the Boston cartridge and the three D.A.S. cartridges are also safe in the hands of the U.S.O.U.S. Attempts to trace "the *samizdat*"—Tine's staff's name for the Entertainment—"place the likely dissemination-point someplace along the U.S. north border, with routing hubs in metro Boston/New Bedford and/or somewhere in the desert Southwest." ("InterLace's two hubs of manufacture and dissemination" are in Phoenix and Boston (p. 33). "Postal codes route the [medical attaché's] package through the desert Southwest," where the A.F.R. is building a "disseminatory Ops base" (pp. 90, 109).) The "possibility of Canadian involvement" and reports "of the thing popping up yet again in metro Boston" (the displays to be seen by Joelle on 7 November?) have brought Tine to Boston.

One of the "test-subjects, volunteers from the federal and military penal systems" (cf. Marathe and Steeply's discussion of subjects and volunteers, Ch. 24.5), was "able to report that the thing apparently opens with an engaging and high-quality cinematic shot of a veiled woman going through a large building's revolving doors and catching a glimpse of someone else in the revolving doors, somebody the sight of whom makes her veil billow." People who have watched the Entertainment are "now all in wards. Docile and continent but blank"; "no other activity or connection could hold their attention."

PLOT AND CHARACTER: U.S.O.U.S., Samizdat
THEME: Fear/Obsess, Secrets, Cycles, Inf/Reg, Recur

The D.E.A. as well as the Academy of Digital Arts and Sciences are with Tine, suggesting that the Entertainment is also being considered a drug by the U.S. government. Tine's penis measurements and associated record keeping are another example of obsessive and secretive routines (recall Tine is a "former O.C.D.-support-group-sponsor," n. 156). The revolving door suggests a cycle, and the people who have watched the Entertainment have regressed to a "deep reptile brain level." There are recurring images here of billowing (Joelle's veil) and of "standing on one foot and then the other."

Chapter 26.4, Section 111, Pages 550-553
9 November Y.D.A.U., 2100h.

This section occurs the night before Pemulis, Hal, Axford, and Kittenplan are called into Tavis's office (Ch. 25.5). Pemulis walks by Rusk's office and overhears her telling Stice that he is experiencing a "delusion of some special agency or control to compensate for some repressed wounded inner trauma having to do with absence of control." Recall that Stice consulted Lyle last night about the unexplained movement of his bed and was advised not to underestimate objects (Ch. 23.4). In response to Ortho's query about whether he is "*over*estimating objects," Rusk states that "there's a very young Ortho in there with some very real abandonment-issues who needs some nurturing and championing from the older Ortho."

Pemulis next enters the administrative reception area, where he can hear Tavis exercising on a StairBlaster in his office (cf. the StairMaster at HmH, p. 253). Pemulis notices that "Tavis's doorknob [has] no insulating rubber sheath" (cf. p. 512). He wears a belt that was "transferred" to him "during a Big Buddy tennis-as-game-of-chance exercise" (cf. pp. 116-7, 120). He enters Avril's "doorless" office to find her "two meters from [John] Wayne, facing him, doing near-splits" in "a little green-and-white cheerleader's outfit" and "pretending to blow [a] whistle." Wayne "wore a football helmet and light shoulderpads and a Russell athletic supporter and socks and shoes and nothing else. He was down in the classic three-point stance of U.S. football" and "growling." "Mrs. Inc seemed frozen in place," and there was "way less time passing in the office than there seemed to be." Pemulis says "Hoping for a second of your time" and "I predict this'll take about two minutes at most."

PLOT AND CHARACTER: E.T.A., Avril
THEME: Inf/Reg, Secrets, Time, Cycles

Rusk references Ortho's "absence of control" before promoting her infantilizing philosophy. Pemulis's irresistible "biting down" on the mint is a compulsion that immediately precedes his self-destructive compulsion to confront Avril and Wayne. It's possible that the meeting in the Headmaster's office the next day would not have been called if not for Pemulis's interruption of Avril and Wayne. Time seems to slow down upon Pemulis's entrance, and he makes statements related to time. Avril and Wayne are in costumes, participating in what is meant to be a secret ritual (although there is no door to Avril's office). Pemulis hears Tavis in the cycle of his exercise routine.

What is the "odd vehicular shape near the north wall's trophy case" (p. 551)? Could it be a wheelchair? Does Wayne's football attire and posture signify anything about Avril's relationship with Orin?

Chapter 26.5, Section 112, Pages 553-559
Notes 230-233, Pages 1037-1038
11 November Y.D.A.U., around 2200h.

The adventures of Lenz (in disguise) and Green continue from Ch. 26.1. Lenz likes Green, but it "kind of enrages Lenz to like somebody" because when you like somebody "it's like you drop something, you give up all your power over it: you have to stand there impotent waiting for it to hit the ground." Although Lenz would like to get back to his issue-resolution routine, he refrains from sending Green away for fear that Green will misinterpret his intentions. Conflicted, Lenz does cocaine "off the top of the toilet-tank" in a stall with a "lockable door" at a Wednesday night meeting, which he believes will help him send Green away but only makes him want to keep Green "right there with him, and to share . . . pretty much every experience and thought he's ever had" and gives him "hemispasm[s] of the mouth and right eye." The variety of effects that the hydrolysis of cocaine has had on Ennet residents, counselors, and staff is discussed in n. 232.

Lenz demonstrates akido in "slo-mo constituent movements" and discusses a "recurving nightmare about a clock with hands frozen eternally at 1830." He tells of a Halloween party in which a "woman with [a] lei of gull-heads and other persons in costumes had ingested hallucinogens and drank mescal and . . . performed circled rituals" around "a Concavity-refugee infant" of "normal-size and unferal . . . but totally without a skull." They were "worshipping the infant, or as they termed it simply *The Infant*, as if there were only One."

PLOT AND CHARACTER: Ennet, AA&R
THEME: Cycles, Secrets, Inf/Reg, Recur

Lenz is in a cycle of rage about liking Green and being powerless to send him away. Lenz wears a disguise and speaks of "persons in costumes" (one with a "necklace made of dead gulls") who "performed circled rituals" in worship of a "Concavity-refugee infant" "without a skull." Lenz "claims to remember some experiences which he says happened to him *in vitro*." Other ideas and images recurring in this section are toilets and dumpsters, "Crows in trees," "cries and screams" in the night, a frightening smile (Lenz's mother's laugh "had sounded like she was being eaten alive"), a "recurving" dream, slow-motion movements, and a frozen clock. Lenz's "phobic fear of time-pieces stems from his [abusive] stepfather."

Chapter 26.6, Section 113, Page 560
11 November Y.D.A.U., lunchtime

It is assumed that this section occurs on the day after the meeting in Tavis's office (Ch. 25.5)—the same day as Lenz's activities in the chapter—before the match Hal plays later today (Ch. 27). It is lunchtime. Hal is "lying on his bunk . . . with his hands laced over his chest," counting his breaths. He is visited by Troeltsch, Pemulis, and Wayne, who doesn't speak.

PLOT AND CHARACTER: E.T.A., Hal
THEME: Non-Action, Cycles

Hal is lying down (inactive) and uses primitive imagery (a gorging beast and his loyal pride) in declining lunch. Counting breaths could be a pre-match ritual, or perhaps Hal is worried about fallout from the meeting with Tavis or the significance of his upcoming match. If Hal decided to stop making visits to the Pump Room after the meeting in Tavis's office (at which the O.N.A.N.T.A. urologist was present), he could be in withdrawal from marijuana (cf. the "psychic fallout" of marijuana-dependency and -detox, pp. 503-4).

Chapter 26.7, Section 114, Pages 560-562
11 November Y.D.A.U., after 2200h.

The adventures of Lenz and Green continue from Ch. 26.5. Lenz continues to regale Green with his knowledge of cults, including Delawareans searching for "a perfect piece of digito-holographic porn"; "a suicidal Nuck cult" that "involved jumping in front of trains" (Marathe lost his legs to a train (p. 108), and Steeply digs at Marathe with a comment about "amputations for daring young train-cultists" (p. 473)); cultists who have ventured in search of "whole packs and herds of feral animals" in the "Concavity to the due northeast, descended reputedly from domestic pets" (cf. p. 93); and cults "existing around belief systems about the metaphysics of the Concavity and annular fusion and . . . radiation-affected fauna and overfertilization and verdant forests with periodic oasises of purported desert."

Infants "the size of prehistoric beasts [roam] the overfertilized east Concavity quadrants, leaving enormous scat-piles and keening for the abortive parents who'd left or lost them in the general geopolitical shuffle of mass migration" (cf. the Concavity Cabinet, pp. 403-4). The infants may have originated "from abortions hastily disposed of in barrels in ditches that got breached and mixed ghastly contents with other barrels that reanimated the abortive feti" (cf. p. 399). "Lenz shudders just at the thought of the raging Powerlessness he'd feel . . . wandering in circles" like the Rastafarian "Infant-cultists" who disappeared into the Concavity "seeking *The Infant* they called it, as if there were only One, and toting paraphernalia for performing a cultish ritual referred to in oblique tones only as *Propitiating The Infant*" (cf. "*propitiate* the divine spell," p. 243).

Lenz refers to himself once in this section as "yrstruly," which he probably picked up from fellow Ennet resident Emil Minty, who narrated Ch. 12.2 as "I" and "yrstruly." At the same time as the events of this section, Day is telling Gately that he sat next to "Emil M." at the meeting he just attended, where the speaker was "looking *right* at yours truly" (p. 1001). Like the narrator for Minty in Ch. 12.2, the narrator for Lenz in this section uses interesting misspellings like "Shrangi-la" and "kamasupra."

PLOT AND CHARACTER: Ennet, AA&R, O.N.A.N.
THEME: Fear/Obsess, Inf/Reg, Waste, Loss, Recur

Lenz lists the obsessions of a variety of cultists. This section features feral infants, perhaps born out of toxic waste, who leave "enormous scat-piles." Green almost steps in vomit. Feral infants in the Concavity—the focus of cultish rituals—keen for their parents and experience a sense of loss or isolation over a parent who does not come. The Infant-cultists are often lost in the Concavity. The "annulated Shawshine River feeds the Charles and tints it . . . blue." Lenz recalls "his stepfather's blue-vested gut."

Chapter 26.8, Section 115, Pages 563-565
11 November Y.D.A.U., before 2330h.

This section is comprised of five "SNIPPETS FROM THE INDIVIDUAL-RESIDENT-INFORMAL-INTERFACE MOMENTS OF D. W. GATELY," separated by a single line-space as in Ch 15.4. These interfaces occur on 11 November "UP TO ABOUT 2329H." See n. 90 for a sixth snippet, of an interface with Geoffrey Day.

Joelle talks again of football as she did earlier in the morning (Ch. 25.7) and mentions that her "mother's dead" (she thought of "her stepmother in the Locked Ward" four nights ago, p. 239) and that one of tonight's speakers seemed fatherly.

Chandler Foss is elected to notify Gately of a potential problem and brings Gately one of Morris Hanley's cookies. Tingley is here spelled with an "e" (cf. Tingly, p. 208).

Ennet toilet-flushing troubles continue (cf. p. 179).

McDade reports cold water coming from the "H-faucet in the shower."

Yolanda makes her first appearance in the novel. Gately advises her to avoid using Randy Lenz as a sponsor, given that Lenz suggests that she "Ask For Help into his fly."

PLOT AND CHARACTER: Ennet, Gately, Joelle
THEME: Cycles

Resident interfaces are routine between meetings and curfew, as are problems with toilets and with residents in general. Hanley bakes routinely (brownies will be made in Ch. 28).

Chapter 26.9, Section 116, Pages 565-567
Notes 234-235, Pages 1038-1044
10 November Y.D.A.U.

In his 1600h. phone call to Hal on 7 November, Orin said he told Steeply he would "consider certain issues very carefully before

[he] responded" (p. 1010). Steeply was "en route" to Enfield (p. 1012) at that time, and Hal said he would let Orin know "when and if" he saw "any journalists" (p. 1010). Steeply was in Enfield on 8 November—Orin presumably was playing football that Sunday; his 1412h. phone message the day before included "professional-locker-room sounds in the background" (p. 1005)—covertly observing the Eschaton debacle (Ch. 22.1) and overtly making arrangements with Avril to visit E.T.A. (cf. n. 147). In this section (assumed to occur on 10 November, cf. the summaries of Chs. 27.26 and 27.29), Steeply has returned to Phoenix and is conducting a final interview with Orin (who volunteered to take Steeply to the airport) before leaving Phoenix again. "TRANSCRIPT-FRAGMENTS" of Orin's part of this interview (Steeply's questions are replaced with "Q"s, as in n. 145) are provided in n. 234 (and meta-narrative comments are provided in nn. 234.a-b), including Orin's attempts to turn the conversation to the "strange bond I feel between us."

Steeply is apparently questioning Orin about his parents' sanity, to which Orin says "what is *insane* supposed to mean." Orin cites Jim's accomplishments with respect to E.T.A. ("In the last five years of his life [April 1999-April 2004] he put together a tennis academy"), his invention of "a new kind of window glass that doesn't fog or smudge from people touching it" (perhaps Avril's writing of a name in the window of the Volvo (cf. p. 999) was habitual), and his managing "the revenues from all his previous patents"; all while "drink[ing] himself blind on a daily basis," "impersonating various kinds of health-care professionals" (cf. Ch. 3), and "*in his spare time*" creating work "that people are still writing doctoral theses on." Orin says that he does not trust or want to associate with his mother. After recounting Avril's various E.T.A. duties, her work with "the Militant Grammarians of Massachusetts," her "thing about never eating until it's late," and her longtime habit of never leaving the E.T.A. grounds (except for "The Stork's funeral"), Orin states that "the only reason she's never been diagnosed or treated" for Obsessive-Compulsive Disorder is that it "doesn't prevent her from functioning." For example, "the Moms solved a lot of her threshold-problems by having no real doors," but Orin says there are "lockable doors" (but cf. Ch. 16.1

commentary) upstairs "in service of other compulsions." Orin says Avril's "four horsemen [are] enclosure, communicational imprecision, untidiness," and the "fourth horseman stays hidden." Presumably the fourth horseman is whatever triggers Avril's sexual compulsions.

In contrast to Avril, Marlon Bain (whose "parents were killed in a grotesque freak accident") was in a "paralysis of compulsive motions that didn't serve any kind of function." Orin speaks of Bain's "constant rituals," his "compulsive sweat" (recall Lyle's reverie, pp. 386-7), and Jim's use of him in *Death in Scarsdale* (cf. p. 987). It "suddenly occurs" to Orin to give Steeply Bain's address ("he's not Inter-Netted"), although Orin told Hal five days ago that he'd "thought of referring her to Bain" (p. 246). Bain's "little greeting-card company [Saprogenic Greetings] has just been bought up by a huge novelty concern" (Acme, cf. n. 204).

Orin tells Steeply that Avril's "got to keep Hal's skull lashed tight to hers" (recall Orin's dream, pp. 46-7) and that Hal is "still obsessed with her approval" ("still performing for her, syntax- and vocabulary-wise," cf. pp. 524-5), is "shut down," and "has no idea he even knows something's wrong." Orin says that he never saw his mother and father fight and that his father "was the victim of the most monstrous practical joke ever played, in my opinion." Orin relates that Avril's father had been "at one time a millionaire potato-baron-type farmer, in Québec" and that her home town "near Maine. Heart of the Concavity" was "wiped off the map." Orin says that Jim would often visit Lyle in Ontario before the advent of E.T.A. and that Jim is buried in "the Moms's family plot."

As an example of Avril's "emotional weather," Orin relates the story of Hal eating the mold in Weston in "early March" when Hal was "four" ("March or early April" when Hal "was around five," p. 10). Orin says that Hal wore "slippers that had those awful Nice-Day yellow smile-faces on both toes." When Avril sees Hal "[e]verything slows waaay down." Hal shows her the mold and says, "I ate this." Avril runs around screaming, and Orin sees his father's "face at the glass door over the deck, palms out and thumbs together to make a frame" and "Mario's face all squished against the glass . . . also trying to make that frame with his hands." Eventually, "Mr. Reehagen next door, who was so-called 'friends' with [Avril came] out and over and finally had to hook up the hose."

At the airport after Steeply's departure, Orin, "with his forehead against the glass of the Weston back door—or rather the Delta gate window," is approached by "a putatively Swiss hand-model." Within days of Hal berating Orin regarding his "rapacious fetish for young married mothers he can strategize into betraying their spouses and maybe damaging their kids for all time" (pp. 1014-5), Orin is in "a sexual mode" with a woman "he hadn't had to ask" (n. 235) to arrange pictures of her family on a dresser in Orin's range of vision. Orin sees this event as a "balancing out of the jacuzzi's dead bird [p. 44] and the frigidly invasive reporter" (n. 235) and as "the universe . . . reaching out a hand to pluck him from the rim of the abyss of despair" (cf. Gately's dream of a smiley-face-circle-masked Sergeant at Arms threatening to pluck him away from the safety of "thin clean clear glass" walls, pp. 358-9).

Orin's interactions with his Subjects are not about "leaving yourself; nor about love or about whose love you deep-down desire, by whom you feel betrayed. Not and never about love, which kills what needs it." They are rather about "the need to be assured that for a moment" "he is the One." It is posited that the reason "one Subject is never enough" is that if there were for Orin "just one, now, special and only," O. would experience "the obliterating trinity of You [U] and I into We [OUI]. Orin felt that once and has never recovered, and will never again." Presumably, Orin felt this with Joelle, "the only really cardiac-grade romantic relationship of Orin's life" (p. 294). The hand model circles Orin's neck with her legs, and "he bears her to bed as would a waiter a tray."

PLOT AND CHARACTER: Orin, Jim, Avril, Hal, Mario, U.S.O.U.S, A.F.R.
THEME: Secrets, His/Father, Fear/Obsess, Cycles, Inf/Reg, Memory, Recur

The putative journalist (Steeply) and the "putatively Swiss hand-model" are both in disguise. Orin's hatred of the women he needs and fears "comes out disguised as a contempt he disguises in the tender attention" he pays his Subjects. Avril wears a "Fukoama microfiltration pollution mask" in the mold story (as at the I.-Day gala supper, n. 148). Avril has a "humiliating little family pet name" for Hal, which Orin keeps secret. Orin says he doesn't want to talk about his family, but for Steeply he is compelled to: "It's like I can't help it." Steeply cycles between Boston and the Southwest, as have Jim, Orin, InterLace, Marathe/A.F.R., and E.T.A. (for the What-aBurger Invitational). Avril's obsessive compulsions and Bain's "constant rituals" are described. As a result of the mold incident, "a corner of the universe suddenly peeled back to reveal what seethed out there just beyond tidiness." For Orin "one Subject is never enough," "hand after hand must descend to pull him back from the endless fall" from a "great height without even idiotic red wings strapped to his back" (cf. pp. 65-6). The hand model's leap to "circle his neck with her legs" is symbolic of Orin's wish for infantile regression. Orin wants the total attention that an infant receives, to be "the One," which resonates with the infant cults discussed by Lenz in this chapter (cf. "as if there were only One"; pp. 559, 562). Orin wants his Subjects "vacuumed of all but his name"; e.g., of memories and "the deaths of pets," which resonates with Lenz's activities in this chapter. Recall that Orin killed his mother's pet dog (p. 1014).

The face-against-glass motif recurs in the mold-story memory (Jim and Mario) and in Orin's moment of confusion at the airport window. Omens of danger recur: the hand model's lids flutter, Hal wears smiley-face slippers, the mold is "*chewed on*," and "There's the tentative chirp of a bird." The tiller "farts some blue smoke." Orin states that Avril has "videophony out the bazoo, though she'd never use a Tableau" (cf. Ch. 13.7). The fact that "clichés earned their status as clichés because they were so obviously true" recalls Gately's AA-inspired philosophy. Orin says Hal is "shut down." Jim thought so in the past (Ch. 3); Hal has taken to lying down and counting breaths in the present (Ch. 26.6); and something appears to be wrong in the future (Ch. 1).

What is the "monstrous practical joke" played on Jim according to Orin? Was Jim's marriage a joke because Avril only married him to get Visas and a Green Card (p. 64)? Was the Wild Turkey bottle with "a large red decorative giftwrappish bow on the neck" found at the scene of Jim's death (p. 250) a practical joke gone wrong? Also, how does the hand-model know of Orin's specific obsessions?

Chapter 26.10, Section 117, Pages 567-574
Notes 236-238, Page 1044
11 November Y.D.A.U.

This dialogue-only section documents a blindfolded Idris Arslanian (one of Hal's Little Buddies, cf. Ch. 11.8) and is assumed to occur on 11 November (Arslanian will be wearing the blindfold at supper later tonight, p. 638). Arslanian first bumps into Ted Schacht, who informs Idris that the weeping he hears is from a depressed Anton Doucette, being bucked up by Lyle while "[s]ome of the crueler guys are in there watching like it's entertainment. I got disgusted. Somebody in pain isn't entertainment." Arslanian is wearing the blindfold in order to train his ear, a response to an "experimental theory" of Thorp's that bases the high ranking of "blind, soft-skulled" Dymphna (cf. pp. 246, 518), "age only nine" (Hal cites Dymphna's age as sixteen in Y.G., p. 17), on his ability "to judge the necessary spot of landing by the intensity of the sound of the ball against the opponent player's string." In the case of Arslanian, however, the blindfold has not improved court play. Help finding the lavatory is being sought from those with whom Idris collides.

After Schacht leaves, Arslanian next bumps into Pemulis, who explains that Doucette's depression is from a fear of expulsion for flunking an Energy survey class that includes lectures on annulation. Doucette has been "dope-slapped by anxiety. I'm saying frozen" (cf. p. 390). Mario, "exploiting a previous like therapeutic bond with the kid from about the mole" (prompted by Lyle, cf. p. 390 and n. 147), explained annulation by telling Doucette "to just imagine somebody doing somersaults with one hand nailed to the ground" (cf. p. 503). Pemulis gives a "thumbnail lecture" on annulation: a "moving right-triangular cycle of interdependence and waste-creation and -utilization" with points in what used to be Montpelier VT ("where the annulated Shawshine River feeds the Charles," p. 561), Methuen MA ("just south of the Concavity"; cf. the "Lowell-Methuen stretch of border," p. 217), and what used to be Presque Isle, ME. (Another triangle with points in Syracuse NNY, Ticonderoga NNY, and Salem MA is referenced in n. 237.)

Pemulis, who saw Avril with Wayne two nights ago (Ch. 26.4) and refers to Jim as "Mrs. Inc's poor cuc[kold]," explains that Jim's contribution to annular fusion was to help design "special holographic conversions [recall that holography may be the basis of *Infinite Jest*'s appeal, cf. p. 490] so the team that worked on annulation could study the behavior of subatomics in highly poisonous environments. Without getting poisoned themselves" (cf. header, p. 393). This allowed the development of "a type of fusion that can produce waste that's fuel for a process whose waste is fuel for the fusion." (The "whole [annular] theory behind the physics" of the fusion was inspired by medicine—as described in a chapter of the same book in which Jim's reminiscence on annulation appeared, written by the man with colorectal neoplastis from Lyle's story to Stice (n. 238, cf. p. 395).) All you need is "access to mind-staggering volumes of toxic material," "placing the natural fusion site in the Great Concavity." However, the "resultant fusion turns out to be so greedily efficient that it sucks every last toxin and poison out of the surrounding ecosystem," resulting in "rapacial feral hamsters and insects of Volkswagen size and infantile giganticism and the unmacheteable regions of forests of the mythic eastern Concavity" (cf. Lenz to Green, Ch. 26.7). Annular fusion requires that toxins be steadily dumped into the Concavity "to keep the uninhibited ecosystem from spreading and overrunning more ecologically stable areas, exhausting the atmosphere's poisons so that everything hyperventilates." Hence, E.W.D.'s catapulting of waste into the region. The eastern Concavity (in contrast to the "barren Eliotical wastes of the western Concavity") goes "from overgrown to wasteland to overgrown several times a month," which seems to Arslanian to be a speeding up of time, but is "actually equivalent to an incredible *slowing down* of time." (If the amount of growth that used occur in one year now occurs in one hour, then that hour must be incredibly slowed down in order for a year's worth of growth to occur in it.)

Pemulis agrees to help Arslanian, who "eschew[s] stimulants [and] depressing compounds [as] prescribed by the holy teachings of [his] faith," to the lavatory in exchange for Arslanian's urine (cf. Ch. 14).

PLOT AND CHARACTER: E.T.A., Tech, O.N.A.N.
THEME: Cycles, Waste, Time, Recur, Fear/Obsess, Phys/Ob, Boundaries

This section contains an explanation of the annulation cycle of "waste-creation and -utilization," which provides another instance of time slowing down (as it did for Poor Tony in the bathroom stall and for Orin during the mold story; cf. Ch. 20.2 and p. 1042). Pemulis, who tells Arslanian that he doesn't need "to go on and on," will utilize the waste created by Arslanian, who "stands first upon one foot then upon another foot." Doucette's anxiety creates physical obstacles in that one half of his face is "spasming around [cf. Lenz on cocaine earlier in the chapter] while the half with the mole just hangs there" (cf. Ch. 25.5 commentary for more on spasming and halves of faces). Arslanian's blindfold serves as a mask and creates opportunities to overcome physical obstacles. The blindfold technique was inspired by "soft-skulled" Dymphna, "one of the infantile natives of Ticonderoga NNY evacuated too late" (p. 518). Dymphna, "age only nine" in Y.D.A.U., is said by Hal to be sixteen in Y.G. (p. 17). Has time somehow slowed for Dymphna, who ages seven years in a one-year period? Pemulis says that without a steady supply of toxins, the ecosystem in the Concavity will spread beyond its boundaries, and he compares the toxification and detoxification that occurs in the Concavity to hyperventilation. On p. 560, Hal is counting his breaths. Has Hal's detoxification from marijuana brought on hyperventilation?

Chapter 26.11, Section 118, Pages 574-575
10 November Y.D.A.U.

More of Orin's first liaison with the putatively Swiss hand-model that he met in Ch. 26.9 will be described in Ch. 26.15. This section occurs immediately after Ch. 26.15. As Orin drives away from this first liaison with the hand-model, he realizes that the "legless surveyer" (cf. Ch. 26.15) with the "same Swiss accent as the hand-model" was "the first wheelchair he'd seen since Hal'd hit him with his theory" ("very shy fans," p. 245) and since "the day before [Steeply] came up"; but that "hours after [Steeply] left," they "were now back, with their shy ruses." (Steeply's quick trip to Enfield and back—during which most of Orin's time would have been spent with the Arizona Cardinals—presumably allowed no time for a "wheelchair" to approach Orin.)

PLOT AND CHARACTER: Orin, A.F.R.
THEME: Cycles

The "cycle of seduction always left Orin stunned and wrung out." Orin goes through a "revolving door" (like Joelle in *Infinite Jest*, p. 549) on his way out of the hotel.

Chapter 26.12, Section 119, Pages 575-589
Notes 239-241, Page 1044
11 November Y.D.A.U., before 2330h.

The adventures of Lenz and Green continue from Ch. 26.7. Lenz relates the story of his mother, who "lost all will to . . . cook or clean, or nurture, or finally even move" upon receiving a settlement from an embarrassing bus incident, after which she sat in a "recliner watching InterLace Gothic Romances" (cf. the medical attaché watching *Infinite Jest* in his "special electronic recliner," p. 34) and eating until she "ruptured and died." Lenz did not receive an inheritance.

"The searing facts of the case of Bruce Green's natural parents' deaths when he was a toddler are so deeply repressed inside Green" that he currently doesn't remember them (except for flashes of "visual memory, contextless and creepy"), but they are described by the narrator of this section. Green's father worked for Acme (owned by the shadowy Albertan mogul; cf. pp. 411, 414, and 1034) and gave Bruce a putative can of Polynesian macadamia nuts to give to his mother for Christmas. Bruce so overwrapped the present that it "seemed mushily to struggle" as if it held "an oversized dachshund" (this image resonates with Lenz's issue-resolution methods). It actually held "a coiled cloth snake" within the can, which literally scared Bruce's mother to death upon opening it. In the aftermath of this event, Bruce's father clunked (due to his uneven legs) around the house "in circles" and was eventually sentenced to death for sending out actual explosives in a case of "Blammo Cigars" (cf. n. 204), which resulted in 28 decapitations. Green went to live with his aunt, who wore a "black mesh veil" for three months. Although he doesn't remember these details and "he compulsively avoids" things associated with them, he is drawn to the Polynesian music he hears which pulls him southwest away from Lenz.

Hearing the Don Ho music reminds Green of a "Beach-Theme Party" he attended during the time when "life with M. Bonk was one big party" (cf. p. 39) at which he "actually *shit* his pants." As Green approaches "the Canadian-refugee-type house" from which the music originates, he notes that Ennet curfew is approaching and sees Lenz there engaging the "full attention" of a dog with Gately's meatloaf. Green observes an address (412 W. Brainerd), "[f]leur-de-lis stickers and slogans in Canadian," a "Montego cammed out into a slingshot dragster," and Hawaiian attire (cf. the F.L.Q., n. 47). Lenz moves in "a melting and wraithlike quality" behind the dog and kills it. The dog's last whine alerts the partygoers to what has happened. As Lenz runs away, three "Nucks" jump into the Montego and give chase. Green observes wheelchaired figures in another house across the street as he stands "breathing into the bark of the tree."

PLOT AND CHARACTER: Ennet, AA&R, A.F.R.
THEME: Loss, His/Father, Memory, Recur, Secrets, Dreams, Time, Fear/Obsess, Waste, Inf/Reg

Green experiences "a moment of deep wrenching loss, of wishing getting high was still pleasurable for him so he could get high." Information about the families of both Lenz and Green are provided in this section. Green has repressed facts about his family, except for flashes of "visual memory." Lenz's "mouth writhes" as he relates Charlotte Treat's "secret dream" to "become a dental hygenist" (cf. Hal's recurring dreams regarding teeth), which dream is rooted in incidents of childhood abuse (n. 239). Concerning the slow movement of time, Green has "one fully developed thought every sixty seconds." Thrust has said it's "like listening to a faucet with a very slow drip." Doocy's (spelled without an "e" (cf. p. 39) here from Green's perspective, cf. p. 179) "snakes [do] not move once in three days, in their tank." Lenz "consumes several minutes and less than twenty breaths" relating the story of his mother who had "anxiety and ensconcement-phobias," who "never once did come to Parent's Day," and whose "shouts for Help" go unanswered in the "human-waste-flinging" bus incident, for which she received a settlement that allowed her to lose all will to live and to sit and eat until she "ruptured and died." (This is reminiscent of the man in *Monty Python's The Meaning of Life* who ate one last wafer-thin mint (cf. also the discussion of projectile vomiting on p. 233). There was also a "Monty Python's Flying Circus" sketch about a joke that was so funny that everyone who heard it died laughing, which is almost analogous to Jim's *Infinite Jest.*) Lenz says "the urban city is . . . one big commode." Green remembers shitting his pants at a party and having to "wipe himself off like a fucking baby." Against the grain of self-obsession and infantile regression, as a child Green was "more excited about his gift's receipt than what he's going to get himself." Lenz is "talking baby-talk" to the dog. The man holding "the expired dog" "staggers in circles."

The Hawaiian-type music is "at once top-volume and far far away" (p. 577). The sounds of cumulative footsteps on "a busy urban sidewalk" are described as "like something getting chewed by something huge and tireless and patient" (p. 578). Another old TV show —"Hawaii Five-O" (p. 584)—is again referenced (cf. Hal's essay, Ch. 13.4). Chinese women with shopping bags are observed (p. 578, cf. p. 224). Green passes the familiar landmarks of The Unexamined Life (p. 581, cf. n. 67) and St. Elizabeth's Hospital (p. 582), the emergency room of which Otis P. Lord recently visited (p. 456). The "white caterpillar" (p. 588) is Lenz's white mustache (cf. p. 539). Three artists are referenced in this section: "a Mondrian of alleys" (p. 577), "a gaily Gauguin-colored can" (p. 578), and "Durer prints" (p. 585). Green's father drank a "Falstaff tallboy" (p. 579), and Green remembers Doocy's "ancient cartridge" as "War of the Welles": actually

"War of the Worlds," written by H. G. Wells and made famous on radio by Orson Welles, an actor well-versed in Shakespeare and at the end of his career a physical match for the role of Falstaff.

Chapter 26.13, Section 120, Pages 589-593
Notes 242-244, Page 1044
11 November Y.D.A.U., before 2330h.

Pages 589-590 describe Mario, who will be nineteen on 25 November, in the days leading up to 11 November. Mario continues to sleep on an air mattress at HmH, as he has done since very late October (Ch. 24.2). "His insomnia worsens as Madame Psychosis's hiatus enters its third week" (one of her final shows was in the first hour of 23 October, Ch. 16.1): "It's weird to feel like you miss someone you're not even sure you know" (cf. Ch. 24.2 summary). "Hal had asked him when he'll start coming back to their room to sleep, which made Mario feel good." Mario has "a neurological deficit whereby he can't feel physical pain very well" and "got a serious burn on his pelvis leaning against a hot stove talking to Mrs. Clarke." Mario is worried because for the first time it is becoming hard to read "Hal's states of mind," and he "can't tell if Hal is sad."

Pages 590-593 describe Mario's 11 November walk after leaving Avril's office (to be documented in Ch. 27.36). Mario didn't tell Avril he would be walking around, because he knows she fears "Mario would be easy prey for just about anybody, physically" (e.g., the U.S.S. Millicent Kent; cf. Ch. 11.9). Mario walks around the grounds of Enfield Marine because he "knows a couple of the E.M. Security officers from when his father [used them in] *Dial C for Concupiscence*" (cf. n. 67). He hears a woman "calling for help without any real urgency" (cf. p. 196). Mario likes "Ennet's House" where the "Headmistress" has a disability (cf. Pat's stroke, p. 465) and has "twice invited Mario in during the day for a Caffeine-Free Millennial Fizzy." Mario likes "Ennet's House because it's very real; people are crying and making noise and getting less unhappy, and once he heard somebody say *God* with a straight face and nobody looked at them or looked down or smiled in any sort of way where you could tell they were worried inside." It confuses Mario that all the older E.T.A. students "get embarrassed" about "stuff that's really real": "It's like there's some rule that real stuff can only get mentioned if everybody rolls their eyes or laughs in a way that isn't happy."

Passing by an open window, Mario hears a sound recording of an old Madame Psychosis show "from the Year of the Wonderchicken, Madame's inaugural year, when she'd sometimes talk all hour and had an accent" (she now has "no accent except under stress," p. 234) and "often spoke on the show as if she were talking exclusively to one person or character who was very important to her." Mario makes a mental note to check with Hal about the etiquette of asking to borrow tapes. Mario loved these old programs "because he felt like he was listening to someone sad read out loud from yellow letters she'd taken out of a shoebox on a rainy P.M. [cf. Mario's shoebox, pp. 1005-7], stuff about heartbreak and people you loved dying and U.S. woe, stuff that was real. It is increasingly hard to find valid art that is about stuff that is real in this way."

Ennet House doesn't allow visitors after 2300 because of the 2330 curfew, so Mario walks on, but as he goes he sees "a wide square-headed boy bent over something he's writing," which is a segue into the next section's description of Gately's pre-curfew duties.

PLOT AND CHARACTER: Mario, Joelle, Ennet
THEME: Dreams, Recur, Phys/Ob

Avril "gets night terrors," and Mario's worry "feels like when you've lost something important in a dream." Like Tavis, Mario "has a dislike of fluorescent lighting" (n. 244). Like Gately, Mario has "a really big head." Unlike Gately, he doesn't kneel when he prays ("it's more like a conversation"), but his "nighttime prayers take almost an hour and sometimes more and are not a chore." Mario misses the connection that it is Joelle herself listening to her old recorded voice. Mario imagines Madame Psychosis as being tall (like his mother) and on a beach in a beach chair. Mario references the "cars everybody has to move at 0000h." (cf. p. 545). Mario's perspective on "real stuff" is reminiscent of the "Irony-free zone" (p. 369) required of Boston AA meeting attendees. Although Mario could be called mentally regressed, he is not spiritually regressed and self-absorbed, like those who passively worship the(ir inner) infant. The "female girl in a little fur coat" might refer to Hester Thrale in a "false fox jacket" (p. 601), but who is the "young person Mario's never seen" that helps him with his police lock?

Chapter 26.14, Section 121, Pages 593-596
Note 245, Pages 1044-1045
11 November Y.D.A.U., before 2330h.

In addition to interfacing with residents (n. 90, Ch. 26.8), Gately performs many other tasks before the 2330 curfew on 11 November, including making log entries (Mario sees him "bent over something he's writing" in the previous section). Kate Gompert "claimed to be too sick to hit AA again tonight and has been in bed in her room more or less steadily for three days" (but cf. her attendance at the 9 November NA meeting, Ch. 25.3). Doony Glynn has diverticulitis and "has to lie fetal" on his bunk. The "newest guy's still sitting in the linen closet" (Tingley, cf. p. 564), and "helpless" Amy Johnson isn't back yet. Gately also orients new resident Ruth van Cleve. (Excising Skull from the list in the Ch. 16.4 summary and adding Burt F. Smith, Joelle, Amy J, Yolanda, and Ruth van Cleve; the Ennet House resident count is now 26, four residents over the capacity stated on p. 137.)

PLOT AND CHARACTER: Ennet, Gately
THEME: Cycles, Waste, Boundaries

This section documents the routine of an Ennet House live-in staffer before curfew. There are other resonances with toilets and waste, powerlessness, and boundaries. Being an Ennet resident has "smashed [Gately's] longstanding delusion that women didn't go to the bathroom with the same appalling vigor that men did." When his night shift ends, Gately will "clean real shit" at the Shattuck Shelter. Ennet House "has a Boundary about the office phone for residents" as well as other rules detailed throughout the section. Amy Johnson is described as "helpless" (powerless). Depressed, suicidal Kate Gompert is reading Sylvia Plath, which Gately sees as Sylvia Plate.

Gately "wonders again what he'll end up doing when his year's staff term is up" (June-July Y.G., given that Gately has been "on live-in Staff here four months now," p. 275) and he "has to leave here and do something back Out There." Unless Gately leaves Ennet House early, he presumably will help Hal dig up Hal's father's head (p. 17) between July and November Y.G.

Chapter 26.15, Section 122, Pages 596-601
10 November Y.D.A.U.

Immediately after the "sexual mode" of Orin's first liaison with the hand-model (Ch. 26.9), he feels "an abrupt loss of hope" and a "contempt he belies . . . with gentleness and caring" (cf. p. 567). When there is a knock at the door, the hand-model—who had begun to ask Orin "to tell her things about his own family"—goes through the ruse of fright and hiding, and Orin goes to the door "ready for anything": "Swiss cuckolds, furtive near-Eastern medical attachés, zaftig print-journalists."

At the door is a man in a wheelchair with "a bald spot" (the leader of the attack on the Antitois, cf. p. 486), who putatively is conducting a survey and asks Orin what he misses. Orin says "I miss TV" and "I miss sneering at something I loved" and "I miss seeing the same things over and over again." When the man suggests that InterLace now provides the option for repeating viewings, Orin says that it's "not the same. The choice, see. It ruins it somehow. With television you were *subjected* to repetition. The familiarity was inflicted." The man glances past Orin and says, "Can return at later time which we specify." Orin's post-interview and post-liaison thoughts were documented in Ch. 26.11.

Plot and Character: Orin, A.F.R.
Theme: Choice, Inf/Reg, Secrets, Cycles, Dreams, Loss, Memory, Recur

Orin wants to "[sneer] at something he loves," and the ability to choose what he watches on TV ruins that opportunity. Orin wants to act on compulsion as he does with his Subjects. He wants to have no choice. Orin has now been fooled by three disguises: Steeply, the hand-model, and the legless surveyer, who joggles his clipboard "a little like an infant." Orin is caught in a cycle: he "can only give, not receive, pleasure" (ironic given Orin's self-absorption) which makes his Subjects think he is "almost a dream-type lover" which fuels his contempt which he cannot show because it would detract from the Subject's pleasure (p. 596). Sneering at his current Subject, Orin feels "the sort of clinical contempt you feel for an insect you've looked down on and seen and know you're going to torture for a while" (recall that Orin asphyxiates roaches in his bathroom, pp. 44-5). Orin also experiences loss. Orin misses the cycle of "seeing the same things over and over again." He is "sad inside" and has a "sense as in dreams of something vital you've forgotten to do." His "rising heart went out" to the legless surveyer, as Mario's went out to the "damaged or askew" in Enfield Marine (p. 590). Another reference to Orin's cruelty is provided: "He tried to remember from Mario's childhood how long under blankets before it got unbearably hot and you started to smother and thrash." This resonates with Lenz's cruelty to animals in this chapter. Orin also remembers old TV characters on p. 600: "Jeannie, Samantha, Sam and Diane, Gilligan, Hawkeye, Hazel, Jed." Orin looks up, "as if memories were always lighter than air." The hand-model's hand moved "like a blind spider." What is the significance of Orin's thinking of the medical attaché?

Chapter 26.16, Section 123, Pages 601-619
Notes 246-256, Page 1045
11-12 November Y.D.A.U.

Gately's pre-curfew activities continue from Ch. 26.14. Lenz "oozes through the door" just as Gately is locking it, which brings the narrative back to where the chapter began with Lenz taking "right up to 2329 to get home" and "Bruce Green and Amy J. separately both missing curfew" (p. 539). Gately decides to let Green in at 2336, "gives him the required ass-chewing," takes a urine sample, decides to discharge Amy J. when she is still not there at 2350 (he has her stuff packed up "in the same Irish Luggage [trashbags; cf. pp. 178, 356, 541] she'd brought it in Monday" and put on the porch), and prepares to get "the residents' cars moved, the night-shift's biggest pain in the ass." Since Y.T.-S.D.B., in metro Boston "only one side of any street is legal for parking, and the legal side switches abruptly at 0000h., and cruisers and municipal tow trucks prowl the streets from 0001h. on, writing $95.00 tickets and/or towing suddenly-illegally-parked vehicles" (cf. pp. 545, 591). Gately has to round up residents with cars (who sometimes resist because "early-recovery Denial makes it impossible for them to imagine their own car getting towed": "It's like a kind of idolatry of uniqueness"), orchestrate the car-switching procedure, and keep an eye on all the residents at the same time.

Gately notices that Lenz's "mouth is writhing" and wants to "pull an immediate urine," but Gately sees restless residents and "tow trucks aprowl" and decides to wait until after the car switching. Gately realizes Doony Glynn can't move his car because he is in the throes of diverticulitis, so Gately has to go back in and find someone with a driver's license (Gately "doesn't have a valid license," cf. pp. 462-3) who can move Glynn's car. Green agrees to do it, but Gately has to go up and get permission from Glynn, who is delirious with fever and unable to tell Gately where his keys are (Glynn, who is in the "2-Man seniorest males' bedroom," presumably just changed rooms today, since Lenz still thinks of Glynn as his roommate; cf. pp. 539, 545). Hester Thrale screams. Green runs upstairs and commands Gately to come outside. "A watercolor of a retrieverish dog cants and then falls from the wall" as Gately races down the staircase. Outside, Gately hears Joelle shouting something down to him and sees Lenz being chased "around and around" a Montego by "two almost Gately-sized bearded guys." When he sees a third guy holding the rest of the residents at gunpoint, everything "slightly slows down," or rather things "break into frames." Gately realizes "the trio Lenz has managed to somehow enrage is Nucks" (cf. Ch. 26.12) and remembers a "Québecer he'd killed by gagging a man with a cold" (cf. Ch. 7.4). Joelle's shouts mix with those of the "Help lady" that Mario heard earlier (Ch. 26.13). She "has cried Wolf for so many years that real shouts for real help are all going to be ignored." Gately approaches the Montego as Lenz runs behind him for protection. The man with the gun (a .44; cf. Lucien Antitoi's gun, p. 480) "sights square on Gately" while keeping the residents in his peripheral vision. Gately's "senses haven't been this keen in over a year." He is aware of the "[s]tar-chocked sky, his breath, faraway horns, [the] low trill of ATHSCMEs way to the north. . . . Motionless heads at #5's windows."

The "Nuck duo" come toward Gately and Lenz; Hester Thrale runs "off into the night"; and more residents come out onto the porch. Gately notices dried blood on Lenz's fingernails, and it "occurs to Gately that if he'd pulled the instant spot-urine he'd wanted on Lenz this whole snafu wouldn't maybe be happening." When one of the Nucks pulls out a knife, "Gately feels adrenaline's warmth spread through him," and he has "no choice now not to fight." He's "just one part of something bigger he can't control."

Lenz runs away from the Nuck charge. Gately breaks the arm of the Nuck who punches him, is stabbed in the calf by the Nuck with the knife, and kicks the Nuck with the knife back onto the hood of the Montego. The Nuck with the gun shoots Gately in the shoulder. Green gets the Nuck with the gun in a half-nelson before he can shoot Gately again. Nell Gunther kicks the Nuck in the face, snapping his head back which breaks Green's nose, but Green doesn't let go. Now "that the Nuck's restrained, notice, here comes Lenz," who "tackles the Nuck and Green both, and they're a roil of clothes and legs on the lawn, the Item [gun] not in sight." Clenette and Yolanda begin "stomping the inert Nuck." Gately beats the head of the now knifeless Nuck into the windshield until "something in the head gives with a sort of liquid crunch." He then goes to the Nuck who originally punched him and stomps on his face "as if he were killing cockroaches."

Joelle has now climbed down from the window and reaches the street "just as Gately decides to lie down." He says, "Just don't try and walk me around" (cf. Gately's story to Joelle earlier this morning, Ch. 25.7). There is a flurry of activity. Gately "does not want to be lying here with a gunshot in shock trying to deal with the Finest [Boston police]." Gately is aware that Joelle smells good, and "from out of nowhere he's all of a sudden sure" that her "odd empty half-accented voice" is "that one Madame lady's voice on no-subscription radio." "[O]ne of the ex-football E.M. Security guys, that spends half his shift down at the Life" (cf. n. 67), arrives drunk; and Joelle orders Erdedy to distract him. The E.M. Security guy gives drunken orders as Lenz and Green and Joelle prepare to move Gately inside.

PLOT AND CHARACTER: Ennet, Gately, Joelle
THEME: Non-Action, Boundaries, Cycles, Time, Recur

Gately's failure to take action against Lenz puts him in a situation he can't control. For most of this section, Erdedy is inactive, frozen with his arms up and keys in his hand. After he is shot, Gately becomes physically passive—his "brain keeps wanting to go away inside himself"—and boundaries begin to blur for him. "The night's so clear the stars shine right through people's heads." In this state of flux he can recognize Joelle as Madame Psychosis. Examples of cycles in this section include detailed descriptions of Gately's live-in staffer routines, the car-switching routine (which happens at midnight, the boundary between days), the Nucks chasing Lenz "around and around" the car, and the "circle of stars' heads' faces" Gately sees ("the stars shine right through people's heads"). Recalling Pemulis and Arslanian's discussion of time in the Concavity in Ch. 26.10, "It's always that everything always speeds up and slows down both." Things "break into frames." Gately's "appraisal's taking only seconds; it only takes time to list it." The slow fall of the petals shed by the Nucks' leis contrasts with the speed of their charge, just as their earlier exit in the Montego left "a wake of white petals that [took] forever to stop falling" (p. 589). Earlier in Pat's car, Gately created a "tornado of waste . . . sustained in its whirl by the strong west breeze" (p. 479).

There are a wealth of recurring images and ideas in this section. McDade is drinking Glynn's Millennial Fizzy; an E.W.D. vehicle is launched; Gately grumbles about a cup of urine (blue-lidded); Day wears a Lone Ranger (old TV character) sleep mask; and Gately sees motionless heads (heads separate from bodies). Another missed connection occurs when the Nucks assume Gately's name is Moose. Sounds "have receded" (p. 613); Hester Thrale is heard receding; and "the sky's depth . . . seems to bulge and recede," recalling an image of a breathing ceiling that recurs for Gately (cf. Herman the Ceiling That Breathed (p. 447) and the baggy sky of p. 478). There are "spidered" stars in the windshield, and Gately says, "You can tell some of the stars are nearer and some far" (cf. another description of stars on pp. 507-8). The A.F.R.'s railroad-spike tactic comes to mind as Clenette and Yolanda (who have come back from the Footprints club, a place in which the smiles are excruciating to see; n. 246) are exhorted to "use the spike heel," leaving "one of their shoes" in the eye of a Nuck. This recalls O'Brien's stamping-foot image to Winston Smith in *1984* (cf. Ch. 18.1 commentary). Shakespeare's character is substituted for Arthur Conan Doyle's in "No shit Shylock" (p. 618), and another famous Monty Python line (from *Monty Python and the Holy Grail*) is used when Gately twice refers to his gunshot as a "Flesh-wound."

The frenetic, quick-cut dialogue at the end of the section echoes the intensity of the administrators' response to Hal in Ch. 1, especially "I just never saw anything *like* that." There are Gately-Orin correspondences in this section. After Gately punts a Nuck into the Montego, "sounds from everybody else have receded to the sounds stands' crowds make" (cf. p. 295); and Gately stomps another Nuck "as if he were killing cockroaches" (cf. Orin's asphyxiations, p. 45). Gately is also clearly smitten by Joelle. Twenty-one of twenty-six current Ennet residents appear in this section. Concerning the other five residents, Gately accounted for Gompert and van Cleve just before the events of this section (Ch. 26.14); and Ewell, Neaves, and Smith were referenced in the first section of the chapter, which begins on the same day as this section.

Chapter 26: Powerless: Compulsion, Secrecy, Ritual, The Cult Of The Infant

Lenz compulsively kills animals in order to address his issues of powerlessness and fear. The killings become a necessary ritual for time-obsessed Lenz, who prefers to accomplish them during a certain interval (2216h. to 2226h.) and in disguise. Lenz's secrecy adds to his feeling of power. Ennet residents are incapable of locking their doors, so their ability to gain power through keeping secrets is diminished. Tine compulsively measures his penis and keeps daily records of the measurements (secret rituals). Tine is tracking a cartridge that renders its viewers powerless by initiating regression to an infantile state. Rusk believes Stice has a repressed (secret, hidden) trauma having to do with "projective infantile omnipotence" and "absence of control." Pemulis eavesdrops (in secret) on Rusk and Stice and on Tavis, but compulsively bites down on a mint before compulsively announcing his presence to Wayne and Avril, who were participating in a compulsive (secret) ritual which included costumes (disguises). Lenz wants to send Green away, but cannot make the choice (is powerless) to do so. Lenz speaks of cults and rituals to Green, especially cults in which participants worship (give power to) infants. Orin is caught in a cycle of seduction and cannot help himself with either Steeply or the hand-model. He laments being given a choice of (the power over) what he watches and needs to be "the One" with all the attention, like an infant.

Hal's anxious counting of his breaths—cycles of inhalation and exhalation—is ritualistic. Mario (on a secret walk) is confused about the anxieties others have about "real stuff." Doucette is frozen in anxiety over his powerlessness to understand the annulation cycle of waste, which Pemulis explains to Arslanian, who chooses to wear a blindfold (taking away his power to see) and suffers the discomfort of not being able to find the lavatory. Pemulis will recycle Arslanian's waste. Green is powerless to remember the trauma of his youth, but is compulsively drawn to the Hawaiian music that he hears which unconsciously (secretly) reminds him of the trauma and overtly reminds him of a party at which he was unable to control his bowels (like an infant). Gately, mired in resident interfaces and other picayune and unpleasant routines, becomes "one part of something bigger he can't control"—having "no choice" not to fight once he sees a knife.

Infinite Jest IV

Around In Circles

The disparate threads of Wallace's narrative are looped as well as intertwined. Marathe and Steeply's conversation always comes back around. Winding its way through the novel, the conversation spreads out over the night of 30 April into the day of 1 May and continues still. Dusk and dawn are neither beginnings nor ends; they are parts of an ongoing cycle. Gately's all-night duty leads directly into his daytime job at the Shattuck Shelter. Conversations loop rather than resolve: Marathe goes round and round with Steeply; Joelle goes round and round with Gately. Marathe and Steeply are meeting for the sixth or seventh time, and Joelle and Gately's conversation is picked up in progress. The past is not over and done; it is readily available in the present via the characters' memories and the fragmented nature of the novel. The novel's present—November Y.D.A.U.—is also its past (because the novel begins a year later in November Y.G.) and its future (because of significant threads involving Marathe and Steeply, Jim, and other characters that occur before November Y.D.A.U.). Jim's memory of seeing "two perfectly circular motions on two distinct axes" in 1963 was published in 2003. Waiting to enter Tavis's office in November, Hal has a vivid memory from August in which he orbited his mother. Characters always come back around: Erdedy (prominently featured in Ch. 2), Roy Tony (significant in Ch. 5.2), and Kate Gompert (prominently featured in Ch. 10.1) join hands in the "huge circle" of the NA meeting in Ch. 25.3. Clenette (prominently featured in Ch. 5.2) leaves Tavis's office as Hal and others enter in Ch. 25.5, at the end of which Wallace leaves the thread of the Eschaton consequences just as something significant is about to occur. The reader need not wonder what happens next, though: there is no ending to miss; the thread will come back around.

Chapter 26 begins with Lenz missing curfew on 11 November and then circles back to follow the thread of Lenz's story (which is intertwined with Green's story) up to that moment, which intertwines with Gately's thread of pre- and post-curfew duties at the end of the chapter. Doors in this chapter are either unlocked or revolving; motion is not impeded. Lenz (and the cultists he describes), Tine, Tavis, Avril and Wayne, Hal, Gately, and Orin participate in rituals (actions that are repeated over and over). Pemulis explicates the annulation cycle of waste-creation and -utilization to Arslanian, who creates waste that Pemulis will use. The circular patterns of the intertwined threads yield simultaneities of past, present, and future and gaps in the narratives. The reader is only privy to snippets of Gately's ongoing conversations with residents. Following Orin's thread, the reader moves from the airport to Orin's post-liaison ride home back to the liaison. A piece of Mario's story that fits between Chs. 27.36 and 27.37 is presented in Ch. 26.13. Beginnings and endings are not easily discerned in this novel; the reader seems always to be in the middle, in orbit. The reader is powerless to resolve the conflicts of Wallace's novel and remains in a cycle of continuous entertainment without beginning or end: a pleasing powerlessness analogous the powerlessness of those who view Jim's cartridge. The narrative tensions of the novel accelerate (bulge) as the reader traces ever-increasing strands of narrative threads on an intertwined loop. To an orbited body, an object in orbit (in a loop) appears to bulge at perigee and recede at apogee. From the perspective of E.T.A. students, Tavis usually recedes but sometimes grows and rushes in. Hal's breaths cause his body to bulge and recede. From Gately's perspective, the sky seemed "to bulge and recede" like the breathing ceiling of his youth. The ongoing narrative tensions of Wallace's novel will bulge before they recede.

Chapter 27

A Kind of Writhing Weave: Horrors, Secrets, Pursuits, Surprises

Chapter 27.1, Section 124, Pages 620-626
Notes 257-258, Page 1045
12 November Y.D.A.U.

This section occurs on "a weekday c. mid-November," probably 12 November Y.D.A.U. (cf. Ch. 27.29 summary). The first nine lines of this section repeat almost exactly the text of Ch. 7.5 (p. 60): a listing of the features, components, capabilities, and accessories associated with a particular Y.D.A.U. model of InterLace teleputer. There are three differences: the words "post-Web" and "ceramic" have been added and the word "couture" is not italicized as it was on p. 60. The detailed listing underscores the societal trends of working at home and of "private watching of customized screens behind drawn curtains in the dreamy familiarity of home. A floating no-space world of personal spectation. . . . Total freedom, privacy, choice." Tawni Kondo's "immensely popular exercise program" is referenced, a program that was viewed briefly by the medical attaché before he chose to watch the unlabeled cartridge (p. 35).

This trend toward privacy has created "the new millennium's passion for standing live witness to things . . . , the priceless chance to be part of a live crowd, watching." "[S]pect-ops" include purse-snatchings, the 0000h. car-switching, and November's annual "drain and scrub [of] the Public Gardens' man-made duck pond for the upcoming winter [at which] long shiny trucks just all of a sudden appear in a ring at the pond's rim." "It seems as if everyone in metro Boston's seen at least one pond-draining," including several Ennet residents, Jim, Hal, and Mario. Recall that the duck pond is

Marathe's "favorite personal place of off-duty" in Boston (p. 427). From an eighth-floor window of "the State House Annex on Beacon and Joy Sts.," Rodney Tine looks down "at the concentric rings of pond and crowd and trucks [as] wind-driven leaves and street-grit [swirl] right outside." The wind is also "möbiusizing" Depend advertising banners strung out behind planes overhead. The people behind Tine include fellow U.S.O.U.S. employees Rodney Tine Jr. and Hugh Steeply, who left Orin at the Phoenix airport on 10 November (cf. Ch. 26.9) and whose activities at E.T.A. on 11 November will be documented as the chapter progresses.

At the bottom of p. 622, narrative focus shifts to the WYYY student engineer who worked with Madame Psychosis on her show (cf. Ch. 16.1). The engineer lies in the November sun on a "NASA-souvenir space blanket" (cf. Hal's NASA glass) amid the "fetal forms" of "the Gardens' permanent residents, sleeping or in stupors of various origin," one of whom "has vomited in his sleep" and another of whom is "on his hands and knees to the engineer's lower left, throwing up." Mario's recent visit to the studio is recounted (cf. n. 180), and the "engineer knows about the ambulance and the Brigham and Women's ICU and the five-day rehab ward" from Molly Notkin, who (still "bearded" and in a "sooty hat," cf. p. 227) came "to retrieve some old tapes of the program [cf. pp. 591-2] for the Madame's personal listening use." Joelle of course entered the five-day ward after overdosing at Molly Notkin's party on 7 November (Ch. 17) and stayed for less than a day before being admitted to Ennet House on 8 November (cf. p. 364, n. 134).

Two white vans have appeared, one at the bottom and one at the top of the hill. A "fleur-de-lis-with-sword-stem-masked" man in a wheelchair (cf. p. 485) exits the van, races down the hill, bumps a grocery cart and sends it rolling, scoops up the engineer, and makes for the "angled ramp [that slid] out like a tongue" from the van at the bottom of the hill, leaving in his wake "the NASA blanket twisting coruscant in the air high above" and "the hunched man, the unwell man who'd been hit by the dislodged cart . . . holding the parts that were hit."

PLOT AND CHARACTER: Art/Ent, Tech, U.S.O.U.S., O.N.A.N., A.F.R.
THEME: Isolation, Non-Action, Cycles, Recur

Citizens of O.N.A.N. prefer to be entertained (and often prefer to work) in the isolation of their homes through the use of their technologically advanced teleputers. Even when they go out, they simply substitute "being part of a live crowd, watching" for "private watching" (non-action). If a waste displacement vehicle goes off course, "the circle of impacted waste [draws] sober and studious crowds, milling in rings around the impact." For the pond-draining, people appear in a ring around the "perfectly round" duck pond to watch. Tine watches the pond-draining from above. The engineer and the "permanent residents" are "supine," "fetal," or "hunched": non-active. Alternately, the anti-O.N.A.N. A.F.R. operative sweeps through the Public Gardens, setting carts, blankets, and people in motion. Does Tine see this, or has he stepped away from the window?

Besides an almost exact recurrence of nine lines of text, the leaves and street-grit that swirl before Tine recall the tornado of waste Gately stirred up outside the Antitois' shop (pp. 479-80). Also, the NASA blanket twists in the air, and Depend banners (note the Glad bags, too; p. 623) möbiusize (like an infinity symbol) in the wind. The engineer lies "at about the angle of a living-room recliner." The recliner is a symbol of non-action, and non-action is often a precursor to danger, as it is for the engineer here and was for the attaché in his recliner. The "hunched man vomiting . . . who'd been hit by the dislodged cart" recalls Lamont Chu "on his hands and knees, throwing up," his "arched form" being hit by Otis P. Lord during Eschaton (p. 342). Tawni Kondo inspires "60 million North Americans" to choose participation in a "mass choreography somewhat similar to those compulsory A.M. tai chi slow-mo exercises in post-Mao China—except that the Chinese assemble publicly together." Compare this with Winston Smith, alone in his room and doing compulsory Physical Jerks at the command of "a youngish woman [on a "telescreen"], scrawny but muscular, dressed in tunic and gym shoes" (Orwell, *1984*: Book One, Ch. 3). Also, "spect-ops" even sounds like newspeak.

Chapter 27.2, Section 125, Pages 627-638
Notes 259-262, Pages 1045-1046
11 November Y.D.A.U., 1810h.

This section occurs at suppertime in the E.T.A. dining hall after an exhibition match called by Schtitt in which Stice unexpectedly almost beat Hal and after a regular match in which Shaw unexpectedly did beat Axford. It is the day after the meeting in Tavis's office (Ch. 25.5), and some E.T.A. students wonder whether possible Eschaton fallout has affected Hal's and Axford's play. Hal's match will be documented as the chapter progresses. "133 kids and thirteen assorted staff" as well as the "enormous peasant-skirted *Moment* soft-profiler" are at supper. Given that 136 students are in attendance at E.T.A. (p. 450), three are not at supper. Possalthwaite is probably in attendance, given that he was at drills on 9 November; so presumably Penn, Lord, and Ingersoll are the other absentees, although Ingersoll will arrive before the section ends (cf. p. 456, n. 266).

Troeltsch has "growing-up domestic confirmed traumas" around powdered milk and worries that E.T.A. has switched to using powdered milk. Troeltsch has a bottle of Seldane with him, purportedly for the cold he also claimed to have on 3 November, eight days ago. Recall this bottle includes Tenuate capsules stolen from Pemulis (p. 60).

Since the "tripod of Mario's near-fatal encounter with the U.S.S. Millicent Kent" (cf. Ch. 11.9), more "inanimate objects have either been moved into or just out of nowhere appearing in wildly inappropriate places around E.T.A. for the past couple of months in a steadily accelerating and troubling cycle." There have been instances of acoustic ceiling-tiles falling from their places, dinette sets in the tunnels, a lawnmower in the kitchen, a ball machine in the Females' Sauna, and squeegees hanging on the wall without apparent means of attachment. Also, "Stice's bed moves around" (cf. p. 394).

Hal, looking "east, out over the hillside and the Enfield Marine complex," sees Didi and Clenette (who was in Tavis's office yesterday and will stomp a Nuck tonight) returning to Ennet House from their jobs at E.T.A. Clenette carries "a bulging backpack on her back, as in bulging maybe with dumpster-pilferage."

Hal, whose "mouth feels like it's overflowing with spit," is "now a whole new Hal, a Hal who does not get high, or hide, a Hal who in 29 days is going to hand his own personal urine over to authority figures." Earlier today Hal had played "as if deep inside some well of his own private troubles." He and Mario know that "the skim milk at E.T.A. has been pre-mixed powdered milk since Charles Tavis assumed the helm four [actually five] years back."

"Stice had a traumatic psychic experience at fourteen when he'd set the weight on the pull-down station too high, and Dr. Dolores Rusk has authorized his exemption from all but very basic weights, pending resolution of his fear of weights" (cf. Rusk to Stice on p. 550 and Lyle's advice about weights on p. 128). This section began with a story about Stice's family, which is linked via a "Phoneless Cord" to a story about Freer's family at the end of the section. Steeply tells a story about his family in the next section.

PLOT AND CHARACTER: E.T.A.
THEME: His/Father, Secrets, Cycles, Waste, Recur

Snippets of Stice, Freer, and Incandenza family histories are recounted here. Hal, who used to get secretly high, knows that the milk is secretly powdered. Stice "has a secret suspicion about a secret" concerning his table (p. 635). "If you could open Stice's head you'd see a wheel inside another wheel." Littler kids run "in tight circles trying to follow the shadow of the ceiling fan." After Makulic throws up, a custodian mops "Makulic's chyme out in a thinning circle." Axford's food "tastes the way vomit smells," and Clenette hauls away "dumpster-pilferage." Concerning other recurring motifs, a "blue dot" has been used to correct the grammar of a milk dispenser sign, and Troeltsch's milk has a "bluish cast." Upon his entrance, there is "a corona around Ingersoll." Half of Struck's face is shadowed (p. 636). Stice tries to "respect [an] object with all his might." When Stice's parents are "on good domestic terms" there are "squeaking springs" behind their locked bedroom door (cf. that Jim never heard his parents' bed squeak, p. 499). Joelle's disfigurement is referenced (p. 634), as well as a "cardboard persona" and Winston Churchill, all three of which are also referenced in Ch. 17.3. Three figures from Greek myth are referenced at the bottom of p. 636. The tennis balls' "sudden anomalous swerves against wind and their own vectors" (p. 637) resonates with Wallace's essay "Derivative Sport in Tornado Alley," from his essay collection *A Supposedly Fun Thing I'll Never Do Again*. Are the anomalous swerves connected to the inappropriate movement of objects at E.T.A.?

Chapter 27.3, Section 126, Pages 628-648
Notes 263-264, Page 1046
1 May Y.D.A.U.

Marathe and Steeply's all-night conversation continues from Ch. 25.6. Steeply relates a story about his father, who was "consumed with a sort of entertainment": the old broadcast television program, "M*A*S*H." It started as an "attachment or habit" and "progressed very slowly" into a "withdrawal from life." He "began writing notes in a notebook" (like the former Navy M.P. of Gately's youth recording each beer he drank and Rodney Tine's recording his penis measurements) as he viewed and "never left the notebook lying around." Steeply recalls "the odor of obsession about the whole thing. The secrecy about the notebook, and the secrecy about the secrecy." "He began a practice of magnetically recording each week's 29 broadcasts and reruns. He stored the tapes, organizing them in baroque systems of cross-reference."

Steeply's mother found letters in the garbage addressed to Major Burns in Seoul, South Korea, associating the character with "some type of cataclysmic, Armageddon-type theme." (Steeply misremembers the name of the actor who played Major Burns. It was Larry Linville, not Maury Linville. Gompert referenced Jack Nicholson as "Nichols" on p. 78.) Later, Steeply's father actually mailed letters, which came back, being undeliverable. Steeply's father "started missing whole weeks at a time from work," and when he did go in customers complained "that the old man kept trying to engage them in bizarre theoretical discussions of the thematics of 'M*A*S*H.'"

When Steeply tells Marathe that his mother "began taking prescription anti-anxiety medication," Marathe thinks "Land of the freely brave."

Eventually, Steeply's father watched tapes constantly and refused to leave his den "even to go to the bathroom," which Marathe diagnoses as "the final enclosing isolation of obsession." Steeply: "He died just before his birthday. He died in his easy chair." Recall that the medical attaché watched the unlabeled cartridge in his recliner just before his birthday (p. 33) and is now in a ward (p. 548). Steeply's father died not of his obsession (Marathe: "The obsessed frequently endure"), but of a heart attack. Based on the expressions in the eyes of his father and of victims of the Entertainment, Steeply describes them as "trapped in some sort of middle. Between two things. Pulled apart in different directions" (as Erdedy was at the end of Ch. 2), not craving anything but "stuck wondering," as if they'd forgotten something.

Marathe politely asks Steeply to leave first as "Tucson AZ resumed once more the appearance of the mirage, as it had appeared when Marathe had first arrived." Now that the "sun was up and pulsing," all "birds and living animals had been silenced . . . and the site's bright loaders had not yet been started in movement" (cf. p. 530). The narrative thread of Marathe and Steeply's long conversation ends with them going round and round over the choice of a single word: misplaced or lost. In August, Steeply's article on Poor Tony will be published (Ch. 13.5); and in November, Steeply will interview Orin and visit E.T.A. Marathe's activities in November will be documented as the chapter progresses.

PLOT AND CHARACTER: Samizdat, U.S.O.U.S., A.F.R.
THEME: His/Father, Fear/Obsess, Secrets, Memory, Inf/Reg, Cycles, Recur

Steeply says of the story of his father's obsession and secret notes, "I'm trying to reconstruct this out of memory." During the tale he misremembers an actor's name, and he says the final episode of "M*A*S*H" ran in "autumn of B.S. 1983." This would be a rebroadcast of the final episode which originally ran on 28 February

1983 ("M*A*S*H," Episode Guides). Steeply's father regresses to "the final enclosing isolation of obsession." When describing his father, Steeply seems "self-enmeshed" and "more young" to Marathe. Completing the cycle of the long conversation, the *Brockengespenstphanom* (wraith-shadow phenomenon) is noted again as it was in the first section of the conversation (p. 641; cf. p. 88, n. 38), and Tucson appears to Marathe as it did when he "had first arrived." Also, Steeply's father was born in Troy NY, recalling references to Helen of Troy throughout the conversation (pp. 105-6, p. 375). There is an "annular pallor" on Steeply's hand, probably from the removal of "a wedding band." Marathe refers to recycling as "recircling."

"M*A*S*H" is another old-TV recurrence. Shadows again change shape as time passes. Marathe's chair makes "small squeaks"; a thought occurs to him "from somewhere blue" (cf. p. 90); and the sky has become "too light blue for his pleasure." Like an addict, Steeply has "several cigarettes going at one time" (cf. Lenz, p. 556), and his "wet and then dried makeup" looks "like a mask of a mentally ill clown." Is Marathe judging Steeply's mother for pill-taking and non-action when he says, "She never complained, however" (p. 646)? Did she allow events to transpire while ignoring their significance, like Gertrude in *Hamlet*?

Chapter 27.4, Section 127, Pages 648-651
13 November Y.D.A.U., 0245h.

This section occurs early on Friday the 13th, about 26 hours after "Wednesday's free-for-all unpleasantness with Lenz and Gately in the streetlet [Ch. 26.16], from which the whole House is still reeling and spiritually palsied." Gompert, Day, Erdedy, and Green are in the living room of Ennet House. "The Mr. Bouncety-Bounce Daily Program" is on, which features the title character in "his old cloth-and-safety-pin diaper and paunch and rubber infant-head mask." This program was also viewed briefly by the medical attaché on 1 April (p. 35). Green is sleeping and dreams of the traumatic childhood incident he cannot remember except in flashes (cf. Ch. 26.12).

Day relates a story from his childhood of the total horror that "rose in me, out of me, summoned somehow by the odd confluence of the fan"—creating vibrations in the glass of the upraised pane of the window in which the fan sat—and notes created by Day on his violin. "As the two vibrations combined, it was as if a large dark billowing shape came billowing out of some corner in my mind." (Recall one administrator's response to Hal's behavior as being like "a time-lapse, a flutter of some sort of awful . . . growth.") Day dropped his violin and ran, and the horror receded. When he returned to his playing, "the black flapping shape rose in my mind again. It was a bit like a sail, or a small part of the wing of something far too large to be seen in totality. It was total psychic horror: death, decay, dissolution, cold empty black malevolent lonely voided space. It was the worst thing I have ever confronted." When Day left the room again, the horror did not recede. "It was as if I'd awakened it and now it was active. It came and went for a year." But even after that year, "[e]very few months it would rise inside me." The last time Day experienced this feeling was during his sophomore year in college, when "he simply could not live with how it felt" and considered jumping out his window until a boy he hardly knew "came up and sat up with [him] until it went away."

Gompert (who spoke of horror on p. 73 and whose crossed legs form a circle) is the only one listening to Day (who spoke to Gately of horror on p. 1002). She says, "And there was this idea underneath that you'd brought it on, that you'd wakened it up. You went back up to the fan that second time. You like despised yourself for waking it up." Although the feeling hasn't returned in over twenty years, Day hasn't forgotten it and says, "If I had to go for any length of time with that feeling I'd surely kill myself."

PLOT AND CHARACTER: Ennet
THEME: Inf/Reg, Fear/Obsess, Dreams

Day relates a story from his childhood. Mr. Bouncety-Bounce, a "capering 130-kilo infant," is another symbol of infantile regression. This section has "a dreamy and almost surreal atmosphere," like an avant-garde film, and is primarily about fear. As Day speaks of his horror, Green dreams of his. Day says the black flapping shape in his mind is the "worst thing" he has ever confronted. Speaking to Winston Smith in Room 101, O'Brien says, "There are occasions when a human being will stand out against pain, even to the point of death. But for everyone there is something unendurable—something that cannot be contemplated" (Orwell, *1984*: Book Three, Ch. 5).

Chapter 27.5, Section 128, Pages 651-662
Notes 265-268, Page 1046
11 November Y.D.A.U.

This section documents the first set of the afternoon exhibition match called by Schtitt between Hal and Ortho Stice. Helen Steeply is in attendance, "accompanied for the first set [actually the first two sets, cf. p. 673] by Aubrey deLint before Thierry Poutrincourt stole his spot on the bleacher." Tavis will not let Steeply talk to Hal yet, even chaperoned. Schtitt's "transom's crow's-nested shadow . . . wheeled around gradually east like some giant hooded shadowed moving presence [and] gave everyone watching the fantods as it elongated along the nets."

An interlude of seven paragraphs (pp. 654-655) documents seven events or facts occurring simultaneously with the match: Gately is sleeping (hours before he will be shot); Poor Tony Krause is in a men's room "getting a whole new perspective on time" (cf. Ch. 20.2); Pemulis and Struck are "library-tossing" (so Pemulis has indeed "let Struck in" on the DMZ, cf. p. 218); Steeply's car is parked legally in the E.T.A. lot (presumably he was not parked legally during Eschaton); Tavis searches for a bathroom scale between appointments with parents; Avril's "whereabouts on the grounds" are unknown; and Orin is "once again embracing a certain 'Swiss' hand-model [in] a different tall hotel (from before) in Phoenix AZ" (different from the hotel of 10 November; cf. Chs. 26.9, 26.15, 26.11). Another two-line interlude (p. 658) refers to boys in a tunnel, whose activities will be documented in Ch. 27.7.

After a gesture of sportsmanship by Hal over a serve too close to call (cf. p. 118), deLint laughs when Steeply remarks that Hal and Stice seem like friends. The laugh reminds Steeply (recently divorced,

p. 375) of a man "hearing his son say his wife claimed no longer to know who he was." Is Steeply thinking of his own father? Was the story of his father's death told to Marathe in Ch. 27.3 a lie?

Steeply asks when he will be able to talk with Hal, and deLint guesses that "she" will not be allowed to talk with Hal, given that no E.T.A. student has ever been interviewed while in training. Recall Hal to Orin: "Schtitt's not going to let any of us here talk to anybody from some glossy rag like *Moment* without him or deLint sitting right there with us" (p. 1012). In response to Steeply's protests, deLint explains that Schtitt's philosophy of "self-transcendence through pain," of students getting "lost in something bigger than them[selves]," and of it "never about being seen" would be compromised by interviews. DeLint says that for Steeply "it's about entertainment and personality" and that "you chew [tennis players] up," but that E.T.A. attempts to teach students to "forget everything but the game" so that "the Show won't fuck them up." Although "they're all dying to throw themselves into" the machine, Schtitt's "teaching them to see the ball out of a place inside that can't be chewed." Steeply says, "It's a secret place." DeLint says that E.T.A. is "carved out to protect talented kids." Steeply counters, "Carved out of what, though, this place?"

PLOT AND CHARACTER: E.T.A., Hal, Art/Ent, U.S.O.U.S.
THEME: Isolation, Time, Fear/Obsess, Recur

E.T.A. practices a philosophy of isolation to protect their student players from the dangers of being seen as entertainers. Stice's moves on his serve seem isolated into frames like a film, and the ball's movement seems an "afterimage" (p. 656). The interludes are like episodic quick-cuts in a film and call attention to the frequent simultaneity of events in the novel. Day's frightening shadow of the previous section is recalled by the on-court shadow in this section. Mario also casts a "weird needly shadow" (p. 652) and will later be described as an "apparition" (p. 678). Gately wears a "Lone-Rangerish sleeping mask" (old TV character), and a cage image is called up by deLint telling Steeply that if he were in command "you'd be pressing your nose between the bars of the gate down there." Compare J. G. Struck

(p. 655) with James Albrecht Lockley Struck Jr. (pp. 118, 1058). In Ch. 1, has Hal gone to the secret place that can't be chewed?

Chapter 27.6, Section 129, Pages 663-665
Note 269, Pages 1047-1052
10-19 November Y.D.A.U.

This section consists of three letters: Steeply seeking permission to ask Marlon Bain questions, Bain granting permission (and misspelling Steeply's name), and placeholders for Steeply's seven questions and associated subquestions. Parts of Bain's answers (in a fourth letter) are documented in n. 269. Orin gave Steeply Bain's address (p. 1043) on the way to the Phoenix airport (p. 565) on 10 November. Presumably, Steeply was with Orin until he got on the plane and then wrote the first letter (which begins "In Phoenix on other business") either on the plane or in Boston. Presumably, Steeply either emailed it to Helen's AZ office and had someone mail it (Bain is "not InterNetted," p. 1043) from there, or he somehow put an AZ postmark on it while he was in Boston. Assuming the next three exchanges involved immediate responses and maximum postal efficiency (perhaps even the use of overnight mail) between MA (Bain) and AZ (Steeply's office), Steeply could read Bain's answers by 19 November. Saprogenic Greetings, Bain's greeting card company, "has just been bought up by a huge novelty concern [ACME]" (p. 1043) owned by "the Québec-sympathetic shadowy Albertan mogul who'd been such a force in the anti-broadcast A.C.D.C." (n. 204; cf. pp. 411-2, 414) and who took over ACME after "the serial Blammo Cigar tragedies" initiated by Bruce Green's father (p. 581).

Bain informs Steeply that he "became a sort of hanger-on at the Incandenza house out in Weston" after his "parents were horribly killed on the Jamaica Way commuter road one morning in the freak crash of a radio traffic-report helicopter." Joelle was unable to remember that it was Bain who was affected by this event (p. 238), and the helicopter was piloted by a soon-to-be-Lateral Alice Moore (p. 510). Although Bain "was one of the first matriculants" at E.T.A., he left "at 17, prior to graduation," citing "negative methoxy-psychedelic experiences [which left him] with certain Disabilities that to this day make normal life an exceptional challenge."

Although in his last interview with Steeply, Orin seemed to defend his father against a charge of insanity (p. 1038), here Bain tells Steeply that Jim was working "on a whole new genre of film-cartridge that Orin at the time claimed was driving Dr. Inc insane." Bain has it from his sister (one of Orin's Subjects, cf. p. 47) "that some incident occurred in the Incandenza's Volvo involving a word [that] cast a conjugal pall in all sorts of directions" (cf. n. 80).

Bain describes Orin as "the *least open man* I know" and says that Orin's apparent sincerity is "a pose of poselessness" and that Orin is not a liar but "has come to regard the truth as *constructed* rather than *reported*." Bain, who acknowledges that his judgments of Orin are "short on charity," believes Orin is attempting to escape the influence of Avril, "the most consummate mind-fucker I have ever met," and that "men who believe they hate what they really *fear* they *need* are of limited interest." Bain cites as evidence "of both Orin's mendacious idiocy and Mrs. Incandenza's unwillingness to countenance an idiotic lie" the story of the killing of the family dog, S. Johnson (Hal cited this incident in his 7 November conversation with Orin, p. 1014). On the day in question, Mario and Avril had been driven to one of Hal's tournaments by a "swarthily foreign-looking monilial-internist medical resident Mrs. Inc had introduced as a so-called 'dear and cherished friend' but hadn't explained how they'd met."

In answering Steeply's final question, Bain progresses from simply misspelling Steeply's name to the following distortions: Steeples, Steeley, Starkly, Starksaddle, and Bainbridge (perhaps because Steeply is using Bain as a bridge to the Incandenzas). Bain reflects on his lack of connection with his father, on his parents' deaths, and on why well-intentioned parents end up raising children with problems (e.g., "lethally self-indulgent" children). In assessing Avril's motives and her influence on Orin, Bain notes that after the S. Johnson incident Avril's "love-and-support-bombardment" of Orin increased. Bain wonders whether this was for Orin's sake or for Avril's "vision of herself as a more stellar Moms than any human son could ever hope to feel he merits." Bain compares Avril to a philanthropist who "views the recipients of his charity not as persons so much as pieces of exercise equipment on which he can develop and demonstrate his own virtue." Bain references Orin's old impression of Avril in which he moved in face-to-face with someone (cf. Orin's dream, pp. 46-7), "a person closing in, arms open wide, smiling" (cf. the indiscriminate huggers of the NA meeting with their "arms out and leaning in," p. 505).

PLOT AND CHARACTER: E.T.A., Orin, Avril, U.S.O.U.S.
THEME: Secrets, His/Father, Inf/Reg, Non-Action

In this section, Bain theorizes about the secret motives of Orin and Avril. Family histories of both the Bains and the Incandenzas are discussed. The phrases "lethally self-indulgent," "love-and-support-bombardment," and "a person closing in, arms open wide, smiling" resonate with *Infinite Jest*; a film that initiates lethal self-indulgence, that features Joelle in a "maternal 'I'm-so-terribly-sorry' monologue-scene" (p. 999), and that is being sent out unlabeled except for a smiley-face. In Ch. 27.3, Steeply describes victims of the Entertainment as "trapped in some sort of middle. Between two things. Pulled apart in different directions [and] stuck wondering" (p. 647). Compare this with the statement that marijuana smokers do not "lose interest in practical functioning, but rather Marijuana-Think themselves into labyrinths of reflexive abstraction [and try] to claw [their] way out of a labyrinth" (n. 269.a). Like Hamlet, abstract thinkers are accused of non-action by those who are unaware of the complexity of their thought processes. The killing of a dog is significant here as it was for Lenz throughout Ch. 26.

Footnotes are used in n. 269 instead of the standard endnotes, perhaps to indicate that the notes are Bain's rather than the narrator's. Compare the "MK Bain" of the letters with the "Marlon R. Bain" credit in *Death in Scarsdale* (p. 987). What is the "vailed warning" of Bain's "postal response" (p. 1048)? Does it have something to do with the "V.D." above Bain's name (p. 664)?

Chapter 27.7, Section 130, Pages 666-673
Notes 270-272, Page 1052
11 November Y.D.A.U., 1625h.

Several of the younger E.T.A. students are "26 meters directly below the Hal/Darkness match's Show Court" in the E.T.A. tunnels with Glad trashbags and flashlights. The boys are on "semi-punitive shit detail" due to their role in the recent Eschaton debacle and have been assigned to remove trash and make notes about "objects too bulky for them to move out of the way," all to clear a path to the Lung Storage Room in preparation for the inflation of the Lung. "With the exception of Kent Blott, every boy down here on this detail is an Eschatonite and a member of the Tunnel Club" (cf. p. 52), an organization founded (p. 899) by a young Heath Pearson ("former tow-truck shareholder," p. 1035), whose "No-Girls exclusion is the only ironclad part of [their] charter."

Because he claimed to have seen either a rat or a feral hamster, Blott is here to "trace the possible routes" of the rodent or to be disciplined "if it turns out he was yanking people's chains." The "rodential squeaking of match play and spectation far above" heightens the intensity of the search. The search is being done without the help of the overhead bulbs, since only a "booger-eating moron would do rat-reconnaissance in the light." The fear factor of feral hamsters is deemed equivalent to that of "mile-high toddlers [and] skull-deprived wraiths . . . in terms of late-night hair-raising Concavity narratives" (cf. p. 93). A feral-hamster sighting could distract from "post-Eschaton reprisals," and "hamster-incursions could be posited to account for the occult appearance of large and incongruous E.T.A. objects in inappropriate places" (cf. Ch. 27.2), making "the Tunnel Club guys something like heroes, foreseeably."

There is "a strange sweet stale burny smell" near the Pump Room (although Hal presumably quit visiting the Pump Room as of yesterday, p. 635). There are "several old broadcast televisions some older kids [kept] around to watch the static." A "bulky old doorless microwave oven" (is this the microwave oven Jim used to kill himself?) is too heavy to lift and marked for later pick-up. Three half-full

Glad bags containing fruit rinds and "old and mostly unlabelled" TP-cartridges found spilt from a single box (the tunnels are connected to Jim's "former optical and film-development facilities", p. 51) are hauled back to the tunnel's start by Blott. Will some of these cartridges end up as "dumpster-pilferage" in Clenette's "bulging backpack" (pp. 633-4), seen by Hal later tonight? Are the cartridges dangerous like Sunstrand's "annular-generated amps . . . waiting underground for anyone who digs" (p. 242)? Finally, a refrigerator with a horrible smell is discovered, which prompts a switch to fast-paced dialogue that intensifies the scene. The opened refrigerator is found to contain maggoty sandwich-meat. The smell expands as the boys run the other way back up the tunnel.

PLOT AND CHARACTER: E.T.A.
THEME: Waste, Recur, Fear/Obsess, Cycles

This section deals primarily with the collection of waste, and there are recurrences of the Glad and Habitant brand names (Habitant was the brand name of the "French-Canadian-type pea soup" in Marathe's example, p. 425) and of rats and feral hamsters as objects of fear. In Day's childhood, an expanding fear is triggered by sound; here an expanding fear is triggered by smell. The maggots and expanding smell add to the eerie quality of a scene played entirely in the dark with only circles of radiance from flashlights (cf. scenes from *Twin Peaks* in which characters visit the woods). The discovery of a feral hamster "would cause simply no end of adult running-in-circles."

Chapter 27.8, Section 131, Pages 673-682
Notes 273-277, Page 1052
11 November Y.D.A.U.

This section documents the third set of the afternoon exhibition match called by Schtitt between Hal and Ortho Stice; the first set was documented in Ch. 27.5. Steeply now sits between deLint and Thierry Poutrincourt, a Québecer who teaches the class on Québecois History that Hal is taking this semester (cf. p. 309). Note the change in English syntax that occurs when Steeply (smooth to rough) and Poutrincourt (rough to smooth) switch to conversing in French (Steeply in Parisian, Poutrincourt in Québecois), which is translated into English for the reader. Steeply's English syntax is smooth in his long meetings with Marathe because those meetings are conducted in English, although Steeply's "Québecois was better than Marathe's English" (p. 89).

Steeply asks Poutrincourt why Tavis has instructed prorectors to be unfriendly to "her." Poutrincourt explains that young players have an advantage in tennis because they are fearless and "do not feel the anxiety and pressure in the way it is felt by adult players." But this advantage dwindles as pressures build because the young tennis player is lavished with money and realizes that he or she is loved for winning. The young tennis player "must keep winning to keep the existence of love and endorsements and the shiny magazines wanting your profile." Therefore E.T.A. creates an environment to prepare the young tennis players to deal with pressure by making players continuously aware of their rank with respect to other players (as they will have to do as professionals) and by educating players about the dangers of the desire for fame.

Steeply notices the Tunnel Club of the previous section "carrying and dragging white plastic bags to the nest of dumpsters" at the rear of the parking lot.

Poutrincourt says that students are doomed if they are not able to transcend the shock of realizing that attaining a goal "does not complete or redeem you" and to transcend success with its attendant profiles and photographs. "Poutrincourt's figured out that Steeply is neither a civilian soft-profiler nor even a female," probably because of the way Steeply lit his cigarette (cf. n. 276; Marathe made a similar observation, p. 93). Schtitt trains students to "map out some path between needing the success and mockery-making of the success." Schtitt has adopted Jim's philosophy that it's "not so much how one sees a thing, but [the] relationship between oneself and what one sees," a concept that Jim translated "numerously across different fields." Poutrincourt summarizes quietly, "So to survive here for later is, finally, to have it both ways."

DeLint contrasts John ("No relation to the real John Wayne") Wayne and Hal with respect to "the head." Whereas Wayne has "everything," Hal's strength is in "constructing a game as much out of what's missing as what's there." Wayne is "pure force" without feeling or flexibility, who has the will to forget points when they are over; Hal remembers points and has an "emotional susceptibility" that, more than any other E.T.A. student, prompts "lapses in concentration . . . like some part of him leaves and hovers and then comes back" (compare deLint's ideas with Hal and Schtitt's dialogue on p. 461).

PLOT AND CHARACTER: E.T.A., Hal
THEME: Choice, Boundaries, Secrets, Cycles, Recur

This section is concerned with the choice between transcending or indulging the pleasures of celebrity. Poutrincourt says that "you cannot both celebrate and suffer, and play is always suffering." Wayne's force, lack of feeling, and "forgetful will" outrank Hal's flexibility, which deLint thinks is compromised by his emotional susceptibility (cf. Hal: "I'm not a machine," p. 12). However, Hal transcends his own boundaries as a player (cf. again Wallace's "Derivative Sport in Tornado Alley," from his essay collection *A Supposedly Fun Thing I'll Never Do Again*, especially given the "freak gust" that blows a ball out of bounds in Hal's match on p. 680) by "constructing a game as much out of what's missing [determined objectively] as what's there [experienced subjectively]." (Readers of this novel, the structure of which is analogous to a Sierpinski Gasket (cf. the Introduction of the study), must fill in holes and construct an interpretation as much out of what's missing as what's there.) Hal capitalizes on the "relationship between oneself [subjective] and what one sees [objective]." Poutrincourt's phrase "Two selves, one [objective, transcendent] not there" is followed by a reference to Steeply's wife, not there for Steeply since the divorce.

DeLint explains the bandage on Possalthwaite's nose as a "soap-and-shower-slipping thing," but Steeply should be aware of the actual origin of the injury since he spied on the Eschaton debacle. Steeply is well disguised as a woman and a journalist, but Poutrincourt sees through these disguises (resonating with Stice's "secret suspicion about a secret," p. 635), which means she must be "an almost professionally hypervigilant and suspicious person" (n. 276). Is Poutrincourt, a Québecer, secretly involved with the A.F.R.? Regarding cycles and recurrences, there are circles beneath Poutrincourt's blue eyes (p. 674), and her hands move in small circles (p. 676). Troeltsch, "hunched over and gesturing and speaking into his empty fist," reports that Hal and Stice have chilly and cold blue eyes (p. 678). Like Gately, "Stice was born with a large head" (p. 678).

Chapter 27.9, Section 132, Pages 682-686
Note 278, Page 1052
14 November Y.D.A.U., after 2215h. (p. 700)

This section features Michael Pemulis's "older brother" (p. 551) Matty, a prostitute eating at a Portuguese restaurant on his twenty-third birthday and overlooking "the heavy foot traffic between Inman and Central Squares," including a bag-lady who defecates on the pavement. Matty also sees "two underweight interracial girls" followed by Poor Tony Krause (how Poor Tony gets from his seizure in Ch. 20.2 to here will be documented in Ch. 27.11).

Matty thinks of his sexually abusive father (recall that Pemulis's "pre-E.T.A. home life was apparently hackle-raising," p. 154), who died "when Matty was seventeen, of pancreatic complaints," spraying Matty with particles of aspirated blood that hung in the air. Mr. Pemulis used to open the door to his sons' bedroom "with the implacable slowness of a rising moon, [his] shadow lengthening across the floor" and with "a smell about him" of malt liquor. While Mr. Pemulis raped Matty, Mick[e]y was "over in a cot by the window always silent as a tomb, on his side, face to the wall and hidden." The brothers didn't speak about the incidents afterwards. The first-person narrator of n. 278 wonders, "Where was *Mrs.* Pemulis all this time, late at night"? Compare this to the AA speaker of p. 372 "lying perfectly still in the next bed," "face turned to the wall," as her adoptive father raped her paralyzed and catatonic adoptive sister. The speaker would then tidy-up her sister in "unspoken complicity."

PLOT AND CHARACTER: AA&R
THEME: His/Father, Memory, Fear/Obsess, Non-Action

In this section, Matty's history as a victim of abuse has an effect on his present actions. Mr. Pemulis chastised Matty for shrinking away from him in fear of impending abuse, "[a]s if the sone were some forty-dollar whore off the docks," and Matty is now a prostitute. Matty had "seen sometimes where persons that had unpleasant things happen to them as children blocked the unpleasantness out in their mentality as adults and forgot it. Not so with Matty Pemulis." Matty does not have the "forgetful will" discussed by deLint in the previous section. Again, fear is accompanied by a slow-moving shadow and a smell. Again, a mother's non-action is called into question. The significance of prostitute Stokely "Dark Star" McNair's nickname is made clear by Mr. Pemulis's smearing of Vaseline "roughly around Matty's rosebud, his dark star." The word "rosebud" is also symbolic of a significant childhood memory in Orson Welles's *Citizen Kane*.

Chapter 27.10, Section 133, Pages 686-689
Note 279, Page 1052
11 November Y.D.A.U.

This section takes place after supper (after Ch. 27.2) on the day of Hal's close match with Stice. Hal seeks insight on his poor play and on "what the exhibition might have signified," and is "chill[ed] to the root" when deLint says that Hal "never quite occurred out there" (cf. the dialogue of Schtitt and Hal at the 9 November drills, p. 461). Afterwards, a depressed Hal watches several "cartridges of his late father's entertainments" in Viewing Room 6, where Hal held his Big Buddy meeting in Ch. 11.8. Hal "hasn't gone over twenty-four hours without getting high in secret for well over a year, and doesn't feel very good at all" (n. 279). Recall the "whole new [Hal] who does not get high" (p. 635) since the 10 November meeting with Tavis.

One of the cartridges Hal views is *Union of Publicly Hidden in Lynn*, which is not listed in n. 24 (but cf. Moore, commentary on draft pp. 610-16). *Valuable Coupon Has Been Removed* is listed as silent in n. 24

(p. 991), but features a maddening monologue according to the narrator for Hal in this section. "Each of the cartridges is a carefully labelled black diskette," which suggests that there is no danger of Hal accidentally watching an unlabeled copy of *Infinite Jest*. An explication of *Wave Bye-Bye to the Bureaucrat* is provided. It is a work about a man who makes a selfless choice and includes a scene "filmed in a glacial slo-mo" and "a clear internal-conflict moment, one of Himself's very few." It "remains Mario's favorite," and "Hal secretly likes it, too." Hal plans to watch *Blood Sister: One Tough Nun*, which unbeknownst to Hal "germinated out of James O. Incandenza's one brief and unpleasant experience with Boston AA."

PLOT AND CHARACTER: Hal, Art/Ent
THEME: His/Father, Memory, Recur, Choice

Hal watches his late father's cartridges as he has no father to go to when he is depressed. Hal struggles to remember the name of the former E.T.A. kid featured in *Wave Bye-Bye to the Bureaucrat* (Smothergill), but cannot. There are recurrences of a slow motion moment in the film and a double-bind for the fictional bureaucrat, who makes an unselfish (not an infantile) choice, which prompts the kid to ask, "Are you Jesus?"

Chapter 27.11, Section 134, Pages 689-691
14 November Y.D.A.U., after 2215h. (p. 700)

Chapter 20.2 ended with Poor Tony Krause in seizure on the T. It turns out that Poor Tony "awoke in the ambulance lizardless and continent and feeling right as rain." Cambridge City Hospital bowed to his "will not to stay" when presented with "a Health Card that [was] expired and not even in [Poor Tony's] name." Krause then resumes his trek toward Antitoi Entertainent, now only blocks away. He has no way of knowing that the Antitois were killed by the A.F.R. six nights ago (Ch. 24.6).

Poor Tony recalls the night that he and five of his fellow prostitutes made up half of a crew of decoys wearing "identical red leather coats and auburn wigs and spike heels." The crew included "the [now] late Stokely ('Dark Star') McNair" (recall that McNair had "got the virus for sure" last Christmas Eve, p. 129). On that night, the crew's job was to "disperse in a dozen different vectors" from a hotel ballroom to facilitate the escape of "an androgynous Québecer insurgent" who "threw foul semi-liquid violet waste from a souvenir miniature waste-displacement barrel in the face of [a] Canadian Minister." The "diversionary aspects" of the operation were the responsibility of the Antitois, "only one of whom could or would speak."

Krause sidesteps "an impressive pile of dog droppings" (actually the droppings of "a bag-lady-type older female," p. 683) and passes both the restaurant in which "his old former crewmate Mad Matty Pemulis" sits and Ryle's Tavern where he first met the Antitois, debating whether to snatch the purses of "the duo interracial" (cf. "the two skinny girls," p. 684). Recall that Poor Tony once snatched a purse containing a heart (Ch. 13.5).

PLOT AND CHARACTER: AA&R
THEME: Memory, Waste, Recur

Poor Tony's memory (of the night he presumably first wore his red leather coat; cf. "the Antitoi brothers' red leather coat," p. 300) involves the flinging of waste. The crew of decoys for the waste-flinger disperses through revolving doors, which recalls the scene in *Infinite Jest* (p. 549). Poor Tony flirts with a "blue-jawed paramedic" (p. 690; cf. Hal's blue-jawed MD, p. 16) and parodies the Minimal Mambo, a dance performed at Molly Notkin's party (p. 229). The end of this section is a recurrence of events in Ch. 27.9 from a different point of view.

Chapter 27.12, Section 135, Page 692
13 November Y.D.A.U.

This section is assumed to occur after Geoffrey Day spoke of his horror in Ch. 27.4. Although Day finds himself "almost missing Lenz," he "would die before he admitted he missed either Lenz or his soliloquies about the Hog, which had been frequent." Penis-naming is a common occurrence among Ennet House's male residents, the Frightful Hog being Lenz's name for his (but cf. that a Texas catheter's "receptacle for his Unit gives Lenz inadequacy-issues," p. 544). "A surprising amount of Day's Recovery Journal is filled with quotations from R. Lenz." Day's journal also contains "a certain amount of comparative-class data." Neither Day nor Ewell nor Erdedy—presumably 3-Man roommates after Lenz's discharge—have named their penises.

PLOT AND CHARACTER: Ennet
THEME: Recur, Loss

Day and Gompert were the focus of the previous Ennet section (Ch. 27.4). Day continues the Ennet thread in this section, which also prepares for the return of Lenz in Ch. 27.23; and Gompert is featured in several sections of the chapter, including the next two. There is a recurrence here of penis obsession and the recording of data (cf. Tine, Ch. 26.3). Day experiences an unexpected sense of loss in the absence of Lenz's company.

Chapter 27.13, Section 136, Pages 692-698
Notes 280-283, Page 1053
13 November Y.D.A.U.

Hal's depression in Ch. 27.10 and Geoffrey Day's sense of loss regarding the absence of Lenz and his Hog in Ch. 27.12 lead into this section (featuring Kate Gompert, last seen with Day on 13 November in Ch. 27.4), which references the sensualist's "beloved Unit" and makes clear the difference between "dead-eyed anhedonia"—the category under which Hal's depression falls—and the "predator-grade" clinical depression experienced by Kate Gompert (cf. Ch. 10.1). This section is narrated in first-person plural (cf. "we" on p. 694, which presumably refers to the narrator and the reader).

Anhedonia is "a kind of emotional novocaine" which involves a "radical abstracting of everything": "The world becomes a map of the world." Contrast this with the Eschaton of 8 November in which the map of a world conflagration became a real-world E.T.A. conflagration. Younger E.T.A.s are "mostly going through the motions when they invoke anhedonia" and misattribute Jim's reasons for "putting his head in the microwave [to] anhedonia." Hal is anhedonic and lonely because he "hasn't had a bona fide intensity-of-interior-life-type emotion since he was tiny." He can "satisfy everyone but himself that he's in there, inside his own hull, as a human being—but in fact he's far more robotic than John Wayne." Contrast this with deLint's analysis of Hal and Wayne (p. 682) and with Hal's analysis of himself one year from now in Ch. 1: "I am in here" (p. 3); "I'm not a machine. I feel and believe" (p. 12).

Once young people enter "spiritual puberty," they will "wear any mask" to avoid "the great transcendent horror [of] loneliness, excluded encagement in the self." The "lively arts of the millennial U.S.A." show them "how to fashion masks of ennui and jaded irony." Jim's *The American Century as Seen Through a Brick* (summarized on p. 695 and featuring Joelle's thumb, cf. p. 297) is about the "U.S. myth that cynicism and naïveté are mutually exclusive. Hal, who's empty but not dumb, theorizes privately that what passes for hip cynical transcendence of sentiment is really some kind of fear of being really human, since to be really human (at least as he conceptualizes it) is probably to be unavoidably sentimental and naïve and goo-prone and generally pathetic [like Mario? cf. Mario's thoughts on "real stuff," p. 592], is to be in some basic interior way forever infantile, some sort of not-quite-right-looking infant dragging itself anaclitically around the map." Hal "despises what it is he's really lonely for: this hideous internal self . . . just under the hip empty mask." He "goes around feeling like he misses somebody he's never even met" (n. 281; cf. Mario's "It's weird to feel like you miss someone you're not even sure you know," p. 589).

"Instead of just an incapacity for feeling, a deadening of soul, the predator-grade depression Kate Gompert always feels as she Withdraws from secret marijuana is itself a feeling. It goes by many names . . . but Kate Gompert, down in the trenches with the thing itself, knows it simply as *It*." *It* is described in detail on pp. 695-6 as "psychic pain," "evil," "poisoning that pervades the self," "nausea of the cells and soul," and "an unnumb intuition in which the world is fully rich and animate and un-map-like and also thoroughly painful and malignant and antagonistic to the self, which depressed self It billows on and coagulates around and wraps in *Its* black folds and absorbs into *Itself*" (cf. Day's horror of Ch. 27.4). A person in It's clutches is in "a sort of double bind in which [any human action or its opposite is] not just unpleasant but literally horrible" and "lonely on a level that cannot be conveyed." The "clinically depressed person cannot even perceive any other person or thing as independent of the universal pain that is digesting her cell by cell" and is therefore "incapable of empathy with any other living thing." Unlike victims of torture, the causes of a depressed person's pain are "undetectable by any outside party." Like a person who jumps from a burning building sees the flames as worse than the fall, a depressed person who attempts suicide sees *It* as worse than death. The fact that people who are not in the grip of *It* cannot understand a depressed person's pain makes the depressed person feel even more alone.

Kate Gompert knows a "permanently psychotically depressed man" whose "fondest dream [is] anhedonia, complete psychic numbing. I.e. death in life." The man—Ernest Feaster, whose "case gave Kate Gompert the howling fantods"—was evaluated for a type of surgery in which "the part of the brain that causes all sentiment and feeling" would be removed. Kate doesn't know if he had the surgery or not.

PLOT AND CHARACTER: E.T.A., Hal, Art/Ent, Ennet
THEME: Fear/Obsess, Isolation, Recur

This section describes the loneliness and the horror associated with two types of depression: anhedonia (abstract) and clinical, psychotic depression (concrete). Recurring images and concepts include encagement, masks, maps, double binds, and the howling fantods. Other works by Wallace relevant to this section are his story "The Depressed Person," from *Brief Interviews with Hideous Men*, and his essay "E Unibus Pluram: Television and U.S. Fiction," from *A Supposedly Fun Thing I'll Never Do Again*. Stephen King's horror novel *It*—at 1137 pages comparable to *Infinite Jest* in length—is about a group of adults who have to deal with a billowing fear from their childhood after one of their members, terrified by the resurfacing of the past, kills himself in his bathtub. Eventually, the group goes back "down in the trenches [like the Tunnel Club] with the thing itself." Critics who fear a charge of "unsophisticated naïveté" for associating Wallace with King may prefer Ch. 6 of Tolstoy's *The Death of Ivan Ilych*, which also references "Caius is Mortal" (cf. p. 693) before describing the pain in Ivan Ilych's side and his consciousness of impending death: "And what was worst of all was that It drew his attention to itself not in order to make him take some action but only that he should look at It, look it straight in the face: look at it and without doing anything, suffer inexpressibly" (Tolstoy, who was referenced on p. 95).

What does it mean that Hal has no idea "yet" of why his father killed himself (p. 694)? What will he learn in the next year? Who is correct in their description of Hal: deLint, who says that Hal unlike Wayne has "emotional susceptibility" (p. 682); or the narrator of this section, who says that Hal although lonely is "more robotic than John Wayne"? Does Hal change between now and next November, when he says "I am in here" (p. 3) and "I'm not a machine. I feel and believe" (p. 12)?

Chapter 27.14, Section 137, Pages 698-700
Notes 284-286, Page 1053
14 November Y.D.A.U., after 2215h. (p. 700)

The "psychotically depressed Kate Gompert" of the previous section walks with Ruth van Cleve on Cleve's "first day off new residents' three-day House Restriction" (cf. "the brand-new Court-Ordered female, Ruth van Cleve," who entered the house on 11 November; p. 595). Van Cleve "is shaping up to be excruciating for Kate Gompert" because van Cleve "talks nonstop into her right ear." Gompert sees "persons in wheelchairs" (A.F.R.?) with "invitations to help them." Van Cleve and Gompert are the women being followed by Poor Tony (cf. Chs. 27.9, 27.11), who eyes their purses.

PLOT AND CHARACTER: Ennet, AA&R
THEME: Boundaries, Recur

Boundaries blur for Gompert, who "hasn't slept in four nights" and who sees reflections in shop windows as "disconnected floating heads." Recurring topics of obsession are found in Gompert's focus on the time she needs to get back before curfew and in van Cleve's request for a toothbrush. Van Cleve has a "projecting beak." Gompert and van Cleve "move in and out of cones of epileptic light" as a man who just had a seizure follows them. Although van Cleve talks obsessively like Lenz, Gompert does not listen with interest like Green. Gompert's concern with a curfew and the "excruciating" poison of van Cleve's words in her ear resonate with the concerns of the ghost in *Hamlet* (I.iv). Contrast the story of van Cleve's baby with the story of the AA speaker's baby in Ch. 22.7. The meta-narrator of n. 285 believes that van Cleve has misused a word.

Chapter 27.15, Section 138, Page 700
11 November Y.D.A.U.

This section is the first of five to address simultaneous events at or near E.T.A. during the evening of 11 November. Troeltsch is alone in the room he shares with Pemulis and Schacht (cf. p. 211) "preparing to call the action" of a pro-wrestling cartridge. He is "surrounded by Seldane-bottles and two-ply facial tissue" (cf. Ch. 7.6).

PLOT AND CHARACTER: E.T.A.
THEME: Time, Fear/Obsess

Like the interludes in Ch. 27.5, Chs. 27.15-19 call attention to the frequent simultaneity of events in the novel. Troeltsch's obsession with pretend-sportscasting and (addiction to?) Seldane (Tenuate?) continues.

Chapter 27.16, Section 139, Page 700
11 November Y.D.A.U.

This section is the second of five to address simultaneous events at or near E.T.A. during the evening of 11 November. Pemulis checks to see if the DMZ is still secure in its hiding place (cf. p. 216).

PLOT AND CHARACTER: E.T.A., AA&R
THEME: Time, Fear/Obsess, Secret

Like the interludes in Ch. 27.5, Chs. 27.15-19 call attention to the frequent simultaneity of events in the novel. Although the drop-ceiling is a "time-tested entrepôt" (p. 216), Pemulis, afraid the DMZ will be gone, obsessively reassures himself that it is still there in its hiding place.

Chapter 27.17, Section 140, Page 700
11 November Y.D.A.U.

This section is the third of five to address simultaneous events at or near E.T.A. during the evening of 11 November. Lyle "hovers" with his "eyes rolled up" in the weight room and seems to be in a trance.

PLOT AND CHARACTER: E.T.A.
THEME: Time, Boundaries

Like the interludes in Ch. 27.5, Chs. 27.15-19 call attention to the frequent simultaneity of events in the novel. Lyle transcends the physical boundaries of gravity by hovering in the weight room and seems to be having a transcendent spiritual experience as well. Compare the description of Lyle in this section with the display Joelle sees on p. 224.

Chapter 27.18, Section 141, Page 701
11 November Y.D.A.U.

This section is the fourth of five to address simultaneous events at or near E.T.A. during the evening of 11 November. Schtitt and Mario—going for ice cream at Low-Temperature Confections on Schtitt's BMW cycle (cf. pp. 79, 83, and 173)—are on a "downhill flight, preparing to whoop when they bottom out."

PLOT AND CHARACTER: E.T.A., Mario
THEME: Time, Recur

Like the interludes in Ch. 27.5, Chs. 27.15-19 call attention to the frequent simultaneity of events in the novel. The downhill flight of this section recalls the A.F.R. swooping up the WYYY engineer in Ch. 27.1.

Chapter 27.19, Section 142, Page 701
11 November Y.D.A.U.

This section is the fifth of five to address simultaneous events at or near E.T.A. during the evening of 11 November. After obtaining the phone number of *Moment* Magazine's business address in AZ, Avril dials her phone, presumably to contact the *Moment* Magazine offices.

PLOT AND CHARACTER: E.T.A., Avril
THEME: Time, Recur, Fear/Obsess

Like the interludes in Ch. 27.5, Chs. 27.15-19 call attention to the frequent simultaneity of events in the novel. Avril has "three or four cigarettes all going at once," a recurring image for addicts or obsessives, and uses "a blue felt pen to stab at the console's keys." Steeply currently is looking for Hal (p. 702). If Avril is calling *Moment*, why is she doing so while Steeply is still at E.T.A.? Has Poutrincourt communicated her suspicion of Steeply, prompting Avril's call? Is Avril calling *Moment* to confirm Steeply's employment? Is she seeking information about Orin?

Chapter 27.20, Section 143, Pages 701-711
Notes 287-295, Pages 1053-1054
11/14 November Y.D.A.U.

Pages 701-6 pick up the narrative thread of Hal's 11 November post-Stice-match cartridge-watching from Ch. 27.10. Pages 707-11 shift focus to Joelle on 14 November, three days after the Gately-Nuck incident (Ch. 26.16). Hal is watching *Blood Sister: One Tough Nun* (as planned, cf. p. 689) with Boone, Unwin, Longley, and Bash, who have now joined him in Viewing Room 6. Longley informs Hal that there is "a totally huge lady [Steeply] cruising the halls looking for [him]." Bash reports "moaning coming from Struck and Shaw's room" over a "paper due for Thierry tomorrow," an assignment already completed by Hal. Longley reports that Pemulis "did something really funny today," but Hal sarcastically deflects any impending anecdote. Arslanian (with his blindfold now around his neck), Possalthwaite, and Blott "all drift in" and "are sucked immediately into *Blood Sister*'s unfolding narrative . . . until after a while Hal's the only person in the room who isn't 100% absorbed."

Pages 704-6 provide an explication of *Blood Sister: One Tough Nun*, a film inspired by Boston AA (n. 289) that includes a scene in which Blood Sister and her charge "compare tattoos" (cf. Ennet House residents in Ch. 16.4). Blood Sister's charge (played by Marla-Dean Chumm, p. 990) is "burn-scarred" and addicted to cocaine: "Whether the girl's hideous facial burn-scars are the result of a free-base accident is never made explicit" (n. 290). Although filmed before Joelle begins working regularly with Jim (cf. n. 24), this character certainly has much in common with present-day Joelle, who will become the focus of this section following the explication. Boone suggests that the "deformed addicted girl" has exchanged "one will-obliterating 'habit' for another, substituting one sort of outlandish head-decoration for another," which is "very close to the way many not-yet-desperate-enough newcomers to Boston AA see Boston AA as just an exchange of slavish dependence on the bottle/pipe for slavish dependence on meetings" until their "double-bound desperation" brings them back to Boston AA.

While the others are focused on *Blood Sister*, Hal, in a "radical loss of concentration that attends THC-Withdrawal," thinks of *Low-Temperature Civics* (Schtitt and Mario are currently en route to Low-Temperature Confections, p. 701), in which the CEO of a sandwich-bag conglomerate "has an ecstatic encounter with Death ([played by 'Madame] Psychosis') and becomes irreversibly catatonic" (p. 991). Around the time of this work, Jim spent a year "in a remote spa off Canada's Northwest coast, where he supposedly met and bonded with Lyle." *Low-Temperature Civics* was Joelle's "first appearance in a James O. Incandenza project" (not counting the use of her thumb in *The American Century as Seen Through a Brick*, p. 297).

On Saturday 14 November, Joelle is attending a Cocaine Anonymous meeting at St. Elizabeth's Hospital (cf. "the St. E's [AA] meeting on Wednesday," p. 362), a "click and a half straight downhill from E.T.A.," "where Don Gately, whom she just got done visiting and mopping the massive unconscious forehead of, is lying in the Trauma Wing in a truly bad way." She "thinks with fearful sentiment" of the delirious Gately, who was "looking at his room's semi-private ceiling like it would eat him." The truthful speaker she is watching tells a story of "money in the pocket and no defense against the urge," in which he gives up rent and grocery money to use cocaine, betraying his wife and child. This event prompted his entry into both the Shattuck Shelter and Cocaine Anonymous. Tonight is the first time Joelle has "felt sure she wants to keep straight no matter what it means facing" and "the first time in a long time [she's] even considered possibly showing somebody [Gately] the face."

PLOT AND CHARACTER: E.T.A., Hal, Art/Ent, Joelle, AA&R
THEME: Inf/Reg, Non-Action, Cycles, Recur, Fear/Obsess

This section balances Jim's rejection of recovery programs like Boston AA (of which *Blood Sister* is an allegory, n. 289) with Joelle's "starting to I.D." with them. The structure of this section invites comparisons between Ennet House and E.T.A. Like the doors in Ennet House (p. 548), the E.T.A. viewing rooms have no locks (since dental stimulators and panatela butts were found in V.R.3, n. 287: cf. Schacht; pp. 117, 395). Addicts "who stick and Hang" (p. 707) recall E.T.A. students who "hang for the long haul" (p. 120). Regarding compulsive passivity, the E.T.A. kids are "sucked immediately into *Blood Sister*'s unfolding narrative," and the addict has "no defense against the urge." The three nuns in *Blood Sister* are part of an ongoing cycle of biker chicks saved by tough ex-biker nuns (p. 704). The cartridge features "combatants [who] circle each other," and Boone watching the cartridge eats "frozen yogurt from a cylindrical carton." There are recurrences of slow-motion movement in the way Hal looks, raises his arm, and spits "slowly" and the way Boone withdraws her yogurt spoon "just as slowly" (pp. 701-2). Hal says that he's "isolating." The desperation of the addict is described as "double-bound." The speaker is yet another addict who has wept. Joelle thought "with fearful sentiment" of Gately, who seemed frightened of the ceiling. After bingeing, the addict said his house's "emptiness pulsed and breathed." The "endless little Xeroxed formalities" read aloud at CA meetings recall the U.H.I.D. flyer read by Joelle on her program (p. 187).

Like *Hamlet*, two of Jim's works discussed in this section are revenge stories: *Blood Sister: One Tough Nun* makes use of "the seductive formulae of violent payback," and *The Night Wears a Sombrero* is "an ambivalent-but-finally-avenging-son story." The addict at the CA meeting makes "all speech a protracted apostrophe to some absent Jim" (n. 294), which recalls Velvet Underground lyrics in drug-related songs like "Sister Ray" ("whip it on me, Jim") and "Heroin" ("all the Jim-Jim's in this town") and perhaps resonates with the E.T.A. students' commentary on the (absent) Jim Incandenza's work. Note that the addict switches from Jim to James (p. 710) after relating his decision to get straight. Foltz called Roy Tŏny "Jim" on p. 507.

Chapter 27.21, Section 144, Pages 711-714
Notes 296-298, Page 1054
11 November Y.D.A.U.

The explication of *Blood Sister* continues from the previous section. Hal remembers the name of the actor (Smothergill) he was trying to remember earlier (cf. p. 687). Possalthwaite and Arslanian (who were not listed in the tunnels earlier, cf. p. 666), have "brought Blott in to speak to Hal about something disturbing they encountered during their disciplinary shit-detail in the tunnels that P.M." Presumably, the "something disturbing" is not a blank cartridge, given that the cartridges were hauled away as trash (although some cartridges may not have made it all the way to the trash, cf. that "the cartridge-cases' sharp edges put holes in their Glad bags" (p. 670)). As Hal looks for a cartridge case in V.R.6, it is reiterated that, unlike most of the cartridges found in the tunnel, all the cases in V.R.6 "are clearly labelled" (cf. p. 689).

PLOT AND CHARACTER: E.T.A., Hal, Art/Ent
THEME: Cycle, Secrets, Recur

Blood Sister, with its convoluted, interconnected plots and ambiguous finale, is described as "narratively prolix and tangled stuff," a description that could apply to *Infinite Jest* as well. There is a long cycle of saved nuns: new girl saved by Blood Sister saved by Vice-Mother Superior "saved" by Mother Superior saved by someone else in a long line back to the Huron nun saved by the "original founder of the Toronto tough-girl-saving order". The Vice-Mother Superior was "suffering a kind of hidden degenerative recidivist soul-rot" which led to her establishment of a secret drug-dealing operation. Blood Sister "knocking [a] toothless head clean off" recalls the disembodied heads seen by Gompert (p. 699). The new girl is found "bluely" dead; Blood Sister rides a Hawg (of a different sort than Lenz's Hog); and Hal remembers a name from "[o]ut of nowhere." Reference is made to Kabuki theatre (p. 712), in which the use of makeup is analogous to a mask.

Chapter 27.22, Section 145, Pages 714-716
Note 299, Page 1054
14 November Y.D.A.U., before 2230h.

As Ch. 27.14 ended, Poor Tony was eyeing the purses of Gompert and van Cleve. As this section opens, Poor Tony (who Gompert sees as "the apparition") has taken their purses and is being pursued by van Cleve. Gompert hit her head on a lightpost during the purse-snatching incident. From Gompert's perspective, a "kind of gargoyle seemed to detach itself from a storefront hardware display and moved in, its motions oddly jerky, as in a film missing frames." The gargoyle turns out to be a smelly old man who declares that he is "a witness." A detailed description of the purse-snatching moment concludes the section.

PLOT AND CHARACTER: Ennet, AA&R
THEME: Time, Recur

The witness's motions are "oddly jerky, as in a film missing frames." The purse-snatching is described like a slow-motion moment in a film. Several recurrences are associated with Gompert here: she sees Poor Tony as an "apparition"; her mouth floods with spit; her swing in a "wide circle" triggers a memory of childhood; and she watches Krause and van Cleve "recede, both seeming to be shrieking for help" (like the woman at the Enfield Marine complex: pp. 196, 590, 608-9).

Chapter 27.23, Section 146, Pages 716-719
14 November Y.D.A.U., before 2215h. (p. 718)

This section marks the first appearance of Randy Lenz since the Gately-Nuck incident of 11-12 November (Ch. 26.16). He is under the influence of cocaine and, like Poor Tony in this chapter, follows two women ("two very small sized Chinese women"; cf. two "Oriental women [with] shopping bags" on Joelle's 7 November walk, p. 224) with an eye towards stealing their bags. Since the "ejection from the House," Lenz is "Alone," is "ever moving," and (analogous to U.H.I.D. members) is "disguised" and "could openly hide."

"The Chinese women and then Lenz all passed a gray-faced woman squatting between two dumpsters, her multiple skirts hiked up" (cf. p. 683). They also pass a man in a "rat-colored suit . . . shooting a suction-cup arrow" at a building and then drawing a circle "around the arrow, and then another circle around that circle, and etc., as in a what's the word." Lenz remembers the word "Bull's-eye" later (like Hal remembering Smothergill, p. 714). Lenz considers the shopping bags, "his adrenaline invisible for all to see." Minutes from now, Matty will see Poor Tony following Gompert and van Cleve (Chs. 27.9, 27.11, 27.14). Poor Tony will rob the women, and van Cleve will give chase (Ch. 27.22).

PLOT AND CHARACTER: Ennet, AA&R
THEME: Time, Recur

Lenz and his Frightful Hog were last referenced by Day in Ch. 27.12, and here Day and the Frightful Hog are both referenced by Lenz. Desperation and drug-use cause Lenz to consider the span of the last 2 ½ days as "several-odd days" (minutes from now, Gompert will think of Lenz's absence as occurring "who knows how many days or weeks ago," p. 700). Rat images and concentric circles recur. Matty saw the squatting woman with multiple skirts defecate in the street (p. 683); Poor Tony sidestepped her droppings (p. 691); and Lenz now sees her squatting between two dumpsters (p. 718). The thread of this woman's action, woven through other narrative threads across a certain time period within the same city, recalls the "Wandering Rocks" chapter of *Ulysses*. Lenz's "ghostly aspect" and reference to the "wandering mad, the walking dead and dying" recall the appearance of the ghost, Hamlet's antic disposition, and Horatio's account of omens in Act I of *Hamlet.*

Chapter 27.24, Section 147, Page 719
8-10 November Y.D.A.U.

This 10-line section picks up the narrative thread of the A.F.R. in the Antitois' shop, where they were on 8 November at the end of Ch. 24.6. The A.F.R. would prefer "to locate and secure a Master copy ["a Copy-Capable copy," p. 321] of the Entertainment on their own" (which is why they are "still here, in the Antitois' shop"), but if necessary will revert to an "indirect route: surveillance and infiltrating the surviving associates of the Entertainment's *auteur*, its actress and rumored performer, relatives—if necessary, taking them and subjecting them to technical interview, leading with hope to the original *auteur's* cartridge."

PLOT AND CHARACTER: Samizdat, A.F.R.
THEME: Secrets, Choice

The A.F.R. is searching for the secret cartridge directly, but is prepared to choose the indirect route if necessary. They do not know that "the original *auteur's* cartridge" was probably one of the cartridges "in fact" buried with Jim (nn. 80, 160). Although "its actress and rumored performer" is presumably a dual reference to a single person (cf. "probable performer," p. 726), recall that there is "someone else in the revolving doors" (p. 549) with Joelle.

Chapter 27.25, Section 148, Pages 719-721
14 November Y.D.A.U., before 2230h.

The purse-snatching thread shared by Matty, Poor Tony, and Gompert and van Cleve (Chs. 27.9, 27.11, 27.14, 27.22) continues from Poor Tony's perspective. Presenting this two-page section as a single paragraph intensifies the chase. Poor Tony thinks of van Cleve as "the Creature" and "the Thing," and of Gompert (who saw Poor Tony as "the apparition," p. 714) as "the other Thing." Poor Tony's "odor preceded him like a shock-wave" (like the smell from the refrigerator in the tunnel, p. 673). When van Cleve grabs hold of it, Poor Tony "sacrifice[s] the boa" that he pulled from the dead mouth of Bobby C (p. 135) over ten months ago. As Poor Tony races toward the Antitois' shop, which presumably is still held by the A.F.R. (cf. previous section), he leaps over "a queerly placed cardboard display for something wheelchaired" (also seen by Joelle a week ago, p. 224). Poor Tony takes a sharp right into an alley of "the homeless supine," one of whom counters van Cleve's order to "*Stop!*" by telling Poor Tony to "*Go.*"

PLOT AND CHARACTER: Ennet, AA&R
THEME: Dreams, Memory, His/Father, Recur

As van Cleve chases him, Poor Tony thinks "the hand and hissed breath just behind him [is] like one of those simply horrid dreams where something unimaginable is chasing you . . . its talons [about to] close on the back of your collar" (cf. "human nails are the vestiges of talons," p. 257). This prompts a memory of his father "scratching at his head where his mask's green strings had dug into the head." Earlier when Gompert hit the pole, it reminded Poor Tony of when his "father had struck himself about the head and shoulders as he grieved for his symbolically dead ["gender-dysphoric," p. 300] son." Poor Tony grieves for his lost boa, which is associated with Bobby C's death. There are a host of additional recurrences associated with Poor Tony in this section: he runs "inclined way forward" (cf. Mario "inclined ever forward," p. 315); he wears a wig, as does Lenz, who, nearby, is also considering bag-snatching (Ch. 27.23); he sees a "cardboard display for something wheelchaired" like Joelle did; near blackout, he sees "rings"; "his breath [comes] in stitches and half-sobs"; his father's address, "412 Mount Auburn Street" (cf. p. 301), recalls the "Hawaiianized Nuck house [at] 412 W. Brainerd" (p. 586); and his father wears a mask. Also, "the homeless supine" in the alley recall the park residents of the first section of this chapter.

Chapter 27.26, Section 149, Pages 721-723
Notes 300-302, Pages 1054-1055
8-10 November Y.D.A.U.

The thread of the A.F.R. in the Antitois' shop continues from Ch. 27.24. Marathe is in the shop with "his A.F.R. superiors Fortier and Broullîme" (p. 420). "Fortier, the son of a Glen Almond glass-blower, had allowed none of the mirrors to be broken or dismantled" (recall that "the happy-masked A.F.R. leader" complimented the Antitois on the craftsmanship of some of their "blown-glass notions," p. 487). CLOSED signs have been placed in the shop, and the Antitoi brothers have been rolled "in construction-plastic" and placed in a storage room. The A.F.R. had "traced their best chances at a copy [of the Entertainment] to the hapless Antitois' establishment," and it takes them "several days to find it there." Tracing the cartridge back from the Antitois leads first to the "sartorially eccentric cranio-facial-pain-specialist" (the "wrinkled long-haired person of advanced years in a paisley Nehru jacket" of p. 481 whose business dealings with Kite will be described on p. 927) and then to Trent Kite, the "young burglar" who robbed DuPlessis with Gately (cf. Ch. 7.4 and nn. 13, 16, 18). Kite was found pawning a Cafe-au-Lait Maker (n. 300, cf. p. 57) at some point during the 14 months since the burglary. Recall that the "kitchen-can waste bag filled with crusty old mossy, boot-and-leg

Read-Only [cartridges from the person of advanced years] appeared to have been stored in a person's rear yard" (p. 482). In the wake of Gately's arrest (p. 444), Kite apparently buried the bag of cartridges until he thought it was safe to sell them. "There was reason to think M. DuPlessis had received his original copies [presumably including the "alleged Master copy from the DuPlessis burglary," p. 489] from [Orin]. Marathe felt [U.S.O.U.S.] felt [Orin] may have borne responsibility for the razzles and dazzles of Berkeley and Boston." Presumably, Marathe is unaware of the situations in New Iberia and Tempe discussed in Ch. 26.3.

Two blank cartridges from "the rival F.L.Q.'s tactical street-display . . . which featured wheelchairs, a smack to the testicles of A.F.R." are found. The Antitois, "spurned by F.L.Q. after DuPlessis's assassination" (p. 480), would have been unaware that the F.L.Q. sponsored the displays. Lucien found the F.L.Q. cartridges—as well as the "old rude person's bartered tapes"—to be "blank beyond static" (p. 483), but Master cartridges require special codes and equipment to run, unlike standard Read-Only cartridges (nn. 205, 301); so it is possible the cartridges—being played on the "consumer TP" that replaced the Antitois' "visually dysfunctional" viewer (cf. p. 483)—are not blank. It is assumed by the A.F.R. that the F.L.Q. is propagating a "hoax" (that the F.L.Q. has no copies of the Entertainment). "Unlike the F.L.Q., [the A.F.R.] had no interest in blackmail or cartographic extortings for the Convexity's return." The A.F.R.'s "real objective [is] a Master cartridge" (cf. p. 719) that can be used to make copies of the Entertainment for mass distribution throughout the United States, incurring "the wrath of a neighbor struck down by its own inability to say '*Non*' to fatal pleasures." Ottawa will then support Québec's secession from Canada so that U.S. wrath will be focused solely on Québec. This description of the A.F.R.'s Separatist mission (p. 722) matches the Steeply-inspired version that Orin discussed with Hal on 7 November (pp. 1007-1022).

Note 302 states that Fortier had been present at the train-cult-related deaths of Marathe's elder brothers and that he suspects Marathe may be nursing "dreams of redress for this." Fortier leaves "in the search's middle" to "help facilitate" the surveillance of Orin (cf. Ch. 26.15). Steeply "had been clinging to [Orin] like a bad odor" since about 3 November. Presumably Orin was playing football with the Arizona Cardinals and remained unavailable to the A.F.R. during Steeply's brief trip to Enfield on Sunday 8 November.

PLOT AND CHARACTER: Samizdat, A.F.R., Orin
THEME: Secrets, Inf/Reg, Recur

After they find a secret cartridge, the A.F.R.'s secret agenda is to initiate widespread infantile regression throughout the United States. Fortier has a secret suspicion about Marathe. Although metaphorical, another instance of "bad odor" is cited here. Wrapping the Antitoi brothers in plastic resonates with one of the earliest images in David Lynch's *Twin Peaks*.

Was the original Master buried with Jim as ordered (nn. 80, 160)? If so, who made copies from Jim's original Master cartridge before it was buried? Were copy-capable copies (other Masters) made? Did DuPlessis receive his copies (note the plural) from Orin or from someone else? Are the F.L.Q. tapes blanks or Masters?

Chapter 27.27, Section 150, Page 723
10 November Y.D.A.U.

This section continues from the previous section and documents Fortier's disgust with the U.S.A. for treating "wheelchaired persons with the solicitude that the weak substitute for respect. As if he were a sickly child, Fortier." He foregoes the use of technologically advanced "attachable legs" on his trip to interview Orin because he prefers this U.S.A. "condescension," which "honed the edge of his senses of purpose."

PLOT AND CHARACTER: Tech, A.F.R.
THEME: Phys/Ob, Inf/Reg

Fortier transcends physical obstacles, either with "attachable legs" or without. U.S.A. citizens treat him like a child.

Chapter 27.28, Section 151, Pages 723-724
14 November Y.D.A.U., before 2300h.

Joelle has returned from her meeting at St. Elizabeth's (Ch. 27.20; cf. the "post-meeting" noise she hears later in this thread, p. 736) and is in her room at Ennet House next to "Kate Gompert's empty bunk" (Gompert and van Cleve have been mugged by Poor Tony, Ch. 27.22). Joelle has "begun to worry obsessively about her teeth," given the effects on the teeth of excessive drug use. She dreams that Gately is a dentist, "leaning in above her" to work on her teeth. She looks into "the little round mirror" on his head and sees the "teeth of a creature that carelessly tears at meat. These are teeth that have been up to things she hasn't known about." The "endless red-stained rows of teeth [lead] back and away down a pitch-black pipe."

PLOT AND CHARACTER: Joelle
THEME: Fear/Obsess, Dreams, Recur

Joelle, like Hal, has fearful dreams about her teeth. Joelle's concern with dental hygiene recalls that of Ruth van Cleve's in this chapter (p. 700). Like Joelle's dream, Jim's *Fun with Teeth* also occurs in a dentist's office (p. 987). Joelle is aware of the cleanliness of her dream environment, where even "the light is sterilely clean." Other recurrences include a "mirror" that is "round" in which Joelle sees an endless regression of teeth when Gately "lean[s] in above her" (recalling the image of Joelle leaning in above the camera in *Infinite Jest*). Joelle's dream of her teeth being those of a "creature that carelessly tears at meat" is another primitive image, like Poor Tony's thought of van Cleve's "talons" (p. 720). In the dream, Gately's "head is massive and vaguely square." Compare Joelle's dream to AA speaker John L.'s description of the Substance as having "a ravening maw, and canines down to here," which is sandwiched between descriptions that also recall the dreams of Gately and Hal (p. 347).

Chapter 27.29, Section 152, Pages 724-728
Note 303, Page 1055
11-13 November Y.D.A.U.

By the time Fortier is "able to return" from his trip to Phoenix on 10 November (cf. Ch. 26.15), the A.F.R. finds (at the cost of two operatives) "a third cartridge emblazoned with the embossed smile and letters disclaiming the need of happy pursuit" (like the two F.L.Q. display cartridges, p. 722). It is "a *samizdat* cartridge of Entertainment" that the A.F.R. presumes was "burglared from the death of DuPlessis" (the A.F.R. would not consider that the F.L.Q. could be the source of the *samizdat* cartridge because they do not believe the hoax-propagating F.L.Q. has any cartridges, p. 722). Recall that, before his death, Lucien Antitoi viewed both of the F.L.Q. display cartridges and "the old rude person's bartered tapes he had removed from the waste bag" ("boot-and-leg Read-Only cartridges," p. 482), which were all "blank beyond static" (p. 483). Presumably the bartered tapes were the ones stolen from DuPlessis (cf. Ch. 27.26 summary). Either Lucien had not finished removing cartridges from the waste bag and the *samizdat* cartridge was found there by the A.F.R., or the *samizdat* cartridge was found elsewhere in the shop. If the latter is true, then how did this cartridge get to the Antitois' shop?

There "was no need yet for the high-rpm hardware of duplication: the found copy was Read-Only" (cf. n. 301). This news "had been expected by Broullîme and Fortier the moment they witnessed the shop's brothers active and alert," because "even the dim brothers Antitoi, seeing the unique case and slightly larger size of a Master," would have obtained the special hardware to view it (n. 303). Presumably then, the blank (p. 483) F.L.Q. cartridges and crusty, mossy, bartered tapes are not Masters (the suspicion of which was generated by n. 205), because they are not the right size to be Masters. They are regular-size blank cartridges played on regular hardware, whereas Masters would be larger-size cartridges only appearing to be blank on regular hardware.

Receiving "the expected bad news" on his return, "Fortier reminded the A.F.R. that they did now encouragingly know the Entertainment of such power did truly exist, for themselves." Recall that when Steeply asked Marathe over six months ago whether the A.F.R. had at least one Read-Only copy, Marathe said (apparently lying), "Yes" (p. 489). Fortier—"forfeiting hopes of securing a Master copy and instead striving to secure the original Master, the *auteur's* own cartridge, from which all Read-Only copies had presumably been copied"—now decides to adopt "the more arduous and risky task of taking for technical interview known persons associated with the Entertainment and locating the original maker's duplicable Master copy." This plan is in line with the A.F.R. objectives as stated on pp. 719 and 722. Fortier gives "numerous orders" to execute this new plan.

Fortier suspends surveillance "on the hated F.L.Q.'s *bureau centrale*, in the poorly disciplined house on Allston's Rue de Brainerd"—cf. "the Hawaiianized [cf. n. 47] Nuck house [at] 412 W. Brainerd" (p. 586)—which means (assuming Fortier's orders would be carried out immediately) that Fortier was probably not "able to return" until 12 November, since Bruce Green saw a wheelchaired person across the street from this house late on 11 November (p. 588). An E.T.A. employee "had been recruited and joined the Canadian instructor and student already inside for closer work of surveillance." (Is Poutrincourt the instructor? Is Wayne the student? Who is the new recruit?) "Inquiries into the composition and travel of the Québecois team" scheduled to play E.T.A. (cf. p. 217) "were under way." Luria P—— continues her surveillance of Orin in "the Desert." "On the day of Fortier's return also," the engineer was scooped up near the duck pond (Ch. 27.1) and interviewed as to the whereabouts of "the Subject" (Joelle). The A.F.R. finds it curious that the engineer says M.I.T. is "defensive in bed" (cf. "M.I.T. is in bed with Defense," p. 186).

"Today" (presumably 13 November, the day after Fortier's other orders were carried out) some A.F.R. operatives, including Fortier and Marathe, begin searching "Substance-Difficulty-Rehabilitation facilities" in the area, while the engineer becomes "the A.F.R.'s first Subject in field-tests of the *samizdat* cartridge's motivational range." Teams of A.F.R. operatives search the streets for "the purpose of acquiring additional Subjects . . . to be acquired publicly with quiet, yet not damaged in the brains or under the influence of the many of the district's intoxicant compounds."

Fortier dislikes fluorescent lighting, as do Mario, Tavis, (cf. n. 244) and Avril (cf. "an ethnic Canadian's horror of fluorescent light," p. 898). Fortier "can smell snow coming." He imagines U.S.A. citizens "fouling their divans and the chairs which may recline" in front of the "blue flicker of expensive digital equipment." Fortier has "wiry hair that tends to bulge unsmoothly around the bare spot" (cf. the bald spot of Lucien Antitoi's interrogator on p. 486 and of Orin's interviewer on p. 598).

PLOT AND CHARACTER: Samizdat, A.F.R.
THEME: Choice, Cycles, Waste

The A.F.R.'s discipline in its choices, actions, and sacrifices is featured in this section. Two operatives watch *Infinite Jest* repeatedly until they "succumb." They "had taken their chances at random in the rotation of viewing." Soon after returning from Phoenix AZ, Fortier visits Phoenix House while "making the rounds" of Boston rehab facilities. Fortier imagines people "fouling their divans," and an A.F.R. operative was saved from seeing *Infinite Jest* because he left the room "to change the bag of his partial colostomy." To watch *Infinite Jest*, the engineer's head is "immobilized with some straps" in another image that recalls *A Clockwork Orange*.

Chapter 27.30, Section 153, Pages 728-729
14 November Y.D.A.U., before 2230h. (p. 728)

At the end of Ch. 27.23, Randy Lenz was considering taking the bags of two Chinese women. We rejoin him now after he has taken the bags. Lenz's bag-snatching happens offstage, just as Poor Tony's purse-snatching happens offstage (between Chs. 27.14 and 27.22). Lenz hears a "tiny crash off somewhere south [which is] Poor Tony Krause rolling the steel waste barrel that tripped up Ruth van Cleve" (presumably shortly after the events of Ch. 27.25). As he looks for a "cleaner" alley in which to sort through the bags, he steps over a "sexless figure" whose hand moves "furiously in its groin" and who chants "Pretty, pretty, pretty."

PLOT AND CHARACTER: Ennet, AA&R
THEME: Recur, Waste, Fear/Obsess

This section weaves together Lenz and Krause threads. There are several recurrences here: "blue light" flickers from the lighter of young boys who use "a M. Fizzy bottle instead of a pipe" and who look "ratty" to Lenz, who notes that the alley "smelled of ripe waste" and "was devroid of cats and rodents both" "between 2224 and 2226h," a time formerly prime for issue resolution (cf. pp. 542, 554). The "junior crack-jockeys" (none of whom "wore watches") and the "sexless figure" with hair in "a clotted mass around its face" masturbating in an alley add to the hellish vision initiated by the "shriek-roused figures" (p. 626) in the first section of this chapter and by the "decayed head" of the alley inhabitant passed by Poor Tony (p. 721).

Chapter 27.31, Section 154, Pages 729-735
Note 304, Pages 1055-1062
14 November Y.D.A.U., before 2300h.

This section opens with a brief dialogue between "two craggy-faced brunette ex-residents . . . talking cults" ("the Ennet graduates" referred to by Lenz on p. 559), to whom Gately "bid goodnight" (p. 601) three nights ago immediately before the incident in which he was shot. Narrative focus then shifts to Marathe, who is "veiled" and searching Ennet House—on his last stop "for this day" (presumably the second day of the A.F.R.'s search, cf. p. 726 and Ch. 27.29 summary)—for Joelle, who is up in her room next to "Gompert's empty bunk" (p. 724). "A person with authority was conducting interviews to fill some vacancies" (Amy Johnson and Randy Lenz were expelled on 12 November). The people in the living room ("residents and visitors and applicants," p. 736; cf. "People from the public can't be in there after 2300," p. 591) are described from Marathe's perspective. These include a woman in a wheelchair like Marathe, "a tormented-appearing man scuttling like the crab" and "two hooligans" playing "a cruel game of jumping over him," a young girl who "seemed to remove her eye from her head and [place] it in her mouth" (Nell Gunther, cf. pp. 362-3), and Geoffrey Day. "A clatter and two shrieks" are heard in the kitchen. Marathe experiences a memory of himself "as a child, with legs" before he became associated with the train cultists. This prompts a reference to n. 304 in which Struck (on 11 November) prepares for the assignment that Hal had already completed (p. 702) by plagiarizing a "wheelchair-killers essay" from Y.W.-Q.M.D. in "a woebegone little marginal archaic" publication "edited by the same-named guy" who wrote the essay, G. T. Day. Recall that Geoffrey Day formerly "manned the helm of a Scholarly Quarterly" (p. 272).

The essay claims that the A.F.R.'s agenda is "the total return of all Reconfigured territories" (p. 1057), an agenda in which the A.F.R. actually has "no interest" (p. 722). The essay concurs "with the thesis that Canadian and other non American Root Cults" revere principles which are "actively *opposed* to the cultists' own individual pleasure." The essay reports that the A.F.R.'s "confinement to their epithetic wheelchairs can be traced" to "The Cult of the Next Train," which originated among miners' sons in the Papineau region of Québec. The object of the game played by the cult is to be "the last of your round's six [players] to jump from one side of the tracks to the other—that is, across the tracks—before the train passes. Your only real opponents are your six's other five. Never is the train itself regarded as an opponent [but rather as the game's] boundary, arena, and reason." A contestant waits "motionlessly to move, wait[s] as one by one the other five quail and save themselves, leap to beat the train." The best contestants "ignore their five competitors completely, concentrating their entire attention on determining the last viable instant in which to leap." "The game's object is to jump last and land still fully limbed upon the opposite embankment." The first contestant to jump is "disgraced and ashamed" but still "has jumped." Not to jump "is unthinkable. Only once . . . has a miners' son not jumped, lost his heart and frozen." This was Bernard Wayne. (Is this John Wayne's father? Recall that John Wayne is the "eldest son" of "an asbestos miner" (p. 262).) Often, contestants die or lose their legs as the result of mistimed jumps. The six survivors of the first round then compete in a final round.

In the Cult of the Next Train's game, does the jumper furthest up the track from the oncoming train have an advantage for jumping last? Would players further up the track need to take a proportional number of steps back from the rail, analogous to what runners at track meets must do? Does Day, who wrote about the A.F.R. three years ago, suspect Marathe? He is "ironic toward Marathe" (pp. 731-2). Note 304 includes both Day's footnotes (nn. 304.4-6) and the narrator's endnotes (nn. 304.a-b).

Back at Ennet, an "addicted man" whose "smell suggested livestock" approaches Marathe. He was Gompert's witness after she was mugged by Poor Tony: compare "One of his eyes had an exploded vein within it" (p. 733) with "One eye had a system of exploded arteries in it. He shook like an old machine. There was a smell involved" (p. 714). The man suggests that most of the people in the room "ain't real," that they are "metal people" with "[h]eads full of parts" (cf. the implants in Jim's head, p. 31). He suggests that only a select few people, including he and Marathe, are real; that all the people they encounter are just a limited number of machines that "play different characters" and "wear different faces"; and that they are fooled by projections: "We're all in one room. The real ones. . . . Everything's pro—jected. . . . The pictures on the wall change so we think we're going places." When Marathe is called into Pat's office, the man encourages him to "pet the dogs!"

PLOT AND CHARACTER: E.T.A., Ennet, A.F.R.
THEME: Recur, Secrets, Memory, Phys/Ob, Boundary, Non-Action, Waste, Fear/Obsess, Inf/Reg

There are several recurring images and ideas in this section. As Marathe waits he hears someone "vomiting" outside. He is approached by a man who "appeared to have several cigarettes burning at one time," whose smile "disclosed what might have once been teeth," and who suggests that people are secretly machines who "wear different faces" (masks). Marathe is veiled and secretly hunting Joelle, but he misses the connection that she is in the building. Struck takes "painstaking care to hide and camouflage [his] plagiarism." "Marathe was mentally memorizing every detail of all things, for both his reports." Marathe has a memory "of his four-limbed childhood." Compare the Next Train philosophy of train-as-boundary (p. 1059) and of a player's "true opponent [being his own] will, mettle, and intuition about the last viable instant in which to leap" (p. 1060) with Schtitt's "[t]he true opponent, the enfolding boundary, is the player himself" (p. 84). Non-action (to remain "frozen" like Bernard Wayne) is considered unthinkable in The Cult of the Next Train. One of the Separatist groups dropped a "12 meter, human waste filled, pie shell onto the rostrum of . . . Gentle's second Inaugural." The "battle of the Endless Kiss" (cf. "Her mouth is glued to his mouth; she is his breath," p. 567) requires "waste utilization" and has imagery in common with Orin's dream (pp. 46-47). Thirty-nine "*Cults of the Unwavering I*" are identified in n. 304.5: a list of obsessions, addictions, and regressions.

The "addicted man" warns that people are machines and that everything is projected (like holograms). On p. 12, Hal states that he is not a machine and that he believes the inventor of holography (Gabor) may have been the Antichrist. Marathe adjusts his breathing to avoid the man's smell like Hal adjusts his breathing to avoid Dr. Zegarelli's bad breath (p. 526). Struck on the 11th, like Fortier on the 13th (p. 728), has a "storm's-on-the-way feeling." A player's jumping "at the last viable instant" to save himself (which sometimes results in lifelong problems) recalls an addict hitting bottom before coming in. In *Hamlet* II.ii, Hamlet calls Polonius a fishmonger and suggests that Polonius could traverse time "if, like a crab, [he] could go backward." Polonius comments on the method inherent in Hamlet's madness and invites Hamlet to walk "out of the air." Here, Marathe compares the addicted man's eyes to "the eye of a fish in a vendor's crushed ice," and there is a man "scuttling like the crab" in the living room of Ennet House. The addicted man's theories, although far-fetched, have thematic unity. One of Marathe's recurring phrases is "from somewhere blue" (from out of the air, in Hamlet's phrase; or "as if from nowhere," p. 1056).

Chapter 27.32, Section 155, Pages 736-747
Notes 305-310, Page 1062
14 November Y.D.A.U., before 2300h.

While Marathe is downstairs looking for her, Joelle remains up in her room undetected. Her scream upon waking from her dream (Ch. 27.28) is "preempted" by the screams of Nell Gunther that Joelle hears from downstairs (where tonight Joelle is "oddly averse" to going), and "she wasn't listening to any YYY tapes" (as she was when Mario heard them outside her window three nights ago, p. 591). Although she has stopped getting high, she still "liked to clean" (cf. p. 225), an activity that "had started with Orin" and now prompts memories of her relationship with him and his relationship with his family. While reflecting on her initial reluctance to Orin's suggestions that she work with Jim, Joelle hears "a howl and a crash from the kitchen, followed by McDade's tubercular laugh." Compare this howl, crash, and laugh with the "clatter and two shrieks" (p. 731) heard by Marathe.

Jim's work is cited as "the work of a brilliant optician and technician who was an amateur at any kind of real communication." His work had "no narrative movement toward a real story; no emotional movement toward an audience." But Joelle occasionally noticed "flashes of something" in the work. For example, in "*The Medusa v. the Odalisque,*" she noticed "the gorgeous combatants' faces, twisted past recognition with some kind of torment . . . as if what their beauty was doing to those drawn to watch it ate them alive." "It was like [Jim] couldn't help putting human flashes in, but he wanted to get them in as quickly and unstudyably as possible, as if they compromised him somehow" (recall Mario's thoughts on people's ability to deal with "real stuff," p. 592). This prompts Joelle's memory of the first boy "ever to approach her in a male-female way," a lineman who "confessed the whole team's paralyzing horror of [Joelle's] prettiness." Orin had been the second boy to approach her. Recall that Orin remembers Joelle approaching him (cf. p. 295 and n. 307). The only other time "Orin has perceived himself as the approachee" is with "the 'Swiss hand-model' on whose nude flank he's been furiously tracing infinity symbols [cf. pp. 47, 289] all during the Moment Subject's absence" (n. 307).

In *Pre-Nuptial Agreement of Heaven and Hell*, there is a seemingly gratuitous "240-second motionless low-angle shot" of Bernini's "Ecstasy of St. Teresa" (significant to Joelle, cf. Ch. 22.4 summary). But Joelle realized that these four minutes were the only time that the alcoholic sandwich-bag salesman's head was not on screen and that this shot signified "[f]reedom from one's own head, one's inescapable P.O.V.," especially given that "the mediated transcendence of self was just what the apparently decadent statue of the orgasmic nun claimed for itself as subject." For Joelle, this film represented "self-forgetting as the Grail" and "presented the self-forgetting of alcohol as inferior to that of religion/art."

Jim told Joelle that he "didn't know how to speak with either of his undamaged sons without their mother's presence and mediation" and that "Hal was so completely shut down in Jim's presence that the silences were excruciating" (cf. Ch. 3). With Mario, who didn't speak until age six, Jim had the "chance to become comfortable in mutual silence."

Joelle recalls her "first interface with the whole sad family unit," her 2001 ("last pre-Subsidized") Thanksgiving dinner with the Incandenzas, after which it "took a long time for Joelle even to start to put a finger on what gave her the howling fantods about Orin's mother." Joelle, unaware of the S. Johnson incident (pp. 1014, 1049-50), noticed "a spotless doggie-dish under the table, but no dog, and no mention was ever made of a dog." At dinner, Jim spoke of Method actors like Brando (as Jim's father did in 1960, pp. 157-8) and "molded his twice-baked potatoes into an intricate futuristic city-scape" (cf. Hal in Y.D.A.U., pp. 628 and 637-8). Joelle found the bow-tied Hal irritating and felt—although she "could detect nothing fake about [Avril's] grace and cheer toward her"—that Avril could have cut her up and eaten food prepared with her remains while the event went "unremarked by all who leaned her way." "[E]verybody at the table was smiling, broadly and constantly, eyes shiny in the plants' odd light." At home that night with Orin "was the first historical time Joelle intentionally did lines of cocaine to keep from sleeping." She "was awake at 0400, cleaning." Weeks later on New Year's Eve, Orin would see Joelle ingest cocaine for the first time (p. 296). Nearly eight years later Joelle, in recovery from her cocaine addiction, is cleaning her room at Ennet House while downstairs Marathe—like Avril, a Canadian and (in his case literally) a veiled threat—seeks her out because of her participation in Jim's work.

PLOT AND CHARACTER: Joelle, Orin, Avril, Jim, Hal, Art/Ent
THEME: Recur, Fear/Obsess, Memory, Cycles, Isolation, Inf/Reg, His/Father

Just as the sound of a crash (p. 728) connects the Krause and Lenz threads, a crash (p. 740)/clatter (p. 731) connects the van Dyne and Marathe threads. Again, characters are in close proximity without contact. Like Avril, whom she fears, Joelle is obsessed with cleaning. As she cleans, she experiences memories ("bubbling up") of her family and of Orin and his family. Joelle's father thought her grandmother hung the moon (p. 738). "Orin described his childhood's mother as his emotional sun" and "the family's light and pulse and the center that held tight." Recall Hal's orbiting of Avril on pp. 521-2. "The whole Thanksgiving table inclined very subtly toward Avril, very slightly and subtly, like heliotropes." Recall one of Jim's production companies was called Heliotrope Films (n. 24). Whereas Avril draws attention, Jim isolates himself. He is "irretrievably hidden" and "almost catatonic." His work is described as "cold" and "hidden." Jim describes Hal as silent in his presence, and Orin says that Jim "barely existed" and that Jim's face was "any room's fifth wall" (Jim says the same thing about his father, p. 31). It is suggested that perhaps Avril's "high-watt maternal love" brought "into sharper relief Jim's remote self-absorption." Orin's regression is more infantile. While dating Joelle, he "liked to sit in the dark and enter what he watched, his jaw slackening, a child raised on multi-channel cable TV." The night before the Thanksgiving dinner, Orin was "vomiting with anxiety"; and Joelle's cleaning was often prompted when she was "seized with anxiety" over strains in her relationship with Orin, brought about in part by the fact that "she was closer to Jim than Orin had ever been." Orin's cruelty to Mario is again referenced: he prepares "to brain the needy infant." Joelle's memories of Orin's issues with his father are mingled with memories of her own father. She often felt relief when her father left the room; because when he was with her, it "was like when she exhaled he inhaled and vice versa," which recalls the battle of the Endless Kiss (pp. 1061-2).

There are a host of other recurrences in this section, including images of Joelle's "writhing mouth when she cleaned high" and "the gorgeous combatants' faces, twisted past recognition with some kind of torment." Charlotte Treat wears a sleep mask, and Avril refers to Jim's face as "*Le Masque*." Joelle reflects that "parodists were no better than camp-followers in ironic masks." Jim's deftness at hailing cabs is again noted. The bed slats in Joelle's room "clotted with dust" recall Jim's childhood memory recounted in Ch. 25.2. The lineman that almost splashed Joelle when he "threw up" leaned against a "blue pine," and at the Thanksgiving dinner "the table's candles' glow [was] a weird bright blue." Joelle notes that everyone's "teeth were dazzling in the candlelight." Joelle envisions Avril stabbing her with a knife. Knives also carry significance for Gately (p. 612) and Hal (p. 16). The large-head (Gately) and head-fills-frame (Lord at the end of Eschaton) motifs are represented here by the alcoholic sandwich-bag salesman's head (recall that Jim's father was the original Man From Glad), which swells "horrendously, until by the film's end its dimensions exceeded the frame." Joelle's thoughts on the lack of emotion in most of Jim's work mirror traditional complaints about postmodern works in general. Jim's taking "the risk of appearing amateurish" to make his work more human recalls the following quote from Wallace's essay "E Unibus Plurum: Television and U.S. Fiction," from *A Supposedly Fun Thing I'll Never Do Again*: "The new rebels might be the artists willing to risk the yawn, the rolled eyes, the cool smile, the nudged ribs, the parody of gifted ironists" (p. 81).

The passing out of dental stimulators places Ted Schacht as one of the "lopsidedly muscular boys" at the 2001 Thanksgiving dinner. Who is Hal's other callused-handed guest? Avril is found to be mysterious and potentially threatening in this section. There are symbolic references to duplicity in that "the Moms" sounds "[a]s if there were more than one of her." Since both of his parents were tall,

Orin "found it secretly odd that none of the brothers were taller." Jim's paternity has been questioned in the case of Mario (p. 451). Is Jim's paternity with respect to Orin and Hal being questioned here?

Chapter 27.33, Section 156, Pages 747-751
Notes 311-313, Page 1062
14 November Y.D.A.U., before 2300h.

Concurrently with Joelle's cleaning and continuing from Ch. 27.31, Marathe is now in Pat's office. Pat is on the phone with her husband, Mars, discussing an untrustworthy "she" who must be told "no" (cf. Pat's remarriage to an "older South Shore like trillionaire with what sounded like psychotic kids," p. 465). Gompert's witness who spoke with Marathe earlier is identified as Selwyn. Marathe, like Orin's hand-model, lists his citizenship as Swiss. When Pat reaches into a cabinet, Marathe notices cartridges inside the cabinet with titles that suggest the cartridges are from E.T.A. Some of the cartridges found and discarded by the E.T.A. Tunnel Club (Ch. 27.7) were presumably taken from the trash by Clenette on 11 November (cf. her "bulging backpack," pp. 633-4) and have now made their way to Pat's office. The cartridges include "two cases of plain brown plastic, blank . . . except maybe for tiny round faces of embossed smiles upon the brown cases." Are these *Infinite Jest* cartridges? Pat informs the veiled Marathe that "we have a U.H.I.D. member in early residency right now," which prompts Marathe to consider "whether he would report truly first to M. Fortier or to [Steeply]." He "could give the fact of the cartridges to Fortier and the veiled girl to Steeply, or oppositely."

PLOT AND CHARACTER: Ennet, A.F.R.
THEME: Secrets, Recur

Ironically, Pat tells "Marathe the false addict that she found his honesty encouraging." Marathe considers what he will tell Fortier and Steeply and what he will keep secret from Fortier and Steeply. When Marathe feels "suddenly the excitement of himself," he thinks of Steeply's recurring phrase "*from somewhere blue*." Recalling Selwyn's philosophy of Ch. 27.31, Marathe imagines "a faint whirring noise coming from the head." Like readers of *Infinite Jest*, Marathe "had the ability of splitting his mind's thinking along several parallel tracks." Marathe "had the great fatigue, a time at which English was straining," which may account for the narrator's use of "utilized" (p. 750, cf. p. 948), a word denigrated by Wallace in *The Oxford American Writer's Thesaurus*.

Chapter 27.34, Section 157, Pages 751-752
14 November Y.D.A.U., before 2300h.

Joelle continues to clean (cf. Ch. 27.32). Ironically, she fears being discovered by Gompert rather than by Marathe, who is currently in Pat's office.

PLOT AND CHARACTER: Joelle
THEME: Secrets, Fear/Obsess, Cycles

The whole Incandenza family was "lousy with secrets," one of which was the "pretense that overt eccentricity was the same as openness." Joelle fears Gompert—who makes her nervous—and is obsessed with cleaning, "wiping in careful rings around objects she wasn't to touch."

Chapter 27.35, Section 158, Pages 752-755
Notes 314-315, Page 1062
14 November Y.D.A.U., before 2300h.

Marathe's interview with Pat continues from Ch. 27.33. Marathe contemplates who he should telephone about the cartridges and Joelle and (analogous to train-cult philosophy) calculates "how long to remain and work for dissemination against when to jump to the safety of American welcome." His A.F.R. colleagues (who he has known since his train-cult days) have not "sensed truly that Marathe has lost the belly for this type of work." It was Marathe who killed Lucien Antitoi (cf. p. 488); afterwards, he had "vomited out into the alley under secrecy."

Johnette Foltz pops in to announce her arrival for the night shift ("Dream Duty," cf. p. 272). Pat tells her that "Clenette H. brought some donie-cartridges down from E.T.A. this afternoon" (presumably taken from E.T.A. on 11 November (cf. pp. 633-4) and brought down from Clenette's room just today, cf. Ch. 28.1 summary) and asks her to screen them to determine their appropriateness. Pat also asks Johnette to "keep Emil and Wade from tormenting David K." This places new resident David K. as the "tormented-appearing man scuttling like a crab" (p. 731) and Emil and Wade as the "two hooligans . . . jumping over him" (p. 731; cf. their "pathetic harassments," p. 178). Marathe asks Pat what *etier* means; and she explains that she is referring to E.T.A., the "private school . . . just up the hill," which prompts a "deep intake" of breath from Marathe.

PLOT AND CHARACTER: Ennet, A.F.R.
THEME: Secrets, Choice, Recur

Marathe continues to consider his choices concerning the secret information he now has on potentially lethal cartridges and on Joelle. He considers moving with his wife "down here among U.S.A.'s confusion of choices, demanding hidden protection from Steeply." Marathe keeps secret from his A.F.R. colleagues his "nausea of the stomach" in the face of violence. In a recurrence of the missed-connection motif, when Pat mentions an Ennet staffer who is "under the weather," Marathe does not realize she is referring to the man who caused the death of DuPlessis. Johnette makes a "curious circle with two of her fingers."

Although Marathe hears Pat say "*etier*" at the top of p. 754, the letters inside her quotation are what she says: "E.T.A." At the bottom of p. 754, the letters inside Pat's quotation now reflect what Marathe hears (living) instead of what Pat says (live-in).

Chapter 27.36, Section 159, Pages 755-769
Notes 316-319, Pages 1062-1063
11 November Y.D.A.U., around 2100h.

This section occurs around 2100h. on 11 November, after Mario and Schtitt have returned from their outing (Ch. 27.18, p. 701), but before Mario's secret walk by Ennet on which he hears the Madame Psychosis tapes (Ch. 26.13). In Schtitt's first-floor room in the Comm.-Ad. Building, Mario has the "Bolex H64 camera strapped to his head" and records Schtitt, who "sleeps only amid excruciatingly loud European opera." On the second floor of the Comm.-Ad. Building, Mario walks by "a study group for Mr. Ogilvie's 'Reflections on Refraction' exam tomorrow" (cf. that this class is "Leith-taught" on p. 511) and "gets a couple seconds of [Felicity] Zweig hurrying away in the towel" she wears. There are "sounds of retching from behind Diane Prins's door." Upon exiting the bathroom on the third floor, Lamont Chu sees Mario and offers to speak into the camera, but then his mind goes blank. Chu asks Mario if "Hal told you what happened" after Hal and Pemulis were seen leaving "Tavis's office with the Association urine-guy holding them both by the ear."

Mario next goes to his mother's well-lit office back on the first floor. "It takes Mario longer to walk down a set of stairs than to walk up." Avril, "a fiend for light," is "listening to someone on the phone" (presumably the party she was dialing in Ch. 27.19, p. 701). "Mario didn't hear her say goodbye to the man as she put down the phone." The "fleur-de-lis pennons on tall sharp polished sticks" in the corner of her office recall the A.F.R. and Lucien Antitoi's death. Are the "carpet-prints in the heavy shag" from Avril's liaison with Wayne two nights ago (Ch. 26.4), or has there been more recent activity? With Chu's questions fresh in his mind, Mario brings up the Eschaton "debracle." Avril tells Mario that she can't find Hal and asks Mario if Hal is with Pemulis, who was seen leaving in their truck earlier (with Struck to research the DMZ, cf. p. 655). Mario says that he hasn't "seen Hal since lunchtime. [But recall that honest Mario filmed the first set of Hal's afternoon match with Stice (p. 652), so by "hasn't seen" he probably means "hasn't talked to."] He said he'd had a tooth thing." Avril has "no problem waiting to hear about Eschaton, teeth, and urine" from Hal, who she trusts will come to her "the moment it's appropriate."

Mario asks, "How can you tell if somebody's sad?" Avril, the militant grammarian, rephrases his question and provides lists of correct answers to his subsequent questions before asking, "Is this about Hal?" Mario replies, "I'm just saying how to be generally sure." Avril explains that sadness could make someone appear to be "not himself": "There are, apparently, persons who are deeply afraid of their own emotions . . . . As if something truly and thoroughly felt would have no end or bottom. Would become infinite and engulf them. . . . [S]uch persons usually have a very fragile sense of themselves as persons. As existing at all." Avril then relates a story of her potato-farmer father (cf. p. 1041) who "told stories of his own father," who was "frozen, and could feel emotion only when he was drunk," which occurred four times a year and resulted in Avril's father being thrown through the living room window. Avril: "My father, of course, could himself tell this story only when *he* was drunk. He never threw anyone through any windows" (but cf. that Avril makes reference to "throwing someone through a living room window out into the flowerbeds she'd so very carefully repaired after the last incident" as an example of how drugs or alcohol "allow some skewed version of the sadness some sort of expression"). Avril describes sad people as "imprisoned in something" and that "the very imprisonment that prohibits sadness's expression must itself feel intensely sad and painful" (cf. Ch. 27.13). Mario asks Avril, "[What if] it's not that he's blank or dead. If he's himself even more than before a sad thing happened. What if that happens and you still think he's sad, inside, somewhere?" Avril, confused, wonders whether Mario is sad and hopes that he would "simply come and tell [her he was] sad. There would be no need for intuition about it."

Outside are "clouds whose movement's pattern has a kind of writhing weave"; "the red rotating tip of the WYYY transmitter, it's spin's ring of red reflected in the visible Charles River"; and "gulls asleep or brooding, bobbing, head under wing."

PLOT AND CHARACTER: E.T.A., Mario, Avril, AA&R
THEME: Cycle, Isolation, Non-Action, His/Father, Waste, Fear/Obsess, Recur

Avril notes the irony of the vicious cycle of sadness in which "the very imprisonment [isolation] that prohibits sadness's expression must itself feel extremely sad and painful." Ironically, Avril notes that this type of "suppression" (being "frozen," unable to take action) might derive "from childhood trauma" but does not consciously admit her own trauma in the drunken-window-throwing cycle of addiction-abuse passed down from her grandfather to her father. In another reference to childhood, "Mario was involuntarily incontinent [unable to take action against waste] up to his early teens." Avril, with her aversion to waste and obsession with cleanliness, was unable to change his diapers and feared Mario's interpretation of her inability to "deal with" his diapers. In redirecting Mario's question about sadness at the end of the section, Avril is a manipulator (one who gulls) who would rather brood, bob (redirect questions), or put her head under her wing than take action (change diapers, deal with sadness, leave E.T.A. grounds). If sad persons feel engulfed, obliterated, and doubtful of their existence (p. 765), then do these traits contribute to the communication problems experienced by Hal in Ch. 1 and Jim in Ch. 3?

Hal's recurring dental problems were inherited from his father (p. 763), and n. 316 relates that Jim's teeth would grind so bad at Tavis's "Opheliac mad monologue of chatter" that "there'd be grit in [his subsequent] throw-up." Other waste references include Diane Prins's retching (p. 757), a locker room odor (p. 758), and the roar of a toilet (p. 759). There is another *Hamlet* resonance in that Avril's catalogue of sadness identifiers (p. 764) are "actions that a man might play," whereas Mario is asking about "that within which passes show" (I.ii.85). Note Lamont Chu's misreference of his own "invitation" to speak as coming from Mario (p. 757). Mario thinks *typhoon* when he means *tycoon* (p. 763). Mrs. Clarke's name is spelled two different ways on p. 765. Compare Avril's word games with Mario in this chapter with her game with Hal on pp. 524-5. There are more references to lights (lamps) and reflections (mirrors). A "ring of red" light is reflected in the blue river; and Mario's "big head," which "moves in a weary circle," is reflected in the window of Avril's office. Other recurrences include Avril's blue chairs and blue pens, a "blue blazer with an O.N.A.N.T.A. insignia" in the corner of Avril's office (like the urologist's, cf. p. 527), a reference to the brooms from "out of nowhere" (cf. the squeegees, p. 632), and the "tiny whir" of Mario's camera mechanism.

The narrator of this section states that Avril's "hair has been pure white since Mario can first remember seeing her looking down at him through the incubator's glass" (p. 761, cf. p. 313); but the narrator of Ch. 25.5 says that "Avril has vividly white hair—as of the last few months before Himself's felo de se" (p. 510). This is a discrepancy of about 13 years.

Chapter 27.37, Section 160, Pages 769-774
Note 320, Page 1063
12 November Y.D.A.U., pre-dawn

Except for the opening sentence—which connects to the end of the previous section by referencing clouds—this section consists entirely of dialogue (and sounds and silences) between Mario and Hal (like Ch. 6.1). Between the previous section and this one, Mario has taken his secret walk by Ennet (Ch. 26.13) and has returned to sleep in his and Hal's room for the first time in about two weeks (Mario felt good when Hal had inquired about his return, p. 590). Hal awakes from another dream about teeth (as Joelle did in Ch. 27.28) to find Mario with him and notes that "The sun won't be up for a while." Mario tells Hal about the Psychosis tapes he heard and requests that Hal show him "how to ask somebody I don't know to borrow tapes." Mario relates both Chu's and Avril's concerns (cf. previous section), but Hal talks of his dream instead. Mario has moved on to other topics when Hal begins to discuss what happened after the meeting in Tavis's office. Hal says that Pemulis convinced the urine guy to give them thirty days before requiring a sample. (But perhaps Avril convinced the urine guy. There are "carpet-prints in the heavy shag" and a blue O.N.A.N.T.A. blazer in her office (cf. pp.

151, 527, 763, 768). Alternately, the carpet-prints might still be there from Avril's liaison with Wayne two nights ago (Ch. 26.4).)

Hal wonders how Mario determines whether he's being lied to and then begins to categorize different types of liars, including Orin and Pemulis. Mario: "You sound like you can always tell." Hal remarks how Pemulis's face was "a brass mask. It was almost frightening" and then says, "The truth is nobody can *always* tell, Boo." Hal says that he "no longer believe[s] in monsters as faces in the floor" (cf. Ch. 7.7). He now believes "the only real monsters might be the type of liar where there's simply no way to tell" and that "they walk among us. Teach our children. Inscrutable. Brass-faced."

PLOT AND CHARACTER: Hal, Mario, Orin, E.T.A.
THEME: Dreams, Memory, Waste, Recur, Secrets

Hal has nightmares about his teeth and references his old nightmares about faces in the floor. Mario is said to have a "phenomenal memory." Urine samples of potential import are forthcoming. There are recurrences in Mario's reference to the sound of the fans "over and over. From very far away." For most of this section, Hal and Mario are out of phase with respect to the topics of conversation (a recurrence of the missed-connection motif). Hal says that Pemulis's face was "a brass mask." This section is an examination of liars in general and of Orin and Pemulis in particular, and links to the next section where two more types of liars are examined: spies (Marathe) and addicts (Gompert).

Chapter 27.38, Section 161, Pages 774-782
14 November Y.D.A.U., after 2300h.

This section is the second of three consecutive sections of dialogue, and joins Kate Gompert's thread (from Ch. 27.22, before 2230h.) with Marathe's thread (from Ch. 27.35, before 2300h.). Marathe and Gompert are in Ryle's Tavern (cf. pp. 479, 691). Gompert came in to escape her witness (cf. p. 714) and to "throw up from getting *mugged*." She confesses that as a recovering drug addict, she should not be drinking. Marathe confesses that his wife is dying at home and that he is "spending a day to find someone I think my friends will kill, all the time I am awaiting the chance to betray my friends, and I come here and telephone to betray them and I see this bruised person who strongly resembles my wife." Marathe doesn't know that the man who spoke to him of machines at Ennet House was Gompert's witness, that Gompert is a resident of Ennet House, and that the person his friends would kill is Gompert's roommate. (Marathe had not decided who to call when he was at Ennet, but now has called and betrayed his friends; therefore, presumably the events of this section occur after Marathe's visit to Ennet.)

Marathe laments the loss of his legs and speaks to Gompert of his "Swiss" heritage and of "neighboring nations" who instituted an "invasion of paper" by "conferring on us gifts of alliance." After the invasion of paper, Marathe spent a lot of time "drinking, alone, wishing for my death, locked inside my pain in the heart." He "roll[ed] about, hoping to be hit by a vehicle of someone else, but at the last minute roll[ed] out of the path . . . unable to will [his] death" (compare this practice with that of The Cult of the Next Train, n. 304). Like Gompert and other depressed people (cf. Ch. 27. 13), Marathe felt "chained in a cage of the self, from the pain. Unable to care or choose anything outside it." Gompert: "The billowing shaped black sailing wing" (cf. Ch. 27.4).

Marathe tells Gompert the story of being saved from this no-choice pain by his future wife when he rescued her from being hit by a truck: "I was allowed to choose something as more important than my thinking of my life. . . . She with one blow broke the chains of the cage of pain at my half a body and nation. . . . I became, then, adult" (compare this with what Steeply and Marathe say about choice and love on p. 108). Marathe explains that his future wife was "born without a skull, from the toxicities in association of our enemy's invasion on paper" and then catalogues her extraordinarily severe medical problems. Marathe thought that he would then "wheel off into [his] new life of uncaged acceptance and choice" by choosing to fight for his nation, but when he tried to roll away from the hospital, he realized that he "needed this woman. Without her to choose over myself, there was only pain and not choosing. . . . It is for her I betray my friends." Although she is dying, she can "live for many more years in a comatose and vegetative state" if she receives (via Marathe's betrayal) a "Jaarvik IX Exterior Artificial Heart," like the one Steeply (who just received the betray-my-friends phonecall from Marathe) reported being stolen in Ch. 13.5 (where the spelling is "Jarvik") by Poor Tony, who just stole Gompert's purse (Ch. 27.22).

Gompert summarizes, "You're spying and betraying Switzerland to try and keep alive somebody with a hook and spinal fluid and no skull in an irreversible coma?" Marathe: "It chains me, but the chains are of my choice." Before saving his future wife, Marathe was bound by "other chains: . . . the chains of not choosing." Gompert and other U.S. citizens "think there is no love without the pleasure, the no-choice compelling of passion"; but this kind of no-choice love "yields none of the pleasure you seek in love." Marathe offers to take the now drunken Gompert "only three streets from here" where she might choose to remove "the pain of the chains and cage of never choosing."

PLOT AND CHARACTER: Ennet, A.F.R.
THEME: Isolation, Choice, Inf/Reg, Phys/Ob, Recur

Isolation is represented again in this section as being "chained in a cage of the self." For Marathe, chains are acceptable if they are chosen. When Marathe made a selfless choice he equated that choice with becoming an adult (as opposed to the no-choice of incessantly succumbing to infantile pleasures). His chosen wife has severe physical obstacles and has regressed to a vegetative state. Marathe isn't aware of Gompert's connections to Selwyn and Joelle. Gompert comes into Ryle's to vomit and speaks to Marathe of sitting in a circle. Marathe, who like the hand-model is not Swiss, again says "Out of a blue place" and speaks of his future wife as hunched, frozen with terror, and incontinent.

Marathe and Gompert have more than the experience of depression in common. On p. 76, "Kate Gompert pretended to sniff instead of engaging in a real sniff" as Marathe does with Steeply. Marathe believes the "fight against the invasion of paper" (the fight to return the Convexity) is "without point." This recalls the Norwegian captain telling Hamlet, "We go to gain a little patch of ground/ That hath in it no profit but the name" (*Hamlet* IV.iv.18-9). Presumably, Fortinbras is using his quest for Polish ground as a ruse to gain his primary objective: access to Denmark; people assume that the A.F.R. wish to make the U.S. take back the Convexity, but their primary objective is to gain secession for Québec (cf. p. 722). Marathe says of his love for his wife that "It was not mad. I had already chosen." Marathe, like Hamlet, says that he is not mad because his rash actions are by choice.

Chapter 27.39, Section 162, Pages 782-785
Note 321, Pages 1063-1066
12 November Y.D.A.U., pre-dawn

Hal divulges his secrets to Mario as their dialogue continues from Ch. 27.37. Hal confesses his secret pump-room rituals (cf. Ch. 7.1) and explains that since "Pemulis publicly dosed his opponent at Port Washington" (cf. Ch. 19.3) and since "[s]ales of Visine bottles of pre-adolescent urine . . . have been noted" (cf. Ch. 14) by "C.T. and the Moms," they suspect Pemulis and want him "gone." Hal: "My urine and Axhandle's urine are just to establish a context of objectivity for Pemulis's urine." Concerning the impending drug screen, Hal says, "The ingenious layer to [Pemulis's] lie was that the [urine] guy thought the thirty days' grace was for Pemulis [but actually Pemulis] did it for me, and I'm not even the one they want." With the proper fluids, it is likely that the marijuana (the "Hope") in Hal's system will be gone in thirty days. Hal is afraid of the consequences of "flunk[ing] a urine," especially given that "this *Moment* lady [is] lumbering around looking for family linen." It would hurt E.T.A. and therefore "Himself's memory" and "it'd *kill* the Moms . . . . The *secrecy* of it. That I hid it from her. . . . Something terrible will happen if she finds out I hid it from her."

Reacting to Mario's kindness, Hal says that it is okay for Mario to be mad at him, given that he has lied to Mario. Hal says that talking to Mario is like "talking to a big poster of some smily-faced guy. Are you *in* there?" Hal fears marijuana withdrawal (cf.

Kate Gompert saying "I fear it more than anything," p. 77) because he's "bats inside" and "can't sleep without more of the horror-show dreams." He feels like he's "stuck halfway down a chimney." Looking on the bright side ("The sun's thinking about coming up"), Mario notes that Hal's toothache is gone. But Hal says, "I feel a hole. It's going to be a huge hole, in a month. A way more than Hal-sized hole." He tells Mario he is afraid and says, "Tell me what you think I should do. . . . Because I do not know what to do." Mario: "I think you just did it. What you should do. I think you just did."

Note 321 features another section of dialogue that occurs after the sun goes down on 12 November (1930h.). Here, Pemulis is helping Hal prepare for his Boards and speaks of "triangles inside triangles" and of "points moving inexorably toward each other until for all practical purposes they're the same point." (Concerning the formula Pemulis uses on p. 1063, cf. Mike Strong's fourth error: "Pemulis states that for the function x^n, the derivative is $nx + x^{(n-1)}$. In fact, the correct expression is $nx^{(n-1)}$.") Hal digresses to discuss his dream that he was "the soldier" who had taken DMZ (cf. p. 214). In his dream, Hal is "screaming for help and everybody's acting as if [he's] singing Ethel Merman covers." Pemulis notes that DMZ is mold-based (cf. p. 170) and doesn't show up on a drug screen and that Struck's research may find that DMZ's "original intent was to induce . . . transcendent experiences in . . . chronic alcoholics in the like 1960s at Verdun Protestant Hospital in Montreal." This prompts Hal to note that "everywhere I turn this fall now everybody's suddenly mentioning Québec in all kinds of radically different contexts." Pemulis tells Hal that his "hinges are starting to squeak" and that taking DMZ "could be just the reconfiguration you need."

Hal tells Pemulis that he might "make a decision" to stop all drug intake. He agrees with Pemulis who says, "You want to quit because you're starting to see you need it." But Pemulis warns, "You lose your mind, Inc. You die inside. What happens if you try and go without something the machine *needs*?" Later, Hal mistakenly believes Pemulis is suggesting Jim's sobriety contributed to his suicide and notes the Wild Turkey bottle by the microwave. Pemulis refers to those he knew who quit as the "walking dead. They loved it so much they needed it and gave it up and now they were waiting to die." (What would Pemulis say if he knew about people like Gately?) Pemulis advises Hal "to look a little further past that second of deciding something I know you won't let yourself take back" and asks Hal to figure out "what part of you's come to *need* it, do you think." Pemulis says that addict is "just a word."

PLOT AND CHARACTER: Hal, Mario, E.T.A., AA&R
THEME: Fear/Obsess, Secrets, Choice, Dreams, Isolation, Recur

Throughout this chapter, shadows have been associated with fear. Mario says of Hal, "When you're on your back you don't have a shadow." While Hal is on his back, he is unafraid to tell Mario everything that is going on, all his secrets. Shortly after Hal says he is afraid, he also says, "I'm up on my elbow again. Tell me what you think I should do." Although afraid, Hal is no longer horizontal (inactive) and therefore ready to take action. He is ready to "make a decision. Forever." Pemulis, like Marathe in the last section, chooses (according to Hal) to act for someone outside himself, which is standard practice for Mario. Hal's dream of being misunderstood after taking the DMZ has "a quality of *loneliness* to it." Compare Hal's "screaming for help" in the dream with the nurse that screams "Help!" (p. 196) and with Avril in the mold story (p. 11). Hal, isolated (lonely?) in Ch. 1, says "I cannot make myself understood, now. . . . Call it something I ate" just before recounting the mold-story. Is there a connection between the mold story and the fact that DMZ is mold based (cf. p. 1064)?

In addition to the usual recurrences of urine, dreams, and toothaches, note Hal's comparison of Mario to a "smily-faced guy" and his asking Mario "Are you *in* there?" (cf. Hal on p. 3: "I am in here"). Hal also refers to his desire for the drug he misses as being "stuck" (cf. Steeply speaking of his father, p. 647). *A Clockwork Orange* is recalled again when Hal speaks of his "horror-show dreams." Pemulis's "triangles inside triangles" recalls the "hand-drawn Sierpinski gasket" on his wall (p. 213). Pemulis's description of the long-term Hope user (p. 1064) resembles Erdedy in Ch. 2. Compare Hal calling

Pemulis Mikey (p. 1063) with the narrator for Matty using Micky and Mickey on p. 684.

Chapter 27.40, Section 163, Pages 785-787
Notes 322-323, Page 1066
17 November Y.D.A.U., just after 0830h.

The narrative of Ch. 27 now shifts from 11-14 November to 17 November. Johnette Foltz has "worked five straight night shifts on Dream Duty," which would place her on Dream Duty in the wee hours of 13-17 November. Recall though that on 11 November Gately was preparing to "confer with Johnette Foltz" (p. 593), who was presumably about to begin the 12 November Dream Duty shift as well. Also, at least part of her 13 November shift was taken over by Eugenio Martinez (p. 648). She was preparing for the 15 November shift in Ch. 27.35 (pp. 753-4), and this section begins at the end of her 17 November shift, just after 0830h.

Johnette talks with "a kid" who has "a weird tan" (recall Hal's complexion, p. 101), an "A.T.E." jacket, and "all [his] teeth"; who "didn't seem like he had enough emotional juice"; whose "talking had a burbly, oversalivated quality"; and who had "the quality of somebody who'd just lately put down the pipe and/or bong." New resident David Krone scuttles by during the conversation. Johnette notes that the kid asks for information about substance anonymous meetings in "the exact same roundabout [way] as persons without teeth." The narrator notes that Johnette "would clearly recall" this boy "[m]uch later, in subsequent events' light."

PLOT AND CHARACTER: Ennet, Hal
THEME: Recur, Secret

This section begins with the sound of a flushing toilet, and it is interesting that the narrator for Johnette (who is "incisorless," p. 795) twice references Hal's complete set of teeth, given that Hal dreams of losing his teeth (most recently on p. 770). Hal has exchanged getting high in secret for seeking meetings in secret. What are the subsequent events Johnette will clearly recall?

Chapter 27.41, Section 164, Page 787
Note 324, Pages 1066-1072
17 November Y.D.A.U., 1420h.

Ch. 27.41 is simply a reference to n. 324, which details the adventures of Michael Pemulis, last seen helping Hal in n. 321 on 12 November. The scene begins in the "E.T.A. males' locker room," which holds "the best mirror in the Academy, intricately lit from all perspectives. Dr. J. O. Incandenza knew his adolescents." Pemulis enters the locker room to find his upcoming opponent Freer at the mirror and Possalthwaite "hunched and weeping" over what Freer unsympathetically reports is fatherly betrayal. Pemulis has a brief memory of his own father. Possalthwaite says "Nothing's fair because nothing's *true*," as "[s]omething old in one of the shower drains sighed and gurgled, a nauseous sound." As Troeltsch (last seen in Ch. 27.15, p. 700) begins his weekly WETA broadcast (cf. p. 308), Pemulis says Possalthwaite is "just reeling from a temporary paternal kertwang" that is "emotion-based and not fact-based." Irritated by Freer, Pemulis tries to imagine Freer being "roundly buggered" before telling Possalthwaite that he remembers "staring down the exact same-type thing, though from a more like philosophicalized kertwang than emotions." Pemulis then advises Possalthwaite that he can trust math, and initiates a paean to its truths, concluding with "Never trust the father you can see."

Pemulis has uncharacteristically taken "pre-match Tenuate," risky "given that he and Inc'd escaped on-spot urinalysis only because Pemulis implied to Mrs. Incandenza that he'd tell the Incster about Avril having some sort of major-sport interlude with John Wayne" (cf. Ch. 26.4), which differs from Hal's understanding of why there was no on-spot urinalysis (cf. pp. 772, 783). Earlier, Pemulis found Wayne standing "over Troeltsch's pharmacopic bedside table" looking for Seldane (Wayne had "a cloth hankie" and kept "wiping his nose" nine days ago, p. 385). Recall Troeltsch's bedside table contains a Seldane bottle with "several Tenuate 75-mg. capsules Troeltsch has incrementally promoted from Pemulis" (p. 60). Now, Stice enters the locker room to report, "Troeltsch's got Wayne on the air and Wayne's lost his mind."

PLOT AND CHARACTER: E.T.A.
THEME: Inf/Reg, His/Father, Recur

The "intricately lit" mirror and Freer's preening reflect infantile self-absorption. Fatherly trust issues ("paternal kertwang"s, the parent who does not come) are considered by Possalthwaite and Pemulis (cf. Ch. 27.9 for more on Pemulis's father). In addition to the recurrence of a mirror, Pemulis also considers math an "honest lamp in the inkiest black." The Antitois acquired the DMZ in barter for a lamp and mirror (p. 481) and then sold DMZ to Pemulis (p. 215). Pemulis's mind is on the DMZ because he thinks of the entrepot (p. 1067; cf. pp. 216, 700) and fantasizes about the effects of DMZ on Freer (p. 1069). There are recurrences of sensory environmental horrors: the "nauseous sound" of the gurgling drain and the "dentalish sweet stink" of catgut strings. Suspecting Kornspan of killing the "two collarless cats whose burnt corpses had been found on the hillside during pre-drill sprints a couple weeks back" is another missed connection since surely it was Lenz who did this. Pemulis's paean to math includes references to philosophers, mathematicians, and notable terms and phrases. "Caius is mortal" is again referenced (cf. p. 693). The myth of Sisyphus is alluded to, and there is allusion to being "directionless in a dark wood" like Dante at the outset of the *Inferno*. The narrator for Pemulis comments about something "Hal would have observed" (p. 1068).

There are recurrences in this endnote (or endnotes to this endnote) specific to other endnotes. Tavis is referred to as "Gretel the Cross-Sectioned [Dairy] Cow" as he was by Bain in n. 269 (p. 1048). In endnote 324.f, the circling and chest-hitting activity of the 16s (presumably in imitation of the apes in *2001: A Space Odyssey*) is again referenced (cf. n. 304, p. 1058). Endnote 324.e references n. 22 (also referenced on p. 60), which helps the reader recall the contents of Troeltsch's Seldane bottle.

Chapter 27.42, Section 165, Pages 787-795
Notes 325-331, Page 1072
17 November Y.D.A.U.

This section is assumed to occur on 17 November only because it is situated between four sections that definitely occur on that date. On 7 November (Ch. 17.5), Molly Notkin hosted the party at which Joelle overdosed in Joelle's old co-op ("passed on to Molly Notkin," p. 227), the brownstone in which *Infinite Jest* was filmed (n. 80). Soon after, Notkin obtained "some old tapes of [Joelle's] program for the Madame's personal listening use" (p. 625) from the since-abducted engineer, tapes which were heard outside Joelle's window by Mario on the 11th (pp. 591-2). Now, Notkin—whose homberg has been removed (cf. p. 227) and who has "a fear of direct light" (p. 220)—is undergoing a technical interview under "a portable high-watt lamp" and "amid dropped luggage in her co-op's darkened and lock-dickied living room." The interview is conducted by R. Tine Jr., who was with his father the day the engineer was abducted (p. 622). This section consists of an introductory paragraph followed by 27 subsequent paragraphs (one of which is simply an ellipsis) in which "Molly Notkin tells the U.S.O.U.S. operatives" "everything she believed she knew" ("(and then some)," n. 326).

Notkin refers to the "lethally entertaining" work as *Infinite Jest (V or VI)*—it was referenced as *Infinite Jest (V?)* in n. 24 (p. 993)—and that "it features Madame Psychosis as some kind of maternal instantiation of the archetypal figure Death, sitting naked, corporeally gorgeous, ravishing, hugely pregnant ["an f/x"], her hideously deformed face either veiled or blanked out" (cf. the "fatally entertaining and scopophiliac thing Jim alleges he made out of [Joelle's] unveiled face," p. 230). The "alleged substance of the Death-cosmology Madame Psychosis was supposed to deliver in a lalating monologue to the viewer, mediated by the very special lens" over which she was "inclined," was that "the woman who kills you is always your next life's mother" (cf. "the weird wobble-lensed maternal 'I'm-so-terribly-sorry' monologue-scene," n. 80). "She may or may not have been holding a knife during this monologue."

Many of Notkin's statements are inaccurate (the narrator of n. 329 calls one statement "complete horseshit"). She says that "the film's Auteur" believed in "a finite world-total of available erections," but she is apparently attributing to Jim the condition of "her one tormented love" (at NYU, p. 220) that she has presumably just come from visiting (cf. that Molly is "fresh off the N.N.Y.C. high-speed rail"). She says that "the Auteur" was "extremely close to his own mother," but this does not seem to be the case, given the minimal interaction between mother and son in Ch. 25.2 (but cf. that she "spent her last few years living in the Marlboro St. brownstone" that was Jim and Avril's first home, p. 953). Notkin says that the Auteur's son's excuse for abandoning his relationship with Madame Psychosis was his "accusing Madame Psychosis of being sexually enmeshed with . . . the Auteur." On pp. 227-8 Notkin "has no idea . . . whether Orin left because [Jim and Joelle] were lovers or what." According to n. 80, Orin knows Jim and Joelle weren't lovers (but cf. Jim's role in "the end [of the relationship]'s start" on p. 297 and Orin's implied jealousy when speaking to Hal at the top of p. 250). Near the end of the section, Notkin attributes Orin's departure to Joelle's "traumatic deformity." Notkin says Jim quit drinking at "Xmas"; Orin told Hal that Joelle said January (p. 249). Notkin says "M.P.'s" abuse-problem was a consequence of guilt over Jim's suicide. This matches the narrator's "Joelle's been in a cage since Y.T.S.D.B." (p. 227), but Joelle was using cocaine in 2001 before Jim's death (p. 747). Notkin often lies to protect her friend. She implies that M.P.'s treatment facility is "someplace far, very far away," even though Notkin presumably took the old tapes she acquired from the engineer to Ennet House. She gives her interviewers false names for both Joelle and Joelle's father and reports that the van Dyne's are from southeast Kentucky rather than near Paducah (cf. p. 296) in southwest Kentucky (cf. that Joelle also speaks of fishing with her father on "the Cumberland" (p. 532), which is presumably Lake Cumberland in south-central Kentucky).

Notkin says that Madame Psychosis was a beneficiary of the Auteur's (cf. n. 80), but did not attend his funeral, which was held "in the L'Islet Province of Nouveau Québec, the birth-province of the Auteur's widow" (cf. p. 65). Notkin asks why the U.S.O.U.S. doesn't "simply go to J.O.I.'s widow and verify directly the existence and location of the purported cartridge" (presumably, a technical interview with Avril is not feasible because she "never leaves the grounds"; pp. 42, 51). Notkin doubts Avril would have anti-American connections, "no matter what the files on her indiscreet youth might suggest" (cf. p. 64), given her consuming interest in "her own individually neurotic agendas." Notkin wonders why Jim kept casting Joelle as a feminine Death-figure "when he had the real thing under his nose, and eminently photogenic to boot." Notkin says that Joelle feels guilty because her request that Jim quit drinking may have left him "unable to withstand the psychic pressures that pushed him over the edge" (cf. Pemulis's advice to Hal, p. 1065). Notkin suspects that Avril may have placed the Wild Turkey bottle (cf. p. 250) in the kitchen, jealous that Jim had given up spirits for someone other than her (but recall that it was Avril who "risked exterior transit and took" Jim to his last detox, p. 249). Notkin references Avril's promiscuity and suspects Avril of incestuous behavior, given Orin's issues with his mother.

Notkin reports that as Madame Psychosis "emerged from puberty as an almost freakishly beautiful young woman," her father began to "behave as if Madame Psychosis were getting younger instead of older" and discouraged her entrance to Boston University and her dating of Orin. Orin came home with Joelle "for the third time" (cf. p. 296 for the first time in 2001) in Y.T.M.P. to have Thanksgiving Dinner on 24 November (but cf. that Thanksgiving Day was on 27 November in 2003). At this dinner, Joelle's father confessed "that he'd been secretly, silently in love" with his daughter (cf. pp. 237 and 239 for hands in laps while eating Crackerjacks) and that his repression of that love had become difficult. This prompts Joelle's mother to confront her denial of her husband's behavior, to confess that her own father "had molested her and her sister all through childhood," and to lament that she had married "the exact same kind of monster." Joelle's mother ran (and was followed by all) to the acid-lab (Joelle's father is "a low-pH chemist") in the cellar with intentions to disfigure herself, but instead hurled the acid at her husband, who along with Orin "reflexively ducked," leaving Joelle "open for a direct facial hit, resulting in the traumatic deformity." Since no one pressed charges,

Joelle's mother was allowed to return home to her kitchen, where she "committed suicide by putting her extremities down the garbage disposal" (cf. that Joelle told Gately her mother was dead, p. 563). It is tempting to wonder whether Joelle's disfigurement actually might be the result of a freebase accident (cf. the AA speaker heard by Joelle on p. 377 and the analysis of Blood Sister in n. 290), but Joelle's thoughts of the "dodger of flung acid extraordinaire" (p. 223) and of cleaning "after the acid" (p. 225) support Notkin's story.

It is unclear whether it was before or after her disfigurement that Joelle played a character whose face was "grotesquely mangled" in *Safe Boating Is No Accident* (pp. 991-2) and a "veiled nun" in *The Night Wears a Sombrero* (p. 992). These were two of the last four films released in Y.T.M.P. (but recall that the listing is "not definitive," p. 986); so if these works were filmed post-trauma, there would have been only five weeks left in the year to film, edit, and distribute them. Joelle apparently began wearing a veil regularly after her disfigurement six years ago, because "she unveiled for" Jim (p. 228) in the last *Infinite Jest* and because Notkin has never seen her unveiled (n. 328). Presumably Joelle was occasionally unveiled (e.g.; at "the graduate wine-tasting party" (p. 534) she spoke of to Gately, which presumably was unattended by Notkin) before she officially joined U.H.I.D. ("don[ned] the veil," p. 534) in Y.P.W., "almost four years" ago (p. 533).

PLOT AND CHARACTER: U.S.O.U.S., Samizdat, Joelle, AA&R
THEME: Secrets, Inf/Reg, Cycles, His/Father, Recur

The structure of this section parallels the structure of the novel in that the opening paragraph (chapter) sets up the subsequent 27 paragraphs (chapters) that occurred earlier. Notkin references Joelle's "secret and hidden substance-abuse problem," and instances of child abuse recur in this section. Joelle's father's secret love for his daughter prompts his "infantilizing conduct": "regressing the child mentally to an age of incontinence and pre-mashed meat." The cycle of Joelle's father's movie-watching with his mother continues in his movie-watching with Joelle. Joelle's mother fears that she has contributed to a cycle of abuse by marrying "the exact same kind of monster" as her father. Recurrences include Joelle's mother's "fear of public spaces," a reference to "indifference to dentition and hygiene," and the interviewers' missed connection that the cartridge for which they are searching was partially created in the very room in which they are conducting their interview. Notkin believes the "myth surrounding the purportedly lethal final cartridge" is an illustration of Deleuze's philosophy (p. 792). The flask that contained the acid that disfigured Joelle also contained "an enormous half-eaten-away skull," which resonates with Hamlet's holding the skull of Yorick, a fellow of infinite jest.

There are parallels in the van Dyne and Incandenza families. Both Joelle's mother and Orin's mother hide or repress abuse by their fathers (cf. pp. 766-7 for Avril's repressed abuse). Both Joelle's mother and Orin's father died in "miraculously" horrific kitchen suicides. Joelle's father and presumably Orin and Avril experience repressed incestuous desires. What is the significance of the mistake Notkin makes when she originally states that Orin accuses Joelle "of being sexually enmeshed with their—here Molly Notkin said that she of course meant to say *his*—father"?

Chapter 27.43, Section 166, Page 795
Note 332, Pages 1073-1076
17 November Y.D.A.U.

Ch. 27.43 is simply a reference to n. 332, which continues the adventures of Michael Pemulis from Ch. 27.41 (n. 321). Pemulis has discovered that his "pilfered Tenuates in [Troeltsch's] Seldane bottle" (cf. n. 5.a) are the reason Wayne "lost his mind" (p. 1072) during Troeltsch's broadcast (cf. Pemulis saying he'd "be *way* into watching Wayne play with distorted senses" on p. 213). Pemulis is currently being questioned in Avril's office by prorectors deLint, Nwangi, and Watson about the Wayne incident and treated to excerpts of Wayne's unflattering descriptions of E.T.A. faculty, students, and administration. Pemulis asks whether "the emerging point" of this interaction will affect his chances to compete in the upcoming Whataburger tournament. The prorectors produce potential drug paraphernalia, including "empty sterile Visine bottles," from Pemulis's room. Pemulis suspects Troeltsch of eating "deal-cutting cheese." Upon Pemulis's third request to see Avril, the prorectors forward Avril's invitation that Pemulis "shout whatever you threatened the administrators to shout about from the highest hill you can find, which pretty soon won't be this one." Pemulis again asks about his chances at the Whataburger, prompting incredulity and "infectious" laughter from the prorectors. Recall that Pemulis's "deepest dread is of academic or disciplinary expulsion and ejection, of having to schlepp back down Comm. Ave. into blue-collar Allston" (n. 211).

PLOT AND CHARACTER: E.T.A.
THEME: Fear/Obsess, Waste, His/Father, Recur

As Pemulis is pushed out of E.T.A. (his deepest dread), he is pushed out of the main text of the novel into the notes. Pemulis's trouble is characterized as the "riffle of the wings of the Shit Fairy, which he privately envisions as a kind of violet incubus with the Da's saggy frown," which resonates with the billowing black wing image and themes of waste, fathers, and abuse. There is a recurrence of a "cornered rodent" image (Wayne speaking of Unwin) and of ominous machine sounds: "Mrs. Inc's ventilator hissed and something up in there whirred a little," masking the "slight whir of [Pemulis's] cortex working at full speed" (cf. "a faint whirring noise coming from [Marathe's] head, p. 751). Dave Harde "pitched forward narcoleptically" onto the "blue" carpet (like Jim's father in Ch. 25.2), and Lateral Alice Moore's stress causes her face to become "blue-tinged." "It was Pemulis, deLint, Nwangi, and Watson . . ." matches the four-droog-introducing syntax of *A Clockwork Orange*. How does Wayne know of Orin's seduction strategy? Did the A.F.R. tell him? Did Avril?

Chapter 27.44, Section 167, Pages 795-808
Notes 333-336, Page 1076
17 November Y.D.A.U., around 1730h.

This section occurs about nine hours after Hal's visit to Ennet in Ch. 27.40. He has used a booklet given to him by Johnette to decide to drive out to a "distant and obscure" NA meeting. Although he is still not taking drugs, his head hurts all day, and he feels "wretched and bereft." Hal hears on the radio that "the Gentle administration had scheduled and then cancelled a special . . . address to the nation on subjects unknown." As Hal nears the location of the meeting, "[s]ome sort of bird shits on his windshield" (is this an omen?). Inside the building, there is a "sick sweet dental sub-odor" and "total silence." "The whole cubular building seems to Hal to hold the tensed menace of a living thing that's chosen to hold itself still." Hal enters the room of the meeting (carrying his NASA glass into which he spits a mixture of tobacco and saliva) to find nine or ten bearded men all sitting the same way and sits down. Hal is acknowledged by Harv, the group leader, who holds a teddy bear; as does Kevin, a crying man near the front, who holds his bear close as a means of prompting his "Inner Infant [to express] his grief and loss." Through tears, Kevin says he feels his Inner Infant crying for his parents who do not come, leaving him alone. "Hal wonders what the etiquette is in NA about getting up and leaving right in the middle of somebody's Infantile revelation of need."

When Kevin explains that his parents weren't there for him because they died from a "falling radio helicopter on the Jamaica Way" (cf. Marlon Bain, p. 1047), Hal, "his mouth oval with horror," realizes that this is Kevin Bain (older brother (p. 1051) of "Orin's old E.T.A. doubles and chemical-mischief partner"), that this is not an NA meeting, and that his meeting-information booklet is nearly two years old. As the emotion intensifies, Harv (through Harv's bear) asks Kevin (through Kevin's bear) "if it [Kevin's bear] would maybe point to the man in the group Kevin Bain would most like to have hold and nurture and love him *in loco parentis*." Kevin points to Jim, a man eating yogurt next to Hal; and Harv surreptitiously indicates that Jim should not speak or move. After Kevin's eleventh request is denied, he begins "projectile-weeping," and Hal observes that "[a]t a certain point hysterical grief becomes facially indistinguishable from hysterical mirth." The group suggests that Kevin "owe[s] it to his Inner Infant to come up with some sort of active way to meet the Infant's needs." Kevin realizes he should "actively go over" to Jim. Following the suggestions of Harv and the group that Kevin move like an infant, he goes to Jim on all fours, "his face unspeakable."

PLOT AND CHARACTER: Hal, AA&R
THEME: Isolation, Inf/Reg, Recur

Hal goes from seeking an isolated spot in which to get high to seeking an isolated spot in which to learn how to stop getting high. Kevin Bain felt isolated because he was left alone with his "teething ring" by his parents ("Nobody's coming"), and he feels his "Inner Infant standing holding the bars of his crib." Kevin, crawling at the end of the section, experiences near-complete infantile regression. Kevin's "hand lies over his face like a spider." Harv makes "a cage of his hands." "Hal can hear the squeak of blood in his head." There is a "framed print of [cubist painter] Picasso's 'Seated Harlequin'" in the menacing "cubular building" in which Hal, seated, has a disorienting experience that is comical, at least to the reader. What was to be the topic of Gentle's address? Why do "walls and [a] ceiling the color of Thousand Island dressing" prompt "unplaceable but uneasy associations for Hal"?

Chapter 27: A Kind Of Writhing Weave: Horrors, Secrets, Pursuits, Surprises

The various threads woven together in this next-to-last chapter—sometimes such that characters in close proximity do not meet, like Hamlet and Fortinbras in *Hamlet* (IV.iv)—are unified by recurring examples of horrors, secrets, pursuits, and surprises (cf. p. 403 of the study).

The thread of Madame Psychosis's engineer is joined to the thread of the A.F.R. when the A.F.R. abducts him in the opening section. The threads of Marathe and Steeply, woven together throughout the novel and into this chapter, now separate. Marathe is at the Antitois' shop with the A.F.R., an organization that has spies at E.T.A. Steeply is in Marathe's favorite park with the U.S.O.U.S. when the engineer is taken by the A.F.R. on the day after Steeply watches a match at E.T.A. (references are made to events that occur simultaneously with the match, and Chs. 27.15-19 explore a set of simultaneous events that occur after the match) in which Hal is almost beaten, after which he is depressed and watches some of his father's old cartridges three days before Joelle—Ennet resident and actress in Jim's films, though not any of the ones Hal watches—visits Don Gately. Steeply is in contact with former E.T.A. student Marlon Bain, but cannot contact current student Hal, who will attend a meeting with Marlon's brother, Kevin. Ennet resident Clenette H. takes cartridges from E.T.A. (probably put in the trash by the E.T.A. Tunnel Club), an event witnessed by E.T.A. student Hal, who later visits Ennet. E.T.A. student Struck reads Ennet resident Day's report on train cults; and later Ennet resident Day, who is surprised that he misses ex-resident Lenz, speaks to train-cultist Marathe. Ennet resident Gompert, who listened to Day speak of total psychic horror and who experiences a more intense depression than Hal, will be robbed by Poor Tony Krause when he reenters the narrative after a long absence. Poor Tony, heading to the Antitois' shop, is seen by old friend Matty Pemulis—brother of E.T.A. student (for now) Michael Pemulis—and makes sounds heard by Lenz (also the instigator of a robbery). Krause's robbery leads to Gompert meeting Marathe, who was just looking for Gompert's roommate, Joelle, at Ennet. Joelle has tapes of her old broadcasts given to her by Notkin, who retrieved tapes from the engineer before he was taken by the A.F.R. and before she was interviewed by the U.S.O.U.S. Joelle was not listening to the tapes on the night Marathe was at Ennet—she was thinking of the Incandenza family—but was listening to the tapes on the night Mario Incandenza of E.T.A. passed by her Ennet House window after talking with Avril and before talking with Hal, who was helped by Pemulis, who will receive no help from Avril.

CHAP	HORRORS	SECRETS	PURSUITS (OF)	SURPRISES
27.1	shriek-roused figures	observation by U.S.O.U.S.	engineer by A.F.R.	engineer by A.F.R.
27.2	objects out of nowhere	powdered milk	answers re: matches, objects	tennis match results
27.3	*Brockengespenstphanom*	M*A*S*H notebook	M*A*S*H theories	M*A*S*H obsession
27.4	Day's total psychic horror	Green's trauma	Day by total psychic horror	Day by total psychic horror
27.5	fantods from court shadow	the inside chew-proof place	Hal by H.S., show by E.T.A.s	Hal's mishit
27.6	accidental death of Bains	motives of Orin and Avril	Bain answers by Steeply	Volvo incident
27.7	smell	the E.T.A. Tunnel Club	rat or feral hamster	maggots in refrigerator
27.8	fame	Steeply and Thierry	transcendence of fame	attainment is not redemption
27.9	abuse of Matty	abuse of Matty	Matty by Mr. Pemulis	Matty by Poor Tony Krause
27.10	deLint's words chill Hal	Hal likes *Wave Bye-Bye* . . .	promptness by bureaucrat	bureaucrat helps boy
27.11	Krause's appearance	the Antitoi decoys	Québecer (diverted by crew)	Krause's recovery
27.12	the Frightful Hog	Day misses Lenz	data for journals	Lenz quotes in Day's journal
27.13	depression and loneliness	source of depression's pain	Gompert by *It*	cynicism, naïveté not mutually exclusive
27.14	van Cleve (to Gompert)	Krause is stalking KG and RvC	Gompert, van Cleve by Poor Tony	Gompert forward without volition
27.15	Troeltsch plan (to roommates)	Tenuate in Seldane-bottle	broadcasting	
27.16		DMZ hiding place	DMZ by Pemulis	
27.17		Lyle's experience	something by Lyle	
27.18			confections, whoops	
27.19		Avril's call	information by Avril	
27.20	house pulsed and breathed	Jim's impulse re: *Blood Sister*	Hal by Steeply	Joelle consideration: show face
27.21	violence in Blood Sister	drug deals at mission	revenge by Blood Sister	Hal remembers name
27.22	apparition (Poor Tony)	KG memory of skating rink	Poor Tony by van Cleve	apparition, lightpost
27.23	Lenz's ghostly aspect	Lenz's surveillance of women	Chinese women by Lenz	Bull's-eye
27.24	A.F.R. in Antitois' shop	location of Master	Master by A.F.R.	A.F.R. still in shop
27.25	PTK's horrid dreams, talons	PTK thoughts of father	Poor Tony by van Cleve	pursuit of Poor Tony by van Cleve
27.26	plastic-wrapped cadavers	cartridge, agenda, suspicion	Master, agenda by A.F.R.	Fortier's call from Southwest ops
27.27	U.S.A. condescension (to Fortier)	Fortier's attachable legs	goals, public transit by Fortier	Fortier's attachable legs
27.28	Joelle's fear of teeth	what teeth have been up to	dental hygiene in Joelle's dream	long rows of all canine teeth
27.29	Antitoi remains, field-tests	A.F.R. operations, operatives	various A.F.R. activities	operatives by *samizdat*
27.30	rot-smelling legs of sexless figure	contents of women's bags	a cleaner alley by Lenz	alley sounds
27.31	Ennet denizens, train victims	Marathe's identity	Joelle by Marathe, honor by cult	clatter and two shrieks
27.32	prettiness, Thanksgiving dinner	what Jim is saying w/ his work	meaning in Jim's work by Joelle	flashes of something in Jim's work
27.33	Pat's dog licking itself	Marathe's true goals	cartridges, Joelle by Marathe	cartridges, U.H.I.D. at Ennet
27.34	Gompert's potential entrance	of the whole Incandeza family	cleanliness by Joelle	potentially, Gompert's entrance
27.35	Lucien's technical interview	Marathe's vomiting	new cartridges for residents	*etier* is E.T.A.
27.36	obliteration, engulfment	abuse of Avril	answers by Mario	Avril by Mario
27.37	liars who give nothing away	Avril's disguise for S. Johnson	a catalogue of liars	Hal by Pemulis's performance
27.38	Marathe's wife's condition	Rémy Marathe is not Swiss	a heart for Marathe's wife	Marathe's offer to Gompert
27.39	Hal's dream	divulged to Mario by Hal	advice by Hal	Hal tells Mario, DMZ discoveries
27.40	Hal's hair and saliva	residents hidden from police	meeting information by Hal	Johnette by Hal
27.41	nothing's true	Tenuate in Seldane-bottle	math as truth	Wayne on the radio
27.42	Thanskgiving dinner Y.T.M.P.	Joelle's father's love for her	answers by U.S.O.U.S.	Notkin by interview, Joelle by acid
27.43	the Shit Fairy (and cf. n. 211)	taken from Pemulis	Pemulis's demise	Pemulis by Avril's invitation
27.44	Bain's Inner Infant	Hal's trip to Natick	needs by Bain	Hal by Kevin Bain

Infinite Jest V

A Writhing Weave

The frenetic chaos, nightmare visions, and participation of a majority of characters in the longest chapter of *Infinite Jest* recall "Circe," the longest chapter of *Ulysses*; the weaving of narrative threads across a certain time period within the same city on the same day (14 November) recalls the "Wandering Rocks" chapter of *Ulysses*. In Ch. 27, Wallace weaves together most of the various threads of the novel; but like Penelope, his activity does not tend toward resolution. The frequent and often brief shifts (weaves) in narrative are analogous to filmic quick-cuts and intensify the action, creating a bulge of narrative tensions and the illusion that the plots are converging toward a unified climax—that the finished cloth will be tightly knit and free of holes.

Analogous to the patterned creation of holes in a Sierpinski Gasket (cf. the Introduction to the study), or to weaving something that is intended to remain incomplete, Wallace creates patterned holes by cutting out pieces of narrative, so that the reader constructs a narrative "as much out of what's missing as what's there" (p. 681). Note that the greater portion of the narrative of the latter half of the novel focuses on every third day in the middle of November: 8, 11, 14, 17, and (in Ch. 28) 20 November. Less focus is given to (there are more holes in the narrative of) 9-10, 12-13, 15-16, and 18-19 November. With the exception of an 11 November quick-cut (p. 654) in which he is sleeping hours before he gets shot, Gately does not "appear" in this chapter, although he is referenced (e.g.; his forehead was mopped by Joelle on 14 November, p. 707). Gately's last conscious appearance (in the first minutes of 12 November) was at the end of Ch. 26; he appears again at the beginning of Ch. 28, leaving a Gately-sized hole in Ch. 27.

Chapter 28

Under the Surface: Hunched, Horizontal, Histories, Hauntings

Chapter 28.1, Section 168, Pages 809-827
Notes 337-341, Page 1076
12-15 November Y.D.A.U.

The narrator for Gately returns for the first time since Ch. 26.16. After being shot in the first minutes of 12 November, Gately was taken to St. Elizabeth's Hospital, where "[t]he ceiling was breathing. It bulged and receded" (when Joelle visits Gately at St. Elizabeth's on 14 November he is "looking at his room's semi-private ceiling like it would eat him if he dropped his guard," p. 707). The ceiling reminds Gately of when he was "like four" and living in "a little beach house" with "a big ragged hole in the roof." The hole was covered with "thick clear polyurethane sheeting" which "bulged and settled" and "seemed like some monstrous vacuole inhaling and exhaling directly over little Gately" (recall "Herman the Ceiling That Breathed," p. 447). The "blurred figure in the next bed . . . seemed to have a box on its head." (Otis P. Lord was "alleged to have come back from the emergency room at St. Elizabeth's [on 8 November] with the Hitachi monitor over his head, still, its removal . . . calling for the sort of esoteric expertise you have to fly in by a private medical jet" (p. 456); so presumably Lord would be returning to the hospital. On 11 November, Mario noted that "Otis Lord's door [had] *Infirmary* next to his name" (p. 757).) Gately has a recurring dream that recalls the DuPlessis incident (Ch. 7.4) but with "an Oriental" with "no nose or mouth" in place of DuPlessis. Gately goes "in and out of consciousness," which "seemed to him more like he kept coming up for air and then being pushed below the surface of something" (recall an earlier dream of Gately's in which he was "under a sort of sea, at terrific depths," p. 449).

Gately is aware of nurses; of a tall, ghostish figure, "slumped and fluttering, appearing to rest its tailbone on the sill of the dark window"; of a "stolid shadow of somebody in a hat . . . just outside the room"; and of Tiny Ewell, who "had been discoursing to him for an unknown length of time [on his] first full night in St. Elizabeth's" (late 12 November, early 13 November). As Gately listens to Tiny, other figures keep "popping in and out of fluttery view," and Gately's eyes keep "rolling up in his head." Tiny tells a story of embezzling his third-grade schoolmates in the early 1970s. It was then that he first "tasted power, the verbal manipulation of human hearts"; but "the power had roused something dark" in his personality. He "lived only to feed the dark thing in [his] personality," which had "grown leathery wings and a beak and turned on [him]." Tiny "lived and moved in the shadow of something dark that hovered just overhead" and drove him "to grandiose wickedness" (compare this with Day's description of total psychic horror in Ch. 27.4). Faced with the "shame and horror" of his actions, Tiny resolved "to toe the virtuous line from then on." The "whole shameful interval . . . was moved to mental storage and buried there," until "the other [i.e., last] night, after the fracas and [Gately's] display of reluctant *se offendendo*" when Tiny dreamed of the third-grade incidents again. (As Tiny speaks of memories becoming unburied, he makes the exact same verbal mistake—although perhaps Gately did act in "self-offense," given his current situation—as the gravedigger in *Hamlet* ("V.i. 9," n. 337), the scene in which Hamlet later uses the words "infinite jest.") Tiny confides, "Don, this buried interval . . . may have informed my whole life." He says, "I don't want to remember despicabilities I can do nothing about. . . . Some things seem better left submerged. No?" (Gately began experiencing unwanted memories "burpling greasily up" in May (cf. pp. 446-449), which was as frightening for him as it is for Tiny.) Gately "starts to short-term recall" now that "[l]ast night's emergency surgery" was to remove fragments of ordnance that had done "great and various damage to soft tissues," prompting "a massive infection" that must be monitored for toxemia. Before surgery, Gately had "made Pat Montesian swear" to make his doctors aware of his "HISTORY OF NARCOTICS DEPENDENCY" and has refused the drugs that his doctors have offered him anyway. He tries to assure Tiny that if he "could just hang in" that "everything would end up alright," but he can't speak.

Gately dreams that a tornado hits the beach of his youth. As "a man with a shepherd's crook" (recall Gately's dream, pp. 358-9) beats his mother, he breaks through his "crib's bars with his head" and runs out to the beach "to deep warm water and submerge[s] himself." His mother comes out "holding a bloody Ginsu knife, calling his name." She couldn't hear Gately's calls to her for the tornado, which sucks her away. Gately awakes in unbearable pain (presumably during the morning of 13 November: "It was daytime"). "Later" someone who might have been Joelle ran a washcloth over his face; the "guy with either the square head or the box on his head had been taken off someplace"; there were "no ghostish figures or figures in the mist"; and "Gately couldn't see any shadows of anybody in a hat." "At some point [either the evening of the 13th or the morning of the 14th] a probably real Pat Montesian came in" to reassure him ("The left side of her face was very kind") "that he'd done the very best he could" and "not to worry." He tries to ask her about "the legal fallout of the other night's thug-fracas," but he cannot speak. Later, Gately dreams or hallucinates "Mrs. Lopate, the objay dart from the Shed that they come and install next to the Ennet House viewer some days, sitting there in a gunmetal wheelchair." ("Objay darts" is a phrase used for "Shed" residents by Enfield Marine security officers (n. 67). Marathe saw Lopate at Ennet on 14 November (p. 730).) Gately realizes "that the catatonic Mrs. L had been the same lady he'd seen touching the tree in #5's [i.e., the Shed's] front lawn" (cf. pp. 196-7). "Then at some later point [probably the evening of the 14th, cf. p. 707] Joelle van Dyne was sitting in a chair just outside the railing of the bed."

"Then at some point [probably during the day on 15 November] Calvin Thrust," throughout the second half of this section, informs Gately of events at Ennet House in the wake of his shooting.

Thrust tells Gately what occurred at Ennet immediately before Gately was taken to the hospital, which includes a report of Green being violent toward Lenz but then refusing "to eat cheese." Lenz took Thrust up on his offer of "voluntarily resigning his Ennet residency" (and so three nights later was able to rob two Oriental women on the streets of Enfield; cf. Chs. 27.23 and 27.30). Pat and Joelle "drove interference" in Pat's Aventura (cf. p. 461) for Thrust, who took Gately to the hospital in his Corvette. Gately "kept blinking rhythmically" in an attempt to find out if any Nucks were dead, if "an A.D.A.-type figure that always wore a hat [had] come in from Essex County" (cf. p. 56 and n. 14 for the A.D.A.'s hat, and cf. Ch. 7.4 for the origin of Gately's concern about the A.D.A.), and if any Ennet residents would be credible "as like legal witnesses." Thrust reports that, in the aftermath of the fracas, the Ennet "House Manager had gone so far as planting herself out in front of the House's locked front door with her not-all-that-small arms and legs spread out, blocking the door" from entry by Boston's "Finest." (The Ennet House Manager is probably Janine (p. 753), described by Marathe to be a "large and clipboarded woman" on p. 735.)

Thrust, a former adult-film actor, has an "air of imminent departure about him" and uses (via the narrator) malapropisms like "embryoglio" and "prosfeces" (or maybe Gately hears these mispronunciations, since he thinks of the "Heineken Maneuver" (p.835) in the next section after Thrust is gone). Thrust informs Gately about recent Ennet residents: Amy J picked up her stuff; Hester Thrale never came back after running off into the night and has had her stuff placed on the porch; there were numerous trashbags in Lenz's room; Gompert is missing (did she take what Marathe offered on p. 782?); and Foss graduated. Thrust informs Gately about all current Ennet residents (now at 23 after the admission of David Krone) except Ken Erdedy and Didi Neaves. Recalling that "[d]ischarged residents' possessions stay on the porch for three days," Gately tries to calculate what day it is (Thrust's report is probably occurring hours after Thrale's 72-hour deadline). Attempts are being made to get Glynn, who still has diverticulitis, into "St. E's," despite the "insurance fraud" on his record (cf. Ch. 13.3). Reasons are given for new resident Dave K.'s scuttling like a crab (to be described by Joelle as "weird limbo-injury posture" on p. 855).

Gately "blinks like mad" when Thrust reports that Clenette and Yolanda are restricted to their room "because of what happened to the map of the Nuck they allegedly stomped." Thrust speaks of the cartridges Clenette "promoted" from E.T.A. and of how residents are bitching because it will "take forever" to preview them for "suitability and sex." (Pat asks Johnette to begin screening cartridges Clenette brought "down from E.T.A. this afternoon [14 November]" (p. 754). However, Clenette has been restricted to her room since the first minutes of 12 November, so these are presumably some of the mostly unlabeled cartridges designated as trash by the Tunnel Club and presumably taken by Clenette on 11 November (cf. the bulging backpack seen by Hal on pp. 633-4), cartridges that Clenette presumably waited three days to give to Pat or that were brought from Clenette's room to Pat.) Green "shouts about nuts and cigars in his sleep" (cf. pp. 579-81). Morris Hanley "has baked some cream-cheese brownies for Gately," but the "nurses' station, like, *impounded* them from Thrust." The residents' depositions "support a justifiable senorio of either self-defense or Lenz-defense." The "biggest problem" for making Gately's self-defense case is the missing ".44 item" with which Gately was shot, dropped by Green and now "vanished from legal view." The Item would also help Yolanda's case, because the shoe with which she gave the owner of the gun "a spike heel right through the eye" was left "protruding from the guy's map." As "the sun was starting to go down" (presumably on 15 November) Gately realized that "[w]hen it starts to get dark out is when the ceiling breathes."

PLOT AND CHARACTER: Gately, Ennet
THEME: His/Father, Fear/Obsess, Memory, Dreams, Phys/Ob, Recur

This section documents an incident from Tiny Ewell's childhood (a history) that "may have informed [his] whole life" and documents events at Ennet House from Gately's absence to 15 November. Like Gately earlier in the year, Ewell is afraid of what he remembers. Gately dreams (of the ceiling's "inhaling maw," winds that sucked a "blue stuffed brontosaurus" from his crib, submersion in water, a bulging and receding tornado, and his mother "bluely backlit") or hallucinates between receiving visitors, with whom he cannot speak (an obstacle). There are recurrences of missed connections in that Gately is unable to communicate with his visitors and is unable to identify what day it is. There are other recurring images of light-cycles, fluttering, shadows, secret vomiting (Tiny, p. 813), cages or bars, knives (Gately's mother on p. 816 and Nell Gunther on p. 827), and eyes rolling up (Gately's on pp. 811 and 822). Another addict cries (Tiny, p. 825). The breathing ceiling, "shiny as a lung," resonates with the impending erection of the E.T.A. Lung. Trouble breathing is indicated by "the Oriental" in Gately's dream with "no nose or mouth" and by Gately's seeming need to come up for air. Completing a cycle, the last four pages of notes (pp. 1076-9) are frequently about specific drugs, as were the first three pages of notes (pp. 983-5). Where is the "Item"? Will the spike(d-heel)-in-the-eye lead the F.L.Q. (comrades of the stomped victim) to suspect that the A.F.R. (who often use the spike-in-the-eye tactic) played a part in the events of early 12 November?

Chapter 28.2, Section 169, Pages 827-845
Notes 342-343, Page 1076
15-16 November Y.D.A.U.

Gately's thread continues from the previous section. When Gately next awakens, "[s]ometime later, at night" (on 15 November), Thrust has been replaced at Gately's side by Day, who is eating one of the cream-cheese brownies brought by Thrust to the nurses' station and "plowing through a long [family] story." Like Ewell, Day is "sucker-punched by an emergent sober memory." The long paragraph of pp. 828-838 begins with another "recurring bad dream" of Gately's, which features another Oriental—an anonymous woman like those who carry multiple shopping bags—looking down at him and a menacing dog in the distance (cf. the women that dog-killer Lenz robbed, Chs. 27.23 and 27.30). He "opens his eyes again," but realizes he is just in another dream when he wakes up to the sound of crying from the deep-voiced patient in the next bed (this could be

Lord, whose voice would sound deeper with a monitor on his head). Before midnight, "the ghostish figure" returns, and it is clear now from the narrative description that the self-described "plain old wraith" (cf. the "skull-deprived wraiths" (p. 670) haunting the Concavity and the practice of Papineau-region Québecers who "let out" (p. 244) buried souls) is Jim Incandenza. Gately "didn't have to speak out loud to be able to interface with the wraith-figure." A wraith "could move at the speed of quanta and be anywhere anytime and hear in symphonic toto the thoughts of animate men, but it couldn't ordinarily affect anybody or anything solid" and "had to use somebody's like internal brain-voice" to communicate. Very few wraiths were willing to stand still for the amount of time it took them to communicate with animate men. Perhaps as proof of his quantum speed, the wraith disappears and then reappears, once with one of Gately's "celebrity photos" (of a pre-presidential Gentle) from Ennet and once with an "Oriental-type" (i.e., from far away) Coke can, which the wraith places on Gately's forehead. Note these are both solid things the wraith has affected.

Words unfamiliar to Gately—many related to Jim's life and work—are placed in Gately's head by the wraith, including "PIROUETTE" ("Gately had [n]ever once seen a ballet," p. 194), "POOR YORICK," "LAERTES," and "LEVIRATEMARRIAGE." (Recall that Hal read a Riverside *Hamlet* under a "print of a detail from the minor and soft-core Alexandrian mosaic *Consummation of the Levirates*" on 4 November (p. 171). A "Levirate marriage" is between a man and his brother's widow.) Gately wonders if the wraith is "a message from a Higher Power about sobriety and death." Gately, who is currently unable to speak, equates being struck dumb with "invisibility and being buried alive [or] being strangled somewhere deeper inside you than your neck." Gately's thoughts prompt the wraith to thoughts of extras in the public scenes of "most pieces of filmed entertainment"—including "old network situation comedies" (Gately remembers several, but especially "Cheers!")—whose "faces would animate and mouths [would] move realistically, but without sound": "human furniture" (cf. Jim Sr. on parents as "Furniture of the world," p. 168), "encaged figurant[s]." The wraith "says he personally spent the vast bulk of his own former animate life as pretty much a figurant [a "term from ballet"], furniture at the periphery of the very eyes closest to him." The wraith informs Gately that the cartridges he made in his animate life featured "the babble of crowds every member of which was the central and articulate protagonist of his own entertainment" (but cf. the "lineless figurant background-extra cops," n. 67), which critics mistook for "some self-conscious viewer-hostile heavy-art directorial pose, instead of radical realism."

Gately tries to concentrate on "the ring on his forehead [from the *Coke* can] that's colder than the feverish skin around it" instead of the pain he is experiencing or the encroaching memory of his beaten mother crawling away from the M.P. who was "hunched drunk over his notebook's record of his Heinekens for the day" (cf. p. 447). Gately may or may not see the "seated shadow of somebody in a hat" in the hall. He wishes Ferocious Francis G. would visit, and the wraith may or may not have looked in on Gehaney and predicted that Gehaney would soon be there to offer "acerbic Crocodilian counsel."

Around "0000h., the switching hour," the wraith reflects on seeing his youngest "son, the one most like him, the one most marvelous and frightening to him, becoming a figurant" right before his death. "No horror on earth or elsewhere could equal watching your own offspring open his mouth and having nothing come out." The wraith says that he spent his "boyhood trying unsuccessfully to convince [his] father that [he] even existed," which included "gesturing wildly through the distilled haze" (cf. the administrators' interpretation of Hal in Ch. 1). The wraith believed "that his son had become what he (the wraith) had feared as a child he (the wraith) was." The wraith laments that "no one else in the wraith and boy's nuclear family would see or acknowledge [that Hal] was disappearing right before their eyes. They looked but did not see his invisibility. And they listened but did not hear the wraith's warning." They believed the wraith "was confusing the boy with his own (the wraith's) boyhood self" or that the wraith was not sober enough to make accurate judgments.

The wraith explains his reasons for making the final version of *Infinite Jest* on pp. 838-839, which are quoted in their entirety here.

The wraith "spent the whole last ninety days of his animate life [cf. that he'd been sober "for 89 days, at the very tail-end of his life" (p. 839) and that a half-full Wild Turkey bottle was found near him on the day of his death (p. 250)] working tirelessly to contrive a medium via which he and the muted son could simply *converse*. To concoct something the gifted boy couldn't simply master and move on from to a new plateau. Something the boy would love enough to induce him to open his mouth and come *out*—even if it was only to ask for more. Games hadn't done it, professionals hadn't done it, impersonation of professionals [cf. Ch. 3] hadn't done it. His last resort: entertainment. Make something so bloody compelling it would reverse thrust on a young man's fall into the womb of solipsism, anhedonia, death in life. A magically entertaining toy to dangle at the infant still somewhere alive in the boy, to make its eyes light and toothless mouth open unconsciously, to laugh. To bring him 'out of himself,' as they say. The womb could be used both ways. A way to say I AM SO VERY, VERY SORRY and have it heard. A life-long dream. The scholars and Foundations and disseminators never saw that his most serious wish was: *to entertain*."

As Gately tries to "fend off uninvited memories" of the M.P., the wraith "responds vehemently that No! *No! Any* conversation or interchange is better than none at all." Gately wonders why the wraith is interfacing with him rather than with the son, but then realizes that "maybe thinking he was seeing his late organic dad as a ghost or wraith would drive the youngest son bats" (one could question whether this happened to Hamlet). Then remembering the M.P., "the sort of person who equated incredibly careful record-keeping with control," Gately wonders why he never asked his mother about her reasons for being with the M.P. at all. Gately tries hard "not to explore why it never occurred to him to step in and pull the M.P. off his mother, even after he could bench-press more than the M.P." Instead, Gately would "raise the volume on the television, not even bothering to look over at the beating, watching 'Cheers!'" The M.P. used to maim flies and leave them "trapped in goo or scuttling in circles on the table," telling Gately that "a well-maimed fly produced tiny little fly-screams of pain and fear," for which Gately would listen.

"What makes Gately most uncomfortable now as he starts to try to wake up in the lemonlight of true hospital morning is that he can't remember putting the maimed flies out of their misery, ever, after the M.P. passed out." He dreams that he is "bent in real close to the maimed head ["of the Hawaiian-dressed Nuck"], his ear to the bleeding face, listening very intently."

Gately wakes with a start (on the 16th), like he used to do when he lived in a high loft and bumped his head on the ceiling every morning, creating a "permanent concavity in the ceiling." He can still feel "a flattish spot in the curve of the top of his forehead" from those days (or is it from the *Coke* can?). He imagines he sees Ferocious Francis G., but instead there are three other White Flaggers in the room—one of whom is Glenn K. (cf. pp. 352, 367). Glenn K. asks, "And who's the fellow in the hat outside?" Gately makes "a dumb-show of polite laughter" at the White Flaggers' Al-Anon jokes, which causes him pain. "It's like a big wooden spoon keeps pushing him just under the surface of sleep and then spooning him up for something huge to taste him, again and again."

PLOT AND CHARACTER: Jim, Art/Ent, Ennet, Gately
THEME: His/Father, Memory, Phys/Ob, Fear/Obsess, Dreams, Non-Action, Time, Loss, Recur, Inf/Reg

Like Ewell, Day speaks of family history and is "sucker-punched by an emergent sober memory." Day's memory is of abusing his little brother, a boy with physical obstacles and a "fear of leaves." This abuse recalls Orin's abuse of his brother-with-physical-obstacles, Mario. Both the wraith and Gately remember (or dream of) family histories as well. Gately tries not to remember his non-action with respect to the M.P.'s cruelty. The wraith's experience of time makes "animate men's actions and motions [appear] to be occurring at about the rate of a clock's hour-hand." Gately imagines the wraith's experience as being "free-seeming, but incredibly lonely." There is a missed connection in that the featured performer in the entertainment the wraith made for his son is Gately's new acquaintance, Joelle—an acquaintance of which the wraith must surely be aware.

There are numerous other recurrences in this long section: old television programs, the significance of the color blue ("the legendary Pulsing Blue Light that AA founder Bill W. historically saw during his last detox, that turned out to be God"), cage imagery, Gately's eyes rolling back in his head, the infant imagery of Gately's "big crib" and of the wraith's intended appeal to "the infant still somewhere alive in the boy," the toothlessness of that infant, the "womb of solipsism," the circles transcribed by the maimed flies (the extended torture of these flies recalls Orin's placing of roaches under glass, p. 45), Gately's feeling of being "under the surface" and his "pain with a queer flavor of emotional loss," the crying of the deep-voiced patient, and the wraith's description of his son's "anhedonia" (cf. Ch. 27.13). The idea of being physically divided occurs in the previous section when "the left side of [Pat's] face was very kind" (p. 817) and again in this section with Jack J.'s "tortured grimace that doesn't affect the other side of his face" and with Gately's experience of pain "on his whole right side—DEXTRAL."

This section reveals the significance of the events of Ch. 3 in that they prompted Jim's decision to make the final version of *Infinite Jest.* Here, the ghost of Hal's father appears not to Hal, but to Gately; the wraith also seems "to prefer night to day" like the ghost of Hamlet's father. To this point, Jim's *Infinite Jest* has been seen as a mechanism to induce infantile regression. Apparently, Jim's intention was to induce a *pro*gression of the inner infant outward into a "life-long dream." Does this make sense, or was Jim insane? Rather than being a victim of regression, does Jim see the viewer of *Infinite Jest* as a "hero of *non*-action" (p. 142)? Recall that Joelle wondered whether the last *Infinite Jest* was "a cage or really a door" (p. 230).

Chapter 28.3, Section 170, Pages 845-846
19 November Y.D.A.U.

Several threads from Ch. 27 are connected in this section. Marathe (last seen with Gompert on 14 November in Ch. 27.38) has rejoined the A.F.R. in the Antitois' shop (last seen there on 13 November in Ch. 27.29). Poor Tony (last seen in Ch. 27.25) and Randy

Lenz (last seen in Ch. 27.30) are now subjects for Broullîme's (the two o-less misspellings on p. 845 of the first edition have been corrected in subsequent editions, but the same misspelling on p. 489 was not changed) "field-tests of viewer willingness" (alas, Poor Tony), even though the "Subjects for suitability" were supposed to be free of "the influence of the many of the district's intoxicant compounds" (p. 727). The bags Lenz stole turn out to be "filled of foreign cookware and extremely small-in-size ladies' undergarments."

"Marathe, who had made his decision and call"—apparently to Steeply since Marathe "reported back negatively for all signs of this veiled performer" and has apparently not mentioned anything about the cartridges he saw at Ennet (cf. pp. 750, 752, 776)—was left in charge of "this finally most drastic of the operations . . . to acquire members of the immediate family of the auteur, perhaps in public" (they knew it might come to this, cf. p. 719). Fortier "departed before incoming weather to attend Mlle. Luria P——" (Tine's "timeless love" (p. 105) is now revealed to be Orin's putatively Swiss hand-model) in the conducting of "a technical interview of more importance" in Phoenix. Marathe sent Balbalis "north into the increasingly heavy snowstorm . . . to acquire and replace the tennis children of Québec, known by the A.F.R. to be even then en route to U.S.A. soil for gala competition with the tennis children" of E.T.A. (cf. pp. 217 and 1064). Balbalis and his "field-detail" intend to "place a large mirror in the deserted road and delude the tennis bus that it must leave the road to avoid impact." This is called "[a]n old F.L.Q. trick," but is attributed to the A.F.R. on pp. 311 (cf. n. 112) and 1056. "Marathe promised to conceive an excellent ruse to explain the wheelchairs and adult beards of the false players."

PLOT AND CHARACTER: Samizdat, A.F.R., Ennet, AA&R
THEME: Recur, Secrets, Waste

There are missed connections in that the A.F.R. does not realize that Krause and Lenz are not free of the influence of intoxicants and that Lenz had hoped that the bags he stole contained valuables. The A.F.R. will (secretly) trick the Québec Jr. squads and then presumably trick all those watching the gala match at E.T.A. On his mission, Balbalis permits "those who [are] incontinent to change their bags."

Is Gompert somewhere in the shop? Has she been or will she be a test-subject for Broullîme? The day after Marathe's 14 November offer to her (p. 782), Thrust reported that she was missing (p. 824). If she watches the cartridge, will she recognize her roommate, Joelle?

Chapter 28.4, Section 171, Pages 846-851
16 November Y.D.A.U.

Gately's thread continues from Ch. 28.2. He dreams of Joelle who "lick[s] the sweat off his lids" and promises him "near-terminal pleasures." (Is the wraith influencing Gately's dream with sensations associated with Lyle and *Infinite Jest*?) When the naked, dream-Joelle presses her "face right up intimately close" to dream-Gately's, it is the face of Winston Churchill, who played a part in the origin of U.H.I.D. (cf. p. 226).

Gately is also "powerless over memories" of a childhood neighbor, Mrs. Waite, who was feared to be a witch by neighborhood kids. Gately sometimes talked with her in her kitchen. She was found dead in her house several weeks after Gately's ninth birthday (cf. p. 449). Mrs. Waite, who "rarely left her house," brought a cake to the "annual mass party" which celebrated the birthdays of several neighborhood kids. "Mrs. Waite had spared Gately the humiliation of putting just his name on the cake," but the cake's "nine candles" were "the private tip-off on who the cake was really for." Mrs. Waite was not invited in, and the kids were not allowed to eat the cake. Gately did not defend Mrs. Waite when speculations were made about the cake's ingredients, but afterwards he did steal cigarettes and put them in her mailbox out of gratitude.

Gately's next dream takes place in Mrs. Waite's kitchen, and "in this dream, Mrs. Waite, who is Joelle, is Death." Joelle is nude and has "the face not of a jowly British P.M. but of a total female angel, not sexy so much as angelic, like all the world's light had gotten together and arranged itself into the shape of a face." "Death is explaining that Death happens over and over, you have many lives, and at the end of each one (meaning life) is a woman who kills you and releases you into your next life. . . . [The] woman that kills you is ["always someone you love, and she's"] always your next life's mother." This is why mothers love selfishly and obsessively: "they're trying to make amends for a murder neither of you quite remember, except maybe in dreams" (cf. Notkin's interview, pp. 788-9). The more Gately understands "the sadder he gets, and the sadder he gets the more unfocused and wobbly becomes his vision . . . it's as if he's seeing [Joelle] through a kind of cloud light, a milky filter that's the same as the wobbly blur through which a baby sees a parental face bending over the crib." When Gately "asks Death to set him free and be his mother," Death (Joelle) says, "Wait."

PLOT AND CHARACTER: Joelle, Art/Ent, Gately
THEME: Memory, His/Father, Dream, Non-Action, Recur

This section includes a memory of Gately's childhood over which he is "powerless." (Of their childhood stories, Tiny said "I don't want to remember" in Ch. 28.1, and Day was "sucker-punched" in Ch. 28.2.) Gately, who dreams throughout the entire section (is asleep, non-active), took no action to defend Mrs. Waite (or his mother or dying flies in Ch. 28.2). Images of *Infinite Jest* recur, as Gately dream-watches scenes in his head reminiscent of *Infinite Jest.* Is the wraith causing this to happen? Could Gately resist the "near-terminal pleasures" of viewing the cartridge like he resists Demerol for his pain? Mrs. Waite has her "face up against the smeared garage window" and later "eliminate[s] her own map," and Gately remembers his mother "passed out in vomit."

Gately remembers the ex-Navy "M.P." and dreams of Joelle (M.P., Madame Psychosis), who in one dream had the face of a "jowly British P.M." (cf. Pat Montesian as P.M. on p. 178). Mathew Pemulis (M.P.) awaits an opportunity to consume DMZ (Madame Psychosis). In this section, Mrs. Waite dies and Death says, "Wait."

Chapter 28.5, Section 172, Pages 851-854
Notes 344-346, Page 1076
20 November Y.D.A.U., before 0500h.

Hal narrates several sections of this last chapter in first person as he did for all the sections of the first chapter. It is the third morning since the Kevin Bain incident (Ch. 27.44). A dream about this incident woke Hal early yesterday. He awakes early today—"the first A.M. without dawn drills since Interdependence Day"—on an excess-saliva-soaked pillow, goes to the window, and stands on one foot as therapy for his ankle. Mario continues sleeping. The Boards and Advanced Placement Tests for which he has been studying are three weeks from tomorrow (cf. "12/12's Boards," p. 218). However, "since the Wayne debacle [17 November, cf. n. 332], the little tutorials had ceased and Pemulis himself had been very scarce." Presumably, these are the tests on which Hal's scores will be "subnormal" and "quite a bit closer to zero than [the Arizona administrators are] comfortable with" (p. 6). "Every November, between I. Day and the WhataBurger Invitational in Tucson AZ, the Academy holds a semipublic exhibition meet for the 'benefit' of E.T.A.'s patrons and alumni and friends in the Boston area. The exhibition is followed by a semiformal cocktail party and dance" (hence, the celebratory *GAUDEAMUS IGITUR* is in the heading for this section, as it was for some sections documenting Interdependence Day events; cf. pp. 321, 343, 380). Recall that this weekend of "no classes" (p. 851) and the "End-of-Fiscal-Year fundraising exhibition" was deemed "the window of opportunity" for taking DMZ (p. 217).

"Sometime during the night heavy snow had begun to fall" (cf. the 19 November snowfall in which the A.F.R. found themselves, p. 846), which prompts Hal to hope for the cancellation of today's matches: "I couldn't remember ever actively hoping not to have to play before. I couldn't remember feeling strongly one way or the other about playing for quite a long time, in fact. . . . I'd neither carried nor squeezed my ball for several days. No one seemed to have noticed." He considers it "improbable that anything [will] be landing on time at Logan in this kind of snow." However, the Québec teams playing in today's exhibition apparently have decided on transportation by bus due to the weather, given the activities of the A.F.R. last night on snow-covered roads (pp. 845-6).

PLOT AND CHARACTER: Hal, AA&R
THEME: Dreams, Loss

In this section, Hal dreams, as Gately did in the previous section. Hal doesn't "feel good," has "a sort of nausea of the head," and "felt for almost a week as if [he] needed to cry." Hal the almost-addict almost cries. Hal is losing his drive to play tennis. His phone message underlines a feeling of disconnection or separation: "This is the disembodied voice of Hal Incandenza."

Chapter 28.6, Section 173, Pages 854-864
Notes 347-351, Pages 1076-1077
16 November Y.D.A.U.

Gately awakes from his dream of Joelle in Ch. 28.4 to find that "the apparently real nondream Joelle van D. is leaning over the bed's crib-railing [did this influence the dreams of the previous section?], wetting Gately's big forehead and horror-rounded lips with a cool cloth" and holding two brownies "liberated from the nurses' station and brought down for him, since Morris H. meant them for him" (and had Thrust bring them to St. E's, cf. p. 826), although "she can see he's in no shape to swallow." Gately has been unable to speak for four days because he has been intubated as a result of being "wounded in service to somebody who did not deserve service." Gately does not remember Joelle's previous visits and forehead moppings (pp. 817-8, 707). The other bed is "empty and the crying guy's chart" has been removed (cf. p. 829). Joelle speaks of "last night's St. Columbkill's Meeting," and "Gately racks his RAM for which fucking night St. Columbkill's is." Of the two possible nights, Joelle has been to the "St. Columbkill Sunday Night Group" (p. 209), rather than the Tuesday night meeting referenced by Lenz (p. 546). When Joelle's head is down, Gately sees her veil as "perfectly smooth and untextured, a smooth white screen with nothing behind it." "Joelle says how last night's was St. Collie's once-a-month format where instead of a Commitment they had that round-robin discussion where somebody in the hall spoke for five minutes and then picked the next speaker." A Kentuckian—who had "a deep diagonal furrow in his face" from being hit with a hatchet by his father (perhaps analogous to the acid incident for Joelle)—had spoken of not remembering the last decade and then picked Joelle to speak next.

Having to speak about her experience helped Joelle realize that she needn't "count the days" of her sobriety: "I don't *have* to do it that way. I get to choose how to do it, and they'll help me stick to the choice. . . . I can do this for one endless day." Gately thinks of Joelle as being "three weeks clean," when today is actually the (forgive the counting) ninth day since her overdose at Molly Notkin's. Gately is reminded of "some evil fucking personal detoxes," especially one in a "Revere Holding cage for 92 days [cf. p. 55]. Feeling the edge of every second that went by. Taking it a second at a time. Drawing the time in around him real tight. . . . The whole first two weeks of it are telescoped in his memory down into like one second—less: the space between two heartbeats. A breath and a second, the pause and gather between each cramp. An endless Now stretching its gull-wings out on either side of his heartbeat. And he'd never before or since felt so excruciatingly alive. Living in the Present between pulses." (Compare this with Kate Gompert's experience on the bottom of p. 74; with Poor Tony's slow experience of time "with a shape and an odor" and "sharp edges" (p. 302); and with Gately's first six months at Ennet, when "he'd felt the sharp edge of every second" (p. 280).) Gately realized that he "could do the dextral pain the same way: Abiding. No one single instant of it was unendurable" (cf. "no single, individual moment is in and of itself unendurable," p. 204). "What was undealable-with was the thought of all the instants all lined up and stretching ahead," including instants in which he would face the consequences of "Nuckslaughter [and] of V.I.P.-suffocation": "everything unendurable was in the head, was the head not Abiding in the Present."

Joelle shows Gately pictures from her photo album ("personal historical snapshots"), and Gately fantasizes about sex and possible futures with—and of escape from "the guy in the hat" without—Joelle. Gately experiences shame over these fantasies, in part because in Boston AA "newcomer-seducing . . . is regarded as the province of true bottom-feeders. It's predation." Newcomers are described as having "their nervous systems still on the outside of their bodies" (analogous to a Jarvik IX Exterior Artificial Heart, p. 142) and wanting "to lay responsibility for themselves at the feet of something as seductive and consuming as their former friend the Substance. To avoid the mirror AA hauls out in front of them" (analogous to the mirrors placed in the road by the A.F.R.). Gately realizes that his fantasies are about "wanting somebody else to take care of his mess, somebody to keep him out of his various cages. . . . His eyes roll up in his head at disgust with himself, and stay there."

PLOT AND CHARACTER: Joelle, Gately, AA&R
THEME: His/Father, Memory, Time, Choice, Recur

Bits of personal history are remembered by the Kentuckian, Joelle, and Gately. The Kentuckian lost ten years of time in a blackout. Gately remembers his withdrawal experiences as directly connected to his experience of time, and both Joelle and Gately consider recovery strategies to be directly related to the choices they make about time and to living in the present. There are recurring images of cages and mirrors and Joelle's "veil billowing mightily in and out." Does Gately's intubation resonate with the method by which Lucien Antitoi was killed (p. 488)?

Chapter 28.7, Section 174, Pages 864-876
Notes 352-353, Page 1077
20 November Y.D.A.U., around 0500h.

Hal continues to narrate in first person from Ch. 28.5. Although the "digital display up next to the ceiling's intercom read[s] **11-18-EST0456**," it is 20 November (cf. p. 851). The snow that fell on the A.F.R. last night (19 November, pp. 844-5) continues: "a white curtain endlessly descending." Hal's marijuana withdrawal began on 10 November, around the time of the meeting in Tavis's office (Ch. 25.5). Before that meeting, Hal had been to the dentist, was drooling, and "wanting very much" to go to the Pump Room (p. 518). On the evening of 11 November (p. 686), Hal had gone over twenty four hours without marijuana for the first time in over a year (n. 279, referenced on p. 688). In the pre-dawn hours of 12 November, Hal had gone without marijuana for "like 40 hours" (p. 785). Now Hal says, "For the past ten days I'd always felt worse in the early A.M., before dawn" (the pre-dawn hours of 11-20 November).

In the E.T.A. hallways, Hal hears "faint sounds of early-morning weeping"; two people "weeping at different pitches behind closed doors," one of whom "was nearly skirling, an inhuman keening sound"; and someone "crying out in a bad dream." Hal encounters Ortho Stice, who "had his forehead up against the [window's] glass." Ortho therefore cannot see Hal, and when he first hears Hal's voice asks if Hal is crying. Hal sees a "figure" sitting outside in the bleachers and "getting buried by snow, just sitting there. It was impossible to tell the person's age or sex."

Stice—hot, sweaty, and unable to sleep—had put his head against the window "just after 0100" when "the forehead was sweated up" and it stuck. Stice compares the situation to a tongue stuck to a metal pole in winter, but Hal says, "This is some freakish occlusive seal. Glass doesn't conduct heat like metal conducts heat." Stice asks Hal if he believes in "Ghosts. Parabnormal shit" and says, "There was somebody standing back there about maybe half and hour back. But he just stood there. Then he went away. Or . . . it." Hal says, "Himself allegedly used to see his father's ghost on stairways sometimes, but then again toward the end he used to see black-widow spiders in his hair, too, and claimed I wasn't speaking sometimes when I was sitting right there speaking to him. . . . And good old Mario says he's seen paranormal figures, and he's not kidding, and Mario doesn't lie." Stice offers to show Hal "some parabnormal shit" about which he's only told Lyle, because he's "sick of the secretness" of not talking about it. When Hal attempts to pull Stice off the window, he sees "what might be considered Stice's real face . . . a narrow, fine-featured, and slightly rodential face, aflame with some sort of revelation."

Troeltsch comes out of Axford's room nearby. "It was as if some tacit agreement had been reached not even to bring up Troeltsch's being in Axford's [single, cf. p. 214] room or where Axford was." Axford, one of this weekend's quartet of potential DMZ users (cf. pp. 216-8) and a member of December's trio of urine-providers (p. 782), has not been documented since supper on 11 November after losing to Shaw (p. 629). However, on Hal's 17 November drive to Natick, the truck's little portable disk player had been detached "by either Pemulis or Axford and not returned" (p. 796). Hal takes his toothbrush (n. 352 documents the prank that prompts this; cf. also one of the reasons the ADA is so angry with Gately, p. 56) and asks Troeltsch to "[k]eep an eye on Stice and my NASA glass" while he goes to seek the janitors' help (Kenkle and Brandt were heard below earlier) in removing Stice from the window.

Brandt's "major attraction for Kenkle seemed to consist in the fact that he neither walked away nor interrupted when Kenkle was speaking" (cf. Green's attraction for Lenz, pp. 546-7). Kenkle has "his doctorate in low-temperature physics." After Brandt and Kenkle helped Jim ("somewhat the worse for wear") home one night, "the duo had ended up being cast as black-veiled Noh-style attendants in Himself's *Zero-Gravity Tea Ceremony*, and had been menially employed at E.T.A. ever since, though always on the graveyard shift." Kenkle addresses "Good prince Hal" and after hearing of Stice's predicament asks Hal what is so amusing: "You can barely get your words out. You're all but slapping your knee." Hal "consciously compose[s his] face into something deadly somber" and asks for another assessment of his demeanor. A scream from Stice is heard; Brandt heads toward the stairwell; and Kenkle says "*mirthful*" before joining Brandt. Hal tries to see his expression in the window, but he "looked sketchy and faint to [him]self, tentative and ghostly against all that blazing white."

PLOT AND CHARACTER: E.T.A., Hal
THEME: Recur

E.T.A.'s "curved" hallways are "dinner-mint blue." "E.T.A.'s annular heating system produced a lubricated hum." Hal hears copious weeping and the sound of a flushed toilet. Stice tells a joke that Schacht heard "at the Cranial place from some B.U. fellow with just terrible facial pain." Stice's face is against glass, and he is "sick of [his] secretness." Although the hunched motif has been associated primarily with vomiting up to this point, here Kenkle speaks of "rear-entry" as being a "*hunched* way to have interface."

Alone, Kenkle might resonate with Falstaff since he addresses "Good prince Hal" (although Hal has more in common with Hamlet, another Shakespearean prince), but Kenkle and Brandt together on the graveyard shift resonate more with *Hamlet*'s gravedigger clowns than with the Japanese theatre's Noh-style attendants they played in Jim's film. Stice thinks Hal is crying; Kenkle thinks Hal is laughing. Coleridge, commenting on *Hamlet* I.v, said that "laughter is equally the expression of extreme anguish and horror as of joy" (Coleridge, p. 410). Recall the narrator's description of Gompert: "She looked either pained or trying somehow to suppress hilarity" (p. 76). Recall the narrator for Hal describing Kevin Bain: "At a certain point hysterical grief becomes facially indistinguishable from hysterical mirth" (pp. 806-7). Is this the beginning of a change in Hal that leads to the events of November Y.G. (Ch. 1)? Hal speaks of his father seeing the ghost of his grandfather and references the events of Ch. 3. Was it the wraith (Jim's "ghost") that stood behind Stice? "What would Troeltsch be doing sleeping in Axhandle's room?" Who is the figure in the bleachers?

Chapter 28.8, Section 175, Pages 876-883
20 November Y.D.A.U.

This section is a "PARTIAL TRANSCRIPT OF [A] WEATHER-DELAYED MEETING" on the "8TH FLOOR [OF THE] STATE HOUSE ANNEX" led by U.S.O.U.S. Chief Rodney Tine, Sr. (who held a meeting here on 12 November, too; cf. p. 622). Also attending are Tine, Jr. (last seen interviewing Notkin on 17 November, cf. Ch. 27.42); InterLace's Maureen Hooley; Glad's Carl Yee; and Tom Veals of Viney and Veals Advertising (cf. Chs. 23.7 and 23.11). All, even those coming from elsewhere in Boston, have experienced trouble getting to the meeting due to the snow. Throughout the meeting Tine Jr. taps on the tabletop with a ruler, which annoys Tine Sr. (who uses a ruler to measure his penis, cf. pp. 548-9) even though Tine Sr. taps a telescoping weatherman's pointer (cf. his use of same on p. 403); Veals fights a cold; and Yee fights the onset of epileptic fits (Tine Jr.'s reaction to one of the fits: "Jesus W. Christ").

The group has assembled to discuss the rough cut of a public-service spot aimed at children and intended to air on the "Mr. Bouncety-Bounce Show" in the Year of Glad. When Yee expresses concern about the cost of the project, Tine Jr. says, "You want the Year of Glad to be the year half the nation stopped doing anything but staring bug-eyed at some sinister cartridge . . . ?" The spot features Fully Functional Phil, "a mule-icon [that] provoked a kind of empathy in response groups. Phil's not coming off as an authority-figure-joy-killer type." Phil is "a goof, an iconic child, but he's *active*. He stands for the attraction of capacity, agency, choice. As versus the spot's animated adult who we see in a recliner ostensibly watching the Canadian cartridge [until he's] just a huge five-o'clock-shadowed head in the recliner, his eyeballs huge and whirling." Phil's message is to warn against "a certain very wicked and sneaky cartridge that even has a little smiling face on the case." The danger of watching the cartridge is equated with being abducted by a (Canadian) stranger, the filmed image of which abduction is called by Veals "Stuff of fucking nightmares." (The narrator for Orin used this phrase in reference to "flying roaches that wanted to get at your eyes, as an infant" on p. 45. For Veals's resume of nightmare images in advertising, cf. Ch. 23.7.) Veal's has also "storyboarded an extremely exciting adolescent-targeted version of Fully Functional Phil."

Tine Jr. notes that it will be "difficult for the transcriber [of the meeting] to transcribe" in the dark, and the section ends as the lights are turned off to view the spot.

PLOT AND CHARACTER: Samizdat, U.S.O.U.S.
THEME: His/Father, Phys/Ob, Choice, Inf/Reg, Recur

Tine Jr. attempts to engage his father, but frequently is cut off and is chastised for his ruler-tapping, presumably done in filial homage to Sr.'s pointer-tapping. The characters face many obstacles in this section: all fought the snow; Tine Jr. can't engage his father; Tine Sr. can't abide the tapping; Veals fights a cold; Yee suffers epileptic fits brought on by stress or embarrassment; and the stenographer can't transcribe in the dark. Fully Functional Phil—although "ironize[d]" to be clumsy and incompetent—promotes choice over passivity, non-action, and infantile regression (but in a spot that will air during a show starring a "capering 130-kilo infant," p. 651). The waste motif recurs when Tine Jr. attempts to express the danger of cartridge-watchers dying "of starvation in the middle of their own exc[re-ment]" before being cut off. The adult in the spot turns into a huge head. The dangerous cartridge is identified as Canadian since its dissemination will be by Canadian terrorists; viewers of the spot will miss the connection that the cartridge of course originated in the very city in which this meeting is being held. Nowhere in the transcript is the connection made that if the terrorists succeed in disseminating the cartridge with "a little smiling face on the case," "Year of Glad" could take on an entirely different, sinister meaning.

In this section, Wallace again creates comedy and a sense of "chaotic stasis" (n. 61) out of a flurry of activity in which several things happen at once, including Yee falling out of his seat (like Struck at Eschaton) and making funny sounds. Again Wallace ends a section at a point of maximum anticipation ("So lights already"), recalling the attempt to move Gately into Ennet House at the end of Ch. 26.16 ("Ready?").

Chapter 28.9, Section 176, Pages 883-896
Notes 354-361, Page 1077
16-18 November Y.D.A.U.

In "the wake of Joelle's visit" (late 16 November, Ch. 28.6), Gately dreams that it is sleeting, that the next bed is empty (it held a crying patient with a deep voice (p. 829) but has been empty since Joelle's visit (p. 856)), that he is given a "notebook and Bic" by "the nurse that had changed the catheter-bag" (p. 861), and that he is visited by Ferocious Francis and by the Pakistani M.D. that had tried to give him a Demerol drip after his surgery "between let's say four and eight days ago" (Gately's surgery occurred in the early hours of 12 November; cf. pp. 810, 814). Gately is concerned about the "ghost-words" in his head, repercussions of the Nuck incident (in Gately's dream, Ferocious Francis calls the incident a fight against "six armed Hawaiians" instead of three Canadians in Hawaiian attire), and the man in the hall wearing a hat. Gately dreams that the M.D. is offering him legal narcotics for pain. "Gately imagines the M.D. smiling incandescently as he wields a shepherd's crook" (cf. pp. 358-9). Gately "tries to draw a skull-and-bones" to communicate the danger of his taking drugs, "but the skull looks more like a plain old smiley-face." Ferocious Francis leaves because Gately's "the only one can decide," but does advise Gately that he "Might want to Ask For Some Help, deciding." Gately grabs the M.D.'s balls to keep him "from offering something Gately knows that he's powerless at this moment to refuse." The M.D.'s scream of pain becomes Gately's scream of pain as Gately wakes up with his arm through the railing of his bed. In the "serious A.M. light" of 17 November, there is no sleet, an empty visitor's chair, and no notebook and pen (unless they're on the floor). "The next bed was still empty and made up tight," though. "He couldn't see anything like a hat-shadow in the hall, but it could have been all the sunlight."

In Gately's extreme pain, "[m]emories of good old Demerol rose up, clamoring to be Entertained." Boston AA has taught Gately to let those thoughts "come as they will, but do not *Entertain* them." Gately Asks For Help and "thinks hard about anything else at all," including the "fish asking about what's water" (cf. p. 445). A "black outside-linebacker of a St. E's nurse rumbles in and checks his drips" (between 1600-2400h. on 17 November, cf. p. 922). Gately remembers that from the first time he had taken Demerol "he'd been a faithful attendant at the goddess Demerol's temple, right to the very finish" (cf. Marathe to Steeply, p. 107). When Gately was "narculated in any way he'd become this totally taciturn withdrawn dead-like person . . . practically lying in this chair whose canvas bulged and legs bowed out, speaking barely at all . . . . He made whoever he got high with feel lonely. He got real, like, interior. . . . Kite used to say it was like Gately shot cement instead of narcotics."

"McDade and Diehl come in around 1100h. [presumably on 18 November] from visiting Doony Glynn," who was still at Ennet during Joelle's 16 November visit (p. 856). D. Glynn, unlike D. Gately, has accepted a codeine compound for his diverticulitis pain and "was sitting up in a lotus position and seemed to be a very happy camper indeed." Gately learns that the pair may not be able to "legally depose for Gately" and that they believe Lenz likely has "the .44 Item" (but if this were true, surely the Item would be included in the list of Lenz's possessions on pp. 717-8). Returning from a meeting recently, Erdedy and Smith had seen Lenz "drunk as a maroon." (The description of Lenz's attire matches what he was wearing on 14 November (p. 717). Lenz will be an A.F.R. subject on 19 November (p. 845).) Diehl "can always tell when it's going to snow" and predicts "flurries for maybe as early as tonight" (there will be a "heavy snowstorm" on the evening of 19 November, p. 846). McDade relates a prank he has planned, and "now Gately knows for sure it was McDade and Minty that put the HELP WANTED sign up under the window of the lady in Unit #4 that shouts for Help" (cf. p. 196). In pain, Gately asks himself, "[W]hat if God is really the cruel and vengeful figurant Boston AA swears up and down He isn't"? McDade and Diehl leave as, to Gately's embarrassment, an exceptionally beautiful nurse enters with a bedpan.

PLOT AND CHARACTER: Ennet, Gately
THEME: Dream, Memory, Time, Recur, Choice

Gately's dreams and memories intertwine, and he has a distorted sense of time. His visitors "never think to tell Gately what day it is." The wraith said to Gately, "[D]eath was just everything outside you getting really slow." Gately dreams that Ferocious Francis moves away with "maddening slow care" and that he "slows down even further at the open door." There are several recurring ideas in Gately's memory of a Demerol buzz: his chest seems "far away"; "inside all is a somnolent hum"; and there is an "easy squeak of your head's blood" ("to hear the squeak" warns of impending danger via the

A.F.R.). On Demerol, Gately felt "gratitude at [his] abstract distance from anything that [did]n't sit inside concentric circles." Demerol tablets are called "Pebbles and Bam-Bams" (cartoon characters from an old TV show). Dilaudid is called "Blues" and "The Blue Bayou." There are other recurrences: "Gately wants to weep about the pain"; the M.D. has a frightening smile and unending teeth; and Gately fears that accepting pain medication will "put him back in the cage." Note also the "traps' little cages of cross-hatched bars, the lobsters' eyes' stalks [cf. a reference by the narrator for Gately to "lobster-waters," p. 271] always poking through the squares so the eyes looked out at open sea" (for more lobster empathy, cf. the titular essay of Wallace's *Consider the Lobster*). The description of the "narculated Gately" recalls the condition of viewers of the Entertainment. Gately's choice not to accept medication that will make him happy (glad, with a smiling face) is equivalent to the choice of not watching the Entertainment cartridge. Gately is successful so far, but Doony Glynn makes the opposite choice and immediately accepts medication. Will U.S.A. children be able to make the difficult choice of avoiding the Entertainment (cf. the previous section)?

In this section, the reader (like Gately) doesn't know Gately is dreaming until Gately wakes up. The notes for this section continue to provide specific drug descriptions, completing the cycle initiated in the novel's first notes; n. 12 is even referenced in n. 354. The climax of this chapter is foreshadowed on p. 886: "Facklemann's eliminated map after the insane scam on Sorkin and a disastrous two nights of Dilaudid." There are a few literary references: Dilaudid is called "Facklemann's Mount Doom"; Gately remembers that "he couldn't even finish *Ethan From*" (note the misspelling by the narrator for Gately; cf. also "tittymount," p. 893); and Gately refers to the Nuck incident as his *se offendendo* (which he heard from Ewell, p. 814), again conjuring the *Hamlet* gravedigger scene (also, dream-Francis's voice "signifying nothing" (p. 888) conjures *Macbeth*). In this section, Gately dreams of symbols that represent his inability to write, remembers a symbol on one of the M.P.'s bumper stickers, and fondly remembers symbols found on Demerol tablets.

Chapter 28.10, Section 177, Pages 896-902
20 November Y.D.A.U.

Hal continues to narrate in first person from Ch. 28.7, where he was last seen checking his expression. He was on his way back to his room to continue doing so (and, among other things, "to listen to Orin's phone messages and then the protracted death-aria from *Tosca*"; cf. p. 41) when he was "hit" with an "[u]nexplained panic": "Everything came at too many frames per second. Everything had too many aspects. But it wasn't disorienting. The intensity wasn't unmanageable [cf. Gately's pain]. It was just intense and vivid. It wasn't like being high, but it was still very: *lucid*. The world seemed suddenly edible, there for the ingesting." However: "Something like a shadow flanked the vividness and lucidity of the world. The concentration of attention did something to it. What didn't seem fresh and unfamiliar seemed suddenly old as stone [cf. Lyle to Lamont Chu: "the world is very old," p. 389]. It all happened in the space of a few seconds. The familiarity of Academy routine took on a crushing cumulative aspect." Compare Hal's experience with Troeltsch's illness and subsequent fugue-state that "came out of nowhere" on 3 November (pp. 60-1).

Hal lies on his back (like Gately at St. E's) "on the carpet of Viewing Room 5," where he "held Big Buddy sessions . . . throughout the month of September" (he was in V.R.6 on 3 November, Ch. 11.8). He has "the NASA glass with [his] toothbrush in it balanced on his chest" (but cf. that on p. 873 Hal asked Troeltsch to keep an eye on Stice and his NASA glass and that Hal has not yet gone back "to see about Stice's defenestration"). Peterson and then Khan look in and speak to Hal; and, although he does not talk to them (cf. Hal's behavior on p. 560), Peterson's question causes Hal to consider the etymology of "blizzard" at some length. Hal is keenly aware of the contents of the room, which include "Himself's films . . . arranged on the third shelf of the entertainment-case." Hal's mind is full of thoughts and memories, often associated with his family: e.g., "Himself's middle name had been Orin, his father's own father's name" (but cf. "Mario had been given the name of Dr. James Incandenza's father's father," p. 313).

On his way home from Natick on Tuesday, Hal thought "that if it came down to a choice between continuing to play competitive tennis and continuing to be able to get high, it would be a nearly impossible choice to make." Hal believes that Pemulis has been avoiding him since Tuesday, but Hal doesn't know about Pemulis's troubling experiences on that day (n. 332). Hal has heard about Wayne's "violent allergic reaction to a decongestant" and that Wayne (like Lord) "had been taken to St. Elizabeth's overnight for observation."

Last night, a woman "had recoiled" from Hal "as if she too had seen something in [his] expression that [he] hadn't known was there." This prompts Hal to think of his father, who "for two years before his death, had had this delusion of silence when [Hal] spoke" (cf. Ch. 3). Hal had mentioned this to Stice earlier (p. 870). This prompts Hal to think of his parents' strained relationship, and he recalls another significant fact: Orin "sometimes observed the smeared prints of nude human feet on the inside of the windshield" of his mother's car (cf. n. 80). Hal then considers that "the Moms herself [who "never leaves" E.T.A.; pp. 42, 51] had apparently stayed by Wayne's side late into the night at St. E's."

Hal's thoughts then shift to a consideration of "this will to give oneself away, utterly. To games or needles, to some other person. Something pathetic about it. A flight-from in the form of a plunging-into. . . . The original sense of *addiction* involved being bound over, dedicated, either legally or spiritually. To devote one's life, plunge in." Hal recalls that Stice had asked whether he believed in ghosts, which prompts the thought that Hamlet "never once doubts the reality of the ghost. Never questions whether his own madness might not in fact be unfeigned." Hal thinks that he really should "go up and check on the Darkness," who "promised something boggling to look at," but "just the thought of getting up made [Hal] glad [he] was lying on the floor . . . completely horizontal."

Hal resumes thoughts of his mother and family. Avril's mother died when Avril was eight. Her father (a "binge-drinker," cf. pp. 766-7) was soon remarried to "an American widow named Elizabeth Tavis," who seemed "to have been a dwarf [with a] huge square head" (like Gately). "C.T. was the infant son she'd brought to the new union, his father a ne'er-do-well killed in a freak accident playing competitive darts." Mrs. Tavis's wedding-photo smile is homodontic. "According to Orin, though, C.T. and the Moms claim Mrs. T was not a true homodont the way—for instance—Mario is a true homodont [cf. n. 119]." (Have the homodontic teeth skipped a generation from Mrs. T to Mario? Are C.T. and the Moms in denial about this possibility?) "The account of the [darts-accident] and dental incongruity comes from Orin [which] shrouded the whole thing in further ambiguity, as far as [Hal] was concerned." Avril's father died when she "was a girl" (p. 766), and her "full name is Avril Mondragon Tavis Incandenza" (cf. p. 46); but "Charles Tavis is probably not related to the Moms by actual blood," and "the Moms and C.T. have never represented themselves as anything other than unrelated but extremely close." (C.T. was originally Avril's step-brother; but since C.T. has been referred to throughout the novel as both Avril's adoptive- and her half-brother, Mrs. T must have adopted Avril after "squire Mondragon's" death. This would make C.T. both Avril's adoptive- and half-brother (cf. "adoptive-slash-half-brother," p. 285); i.e., post-adoption, Avril and C.T. have the same "mother," but different fathers.)

Hal is overwhelmed with the "intense horizontality" of the objects in the Viewing Room. He "was the meat in the room's sandwich." He "felt denser now . . . more solidly composed . . . impossible to knock down."

PLOT AND CHARACTER: Hal, Avril, Jim, E.T.A.
THEME: Phys/Ob, Non-Action, Waste, His/Father, Choice, Recur

Hal and Gately are both experiencing obstacles to their movement; they are physically non-active, horizontal (each a "hero of *non*-action" (p. 142)?). However, both are quite mentally active and are at least physically active enough to generate waste: Gately "needed to take a shit" (p. 890); Hal "needed to fart" (p. 898). Family histories are on both of their minds. Both face the hard choice of abstaining from drugs. There are recurrences: there is "a shadow" on p.

896; "excrement," "hunched," and "blue" all occur within six lines on p. 897; Avril has "an ethnic Canadian's horror of fluorescent light" on p. 898 (cf. that Fortier detests fluorescence, p. 727); a triple reference to "hunch" (and variants) occurs on p. 899; there is a reference to "real beaks and claws" on p. 900; the "original sense of *addiction* involved being bound over [hunched?], dedicated, either legally or spiritually" (p. 900); *Hamlet* is referenced again on p. 900; and "horizontal" becomes a significant word in the last pages of the section.

Chapter 28.11, Section 178, Pages 902-906
Notes 362-365, Page 1077
18 November Y.D.A.U.

Since the bedpan incident of Ch. 28.9, Gately has begun thinking-dreaming about his life again. This section chronicles the decline of Gately's football prospects and the rise of his substance abuse from ages 9 to 17. In football, Gately's "biggest asset was his outsized head. . . . It was like it had no nerve endings or pain receptors or whatever. Gately amused teammates by letting them open and close elevator doors on the head" (cf. pp. 55, 476). "His left ear is permanently kind of gnarled from elevator-door impacts."

Gately "smoked his first duBois at age nine" while (as he remembers it) watching the aftermath of the Rodney King verdict. Then Gately experiences "his first real drunk a few months later with an Orkin man that liked to get kids all blunt on screwdrivers." "Gately's whole recall of [this time] tends to telescope into one memory of pissing orange juice into the Atlantic." On 6 November, Gately was "almost twenty-nine" (p. 277); on 8 November, Gately was "age twenty-nine" (p. 478; but cf. that the wraith believes Gately to be twenty-eight on 15 November, p. 834). Therefore, Gately probably was born in November 1980 and was nine for most of 1990. Rodney King was videotaped in 1991, and the riots in the aftermath of the King verdict occurred in 1992. Gately's telescoped memory accounts for this chronological discrepancy.

From ages 13-15, although Gately continued to play football, he began associating with "a whole new rather more sinister and less athletic social set." Gately met Trent Kite, who would later regret the DuPlessis burglary "exponentially more than Gately did, once the A.F.R. got through with him" (n. 363; cf. the "fatal technical interview of the young burglar," p. 721). Kite could construct "a rudimentary pharmaceutical laboratory" and "turn plain old Sominex" into "Quaalude-isotopes" called "QuoVadis" by Kite, who was introduced to the reader in n. 13 as having that nickname. "Quaaludes and 16-oz. Hefenreffers awakened Gately and his new droogs" to the danger of sidewalks: "you're walking innocently along down a sidewalk and out of nowhere the sidewalk comes rushing up to meet you." During this time, the ex-M.P. left "in his sticker-covered Ford" (like Steeply's?).

"During football season [Gately] ruled himself with an iron hand until the sun set, then threw himself on the mercy of sidewalks and the somnolent hum." Gately slept in class and played football on academic probation as a freshman. His grades made him ineligible to play as a sophomore, so he withdrew from school. His "sixteenth year is still mostly a grey blank." Gately does remember "a pharmacist's assistant with disfiguring eczema and serious gambling debts." When Gately returned to school for his "sophomore year of class and junior year of ball at seventeen [1998]," he had to take drugs (hidden in a Tylenol bottle, analogous to Troeltsch's hiding Tenuate in a Seldane bottle) to get through the day. Kite was not there to tutor him (as Gately remembers it, Kite was "gone by that last September of Unsubsidized Time"; but Gately's telescoping memory is combining this time (1998) with the time of his next significant football memory (2001), coming up on p. 916), and he "lost his starting spot in the third game." Then his mother "suffered her cirrhotic hemorrhage and cerebral-blood thing in late October" (cf. pp. 448-9). Gately never went back to high school or "played organized ball again."

PLOT AND CHARACTER: Gately, AA&R
THEME: Memory, Boundaries, Time, Recur

In this section, Gately's recall "tends to telescope into one memory." Gately blurs the boundaries of time (as he has been blurring the boundaries of waking and sleeping) with his thoughts. Gately is horizontal in his hospital bed (like Hal is horizontal in V.R.5) and remembers being horizontal against the sidewalk. There are recurrences of waste (pissing in the Atlantic), of the "somnolent hum" of Gately's buzz, and of blue: "Bored-eyed guys in white cotton blew blue bubbles and loaded [Gately's mother] in the back of a leisurely sirenless ambulance." Gately's "new droogs" is another reference to *A Clockwork Orange.*

The narrator for Gately spells as Gately spells (aveil, 'Water Lou,' and *Ethan From* at the bottom of p. 905), which calls attention to the fluidity of language and meaning. Just before racial slurs and references to white supremacy occur in the narrative, Gately thinks of his first joint as his first "duBois." Is this intended to resonate with the name of W. E. B. DuBois, balancing the racial slurs in Gately's memory with reference to an African American hero? Does the white supremacist's being an Orkin man (an exterminator, but not from Terminex and not Public Enemy's Terminator X) resonate with the idea of roaches, both in terms of marijuana and of the extermination of roaches by Or[k]in. Orin calls on Terminex for the extermination of "widows" (p. 45); he began his football career after Gately's ended; and his December 2001 punt affected both Gentle (p. 442) and Gately (coming up on p. 916).

Chapter 28.12, Section 179, Pages 906-911
Note 366, Page 1077
20 November Y.D.A.U.

Hal continues to narrate in first person from Ch. 28.10. Like Gately, he "might have been dozing." Hal continues to think of one of his father's cartridges, *Good-Looking Men in Small Clever Rooms* (cf. p. 900), and also thinks "of C.T.'s misadventure at Himself's funeral." There is still a question as to whether Hal is in control of his expressions. Pemulis—who Hal hasn't seen in days and who doesn't "look very good"—comes in, uses Hal's greeting ("Mmyellow"), and says that Petropolis Khan "mentioned hysterics" in reference to Hal. Later Freer enters to report "human flesh [Stice's] on the hall window upstairs" and chides Hal with "This is nothing to laugh at."

Pemulis asks Hal to talk with him "someplace discreet," presumably about his situation in the wake of Tuesday's events ("either finish out the term for credit or you can hit the trail," p. 1075). Pemulis asks if Hal has seen Avril. Hal hasn't seen Avril or Tavis all week. Hal assumes they are arranging "a weather-venue" for today's match. Hal "couldn't decide" whether to go with Pemulis and "choose[s] almost at random" not to go with him. Hal tells Pemulis that the "synthetic bacchanal" (scheduled for this weekend) with the DMZ (the "*tu-savez-quo*i"; cf. "*tu-sais-quoi*," p. 482) is "definitely off." Pemulis says "That's part of what we need to interface about" and—in response to Hal's praise of his miraculous blarney (cf. p. 783)—says "Blarney wasn't why we got [the thirty days], Inc, is the thing." (Why did they get the thirty days? Pemulis presumably thinks it has something to do with his seeing Avril and Wayne in Ch. 26.4. But did Avril get the thirty days from the urologist? Does the blue blazer in her office (p. 768) belong to the urologist, or do all tennis academy employees have blue O.N.AN.T.A. blazers (cf. Tavis's blue blazer at Jim's funeral)?) Then Freer and McKenna interrupt the conversation.

Pemulis, unable to engage Hal at present (Hal: "I was bored. I couldn't remember a time when Pemulis had bored me."), mentions that he can come up later if Hal is going to "stand on one foot [cf. p. 851] with that opera thing on [cf. p. 846] at some point." Hal asks Pemulis to cue up the cartridge he has been thinking of, which is "on the third shelf down in the entertainment-case" (cf. p. 898). Hal tells Pemulis specifically where he should cue the cartridge and seems to have the ability to list his father's work alphabetically. The cartridges on the shelf are "supposed to be alphabetized." Pemulis realizes that he is unfamiliar with much of Jim's work, even though he uses "the poor guy's lab" (cf. pp. 154-5). As Pemulis cues the film, Hal thinks of Jim's funeral, at which "a circling gull scored a direct white hit on the shoulder of C.T.'s blue blazer [and] a large blue-bodied fly flew right into [C.T.'s] mouth."

Jim's funeral was "held on 5 or 6 April [it "was twice delayed by annular hyperfloration cycles" (p. 65), cf. n. 160.a] in St. Adalbert ["in the Mondragon-family-plot" (n. 160.a); cf. Orin's misnaming Avril's home town, which was "wiped off the map. Bad ecocycles, real machete-country" (p. 1041)], a small town built around spud-storage facilities fewer than five clicks west of the Great Concavity." Recall that "three-quarters of the Concavity's northern border runs contiguous to Québec" (p. 1017). The northern border runs from Ontario northeast into western New Brunswick (p. 1017), presumably in a relatively straight line and south of major cities like Ottawa, Montreal, and Québec. The spud-storage facilities are just west of (outside) this line; Jim's grave is just east of (inside) it. The curve of the Concavity runs in a jagged line (if the representation in Mario's film is accurate, p. 403) from Ontario through what used to be upper New York (making a near-right-angle at Ticonderoga, p. 403), Vermont, New Hampshire, and Maine (which was lost altogether (n. 318), is no longer represented on the "49-star U.S.A. flag" (p. 761), and is now the heart of the Concavity (p. 1041)), meeting the northern border in western New Brunswick, the eastern coast of which is apparently in bad shape, given that it "was a mercy" cloud-cover prevented Hal from seeing it on the way to Jim's funeral.

In *Good-Looking Men in Small Clever Rooms*, actor Paul Anthony Heaven reads a lecture to students "in the deadening academic monotone that Himself so loved." Heaven says, "We thus become, in the absence of death as teleologic end, ourselves desiccated, deprived of some essential fluid, aridly cerebral, abstract, conceptual, little more than hallucinations of God." Heaven speaks of reactions to the dead ancestor: "to revive or revise," "to repress," and "the battle-to-the-death with the loved dead." Critics believe that the dumb, inappreciative, or victimized "audiences inside Himself's films" reflect "hostility on the part of an '*auteur*' pegged as technically gifted but narratively dull and static and plotless and not entertaining enough"; but the critics' arguments do not explain "the incredible pathos of Paul Anthony Heaven reading his lecture to a crowd of dead-eyed kids . . . in a monotone as narcotizing as a voice from the grave—and yet all the time weeping."

PLOT AND CHARACTER: E.T.A., Hal, Art/Ent
THEME: His/Father, Choice, Recur

Hal thinks of his father's funeral and views his father's work, another critical assessment of which is given in this section. Hal can't "decide" in this section and makes a choice "almost at random." Hal hears "a whoop and two crashes"; his eyes roll up (like Gately's and Lyle's); and he makes a cage of his hands. "Petersen's *The Cage*," which like Incandenza's *Infinite Jest* makes use of a "distorted lens" (Meranda), is featured in the cartridge Hal screens. Before the cartridge played, the "huge screen hummed in a low pitch [and took] on a milky blue aspect like the eye of a dead bird." A "circling gull" deposits waste on C.T.'s "blue blazer," and a "blue-bodied fly" enters his mouth. Heaven's character, who weeps, is unable to connect with his students. What is the significance of the section-ending sentence: "Then this too began to seem familiar"?

Chapter 28.13, Section 180, Pages 911-916
Notes 367-371, Pages 1077-1078
18-19 November Y.D.A.U.

Gately continues to think-dream about his life. At the end of Ch. 28.11, 17-year-old Gately had decided upon a "bailout from school," after which he worked (from "age like eighteen to twenty-three") full-time and then (after he became primarily a burglar) part-time for Whitey Sorkin (who "owned several titty clubs down Rte. 1 in Saugus," perhaps the one referenced by the AA speaker on p. 370, whose "vegetable-kingdom sister" is referenced on p. 923). Gately's partner was Eugene Facklemann (Gately has had Facklemann on his mind since being shot; cf. pp. 614, 886, 892-3), who met Sorkin "through the same eczematic, gamble-happy pharmacist's assistant Gately had first met Sorkin through" (cf. p. 906). "Sorkin referred to Gately and Facklemann as his Twin Towers. They were more or less Sorkin's paid muscle," although the job required more listening to "sob-story-one-more-chance-types" than "actual hands-on coercion." The debtors would "look into Gately's eyes and lie and believe their own lies . . . . These types were Gately's first exposure to the concept of real addiction and what it can turn someone into." Debtors caused Sorkin "cluster headaches and terrible cranio-facial neuralgia," which required "visits to Enfield MA's National Cranio-Facial Pain Foundation" (the organization that supported the Nunhagen Aspirin ads, p. 412). Facklemann was called in for the "first round" of violence "because he had a controlled restraint Gately lacked," and "Gately's internal out-of-control slope of ferocity" was reserved for "an extreme point."

Gately and Facklemann "copped as a unit, as in together." "Gately would do Blues [Dilaudid, favored by Facklemann], which had to be injected, only when no oral narcs were to be got and he was face to face with early Withdrawal." When injected with Dialudid, Gately would experience a "hallucination where he was a gargantuan toddler in an XXL Fisher-Price crib in a sandy field under a storm-cloudy sky that bulged and receded like a big gray lung." Facklemann would "watch Gately's eyes roll up . . . while his huge hands throttled the air in front of him just like a toddler shakes at the bars of his crib. Then after five or so seconds the Dilaudid would cross over and kick, and the sky stopped breathing and turned blue." When "Gately brought Kite into the crew . . . Kite and Facklemann swiftly fell into the I.D.-, credit-history-and-furnished-luxury-apartment-scam [cf. pp. 892-3], in which by this time Gately involved himself pretty much only as a hobby."

"Gately lay in the Trauma Ward in terrific infected pain," presumably now in the light of the morning of 19 November, because he is "remembering a blinding white afternoon just after Xmas" and "winter daylight." On this afternoon, Gately was "laminating some false MA drivers licenses rush-ordered by rich . . . kids for what turned out to be the last New Year's Eve of Unsubsidized Time." Gately sees the multi sponsored bowl featuring Orin, who "had the potential to be a lock for a pretty much limitless pro ball career if he bore down and kept his eye on the carrot" (cf. coaches to Gately (p. 902) and about Gately's replacement (p. 906)). Gately began "to cry like a babe . . . out of emotional nowheres all of a sudden" over several things, including "the loss of organized ball" and "his failure after four years" to visit his mother (actually, three years and two months (since October 1998), cf. p. 906). "It was two days later" that he was pinched for assault "and three months after that that he went to Billerica Minimum."

So three months into Y.W. (when he was 21), Gately entered Billerica Minimum to stay for 17 months and therefore left Billerica around August Y.T.M.P., when he was almost 23 (cf. p. 463: "At twenty-four he'd done 17 months at Billerica"). Presumably, Gately reconnected briefly with Sorkin when he got out of prison before moving on to other contacts, primarily Kite (although no post-prison interaction with Sorkin is documented in the novel). Gately also switched from Percocet to Demerol shortly after release from prison (in "his twenty-third summer," pp. 891-2). Gately's use of "Bam-Bams," specifically cited as referring to Demerol tablets on p. 891 and in n. 189, is cited as a challenge to Gately's memory while working with Sorkin in n. 367. But n. 367 refers to Gately's work with Sorkin when Facklemann was alive (cf. "Facklemann's final demise" (p. 924), which occurs while Gately is "out on bail" (p. 917)); i.e., in the Percocet era. Gately's telescoping memory is blurring the boundaries of these eras. Reference is also made to the use of Percocets and Bam-Bams (p. 914) at a time when Facklemann is still alive. Gately also remembers being told about his mother's condition from a "Pakistani M.D." Is he confusing that doctor with one of his current doctors (cf. pp. 885-9)?

PLOT AND CHARACTER: Gately, AA&R
THEME: Recur, Memory, Inf/Reg, Loss

For five sections, narrative perspective has toggled between Gately and Hal, both horizontal and either dreaming or remembering. The Twin Towers of Gately and Facklemann recall Pemulis's "twin-towered AM cowlick" of the previous section (p. 907). Gately's use (p. 915) of Dilaudid (blues) involves "eyes roll[ing] up," "a toddler shak[ing] at the bars of his crib," and a "sky that bulged and receded" but then turned "blue." The "winter daylight" that "fell across the viewer's big flat screen" made the players in the bowl game "look bleached and ghostly." They are ghosts now, conjured by Gately's memory. As Gately watches O. play, "in the distance was the

Atlantic O." The multi-sponsored bowl game prompted significant reactions from both Gentle (p. 442) and Gately. Gately experiences loss from "out of emotional nowheres all of a sudden."

Chapter 28.14, Section 181, Page 916
20 November Y.D.A.U.

After talking with Hal in Ch. 28.12, Pemulis goes to retrieve the DMZ from its hiding place (cf. p. 700), but discovers "the relevant panel" is one of "at least eight panels of the drop-ceiling" that are now on the floor. "No old sneaker is in evidence" (cf. p. 216). Pemulis looks "up into the darkness of the struts' lattice."

If neither Hal nor Pemulis has the DMZ, presumably only Struck or Axford could have taken it, since they are the only others who know about it. Axford seemed excited about the DMZ's monetary value on p. 212. However, it is unlikely that the paranoid Pemulis would share the location of his hiding place with anyone else; and recall that objects have been found mysteriously out-of-place of late at E.T.A., including "acoustic ceiling-tiles [that have fallen] from their places in the subdorms' drop ceilings" (p. 632). After the tiles fell, dislodging the old sneaker, anyone could have happened upon the sneaker and taken it without knowing the potency of its contents.

PLOT AND CHARACTER: E.T.A., AA&R
THEME: Boundaries, Secrets, Loss

The protective boundary of the secret place has been breached. Pemulis's secret, his DMZ, is lost.

Chapter 28.15, Section 182, Pages 916-934
Notes 372-376, Page 1078
19-20 November Y.D.A.U.

Gately's thread continues from Ch. 28.13. Gately thinks of "the three months [he] was out on bail" (Jan.-Mar. Y.W.), during which time the "scam with Eighties Bill and Sixties Bob" occurred. This prompts Gately to remember "a bad-news new guy Sorkin had lately befriended and put to work . . . that went by the moniker Bobby C or just 'C,'" who (recall) dies in a dumpster with Poor Tony's boa in his mouth on Christmas Eve Y.D.P.A.H. (pp. 134-5). Sorkin's (or C's) "Nuck/fag crew" probably includes Poor Tony but presumably does not yet include current Ennet resident Emil Minty—the yrstruly of Ch. 12.2—because no mention has been made of Gately knowing Minty before Minty entered Ennet (the Nucks are DesMont[e]s and Pointgravè[s], cf. n. 369 and p. 975).

Between 1200-1600h. (in the "winter-P.M. light"), the "R.N. [Cathy or Kathy, whose shift ends at 1600h.] that'd flushed his colon while Gately wept with shame [cf. pp. 895-6] is now back in the room with an M.D. Gately hasn't seen before [Pressburger or Prissburger]." They attach "something to the room's other bed" (the "former kid's bed") that is "metally complex." (Is this attachment for Lord's impending operation? Recall the patient with "a box on its head" (p. 809).) It's "spitting a little goopy sleet." Gately "can smell himself," and there is "greasy sweat purling all over his scalp." The R.N. says she'll try to fit in a sponge bath before going off shift, but Gately hopes to avoid getting "an uncontrolled woodie" by having the sponge bath come from K/Cathy's "linebacker of a replacement" (cf. p. 891) in the 1600-2400h. shift. Time is running together for Gately, who experiences an addict's "late-day dread" and compares himself to a catatonic—"a figurant, mute and unmoving and blank." In the space of pp. 922-3, Gately recalls events or memories or hallucinations he has experienced since his admission to St. E's: "Joelle's visit and show-and-tell with the snapshots," the man in the hat, "innerdicted M.-Hanley-brownies," Herman the Ceiling That Breathed, Gately the frightened toddler who "cannot get anybody to come," and the "figuranted wraith" who "appeared yesterday. Assuming that was yesterday." Now "memories of Gene Facklemann's [Fax's] final demise" and Pamela Hoffman-Jeep (cf. p. 465), who was involved with Gately and staying with Gately and Fax at the time of Fax's demise, come "bubbling up out of nowhere." Gately "never once saw P.H.-J. actually get from one spot to another under her own power. . . . She made passivity and unconsciousness look kind of beautiful."

Gately found out about Facklemann's "historical proclavity for fraudulent scams" on Sorkin via "the not at all small scam with Eighties Bill and Sixties Bob." Gately remembers having to drop ice down the dress of Pamela Hoffman-Jeep to get the details of the scam, because "[l]ike most incredibly passive people, the girl had a terrible time ever separating details from what was really important to a story." The six-page description of the scam (by the narrator for Gately-remembering-P.H.-J.) and its impending consequences (by the narrator for Gately-remembering-Gately-after-P.H.-J.-goes-to-sleep) has been put into outline form below.

- Eighties Bill, a Yale alumnus, regularly bet on Yale through Sorkin
- Yale's next basketball game was against Brown
- Yale's star player had been diagnosed with Post-Coital Vestibulitis (p. 928)
- Eighties Bill was attempting to do business with a rabid Brown alumnus
- To "cozy up," Bill tipped Brown's staff off about the Yale player's condition
- Eighties Bill makes a bet with Fax that Brown will come within 2 points of Yale
- When Fax calls in the bet, Sorkin is at the Cranio-Facial Pain Foundation
- Sorkin is being treated by Sixties Bob
- Sixties Bob knows Kite (and bartered with the Antitois; cf. pp. 481, 721, 927)
- Sorkin's secretary Gwen, "cranially soft as a fucking grape," takes Fax's call
- Gwen puts Bill's $125K on Yale to come within 2 points, not Brown
- School-spirited hetero Brown coeds are recruited to fluster the Yale player
- Offended feminist groups stage an in-game ambush at the first time-out
- Pantyless "cheerleaders, Pep Squad and comely Brown U. sirens" are taken out
- The Yale player's "delicate nervous system" remains intact
- Two Brown U. players are felled in the melee
- Yale wins by "upwards of 20" points
- Eighties Bill thinks he lost because Brown didn't come within 2 points
- Eighties Bill pays Facklemann (with "pre-O.N.A.N. scrip" in early Y.W.)
- Sorkin thinks Bill won because Yale did better than come within 2 points
- Before Fax can pay Sorkin, Sorkin gives Fax payment for Eighties Bill (cf. "5% vig on the 10% vigorish" (p. 914) to follow Fax's math on pp. 929-30)
- Fax imagines a life of ease and endless Dilaudid and keeps his "map shut"
- Fax goes to buy Dilaudid from Dr. Wo with the $250K
- Fax approaches Kite to be his partner
- Kite knows Eighties Bill is the son of Sixties Bob, Sorkin's migrainologist
- Sorkin thug C makes regular purchases from Dr. Wo (cf. Ch. 12.2)
- Even if somehow Sorkin doesn't hear from Sixties Bob, he will hear from C
- Kite tells Facklemann that Facklemann is "already dead"

Gately understands "that the Faxter'd done what any drug addict in possession of his Substance would do when faced with fatal news and attendant terror: [take] staggering quantities of Dilaudid, trying to mentally blot out the reality of the fact that he was going to get demapped if he didn't take some kind of decisive remedial action at once." Indeed, for "two weeks Facklemann had been squatting sweatily in a corner . . . over his Sterno cooker and incredible twin hills of sky-blue Dilaudid . . . , just sitting there hunched and plump and glistening like some sort of cornered toad." This was "the first time it really ever dawned on [Gately] that a drug addict was at root a craven and pathetic creature: a thing that basically hides." It is bothersome to Gately that he "had lumbered so automatically out to Facklemann under the pretense [to himself] that he was just going to check on poor Facklemann, to maybe try and convince him to take some kind of action." But Gately knew Fax would "invite Gately to hunker on down," and the "need for action had [not] even been brought up, so intent were they on the Blues' somnolent hum, blotting everything out, while Pamela Hoffman-Jeep lay wrapped tight in the other room dreaming of damsels and towers."

Now, presumably in the early hours of 20 November, Gately's "feverish dreams punctuate memories and being conscious, like." Gately is on a bus and passes "the same gutted cottages and expanse of heaving sea" (Gately has twice dreamed of being submerged in seawater: pp. 449, 816). Gately "comes sharply around when he feels the little rough tongue on his forehead—not unlike Nimitz [cf. p. 448] the M.P.'s little pet kitten's hesitant tongue." "When Gately gets his eyelids unstuck, though, the . . . wraith is back, . . . except now with him is another, younger, way more physically fit wraith" (cf. Lyle's tongue "like a kitty's" (p. 128) and the wraith-word *LISLE* on p. 919), licking his forehead (Gately dreamed Joelle licked his forehead earlier, cf. p. 847). Gately "reflexively strikes out" at the new wraith as "both wraiths vanish and a blue forked bolt of pain" hits him, making his eyes roll back. He dreams of a mirror and of the color blue. "He's both in a bag and holding a bag."

Gately "dreams he's with a very sad kid [Hal] and they're in a graveyard digging some dead guy's head up [the head (cf. pp. 16-7) of

Hal's father, the wraith of whom just left Gately] and it's really important . . . . [T]he sad kid is trying to scream [he has trouble speaking, cf. Ch. 1] at Gately that the important thing was buried in the guy's head [whose contents one year before his death were a "gyroscopic balance sensor and *mise-en-scene* appropriation card and priapistic-entertainment cartridge" (p. 31)] and to divert the continental Emergency [by means of obtaining the Master (or its rumored antidote, p. 126), which perhaps replaced or was added to the previous contents of Jim's head on his film-related business trip just before his death (p. 249) and somehow survived the microwave] to start digging the guy's head up before it's too late, but the kid moves his mouth but nothing comes out [he has trouble speaking], and Joelle van D. appears [although she supposedly is not one of the visitors who currently "flit in and out" of Gately's room] with wings and no underwear [like the Brown U. girls who are carried off over shoulders both feminine and burly; which is analogous to Joelle being carried off by the burly, feminized Steeply between Chs. 28.16 and 28.18] and asks if they knew him, the dead guy with the head ["Alas, poor Yorick. I knew him, Horatio, a fellow of infinite jest," *Hamlet* V.i.178-9], and Gately starts talking about knowing him [the wraith] even though deep down he feels panic because he's got no idea who they're talking about [Jim], while the sad kid holds up something terrible by the hair [presumably Jim's post-microwave head, buried six years by this time] and makes the face [he has trouble speaking] of somebody shouting in panic: *Too Late*."

PLOT AND CHARACTER: Gately, AA&R, Jim, Hal, Joelle
THEME: Time, Memory, His/Father, Dreams, Cycles, Isolation, Inf/Reg, Non-Action, Waste, Recur

Time runs together for Gately (the narrator of n. 376 gives Y.W.-Q.M.D. Dilaudid prices ($666) for the Y.W. Dilaudid Facklemann is considering in Gately's Y.D.A.U. memory), who lies horizontal in his bed at St. E's "pinwheel-eyed from pain and efforts to Abide via memory." Gately's "deep-focus memories" of Fax's demise bubble "up out of nowhere." "Gately wonders if his organic father the iron-worker is not now maybe dead and dropping in and standing very still from time to time for a communiqué." Gately's "dream goes on and on, without any kind of resolution or arrival, and he weeps and sweats as he lies there, stuck in it." Gately is isolated, "trapped inside his huge chattering head." He is "Alone, worse off than a toddler that could at least bellow and yowl, rattling the bars of its playpen in terror that nobody tall was in any shape to hear him" (cf. the image of Gately-on-Dilaudid shaking "the bars of his crib," p. 915). The infant image is reinforced by Mr. Bouncety-Bounce (who wears an infant-head mask, p. 648), watched by addicts Gately and Fax. When high, Gately and Fax regress to a state of non-action, like sleeping infants. Pamela Hoffman-Jeep is described as passive, horizontal, fetal, a sleeping baby, and yawning an infant's little milky yawn in the paragraph on pp. 924-5 (cf. Joelle, "uprightly fetal" on p. 239). Fax fantasizes about drug-induced regression to a non-active state, which leads to his compulsion to deceive Sorkin. Gately deceives himself and gets high with Fax rather than acting to help him. Gately obsesses over waste: K/Cathy helping him with his bowel movements, his smell, and the continence of P.H.-J. upon first meeting her. There are a host of recurrences in this section: Sorkin wears a Lone Ranger-type mask (cf. Gately's mask, p. 654); Sorkin and Gately both weep (Gately in a dream of the sea); sleet sounds like sand "from real far away"; Gwen has a soft skull; Sorkin wears goggles that "look like lobsters' eyes on stalks"; Fax is "hunched" over "twin hills of sky-blue Dilaudid"; Gately has a "blue forked bolt of pain" (which makes his eyes roll back); Gately dreams of the color blue and of a mirror; and another painter (Turner) is referenced. What is the significance of Lyle's appearance as a wraith? What does it mean that Gately's "both in a bag [cf. "in the bag" as drunk, p. 448] and holding a bag"?

There are several potential correspondences in this section. The kitten in the garbage disposal recalls Joelle's mom (p. 795) and Lenz's bird (p. 547). Lenz also went on a binge after a scam went wrong (p. 276). Gately's attention to hairless patches of Lenz's forearm shaved with a knife (p. 276) may derive from Bobby C's habit. K/Cathy is "the eye of a storm of sexual tension" like Joelle; watching P.H.-J. makes "passivity and unconsciousness look kind of beautiful," like watching Joelle in *Infinite Jest*. P.H.-J.'s medieval associations recall Gately's childhood "Sir Osis." The complicated details of the scam recall the complicated details of the spy games played by Marathe and Steeply.

In this section of the last chapter of *Infinite Jest*, there are three resonances with the last act of *Hamlet*. The graveyard scene and "infinite jest" monologue are again recalled in Gately's dream. Gately has a time-lapse vision of P.H.-J., in which he sees her "losing her looks through her twenties and her face starting to slide over off her skull," which recalls Hamlet saying "to this favor she must come" in the same monologue. A significant event in the last act of *Hamlet* is the "fraudulent scam" perpetrated by Claudius (and Laertes) on Hamlet under the ruse of a friendly wager, which results in the map of Claudius being "eliminated for keeps" at the hands of a vengeful Hamlet. Facklemann's map will be "eliminated for keeps" at the (hired) hands of a vengeful Sorkin. Although the wager presented to Hamlet by Osric is less detailed than the wager documented in this section, it is complicated enough to prompt almost four pages of commentary in the second series of the Arden edition of *Hamlet*.

Chapter 28.16, Section 183, Page 934
20 November Y.D.A.U.

Joelle (whose 16 November visit to Gately was documented in Ch. 28.6) had "come out of the St. E's doors and turned right for the quick walk back up to Ennet" when she was grabbed by "a grotesquely huge woman" (Steeply in disguise). Surely it is 20 November, given that Joelle later walks (presumably on the same day) to Enfield Marine "in the snow" (p. 958). Although in the previous section Joelle is said not to be in Gately's room (on what is presumably the morning—or at least the wee hours—of the 20th), it could be that Gately just doesn't remember her being there. The winged Joelle in Gately's dream could have been prompted by an actual Joelle visit, or Gately's dream of Joelle could have occurred before Joelle arrived later that morning. Steeply tells Joelle that she is "in almost mind-boggling danger." Presumably, Steeply knows from Marathe about the A.F.R.'s mission to find Joelle; but as of 19 November, the A.F.R. have shifted the primary focus of their mission (cf. p. 845).

PLOT AND CHARACTER: Joelle, U.S.O.U.S.
THEME: Secrets

Joelle, who wears a veil, is taken by Steeply, who wears a feminine disguise. Steeply's putative resume (Ch. 17.4) appeared in the midst of a chapter almost exclusively Joelle's, perhaps foreshadowing this meeting.

Chapter 28.17, Section 184, Pages 934-938
Note 377, Page 1078
20 November Y.D.A.U.

The saga of Gately's memory of Facklemann's demise continues from Ch. 28.15. Gately has joined Facklemann on a Dilaudid binge. They are "moving like men deep under water, heads wobbling on strengthless necks, the empty room's ceiling sky-blue and bulging and under it hanging on the wall overhead to their right the apartment's upscale TP's viewer ["the high-def viewer now always the last luxury furnishing to be fenced," p. 915] on a recursive slo-mo loop" of Jim's *Various Small Flames* (or Ruscha's *Various Small Fires*, cf. p. 988).

"[A]t maybe 0830h." Pamela Hoffman-Jeep got ready and left for work. "As the A.M. sun got higher and intolerable, instead of taking action and nailing a blanket or something over the window they opted instead to obliterate the reality of the eye-scalding light and began truly bingeing on Blues, flirting with an O.D." The narrator says, "You have to picture all the binge's verbal exchanges as occurring like very slowly, oddly distended, as if time were honey." "Each exhalation of laughter seemed to take several minutes." They do not respond to phone rings or door buzzers. Both men wet their pants and watch urine spread out and corrode the hardwood floor. Instead of going to the kitchen for more distilled water with which to cook up the Dilaudid, they use urine off the floor sopped up with cotton. Facklemann "had a small convulsion and a bowel movement in his pants and Gately hadn't had the coordination to go to Facklemann's side during the seizure."

Gately dreams of the same bus he will dream of later at St. E's (cf. p. 933). "In his stuporous recall over four years later [actually, over seven and a half years later]" he "has the sickening realization that the connection between the two buses is itself a dream, or is in a dream." At this point, Gately's fever rises which affects his heart monitor "which makes an amber light flash at the nurse's station down the hall."

Although the sun "seemed to go up and down like a yo-yo," it was probably later that same night when Pamela Hoffman-Jeep rang the buzzer. "Gately reached in the dark for the bars of his playpen" but was unable to go far before falling down again, shaking the whole room and causing the viewer to fall and "cast ruddled flames on the ceiling," which "bulged and receded." Gene Facklemann held his hand in the shape of a spider out to Gately "for his inspection." (Years later, when counseling Gately, Gene M will use The Spider as a metaphor for addiction, cf. p. 274.)

PLOT AND CHARACTER: Gately, AA&R
THEME: Time, Boundaries, Memory, Dreams, Non-Action, Recur

In this section, there are several references to an addict's experience of time in slow-motion. In Gately's memory, the time of one day passes slowly enough to seem like many days. At St. E's, several days seems to blend into one day, or at least it is hard for Gately to determine what day it is. The boundaries of time, memory, dream, and reality are blurred. Gately experiences the bus dream in both the past and the present, continually slips from memory to dream to reality, and sees wraiths—an "unreal" phenomenon that Gately is presumably actually experiencing (like Hamlet). Reality blurs in the past such that blinding light, ringing phones, and urine are just part of the environment rather than something to take action against. There are recurrences of hunching, vomiting, ceilings that bulge and recede, human waste, Gately being assaulted by the floor (cf. pp. 904-5), and a potential missed connection if the film Gately remembers was made by the wraith. Perhaps Gately's dreams of the bus in Y.W. and Y.D.A.U. are prompted by near-death experiences.

Chapter 28.18, Section 185, Pages 938-941
20 November Y.D.A.U.

Joelle, grabbed by Steeply in Ch. 28.16, has been taken somewhere and is now in the middle of a U.S.O.U.S. interview with Steeply (Joelle's friend Molly Notkin was interviewed by Tine, Jr. in Ch. 27.42). Steeply's questions are represented by Q's in this section as they were in n. 145, n. 234, and in Steeply's last letter to Bain (p. 665), the answers to which Steeply has probably read by this date. The interview transcript begins as Joelle starts to discuss *Infinite Jest.*

Joelle tells Steeply she "was in two scenes." In the first (cf. p. 549), she has a "random chance" meeting with someone she hasn't seen in a long time. Both characters register a look of shocked recognition and make "several whirls" in a "glass revolving door," each attempting to follow the other. Joelle assumes Steeply "can Identify" with the other character, who was "epicine. . . . Hermaphroditic. Androgynous." The other scene "had the camera bolted down inside a stroller or bassinet. [Joelle] wore an incredible white floor-length gown [recall Notkin said she was nude and pregnant, p. 788] . . . and leaned in over the camera in the crib and simply apologized." Joelle says that she was "[n]ot exactly veiled" and describes the "crib's-eye view" of the camera and its "auto-wobble" lens that made a "tiny whirring noise" when it moved and "looked more like an eye-stalk or a night-vision scope than a lens." The "lens was supposed to reproduce an infantile visual field. . . . [Joelle's] face wasn't important. You never got the sense it was meant to be captured realistically by this lens."

Joelle says that she "never saw" the film or Jim's will but that "the Masters of everything unreleased" were supposed to be buried with him. Joelle says that Jim "couldn't take" not "being drunk all the time" and that was what killed him; the film "had nothing to do with killing himself." Joelle wonders whether there even was a "finished Master. That's *your* story" (cf. "what's *your* story?" p. 17). She says Jim "talked about making something quote too perfect. But as a *joke*" and that "he never talked about an anti-version or antidote." "When he talked about this thing as a quote perfect entertainment, terminally compelling—it was always ironic—he was having a sly little jab at me. I used to go around saying the veil was to disguise lethal perfection, that I was too lethally beautiful for people to stand. It was a kind of joke I'd gotten from one of his entertainments, the Medusa-Odalisk thing. That even in U.H.I.D. [i.e., even when she joined U.H.I.D. over a year and a half later; cf. p. 533] I hid by hiddenness, in denial about the deformity itself. So Jim took a failed piece and told me it was too perfect to release—it'd paralyze people. It was entirely clear that it was an ironic joke. To me" (but cf. what the wraith tells Gately, pp. 838-9). Joelle says "If it got made and nobody's seen it, the Master, it's in there with him" but that where Jim's "buried is *itself* buried, now [cf. Orin to Steeply: "The Moms's home town's wiped off the map" (p. 1041)]. It's in your annulation-zone [cf. that the funeral was "delayed by annular hyperfloration cycles" (p. 65, cf. n. 160.a)]. It's not even your *territory*. And now if you want the thing—he'd enjoy the joke very much, I think."

PLOT AND CHARACTER: Joelle, Samizdat, U.S.O.U.S.
THEME: Cycles, Recur, Inf/Reg, Loss

The characters in Joelle's first scene are in a cycle in which they do not connect. Jim, who invented annulation, is now buried in an annulation-zone. There is another missed connection in that Joelle doesn't know that Steeply spent several days at the beginning of the month interviewing her ex-boyfriend, Orin. Recall Hal's private theory that "to be really human. . . is probably to be unavoidably sentimental and naïve and goo-prone and generally pathetic, is to be in some basic interior way forever infantile" (pp. 694-5). Watching *Infinite Jest* is similar to bingeing on Dilaudid in that both of these choices induce infantile regression. Perhaps the lure of these activities which reduce one to an infantile state arises from a desire "to be really human." Also, when creating *Infinite Jest*, Joelle and Jim were both experiencing extreme loss and pain. Joelle had just learned that her father had "been secretly, silently in love" with her. Immediately afterwards she was disfigured; her mother killed herself; and her relationship with Orin ended (pp. 793-5). Jim was making the film because he feared for Hal (pp. 838-9) and was experiencing the (suicidal, according to Joelle in her interview) depression of withdrawal as a condition of filming it. He had seen the name of one of Avril's lovers in the steamed-up window of the Volvo on the way to shoot Joelle's apology scene (n. 80). Perhaps the honesty and raw vulnerability of its suffering creators endowed *Infinite Jest* with a quality that forces its viewers to drop "the weary cynicism that saves us from gooey sentiment" (p. 694); but the viewers, used to "masks of ennui and jaded irony" (p. 694), are so unprepared for the intensity and honesty of the experience—an experience that appeals to their secret need "to be really human" (cf. Mario's "real stuff," p. 592)—that they become "forever infantile" and, as Jim predicted, paralyzed.

Chapter 28.19, Section 186, Pages 941-958
Notes 378-382, Pages 1078-1079
20 November Y.D.A.U.

Hal continues to narrate in first person from Ch. 28.12. He has left V.R.5, where he was watching one of his father's works, and has now returned to his room, where Mario and Kyle Coyle are watching another of his father's works, "*Accomplice!*, a short melodrama with Cosgrove Watt and a boy no one had ever seen before or since" (Stokely "Dark Star" McNair (cf. p. 992), a late acquaintance of Poor Tony's, who "died in a Fenway hospice" (p. 300) earlier this year). Coyle has informed Mario that "Jim Troeltsch tore some of Ortho's face off trying to pull him off a window" and then with Kenkle put a whole roll of "toilet tissue on the ripped parts." Stice has now locked himself in his room. Hal discovers that "Troeltsch apparently [switched] room-assignments with Trevor Axford" (cf. p. 872).

Before Coyle left his room this morning, he discovered Stice's bed "up near the ceiling of their room" (cf. Stice's reference to "parabnormal shit," p. 871). According to Coyle, Stice thinks he's being "haunted or possessed by some kind of beneficiary or guardian ghost that resides in and/or manifests in ordinary physical objects, that wants to teach the Darkness how to not underestimate ordinary objects and raise his game to like a supernatural level." Stice bet Coyle "he could stand on his desk chair and lift it up at the same time" (cf. Lyle's story to Stice, p. 395). Coyle says to Hal "I don't see what's so funny about it," and Mario asks Hal if he is sad.

In his work, Jim liked to use "*non*actors to achieve [a] stilted artificial I'm-only-acting-here quality," but "in his last several projects he'd been so desperate to make something ordinary U.S. audiences might find entertaining . . . that he had had professionals and amateurs alike emoting all over the place." Hal and Mario disagree about Jim's success in "[g]etting emotion out of either actors or audiences." "Cosgrove Watt was a pro but he wasn't very good." Jim discovered Watt acting as "the Dancing Gland in a series of spots" and wearing "a bulbous white costume, white toupee, and . . . white tap shoes" (compare this to Jim's father's outfit as the Man from Glad, p. 492).

Accomplice! was filmed in the same apartment in which *Infinite Jest* was filmed and features Watt and a "fragile and epicene" boy (Joelle described her *Infinite Jest* co-star (McNair?) as "epicene" on p. 939). "The sad and beautiful Aryan-looking boy [a prostitute] agrees to seduction by the dissipated old specimen, but only on the condition that the man wear protection. The boy, who is inarticulate, nevertheless makes this stipulation extremely clear." The old man takes the request as an insult and contrives to use a razor blade to slice "into both condom and erect phallus on each outthrust." However, it is revealed that the boy has "a vivid purple splotch" of Kaposi's Sarcoma in "eight spidery tentacles" at "the crease of his bum and upper hamstring." The final third of the film features "the racked repetition" of the word "*Murderer!*" by the sobbing boy, who considers that "the depraved old homosexual has made him—the prostitute—a murderer." There is both familial and critical debate as to whether the ending of *Accomplice!* was made "for some theoretical-aesthetic end" or simply reflected Jim's poor editing skills. There is no mention of the significance of an inarticulate boy suddenly speaking for over eight minutes. Recall Jim's concern with Hal's silence since the professional conversationalist incident (Ch. 3), which occurred in Y.T.M.P., the year Jim made *Accomplice!* Recall that McNair's philosophy is different than that of his *Accomplice!* character. Upon learning that he has "the Virus for sure" in Y.D.P.A.H. (five years after *Accomplice!* was filmed), McNair (according to Purpleboy) "said how if he was going down he didnt' give a shit and wasnt' going to give a shit if he gave some others the Virus thru trancemission" (p. 129).

After Mario and Coyle leave, Hal—"in a horizontal position on the bedroom floor"—watches "InterLace's Spontaneous Disseminations for New New England" weather. "Pedestrians were shown bent over and floundering." Tires were spinning, "shuddering in stasis." "ATHSCME fans atop the wall of Ticonderoga NNY were shown making horizontal cyclones of snow in the air." Comparing this storm to previous blizzards, a reporter noted that an "unwelcome old acquaintance was back." During this Hal remembers that "Otis P. Lord had undergone a procedure for the removal of the Hitachi monitor on Thursday." (Otis was in St. E's with "a box on [his] head" next to Gately on Thursday the 12th (p. 809). Presumably the removal of the "box" occurred one week later on Thursday the 19th. Recall the preparation of a metal contraption on "the room's other bed" on the afternoon of the 19th (pp. 918 and 920).) Hal "could barely recall the [March] '98 blizzard ["the second-worst since B.S. 1993" (cf. p. 482)]. The Academy had been open for only a few months" and "final construction [was] delayed by some nasty piece of litigation from the VA hospital below" (cf. pp. 198, 991). "It took almost a year to complete the move from Weston to E.T.A."

1998: hill shaved (cf. p. 241), E.T.A. open, move from Weston begins
1999: move to E.T.A. complete (Hal "in residence at [E.T.A.] since age seven," p. 4)
E.T.A. accredited ("in accredited operation for three pre-Subsidized years and then eight Subsidized years," p. 63)
2000: final construction of E.T.A. complete ("erected [in the summer of 2000] when Mario was nine and Hallie eight and Orin seventeen," p. 314)

Hal "lay flat on [his] back on [his] room's carpet and tried to recall the details of [his] home in Weston" (just as Gately has been recalling his childhood home flat on his back at St. E's). The carpet was "an oversized corruption of the carpet page from the Lindistairne Gospels" (cf. p. 171) and included "tiny pornographic scenes in the Byzantine weave." The carpet goes with the print on the wall over Hal's bed from "the really prurient part of *Consummation of the Levirates*" (cf. p. 171), which features "people broken into pieces and trying to join" (cf. p. 29 for another reference to Hal's interest in Byzantine erotica). Hal "realized [he] could not distinguish [his] own visual memories of the Weston house from [his] memories of hearing Mario's detailed reports of his memories" (cf. that Hal remembers Orin's report of the mold incident on pp. 10-11). Hal's memories of Weston "seemed more like snapshots than film" and include a "surreal memory of a steamed lavatory mirror with a knife sticking out of the pane" (cf. that in Y.G. Hal "once saw the word KNIFE finger-written on the steamed mirror of a nonpublic bathroom" (p. 16) and looks like a "writhing animal with a knife in its eye" to the administrators, p. 14). Some of Hal's memories "have to be confabulated or dreamed" (which recalls Gately's flux between memory and dream).

One of the many items moved from Weston to E.T.A. was a coffee table "on whose corner Mario knocked out a tooth after what Orin swore up and down was an accidental shove. . . . The table had been a wedding gift from Himself's mother." Orin had liked to do impersonations of his grandmother's "spooky kyphotic hunch" and "claw" (which recalls Facklemann on p. 938). Hal recalls that his mother's father died when she was a sophomore and that "the original L'Islet potato farm [was] now part of the Great Concavity and forever lost." Hal has witnessed his mother's "gradual withdrawal and reluctance to leave the grounds" since his father's funeral "four" (actually five and a half) years ago. If asked by Harv (Ch. 27.44) or the grief-therapist what witnessing Avril's aging made Hal feel, he would have to lie because the unacceptable (to them) "truth is Nothing At All . . . . The brutal questions are the ones that *force* you to lie."

Hal has a brief fantasy of hurting himself so that he would be unable to play if the meet occurs, and then "out of nowhere" he remembers "the moving thing Himself had said to Orin . . . concerning 'adult' films." Jim—who Hal remembers "teaching Orin to shave against the grain, upward" (recall that Orin shaves "as he was taught," p. 49)—had given Orin "a lemon soda" (cf. p. 27), warned Orin that watching a pornographic film might give Orin "the wrong idea about having sex," and advised Orin to wait until he experienced sex as a "profound and moving thing" before watching a film that presented sex as "emotionless, terribly lonely." Orin was moved that his father still thought him a virgin, and Hal is sorry that Orin missed Jim's point. Hal thinks "It was the most open I'd ever heard of Himself being with anybody" and "I'd never once had a conversation nearly that open or intimate with Himself" before having an intimate memory of his father carrying him upstairs to bed. Hal wonders why no one has ever asked Mario how open Jim was with him.

John Wayne enters the room but does not speak (cf. p. 560). Hal references Wayne's "complete utilization of each breath" (cf. the Cult of the Endless Kiss, pp. 1061-2). This prompts Hal to have "a sudden and lucid vision of the Moms and John Wayne locked in a sexual embrace." The "expatriates" had been involved "since roughly the second month after [Wayne's] arrival." Hal imagines sex "between the Moms and C.T." as "both frenetic and weary." In sexual encounters—with "Bain [this may explain Marlon's bitterness toward Avril in his response to Steeply, n. 269], graduate students, grammatical colleagues, Japanese fight-choreographers [Kenjiru Hirota, cf. p. 397 and '*The Medusa v. the Odalisque*' (p. 988)], the hairy-shouldered Ken N. Johnson [cf. *Various Small Flames*, p. 988], [and] the Islamic M.D. Himself found so especially torturing [cf. Jim to Hal (p. 30) and *Dial C for Concupiscence* (p. 992) for Jim's obsession with this man]"—Hal "tended to imagine the Moms staring expressionlessly at ceilings throughout. The complicit passion would have come after, probably, with her need to be sure the encounter was hidden" (cf. Hal's Pump Room activities). Hal "wondered about some hazy connection between this passion for hiddenness and the fact that Himself made so many films titled *Cage*, and that the amateur player he became so attached to was the veiled girl, Orin's love" (also referred to as "Orin's fiancée"). Hal thinks that his image of Avril and Wayne is "not very erotic" and seems "stilted, as if composed."

PLOT AND CHARACTER: E.T.A., Art/Ent, Hal, Orin, Jim, Avril
THEME: Isolation, Memory, Non-Action, His/Father, Phys/Ob, Cycles, Secrets, Recur

This section comments on the isolation and disconnectedness of pornographic sex and is rife with sexual images. Jim advised that pornographic films were "emotionless, terribly lonely," and best not seen by those who are sexually inexperienced; but note that Jim's pornographic film *Accomplice!* is viewed by young boys in this section and that as a boy Hal had an interest in Byzantine erotica, an example of which he characterizes as "people broken into pieces and trying to join." Young Hal also is aware of his mother's extramarital sexual encounters, but imagines they are passionless and seems, unlike Hamlet, not to be judgmental about his mother's sexual conduct.

Hal, horizontal (nonactive) throughout this section, continues to remember family history, including Jim's choice to use "*non*actors" in his work. Hal's memories are "more like snapshots than film": more like stills than pictures in motion. The new blizzard is referenced as an "unwelcome old acquaintance," but this term might apply to memories as well, figurative ghosts. Images of the late Stokely "Dark Star" McNair are captured in Jim's film, like images of C and Facklemann (both also late) are captured in (the also horizontal) Gately's memory. Was it a literal ghost (wraith-Jim) that moved Stice's bed, a "guardian ghost that resides in and/or manifests in ordinary physical objects"? The wraith only moved small items at St. E's: a coke can, a photograph. In the blizzard, the tires of cars are "shuddering in stasis," and ATHSCME fans make "horizontal cyclones of snow in the air." Hal's memories of Weston late in the novel balance his memory of Weston early in the novel (pp. 10-11). Other examples of cycles are in Hal's memories of Jim passing down his shaving method to Orin (from father to son), S. Johnson's "running around and around the pen" ("S.J.'s orbit"), E.T.A.s counting "interwoven circles" on the ceiling, and C.T. "talking around and around whatever was taking place" during sex while Avril stared at the ceiling. Avril, like Hal in the Pump Room and Joelle behind her veil, could be said to have a "passion for hiddenness" (secrets).

Sex in *Accomplice!* is described as "extravagantly hunched" (cf. Kenkle to Brandt, pp. 874-5); the boy's horrific disease (signaled by "spidery tentacles" of Kaposi's Sarcoma) is referenced as "*It*" (as were the horrors of depression in Ch. 27.13); and there is a missed connection in that the old man mistook the boy's request as a judgment rather than as a warning. Hal again experiences "tip-of-the-tongue inaccessibility" until he stops trying to recall what he wants to remember and it comes to him. Describing a Weston church, Hal says "a parabolic poured-concrete shape billowed and peaked like a cresting wave." Other recurrences include the "blue-and-white" motif in the Weston home, an instance of Orin's cruelty to Mario, and Jim's offering lemon soda to prompt conversation (cf. p. 27). Yet again, the five years since Jim's death is remembered as four years (p. 954 and n. 381). Another actor's name (Kyle MacLachlan, of *Twin Peaks*) is misspelled, and David Lynch (co-creator, *Twin Peaks*) is referenced (p. 944).

Why have Troeltsch and Axford switched rooms (cf. Bucher)? Why has Avril kept the *Metropolis* print (p. 951, n. 381; cf. p. 193)? Who was the foreign adult in Weston that Hal didn't recognize (p. 952)? Who was the "unidentified woman" in the Weston kitchen (p. 954)?

Chapter 28.20, Section 187, Page 958
20 November Y.D.A.U.

Joelle heads back to Ennet House after her interview with Steeply (Ch. 28.18) and considers it likely that she is being followed. After taking "one of the last trains before they closed the T, probably" (earlier this morning, Hal believed the T would suspend routes "before long," p. 868), she walks "in the snow, and melt soaked the veil and made it adhere to the features below. She'd been close to removing the veil to get away from [Steeply]." She hopes Pat will quarantine her "with Clenette and Yolanda," and she will "tell Pat about the wheelchairs" (one of whom Pat interviewed six days ago; cf. though that the A.F.R. are no longer actively looking for Joelle, p. 845). When Joelle arrives at the House, she sees "the Middlesex County Sheriff's car" parked outside. Lowell, Tewksbury, Billerica, and Concord (cf. pp. 462-3) are all in Middlesex County: "it's only a matter of time [before] Gately has to do the bit [for "driving with a DUI-suspended license"] at someplace MCI-Minimum like Concord or Deer Island" (p. 463).

PLOT AND CHARACTER: Joelle
THEME: Recur

There is a missed connection in that Joelle believes the "wheelchairs" are looking for her, but the A.F.R. have shifted the focus of their mission (p. 845) and presumably are not looking for Joelle as actively as they were. Although the sheriff is presumably at Ennet on old business and unconcerned with Joelle, Joelle presumably does not want to risk making contact with a police officer after her experience with Steeply (cf. the summary of the next section). The sheriff's car's lights are "going bluely."

Chapter 28.21, Section 188, Pages 958-960
20 November Y.D.A.U.

This section is presumed to occur on 20 November and documents the narrative of one Mikey, in recovery for a tendency to "light up" people. Mikey recently was denied permission to see his son ("who he just got the cast off") by his sister and mother. After cursing his family, he realizes he must go back "and try and say I'm sorry"; and when he does, his apology is not accepted. Mikey says, "I got to accept her word and don't even know for sure if the cast is even off. But why I needed to share I think is it [my temper] scared me. *I* scared me."

Mikey is "blurred a bit through the linen [veil, cf. p. 220]," which presumably means that this section is presented from Joelle's perspective and that she has decided to attend this meeting rather than enter the House while the sheriff's car was outside (cf. previous section). It is "another of these round-robin-speaker deals," like the meeting Joelle described to Gately on 16 November (cf. pp. 856-7), except that this meeting is held at "lunchtime" rather than at night. Another less likely possibility of a veiled attendee exists. Gately, whose memory is not always exact, knows "this one male veiled U.H.I.D. guy that's an active White Flagger, Tommy S. or F." (p. 364, cf. also p. 534); and Mikey calls on one "Tommy E." to be the next speaker. But just as the "Vinnie" who hosts this meeting is not the late Vinnie Nucci (cf. p. 892) of Gately's memory, so Tommy E. is most likely not Tommy S. (or F.)

PLOT AND CHARACTER: Joelle, AA&R
THEME: Cycles

At "another of these round-robin-speaker deals," Mikey is scared of the cycle he might get stuck in if he doesn't control his temper. (Mikey does get stuck in a conjunction loop: "But and so and but so.") Although here at the end of the novel the reader is likely paying more attention to the stories of Hal and Gately, it is important to note that the cycle of addiction and recovery continues everywhere and for people to whom we are not paying attention. Joelle entered the novel anonymously (as Madame Psychosis, Ch. 16.1), and now her exit (if this section is from her perspective) is also anonymous.

Chapter 28.22, Section 189, Pages 960-964
Note 383, Page 1079
14-15 November Y.D.A.U.

On his "first full night" in St. E's, Gately noticed "the shadow of somebody in a hat" (p. 810), placing the A.D.A. at St. E's on the night of 12 November (the description of the A.D.A.'s hat in this section matches that of n. 14). Pat's visit to Gately presumably occurred on 13 November, at which point Gately—who "couldn't see any shadows of anybody in a hat"—recalled that he had not told Pat about "the remorseless A.D.A." (pp. 817-8). The A.D.A. had been at St. E's "off and on for three days" before deciding to go "just down the hill" to Ennet House, which means his conversation with Pat in this section occurs either just before all the 14 November activity at Ennet described in Ch. 27 or, more likely, on (the presumably quieter) 15 November. The A.D.A. "for Suffolk County" (in his delirium, Gately assigned the A.D.A. to Essex County on p. 821) met Pat and her husband—"at the Marblehead Regatta for the McDonald's House thing for children, not this summer but [one summer]"—perhaps on the very night that Gately and Kite burglarized the A.D.A.'s home and took the toothbrush-in-bottom pictures (cf. pp. 55-6) that caused his wife Tooty's "oral-dental-hygienic-violation issues" (stemming from a dysfunctional childhood) to "reflare." The A.D.A. tells Pat that he has "harbored a resentment" against Gately over this incident and that his last chance at revenge on Gately (the death of DuPlessis, Ch. 7.4) "went federal and then fizzled."

Now, the A.D.A. is in a program "for codependency-issues surrounding loved ones who [a]re cripplingly phobic or compulsive, or both." Although the recent "incident with the Canadian assault, the alleged firearm, [and] the witnesses who can't depose"—which occurred in Enfield, part of Suffolk County—has provided him with another opportunity for revenge on Gately, his Group has said that he will be doomed if he acts on his resentment. The A.D.A., although he cannot say so publicly, has "already tossed the file." So, ironically, Gately's "going to two-step out of at the very least a probation-violation and prosecution on all his old *highly* convictable charges [except presumably the DUI bit (p. 463), which may be the reason the Middlesex County sheriff is at Ennet on 20 November (p. 958)] because I have to pitch the [new] case, for the sake of my own recovery." He says, "I have to make direct amends, put out my hand and say that I'm sorry and ask the man's forgiveness for my own failure to forgive. This is the only way I'll be able to forgive him. And I can't detach with love from Tooty's phobic compulsion until I've forgiven the b— the man I've blamed in my heart. . . . Whether he forgives or not is not the issue. It's my own side of the street I need to clean."

The A.D.A. is not sure why he is at Ennet, other than that Ennet is where Gately lives (Pat does not confirm this) and is just down the hill from the hospital. He tells Pat, "I couldn't simply leave again and drive home. Yesterday [Tooty]'d been at her tongue with one of those NoCoat LinguaScraper appliances [cf. pp. 413-4] until it bled. I can't go home and look on that again without having cleaned house. . . . I believe I have no choice. But I can't do it. I haven't been able to do it. . . . Yet. I wish to emphasize *yet*."

Gately notices the "seated shadow of somebody in a hat" on what is presumably the night of 15 November (p. 836); and Glenn K., who visits on what is presumably the morning of 16 November, asks (p. 844), "[W]ho's the fellow in the hat outside?" As of the morning of 20 November, the A.D.A. still has not confronted Gately.

PLOT AND CHARACTER: Ennet, Gately, AA&R
THEME: Non-Action, Fear/Obsess, Cycles, Recur, Waste

The A.D.A., like Mikey in the previous section, has trouble saying I'm sorry (although Mikey is able to do so and the A.D.A. is not). Although the A.D.A. believes he has "no choice" but to apologize, he is unable to take action against his desire for revenge, which puts him in an obsessive cycle of thought and non-action (cf. also "time passes and nothing moves forward," p. 963) with respect to this situation, which recalls an addict's wanting to quit and being unable to do so. Tooty's dental-hygiene obsession, stemming from childhood abuse, is quite severe and creates physical as well as mental problems. There are missed connections in that Gately could not have known the degree to which his revenge-prank would affect Tooty, and that currently Gately fears the A.D.A. because he mistakenly believes the A.D.A. is still out for revenge. The waste motif recurs in references to the toothbrush-in-bottom "incident," the A.D.A.'s "defecatory posture" (cf. p. 9), and the flagellant resonance of "Tooty." The A.D.A.'s appearance late in this chapter links this section to the first section of the chapter (cf. pp. 818, 821); his appearance late in the novel loops Gately's thread back to its beginning early in the novel (pp. 55-60); and his defecatory posture links p. 962 to p. 9.

Chapter 28.23, Section 190, Pages 964-971
Note 384, Page 1079
20 November Y.D.A.U.

The E.T.A. thread continues from Ch. 28.19. The first-person narration is now from the perspective of someone other than Hal. Usual gala guests at E.T.A.'s November exhibition (cf. p. 265) include the Gartons (a Dr. Garton was referenced by Kate Gompert on pp.

73 and 776), the Chawafs and Heavens (Soma Chawaf and P. A. Heaven are featured in Jim's work, cf. n. 24; and Soma Chawaf is a teacher at E.T.A., p. 154), and the Reehagens (a Mr. Reehagen was the Incandenza's next door neighbor in Weston, p. 1044). This year, after "the cancellation of the previous cancellation," the gala has been moved to the M.I.T. Student Union (home of the Madame Psychosis radio show, cf. p. 182). Matches will be played on "courts somewhere in the deep-brain tissue of the M.I.T. Student Union" (cf. Hal to Schtitt: "The human head [is w]here I'm going to occur as a player," p. 461). E.T.A. players are going through their traditional pre-match rituals. Arslanian still wears a blindfold. Pemulis has not been seen since this morning, but Doucette saw him by some dumpsters looking "anxiously depressed." Otis P. Lord, "out of post-op" (cf. p. 948), arrives to cheers, but will not play today. "An hysterical rumor" of "Québec adult *wheelchair*-tennis" squads flies "wildly around the locker room." Poutrincourt "looked to be AWOL." Hal is being taped by Head Trainer Barry Loach. Traub and Whale later said "Hal was being weird. Like they said asking Loach if the pre-match locker room ever gave him a weird feeling, occluded, electric, as if all this had been done and said so many times before it made you feel it was recorded" (cf. "they've all been just here before, just like this, and will be again tomorrow," p. 104). "But also, as a consequence, erasable." Hal's "face today has assumed various expressions ranging from distended hilarity to scrunched grimace, expressions that seemed unconnected to anything that was going on."

"One E.T.A. tradition" is a Big-Buddy-to-Little-Buddy recounting of "the Loach saga," which is given here in "outline form" on pp. 967-71. In the saga, Loach (inspiration for one of Orin's seduction strategies, cf. p. 1009) attempts to restore his older brother's spirit and faith in man so that the older brother will stay in seminary school and thereby exempt Loach from fulfilling their mother's wish that one of her children enter the clergy. "Loach challenges his brother to let him prove somehow . . . that the basic human character wasn't as unempathetic and necrotic as the brother's present depressed condition was leading him to think. . . . The spiritually despondent brother basically challenges Loach to not shower or change clothes for a while [and then to stand with] the downtown community's lumpen dregs [and] simply ask passerby to touch him [and thereby] extend some basic human warmth and contact." After nine months, Loach was in spiritual crisis himself and "dangerously close to disappearing forever into the fringes and dregs of metro Boston street life and spending his whole adult life homeless," when his appeal to be touched was granted "by E.T.A.'s own Mario Incandenza," who'd been sent on an errand by Jim, who was filming *Pre-Nuptial Agreement of Heaven and Hell* in "the Back Bay co-op" where *Infinite Jest* would be filmed (this filming places the incident circa 2001, when Mario would have been age ten or eleven, not age fourteen as stated). Mario's handshake "led through a convoluted but kind of heart-warming and faith-reaffirming series of circumstances to B. Loach, even w/o an official B.A.," being given a job at E.T.A. (cf. p. 316).

PLOT AND CHARACTER: E.T.A.
THEME: His/Father, Cycles, Recur

This section documents E.T.A. traditions: the pre-Thanksgiving gala, pre-match locker room rituals, and the telling of the Loach saga (another family history). Most E.T.A. players were first introduced via the locker room rituals of 3 November (Chs. 11.4, 11.6)—which began with Wayne farting and Schacht in his stall (p. 95)—and via subsequent Buddy meetings (Ch. 11.8). Here, after Schacht enters his stall and Wagenknecht is said to have really farted, a Buddy tradition (the Loach saga) is described. Hal has a feeling "as if all this had been done and said so many times before." The word "hunched" appears in reference to Wayne's ritual. The distraction of Loach's brother's pitching "playing cards into a wastebasket" while Loach talks to him recalls Hal's distracting Orin by "clipping [his] toenails into a wastebasket" (p. 242) during their 5 November phone conversation. There is a mythological reference to Camilla and a literary reference to *The Brothers Karamazov* (Does "the good old *Brothers K.*" recall the droogish syntax of *A Clockwork Orange*?) by Fyodor Dostoevsky (Wallace comments on "Joseph Frank's Dostoevsky" in his essay collection *Consider the Lobster*). For more philosophical debate on human resistance to self-sacrifice, cf. Marathe and Steeply in Ch. 21.3.

Chapter 28.24, Section 191, Pages 971-972
20 November Y.D.A.U.

The putatively Swiss hand-model that Orin met on 10 November (Chs. 26.9, 26.15) and was with again on 11 November (p. 655) and 14 November (n. 307) was revealed (p. 845) to be "one Mlle. Luria Perec, of Lamartine, county L'Islet, Québec," Tine's stenographer who "had long doubled" as DuPlessis's stenographer (p. 92). L'Islet is the same county in which Jim was buried (p. 65) in Avril's family plot (pp. 1030, 1041). Earlier this morning, there were phone messages from Orin on Hal's machine (p. 896). Now, Orin is being interviewed by Luria and Fortier, "the A.F.R. leader" who interviewed Orin on 10 November, who offered to "return at later time" (p. 601), and who left Enfield yesterday to get to this interview (p. 845).

Orin wakes up to discover that he is trapped inside a "huge and upside-down" "bathroom-type tumbler" "the size of a cage" (cf. Orin's treatment of bathroom roaches, p. 45). The light inside the tumbler "was the watery dancing green of extreme ocean depths." Orin has "possibly broken the leg's foot" trying to "kick his way out." "There were now smeared footprints on the glass" (like the footprints Orin saw on the inside of the windshield of his mother's car, p. 899). "Every few seconds Orin wiped the steam of his breath away from the thick glass." Orin can see the "hand-model" and the "handicapped fan" behind the glass. Orin tries to deny that this is "pretty clearly not one of his bad dreams." A voice through a small screen demands to know "Where Is The Master Buried." (Orin doesn't know that "perhaps half a dozen . . . cartridge-Masters" were buried with Jim (n. 160). How does the A.F.R. know to ask where the Master is buried rather than where it is hidden? Is it simply a French-to-English translation error, or is it more significant? Anyone that could have told the A.F.R. that the Master was buried with Jim could have told them where it was buried.) Then "the speaker's screen was withdrawn and the sewer roaches ["Orin's special conscious horror," p. 45] began pouring blackly and shinily through." As Orin "splayed [himself] against the tumbler's glass and pressed [his] face" flat against it (like Stice earlier this morning at E.T.A), he shrieked "Do it to her! *Do it to her!*"

PLOT AND CHARACTER: Orin, A.F.R.
THEME: Fear/Obsess, Recur

Orin's fear of roaches is described in his introduction into the novel (Ch. 6.3) and now surfaces to terrify him in his final appearance. Roaches are to Orin as rats are to Winston Smith in *1984*, but Winston actually names the person he betrays (Julia). Whom does Orin betray? It could be Luria or Avril, both natives of L'Islet County; but it is probably Joelle. Orin knows Joelle is in *Infinite Jest* and presumably has figured out that the A.F.R. is looking for the *Infinite Jest* Master, and it was Joelle that Orin presumably loved most.

Like Gately and Hal in this chapter, Orin is unsure if he is dreaming or awake. The cage and ocean images associated with Gately in this chapter are associated with Orin in this section. Orin has his face against glass. Orin wipes steam off glass, which recalls the name that upset Jim in a steamed window (n. 80) and Hal's "surreal memory of a steamed lavatory mirror with a knife sticking out of the pane" (p. 951). In Gately's dream of the smily-faced Sergeant at Arms with a shepherd's crook, the "walls were of like this weird thin clean clear glass" (p. 358). Orin sees Luria as the Subject; Luria sees Orin as the Subject. There is a missed connection in that the Master for which Luria is looking presumably is buried in her native county (n. 160).

Chapter 28.25, Section 192, Pages 972-981
Notes 385-388, Page 1079
20 November Y.D.A.U.

In Ch. 28.17, Gately's fever returned, and his erratic heart monitor caused an amber light to flash at the nurse's station (p. 937). Now, there is a flurry of activity in Gately's room. Presumably, Gately is experiencing the hemorrhage feared on p. 921. Gately, who feels "physically hotter than he'[s] ever felt," perceives that the "recently graduated" Chandler Foss and the Ennet House House Manager are there. "A voice that sounded like his own brain-voice with an echo said to never try and pull a weight that exceeds you" (is this wraith-Lyle?). Gately "gurgled and mooed, saying *addict*. Which was the truth, that he was, he knew." A "voice down the hall was weeping like its heart would break." "It occurred to [Gately] if he died everybody would still exist and go home and eat and X their wife and go to sleep" (compare this to Hal's thoughts on the repetitive cycle of day-to-day activities, p. 966). Gately overhears a conversation about homosexuals. "He saw the A.D.A. with his head bowed and his hat against his chest." "Somebody overhead asked somebody else if they were ready . . . and then he felt an upward movement deep inside that was so personal and horrible [the removal of the device from his throat] he woke up" (actually he returns to his dream-memory of Facklemann's demise).

Pamela Hoffman-Jeep has now climbed a tree and is looking in the window. She falls and is replaced by Bobby C in the window, who breaks in as the "fallen TP screen continued to show shots of small flames." Bobby C kicks Gately in the testicles to keep him from attempting to help Fax escape, which made Gately throw up. Soon there are fourteen people in the room: Fax; Gately; Bobby C; Des-Monts and Pointgravè (Sorkin's "Québecer muscleboys," cf. n. 369); the eczematic pharmacist's assistant; three "big unfamiliar girls . . . with red leather coats and badly laddered hose" and Adam's apples (Presumably one of the three "girls" is Poor Tony, who crews with C at the time of C's death over seven and a half years after these events. There are five other "girls" who "wear identical red leather coats" on p. 690, including Equus Reese, who Gately names on p. 887.); two Oriental punks in shiny leather jackets (cf. C's "crewing with slopes on the North Shore for Whity Sorkin in the days of his youth," p. 131) who carry in Pamela Hoffman-Jeep ("a white stick of bone protruding from her shin"); a "bland groomed corporate guy"; and a "small grim woman with a tight gray bun and sensible shoes."

The corporate guy rehung the teleplayer and inserted a new cartridge that was a "continuous still" of a "portrait Sorkin had let some neuralgic painter do of him having a cluster headache . . . for a series for an ad for aspirin" (cf. pp. 412-3; presumably this is the painting that upset "nine-year-old Hal," n. 162). Many of the people were drinking bourbon, and two of the "transvestals" were pulling grass from a "Glad bag." The "psoriatic assistant" shot up Facklemann with Narcan to counter the effects of the Dilaudid. Facklemann made sounds "like a long-submerged man coming up for air." From the corporate guy's CD player came extracted tracks of just "Linda McCartney singing backup and playing tambourine," which to Gately was "unspeakably depressing" as he imagined her "lost in the sea of her husband's pro noise, feeling low esteem and whispering off-key, not knowing quite when to shake her tambourine . . . . Two of the transvestals were doing the Swim to the awful tape." The pharmacist's assistant then shot up Gately with Sunshine (Canadian Talwin, the "third-hardest thing to street-cop after raw Vietnamese opium and the incredibly potent DMZ" (n. 387); cf. p. 170).

Gately hears Facklemann scream and sees that "the librarian-type lady [is] sewing Facklemann's eyelids open to the skin," like in the "movie the M.P.'d liked," the "one about ultraviolence and sadism" (the oft-referenced *A Clockwork Orange*). For Gately, the "very air of the room bulged. It ballooned"; "red coats were aflame"; and the "passing window exploded with light." Gately noticed one of the Québecers vomiting and the other bringing the TP with Sorkin's image over toward Facklemann. C moved around Gately "like a dancer to slow the fall" (the "[a]ttack of floors and sidewalks"). "A transvestal had P.H.-J.'s torn hem hiked up and a spiderish hand on her flesh-colored thigh. . . . Gately felt . . . disembodied. . . . His head left his shoulders. Gene and Linda were both screaming."

"The last rotating sight was the chinks coming back through the door holding big shiny squares of the room. As the floor wafted up and C's grip finally gave, the last thing Gately saw was an Oriental bearing down with the held square and he looked into the square and saw clearly a reflection of his own big square pale head with its eyes closing as the floor finally pounced. And when he came back to, he was flat on his back on the beach in the freezing sand, and it was raining out of a low sky, and the tide was way out."

PLOT AND CHARACTER: Gately, AA&R
THEME: Recur, Cycles, Memory, Dreams, Waste, Inf/Reg, Isolation

This chapter begins with a bulging ceiling and ends in a room in which "the very air" bulged; it begins and ends with Gately's memories of beaches. In Ch. 28.1, Gately learns that Chandler Foss has graduated Ennet; here Gately sees Foss in his room. As several people enter Gately's room at St. E's and he hears a discussion about homosexuals, several people (including "transvestals") enter the room of his dream-memory. The last thing Gately heard before waking up in St. E's was "Ready?" (p. 619), and the last thing he hears before he returns to his dream-memory in this section is "ready" (p. 974). Gately's dream-memory (prefaced by the heartbreaking weeping down the hall) is nightmarish. The room contains human waste (urine, a bowel movement, vomit). P.H.-J.'s bone sticks out of her skin, and she is touched with a "spiderish hand." "Everybody in the room's shadows were moving around on the west wall." Sorkin's image is scary, and the music is "unspeakably depressing." Gately's dream-memory late in the chapter—"They were small, the Orientals, and they were looking down at him, but neither had bad skin"—recalls a dream from early in the chapter of a "tiny acne-scarred Oriental woman looking down at him" (p. 828).

Gately feels disembodied, as if his head is separate from his body (analogous to seeing just a head in a TV or a mirror). Gately passes out looking at his big square head in a big square mirror (self-absorption). Facklemann will die after being forced to look at a big square screen with a huge image of Sorkin in pain. (Back in Y.D.A.U., Otis P. Lord's head has been freed of its monitor, but Poor Tony's head is now absorbed by screenings of *Infinite Jest*.) Other TV references include the "vertical hold" of Gately's vision and "Gene Gene the Fax Machine," which is an emendation of "Gene Gene the Dancing Machine" from the old TV Gong Show. There are references to water, cycles, dancing, and horizontality throughout this section: Facklemann "coming up for air" (ascending out of a stupor; cf. Joelle, pre-overdose, "like a diver preparing for a long descent" on p. 239), McCartney "lost in the sea," the transvestals dancing the Swim, Gately spinning to the floor (cf. his "rotating sight"), "C moving around him like a dancer to slow the fall," and Gately coming to "flat on his back" (like he is at St. E's) "on the beach."

Analogous to Molly Bloom in *Ulysses*, Gately ends *Infinite Jest* with a long, detailed sequence of dream-memories that moves to an intense climax; but Molly (in bed like Gately) drifts to sleep on a rising affirmation of her happiest memory of her husband, while Gately adds to his horrific dream-memories a coda in which he wakes up alone, like driftwood on a beach. (Gately's final look into the mirror was one of self-absorption rather than one of self-reflection. He "wrecks" instead of stopping, like the drivers duped by the mirrors of the Canadian terrorists.) Although this Y.W. event can be viewed as Gately's bottom, his recovery is delayed. He will soon enter prison, and when he gets out he will go back to drugs and burglary, only getting clean when he goes to Ennet in the wake of the DuPlessis incident over six years later. Gately used to dream that he was "under a sort of sea" (p. 449). However, "when he came back to" in this Y.D.A.U. dream-memory, "the tide was way out." Although Gately's eyes now "looked out at open sea" (p. 891), he knows that like the lobsters of his memory, he is still caged. Before descending into a horrific death at the novel's midpoint, Lucien Antitoi's "face's transparent image fills the glass" (p. 484), analogous to Gately's face filling a mirror at the novel's end. Lucien's descent, like Gately's, includes memories of water; after his death, Lucien ascends "newly whole, clean and unimpeded, . . . free, catapulted home" (p. 489). Since Lucien has died, he soars north "at desperate speeds" (p. 489); Gately's living ascent will be much slower. Gately's Y.W. descent into horror is documented at the end of the novel because it is from this low point that Gately will slowly ascend into sobriety. Gately's ascent is balanced by Hal's gradual "fall into the womb of solipsism, anhedonia, death in life" (p. 839), which accelerates as his dependence on marijuana grows.

Chapter 28: Under The Surface: Hunched, Horizontal, Histories, Hauntings

After the writhing weave of the previous chapter, this chapter focuses on the stillness—the horizontality—of Gately and Hal, heroes of non-action in this chapter who carry much of the narrative inside their heads. Haunting personal memories and family histories lie just under the surface of consciousness with the potential to erupt. The E.T.A. thread culminates in preparation for a gala inside a "brain" which is likely to erupt in a terrorist act. The word "hunched" is associated with tension before violent release and is linked to obsession, addiction, and sex throughout the chapter. The M.P. is "hunched drunk over his notebook's record of his Heinekens for the day," which often led to the beating of Gately's mother. "The original sense of addiction involved being bound over, dedicated, either legally or spiritually. To devote one's life, plunge in" (p. 900); which resonates with Facklemann, hunched before Mt. Dilaudid. The old decadent character is hunched over McNair's character in *Accomplice!* Wayne is hunched on his bench in a pre-match ritual.

Dreams and memories in this chapter are often of family histories, especially those of Gately and Hal; but there are also stories about Ewell, Day, Joelle, Kenkle and Brandt, Avril, Jim's work, the scam on Sorkin, Mikey, the A.D.A., and Loach. There is a haunted quality to the chapter, with its nightmare visions and wraiths. Stice screams when his face is torn away from glass. Orin puts his face to glass and shrieks. As Gately passes out, Facklemann and Linda McCartney are screaming. Many of the characters featured in this chapter will be dead (ghosts of memory) by the Year of Glad: Mrs. Waite, Kite, Facklemann, Bobby C, Stokely McNair, ("the late," p. 16) Cosgrove Watt, and presumably Poor Tony.

Images and phrases that resonate with the sea or submersion can be found throughout the chapter. Gately and Hal are submerged in their dreams and memories. Gately often dreams of the sea. Tiny Ewell relates an emerging memory of a "buried interval." Gately thinks of AA sexual predation as being a choice of "bottom feeders." In the "wake" of Joelle's visit, memories rise to the surface. Facklemann and Gately on Dilaudid are like men underwater. Facklemann's reaction to the Narcan is "like a long-submerged man coming up for air." The final phrase of the novel is "the tide was way out."

Infinite Jest VI
Underworld

The last chapter of *Infinite Jest* is infused with the imagery of underworlds. The characters are haunted by wraiths or by the ghosts of memory: by those now in the underworld, the land of the dead. Facklemann and Gately, participants in Boston's underworld crime network, are like men underwater under the influence of Dilaudid. For much of the chapter, Gately and Hal recede under the surface of consciousness into the underworld of memory, of the past. *Infinite Jest* begins in November 2010, chronicles various events up to November 2009 in episodic and chronologically fragmented fashion, and ends in flashbacks to 2001 (Loach, Ch. 28.23) and 2002 (Facklemann's demise, Ch. 28.25). "It is all falling indelibly into the past" is the last sentence of the prologue to Don DeLillo's *Underworld* (1997). The thread of DeLillo's prologue, set in 1951, is picked up in interludes following Parts 1, 3, and 5 of the novel, which begins in 1992 and cycles its way back to 1951-2 in Part 6. The last paragraph but six of DeLillo's epilogue, which completes another cycle by returning to the 1990s, is: "Everything is connected in the end" (cf. "the connectedness of all events," p. 96). In the last episode but five (Episode 68) of Pynchon's *Gravity's Rainbow* (1973), characters inject a powerful drug ("a CNS depressant") that causes people to experience "hauntings [of] a definite narrative continuity," "the presence of the dead," and "the discovery that *everything is connected*" (Pynchon). The lineage of DeLillo's *Underworld* (1997) and Wallace's *Infinite Jest* (1996)—twin towers (cf. *Underworld*'s cover) of complex, elegant fiction—can be traced through the past to works by Pynchon and Barth and Gaddis and Joyce and Melville and Sterne and on and on and on.

The bulging narrative tensions of *Infinite Jest* are balanced by recessions into the past, and the writhing weave of the various narrative threads stabilizes as those threads complete their cycles. Images at the end of both the E.T.A. and Orin threads resonate with images at the beginning of those threads. The reader was unaware of Joelle's entrance into the novel as Madame Psychosis, and now is not sure if it is Joelle behind the veil at Mikey's talk. The A.D.A. figured prominently at the beginning of Gately's thread, and is a consistent presence at the end of that thread. Also, the transvestals have a Glad bag at the novel's end, which signifies a connection back to the novel's beginning in the Year of Glad. (In the first edition, there is an incomplete circle escaping from the bottom right corner of p. 981. Is it leading us back to p. 3?) The end of *Infinite Jest* brings us back to the beginning. At the end of the novel, Gately is unable to communicate; at the beginning of the novel, Hal is unable to communicate. We can begin the cycle again and follow Gately's narrative thread through the DuPlessis incident and recovery and gunshot wound and memories of substance abuse. We can try to better understand Hal and to discern the reasons for his behavior in the Year of Glad. But there will always be a gap of one year (between November Y.D.A.U. and November Y.G., cf. this study's More Questions) in these elegant, complex narrative cycles that we must navigate by leaps of imagination. With each cycle of our reading, the gap will seem less daunting; but it will always remain open. As we read, we must continue to join the narrative threads—we must connect everything—in the nebulous underworld of our minds.

More Questions

How were copies of *Infinite Jest* obtained? Who is disseminating *Infinite Jest*?

Jim "ordered the cartridge's burial in the brass casket w/ him" (n. 80). "As far as can be determined, only [Jim's] lawyers, Avril, Disney Leith, and perhaps Mario, know that [some] cartridges were, in fact" buried with Jim (n. 160) in April Y.T.-S.D.B. (p. 910). Joelle says, "If it got made and nobody's seen it, the Master, it's in there with him. Buried. That's just a guess. But I bet you" (pp. 940-1). If the Master was buried with Jim, then either that Master was exhumed after his death or a Master copy was (or Master copies were) made—or multiple Read-Only copies were made—in the film lab before or when Jim went away for three days in March Y.T.-S.D.B. or during the "two-day purge and detox" a week later immediately before his death (p. 249), or during the funeral's delay (p. 65, n. 160.a). If a Master secretly was made in the lab, then new Read-Only copies could be made in the lab at any time. But who would make a copy (or copies) and why? Would Leith? He was Joelle's mentor when she first got interested in film (p. 297) and a teacher of "high-level esoteric Optics things" (p. 96). Would Avril? Her regular route from HmH to Comm.-Ad. presumably takes her through the film lab (cf. p. 51). Molly Notkin thinks Avril may have been jealous of Joelle (p. 791, cf. also n. 80), and it is unclear the extent to which Avril currently may be associated with Québecois terrorism. The A.F.R. does not seem to have direct access to Avril, although Wayne and Poutrincourt may be spies (p. 726). Jim linked his family with DuPlessis and Perec (p. 30). If Avril was involved with DuPlessis, then anytime after Jim's funeral Avril could have sent a copy (or copies) to DuPlessis when the cartridge's significance as a potential object of terror became known to her. Whoever made a copy (or copies) must have known not to view the cartridge(s). On 11 November Y.D.A.U. the cartridges in the tunnel under E.T.A. (p. 670) may have been copies of *Infinite Jest.* (But who would have just left these cartridges lying around? Were they hidden in an old box in the lab and accidentally thrown out?) The Tunnel Club took the cartridges to the trash; Clenette took cartridges from the trash to Ennet; Marathe saw cartridges in Pat's office and thought there might be "embossed smiles" on two of them (p. 750); and Johnette was asked to begin screening them on 14 November.

There seems to have been no dissemination of an *Infinite Jest* cartridge for two years after Jim's death. Then "ultimate cartridge-as-ecstatic-death" rumors began in "Dishmaster" (p. 233), and the following year (YUSHITYU) the D.E.A. and Academy of D.A.S. approached the U.S.O.U.S. ("two summers" before Y.D.A.U., p. 548) about the cartridge. Over the next two years (cf. pp. 548-9), cartridges appeared in Berkeley NCA, New Iberia LA, Tempe AZ, and Boston MA (the medical attaché incident). The Berkeley cartridge was stolen (by Canadian terrorists? cf. the "flannel fibers" at the scene of the crime (p. 549) and that "a good bit of Berkeley isn't answering their phone" in November Y.D.A.U. (p. 233), perhaps because the stolen cartridge has been put back in play); the New Iberia and Tempe cartridges are vaulted; and the U.S.O.U.S. presumably is studying the Boston cartridge. In addition, "[t]hree members of the Academy of D.A.S. had received unlabelled copies in the mail." Presumably these are also in safekeeping. In November Y.D.A.U. Tine is attempting to determine whether the cartridge has appeared again in Boston and whether Canadians are involved.

Shortly after the attaché incident of April Y.D.A.U., Steeply said, "Nobody has this mysterious Master ["this alleged Master copy from the DuPlessis burglary"], but we've all got Read-Only's—all the anti-O.N.A.N. cells have at least one Read-Only, we're pretty sure" (p. 489). But the A.F.R. only found out for sure that the cartridge existed when they discovered a Read-Only copy in the Antitois' shop (p. 725) in November Y.D.A.U. and therefore could not have sent the cartridge to the attaché, which matches Marathe's claim (p. 91), but recall that Marathe wants Steeply to think the A.F.R. has a cartridge (p. 489). The F.L.Q. cartridges (regular size and therefore not Masters, n. 303) were blank, a "hoax" (p. 722). The found Read-Only copy is assumed to be the one "burglared from the death of DuPlessis"; but (at least some of) the DuPlessis-to-Kite-to-Sixties-Bob-to-Antitoi cartridges had been examined by Lucien and found to be blank (cf. Ch. 27.29 summary), casting some doubt that the found Read-Only cartridge can be traced definitively to DuPlessis.

"There was reason to think M. DuPlessis had received his original copies from [Orin, and] Marathe felt [U.S.O.U.S.] felt [Orin] may have borne responsibility for the razzles and dazzles of Berkeley and Boston" (p. 723). Why would the A.F.R. suspect Orin? Jim alludes to his "family's sordid liaison with" DuPlessis and Perec (p. 30); but this seems to apply more to Avril than to Orin, given Avril's "involvement" with "the Québecois-Separatist Left while in graduate school" (p. 64) and that Orin doesn't recognize the hand-model as Perec. Recall Avril is from the same county as Luria Perec (p. 92). The locations in which the Entertainment has "popped up" might suggest Orin as a link. New Iberia LA is across the state from New Orleans where Orin played football before being traded to the Arizona Cardinals (pp. 45-6), but there seems to be no motive for Orin to send a cartridge there. Sending the cartridge to a "film-scholar" in Berkeley, to an "avant-garde film festival" (p. 548) in Tempe (near Phoenix where Orin lives), and to "members of the Academy of D.A.S." (pp. 548-9) could be a revenge scheme by Orin, who is knowledgeable of his father's critics (n. 145). Duquette was "in on" (n. 145) Jim's Found Drama joke and co-author of the Incandenza filmography (n. 24). If Orin is responsible for a new razzle in Berkeley, Duquette presumably would be exempt from revenge and therefore able to note that "a good bit of Berkeley isn't answering their phone" (p. 233), assuming Duquette's comment isn't a new joke.

The "*HAPPY ANNIVERSARY!*" cartridge sent to the Near Eastern medical attaché (one of his mother's lovers) on the anniversary of his father's death (cf. pp. 36, 249) could also be a revenge scheme on Orin's part. On the day Orin killed S. Johnson, Avril's ride away from E.T.A. was with the "swarthily foreign-looking monilial-internist medical resident" (p. 1049). Although Orin would be as aware as Hal that Jim found this man "especially torturing" (p. 957; cf. pp. 30, 992), this man's name is probably not the word Avril traced on the Volvo's window (pp. 999, 1048). In Y.D.A.U. the medical attaché is on "his first trip back to U.S.A. soil since completing his residency eight years ago [2001]" (p. 33). During filming of *Infinite Jest* in early 2004, "Avril had been with someone (Orin would not say who or whether he knew who) in the Volvo and had . . . presumably post-coitally idly written the person's first name in the steam of the steamed-up car window" (p. 999). If the name seen by Jim in the Volvo was the attaché's, Avril must have been thinking post-coitally of the attaché instead of the person with whom she was just in coitus. However, Avril could have continued her affair with the attaché, meeting on Canadian soil between 2001 and 2004. She presumably didn't stop leaving E.T.A. grounds until after Jim's funeral (p. 954). If the affair was ended by the attaché after Jim's death—due to a new relationship that would culminate in his October 2005 marriage (p. 36)—Avril might have more of a motive for sending the cartridge than Orin, especially if she prompted Jim's suicide by giving him the Wild Turkey (as Notkin suggests) to pave the way for a union with the attaché. But recall that it was Avril who drove Jim to the "two-day purge and detox" immediately before his death (p. 249). As with Gertrude in *Hamlet*, we cannot know the extent of Avril's complicity with respect to the death of her husband.

Although Avril may have had a motive for sending the cartridge to the attaché, the package sent to the attaché is "postmarked suburban Phoenix area" (p. 36, cf. p. 90), where Orin lives. The medical attaché is "migrating with the Prince and his retinue between InterLace's two hubs of manufacture and dissemination in Phoenix . . . and Boston" (p. 33), so if Phoenix-resident Orin was seeking revenge and looking for the medical attaché he could have been aware that the attaché was back in the country. Orin (or Avril) would have had a problem sending a cartridge to the attaché, given that the attaché was staying "in districts far from [the Prince's] legation's normal" lodgings (p. 34). Of course, an InterLace receptionist would know how to route a package to the attaché and could be easily influenced by Orin to give up an address. The package was sent with "routine O.N.A.N. postage" rather than "a diplomatic seal" (p. 36). Orin's strange phone conversation with Hal just over five weeks after the attaché incident (p. 32) is also suspicious. But if Orin sent the cartridge why would he be "ready for" (p. 597) a near-Eastern medical attaché to appear at his hotel door in November?

If Orin is sending copies, how did he get them? He probably has not been back to E.T.A. since his father's death (cf. Ch. 20.1 summary) and definitely not since Y.P.W. (p. 1015). Apparently, he continued to correspond with his family via mail and phone until YUSHITYU (pp. 244, 249), although the final mailings were "pseudo-form replies" (p. 244, cf. p. 1007). Presumably, Avril could have sent Orin a cartridge up until YUSHITYU if he had asked. If Orin somehow got the Master (or a Master copy), he would have had to clear hurdles to obtain the 585 r.p.m. cartridge-drive (n. 301) required to make copies, which would probably not be difficult for him; but note he is using a 450 r.p.m. drive to watch clips in his junior year at B.U. (p. 298). Orin seems to know nothing about the Master in his 20 November technical interview (Ch. 28.24).

Regarding cartridges sent through the mail, recall that Jim arranged for Mario's camera to be "forwarded from the offices of [his] attorney" (p. 315) after his death. Did Jim arrange for anything else to be mailed after his death? "HAPPY ANNIVERSARY!" is written on the attaché's cartridge in all-cap italics like the words the wraith puts in Gately's head (cf. p. 832). At what point did Jim's wraith enter the picture? Has someone already exhumed cartridges from Jim's coffin, letting out Jim's soul in the process (cf. 244)? Wraiths "couldn't ordinarily affect anybody or anything solid" (p. 831), so it seems unlikely that the wraith has anything to do with dissemination of the cartridges. But the wraith brought objects to show Gately; and objects (like Stice's bed) have been moving around mysteriously at E.T.A., activities which could be attributed to a wraith. However, (unlike the ghost of Hamlet's father) the wraith doesn't seem bent on revenge. In his interaction with Gately, he espouses "conversation or interchange." His "most serious wish was: *to entertain*" (p. 839). What could be more entertaining than a novel that espouses conversation and interchange about interesting questions that are difficult to answer definitively, thereby promoting the ongoing connection of the participants in those conversational interchanges?

What happens from late November Y.D.A.U. to late November Y.G.?

In the Year of Glad, Hal says, "At the only other emergency room I have ever been in, almost exactly one year back, the psychiatric stretcher was wheeled in and then parked beside the waiting-room chairs" (p. 16). (Is it significant that a woman with "an almost parodic Québecois accent" (p. 16) speaks to him?) What brings Hal to the emergency room in November Y.D.A.U.? It seems possible that the infiltrating A.F.R. might have attacked Hal. Hal has a "surreal memory [perhaps a premonition] of a steamed lavatory mirror with a knife sticking out of the pane" (p. 951) and (in Y.G.) "once saw the word *KNIFE* finger-written on the steamed lavatory mirror of a nonpublic bathroom" (p. 16). Perhaps the wraith (who communicates in all-cap italics in Gately's thread; c.f. p. 832) tried to warn Hal by "writing" in the mirror before an A.F.R. knife came at Hal (because the attacker is in a wheelchair, only the knife is high enough to be seen by Hal in the mirror, like Pemulis's spit on p. 95) at the 20 November gala. (Would a bathroom near the courts in the M.I.T. Student Union be considered nonpublic, though?) If Hal was successfully abducted and unable to provide the information the A.F.R. required, he may have been forced to watch *Infinite Jest.* Both the abduction and the viewing are highly unlikely, though. If the A.F.R. tried to attack Hal, they presumably were interrupted. Hal has come into the hospital on a psychiatric stretcher (perhaps from the trauma of almost being stabbed), which means he probably does not have a serious physical injury. Although Jim made *Infinite Jest* for Hal, the effect it would have on Hal presumably would be the same as on other people; therefore, since Hal is not asking to watch the cartridge in Y.G., he presumably has not ever watched the cartridge. Recall that at E.T.A. all of the cartridges in V.R.6 are carefully labeled (pp. 689, 714; *Infinite Jest* is always identified as an unlabeled cartridge) and that the cartridges in V.R.5 are usually in alphabetical order (p. 910), which presumably means they all have labels.

It is also unlikely that Hal has consumed the DMZ. Hal has sworn off drugs (p. 908), at least until he has passed his December Y.D.A.U. drug test. Anyone wanting to slip Hal the drug would be thwarted, because on the morning Pemulis notices that the DMZ is gone (taken by whom? cf. Ch. 28.14 summary) Hal is carrying his toothbrush with him at all times to guard against pranks involving accidental ingestion of unwanted substances. However, there are two things to consider with respect to the Hal's potential ingestion of DMZ or some other substance. First, Hal left his toothbrush and NASA glass with Troeltsch and Stice on p. 873. On his way back "to see about Stice's defenestration" (p. 896), he is hit with a panic attack. However, he has his toothbrush and NASA glass again on p. 897, so presumably someone brought Hal's toothbrush and NASA glass back to him. Therefore, something sinister could have occurred unbeknownst to Hal and the reader between p. 873 and p. 896. Second, the lead-in to the mold story in Y.G.—"I cannot make myself understood, now. . . . Call it something I ate" (p. 10)—seems to imply that Hal may have been affected by the mold he ate as a child or by the mold-based (p. 170) DMZ. However, Hal's inability to make himself understood is surely caused by his retreat into himself—his isolation. Hal's withdrawal from marijuana triggers and intensifies a realization that he has felt isolated since childhood. "Call it something I ate" presumably means that Hal associates eating with the earliest causes of his tendency to isolation. Eating cereal dosed by his mother with steroids (p. 30) may have contributed to Hal's superior intellect (cf. n. 76), a trait that might have exacerbated his social isolation. Even more likely, Hal may associate the beginning of his isolation and trust issues with the day he could not get his mother to come to him when he was scared and needed to be comforted after eating the mold (although recall that Hal doesn't remember this event and describes Orin's account of it). Hal is experiencing an extreme case of the type of loneliness that you and I might easily feel, not as victims of mind-altering drugs or entertainment, but just by being members of a culture that promotes self-obsession and discourages honest self-awareness.

Hal's behavioral changes in November Y.D.A.U. are most likely caused by his withdrawal from marijuana. After Hal quits marijuana, people at or near E.T.A. perceive him to have extreme reactions of joy or sadness (cf. Kate Gompert in withdrawal on p. 76 and in the throes of anhedonia in Ch. 27.13). Pemulis warned Hal that those who quit become the "walking dead" (p. 1066), and Joelle thinks withdrawal from alcohol led Jim to suicide. Hal seems to be falling into "the womb of solipsism, anhedonia, death in life" on which Jim's *Infinite Jest* was intended to "reverse thrust" (p. 839). Hal's communication problem in the Year of Glad may have begun on 20 November Y.D.A.U. and prompted a visit to the hospital on a psychiatric stretcher. It seems likely that withdrawal from marijuana, the onset of anhedonia, the pressures of competitive tennis, and Hal's (and his family's) obsessive nature have driven Hal to retreat internally, to regress to a state of incommunicability with others. In Y.D.A.U. Hal theorizes that "to be really human . . . is to be in some basic way forever infantile" (p. 695). In Y.G. Hal says "I have become an infantophile" (p. 16) and implies that a paper "from the last year [would look] like some sort of infant's random stabs on a keyboard" (p. 9). Hal makes the fluttering, incommunicative noises of an infant, which are terrifying to the administrators. However, Hal is able to express himself to the reader, and Hal's tennis game is excellent. "On court he's gorgeous. Possibly a genius," and his "ankle hasn't ached once this whole year" (p. 16). Hal's ankle began hurting at age 15 (p. 457), around the time he first smoked marijuana (p. 67). Although Hal has retreated so far into his head that his mind has trouble controlling (is distanced from) his body, his E.T.A.-trained body can still instinctively play tennis, a game which is "largely mental" (p. 269).

Lord and Wayne have both been treated at St. Elizabeth's in the days leading up to the gala. Hal is presumably taken there, too, and perhaps assigned the bed next to Gately recently vacated by Lord, who was out of post-op on the morning of 20 November (p. 965). Assuming Gately makes a full recovery from the medical problems he is experiencing at the end of the novel, he might meet Hal—who presumably is no longer able to communicate verbally—in the hospital. Assuming they meet, Gately should recognize Hal as the sad kid from his dream and might inform Hal (assuming Gately, no longer intubated, can now speak) that he has seen a wraith that claimed to be Hal's father (like Horatio informed Hamlet). Gately might tell Hal that Jim made his last film for Hal. Presumably Joelle goes back to Ennet after the Middlesex County sheriff leaves, tells Pat about the wheelchairs, and asks Pat to quarantine her (cf. p. 958). Pat could then inform Joelle that a veiled wheelchaired person (Marathe) applied for Ennet House on 14 November and didn't come back. If Joelle leaves quarantine to visit Gately while Hal is at St. E's, she should recognize Hal. Joelle might inform Hal that both the U.S.O.U.S. and the A.F.R. are searching for *Infinite Jest* and that she believes his father ordered the Master buried with him.

If Joelle does not visit, Hal might be able to deduce that there is an impending Continental Emergency from the Fully Functional Phil spots (Ch. 28.8), which presumably begin airing shortly after 20 November. Or Hal could find out from Orin, who apparently survives his technical interview, given that he is referenced in Y.G. ("The brother's in the bloody NFL for God's sake," p. 14). Given Hal's memory (Ch. 1.5) and Gately's dream (Ch. 28.15), Hal and Gately presumably meet at some point after they each leave the hospital and decide to do something about the Continental Emergency (or at least to retrieve something from Jim's grave). Gately might be motivated to protect Joelle from the "wheelchairs." Hal might feel a sense of responsibility as the son of the *auteur*. If Hal learns that Gately works at Ennet House, where Hal spoke with Johnette Foltz on 17 November (Ch. 27.40), he might decide to ask Gately for help with his marijuana withdrawal. Hal might also see Joelle at Ennet if he did not see her at the hospital. Given Johnette's recall of Hal "[m]uch later, in subsequent events' light" (p. 787), something ominous concerning Hal happens at Ennet House. Perhaps he is just there seeking information about recovery, and Johnette reacts to him the way the Arizona administrators do; but it is also possible that he is at Ennet (called there by Gately or Joelle?) because the Tunnel-Club-to-trash-to-Clenette cartridges turned out to be copies of *Infinite Jest* and are causing a problem at Ennet.

At some point Hal presumably learns that the Master was supposed to be buried with his father (nn. 80, 160) and goes to his father's grave. But Hal is apparently looking for something in his father's head rather than looking through the cartridges that should be in the casket unless someone has taken them. In Gately's dream, Hal is "trying to scream at Gately that the important thing was buried in the guy's head and to divert the Continental Emergency to start digging the guy's head up before it's too late." Hal "holds something terrible up by the hair and makes the face of somebody shouting in panic: *Too Late*" (p. 934). Exactly one year before his death, Jim told Hal that he had a "gyroscopic balance sensor and *mise-en-scene* appropriation card and priapistic-entertainment cartridge implanted" in his head (p. 31). During the editing process of *Infinite Jest* (Hal tells Orin) Jim "[flew] off somewhere for three days, for what the impression I get was work-related business. Film-related. If Lyle didn't go with him Lyle went somewhere, because he wasn't in the weight room. I know Mario didn't go with him and didn't know what was up" (p. 249). Perhaps Jim was having those items removed from his head and having the *Infinite Jest* Master (or the rumored antidote to *Infinite Jest*) installed in his head (if this is true, then presumably copies of *Infinite Jest* were made earlier without Jim's knowledge and eventually distributed). If anything was in Jim's head, it could have been damaged by microwave pressure. Given that Hal believes they are too late, either the A.F.R. have beaten them to the grave (but how would they know to take something from Jim's head?) or Hal is mistaken about how to divert the Continental Emergency. If *Infinite Jest*'s appeal is due to holography (p. 490) and *Infinite Jest* has caused a Continental Emergency, this may be why Hal considers the inventor of holography, Dennis Gabor, a potential Antichrist (p. 12). Perhaps Hal is attempting to alleviate his father of some of the culpability for the Emergency.

John Wayne is "standing watch in a mask" as Hal and Gately dig up Jim's head. This might be a smiley-faced A.F.R. mask; but if Hal is trying to divert the Continental Emergency, why would an A.F.R. operative be there, presumably supporting the diversion? If Wayne was originally a spy, perhaps he changed his mind. Perhaps he was attempting to engage Hal about his change of mind on the two occasions he looked in on Hal but didn't speak. But then why is Wayne wearing a mask? Why isn't Wayne competing in the What-aBurger in Y.G.? Recall that there is "very little doubt" in Hal's mind "that Wayne would have won" (p. 17). What roles, if any, do others associated with E.T.A.—like the AWOL Poutrincourt or the unknown spy or Avril—play in the Continental Emergency? If the Emergency was not diverted, then what were/are the consequences? What is the significance of the Year of Glad being "the very last year of O.N.A.N.ite Subsidized Time" (n. 114)?

Interpretation

Our ability to connect with other people is compromised by our inclination to self-obsession and self-absorption. We are all on some level dreamers, addicts, and deceivers: vulnerable to our compulsive tendencies. Although our social systems are built around the ideal of achieving the greatest good for the greatest amount of people, technological advances often promote isolation and self-focus rather than communication with others. We are generally focused on practicalities, on personal gain, and on the details and patterns of our daily lives; and our stories and conversations generally lead back to ourselves. We are anxious about the vulnerability inherent in our dependency on each other, which causes us to mask our true selves and drives us to physical, mental, and spiritual isolation. We are creatures of habit, of cycles and rituals and routines, often powerless against our compulsions and resistant to change, preferring to discount simple truths as naïve clichés rather than trusting the wisdom of those truths to guide us through the effort of honoring them. Isolation and denial intensify the loneliness of our pursuits and the horrors, secrets, and surprises that always loom for us; but the truth of our remembered experiences—that our histories are shaped by our families and by other people—lies just under the surface of consciousness to haunt us if we persist in our denials.

However, we are capable of making choices: of recognizing that substances and entertainment and other habitual compulsions distract us from simple but difficult truths and that "we (who are mostly not small children) know it's more invigorating to *want* than to *have*" (p. 694; cf. p. 205); of choosing awareness over denial; of reversing our retreat into ourselves; of honoring the reality and the necessity of our dependence on each other; of risking connection with other people; and of choosing action over stasis. Even if that action seems repetitive and pointless, it is better to abide moment-to-moment than to succumb to the passivity of paralyzed stasis. Making these choices does not diminish our compulsive and selfish tendencies. Therefore, keeping these choices in mind and acting on them is forever difficult, and there is no guarantee that we will maintain the discipline to act on these choices each day. But once we have acknowledged truths that are as sobering and undeniable as the fact of our mortality, it is better to look for comfort or humor in those truths than to hide from them. "Now get you to my lady's chamber and tell her, let her paint an inch thick, to this favor she must come. Make her laugh at that" (*Hamlet*, V.i.186-9).

Outline

Pages 489-92 present a thematic outline of *Infinite Jest*. Each of the 192 sections of the novel has been titled with a phrase (or phrases) from the text or notes of that section. The chapter titles (most of which are also derived from the text or notes) and unit titles are those that have been used throughout the study. Each section is identified by its chapter or subchapter, page numbers, notes, and most prominent characters (or occasionally by its plot or setting). Readers may wish to compare this thematic outline with the plot-based outlines of K. O'Neill and Steve Russillo.

This outline was constructed as an attempt to discover the essential ideas of the novel and to represent those ideas succinctly. For readers who prefer using poetry to get at the essence of things, the 13th section of Wallace Stevens's *Esthetique du Mal* is an excellent poetic complement to *Infinite Jest*. In the poem, "a man,/Reclining, eased of desire" is "sure of a reality/Of the longest meditation, the maximum"; and "The force that destroys us is disclosed, within/This maximum, an adventure to be endured/With the politest helplessness. Ay-mi!/One feels it action moving in the blood." Readers who prefer a critical essay on the thematic scope of *Infinite Jest* are directed to Ch. 4 of Marshall Boswell's *Understanding David Foster Wallace*, which also cites text by Wallace Stevens.

Sec.	Chap.	Pages	Notes	Plot/Character	Outline
				I. DISCONNECTED: DANGERS, ADDICTIONS, DECEPTIONS, BOUNDARIES, BAD DREAMS	
	1				**Surrounded By Heads And Bodies**
1	1.1	3-10		Hal	I Am In Here
2	1.2	10-11		Hal	I Ate This
3	1.3	11-13		Hal	I Am Not Just A Boy Who Plays Tennis
4	1.4	13-15		Hal	I Simply Lie There, Listening
5	1.5	15-17		Hal	I Have Become An Infantophile
6	2	17-27	1	Erdedy	**An Immobility That Seemed Like The Gathering Of A Force**
7	3	27-31		Hal/Jim	**Are You Hearing Me Talking, Dad?**
8	4	32-33		Hal/Mario/Orin	**The Connection Was Cut**
	5				**Fatally Pretty**
9	5.1	33-37		Attaché	Without Having To Remove His Eyes
10	5.2	37-38		Clenette	Sick Down In My Insides To Look At It
11	5.3	38-39		Green	A Vision In A Sundress And Silly Shoes
	6				**After Himself Passed Away**
12	6.1	39-42		Hal/Mario	From Either Side Of Some Unbridgeable Difference
13	6.2	42		Attaché	Still Watching
14	6.3	42-49	2	Orin	A Kind Of Desiccated Circle
	7				**Overlooked**
15	7.1	49-54	3-10	Hal	Attached To The Secrecy
16	7.2	54	11	Attaché	He Sits There, Attached
17	7.3	54-55		Mario	Show The Tapes
18	7.4	55-60	12-20	Gately/DuPlessis	Bound To His Chair
19	7.5	60		Tech	Killer Apps
20	7.6	60-61	21-22	Troeltsch	You Can't Escape Looking
21	7.7	61-63		Hal	A Face In The Floor
	8				**A Great Loss In At Least Three Worlds**
22	8.1	63-65	23-25	Jim	The Man's Very Gradual Spiral
23	8.2	65-66		Orin	He Doesn't Loop Or Spiral
	9				**The Lines That Bound And Define Play**
24	9.1	66-67		Pemulis	A Kind Of Semi-Sleep Like Trance
25	9.2	67-68	26-27	Hal	A Kind Of Psychodysleptic Sominex
	10				**Paralyzed Stasis**
26	10.1	68-78	28-30	Gompert	A Frightening Smile
27	10.2	78-79		Attaché	His Rictus Of A Face
28	10.3	79-85	31-36	Schtitt/Mario	The Happy Pleasure Of The Person Alone
29	10.4	85-87		Ewell	Little Smiles And Grimaces
30	10.5	87		Attaché	Not One Bit Distressed Or In Any Way Displeased
	11				**Limits And Rituals**
31	11.1	87-92	37-41	Marathe/Steeply	Shadow-Play
32	11.2	93		O.N.A.N.	Protective Walls
33	11.3	93-95	42	Marathe/Steeply	This Little Interface Of You And Me
34	11.4	95-97		E.T.A.	The Connectedness Of All Events
35	11.5	97		Marathe/Steeply	Night, Emerging
36	11.6	97-105	43	E.T.A.	A Grief Felt In The Bones
37	11.7	105-109	44-45	Marathe/Steeply	Attached, Fanatically; A Citizen Of Nothing
38	11.8	109-121	46	E.T.A.	Deeply Alone
39	11.9	121-126		Mario/Hal	Secret Minutes Alone
40	11.10	126-127	47-48	Marathe/Steeply	Some Sort Of Game
41	11.11	127		Marathe/Steeply	Your Walled Nation
	12				**A Weight Greater Than Their Own Weight**
42	12.1	127-128		Lyle	Off The Sweat Of Others
43	12.2	128-135		Poor Tony	Wet Work
	13				**Working Alone**
44	13.1	135-137		Orin/Hal	About Separation
45	13.2	137-138	49-51	Ennet	Tradition Of Anonymity
46	13.3	138-140		Glynn	Trying To Do The Job Alone
47	13.4	140-142		Hal	Riding Lonely Herd In Paradise
48	13.5	142-144		Steeply/Poor Tony	Kept From The Light Of Public Knowledge
49	13.6	144		Anti-O.N.A.N.	Opposition To Interdependence
50	13.7	144-151		Tech	Reluctant To Leave Home
51	14	151-156	52-55	Pemulis/Mario/Hal	**Closely Monitored**
	15				**Managed Fear**
52	15.1	157-169		Jim	Desperately Forward Toward The Net
53	15.2	169-171	56-57	Pemulis/Hal	Kinetic Even In Stasis, Plowing Temporally Ahead
54	15.3	172-176		Hal	Fall Forward Into The Court
55	15.4	176-181	58-59	Ennet	How Come I Can't Stop, If I Want To Stop

Sec.	Chap.	Pages	Notes	Plot/Character	Outline
				II. DETAILS, PATTERNS	
	16				**Circulars and Catalogues**
56	16.1	181-193	60-66	WYYY/HmH	Over Time Some Kind Of Pattern Emerges, A Trend Or Rhythm
57	16.2	193-198	67	E.M.P.H.H./Gately	Seven Moons Orbiting A Dead Planet
58	16.3	198-200	68	E.T.A.	Various Resistance-Systems
59	16.4	200-211	69-72	Ennet	More Exotic New Facts, Intoxicated Impulses
60	16.5	211-219	73-77	Pemulis/Axford/Hal	The Window Of Opportunity
	17				**Veiled Veils**
61	17.1	219-223		Joelle	She's Lost The Ability To Lie To Herself
62	17.2	223	78	O.N.A.N.	Subsidized Time
63	17.3	223-226	79	Joelle	Unconstrained Concealment
64	17.4	227		Steeply	Helen P. Steeply
65	17.5	227-240	80-81	Joelle	The Encaged Rapacious Thing Inside
	18				**Probing For Details**
66	18.1	240-242		Enfield	Waiting Underground For Anyone Who Digs
67	18.2	242-258	82-84	Hal/Orin/Jim	Stained-Family-Linen-Type Questions
	19				**Trying To Locate Patterns In Each Other's Rhythms**
68	19.1	258-270	85-89	E.T.A./Schacht	Competitive Tennis Is Largely Mental
69	19.2	270-281	90-91	Ennet/Gately	The Disease Makes Its Command Headquarters In The Head
70	19.3	281-283	92	E.T.A.	The Whole Mammoth Travelling Squad
	20				**Both Destiny's Kisses And It's Dope-Slaps**
71	20.1	283-299	93-101	Orin	The Roar Gathering, Tidal, Amniotic
72	20.2	299-306	102-103	Poor Tony	A Rushing Train Roar That Was No Train On Earth
	21				**The Only Thing Of Importance, Choosing**
73	21.1	306-312	104-112	E.T.A./Hal/Orin/A.F.R.	Separation And Return's Real Meaning
74	21.2	312-317	113-119	Mario	Buttressed On Sets Himself Had Him Help Erect
75	21.3	317-321		Marathe/Steeply	Not Someone Outside You, This Enemy
				III. INTERDEPENDENCE	
	22				**Triggering Situation**
76	22.1	321-342	120-130	E.T.A./Eschaton	Degenerating Into Chaos
77	22.2	343-367	131-141	AA&R/Gately	This Cliffish Nexus Of Exactly Two Total Choices
78	22.3	367		O.N.A.N.	Changed Each 1 Jan.
79	22.4	367-375	142-143	AA&R	One Particular Seminally Scarring Night
80	22.5	375		Marathe/Steeply	Back In The Field Of Duty
81	22.6	375-376	144-145	Jim/Lyle/Orin	Found Drama
82	22.7	376-379		AA&R	The Arrow Of Responsibility
83	22.8	379	146	Jim/Lyle/Mario	The Odd Couple Of Libations
	23				**Hygienic Stress**
84	23.1	380-386	147-151	E.T.A./O.N.A.N.	Sucrotically Mad, The Gala But Rather Ironic Annual Celebration
85	23.2	386-390	152-153	Lyle/E.T.A.	Stunted Desire, Snared By Something Untrue
86	23.3	391-394		O.N.A.N.	Historical Headers, A Whole Bright Spanking New Millennium
87	23.4	394-395		Lyle/E.T.A.	Do Not Underestimate Objects
88	23.5	395-398	154-155	Hal/Jim	Severe Compulsion-Issues, Audience-Obsessed Pieces
89	23.6	398-410	156-160	O.N.A.N./E.T.A.	Willing To Eliminate Own Map Out Of Sheer Pique
90	23.7	410-418	161-168	Hal/O.N.A.N.	The Vulnerable Psyche Of An Increasingly Hygiene-Conscious U.S.A.
91	23.8	418-430	169-174	Marathe/Steeply	Knowledgeable Choices About Pleasure And Delay
92	23.9	430-434	175	E.T.A.	The Clipperton Suite
93	23.10	434-436		Gately	Human Waste In The Showers
94	23.11	436-442	176-177	E.T.A./O.N.A.N.	A Desolate Late-Day Hysteria
	24				**The Human Head**
95	24.1	442-449	178-179	Gately	Burpling Greasily Up Into Memory
96	24.2	449-450	180	Hal	Like Somebody's Mind Coming Apart
97	24.3	450-461	181-187	E.T.A.	The Game's Two Heads' One World
98	24.4	461-469	188-197	Gately	Like Your Mind Wasn't In Possession Of Your Body
99	24.5	470-475	198	Marathe/Steeply	The Department of Euphoria, So To Speak, Within The Human Brain
100	24.6	475-489	199-207	Gately/A.F.R.	Lucien's Leonine Head Is Tilted Back
				IV. AROUND IN CIRCLES	
	25			**Cycles: Orbits, Annulation, Attraction, Repulsion**	
101	25.1	489-491		Marathe/Steeply	A Ring Of Smaller And Palsied Fires, Hologrammatical Activity
102	25.2	491-503	208	Jim/Tech	Somersaults With One Hand Nailed To The Floor
103	25.3	503-507		AA&R/Ennet	NA's Traditional Huge Circle, Indiscriminate Hugging
104	25.4	507-508		Marathe/Steeply	The Stars' Light Had Paled, Empty Of Intent
105	25.5	508-527	209-221	Hal/Avril/E.T.A.	Seeming To Recede, Pulsing With Swollen Proximity
106	25.6	528-530	222-223	Marathe/Steeply	False Dawns, A Stillness, Just Below The Ring Of Night
107	25.7	531-538		Gately/Joelle	Around In Circles, Annular And Insidious, Deformed With Beauty

Sec.	Chap.	Pages	Notes	Plot/Character	Outline
	26			**Powerless: Compulsion, Secrecy, Ritual, The Cult Of The Infant**	
108	26.1	538-547	224-227	Lenz	A Panoply Of Strange Compulsive Habits
109	26.2	548		Ennet	None Of The Doors Inside Ennet House Have Locks
110	26.3	548-549	228-229	Tine	No Other Activity Or Connection Could Hold Their Attention
111	26.4	550-553		Pemulis/Avril	Absence Of Control
112	26.5	553-559	230-233	Lenz/Green	Give Up All Of Your Power
113	26.6	560		Hal	Over 200 Breaths
114	26.7	560-563		Lenz/Green	Propitiating The Infant
115	26.8	563-565		Gately	Individual-Resident-Informal-Interface Moments
116	26.9	565-567	234-235	Orin	The One
117	26.10	567-574	236-238	Pemulis	An Incredible Slowing Down Of Time
118	26.11	574-575		Orin	Cycle Of Seduction
119	26.12	575-589	239-241	Lenz/Green	Getting Chewed By Something Huge And Tireless And Patient
120	26.13	589-593	242-244	Mario	Real Stuff
121	26.14	593-596	245	Gately	The Picayune And The Unpleasant
122	26.15	596-601		Orin	Emotions Of Mastery And Control And Superiority And Pleasure
123	26.16	601-619	246-256	Gately	One Part Of Something Bigger He Can't Control
				V. A WRITHING WEAVE	
	27			**A Kind Of Writhing Weave: Horrors, Secrets, Pursuits, Surprises**	
124	27.1	620-626	257-258	Engineer/A.F.R.	Look Out Below, Shriek-Roused Figures
125	27.2	627-638	259-262	E.T.A.	Sudden Anomalies
126	27.3	638-648	263-264	Marathe/Steeply	Pulled Apart In Different Directions
127	27.4	648-651		Day/Gompert	Total Psychic Horror
128	27.5	651-662	265-268	E.T.A.	A Place Inside That Can't Be Chewed
129	27.6	663-665	269	Orin/Avril	Closing In, Arms Open Wide, Smiling
130	27.7	666-673	270-272	E.T.A.	Underground For No Good Or Clear Reason
131	27.8	673-682	273-277	E.T.A./Hal	Forgetful Will
132	27.9	682-686	278	Matty	Unable Not To Be Afraid
133	27.10	686-689	279	Hal	A Clear Internal-Conflict Moment
134	27.11	689-691		Poor Tony	A Deceptive Feeling Of Well-Being
135	27.12	692		Day	The Frightful Hog
136	27.13	692-698	280-283	Gompert/Hal	The Great Transcendent Horror
137	27.14	698-700	284-286	Gompert	Psychotically Depressed
138	27.15	700		Troeltsch	Preparing To Call The Action
139	27.16	700		Pemulis	Careful Not To Let It Fall
140	27.17	700		Lyle	Eyes Rolled Up
141	27.18	701		Mario/Schtitt	Downhill Flight, Preparing To Whoop
142	27.19	701		Avril	All Going At Once
143	27.20	701-711	287-295	Hal/Joelle	Double-Bound Desperation
144	27.21	711-714	296-298	E.T.A.	Narratively Prolix And Tangled Stuff
145	27.22	714-716	299	Gompert	Right Up Close, Looming In
146	27.23	716-719		Lenz	Another Circle Around That Circle
147	27.24	719		A.F.R.	Turning All The Stones
148	27.25	719-721		Poor Tony	Something Unimaginable Is Chasing You
149	27.26	721-723	300-302	A.F.R.	The Wrath Of A Neighbor Struck Down, Fatal Pleasures
150	27.27	723		Fortier	Senses Of Purpose
151	27.28	723-724		Joelle	A Fear Of Her Teeth
152	27.29	724-728	303	A.F.R.	Happy Pursuit
153	27.30	728-729		Lenz	A Kind Of Second City
154	27.31	729-735	304	Marathe/Day/Struck	A Clatter And Two Shrieks, Heads Full Of Parts
155	27.32	736-747	305-310	Joelle	The Second-Saddest Family Joelle'd Ever Seen
156	27.33	747-751	311-313	Marathe	Thinking Along Several Parallel Tracks
157	27.34	751-752		Joelle	Careful Rings
158	27.35	752-755	314-315	Marathe	Confusion Of Choices
159	27.36	755-769	316-319	Mario/Avril	A Kind Of Writhing Weave
160	27.37	769-774	320	Hal/Mario	Real Monsters
161	27.38	774-782		Marathe/Gompert	The Pain Of The Chains And Cage Of Never Choosing
162	27.39	782-785	321	Hal/Mario/Pemulis	Points Moving Inexorably Towards Each Other
163	27.40	785-787	322-323	Ennet/Hal	The Kid At The Door
164	27.41	787	324	Pemulis	Never Trust The Father You Can See
165	27.42	787-795	325-331	Notkin/U.S.O.U.S.	The Exact Same Kind Of Monster, A Direct Facial Hit
166	27.43	795	332	Pemulis	Close-Mouthed And Breathing With Terrible Ease
167	27.44	795-808	333-336	Hal	Tensed Menace, A Living Thing That's Chosen To Hold Itself Still

Sec.	Chap.	Pages	Notes	Plot/Character	Outline
				VI. UNDERWORLD	
	28			**Under The Surface: Hunched, Horizontal, Histories, Hauntings**	
168	28.1	809-827	337-341	Gately/Ennet	The Shadow of Something Dark
169	28.2	827-845	342-343	Gately/Jim	Feelings Of Communicative Impotence And Mute Strangulation
170	28.3	845-846		A.F.R.	A Brief Period Of The Tension
171	28.4	846-851		Gately	More Dark Myth
172	28.5	851-854	344-346	Hal	Standing On One Foot In The Dark
173	28.6	854-864	347-351	Gately/Joelle	Personal Historical Snapshots
174	28.7	864-876	352-353	Hal/E.T.A.	His Forehead Up Against The Glass
175	28.8	876-883		U.S.O.U.S.	Stuff Of Fucking Nightmares
176	28.9	883-896	354-361	Gately	Let Them Come As They Will, But Do Not Entertain Them
177	28.10	896-902		Hal	Real Beaks And Claws, Intense Horizontality
178	28.11	902-906	362-365	Gately	Out Of Nowhere The Sidewalk Comes Rushing Up To Meet You
179	28.12	906-911	366	Hal/Pemulis	Desiccated, Deprived Of Some Essential Fluid
180	28.13	911-916	367-371	Gately	Real Addiction And What It Can Turn Someone Into
181	28.14	916		Pemulis	Looking Up Into The Darkness
182	28.15	916-934	372-376	Gately	A Thing That Basically Hides
183	28.16	934		Joelle/Steeply	Almost Mind-Boggling Danger
184	28.17	934-938	377	Gately	Like Men Deep Under Water
185	28.18	938-941		Joelle/Steeply	Terminally Compelling
186	28.19	941-958	378-382	Hal/E.T.A.	People Broken Into Pieces And Trying To Join
187	28.20	958		Joelle	A Linen-Pale Version Of What She Really Looked Like
188	28.21	958-960		AA&R/Joelle	Another Of Those Round-Robin-Speaker Deals
189	28.22	960-964	383	Ennet	Time Passes And Nothing Moves Forward
190	28.23	964-971	384	E.T.A./Loach	Postures And Little Routines, Begging For One Touch Of A Human Hand
191	28.24	971-972		A.F.R./Orin	Pretty Clearly Not One Of His Bad Dreams
192	28.25	972-981	385-388	Gately	Like A Long-Submerged Man Coming Up For Air

Chronologies

Pages 494-6 present a more-or-less chronological ordering of *Infinite Jest* by subchapters. Although this ordering is intended to serve as a timeline to orient the reader, care was taken to list subchapters in a way that would support a more-or-less chronological reading of the novel. Subchapters without a heading and for which a year and date cannot be determined from the text are designated "unspecified" and are assumed to occur as of or by Y.D.A.U. Subchapters occurring in Y.D.A.U. for which a more specific date cannot be determined from the text are designated "unspecified Y.D.A.U." and are placed after the sections occurring as of or by Y.D.A.U. Occasionally dates have been assumed to facilitate a more-or-less chronological reading of the novel. Notes have been listed in the chronology when the date of the note is different than the date of the subchapter in which the note was referenced. Subchapters in parentheses have been referenced twice in the timeline.

Partial chronologies are provided for Gately (pp. 496-7), for Joelle (pp. 497), and for events in November Y.D.A.U. (pp. 498). Readers may wish to compare the chronologies of this study with Stephen Burn's chronology (Burn, pp. 81-92).

A More-Or-Less Chronological Ordering Of *Infinite Jest* By Subchapters

Subsidy	Year	Date	Subchapters
B.S.	1960	Winter	Ch. 15.1
B.S.	1963	Winter	Ch. 25.2
B.S.	early '90s	unspecified	n. 76 [Hal is a toddler]
B.S.	1997	March-early April	(Ch. 1.2) [flashback from late November Y.G.; Hal is 4, almost 5]
B.S.	c. '99-'01	unspecified	Ch. 22.8
Y.W.	2002	Winter	Ch. 22.6
Y.T.M.P.	2003	April 1	Ch. 3
Y.T.-S.D.B.	2004	unspecified	Ch. 5.2
		April-May	Ch. 7.7 [flashback from unspecified, Hal is almost 12]
Y.P.W.	2005	February 21	Ch. 13.4
Y.W.-Q.M.D.	2006	June	n. 110.2-3
YUSHITYU	2007	April	Ch. 15.3
Y.D.P.A.H.	2008	unspecified	Ch. 9.2 [flashback from unspecified, Hal is almost 16]; Ch. 18.1
		June 26	Ch. 13.3
		Autumn	Ch. 7.4
		December 24	Ch. 12.2
unspecified		unspecified	Ch. 5.3; Ch. 11.2; Ch. 13.2,6; Ch. 22.3; Ch. 26.2
Y.D.A.U.	2009	As Of, By	Ch. 8.1; Ch. 13.7
		unsp. Y.D.A.U.	Ch. 2; Ch. 6.1; Ch. 7.5; Ch. 9.1; Ch. 10.1,3; Ch. 12.1; Ch. 17.2,4; Ch. 20.1; Ch. 21.2
Y.D.A.U.	2009	April 1-2	Ch. 5.1; Ch. 6.2; Ch. 7.2; Ch. 10.2,5
		April 30-May 1	Ch. 11.1,3,5,7,10-11; Ch. 21.3; Ch. 22.5; Ch. 23.8; Ch. 24.5; Ch. 25.1,4,6; Ch. 27.3
		May 9	Ch. 4
		May	Ch. 7.3
		July	Ch. 24.1
		August 10	Ch. 13.5

A More-Or-Less Chronological Ordering Of *Infinite Jest* By Subchapters

Subsidy	Year	Date	Subchapters
Y.D.A.U.	2009	October	Ch. 6.3
		October	Ch. 7.1 [after Hal's 17th birthday]
		mid October	Ch. 11.9
		October 15	Ch. 14
		October 22-23	Ch. 16.1
		very late October	Ch. 24.2
		Sunday, Nov. 1	Ch. 8.2
		Tuesday, Nov. 3	Ch. 7.6; Ch. 11.4,6,8; n. 145; Ch. 13.1
		early November	Ch. 10.4; Ch. 16.2; Ch. 26.3
		Wed., Nov. 4, E.T.A.	Ch. 15.2
		Wed., Nov. 4, Ennet	Ch. 15.4
		beginning November 4	Ch. 16.4
		November 4-5	Ch. 16.5
		Thursday, Nov. 5	Ch. 18.2
		Friday, Nov. 6, Ennet	Ch. 19.2
		Friday, Nov. 6, E.T.A.	Ch. 16.3; Ch. 19.1,3
		Saturday, Nov. 7	Ch. 21.1; Ch. 17.1,3,5
		Sunday, Nov. 8	Ch. 22.1; Ch. 24.4,6; Ch. 23.1-7,9,11; Ch. 22.2,4,7
		Monday, Nov. 9	Ch. 23.10; Ch. 24.3; Ch. 25.3; Ch. 26.4
		Tuesday, Nov. 10	Ch. 25.5
		November 8-10	Ch. 27.24,26-27; Ch. 26.9; Ch. 26.15; Ch. 26.11
		November 11-12, Ennet	Ch. 25.7; Ch. 26.1,5,7; n. 90; Ch. 26.8,12,14,16
		November 11-12, E.T.A.	Ch. 26.6,10; Ch. 27.5,7-8; Ch. 27.2,10,15-19; n. 304; (Ch. 27.20); Ch. 27.21,36 Ch. 26.13; Ch. 27.37,39; n. 321
		Friday, Nov. 13	Ch. 27.4,12-13
		November 11-13	Ch. 27.1,29

A More-Or-Less Chronological Ordering Of *Infinite Jest* By Subchapters

Subsidy	Year	Date	Subchapters
Y.D.A.U.	2009	Saturday, Nov. 14, AA&R	Ch. 20.2; Ch. 27.23; Ch. 27.14; Ch. 27.11; Ch. 27.9; Ch. 27.22,25,30
		Saturday, Nov. 14, Joelle	(Ch. 27.20); Ch. 27.28,32,34
		Saturday, Nov. 14, A.F.R.	Ch. 27.31,33,35,38
		November 12-16	Ch. 28.1; Ch. 28.22; Ch. 28.2,4,6
		Tuesday, Nov. 17	Ch. 27.40-44
		November 10-19	Ch. 27.6
		November 16-19	Ch. 28.9,11,13
		Thursday, Nov. 19	Ch. 28.3
		Friday, Nov. 20, U.S.O.U.S.	Ch. 28.8
		Friday, Nov. 20, E.T.A.	Ch. 28.5,7,10,12, 14,19,23
		November 19-20	Ch. 28.15,17
		Friday, Nov. 20, Joelle	Ch. 28.16,18,20-21
		Friday, Nov. 20, A.F.R.	Ch. 28.24
		Friday, Nov. 20, Gately	Ch. 28.25 [includes flashback to early Y.W.]
Y.G.	2010	late November	Ch. 1.1; (Ch. 1.2); Ch. 1.3-5

Partial Chronology: Gately

Year	Age	Event
1980		Estonian immigrant father Bulat (p. 447) leaves before birth (p. 446) born (in November?); given mother's maiden name, only child (p. 446)
1985	04	lives in beach house off a public beach in Beverly (p. 809) at age "like four" names the ceiling Herman (pp. 447, 809)
1990	09	Mrs. Waite dead, Mom first diagnosed (pp. 449, 848-9) first duBois, first real drunk a few months later (p. 903)
1991-2	10-11	nightly Stolichnaya routine (pp. 447-8)
1993	12	puberty (p. 902)
1994-6	13-15	The Attack of the Killer Sidewalks, ex-M.P. leaves (pp. 904-5) meets Kite, begins narcotics (p. 904)
1997	16	this year is mostly a grey blank (p. 906)
1998	17	last season of football, Mom admitted to L.T.I. in Oct. (pp. 449, 906)
1999	18	begins working for Sorkin (pp. 911-2)
2001	20	slept in loft in Malden (p. 843) becomes involved with Pamela Hoffman-Jeep (p. 924)
	21	sees Orin in bowl game, pinched for assault in late Dec. (pp. 915-6)
2002	21	Gately out on bail, Fackleman's demise, Jan.-Mar. (p. 917) enters Billerica, Mar.-Apr. (p. 916)
2004	23	leaves Billerica 17 months later, Aug.-Sept. (p. 463) Kite signs on "as Gately's new trusted associate for B&Es" (p. 918) first uses Demerol (pp. 891-2)
2005	24	pleuritic laryngitis, sleeping on the cold beach in Gloucester (p. 833)
2006	25	pinched on a DUI in Peabody, loses license (p. 462)
2008	27	Autumn [technically late Summer], death of DuPlessis (Ch. 7.4) Probie drives Gately to Ennet from Peabody Holding (p. 444) 12 September, begin 421 days of Gately clean (p. 274)

Partial Chronology: Gately

Year	Age	Event
2008	27	October, gets job (p. 435), at 30 days clean spews vitriol at meeting (pp. 352-3)
		Francis G. sponsors, Gene M. counsels, epiphanic dream (pp. 357-9)
2009	28	Jan.-Feb., 4-5 months, desire for narcotics removed (pp. 349, 466-7)
		April, 7 months, cracks tabletop with head (p. 468)
		May, 8 months, nears end of Ennet residency (p. 446)
		May (p. 447), 8 months, memories burpling greasily up (p. 448)
		June, 9 months, period of residency and treatment ends (p. 137)
		June-July, graduates treatment, takes job of live-in Staffer (p. 196)
		July (p. 442), 10 months (p. 443)
		13 September, the one-year cake (p. 468)
		6 November, on live-in staff four months (p. 275)
		6 November, 421 days clean (p. 274), almost twenty-nine (p. 277)
		8 November, age twenty-nine (p. 478), age thirty approaches (p. 346)
		15 November, age twenty-eight (p. 834)
2010	29	Jan., approached by Tiny near end of two-month tatt obsession (p. 210)
		June-July, "his year's Staff term is up" (p. 594)
		digs up Jim's head with Hal (p. 17)

Partial Chronology: Joelle

Year	Time	Event
2001	Fall	begins sophomore year at B.U. (p. 289)
	Columbus Day	begins dating Orin (p. 295) for 26 months (p. 229)
	Thanksgiving	dinner with Incandenzas, later uses cocaine (p. 747)
	after Thanksgiving	thumb filmed (p. 297)
	New Years Eve	with Orin, uses cocaine (p. 296)
2003	May/June	Joelle begins working with Jim (p. 297) for 21 months (p. 229) [actually 9 months, cf. Ch. 20.1 summary]
		roles include Death, mangled-faced fiancée, veiled nun (pp. 990-3)
	Thanksgiving	disfigured, Mom's death (p. 795)
	December	stops dating Orin, end of 26 months with Orin
		agrees not to call Orin (p. 249)
2004	Jan./Feb.	finishes *Infinite Jest*, "unveiled for" Jim (p. 228)
		end of 21 months [actually 9 months] with Jim
		"after the acid, after first Orin left and then [*Infinite Jest*], after taking the veil, for a while she like to get really high and clean" (p. 225)
2004/2005		graduates B.U.
		starts grad school at M.I.T. in Film & Film-Cartridge Theory (p. 220)
		graduate wine-tasting party, improbably deformed (pp. 531, 535)
		meets Notkin "before her retreat into broadcast sound" (p. 220)
		never unveils for Notkin (n. 328)
2005		begins Madame Psychosis show (p. 591)
	November	dons the veil as a new U.H.I.D. (p. 533-4)
2006		opening phrase of Madame Psychosis show is set (p. 184)
2007		"J. van Dyne, M.A.'s one and only published film-theory monograph" (p. 234, n. 81)
		retreats into broadcast sound instead of obtaining Ph.D.
		"feared for quitting instead of failing" (p. 231)
2009	23 October	one of the last Madame Psychosis shows (Ch. 16.1)
		"she says what she's said for three years of midnights" (p. 184)
	07 November	Notkin's party (Ch. 17)
	08 November	enters Ennet House (n. 134)
	11 November	"almost four years in" U.H.I.D. (p. 533)
		hiatus from Madame Psychosis show enters third week (p. 589)

Partial Chronology: November Y.D.A.U.

by 3 November	Steeply begins interviewing Orin (n. 145)
	A.F.R. temporarily stops surveillance of Orin (p. 574)
3, 5 November	Orin calls Hal (Chs. 13.1, 18.2)
7 November	Steeply "en route" to E.T.A. (p. 1012)
	1412h., Orin leaves message w/ locker-room sounds (p. 1005)
	1600h.; Orin calls Hal, preps answers for Steeply (n. 110.4)
8 November	Orin with Arizona Cardinals; Steeply at Eschaton, then back to Orin
	A.F.R. at Antitois, search for cartridge begins
10 November	Fortier leaves in the search's middle to interview Orin (p. 723)
	Orin takes Steeply to airport, gives Steeply M. Bain's address
	Steeply begins correspondence with M. Bain
	Luria meets Orin (Ch. 26.9)
	Hours after Steeply leaves (p. 574), Fortier interviews Orin
11 November	Steeply at E.T.A., Luria with Orin again (p. 655)
	A.F.R. finds cartridge
12 November	Engineer nabbed, Fortier is able to return
13 November	A.F.R. begins searching halfway houses for Joelle
14 November	Luria with Orin again (n. 307)
14 November	
before 2200	Poor Tony's seizure (Ch. 20.2)
until 2200	Joelle in St. E's meeting (Ch. 27.20)
before 2215	Joelle takes "the quick walk" (p. 934) from St. E's to Ennet
	Lenz (Ch. 27.23, p. 718)
after 2215	Gompert and van Cleve (Ch. 27.14, p. 700)
	Poor Tony walks by Matty (Chs. 27.11, 27.9)
before 2230	van Cleve after Poor Tony, Selwyn with Gompert (Ch. 27.22)
	Poor Tony (Ch. 27.25)
	Lenz (Ch. 27.30, p. 728)
before 2300	Joelle in her room at Ennet (Chs. 27.28, 27.32, 27.34)
	Selwyn and Marathe at Ennet (Chs. 27.31, 27.33, 27.35)
after 2300	"People from the public can't be" at Ennet (p. 591)
	Marathe with Gompert (Ch. 27.38)
after 2330	Gompert missing from Ennet House (p. 824)
17 November	Hal at Ennet, then to K. Bain
by 19 November	M. Bain answers get to Steeply
19 November	A.F.R. shifts focus of operation after no sign of Joelle (p. 845)
19 November	Fortier leaves for 2nd interview, A.F.R. hijack tennis teams
20 November	Joelle interviewed by Steeply, A.F.R. at Ennet
	Fortier and Luria interview Orin

E.T.A. Spatial Orientation

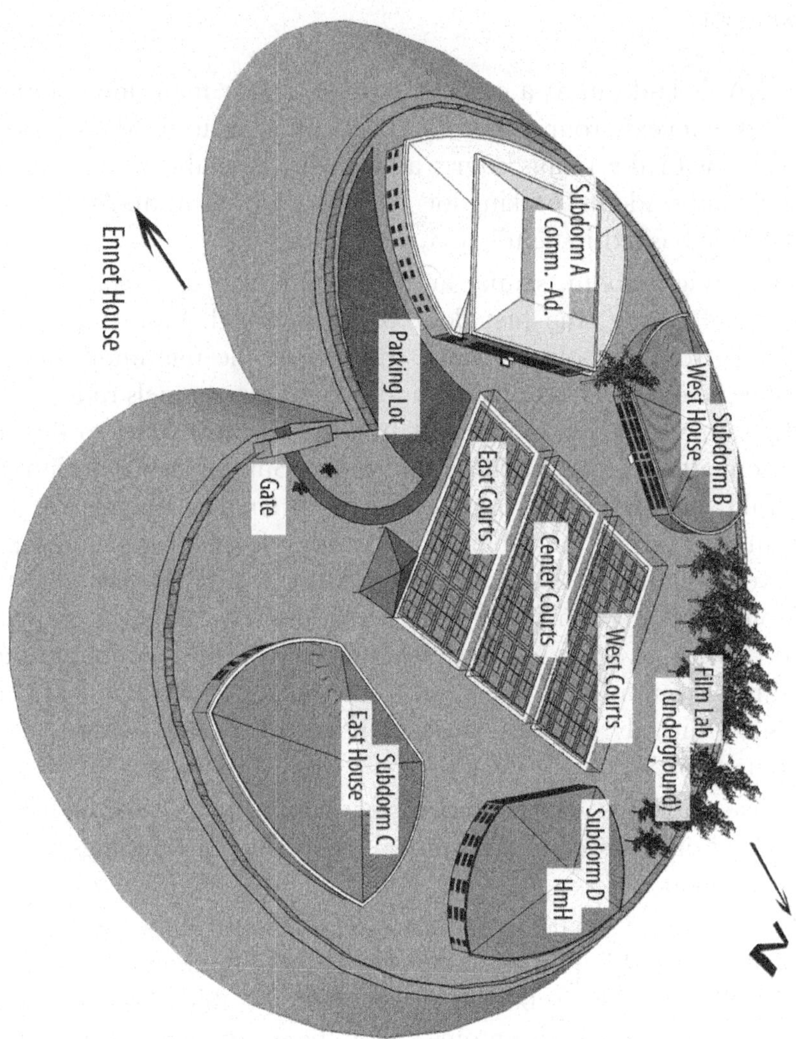

The diagram above will work for the citations that follow if it is assumed that the narrator of p. 51 meant "north and west" rather than "south and east" when referencing the tunnels off the sauna below the first floor of Comm.-Ad. (cf. the 2nd citation below) and if the narrator of n. 266 meant to reference the "East Courts' south fence" rather than the "West Courts' south fence" as the fence nearest the parking lot.

- "E.T.A. is laid out as a cardioid, with the four main inward-facing bldgs. convexly rounded at the back and sides to yield a cardioid's curve, with the tennis courts and pavilions at the center and the staff and students' parking lots in the back of Comm.-Ad. forming the little bashed-in dent" (n. 3, p. 983).
- The "weight room, sauna, and locker/shower areas [are] on the sublevel below" the first floor of Comm.-Ad. One large tunnel "leads from just off the boys' showers to the mammoth laundry room below the West Courts, and two smaller tunnels radiate from the sauna area south and east [read north and west] to the subbasements" of the buildings that house Subdorms D (presumably HmH) and B (West House). Two even smaller tunnels "in turn connect each of the subbasements to the former optical and film-development facilities . . . below and just west of the Headmaster's House (from which facilities there's [a tunnel] that goes straight to the lowest level [i.e., below the sublevel] of the Community and Administration Bldg. . . .) and to the offices of the Physical Plant, almost directly beneath the center row of E.T.A. outdoor tennis courts" (p. 51).
- Unlike sublevels and subbasements, subdorms are located above ground on the second and third floors of E.T.A. buildings (cf. citations below).
- "Dr. and Mrs. I's marriage's third and final home at the northern rear of the grounds" (p. 314) was in HmH, now the home of Avril and C.T. Presumably, Subdorm D occupies the third floor of HmH, since Avril's and Tavis's rooms are on the second floor (p. 191). From HmH, Tavis looks "southeast past West and Center Courts" (p. 451).
- V.R.6 is "one of the three little Viewing Rooms on the second floor of the Comm.-Ad. Bldg., two flights up from the locker areas and three from the main tunnel's mouth" (p. 109). The main tunnel is the tun-

nel between the film lab and the lowest level of Comm.-Ad. (p. 153). V.R.5 is "Two curves down the hall" (p. 115). Presumably, V.R.4 is the third Viewing Room located on the second floor of Comm.-Ad.

- Presumably all Viewing Rooms are found in groups of three. The second floor of "East House, the structure nearest the front gate" of E.T.A. (p. 432), is the location of Viewing Rooms 1-3; and the third floor of East House is the location of Viewing Rooms 7-9 and the Clipperton Suite, an "unused top-floor room in Subdorm C of East House" (p. 432). Consider the following from pp. 116-7: "Pemulis says in V.R.2, subdorm C"; "Ted Schacht in V.R.3"; and "Troeltsch holds court in his, Pemulis and Schacht's room in Subdorm C." "Two levels down" from Struck in V.R.8, Ortho Stice holds his meeting in the "foyer off the front door [of East House which is the front door] to subdorm C" (pp. 118-9).
- "Pemulis, Troeltsch, and Schacht's triple-room is in subdorm B in the back north part of the second floor of West House and so superjacent to the Dining Hall" (p. 171). This room assignment conflicts with "Subdorm C" (p. 117, cf. previous citation), but supports "Rm. 204, Subdormitory B: Jim Troeltsch" (p. 60).
- The "east wall of windows [in the dining hall in West House] faces Comm.-Ad." (p. 387). The "room's big windows face east, out over the hillside and the Enfield Marine complex that the Academy has bathed in shadow." Hal sees Clenette and Didi "making their way down the steep hillside's unauthorized path back down to the halfway-house" (p. 633).
- Mario goes from Schtitt's room in 106 Comm.-Ad. to the second floor where the girls' rooms are to the third floor where the boys' rooms are (pp. 755-7). In West House, the boys' rooms are on the second floor (cf. Pemulis, Troeltsch, and Schacht; p. 171).
- Hal leaves his room on the third floor of Comm.-Ad., walks "along the subdorm halls," and looks out a bathroom window at the East Courts (p. 864). Kenkle and Brandt are "right below" (p. 868) on the second floor. After speaking with Kenkle and Brandt, Hal wanted to go "back up" to his floor, but was hit with panic and stayed in "Viewing Room 5, still on the second floor" (p. 897).

Character Associations

Below is an Incandenza family tree. Pages 503-7 provide partial lists of characters associated with E.T.A., with Ennet House, and with O.N.A.N. and anti-O.N.A.N. groups. Partial lists of E.T.A. teams and rankings and a partial roster of Ennet House room assignments are also provided. Readers researching characters in *Infinite Jest* may wish to consult the chapter on Minor Characters and Real People provided by Dowling and Bell, Tim Ware's *Infinite Jest* Index, and other resources on the *Infinite Jest* page at www.thehowlingfantods.com/dfw.

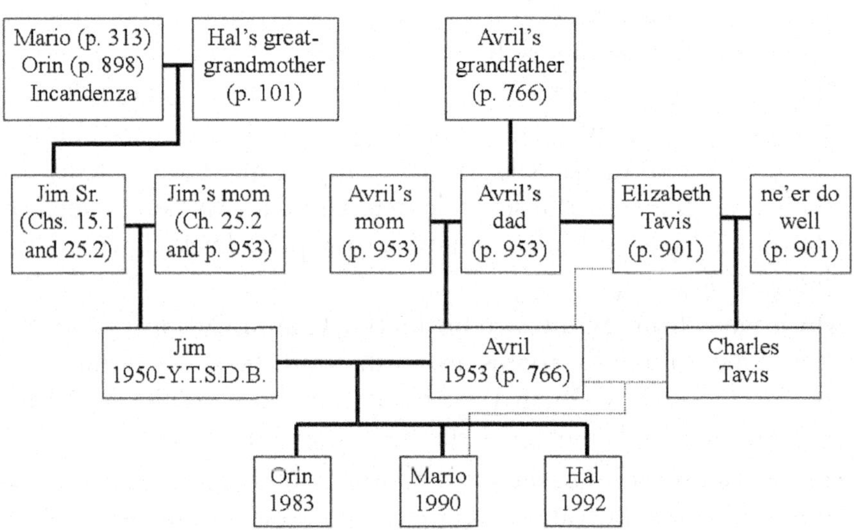

THE ENFIELD TENNIS ACADEMY

JOI FILM
Heaven, P. A.
Johnson, Ken
Watt, Cosgrove

CRITICS
Comstock
Duquette
Posner/Poesner
Sperber

FILM/TEACHERS
Chawaf, Soma
Heath, Pam
Leith, Disney R.
Ogilvie, Urquhart
Pricket, Mrs.

TEACHERS
P. 254
Flentriss
Flottman
Lingley
Pettijohn

FILM/JANITORS
Brandt, Otto
Kenkle, E. J.

JANITOR
Harde, Dave

STAFF
Clarke, Mrs.
Lyle
Rusk, Dolores

ADMIN
Incandenza, Jim (founder, 1st Hm)
Incandenza, Avril
Moore, Lateral A.
Tavis, Charles (2nd Hm)

DESIGNER
Rickey, A.Y.

COACH
Schtitt, Gerhardt

PRORECTORS
8 MALE
Cantrell (former)
deLint, Aubrey
Dunkel, Rik
Hartigan, Neil
Nwangi, Tony
Thorp, Corbett
Watson, Tex

PRORECTORS
4 FEMALE
Carolyn (p. 1006)
Poutrincourt, T.
Stott, Donnie
Thode, Mary E.

TRAINER
Loach, Barry

NON-E.T.A.
Grief-Therapist
Urologist
Zegarelli, Dr.

THE ENFIELD TENNIS ACADEMY

FORMER E.T.A.
Bain, Marlon
Flechette
Mackey
Pearson, Heath
Penn, Miles
Reat, Ross
Smothergill, P. T.
Vandervoort
Incandenza, Orin

NON-E.T.A.
TENNIS
Clipperton, Eric
Dymphna
Polep (p. 17)
Veach (p. 259)

BAIN
Bain, Kevin
Bain's sister

E.T.A.
Incandenza, Mario

E.T.A. STUDENTS
GIRLS
Bash, Jennie
Boone, Bridget
Clow, Lori
Criess, Jolene
Echt, Tina
Holt, Gretchen
Kent, Millicent
Kittenplan, Ann
Longley, Bern
Prins, Diane
Siress, Erica
Spodek, Carol
Unwin, Frannie
Vaught, Caryn
Vaught, Sharyn
Wingo, Amy
Zweig, Felicity

E.T.A. STUDENTS
BOYS
Axford, Trevor
Cisne (p. 264)
Cs/yi, Zoltan
Coyle, Kyle D.
Doucette, Anton
Freer, Keith
Gloeckner
Incandenza, Hal
Khan, Petropolis
Kornspan, Eliot
Makulic, Bernard
Pemberton
Pemulis, Michael
Penn, J. J.
Rader, Graham
Redondo (p. 759)
Reynes (p. 759)
Schacht, Ted
Shaw, Tall Paul
Stice, Ortho
Stockhausen
Struck, James
Troeltsch, Jim
van Slack, Duncan
Virgilio (p. 757)
Wax, Jeff (p. 457)
Wayne, John
Yardley (p. 102)

E.T.A. STUDENTS
LITTLE BUDDIES
AXFORD LB
Possalthwaite/p.98

HAL LB
Arslanian, Idris
Beak, Peter
Blott, Kent
Ingersoll, Evan

PEMULIS LB
Lord, Otis P.
Possalthwaite/p.117
Sweeny, Chip

STICE LB
Wagenknecht

STRUCK LB
Gopnik, Josh
Tallat-Kelpsa
Traub, Philip
Whale, Carl

WAYNE LB
Chu, Lamont
McKenna, Kieran
Peterson, T. P.
van Vleck, Brian

THE ENFIELD TENNIS ACADEMY

E.T.A. TEAMS/RANKINGS
Most Rankings: Port Washington (Ch. 19.1), Troeltsch broadcast (Ch. 21.1)

BOYS	BOYS	BOYS	GIRLS
18A	18B		18A
1 Wayne	1 Freer (five slots under Hal, p. 112)		1 Longley
2 Incandenza	2 Troeltsch (p. 60; over [read under] Freer, p. 112)		2 Prins
3 Coyle	3 Schacht	18C	3 Boone
4 Axford		Gloeckner (p. 1010)	
Struck (p. 112)		Stockhausen (p. 281)	
6 Shaw	6 Pemulis	van Slack (p. 1010, cf. p. 1071)	
16A	16B	16C	16s
1 Stice	Doucette (p. 390)		Al Kent (p. 121)
Kornspan (p. 282)			Spodek (p. 395)
14A		14C	14A
1 Chu		Makulic (p. 634)	
2 Penn			
3 Beak (12)			3 Zweig
4 Arslanian (14)	6 Nov. ranks, p. 309		4 Holt
5 Possalthwaite	cf. 3 Nov. ranks, p. 112		5 Kittenplan
Ingersoll (11)	boys ages, pp. 96-7		6 Criess
OTHER A's (9 Nov. drills, Ch. 24.3)		12s	12s (p. 524)
Khan		Blott (10)	Echt (7)
Rader			
Sweeny			
van Vleck			
Wagenknecht			
Wax			

ENNET HOUSE

FOUNDER
Guy Who Didn't Even Use His First Name

ADMINISTRATION
Montesian, Pat: Executive Director (p. 278)
Parrot, Annie: Asst. Dir./Mgr. (pp. 279, 434)
Janice: House Manager (pp. 735, 753, 822)

RESIDENTS
Belbin, Jennifer
Cortelyu, April
Day, Geoffrey
Diehl, Gavin
Erdedy, Ken
Ewell, Tiny
Foss, Chandler
Glynn, Dwayne
Gompert, Kate
Green, Bruce
Gunther, Nell
Hanley, Morris
Henderson, Clenette
Johnson, Amy
Krone, David
Lenz, Randy
McDade, Wade
Minty, Emil
Neaves, Didi
Parias-Carbo, Alfonso
Smith, Burt F.
Thrale, Hester
Tingley
Treat, Charlotte
van Cleve, Ruth
van Dyne, Joelle
Willis, Yolanda

LIVE-IN STAFF
Foltz, Johnette
Gately, Don

COUNSELORS
Martinez, Eugenio
N, Maureen (p. 826)
Steenbok, Danielle
Thrust, Calvin

GREEN
Bonk, Mildred
Bonk-Green, Harriet

C, Bobby

JOELLE
engineer, WYYY
Notkin, Molly

GATELY/Ennet
Lobokulas, Stavros
Gehaney, Francis

DEALERS
Doocey, Tommy

Roy Tony

Wo, Dr.

Delphina, Lady

GATELY/Sorkin
A.D.A., Revere
Kite, Trent
Fackleman, Gene
H.-Jeep, Pamela
Sorkin, Whitey
Eighties Bill
Sixties Bob

PROSTITUTES
Cheese, Susan T.
Krause, Poor Tony
Lolasister
McNair, Stokely
Pemulis, Matty
Purpleboy
Reese, Equus
Tenderhole, B.
Vinoy, Kely

ENNET ROOM ASSIGNMENTS

4 NOVEMBER	6 NOVEMBER	11 NOVEMBER	13 NOVEMBER
		2 MAN ROOM	
		Glynn (p. 606)	
	3 MAN (p. 279)	3 MAN (p. 539)	3 MAN? (p. 692)
		Glynn	Day
	Lenz	Lenz (out 12 Nov.)	Erdedy
	Day	Day	Ewell

5 MAN ROOM (p. 209)
Lenz
Day (in six days on 6 Nov., p. 272)
Erdedy (at Ennet about a month (p. 360), but Day moves up first (p. 539))
Skull (lasted like four days, p. 208)
Ewell (at Ennet by 4 Nov.; pp. 86, 177, 205)

O.N.A.N. AND ANTI-O.N.A.N. GROUPS

QUÉBEC/A.F.R.
Antitois
DuPlessis, G.
Broullîme, M.
Fortier, M.
Marathe, Rémy
Perec, Luria

U.S.A./U.S.O.U.S.
Steeply, Hugh
Tine, Rodney, Sr.
Tine, Rodney, Jr.

U.S.A. BUSINESS
Lace-Forche, N.
Veals, P. Tom
Viney

PRESIDENT/CABINET
Gentle, J.
Pres. Mex.
P. M. Can.
Sec. Treas. (Chet)
Sec. Int. (Blaine)
Sec. State (Billingsley)
Sec. Transp. (Marty)
Sec. H.E.W. (Trent)
Sec., Press (Jay)
Sec. H.U.D. (Mr. Sivnik)
Sec. Def. (Ollie)

References

The page numbers below identify where these sources are referenced in the study.

Primary Web References

Maniatis, Nick. *The Howling Fantods.* www.thehowlingfantods.com/dfw pp. 16, 502
This comprehensive website is a nexus for Wallace-related material. The *Infinite Jest* page at this site contains links to several of the web-based references listed below.

Wallace-L. waste.org/mail/?list=wallace-l pp. 5, 16
This listserv regularly features commentary on *Infinite Jest* and a wide range of other topics.

Other Web References

Amazon.com's Search Inside feature for *Infinite Jest.* www.amazon.com
This feature allows readers to search the text of *Infinite Jest.*

Bourke, Paul. "Sierpinski Gasket." March 1993. local.wasp.uwa.edu.au/~pbourke/fractals/gasket p. 20

Bucher, Matt. "*Infinite Jest* Character Profiles: Trevor Axford." www.geocities.com/Athens/Acropolis/8175/profiles.htm p. 459

"M*A*S*H," Episode Guides. www.mash4077.co.uk/guides.html pp. 333-4

Meranda, Yoel. "The Lead Shoes." *UbuWeb: Film and Video.* www.ubu.com/film/peterson.html p. 439
This site provides links to a great variety of experimental films, including Peterson's *The Lead Shoes.*

Mikkelson, Barbara. "The Barrel of Bricks." *Urban Legends Reference Pages.* 24 October 2004. www.snopes.com/humor/letters/bricks.asp p. 106

Moore, Steven. "The First Draft Version of *Infinite Jest*." www.thehowlingfantods.com/ij_first.htm pp. 18-9, 36, 346-7

O'Neill, K. "*Infinite Jest*: a scene-by-scene guide." web.archive.org/web/20060321052141/http://www.english.uga.edu/~koneill/IJ.htm p. 488

Russillo, Steve. "Steve's *Infinite Jest* Utilities Page." members.aol.com/russillosm/ij.html p. 488

Strong, Mike. "Dubious Math in *Infinite Jest*." www.thehowlingfantods.com/IJmath.htm pp. 165, 204, 389

Wallace, David Foster. Interviewed by Michael Silverblatt on *Bookworm*. April 11, 1996. www.kcrw.com p. 20
This public radio program airs on KCRW, which is affiliated with Santa Monica College. Type "David Foster Wallace" under the "SEARCH KCRW" heading at www.kcrw.com and select the 1996 interview to listen.

Ware, Tim. "*Infinite Jest* Index." members.aol.com/russillosm/ijndx.html p. 502

Selected References to Television, Film, and Music

2001: A Space Odyssey. Stanley Kubrick, director. pp. 49, 393

Beatles. *Revolver*. p. 40

Blue Velvet. David Lynch, director. p. 236

Citizen Kane. Orson Welles, director. pp. 346
Orson Welles is also referenced on p. 313-4.

A Clockwork Orange. Stanley Kubrick, director. pp. 49, 93, 102, 369, 390, 399, 436, 465, 469

"Hill Street Blues." Steven Bochco and Michael Kozoll, co-creators. pp. 107-8

Monty Python and the Holy Grail. Terry Gilliam and Terry Jones, directors. p. 322

"Monty Python's Flying Circus." Monty Python, creators. p. 313

Monty Python's The Meaning of Life. Terry Gilliam and Terry Jones, directors. p. 313

Requiem for a Dream. Darren Aronofsky, director. p. 153

"Twin Peaks." David Lynch and Mark Frost, co-creators. pp. 87, 255, 275, 285, 342, 365, 459

Velvet Underground. "Heroin." *Andy Warhol.* pp. 358

Velvet Underground. "Sister Ray." *White Light, White Heat.* pp. 358

References to Books, Plays, and a Poem

Appignanesi, Richard, et al. *Introducing Postmodernism*, 2nd edition. UK: Icon, 2003. p. 202

Beckett, Samuel. *Company*. p. 108

Beckett, Samuel. *The Unnamable*. p. 108

Blake, William. *The Marriage of Heaven and Hell.* p. 221

Blamires, Harry. *The New Bloomsday Book: A Guide Through Ulysses*, third edition. London: Routledge, 1996. pp. 5, 16, 67

Boswell, Marshall. *Understanding David Foster Wallace.* University of South Carolina Press, 2003. pp. 15, 16, 488

Burgess, Anthony. *A Clockwork Orange*. pp. 49, 93, 102, 369, 390, 399, 436, 465, 469

Burn, Stephen. *David Foster Wallace's Infinite Jest: A Reader's Guide.* New York: Continuum, 2003. pp. 16, 157, 275, 493

Clarke, Arthur C. *2001: A Space Odyssey*. pp. 49, 393

Coleridge, Samuel Taylor. Commentary on *Hamlet* I.v in *The Bedford Introduction to Drama*, 5th edition (2005), edited by Lee A. Jacobus and published by Bedford/St. Martin's. p. 425

Danielewski, Mark Z. *House of Leaves*. New York: Pantheon, 2000. p. 285

Dante. *Inferno*. p. 394

DeLillo, Don. *Underworld*. New York: Scribner, 1997. p. 473

DeLillo, Don. *White Noise*. New York: Viking Penguin, 1985. p. 88

Dostoevsky, Fyodor. *The Brothers Karamatzov*. p. 465

Dowling, William and Robert Bell. *A Reader's Companion to Infinite Jest.* Xlibris, 2005. pp. 16, 25, 157, 502

Faulkner, William. *The Sound and the Fury*. pp. 146, 285

Gaddis, William. *The Recognitions*. New York: Harcourt, Brace, 1955. pp. 88, 154-5

Graves, Robert. *The Greek Myths*, combined edition. London: Penguin, 1992. p. 180

Homer. *The Odyssey*. Penelope is referenced on p. 404.

Joyce, James. *Ulysses*. pp. 16, 19, 20, 67, 95, 112, 179, 229, 361, 404, 470

King, Stephen. *It*. pp. 351-2

Miller, Frank and Dave Gibbons. *Give Me Liberty*. p. 236

Miller, Frank and Geoff Darrow. *Hardboiled*. p. 236

Miller, Frank. *Sin City*. p. 236

Moore, Alan and Dave Gibbons. *Watchmen*. p. 236

Munem, Mustafa A. and David J. Foulis. *Calculus with Analytic Geometry*. New York: Worth, 1978. p. 204

Orwell, George. *1984*. pp. 19, 146, 157, 228, 255, 276, 322, 329, 336, 467

Pynchon, Thomas. *Gravity's Rainbow*. New York: Viking. 1973. pp. 82, 473

Shakespeare, William. *Hamlet*. Citations in this study refer to the second series of the Arden edition (1982), edited by Harold Jenkins. pp. 19, 30-1, 37-8, 47, 49, 54, 60, 65, 67, 76, 82, 109, 122, 123, 146, 150-1, 154, 160-1, 162, 164, 179, 189, 276, 334, 340, 353, 358, 361, 373, 383, 387-8, 398, 401, 406, 411, 413, 415, 425, 430, 432, 434, 446, 448, 450, 458, 478, 479, 483, 487

Shakespeare, William. *Henry IV*. Prince Hal and/or Falstaff are referenced on pp. 313-4 and 425.

Shakespeare, William. *Henry V*. p. 179

Shakespeare, William. *Macbeth*. p. 430

Shakespeare, William. *The Merchant of Venice*. Shylock is referenced on p. 322.

Stevens, Wallace. *Esthetique du Mal*, XIII. p. 488

Tolstoy, Leo. *The Death of Ivan Ilych*. p. 352

Wallace, David Foster. *A Supposedly Fun Thing I'll Never Do Again*. Boston: Little, Brown, 1997.

"Derivative Sport in Tornado Alley": pp. 259, 332, 344

"E Unibus Pluram: Television and U.S. Fiction": pp. 92, 351, 377

"David Lynch Keeps His Head": pp. 87, 195

Wallace, David Foster. *Brief Interviews with Hideous Men*. Boston: Little, Brown, 1999.
"Brief Interviews with Hideous Men": pp. 182 ("B. I. #42"), 219
"The Depressed Person": p. 351
Wallace, David Foster. *The Broom of the System*. New York: Viking Penguin. 1987. pp. 35, 83, 142
Wallace, David Foster. *Consider the Lobster*. Boston: Little, Brown, 2005.
"Authority and American Usage": p. 27
"The View from Mrs. Thompson's": p. 226
"Consider the Lobster": p. 430
"Joseph Frank's Dostoevsky": p. 465
Wallace, David Foster. *Everything and More: A Compact History of* ∞. New York: Norton, 2003. p. 77
Wallace, David Foster. *Girl with Curious Hair*. New York: Norton, 1989. pp. 35, 102
Wallace, David Foster. *Infinite Jest*. Boston: Little, Brown, 1996.
Wallace, David Foster. "Kenyon Commencement Speech" in *The Best American Nonrequired Reading 2006*, edited by Dave Eggers and published by Houghton Mifflin. p. 255
Wallace, David Foster. *Oblivion*. Boston: Little, Brown, 2004.
"Mister Squishy": p. 190
"Incarnations of Burned Children": p. 195
"The Suffering Channel": p. 87
Wallace, David Foster, contributing editor. *Oxford American Writer's Thesaurus*. Oxford University Press, 2004. p. 379

CPSIA information can be obtained
at www.ICGtesting.com
Printed in the USA
BVOW06s1022040118
504458BV00014B/353/P